Rick Steves'

GREAT
BRITAIN
2008

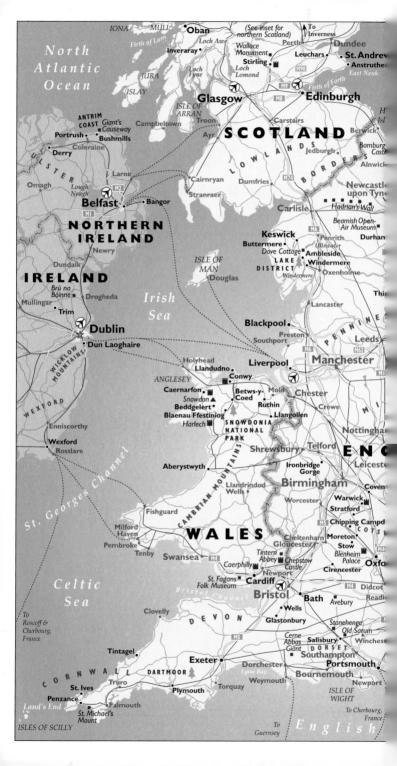

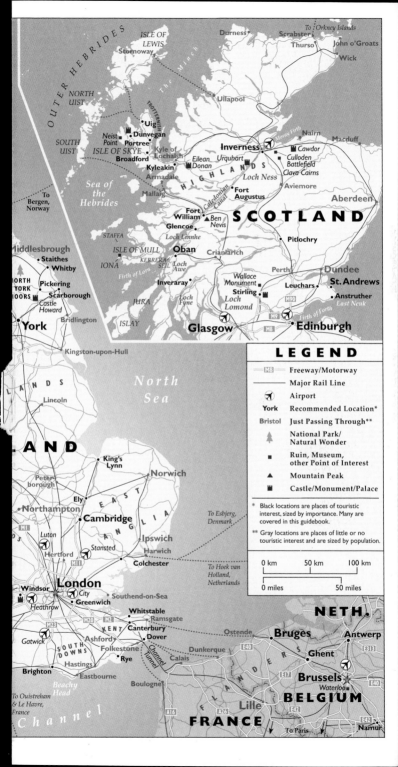

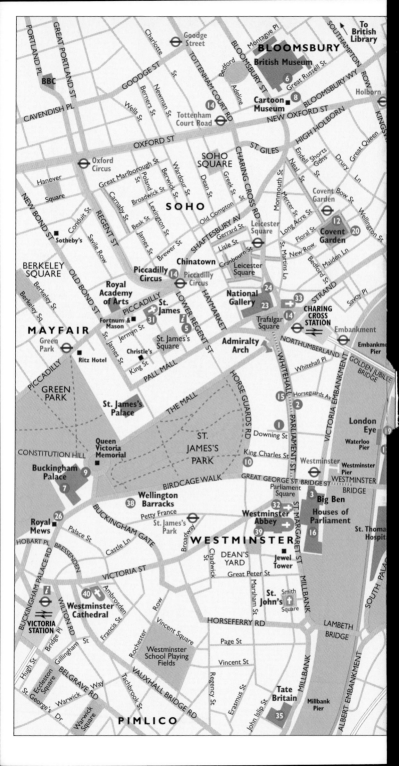

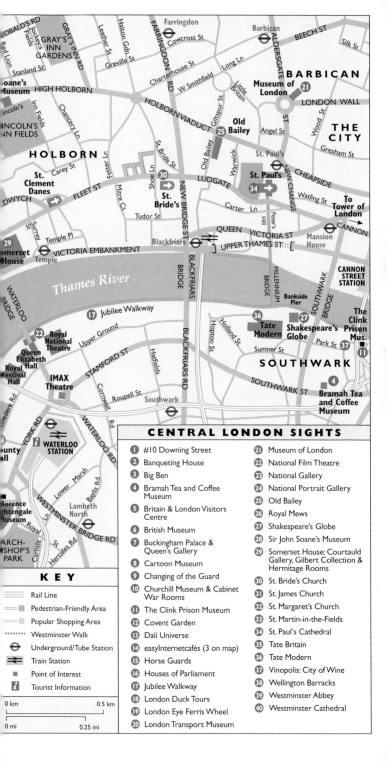

Map labels (reading across the map):

EOBALD'S RD · Dockers Fields · Red Lion · GRAY'S INN GARDENS · GRAY'S INN RD · Leather St · Halton Gdn · FARRINGDON · Farringdon · Cowcross St · Barbican · ALDERSGATE · BEECH ST · Silk St

oane's Museum · HIGH HOLBORN · Stanland St · Greville St · Charterhouse St · W Smithfield · Long Ln · Little Britain · Museum of London · 21 · BARBICAN · LONDON WALL · Wood St

incoln's · INCOLN'S NN FIELDS · Chancery Ln · HOLBORN VIADUCT · Gloucester St · Old Bailey · 25 · Angel St · ST · THE CITY · Gresham St

HOLBORN · St. Clement Danes · Carey St · S · St. Paul's · St. Paul's · CHEAPSIDE · NEW CHANGE · Watling St · To Tower of London

DWYCH · FLEET ST · Fetter Ln · Mitre Ct · Shoe Ln · S Bride St · New Bridge St · 30 · St. Bride's · LUDGATE · Warwick · Old Bailey · Carter Ln · Peter's Hill · 34 · St. Paul's Cathedral

Surrey · Temple Pl · Tudor St · QUEEN VICTORIA ST · UPPER THAMES ST · Mansion House · CANNON

29 · omerset House · VICTORIA EMBANKMENT · Temple · Blackfriars · BLACKFRIARS BRIDGE · MILLENNIUM BRIDGE · SOUTHWARK BRIDGE · CANNON STREET STATION

Thames River · 17 Jubilee Walkway · Bankside Pier · 36 Tate Modern · 27 Shakespeare's Globe · Park St · 37 · The Clink Prison Mus. · 11

WATERLOO BRIDGE · 22 Royal National Theatre · Upper Ground · Holland St · Hopton St · Sumner St · SOUTHWARK

Queen Elizabeth Hall · Royal Festival Hall · IMAX Theatre · STAMFORD ST · Hatfields · BLACKFRIARS RD · SOUTHWARK ST · 4 Bramah Tea and Coffee Museum

belvedere Rd · YORK RD · Cornwall Rd · Roupell St · Southwark · WATERLOO RD

ounty all · WATERLOO STATION · WESTMINSTER BRIDGE RD · Lower Marsh · Baylis Rd · Lambeth North

lorence ightengale useum · Royal St · Hercules Rd · Carlisle · St

ARCH-ISHOP'S PARK

KEY

- ═══ Rail Line
- ▬ Pedestrian-Friendly Area
- ▬ Popular Shopping Area
- ⋯⋯⋯ Westminster Walk
- ⊖ Underground/Tube Station
- ⇄ Train Station
- ■ Point of Interest
- 𝒊 Tourist Information

0 km	0.5 km
0 mi	0.25 mi

CENTRAL LONDON SIGHTS

1. #10 Downing Street
2. Banqueting House
3. Big Ben
4. Bramah Tea and Coffee Museum
5. Britain & London Visitors Centre
6. British Museum
7. Buckingham Palace & Queen's Gallery
8. Cartoon Museum
9. Changing of the Guard
10. Churchill Museum & Cabinet War Rooms
11. The Clink Prison Museum
12. Covent Garden
13. Dalí Universe
14. easyInternetcafés (3 on map)
15. Horse Guards
16. Houses of Parliament
17. Jubilee Walkway
18. London Duck Tours
19. London Eye Ferris Wheel
20. London Transport Museum
21. Museum of London
22. National Film Theatre
23. National Gallery
24. National Portrait Gallery
25. Old Bailey
26. Royal Mews
27. Shakespeare's Globe
28. Sir John Soane's Museum
29. Somerset House: Courtauld Gallery, Gilbert Collection & Hermitage Rooms
30. St. Bride's Church
31. St. James Church
32. St. Margaret's Church
33. St. Martin-in-the-Fields
34. St. Paul's Cathedral
35. Tate Britain
36. Tate Modern
37. Vinopolis: City of Wine
38. Wellington Barracks
39. Westminster Abbey
40. Westminster Cathedral

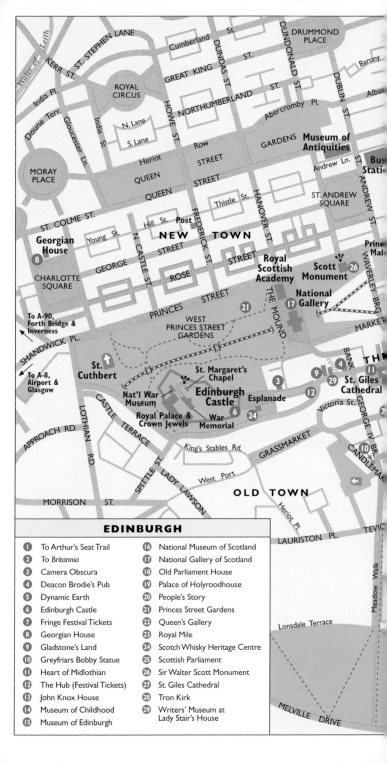

EDINBURGH

❶	To Arthur's Seat Trail	⓰	National Museum of Scotland
❷	To *Britannia*	⓱	National Gallery of Scotland
❸	Camera Obscura	⓲	Old Parliament House
❹	Deacon Brodie's Pub	⓳	Palace of Holyroodhouse
❺	Dynamic Earth	⓴	People's Story
❻	Edinburgh Castle	㉑	Princes Street Gardens
❼	Fringe Festival Tickets	㉒	Queen's Gallery
❽	Georgian House	㉓	Royal Mile
❾	Gladstone's Land	㉔	Scotch Whisky Heritage Centre
❿	Greyfriars Bobby Statue	㉕	Scottish Parliament
⓫	Heart of Midlothian	㉖	Sir Walter Scott Monument
⓬	The Hub (Festival Tickets)	㉗	St. Giles Cathedral
⓭	John Knox House	㉘	Tron Kirk
⓮	Museum of Childhood	㉙	Writers' Museum at
⓯	Museum of Edinburgh		Lady Stair's House

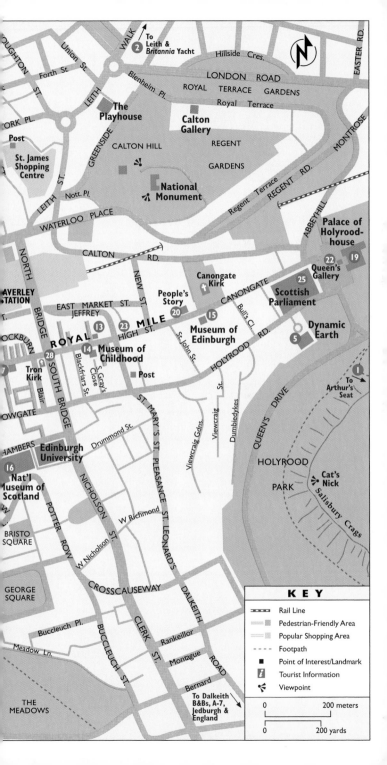

To Leith &
Britannia Yacht

Hillside Cres.

LONDON ROAD

ROYAL TERRACE GARDENS

Royal Terrace

Blenheim Pl.

The Playhouse

Calton Gallery

CALTON HILL

REGENT

GARDENS

National Monument

Regent Terrace

REGENT RD.

ABBEYHILL

Palace of Holyrood-house

Queen's Gallery

Scottish Parliament

Canongate Kirk

CANONGATE

People's Story

Bull's Cl.

Dynamic Earth

Museum of Edinburgh

HOLYROOD RD.

St. John St.

ROYAL MILE

HIGH ST.

NEW ST.

EAST MARKET ST.

JEFFREY

Museum of Childhood

Blackfriar's Close

S. Gray's Close

Post

Tron Kirk

SOUTH BRIDGE

Blair

COCKBURN

COWGATE

CHAMBERS

Edinburgh University

Drummond St.

Nat'l Museum of Scotland

ST. MARY'S ST.

PLEASANCE

ST. LEONARD'S

Viewcraig Gdns.

Viewcraig St.

Dumbiedykes

To Arthur's Seat

QUEEN'S DRIVE

HOLYROOD

PARK

Cat's Nick

Salisbury Crags

NICHOLSON

POTTER ROW

W. Nicholson St.

W Richmond

BRISTO SQUARE

GEORGE SQUARE

CROSSCAUSEWAY

DALKEITH

CLERK ST.

Buccleuch Pl.

BUCCLEUCH ST.

Meadow Ln.

Rankeillor

Montague

Bernard

BERNARD ROAD

To Dalkeith B&Bs, A-7, Jedburgh & England

THE MEADOWS

WALK

Union St.

Forth St.

LEITH ST.

GREENSIDE

LEITH ST.

Nott. Pl.

WATERLOO PLACE

CALTON RD.

NORTH BRIDGE

AVERLEY STATION

ST. JAMES
Post
St. James Shopping Centre

York Pl.

Broughton St.

EASTER RD.

MONTROSE

CALTON RD.

KEY

- - - Rail Line
Pedestrian-Friendly Area
Popular Shopping Area
- - - Footpath
■ Point of Interest/Landmark
i Tourist Information
Viewpoint

0   200 meters

0   200 yards

Rick Steves'

GREAT BRITAIN

2008

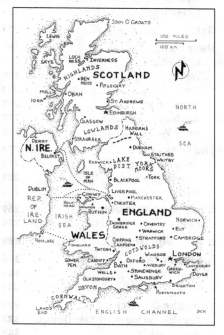

AVALON
TRAVEL

CONTENTS

Top Destinations in Great Britain

INTRODUCTION

Watch a world-class Shakespeare play, do the Beatles blitz in Liverpool, and walk along a windswept hill in the footsteps of Wordsworth. Climb cobblestone streets as you wander Edinburgh's Royal Mile. Try your tongue at a few Welsh phrases, taste "candy floss" by the beach, and enjoy evensong at Westminster Cathedral. Stroll through a cute-as-can-be Cotswold town and sail along the Thames past Big Ben. Great Britain has it all.

This book breaks Britain into its top big-city, small-town, and rural destinations. It gives you all of the information and opinions necessary to wring the maximum value out of your limited time and money in each of these locations. If you plan a month or less for Britain and have a normal appetite for information, this book is all you need. If you're a travel-info fiend, this book sorts through all the superlatives and provides a handy rack upon which to hang your supplemental information.

Experiencing British culture, people, and natural wonders economically and hassle-free has been my goal for three decades of traveling, tour guiding, and travel writing. With this new edition, I pass on to you the lessons I've learned, updated for your trip in 2008. Note that Northern Ireland—which is part of the UK—is covered in my book *Rick Steves' Ireland*.

While including the predictable biggies (such as Big Ben, Stratford-upon-Avon, and Stonehenge), the book also mixes in a healthy dose of Back Door intimacy (windswept Roman lookouts, angelic boys' choirs, and nearly edible Cotswold villages). I've been selective. For example, there are plenty of great countryside palaces; again, I recommend just the best—Blenheim.

The best is, of course, only my opinion. But after spending half of my adult life researching Europe, I've developed a sixth

Introduction

sense for what travelers enjoy. The places featured in this book will knock your spots off.

About This Book

Rick Steves' Great Britain 2008 is a personal tour guide in your pocket. This book is organized by destination, each one a mini-vacation on its own, filled with exciting sights and homey, affordable places to stay. In the following chapters, you'll find:

Planning Your Time, a suggested schedule with thoughts on how best to use your limited time.

Orientation includes tourist information, tips on public transportation, local tour options, helpful hints, and an easy-to-read map designed to make the text clear and your arrival smooth.

Self-Guided Walks take you through interesting neighborhoods, as if you had a local guide showing you around.

Sights provides a succinct overview of the most important sights, arranged by neighborhood, with ratings:

▲▲▲—Don't miss.

▲▲—Try hard to see.

▲—Worthwhile if you can make it.

No rating—Worth knowing about.

Sleeping describes my favorite hotels, from budget deals to splurges.

Eating serves up good-value restaurants, ranging from inexpensive pubs to fancier options.

Transportation Connections to nearby destinations by train, bus, and plane, and route tips for drivers.

The **appendix** is a traveler's tool kit, with a handy packing checklist, recommended books and films, instructions on how to use the telephone, useful phone numbers, and the procedure for dealing with lost credit cards. You'll also find a climate chart, festival list, hotel reservation form, and a fun British–Yankee vocabulary list.

Browse through this book and choose your must-see sights. Then have a brilliant trip! Traveling like a temporary local, you'll get the absolute most out of every mile, minute, and dollar. As you visit places I know and love, I'm happy you'll be meeting my favorite British people.

PLANNING

Trip Costs

Five components make up your trip cost: airfare, surface transportation, room and board, sightseeing and entertainment, and shopping and miscellany.

Airfare: A basic round-trip flight from the US to London costs

$800 to $1600 (even cheaper in winter), depending on where you fly from and when. If your trip extends beyond Great Britain, consider saving time and money by flying "open jaw" (into one city and out of another; for instance, into London and out of Edinburgh).

Surface Transportation: For a three-week whirlwind trip of all my recommended British destinations, allow $600 per person for public transportation (train pass and key buses) or $900 per person for car rental (based on two people sharing a three-week rental), including gas and insurance. Car rental is cheapest if arranged from the US. Train passes are normally available only outside of Europe (although you can buy a bus pass in Britain). You may save money by simply buying tickets as you go (see "Transportation," page 645).

Room and Board: You can manage well in Britain on an average of $120 per day per person for room and board (allow less for villages). A $120-per-day budget allows $15 for lunch, $20 for dinner, $5 for snacks and ale, and $80 for lodging (based on two people splitting a $160 double room that includes breakfast). Students and tightwads can do it on $50 ($35 for hostel bed, $15 for groceries).

Sightseeing and Entertainment: Figure on paying roughly $15–30 apiece for the major sights that charge admission (Stonehenge-$12, Shakespeare's Birthplace in Stratford-$14, Westminster Abbey-$20, Tower of London-$32), $4 for minor ones (climbing church towers), $12 for guided walks, and $30 for bus tours and splurge experiences (Welsh and Scottish folk evenings). For information on the various passes that are available for British sights, see page 17.

Fortunately, many of the best sights in London are free, including the British Museum, National Gallery, National Portrait Gallery, Tate Britain, Tate Modern, Victoria & Albert Museum, and the British Library (though they usually request donations). An overall average of $30 a day works for most. Don't skimp here. After all, this category is the driving force behind your trip—you came to sightsee, enjoy, and experience Britain.

Shopping and Miscellany: Figure roughly $2 per postcard, tea, or ice-cream cone, and $5 per pint of beer. Shopping can vary in cost from nearly nothing to a small fortune. Good budget travelers find that this category has little to do with assembling a trip full of lifelong and wonderful memories.

When to Go

For England and Wales, July and August are peak season—my favorite time—with very long days, the best weather, and the busiest schedule of tourist fun. For Scotland, the weather is best in May and June.

Britain's Best Three-Week Trip by Car

Day	Plan	Sleep in
1	Arrive in London, bus to Bath	Bath
2	Bath	Bath
3	Pick up car, Avebury, Wells, Glastonbury	Bath
4	South Wales, St. Fagans, Tintern	Chipping Campden
5	Explore the Cotswolds, Blenheim	Chipping Campden
6	Stratford, Warwick, Coventry	Ironbridge Gorge
7	Ironbridge Gorge, Ruthin banquet	Ruthin (if banquet) or Conwy
8	Highlights of North Wales	Ruthin or Conwy
9	Liverpool, Blackpool	Blackpool
10	South Lake District	Keswick area
11	North Lake District	Keswick area
12	Drive up west coast of Scotland	Oban
13	Highlands, Loch Ness, Scenic Highlands Drive	Edinburgh
14	Edinburgh	Edinburgh
15	Edinburgh	Edinburgh
16	Hadrian's Wall, Beamish, Durham's Cathedral and evensong	Durham
17	North York Moors, York, turn in car	York
18	York	York
19	Early train to London	London
20	London	London
21	London	London
22	Whew!	

While the three-week itinerary outlined above is designed to be done by car, it can be done by train and bus or, better yet, with a BritRail & Drive Pass (best car days: the Cotswolds, North Wales, Lake District, Scottish Highlands, Hadrian's Wall). For three weeks without a car, I'd probably cut back on the recommended sights with the most frustrating public transportation: South and North Wales, Ironbridge Gorge, and the Scottish Highlands. (Drivers can save a couple of days and a lot of miles by going directly from the Lake District to Edinburgh and skipping the long ride through the Highlands.) Lacing together the cities by train is very slick. With more time, everything is workable without a car.

Major Holidays and Weekends

Popular places are even busier on weekends...and inundated on three-day weekends, when hotels, trains, and buses can get booked up before, during, and after the actual holiday. Holidays can bring many businesses to a grinding halt. Plan ahead and reserve your accommodations and transportation well in advance.

A few national holidays jam things up, especially Bank Holiday Mondays. Mark these dates in red on your travel calendar: New Year's Day, Good Friday through Easter Monday (March 21–24 in 2008), the Bank Holidays that occur on the first and last Monday in May (May 5 and 26), the first Monday in August (Aug 4, Scotland only), the last Monday in August (Aug 25, England and Wales only), Christmas, and December 26 (Boxing Day).

Many businesses, as well as many museums, close on Good Friday, Easter, and New Year's Day. On Christmas, virtually everything closes down, even the Tube in London (taxi rates are high). Museums are also generally closed December 24 and 26.

Also check the list of festivals and holidays on page 658 of the appendix.

Prices and crowds don't go up during peak times as dramatically in Britain as they do in much of Europe, except for holidays and festivals (see "Major Holidays and Weekends" sidebar on this page). Shoulder-season travelers get minimal crowds, decent weather, the full range of sights and tourist fun spots, and the ability to grab a room almost whenever and wherever they like—often at a flexible price. Winter travelers find absolutely no crowds and soft room prices, but shorter sightseeing hours. Some attractions are open only on weekends or are closed entirely in the winter (Nov–Feb). The weather can be cold and dreary, and nightfall draws the shades on sightseeing well before dinnertime. While rural charm falls with the leaves, city sightseeing is fine in the winter.

Plan for rain no matter when you go. Just keep traveling and take full advantage of "bright spells." The weather can change several times in a day, but rarely is it extreme. As the locals say, "There is no bad weather, only inappropriate clothing." Bring a jacket and dress in layers. Temperatures below 32°F cause headlines, and days that break 80°F—while increasing in recent years—are still rare. (For more information, see the climate chart in the appendix.) July and August are not much better than shoulder months. May and June can be lovely anywhere in Britain. While

Get It Right

Americans tend to use "England," "Britain," and "UK" interchangeably, but they're not the same:

- **England** is in the southeast part of Britain.
- **Britain** is the name of the island.
- **Great Britain** is the political union of England, Scotland, and Wales.
- The **United Kingdom** adds Northern Ireland.
- The **British Isles** (not a political entity) also includes the independent Republic of Ireland.
- The **British Commonwealth** is a loose association of possessions and former colonies (including Canada, Australia, and India) that profess at least symbolic loyalty to the Crown.

sunshine may be rare, summer days are very long. The summer sun is up from 6:30 until 22:30. It's not uncommon to have a gray day, eat dinner, and enjoy hours of sunshine afterward.

Sightseeing Priorities

Depending on the length of your trip, here are my recommended priorities:

3 days:	London
5 days, add:	Bath, Cotswolds
7 days, add:	York
9 days, add:	Edinburgh
11 days, add:	Stratford, Warwick, Blenheim
14 days, add:	North Wales, Wells/Glastonbury/Avebury
17 days, add:	Lake District, Hadrian's Wall, Durham
21 days, add:	Ironbridge Gorge, Blackpool, Scottish Highlands
24 days, add:	Choose two destinations among the following—St. Andrews, Glasgow, Cambridge, South Wales

(This includes virtually everything on the "Britain's Best Three-Week Trip by Car" itinerary and map on pages 4 and 5, respectively.)

Travel Smart

Your trip to Britain is like a complex play—easier to follow and to really appreciate on a second viewing. While no one does the same trip twice to gain that advantage, reading this book in its entirety before your trip accomplishes much the same thing. Reread it as you travel. London's British Museum is much more entertaining, for instance, if you've boned up on mummies the night before.

Most people fly into London and remain there for a few days.

Know Before You Go

Your trip is more likely to go smoothly if you plan ahead.

Since **airline carry-on restrictions** are always changing, visit the Transportation Security Administration's website (www.tsa.gov/travelers) for an up-to-date list of what you can bring on the plane with you...and what you have to check. Remember to arrive with plenty of time to get through security. When leaving Britain, you're allowed only one carry-on (no extras such as a purse or backpack); check Britain's website for the latest (www.dft.gov.uk).

Call your **debit and credit card companies** to let them know the countries you'll be visiting, so that they'll accept (and not deny) your international charges. Confirm what your daily withdrawal limit is; consider asking to have it raised so you can take out more cash at each ATM stop.

Be sure that your **passport** is valid at least six months after your ticketed date of return to the US. If you need to get or renew a passport, it can take up to three months (for more on passports, see www.travel.state.gov).

Book your rooms well in advance if you'll be traveling during any major **holidays** (see "Major Holidays and Weekends," page 6). In general, it's smart to reserve rooms in peak season (particularly for B&Bs in June, July, and August), and definitely for your first night.

If you're planning on **renting a car** in Great Britain, it's recom-

Instead, consider a gentler small-town start in Bath (the ideal jet-lag pillow), and let London be the finale at the end of your trip, when you'll be more rested and ready to tackle Britain's greatest city. Heathrow Airport has direct bus connections to Bath and other cities. (Bristol Airport is also near Bath.)

Design an itinerary that enables you to visit the various sights at the best possible times. As you read this book, make note of festivals, colorful market days, and days when sights are closed. Treat Saturday as a weekday, except for transportation connections outside of London (which can be less frequent than on Mon–Fri, and downright meager on Sun). Be aware of upcoming holidays that could affect your trip (see page 6). Sights normally closed on Monday are often open on Bank Holiday Mondays. Popular destinations attract more crowds on weekends, especially sunny weekends, which are sufficient cause for an impromptu holiday in this soggy corner of Europe.

To give yourself a little rootedness, minimize one-night stands. It's worth a long drive after dinner to be settled into a town for two nights. B&Bs are also more likely to give a better price to

mended—though not required—that you carry an International Driver's Permit (available at your local AAA office for $15 plus two passport photos; www.aaa.com). Confirm pick-up hours—many car-rental offices close Saturday afternoon and all day Sunday.

If you'll be in London or Stratford and want to **see a play,** check theater schedules ahead of time. For simplicity, I book plays while in Britain, but if there's something you have to see, consider buying tickets before you go. For the current schedule of London plays and musicals, visit www.officiallondontheatre.co.uk. For Stratford, check www.rsc.org.uk (even though Stratford's major Shakespeare theaters are closed for renovation, the town will still host productions by the Bard in 2008).

To attend the **Edinburgh Festival** (Aug 8–31 in 2008), you can book tickets in advance (for details, see page 487).

If you want to **golf at St. Andrews' famous Old Course,** reserve a year ahead, or for other courses, reserve at least two weeks ahead. You can also try for a tee time when you arrive, but to play the Old Course, you'll need a golf handicap certificate (see page 514).

If you want to attend the pageantry-filled **Ceremony of the Keys** in the Tower of London, write for tickets (see page 94).

If you'll be **day-tripping to Paris** on the Eurostar train, consider ordering a ticket in advance (or buy it in Britain); for details, see "Crossing the Channel," page 150.

someone staying more than one night.

Be sure to mix intense and relaxed periods in your itinerary. Every trip (and every traveler) needs at least a few slack days. Pace yourself. Assume you will return.

Reread this book as you travel, and visit local tourist information offices. Upon arrival in a new town, lay the groundwork for a smooth departure; write down the schedule for the train or bus you'll take when you depart.

Plan ahead for laundry, picnics, and Internet stops. Get online at Internet cafés or your hotel to research transportation connections, confirm events, check the weather, and get directions to your next hotel. Use the phone to make reservations, reconfirm hotels, book tours, and double-check hours of sights.

Connect with the culture. You speak the language—use it! Slow down and ask questions—most locals are eager to point you in their idea of the right direction. Keep a notepad in your pocket for organizing your thoughts. Wear your money belt, and learn the local currency and how to estimate prices in dollars. Those who expect to travel smart, do.

Britain Almanac

Official Name: The United Kingdom of Great Britain and Northern Ireland (locals say "the UK" or "Britain").

Population: Britain's 60 million people (nearly twice that of California) are a mix of Celtic DNA, plus about 3 percent recent immigrants, largely from India, Pakistan, and Eastern Europe. Seven in 10 British call themselves Christian (half of those are Anglican), but in any given week, more Brits visit a mosque than an Anglican church.

Latitude and Longitude: 54°N and 2°W. The latitude is similar to Alberta, Canada. Britain sits a mere 21 miles northwest of France.

Area: From "Britannia's" 19th-century peak of power, when it dominated much of the globe, the British Empire lost colonies and fought two world wars, shrinking to a quarter of its former size. Today, this nation is 95,000 square miles (about the size of Oregon or Michigan). It's comprised of one large island, a chunk of another large island, and many small ones.

Geography: Most of the British isles consist of low hills and rolling plains. The climate is generally moderate; about every other day, the TV weather channel shows clouds blowing in from the southwest. The country's highest point is 4,400-foot Ben Nevis in western Scotland. Britain's longest river, the Severn, loops 220 miles from the mountains of Wales east into England, then south to the Bristol Channel. The Thames River runs 215 miles east–west through the heart of southern England (including London).

Biggest Cities: London is the capital, with 8.5 million people. Industrial Birmingham has 2.6 million, Glasgow has 2.1 million, and the port of Liverpool has 500,000.

Economy: The Gross Domestic Product is $1.9 trillion (slightly more than California), and the GDP per capita is $31,800. Money-makers include banking and insurance, meat-and-potatoes

PRACTICALITIES

Red Tape: You need a passport—but no visa or shots—to travel in Britain. It must be valid for at least six months beyond the time you leave Britain. Pack a photocopy of your passport in your luggage in case the original is lost or stolen.

Time: In Britain—and in this book—you'll use the 24-hour clock. It's the same through 12:00 noon, then keep going: 13:00, 14:00, and so on. For anything over 12, subtract 12 and add p.m. (14:00 is 2:00 p.m.).

Britain is one hour earlier than most of continental Europe. It's also five/eight hours ahead of the East/West Coasts of the US;

farming, shipping, trade with the US and Germany, and energy production. Heavy industry—the engine that once drove the Industrial Revolution—is now in decline. The economy and pound sterling are strong, and most Brits oppose joining the euro monetary system. The military commitment in Iraq has pinched government spending on social services, while one in six Brits lives in poverty.

Government: Queen Elizabeth II officially heads the country, but in practice it's Prime Minister Gordon Brown who leads the majority party in Parliament. The British House of Commons has 659 seats. (The upper-house House of Lords is now a mere advisory body.) Britain's traditional two-party system—Labour and Conservatives ("Tories")—now has a smaller third player, the Liberal Democrats. Britain is a member of the European Union (but not the euro system) and is one of the five permanent members (with veto power) of the UN Security Council. In 1999, Scotland, Wales, and Northern Ireland were granted their own parliament.

Flag: The "Union Jack" combines two red crosses on a field of blue: the English cross of St. George and the X-like Scottish cross of St. Andrew.

The Average Brit: Eats 35 pounds of pizza and 35 pounds of chocolate a year, and weighs 12 stone (170 pounds). He or she is 39 years old, has 1.66 children, and will live to age 78. He/she drinks 2.5 cups of tea a day and 2.5 glasses of wine a week (Americans drink less than half that). He/she works a month more each year than the average German, has free healthcare, and gets 23 vacation days a year (versus 12 in the US and 39 in France). He/she sleeps 7.5 hours a night, and throws out 1,500 pounds of trash a year. The average Brit speaks one language and, when quizzed, can name three of the seven continents.

the exceptions are the beginning and end of Daylight Saving Time. Britain and Europe "spring forward" the last Sunday in March (two weeks after most of North America), and "fall back" the last Sunday in October (one week before North America). For a handy online time converter, try www.timeanddate.com/worldclock.

Business Hours: Most stores throughout Britain are open Monday through Saturday from roughly 10:00–18:00. In London, stores stay open later on Wednesday or Thursday (until 19:00 or 20:00), depending on the neighborhood. On Sunday, when some stores are closed, street markets in London are lively with shoppers.

Watt's Up? Britain's electrical system is different from North America's in two important ways: the shape of the plug (three

Just the FAQs, Please

Whom do I call in case of emergency?
Dial 999 for police or medical emergencies.

What if my credit card is stolen?
Act immediately. See "Damage Control for Lost Cards," page 635, for instructions.

How do I make a phone call to, within, and from Great Britain?
For detailed dialing instructions, refer to page 642.

How can I get tourist information about my destination?
Britain has a national tourist information office in the US (see page 627), an excellent office in London (see page 44), and offices in virtually every destination covered in this book. Note that Tourist Information is abbreviated **TI** in this book.

What's the best way to pack?
Light. For a recommended packing list, see page 665.

Does Rick have other resources that could help me?
For more on Rick's guidebooks, public television series, free audio tours, public radio show, website, guided tours, travel bags, accessories, and railpasses, see page 627.

Are there any updates to this guidebook?
Check www.ricksteves.com/update for changes to the most recent edition of this book.

Can you recommend any good books or movies for my trip?
For suggestions, see pages 630–631.

square prongs—not the two round prongs used in continental Europe) and the voltage of the current (220 volts instead of 110 volts). For your North American plug to work in Britain, you'll need a three-prong adapter plug, sold inexpensively at travel stores in the US. As for the voltage, most newer electronics or travel appliances (such as hair dryers, laptops, and battery chargers) automatically convert the voltage—if you see a range of voltages printed on the item or its plug (such as "110–220"), it'll work in Great Britain and Europe. Otherwise, you can buy a converter separately in the US (about $20).

News: Americans keep in touch via the *International Herald*

Do you have information on driving, train travel, and flights?
See page 645 of the appendix.

How much do I tip?
Relatively little. For tips on tipping, see page 635.

Will I get a student or senior discount?
While discounts (called "concessions" in Britain) are not listed in this book, many British sights are discounted for seniors (loosely defined as those who are retired or willing to call themselves a senior), youths (ages 8–18), students, groups of 10 or more, and families.

You might see a "Gift Aid" admission price listed at sights. British taxpayers can choose to pay this slightly inflated admission price and then take a tax deduction (which US tourists are not eligible for).

How can I get a VAT refund on major purchases?
See the details on page 636.

Does Britain use the metric system?
Britain uses a mix of the metric system and "our" system (which they call "Imperial"). Weight and volume are typically calculated in metric: A kilogram is 2.2 pounds and a liter is about a quart. The weight of a person is measured in "stone" (one stone equals 14 pounds). On the road, Brits use miles instead of kilometers. Temperatures are generally given in both Celsius and Fahrenheit. For more metric conversions, see page 661.

Tribune (published almost daily via satellite throughout Europe). Every Tuesday, the European editions of *Time* and *Newsweek* hit the stands with articles of particular interest to travelers. Sports addicts can get their daily fix online or from *USA Today*. Good websites include http://news.bbc.co.uk and www.europeantimes .com. Many hotels have BBC (of course) and CNN television channels.

MONEY

Banking

Throughout Europe, cash machines (ATMs) are the standard way for travelers to get local currency. Bring plastic—credit and/or debit cards—along with several hundred dollars in hard cash as an emergency backup. It's smart to bring two cards, in case one gets demagnetized or eaten by a temperamental machine. Traveler's checks are a waste of time (long waits at slow banks) and a waste of money (in fees).

Cash from ATMs

To use a cash machine to withdraw money from your account, you'll need a debit card (ideally with a Visa or MasterCard logo for maximum usability), plus a PIN code. Know your PIN code in numbers; there are only numbers—no letters—on European keypads.

Before you go, verify with your bank that your card will work overseas, and alert them that you'll be making withdrawals in Europe; otherwise, the bank may not approve transactions if it perceives unusual spending patterns.

Try to take out large sums of money to reduce your per-transaction bank fees. If the machine refuses your request, try again and select a smaller amount.

Even in jolly olde England, you'll need to keep your cash safe. Use a money belt—a pouch with a strap that you buckle around your waist like a belt, and wear under your clothes. Thieves target tourists. A money belt provides peace of mind, allowing you to carry lots of cash safely. Don't waste time every few days tracking down a cash machine—withdraw a week's worth of money, stuff it in your money belt, and travel!

Credit and Debit Cards

For purchases, Visa and MasterCard are more commonly accepted than American Express. Just like at home, credit or debit cards work easily at larger hotels, restaurants, and shops, but smaller businesses prefer payment in local currency (in small bills—break large bills at a bank or larger store).

Credit and debit cards—whether used for purchases or ATM withdrawals—often come with additional, tacked-on "international transaction" fees of up to 3 percent plus $5 per transaction. To avoid unpleasant surprises, call your bank or credit-card company before your trip to ask about these fees.

Using a new scheme called "dynamic currency conversion," some merchants might charge you in dollars for credit-card transactions—but they set their own exchange rate, which is almost always a much worse deal than if you simply pay in pounds. According to Visa, you have the right to decline this "service" and be charged in pounds.

Recently the British began using debit cards with embedded "smart chips." You may see signs or keypads referring to this technology, called "Chip and PIN." British cardholders must enter a

Exchange Rate

I list prices in pounds (£) throughout this book.

1 British pound (£1) = about $2

While the euro (€) is now the currency of most of Europe, Britain is sticking with its pound sterling. The British pound (£), also called a "quid," is broken into 100 pence (p). Pence means "cents." You'll find coins ranging from 1p to £2 and bills from £5 to £50.

London is so expensive that some travelers try to kid themselves that pounds are dollars. But when they get home, that £1,000-pound Visa bill isn't asking for $1,000...it wants $2,000. To avoid this shock, double British prices to estimate dollars.

Scotland and Northern Ireland issue their own currency in pounds, worth the same as an English pound. English, Scottish, and Northern Ireland's Ulster pounds are technically interchangeable in each region, although Scottish and Ulster pounds are "undesirable" in England. Banks in any of the three regions will convert your Scottish or Ulster pounds into English pounds for no charge. Don't worry about the coins, which are accepted throughout Britain.

PIN in order to use these chip-embedded cards in retail stores. In most cases, you can still use your credit or debit card at the cashier and sign the receipt the old-fashioned way. One exception is that US credit or debit cards often don't work at automated machines (such as ticket machines in a train or Tube station, or a pay-at-the-pump gas station). But in most of these situations, there's a cashier nearby who can take your credit or debit card and make it work.

If your cards are lost or stolen, see page 635 for advice on what to do.

SIGHTSEEING

Sightseeing can be hard work. Use these tips to make your visits to Britain's finest sights meaningful, fun, fast, and painless.

Plan Ahead

Set up an itinerary that allows you to fit in all your must-see sights. Most sights keep stable hours, but you can easily confirm the latest by checking with the local TI.

Don't put off visiting a must-see sight—you never know when a place will close unexpectedly for a holiday, strike, or restoration.

If you'll be visiting during a holiday, find out if a particular sight will be open by phoning ahead or visiting its website.

When possible, visit key museums first thing (when your energy is high) and save other activities for the afternoon. Hit the highlights first, then go back to other things if you have the stamina and time.

Depending on the sight, there are ways to avoid crowds. This book offers tips on specific sights. Try visiting very early, at lunch, or very late. Evening visits are usually peaceful, with fewer crowds. For specifics on London, see "London for Early Birds and Night Owls" on page 78.

At the Sight

All sights have rules, and if you know about these in advance, they're no big deal.

Some important sights have metal detectors or conduct bag searches that will slow your entry.

Most museums require you to check daypacks and coats. They'll be kept safely. If you have something you can't bear to part with, stash it in a pocket or purse. If you don't want to check a small backpack, carry it under your arm like a purse as you enter... and hope the guards don't notice.

Cameras are normally allowed, but not flashes or tripods (without special permission). Flashes damage oil paintings and distract others in the room. Even without a flash, a handheld camera will take a decent picture (or buy postcards or posters at the museum bookstore). Video cameras are usually allowed.

Some museums have special exhibits in addition to their permanent collection. Some exhibits are included in the entry price, while others come at an extra cost (which you may have to pay even if you don't want to see the exhibit).

Many sights rent audioguides, which generally offer excellent recorded descriptions of the art (about £3.50). If you bring along your own pair of headphones and a Y-jack, two people can sometimes share one audioguide and save. Guided tours (usually £4 and widely ranging in quality) are most likely to occur during peak season.

Expect changes—paintings can be on tour, on loan, out sick, or shifted at the whim of the curator. To adapt, pick up any available free floor plans as you enter, and ask museum staff if you can't find a particular painting.

Most important sights have an on-site café or cafeteria (usually a good place to rest and have a snack or light meal). The WCs are free and generally clean.

Museums have bookstores selling postcards and souvenirs. Before you leave, scan the postcards and thumb through the biggest guidebook (or skim its index) to be sure you haven't overlooked something that you'd like to see.

Most sights stop admitting people 30–60 minutes before closing time, and some rooms close early (generally about 45 minutes before the actual closing time). Guards usher people out, so don't save the best for last.

Every sight or museum offers more than what is covered in this book. Use the information in this book as an introduction—not the final word.

Sightseeing Pass and Memberships

Many sights in Britain are covered by the Great British Heritage Pass or these memberships: English Heritage or National Trust. If you're a whirlwind sightseer, seriously consider the Great British Heritage Pass, which covers the most sights.

The Great British Heritage Pass: The best deal for most travelers, this pass covers all of the major English Heritage and National Trust sights, plus many others (including several major attractions in Scotland, Wales, and Northern Ireland). Covering about 600 historic sights, this pass is good for a certain number of consecutive days (£28 for 4 days, £39 for 7 days, £52 for 15 days, £70 for 30 days; £62/£86/£114/£154 family pass also available for up to 2 adults and 3 kids aged 5–15, though note that kids already get discounts at sights; for more information, call 0870-242-9988 or see www.britishheritagepass.com). You can buy this pass online (£6.50 extra for shipping) or at about 50 tourist information centers in Britain; for example, in London, this pass is sold by the Britain and London Visitors Centre on Lower Regent Street. Although the pass is a good deal, note that it doesn't cover many sights in London and isn't worthwhile for a London-only trip.

Memberships: Many sights in Britain are managed by either the English Heritage or the National Trust. Both sell annual memberships that allow free or discounted entry to the sights they supervise (which don't overlap). You can become a member of the National Trust or English Heritage online (see websites below), or at just about any of their sights.

Membership in **English Heritage** includes free entry to over 400 sights in England, and half-price admission to about 100 more sights in Scotland and Wales (£40 for one person, £69 for two people, good for one year; senior, student, and couple discounts; children under 19 free, tel. 0870-333-1182, www.english-heritage .org.uk/membership).

Membership in the **National Trust** is best suited for garden-and-estate enthusiasts, ideally traveling by car. It covers more than 300 historic houses, manors, and gardens throughout Great Britain (£43.50 for one year, student and couple discounts, children under 5 free, www.nationaltrust.org.uk).

The Bottom Line: These deals can save a busy sightseer money...but only if you choose carefully. Make a list of the sights you plan to see, check which sights are covered (visit the websites listed above), and then add up the total if you paid admission to the covered sights. Compare the total to the cost of the pass or membership. Keep in mind that an advantage to any of these deals is that you'll feel free to dip into lesser sights that normally wouldn't merit paying admission.

Fine Points: If you have children, consider the Great British Heritage family pass if you're all avid sightseeers; otherwise don't get a pass or membership for them, because they get in free or cheap at most sights. Similarly, people over 60 also get "concessions" (discounted prices) at many English sights (and can get a senior discount on an English Heritage membership). If you're traveling by car and can get to the more remote sights, you're more likely to get your money's worth out of a pass or membership, especially during peak season (Easter–Oct). If you're traveling off-season (Nov–Easter) when many of the sights are closed, these deals are a lesser value.

SLEEPING

I favor accommodations (and restaurants) handy to your sightseeing activities. Rather than list hotels scattered throughout a city, I choose two or three favorite neighborhoods and recommend the best accommodations values in each, from $20 bunk beds to fancy-for-my-book $300 doubles. Outside of London, you can expect to find good doubles for $80–180, including breakfast and tax. (For specifics on London, see page 115.)

I look for places that are friendly; clean; a good value; located in a central, safe, quiet neighborhood; and not mentioned in other guidebooks. I'm more impressed by a handy location and a fun-loving philosophy than hair dryers and shoeshine machines.

Hearty British or generous buffet breakfasts are included unless otherwise noted, and TVs are standard in rooms, but may come with only the traditional four British channels (no cable).

I've described my recommended accommodations using a Sleep Code (see sidebar). Prices listed are for one-night stays in peak season and assume you're booking directly and not through a TI. Official "rack rates" (the highest rates a hotel charges) can be misleading, since they often omit cheaper oddball rooms and special clearance deals. (Some fancy £120 rooms can rent for a third off if you arrive late on a slow day and ask for a deal.) Always mention that you found the place through this book—many of the hotels listed offer special deals to our readers.

When establishing prices with a hotelier or B&B owner,

Sleep Code

(£1 = about $2, country code: 44)

To help you easily sort through these listings, I've divided the rooms into three categories, based on the price for a double room with bath:

$$$ **Higher Priced**
$$ **Moderately Priced**
$ **Lower Priced**

To give maximum information in a minimum of space, I use this code to describe accommodations listed in this book. Prices in this book are listed per room, not per person. Unless otherwise noted, credit cards are accepted and breakfast is included.

S = Single room, or price for one person in a double.

D = Double or twin room. (I specify double- and twin-bed rooms only if they are priced differently, or if a place has only one or the other. When reserving, you should specify.)

T = Three-person room (often a double bed with a single).

Q = Four-person room (adding an extra child's bed to a T is usually cheaper).

b = Private bathroom with toilet and shower or tub.

s = Private shower or tub only. (The toilet is down the hall.)

According to this code, a couple staying at a "Db-£80, cash only" hotel would pay a total of £80 (about $160) per night for a room with a private toilet and shower (or tub). This hotel does not accept credit cards—cash only.

confirm if the charge is per person or per room (if a price is too good to be true, it's probably per person). Because many places in Britain charge per person, small groups often pay the same for a single and

a double as they would for a triple. Note: In this book, room prices are listed per room, not per person.

"Twin" means two single beds, and "double" means one double bed. If you'll take either one, let them know, or you might be needlessly turned away. Most hotels offer family deals, which means that parents with young children can easily get a room with an extra child's bed or a discount for larger rooms. Call to negotiate the price. Teenage kids are generally charged as adults. Kids under five sleep almost free.

Smoke-Free Great Britain

Britain's public places are now smoke-free. Hotels, B&Bs, and restaurants are required to be non-smoking (though hoteliers are permitted to designate specific rooms for smokers). While it's too early to know how successfully this ban will be implemented, an earlier ban in Scotland has been rigidly enforced. In the "Sleeping" sections of each chapter, I've listed the rare instance where a hotel has smoking rooms—but for the most part, the smoke truly is clearing in Britain.

Many places listed have three floors of rooms and steep stairs; expect good exercise and be happy you packed light. Elevators are rare except in the larger hotels. If you're concerned about stairs, call and ask about ground-floor rooms or pay for a hotel with a lift (elevator).

Be careful of the terminology: An "en suite" room has a bathroom (toilet and shower/tub) actually inside the room; a room with a "private bathroom" can mean that the bathroom is all yours, but it's across the hall; and a "standard" room has access to a bathroom down the hall that's shared with other rooms. Figuring there's little difference between "en suite" and "private" rooms, some places charge the same for both. If you want your own bathroom inside the room, request "en suite."

If money's tight, ask for a standard room. You'll almost always have a sink in your room. And, as more rooms go "en suite," the hallway bathroom is shared with fewer standard rooms.

Note that to be called a "hotel," a place technically must have certain amenities, including a 24-hour reception (though this rule is loosely applied). A place called "townhouse" or "house" (such as "London House") is like a big B&B or a small family-run hotel—with fewer amenities but more character than a "hotel."

Britain has a rating system for hotels and B&Bs. These diamonds and stars are supposed to imply quality, but I find that they mean only that the place sporting these symbols is paying dues to the tourist board. Rating systems often have little to do with value.

If you're traveling beyond my recommended destinations, you'll find accommodations where you need them. Any town with tourists has a TI that books rooms or can give you a list and point you in the right direction. In the absence of a TI, ask people on the street or in pubs or restaurants for help. Online, visit www.smoothhound.co.uk, which offers a range of accommodations for towns throughout the UK (searchable by town, airport, hotel name, or price range).

B&Bs

Staying in B&Bs can be a great way to save money over sleeping in a bigger (and more expensive) hotel. B&Bs range from large guest houses with 15–20 rooms to small homes renting out a spare bedroom, but they typically have six rooms or fewer. The philosophy of the management determines the character of a place more than its size and facilities. I avoid places run as businesses by absentee owners. My top listings are run by people who enjoy welcoming the world to their breakfast tables.

If you have a reasonable but limited budget, skip hotels and go the B&B way. If you can use a telephone and speak English, you'll enjoy homey, friendly, clean rooms at a great price by sticking to my listings. Always call first.

B&Bs come with their own etiquette and quirks. Keep in mind that B&B owners are at the whim of their guests—if you're getting up early, so are they; and if you check in late, they'll wait up for you. It's polite to call ahead to confirm your reservation the day before, and to give them a rough estimate of your arrival time. This allows them to plan their day and run errands before or after you arrive...and also allows them to give you specific directions for driving or walking to their place.

A few tips: B&B proprietors are selective as to whom they invite in for the night. At some B&Bs, children are not welcome. Risky-looking people (two or more single men are often assumed to be troublemakers) find many places suddenly full. If you'll be staying for more than one night you are a "desirable." In popular weekend-getaway spots, you're unlikely to find a place to take you for Saturday night only. If my listings are full, ask for guidance. (Mentioning this book can help.) Owners usually work together and can call up an ally to land you a bed.

B&Bs serve a hearty "English fry" breakfast (for more about B&B breakfasts, see page 26). You'll figure out quickly which parts of the "fry" you like and don't like. B&B owners prefer to know this up front, rather than serve you the whole shebang and have to throw out uneaten food. Because your B&B owner is also the cook, there's usually a quite limited time span when breakfast is served (typically about an hour, starting usually around 8:00). It's an unwritten rule that guests shouldn't show up at the very end of the breakfast period and expect a full cooked breakfast—instead, aim to arrive at least 10 minutes before breakfast ends. If you do arrive late (or if you need to leave before breakfast is served), most B&B hosts are happy to let you help yourself to cereal, fruit, and coffee; ask politely if it's possible.

B&Bs are not hotels: If you want to ruin your relationship with your hostess, treat her like a hotel clerk. Americans often assume they'll get new towels each day. The British don't, and neither will you. Hang them up to dry and reuse.

In almost every B&B, you'll encounter unusual bathroom fixtures. The "pump toilet" has a flushing handle that doesn't kick in unless you push it just right: too hard or too soft, and it won't go. Be decisive but not ruthless. There's also the "dial-a-shower," an electronic box under the shower head where you'll turn a dial to select the heat of the water, and (sometimes with a separate dial or button) turn on or shut off the flow of water. Virtually all rooms have sinks.

Some B&Bs stock rooms with a hot-water pot, cups, tea bags, and coffee packets (if you prefer decaf, buy a jar at a grocery, and dump into a baggie for easy packing). Electrical outlets sometimes come with switches on the outlet to turn the current on or off; if your electrical appliance isn't working, flip the switch.

Most B&Bs come with thin walls and doors. This, combined with people walking down the hall to use the bathroom, can make for a noisy night. If you're a light sleeper, bring earplugs. And please be quiet in the halls and in your rooms (talk softly, and keep the TV volume low)...those of us getting up early will thank you for it.

Your B&B bedroom generally won't include a phone. In the mobile-phone age, street phone booths can be few and far between. Some B&B owners will allow you to use their phone (with an international phone card), but many are disinclined to let you ring up charges. If you must use their phone, show them your calling card and keep the call short (5-10 minutes max). If you plan to be staying in B&Bs and making frequent calls, consider buying a British mobile phone (see page 638).

Many B&B owners are also pet owners. And, while pets are rarely allowed into guest rooms, and B&B proprietors are typically very tidy, those with pet allergies might be bothered. I've tried to list which B&Bs have pets, but if you're allergic, ask about pets when you reserve.

Making Reservations

Given the quality of the gems I've found for this book, I'd recommend that you reserve your rooms in advance, particularly if you'll be traveling during peak season. Book several weeks ahead, or as soon as you've pinned down your travel dates. Note that some national holidays merit your making reservations far in advance (see "Major Holidays and Weekends" on page 6). Just like at home, Monday holidays are preceded by busy weekends, so book the entire weekend in advance.

Some travelers make reservations as they travel, calling hotels or B&Bs a few days to a week before their visit. If you prefer the flexibility of traveling without any reservations at all, you'll have greater success snaring rooms if you arrive at your destination early in the day. When you anticipate crowds, call hotels around 9:00 on the day you plan to arrive, when the hotel clerk knows who'll be checking out and just which rooms will be available.

To make a reservation in advance, contact hotels directly by email, phone, or fax. Email is the clearest and most economical way to make a reservation. In addition, many hotel websites now have online reservation forms. If phoning from the US, be mindful of time zones (see page 10). To ensure you have all the information you need for your reservation, use the form in this book's appendix (also at www.ricksteves.com/reservation). If you don't get a reply to your email or fax, it usually means the hotel is already fully booked.

When you request a room for a certain time period, use the European style for writing dates: day/month/year. Hoteliers need to know your arrival and departure dates. For example, a two-night stay in July would be "2 nights, 16/07/08 to 18/07/08." Consider in advance how long you'll stay; don't just assume you can extend your reservation for extra days once you arrive.

If the response from the hotel gives its room availability and rates, it's not a confirmation. You must tell them that you want that room at the given rate.

The hotelier will sometimes request your credit-card number for a one-night deposit. While you can email your credit-card information (I do), it's safer to share that personal info via phone call, fax, or secure online reservation form (if the hotel has one on its website).

If you must cancel your reservation, it's courteous to do so with as much advance notice as possible (simply make a quick phone call or send an email). Family-run hotels and B&Bs lose money if they turn away customers while holding a room for someone who doesn't show up. Understandably, some hoteliers bill no-shows for one night. Hotels in larger cities such as London sometimes have strict cancellation policies (for example, you might lose a deposit if you cancel within two weeks of your reserved stay, or you might be billed for the entire visit if you leave early); ask about cancellation policies before you book.

Always reconfirm your room reservation a few days in advance from the road. Most places will hold a room until 16:00, but if you'll be arriving later, let them know.

On the small chance that a hotel loses track of your reservation, bring along a hard copy of their emailed or faxed confirmation.

Most TIs in Britain can book you a room in their town, and also often in nearby towns. Most often, they charge a £3 fee, and you'll pay a 10 percent "deposit" at the TI and the rest at the B&B

Introduction

(meaning that both you and the B&B pay extra). While this can be useful in a pinch, it's a better deal for everyone (except the TIs) to book direct, using the listings in this book. Also, don't have the tourist office reconfirm rooms for you; they'll take a commission.

Looking for Hotel Deals Online

Given the high hotel prices and relatively weak dollar, consider turning to the Internet to help score a hotel deal. Various websites list rooms in high-rise, three- and four-star business hotels. You'll give up the charm and warmth of a family-run establishment, and breakfast will probably not be included, but you might find the price is right.

Auction-type sites (such as www.priceline.com) can be great for matching flexible travelers with empty hotel rooms, often at prices well below the hotel's normal rates. Don't feel you have to start as high as the site's suggested opening bid. (For more about the complicated world of online bidding strategies and success stories from other travelers, see www.biddingfortravel.com or www.betterbidding.com.) Warning: Scoring a deal this way may require more patience and flexibility than you have, but if you enjoy shopping for cars, you'll probably like this, too.

Check the "Graffiti Wall" at www.ricksteves.com/graffiti for the latest tips and discoveries. For recommendations on online hotel deals in London, see page 116.

Big, Cheap, Modern Hotels

Hotel chains—popular with budget tour groups—offer predictably comfortable, no-frills accommodations at reasonable prices. These hotels are popping up in big cities in Britain. Some are located near the train station, on major arterials, and outside the city center. What you lose in charm, you gain in savings.

These hotels are ideal for families, offering simple, clean, and modern rooms for up to four people (two adults/two children) for £60–90, depending on the location. Note that couples or families (up to four) pay the same price for a room. Most rooms have a double bed, single bed, five-foot trundle bed, private shower, WC, and TV. Hotels usually have an attached restaurant, good security, an elevator, and a 24-hour staffed reception desk. Of course, they're as cozy as a Motel 6, but many travelers love them. You can book over the phone (or online) with a credit card, then pay when you check in. When you check out, just drop off the key, Lee.

If you choose to stay in these, book through their websites, as the room rates are often dramatically less for online bookings. The biggies are Travelodge (reservations tel. 0870-085-0950, www.travelodge.co.uk) and Premier Travel Inn (reservations tel. 0870-242-8000, www.premiertravelinn.co.uk). The Irish chain

Jurys Inn also has some hotels in Britain (book online at www .jurys.com).

Couples could also consider Holiday Inn Express, spreading throughout Britain. These are like a Holiday Inn Lite, with cheaper prices and no restaurant. Many of their hotels allow only two people per room, but some take up to four (doubles cost about £60–100, make sure Express is part of the name or you'll pay more for a regular Holiday Inn, reservations tel. 0870-400-9670, www .hiexpress.co.uk).

Hostels

If you're traveling alone, hosteling is the best way to conquer hotel loneliness. Hostels are also a tremendous source of local and budget travel information. You'll pay an average of £15–18 for a bed and £3 for breakfast. Anyone of any age can hostel in Britain. While there are no membership concerns for private hostels, International Youth Hostel Federation (IYHF) hostels require membership. Those without cards simply buy one-night guest memberships for £3.

Britain has hundreds of hostels of all shapes and sizes. Choose your hostel selectively. Hostels can be historic castles or depressing tenements, serene and comfy or overrun by noisy school groups. Unfortunately, many of the IYHF hostels have become overpriced and, in general, I no longer recommend them. The only time I do is if you're on a very tight budget, want to cook your own meals, or are traveling with a group that likes to sleep on bunk beds in big rooms. But many of the informal private hostels are more fun, easygoing, and cheaper. These alternatives to the IYHF hostels are more common than ever, and allow you to enjoy the benefits of hosteling. Good listings are plentiful at Hostels of Europe (www .hostelseurope.com) and Hostels.com, and you can also book online for many places (for London: www.hostellondon.com; for England and Wales: www.yha.org.uk; and for Scotland: www .hostel-scotland.co.uk).

EATING

Britain's reputation for miserable food is now dated, and the British cuisine scene is lively, trendy, and pleasantly surprising. (Unfortunately, it's also expensive.) Even the basic, traditional pub grub has gone "up market," and you'll generally find fresh vegetables rather than soggy fries and mushy peas.

All British eateries are now smoke-free. Restaurants and pubs that sell food are non-smoking indoors; establishments keep their smokers contented by allowing them to light up in doorways and on outdoor patios.

The Great British Breakfast

The traditional "fry," often included in the cost of your room, is famous as a hearty way to start the day. Also known as a "heart attack on a plate," the breakfast is especially feast-like if you've just come from the land of the skimpy continental breakfast across the Channel.

The breakfast gets off to a healthy start with juice and cereal or porridge. (Try Weetabix, a soggy British cousin of shredded wheat.) Next, with tea or coffee, you get a heated plate with a fried egg, lean Canadian-style bacon, a bad sausage, a grilled tomato, and often a slice of delightfully greasy pan toast and sautéed mushrooms. Toast comes on a rack (to cool quickly and crisply) with butter and marmalade or jam. Try kippers (herring fillets smoked in an oak fire). To avoid wasting food, remember to order only what you'll eat. There's nothing wrong with skipping the fry—few locals actually start their day with this heavy breakfast. Many progressive B&B owners offer vegetarian, organic, or other creative variations on the traditional breakfast.

These days, the best coffee is served in a *cafetière* (also called a "French press"). When your coffee has steeped as long as you like, plunge down the filter and pour. To revitalize your brew, pump the plunger again.

Tips on Budget Eating

You have plenty of inexpensive choices: pub grub, daily specials, ethnic restaurants, cafeterias, fast food, picnics, fish-and-chips, greasy-spoon cafés, pizza, and more.

Pub grub is the most atmospheric budget option. You'll usually get fresh, tasty buffets under ancient timbers, with hearty lunches and dinners priced at £6-8 (see "Pub Grub and Beer," page 28).

At **classier restaurants,** lunch is usually cheaper than dinner; a top-end, £25-for-dinner-type restaurant often serves the same quality two-course lunch deals for £10. Look for early-bird dinner specials, allowing you to eat well and affordably, but early (about 17:30–19:00, last order by 19:00).

Ethnic restaurants from all over the world add spice to Britain's cuisine scene. Eating Indian or Chinese is cheap (even cheaper if you take it out). Middle Eastern stands sell gyros sandwiches, falafel, and *shwarmas* (lamb in pita bread). An Indian samosa (greasy, flaky meat-and-vegetable pie) costs £1, can be microwaved, and makes a very cheap, if small, meal. (For more on Indian food, see page 30.)

Most large **museums** (and some churches) have reasonable cafeterias.

Fast food places, both American and British, are everywhere.

Cheap chain restaurants, such as steak houses and pizza places, serve no-nonsense food in a family-friendly setting (steak-house meals about £10; all-you-can-stomach pizza around £5). For specific chains to keep an eye out for, see "Good Chain Restaurants," below.

Picnicking saves time and money. Fine park benches and polite pigeons abound in most neighborhoods. You can easily get prepared food to go. Munch a relaxed "meal on wheels" picnic during your open-top bus tour or river cruise to save 30 precious minutes for sightseeing.

Bakeries sell yogurt, cartons of "semi-skimmed" milk, pastries, and pasties (PASS-teez). Pasties are "savory" (not sweet) meat pies that originated in the Cornish mining country; they had big crust handles so miners with filthy hands could eat them and toss the crust.

Good **sandwich shops** and corner **grocery stores** are a hit with local workers eating on the run. Try boxes of orange juice (pure, by the liter), fresh bread, tasty English cheese, meat, a tube of Colman's English mustard, local eatin' apples, bananas, small tomatoes, a small tub of yogurt (drinkable), trail mix, nuts, plain or chocolate-covered digestive biscuits, and any local specialties. At **open-air markets** and **supermarkets,** you can get produce in small quantities (3 tomatoes and 2 bananas cost me 90p). Supermarkets often have good deli sections, even offering Indian dishes, and sometimes salad bars. Decent packaged sandwiches (£2–3) are sold everywhere.

Good Chain Restaurants

I know, I know—you're going to Britain to enjoy characteristic little hole-in-the-wall pubs, so mass-produced food is the farthest thing from your mind. But several excellent chains with branches across the UK can be a nice break from pub grub. I've recommended these restaurants throughout this book, but if you see a location that I haven't listed...go for it.

Wagamama is a mod noodle bar serving up reliably delicious pan-Asian dishes, usually with long shared tables and busy servers toting high-tech handheld ordering computers (typically £6–10 main dishes).

At **Yo! Sushi,** freshly prepared sushi dishes trundle past on a conveyor belt. Color-coded plates tell you how much each dish costs (£1.50–5), and a picture-filled menu explains what you're eating. Just help yourself.

Marks & Spencer Simply Food, an offshoot of the department-store chain, is a picnicker's and budget traveler's heaven. They have a wide range of tasty, high-quality pre-prepared salads, sandwiches, and more, all ready to take away (no seating, but plasticware is provided). Most Marks & Spencer (M&S) department stores have a grocery store in the basement—with the same delicious packaged items as in the Simply Food outlets—and sometimes an inexpensive Café Revive on the top floor.

Ask and **Pizza Express** restaurants serve quality pasta and pizza in a pleasant, sit-down atmosphere that's still family-friendly.

On the High Street of most British cities you'll find an array of healthier-than-expected fast food. **Pret A Manger** and **Eat** offer inexpensive and generally good sandwiches and salads.

Afternoon Tea

People of leisure punctuate their afternoon with a "cream tea" at a tearoom. You'll get a pot of tea, small finger foods (like cucumber sandwiches), homemade scones, jam, and thick clotted cream. Tearooms, which often serve appealing light meals, are usually open for lunch and close at about 17:00, just before dinner. For more on this most English of traditions, see "Taking High Tea in London" on page 142.

Pub Grub and Beer

Pubs are a basic part of the British social scene, and, whether you're a teetotaler or a beer-guzzler, they should be a part of your travel here. "Pub" is short for "public house." It's an extended living room where, if you don't mind the stickiness, you can feel the pulse of Britain. Smart travelers use the pubs to eat, drink, get out of the rain, watch the latest sporting event, and make new friends. Unfortunately, many city pubs have been afflicted with an excess of brass, ferns, and video games. Most traditional atmospheric pubs are in the countryside and smaller towns.

Pub grub gets better each year. In London, it offers the best eating value. For £6–8, you'll get a basic, budget, hot lunch or dinner in friendly surroundings. The *Good Pub Guide*, published annually by the British Consumers Union, is excellent. Pubs that are attached to restaurants, advertise their food, and are crowded with locals are more likely to have fresh food and a chef than to be serving lukewarm microwaved snacks.

Pubs generally serve traditional dishes, such as fish-and-chips, vegetables, "bangers and mash" (sausages and mashed potatoes), roast beef with Yorkshire pudding (batter-baked in the oven), and assorted meat pies, such as steak-and-kidney pie or shepherd's pie (stewed lamb topped with mashed potatoes). Side dishes include salads (sometimes even a nice self-serve salad bar), vegetables, and—invariably—"chips" (French fries). "Crisps" are potato chips. A "jacket potato" (baked potato stuffed with fillings of your choice) can almost be a meal in itself. A "ploughman's lunch" is a modern "traditional English meal" of bread, cheese, and sweet pickles that

Sounds Bad, Tastes Good

The British have a talent for making delicious treats sound disgusting. Here are a few examples:

Toad in the Hole: Sausage dipped in batter and fried

Bubble and Squeak: Leftovers, usually potatoes, veggies, and meat, all fried up together

Bap: Small roll

Treacle: Golden syrup, similar to light molasses

Spotted Dick: A communicable dessert

nearly every tourist tries…once. These days, you'll likely find more Italian pasta, curried dishes, and quiche on the menu than traditional fare.

Meals are usually served from 12:00 to 14:00 and from 18:00 to 20:00, not throughout the day. There's usually no table service. Order at the bar, then take a seat and they'll bring the food when it's ready (or sometimes you pick it up at the bar). Pay at the bar (sometimes when you order, sometimes after you eat). Don't tip unless it's a place with full table service. Servings are hearty, service is quick, and you'll rarely spend more than £8. A beer or cider adds another couple of pounds. (Free tap water is always available.)

The British take great pride in their **beer.** They think that drinking beer cold and carbonated, as Americans do, ruins the taste. Most pubs will have lagers (cold, refreshing, American-style beer),

ales (amber-colored, cellar-temperature beer), bitters (hop-flavored ale, perhaps the most typical British beer), and stouts (dark and somewhat bitter, like Guinness). At pubs, long-handled pulls are used to pull the traditional, rich-flavored "real ales" up from the cellar. These are the connoisseur's favorites: fermented naturally, varying from sweet to bitter, often with a hoppy or nutty flavor. Notice the fun names. Short-hand pulls at the bar mean colder, fizzier, mass-produced, and less interesting keg beers. Mild beers are sweeter, with a creamy malt flavoring. Irish cream ale is a smooth, sweet experience. Try the draft cider (sweet or dry)…carefully.

Order your beer at the bar and pay as you go, with no need to tip. An average beer costs £3. Part of the experience is standing before a line of "hand pulls," or taps, and wondering which beer to choose.

Drinks are served by the pint (20-ounce imperial size) or the half-pint. (It's almost feminine for a man to order just a half; I order mine with quiche.) Proper British ladies like a shandy (half-beer and half-7-Up, surprisingly tasty).

Besides beer, many pubs actually have a good selection of wines by the glass, a fully stocked bar for the gentleman's "G and T" (gin and tonic), and the increasingly popular bottles of alcohol-plus-sugar (such as Bacardi Breezers) for the younger, working-class set. Pimm's is a refreshing and fruity summer cocktail, traditionally popular during Wimbledon. It's an upper-class drink...a rough bloke might insult a pub by claiming it sells more Pimm's than beer. Teetotalers can order from a wide variety of soft drinks. Children are served food and soft drinks in pubs, but you must be 18 to order a beer.

Pub hours vary. Pubs generally serve beer Mon–Sat 11:00–23:00 and Sun 12:00–22:30, though many are open later, particularly on Fri–Sat. As it nears closing time, you'll hear shouts of "last orders." Then comes the 10-minute warning bell. Finally, they'll call "Time!" to pick up your glass, finished or not, when the pub closes.

A cup of darts is free for the asking. People go to a public house to be social. They want to talk. Get vocal with a local. This is easiest at the bar, where people assume you're in the mood to talk (rather than at a table, where you're allowed a bit of privacy). The pub is the next best thing to having relatives in town. Cheers!

Indian Food

Eating Indian food is "going local" in cosmopolitan, multi-ethnic Britain. You'll find recommended Indian restaurants in most British cities—and even small towns. Take the opportunity to sample food from Britain's former colony. Indian cuisine is as varied as the country itself, featuring more exotic spices than British or American cuisine—some hot, some sweet. Indian food is very vegetarian-friendly, offering many dishes to choose from on any given menu.

For a simple meal that costs about £10–12, order one dish with rice and naan (Indian bread that can be ordered plain, with garlic, or various other ways). If your budget allows, you can make a mix-and-match platter out of several sharable dishes, including dal (lentil soup) as a starter; one or two meat or vegetable dishes with sauce (for example, chicken curry, chicken *tikka masala* in a creamy tomato sauce, grilled fish tandoori, chickpea *chana masala*, or the spicy vindaloo dish); *raita* (a cooling yogurt that's added to spicy dishes); rice; naan; and an Indian beer (wine and Indian food don't really mix) or chai (a cardamom- and cinnamon-spiced tea). A meal like this—which may also be offered as a fixed-price combo plate—will cost about £20.

British Chocolate

My chocoholic readers are enthusiastic about British chocolates. Like other dairy products, chocolate seems richer and creamier here than it does in the US, so even the basics like Kit Kat and Twix have a different taste. Some favorites include Cadbury Gold bars (filled with liquid caramel), Cadbury Crunchie bars, Nestle's Lion bars (layered wafers covered in caramel and chocolate), Cadbury's Boost bars (a shortcake biscuit with caramel in milk chocolate), and Galaxy chocolate bars (especially the ones with hazelnuts). Thornton shops (in larger train stations) sell a box of sweets called the Continental Assortment, which comes with a tasting guide. The highlight is the mocha white-chocolate truffle. British M&Ms, called Smarties, are better than American ones. For a few extra pence, adorn your ice cream cone with a "flake"—a chocolate bar stuck right into the middle.

Desserts (Sweets)

To the British, the traditional word for dessert is "pudding," although it's also referred to as "sweets" these days. Sponge cake, cream, fruitcake, and meringue are key players.

Trifle is the best-known British concoction, consisting of sponge cake soaked in brandy or sherry (or orange juice for children), then covered with jam and/or fruit and custard cream. Whipped cream can sometimes put the final touch on this "light" treat.

Castle puddings are sponge puddings cooked in small molds and topped with Golden Syrup (a popular brand and a cross between honey and maple syrup). Bread and butter pudding consists of slices of French bread baked with milk, cream, eggs, and raisins (similar to the American preparation), served warm with cold cream. Hasty pudding, supposedly the invention of people in a hurry to avoid the bailiff, is made from stale bread with dried fruit and milk. Queen of puddings is a breadcrumb pudding topped with warm jam, meringue, and cream. Treacle pudding is a popular steamed pudding whose "sponge" mixture combines flour, suet (animal fat), butter, sugar, and milk. Christmas pudding (also called plum pudding) is a dense mixture with dried and candied fruit served with brandy butter or hard sauce. Banoffee pie is the British answer to banana cream pie.

Spotted Dick is a sponge pudding with currants. How did it get its name? Some say it looks like a spotted dog, and dogs were often called Dick. Another theory suggests that "Dick," "duff," and "dog" are all variants of the word "dough." One thing's for

> ## How Was Your Trip?
>
> Were your travels fun, smooth, and meaningful? If you'd like to share your tips, concerns, and discoveries, please fill out the survey at www.ricksteves.com/feedback. I value your feedback. Thanks in advance—it helps a lot.

sure: The stuff isn't selling very well today. Grocers are considering renaming it "Spotted Richard."

The British version of custard is a smooth, yellow liquid. Cream tops most everything custard does not. There's single cream for coffee. Double cream is really thick. Whipped cream is familiar, and clotted cream is the consistency of whipped butter.

Fool is a dessert with sweetened pureed fruit (such as rhubarb, gooseberries, or black currants) mixed with cream or custard and chilled. Elderflower is a popular flavoring for sorbet.

Scones are tops, and many inns and restaurants have their secret recipes. Whether made with fruit or topped with clotted cream, scones take the cake.

TRAVELING AS A TEMPORARY LOCAL

We travel all the way to Europe to enjoy differences—to become temporary locals. You'll experience frustrations. Certain truths that we find "God-given" or "self-evident," such as cold beer, ice in drinks, bottomless cups of coffee, hot showers, and bigger being better, are suddenly not so true. One of the benefits of travel is the eye-opening realization that there are logical, civil, and even better alternatives.

If there is a negative aspect to the image the British have of Americans, it's that we are big, loud, aggressive, impolite, rich, superficially friendly, and a bit naive.

Given our reluctance to work with the world on climate change issues, the British don't respond well to Americans complaining about being too hot or too cold. Bring a sweater in winter, and in summer, be prepared to sweat a little like everyone else.

Americans tend to be noisy in public places, such as restaurants and trains. My British friends place a high value on speaking quietly in these same places. Listen while on the bus or in a restaurant—the place can be packed, but the decibel level is low. Try to remember this nuance, and soften your speaking voice as a way of respecting their culture.

While the British look bemusedly at some of our Yankee excesses—and worriedly at others—they nearly always afford us individual travelers all the warmth we deserve. Judging from all the happy feedback I receive from travelers who have used this book, it's safe to assume you'll enjoy a great, affordable vacation—with the finesse of an independent, experienced traveler.

Thanks, and have a brilliant holiday!

BACK DOOR TRAVEL PHILOSOPHY
From *Rick Steves' Europe Through the Back Door*

Travel is intensified living—maximum thrills per minute and one of the last great sources of legal adventure. Travel is freedom. It's recess, and we need it.

Experiencing the real Europe requires catching it by surprise, going casual..."Through the Back Door."

Affording travel is a matter of priorities. (Make do with the old car.) You can travel—simply, safely, and comfortably—nearly anywhere in Europe for $100 a day plus transportation costs (allow more for London). In many ways, spending more money only builds a thicker wall between you and what you came to see. Europe is a cultural carnival, and, time after time, you'll find that its best acts are free and the best seats are the cheap ones.

A tight budget forces you to travel close to the ground, meeting and communicating with the people, not relying on service with a purchased smile. Never sacrifice sleep, nutrition, safety, or cleanliness in the name of budget. Simply enjoy the local-style alternatives to expensive hotels and restaurants.

Extroverts have more fun. If your trip is low on magic moments, kick yourself and make things happen. If you don't enjoy a place, maybe you don't know enough about it. Seek the truth. Recognize tourist traps. Give a culture the benefit of your open mind. See things as different but not better or worse. Any culture has much to share.

Of course, travel, like the world, is a series of hills and valleys. Be fanatically positive and militantly optimistic. If something's not to your liking, change your liking. Travel is addictive. It can make you a happier American as well as a citizen of the world. Our Earth is home to six and a half billion equally important people. It's humbling to travel and find that people don't envy Americans. Europeans like us, but, with all due respect, they wouldn't trade passports.

Globe-trotting destroys ethnocentricity. It helps you understand and appreciate different cultures. Regrettably, there are forces in our society that want you dumbed down for their convenience. Don't let it happen. Thoughtful travel engages you with the world—more important than ever these days. Travel changes people. It broadens perspectives and teaches new ways to measure quality of life. Rather than fear the diversity on this planet, travelers celebrate it. Many travelers toss aside their hometown blinders. Their prized souvenirs are the strands of different cultures they decide to knit into their own character. The world is a cultural yarn shop, and Back Door travelers are weaving the ultimate tapestry. Join in!

ENGLAND

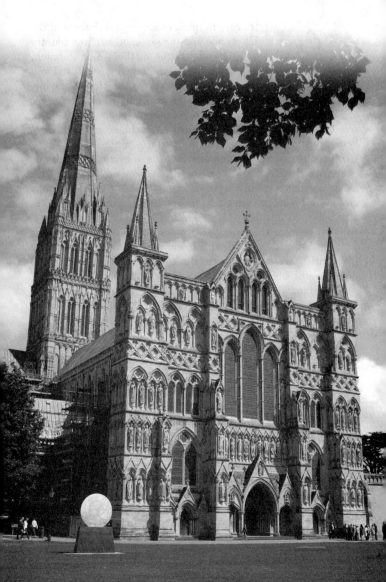

ENGLAND

 It's easy to think of England, Britain, and the UK as one and the same, because the country of England was the birthplace of so much. Even today, England remains a cultural and linguistic touchstone for the almost one billion humans who speak English. It's the center of the UK in every way: home to four out of five UK citizens, the seat of government, the economic powerhouse, the center of higher learning, and the cultural heart.

For the tourist, England offers a little of everything we associate with Britain: castles, cathedrals, and ruined abbeys; chatty locals nursing beers in village pubs; mysterious prehistoric stone circles and Roman ruins; tea, scones, and clotted cream; hikes across unspoiled, sheep-speckled hillsides; and drivers who cheerfully wave from the wrong side of the road. And then there's London, a world in itself, with monuments (Big Ben), museums (the British Museum), royalty (Buckingham Palace), theater and nightlife, throbbing with the pulse of the global community.

England (pop. 50 million) is a hilly country the size of Louisiana (50,346 square miles) located in the lower two-thirds of the isle of Britain. Scotland is to the north and the English Channel to the south, with the North Sea to the east and Wales (and the Irish Sea) to the west. Fed by ocean air from the southwest, the climate is mild, with a chance of cloudy, rainy weather almost any day of the year.

North England tends to be hilly with poor soil, so the traditional economy was based on livestock (grazing cows and sheep). Today it has some of England's most beautiful landscapes, but in the 19th century, the landscape was dotted with belching smokestacks as its major cities and heartland became centers of coal and iron mining and manufacturing. Now its working-class cities and ports (such as Liverpool) are experiencing a comeback, buoyed by higher employment, tourism, and vibrant art scenes.

South England, including London, has always had more people and more money than the north. Blessed with rolling hills, wide plains, and the River Thames, in the past this area was rich with farms, its rivers flowed with trade, and high culture

England

flourished around the epicenter in London.

England was traditionally very class-conscious—the wealthy landed aristocracy, the middle-class tradesmen, and the lower-class farmers and factory workers. And, while social stratification is fading with the new global economy, other regional differences remain strong. Locals can often identify where someone is from by their dialect or local accent—Geordie, Cockney, or Queen's English.

England has an economy that can stand alongside many much larger nations. It boasts high-tech industries (software, chemical, aviation), international banking, textile manufacturing, and is a major exporter of beef. Once a land of farms and villages, England is now an urban, industrial, and post-industrial colossus.

The English people have a worldwide reputation (or stereotype) as cheerful, courteous, and well-mannered. Cutting in line is very gauche. On the other hand, English soccer fans can be notorious "hooligans." The English are not known for being touchy-feely or physically demonstrative (hugging and kissing), but they sure do love to talk. When times get tough, they persevere with a stiff upper lip. The understated British wit is legendary—if someone dies, it's "a bit of a drag" (but if the tea is cold, it's "ghastly!").

As a tourist, you can trace England's illustrious history by roaming the countryside. Prehistoric peoples built the mysterious stone circles of Stonehenge and Avebury. Then came the Romans,  who built baths at Bath and Hadrian's Wall. Viking invaders left their mark in York, and the Normans built the Tower of London. As England Christianized and unified, the grand cathedrals of Salisbury, Wells, and Durham arose. Next came the castles and palaces of the English kings (Windsor and Warwick) and the Shakespeare sights from the era of Elizabeth I (Stratford-upon-Avon). In following centuries, tiny England became a maritime empire (the *Cutty Sark* at Greenwich) and the world's first industrial power (Ironbridge Gorge). England's Romantic poets were inspired by the unspoiled nature and time-passed villages of the Lake District and the Cotswolds. In the 20th century, the gritty urban world of 1960s Liverpool gave the world the Beatles (and the tacky tourist  world of Blackpool). Finally, end your journey through English history in London—on the cutting edge of 21st-century trends.

For a thousand years, England has been a major cultural center. Parliamentary democracy, science (Isaac Newton), technology (Michael Faraday), and education (Oxford and Cambridge) were nurtured here. In literature, England has few peers in any language, producing some of the greatest legends (King Arthur, Beowulf, and The Lord of the Rings), poems (by Chaucer, Wordsworth, and Byron), novels (Dickens, Austen, and J.K. Rowling), and plays (William Shakespeare, England's greatest writer). London rivals Broadway as the best scene for live theater. England is a major exporter of movies and movie actors—Ian McKellen, Kate Winslet, Keira Knightley, Judi Dench, Ralph Fiennes, Hugh Grant, and on and on.

In popular music, England remains almost America's equal. It started in the 1960s with the "British invasion" of bands that re-infused rock and blues into America—the Beatles, the Rolling Stones, the Who. Then came successive waves in the 1970s (Elton John, Led Zeppelin, David Bowie, Queen, and the Sex Pistols); the '80s (Dire Straits, The Clash, The Cure, Elvis Costello, The Smiths, The Police, and Duran Duran); the '90s (Oasis, Spice Girls, and the rave scene); and into the 21st century (Coldplay, Amy Winehouse, Lily Allen, Gorillaz, and Radiohead).

On the other hand, when it comes to cuisine, Britain has given the world...fish-and-chips. Bad, bland British food has become almost a universal joke, headed by dishes with funny names like "bubble and squeak" and "toad in the hole." Traditionally, England was known for heavy, no-nonsense meals. The day started with eggs and bacon, followed by meat pies and beer for lunch, and finished with a heavy meal of red meat and thick sauces.

But the cuisine has changed in recent years. The English have added fresh fruits and vegetables to their diet and have opened up to foreign influences. Indian and Chinese imports are especially popular, having been adapted to local tastes. But one distinctive

English tradition remains popular: afternoon tea served with biscuits, cookies, or little sandwiches. This four o'clock break is part pick-me-up and part social ritual.

One thing that sets England apart from its fellow UK countries (Scotland, Wales, Northern Ireland) is its ethnic makeup. Traditionally, those countries had Celtic roots, while the English mixed in Saxon and Norman blood. In the 20th century, England welcomed many Scots, Welsh, and Irish as low-wage workers. More recently, it's become home to immigrants from former colonies of its worldwide empire—particularly from India/Pakistan/Bangladesh, the Caribbean, and Africa—and to many workers from poorer EU countries in Eastern Europe. These days it's not a given that every "English" person speaks English. Nearly one in three citizens does not profess the Christian faith. As the world becomes interconnected by electronic devices, it's possible for many immigrants to physically inhabit the country without truly assimilating into English culture.

This is the current English paradox. England—the birthplace and center of the extended worldwide family of English-speakers—is losing its traditional Englishness. Where Scotland, Wales, and Northern Ireland have cultural movements to preserve their local languages and customs, England does not. Politically, there is no "English" party in the UK Parliament. In fact, Scotland, Wales, and Northern Ireland now have their own parliaments to decide local issues; England must depend on the decisions of the UK government at large. Except for the occasional display of an English flag at a soccer match (the red St. George cross on a white background), most English people don't really think of themselves as "English"—more as "Brits," a part of the wider UK.

Today, England tries to preserve its rich past as it races forward as a leading global player. There are still hints of its legacy of farms, villages, Victorian lamplighters, and upper-crust dandies. But it's also a jostling world of unemployed factory workers, investment bankers, soccer matches, and faux-Tudor suburbs. Modern England is a culturally diverse land in transition. Catch it while you can.

LONDON

London is more than 600 square miles of urban jungle. With nine million people—who don't all speak English—it's a world in itself and a barrage on all the senses. On my first visit I felt extremely small.

London is more than its museums and landmarks. It's a living, breathing, thriving organism...a coral reef of humanity. The city has changed dramatically in recent years, and many visitors are surprised to find how "un-English" it is. Whites are now a minority in major parts of the city that once symbolized white imperialism. Arabs have nearly bought out the area north of Hyde Park. Chinese take-outs outnumber fish-and-chips shops. Eastern Europeans pull pints in British pubs. Many hotels are run by people with foreign accents (who hire English chambermaids), while outlying suburbs are home to huge communities of Indians and Pakistanis. With the English Channel Tunnel making travel between Britain and the Continent easier than ever, many locals see even more holes in their bastion of Britishness. London is learning—sometimes fitfully—to live as a microcosm of its formerly vast empire.

With just a few days here, you'll get no more than a quick splash in this teeming human tidal pool. But with a good orientation, you'll find London manageable and fun. You'll get a sampling of the city's top sights, history, and cultural entertainment, and a good look at its ever-changing human face.

Blow through the city on the open deck of a double-decker orientation tour bus, and take a pinch-me-I'm-in-London walk through the West End. Ogle the crown jewels at the Tower of London, hear the chimes of Big Ben, and see the Houses of Parliament in action. Cruise the Thames River, and take a spin on the London Eye Ferris wheel. Hobnob with the tombstones in Westminster Abbey, and visit with Leonardo, Botticelli, and Rembrandt in the National Gallery. Enjoy Shakespeare in a replica of the Globe Theatre, then marvel at a glitzy, fun musical at a modern-day theater. Whisper across the dome of St. Paul's Cathedral, and rummage through our civilization's attic at the British Museum. And sip your tea with pinky raised and clotted cream dribbling down your scone.

Planning Your Time

The sights of London alone could easily fill a trip to Britain. It's a great one-week getaway. On a three-week tour of Britain I'd give it three busy days. If you're flying in, consider starting your trip in Bath and making London your British finale. Especially if you hope to enjoy a play or concert, a night or two of jet lag is bad news.

Here's a suggested schedule:

Day 1: 9:00–Tower of London (Crown Jewels first, then Beefeater tour, then White Tower); 12:00–Munch a sandwich on the Thames while cruising from the Tower to Westminster Bridge; 13:00–Follow the self-guided Westminster Walk (see page 63) with a quick visit to the Churchill Museum and Cabinet War Rooms; 15:30–Trafalgar Square and National Gallery; 17:30–Visit the Britain and London Visitors Centre near Piccadilly, planning ahead for the rest of your trip; 18:30–Dinner in Soho. Take in a play or 19:30 concert at St. Martin-in-the-Fields.

Day 2: 8:30–If you'll be traveling around Britain, spend 30 minutes in a phone booth getting all essential elements of your trip nailed down. If you know where you'll be and when, call those B&Bs now. 9:00–Take a hop-on, hop-off bus tour (start at Victoria Street and hop off near the end for the Changing of the Guard); 11:30–Buckingham Palace (guards change most days, but worth confirming); 13:00–Covent Garden for lunch and people-watching; 14:30–Tour the British Museum. Have a pub dinner before a play, concert, or evening walking tour.

Days 3 and 4: Choose among these remaining London highlights: Tour Westminster Abbey, British Library, Imperial War Museum, the two Tates (Tate Modern on the south bank for modern art, Tate Britain on the north bank for British art), St. Paul's Cathedral, or the Museum of London; take a spin on the London Eye or a cruise to Kew or Greenwich; do some serious shopping at one of London's elegant department stores or open-air markets; or take another historic walking tour.

After considering nearly all of London's tourist sights, I have pruned them down to just the most important (or fun) for a first visit of up to seven days. You won't be able to see all of these, so

London's Neighborhoods

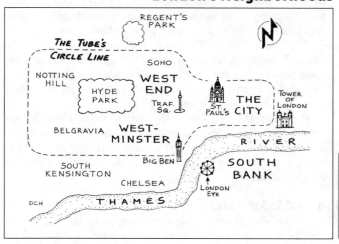

don't try. You'll keep coming back to London. After dozens of visits myself, I still enjoy a healthy list of excuses to return.

ORIENTATION

(area code: 020)

To grasp London more comfortably, see it as the old town in the city center without the modern, congested sprawl. The Thames River runs roughly west to east through the city, with most of the visitor's sights on the north bank. Mentally, maybe even physically, trim down your map to include only the area between the Tower of London (to the east), Hyde Park (west), Regent's Park (north), and the South Bank (south). This is roughly the area bordered by the Tube's Circle Line. This three-mile stretch between the Tower and Hyde Park (about a 90-min walk) looks like a milk bottle on its side (see map above), and holds 80 percent of the sights mentioned in this chapter.

London is a collection of neighborhoods:

The City: Shakespeare's London was a walled town clustered around St. Paul's Cathedral. Today, "The City" is the modern financial district.

Westminster: This neighborhood includes Big Ben, Parliament, the Churchill Museum and Cabinet War Rooms, Westminster Abbey, and Buckingham Palace, the grand government buildings from which Britain is ruled.

The West End: Lying between Westminster and The City (that is, at the "west end" of the original walled town), this is the center of London's cultural life. Trafalgar Square has major museums.

Piccadilly Circus and Leicester Square host tourist traps, cinemas, and nighttime glitz. Soho and Covent Garden are thriving people-zones housing theaters, restaurants, pubs, and boutiques.

The South Bank: Until recently, the entire south bank of the Thames River was a run-down, generally ignored area, but now it's the hottest real estate in town, with upscale restaurants, major new sightseeing attractions, and pedestrian bridges allowing easy access from the rest of London.

Residential Neighborhoods to the West: Though they lack major tourist sights, the neighborhoods of Mayfair, South Kensington, Notting Hill, Chelsea, and Belgravia are home to the city's wealthy and trendy, as well as many shopping streets and enticing restaurants.

Tourist Information

The Britain and London Visitors Centre, just a block off Piccadilly Circus, is the best tourist information service in town (Mon–Fri 9:00–18:30, Sat–Sun 10:00–16:00, phone not answered after 17:00 Mon–Fri and not at all Sat–Sun, 1 Lower Regent Street, tel. 020/8846-9000, www.visitbritain.com, www.visitlondon.com). This TI has many different departments, all with their own sales desks (theater tickets, sightseeing passes, and more). Bring your itinerary and a checklist of questions.

At the London desk, pick up these free publications: *London Planner* (a great free monthly that lists all the sights, events, and hours), walking-tour schedule fliers, a theater guide, *London Buses: Central London* map, and the Thames River Services brochure. After you've grazed through the great leaflet racks, head upstairs for the inviting tables and Internet access (small fee, with disk-burning service).

The "pink desk" sells long-distance bus tickets and passes, train tickets (convenient for reservations), and **Fast Track tickets** to some of London's attractions (at no extra cost), allowing you to skip the queue at the sights. These are worthwhile for places that sometimes have long ticket lines, such as the Tower of London, London Eye, and Madame Tussauds Waxworks. (If you'll be going to the Waxworks, buy tickets here at the TI, since they're cheaper than at the sight itself.)

While the Visitors Centre books rooms, you can avoid their £5 booking fee by calling hotels direct (see "Sleeping," page 115). The entertainment desk to the left of the pink desk sells tickets to plays (20 percent booking fee).

The Britain tourism desk, located at the back of the TI, sells the various sightseeing deals, including the London Pass (skip it; remember that many of London's big attractions are free to enter). Busy sightseers taking far-flung trips could consider the British

Heritage Pass, or English Heritage or National Trust memberships; for details on these, see page 17.

Nearby you'll find the **Scottish Tourist Centre** (Mon–Fri
8:00–20:00, Sat 9:00–17:30, Sun 10:00–16:00, Cockspur Street,
tel. 0845-225-5121, www.visitscotland.com) and the slick **French
National Tourist Office** (Mon–Fri 10:00–18:00, Sat until 17:00,
closed Sun, 178 Piccadilly Street, tel. 0906-824-4123).

Unfortunately, **London's Tourist Information Centres** (which
represent themselves as TIs at major train and bus stations and airports) are now simply businesses selling advertising space to companies with fliers to distribute. For solid information, visit the Britain
and London Visitors Centre, mentioned on the previous page.

Time Out **Magazine:** Newsstands sell this excellent weekly
entertainment magazine, which has good maps and a concise and
opinionated rundown on sightseeing, shopping, entertainment,
and eats (£2.50, www.timeout.com/london).

London Websites: Try www.londontouristboard.com, www
.thisislondon.com, and www.londontown.com.

Arrival in London

By Train: London has eight train stations, all connected by the
Tube (subway) and all with ATMs, exchange offices, and luggage
storage. From any station, ride the Tube or taxi to your hotel. For
more information, see "Getting Around London," page 48.

By Bus: The bus ("coach") station is one block southwest of
Victoria Station (which has a TI and a Tube entrance).

By Plane: For information on getting from London's airports
to downtown London, see "Transportation Connections," page 144.

Helpful Hints

Theft Alert: The Artful Dodger is alive and well in London. Be
on guard, particularly on public transportation and in places
crowded with tourists. Tourists, considered naive and rich,
are targeted. More than 7,500 handbags are stolen annually at
Covent Garden alone. Wear your money belt.

US Embassy: It's at 24 Grosvenor Square, just east of Hyde Park
(for passport concerns, open Mon–Fri 8:30–17:30, closed
Sat–Sun and for American and British holidays, Tube: Bond
Street, tel. 020/7499-9000, www.usembassy.org.uk).

Pedestrian Safety: Cars drive on the left side of the road, so before
crossing a street, I always look right, look left, and then look
right again just to be sure. Many crosswalks are even painted
with instructions, reminding their foreign guests to "Look
right" or "Look left."

Medical Problems: Local hospitals have 24-hour-a-day emergency care centers where any tourist who needs help can drop

Affording London's Sights

London is, in many ways, Europe's most expensive city, with lots of pricey sights but—fortunately—lots of freebies, too.

Many of the city's biggest and best museums won't cost you a dime. Free sights include the British Museum, British Library, National Gallery, National Portrait Gallery, Tate Britain, Tate Modern, Wallace Collection, Imperial War Museum, Victoria and Albert Museum, Natural History Museum, Science Museum, National Army Museum, Sir John Soane's Museum, the Museum of London, and on the outskirts of town, the Royal Air Force Museum London.

Some museums, such as the British Museum, request a donation of two or three pounds, but whether you contribute is up to you. Many offer essential audioguides for around £3.50. If I spend the money on an audioguide, I feel fine about not otherwise donating.

Other freebies to consider: You can get into the Tower of London by attending the Ceremony of the Keys (which requires a reservation made long in advance—see page 94) or by attending Sunday services in the Tower's chapel (chapel access only). You can view the legal action at Old Bailey and the legislature at work in the Houses of Parliament. There are plenty of free performances, such as the lunch concerts at St. Martin-in-the-Fields. You can also enjoy the pageantry of the Changing of the Guard and the people-watching scene at Covent Garden.

Smaller churches let worshippers in free (even tourist worshippers), having given up on asking for donations. The big sightseeing churches—Westminster Abbey and St. Paul's—charge about £10 for admission, but offer free evensong services virtually daily. Westminster Abbey offers free organ recitals on Sunday at 17:45.

When budgeting your sightseeing money, consider the £6 city walking tours as some of the best deals going. The hop-on, hop-off big-bus tours (£19–22), while expensive, provide a great overview, and include boat tours as well as city walks, depending on the company you choose (see page 57). A one-hour Thames ride costs about £7 one-way, but generally comes with an enter-

in and, after a wait, be seen by a doctor. Your hotel has details. St. Thomas' Hospital, immediately across the river from Big Ben, has a fine reputation.

Changing Money: ATMs are the way to go. While regular banks charge several pounds to change traveler's checks, American Express offices offer a fair rate, and will change any brand of traveler's checks for no fee. Handy AmEx offices are at Heathrow's Terminal 4 Tube station (daily 7:00–19:00) and

taining commentary (see page 61). A three-hour bicycle tour is roughly £18 (see page 61).

The queen charges big time to open her palace to the public: Buckingham Palace (£15, open Aug–Sept only) and her art gallery and carriage museum (adjacent to the palace, about £7 each) are interesting but expensive. While Kensington Palace (£12) and Hampton Court Palace (£13) are pricey, they are well-presented and a reasonable value if you have a real interest in royal history.

Gimmicky private enterprises can charge sky-high prices, such as the disappointing London Dungeon (£20) and the fun, popular, and overpriced Madame Tussauds Waxworks (£25, but £16 after 17:00). The privately run Dalí Universe capitalizes on its location next to the popular London Eye, but for £12, it's a bad value.

Big-ticket sights worth their admission fees are Kew Gardens (£12.25), Shakespeare's Globe (£9, also offers plays), and the Cabinet War Rooms, with its fine Churchill Museum (£12). The London Eye is an unforgettable experience (£14.50), and the Vinopolis wine museum provides a classy way to get a buzz and call it museum-going (£16 entry includes five small glasses of wine).

Many smaller museums cost around £5. My favorites include the three Somerset House museums (Courtauld Gallery, Heritage Rooms, and the Gilbert Collection) and the Wellington Museum at Apsley House.

Seek out the freestanding "tkts" booth at Leicester Square to get discounted tickets to London's famous shows. Theater tickets are sold for that day only, and the booth tacks on a £2.50 service charge. But it's still a good deal, offering discounts from 25 to 50 percent (see page 109).

A £5 "groundling" ticket for a play at Shakespeare's Globe is the best deal in town (see page 112). Tickets to the Open Air Theatre at Regent's Park start at £10 (see page 113).

These days, London doesn't come cheap. But with its many free museums and affordable plays, this cosmopolitan, cultured city offers days of sightseeing thrills without requiring you to pinch your pennies (or your pounds).

near Piccadilly (Mon–Sat 9:00–18:00, Sun 10:00–17:00, 30 Haymarket, tel. 020/7484-9610; refund office 24-hour tel. 0800-521-313). Marks & Spencer department stores give good rates with no fees.

Avoid changing money at exchange bureaus. Their latest scam: They advertise very good rates with a same-as-the-banks fee of 2 percent. But the fine print explains that the fee of 2 percent is for buying pounds. The fee for *selling* pounds is 9.5 percent. Ouch!

Internet Access: The **easyInternetcafé** chain offers up to 500 computers per store, and is open long hours daily. Depending on the time of day, a £2 ticket buys anywhere from 80 minutes to six hours of computer time. The ticket is valid for four weeks and multiple visits at any of their branches, including: Trafalgar Square (456 Strand), Tottenham Court Road (#9–16), Oxford Street (#358, opposite Bond Street Tube station), and Kensington High Street (#160–166). They also sell 24-hour, 7-day, and 30-day passes (www.easyinternetcafe .com). **Access Printers,** across the street from Victoria Station (next to the Apollo Victoria Theatre), has plenty of terminals (£1/30 min, open long hours daily). You'll find an Internet café in the **Whiteleys Mall Food Court** in the Notting Hill neighborhood (see page 140).

Travel Bookstores: Located in Covent Garden, **Stanfords Travel Bookstore** is good, and stocks current editions of my books (Mon, Wed, and Fri 9:00–19:30, Tue 9:30–19:30, Thu 9:00–20:00, Sat 10:00–19:00, Sun 12:00–18:00, 12–14 Long Acre, Tube: Covent Garden, tel. 020/7836-1321, www .stanfords.co.uk). Two impressive **Waterstone's** bookstores have the biggest collection of travel guides in town: on Piccadilly (Mon–Sat 10:00–22:00, Sun 12:00–18:00, 203 Piccadilly, tel. 020/7851-2400) and on Trafalgar Square (Mon–Sat 9:30–21:00, Sun 12:00–18:00, with Costa Café on second floor, tel. 020/7839-4411).

Harry Potter's London: Calling all wizards! For filming sites and real-life London landmarks referenced in the books, see page 632.

Left Luggage: As security concerns heighten, train stations have replaced their lockers with left-luggage counters. Each bag must go through a scanner (just like at the airport), so lines can be long. Expect a wait to pick up your bags, too (each item-£6/24 hrs, daily 7:00–24:00). You can also check bags at the airports (£5/day). If leaving London and returning later, you may be able to leave a box or bag at your hotel for free—assuming you'll be staying there again.

Time Zone Difference: Remember that Britain is one hour earlier than most of continental Europe.

Getting Around London

To travel smart in a city this size, you must get comfortable with public transportation. London's excellent taxis, buses, and subway (Tube) system make a private car unnecessary. In fact, the "congestion charge" of £8 levied on any private car entering the city center has been effective in cutting down traffic jam delays and bolstering

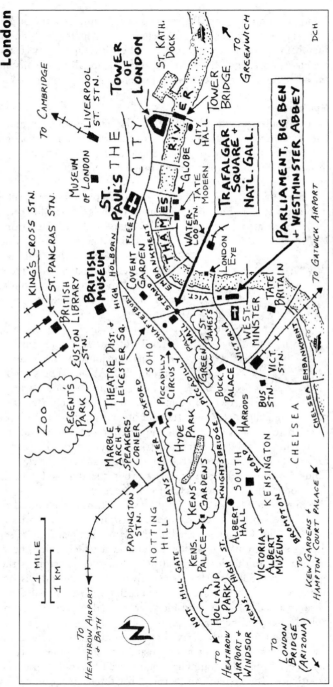

London

London's public transit. The revenue raised subsidizes the buses, which are now cheaper, more frequent, and even more user-friendly than before. Today, the vast majority of vehicles in the city center are buses, taxis, and service trucks. (Drivers, for all the details on the congestion charge, see www.cclondon.com.)

By Tube
London's subway system (called "the Tube" or "the Underground," but never "subway," which refers to a pedestrian underpass) is one of this planet's great people-movers, and often the fastest long-distance transport in town (runs Mon–Sat about 5:00–24:00, Sun about 7:00–23:00).

Start by studying a Tube map. You can pick up a free Tube map at any station. Each line has a name (such as Circle, Northern,

or Bakerloo) and two directions (indicated by the end-of-the-line stops). Find the line that will take you to your destination, and figure out the direction (north, south, east, or west) you'll need to go to get there.

You can use paper tickets, Travelcards, or an Oyster card to pay for your journey (see sidebar on page 52). At the Tube station, feed your paper ticket or Travelcard into the turnstile, reclaim it, and hang onto it—you'll need it to get through the turnstile at the end of your journey. Try not to crease paper tickets or cards, as they may become unreadable by the machines. If you are using a plastic Oyster card, touch the card to the yellow card reader both when you enter and exit the station. Find your train by following signs to your line and the (general) direction it's headed (such as Central Line: east).

Since some tracks are shared by several lines, you'll need to double-check before boarding a train: First, make sure your destination is one of the stops listed on the sign at the platform. Also, check the electronic signboards that announce which train is next, and make sure the destination (the end-of-the-line stop) is the one you want. Some trains, particularly on the Circle and District lines, split off for other directions, but each train has its final destination marked above its windshield. When in doubt, ask a local or a blue-vested staff person for help.

Trains run roughly every three to ten minutes. If one train is absolutely packed and you notice another to the same destination is coming in three minutes, you can wait to avoid the sardine experience. The system can be fraught with construction delays and breakdowns, so pay attention to signs and announcements explaining necessary detours. The Circle Line is notorious for problems. Rush hours (8:00–10:00 and 16:00–19:00) can be packed and sweaty. Bring something to do to make your waiting time productive. If you get confused, ask for advice at the information window located before the turnstile entry.

Remember that you can't leave the system without feeding your ticket or Travelcard to the turnstile or touching your Oyster card to an electronic reader. If you have a single-trip paper ticket, the turnstile will eat your now-expired ticket; if it's a Travelcard, it will spit your still-valid card back out. Save walking time by choosing the best street exit—check the maps on the walls or ask any station personnel. For Tube and bus information, visit www .tfl.gov.uk (and check out the journey planner).

Any ride in Zone 1 (the center of town) costs a steep £4 for adults paying cash, while trips out to Zones 5 or 6 (e.g., to Heathrow Airport) cost more. If you plan to ride the Tube and buses more than twice in one day, you'll save money by getting a Travelcard (or for four or more days, an Oyster card).

If you do buy a single Tube ticket, you can avoid ticket-window lines in stations by using the coin-op or credit-card machines; practice on the punchboard to see how the system works (hit "Adult Single" and your destination). These tickets are valid only on the day of purchase.

Tube Etiquette
- When waiting at the platform, get out of the way of those exiting the train. Board only after everyone is off.
- Avoid using the hinged seats near the doors of some trains when the car is jammed; they take up valuable standing space.
- In a crowded train, try not to block the exit. If you're blocking the door when the train stops, step out of the car and to the side, let others off, then get back on.
- Talk softly in the cars. Listen to how quietly Londoners communicate and follow their lead.
- On escalators, stand on the right and pass on the left (even though Brits do the opposite behind the wheel). But note that in some passageways or stairways, you might be directed to walk on the left (like cars).
- When leaving a station, hold the door for the person behind you.

By Bus
Riding city buses doesn't come naturally to many travelers, but if you make a point to figure out the system you'll swing like Tarzan

Oyster Cards and Travelcards

London has the most expensive public transit in the world—you will definitely save money on your Tube and bus rides using a multi-ride pass. There are two similar but distinct options: Oyster cards and Travelcards (details online at www.tfl.gov.uk, click "Tickets").

Oyster Cards

Oyster cards—hard plastic transit cards embedded with computerized information—are the standard, smart way to ride the Tube and buses economically. Tube fares are heavily discounted with Oyster cards (£1.50–2 per ride in Zones 1–6 off-peak, instead of £4 per ride if you pay cash). Bus fares are also discounted with an Oyster card (£1 in Zones 1–6 at any time, instead of £2 if you pay cash). They're worth considering if you'll be in London for longer than a few days.

Buy Oyster cards at Tube station ticket offices. They can be used on the Tube, buses, and Docklands Light Railway (DLR). On each type of transport, you simply touch the card to the yellow card reader, it flashes green, and you're good to go. With the standard **pay-as-you-go Oyster card,** you load up your Oyster with credit (no minimum, but start with £10), and fares are then deducted as you ride. A price cap guarantees you'll never pay more than the One-Day Travelcard price within a 24-hour period (see "One-Day Travelcard," below). You pay a £3 one-time, refundable fee for the card itself. Pay-as-you-go Oyster balances never expire (but after a two-year-period, you do need to call the Oyster helpline to have the card's validity extended; tel. 0845-330-9876). You can lend your card to someone, but you can't use the card to cover two or more simultaneous trips. When your balance gets low, add another £5 or £10 to keep riding.

To see how much credit remains on your card, swipe it at any automatic ticket machine. You can also see a record of all your travels (and what you paid). Try it.

The **Seven-Day Oyster card** is a good option, even for as few as four days. The least expensive version is £23.20, and covers unlimited, peak-time travel through Zones 1 and 2 (no deposit required, cards covering more zones are also available).

Travelcards

A paper Travelcard works like a traditional ticket: You buy it at any Tube station ticket window or machine, then feed it into a turnstile (and retrieve it) to enter and exit the Tube. On a bus, just show it to the driver when you get on. If you take at least two rides a day, a Travelcard is a better deal than buying individual tickets. Like the Oyster card, Travelcards are valid on the Tube, buses, and Docklands Light Railway. The following fares are for Zones 1 and 2; pricier versions covering more zones are also available. Note that you can use any Travelcard to get a 33 percent discount on most Thames cruises.

The **One-Day Travelcard** gives you unlimited travel for a day. The regular price is £6.60, but an "off-peak" version is £5.10 (good for travel starting after 9:30 on weekdays and anytime on weekends). A One-Day Travelcard for Zones 1 through 6, which includes Heathrow Airport, costs £13.20; the restricted off-peak version costs £6.70.

The **Three-Day Travelcard** for £16.40 costs 20 percent less than three One-Day "peak" Travelcards, and is also good any time of day. Most travelers staying three days will easily take enough Tube and bus rides to make this worthwhile. Three-Day Travelcards are not available in an "off-peak" version. Buying three separate One-Day "off-peak" Travelcards will save you £1.10, but you'll only be able to travel after 9:30 on weekdays.

Which Pass to Buy?

Trying to decide between an Oyster and a Travelcard? Here's what I recommend:

- For one to two days, get a One-Day Travelcard each day.
- For three consecutive days, buy a Three-Day Travelcard.
- For four consecutive days, either buy a Three-Day Travelcard plus an extra One-Day Travelcard as needed (total £23), or a Seven-Day Oyster card (£23.20).
- For five or more days in a row, a Seven-Day Oyster card is your best bet. If you won't be riding public transport every day, get the pay-as-you-go Oyster card instead.

Other Discounts

Groups: Ten or more adults can travel all day on the Tube for £3.50 each (but not on buses). Kids 12–17 pay £1 when part of a group of 10.

Families: A paying adult can take up to four kids (age 10 and under) for free on the Tube and Docklands Light Railway all day, every day. In the Tube, use the manual gate, rather than the turnstiles, to be waved in. Families with children 11–15 also save with the "Kid for a Quid" promotion: Any adult with a Travelcard can buy an off-peak One-Day Travelcard for up to four kids 15 or younger for only £1 (a "quid") each.

London

Handy Buses

Since London instituted a "congestion charge" for cars, the bus system has gotten faster, easier, and cheaper than ever. Tube-oriented travelers need to make a point to get over their tunnel vision, learn the bus system, and get around quickly and easily.

Here are some of the most useful routes:

Route #9: Knightsbridge (Harrods) to Hyde Park Corner to Piccadilly Circus to Trafalgar Square.

Routes #11 and #24: Victoria Station to Westminster Abbey to Trafalgar Square (#11 continues to St. Paul's).

Route #RV1: Tower of London to Tower Bridge to Tate Modern/ Shakespeare's Globe to London Eye/ Waterloo Station/County Hall Travel Inn accommodations to Trafalgar Square to Covent Garden (a scenic joyride).

Route #15: Paddington Station to Oxford Circus to Regent Street/TI to Piccadilly Circus to Trafalgar Square to Fleet Street to St. Paul's to Tower of London.

Route #168: Waterloo Station/London Eye to Covent Garden and then near British Museum and British Library.

In addition, several buses (including #6, #13, #15, #23, #139, and #159) make the corridor run from Trafalgar, Piccadilly Circus, and Oxford Circus to Marble Arch.

through the urban jungle of London. Pick up the free *London Buses: Central London* at a transport office, TI, or some major museums for a fine map listing all the bus routes best for sightseeing.

The first step in mastering the bus system is learning how to decipher the bus-stop signs. Find a bus stop and study the signs mounted on the pole next to the stop. You'll see a chart listing (alphabetically) the destinations served by buses that pick up at this spot or nearby; the names of the buses; and letters that identify exactly where the buses pick up. After locating your destination, remember or write down the bus name and bus stop letter. Next, refer to the neighborhood map (also on the pole) to find your bus stop. Just match your letter with a stop on the map. Make your way to that stop—you'll know it's yours because it will have the same letter on its pole—and wait for the bus with the right name to arrive. Some fancy stops have electric boards indicating the minutes until the next bus arrives; but remember to check the name on the bus before you hop on. Crack the code and you're good to go.

Handy Bus Routes

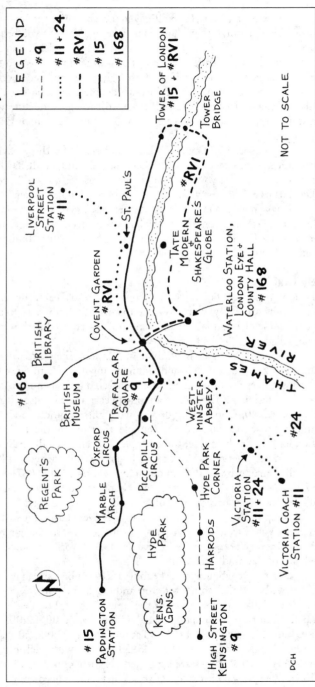

LEGEND
- – – #9
- ..... #11 + 24
- – – # RVI
- #15
- #168

London

NOT TO SCALE

TOWER OF LONDON #15 + #RVI

TOWER BRIDGE

#RVI

TATE MODERN + SHAKESPEARE'S GLOBE

WATERLOO STATION, LONDON EYE + COUNTY HALL #168

THAMES RIVER

LIVERPOOL STREET STATION #11

ST. PAUL'S

COVENT GARDEN #RVI

BRITISH LIBRARY

#168

BRITISH MUSEUM

TRAFALGAR SQUARE

OXFORD CIRCUS

WEST-MINSTER ABBEY

PICCADILLY CIRCUS

HYDE PARK CORNER

#24

VICTORIA STATION #11 + 24

VICTORIA COACH STATION #11

REGENT'S PARK

MARBLE ARCH

HYDE PARK

HARRODS

KENS. GDNS.

HIGH STREET KENSINGTON #9

N

#15 PADDINGTON STATION

DCH

On almost all buses, you'll pay at a machine at the bus stop (exact change only), then show your ticket (or pass) as you board. You can also use Travelcards and Oyster cards (see sidebar on page 52). If you're using an Oyster card, don't forget to touch it to the electronic card reader as you board, though there's no need to do so when you hop off. On a few of the older double-decker buses (serving "Heritage" routes #9 and #15), you still pay a conductor; take a seat and he or she will come around to collect your fare or verify your pass.

Any bus ride in downtown London costs £2 for those paying cash. A six-pack of Bus Saver tickets costs £6 and an all-day bus pass costs £3.50. If you're staying longer, consider the £14 Seven-Day bus pass. The best views are upstairs on a double-decker.

If you have a Travelcard or Oyster card, get in the habit of hopping buses for quick little straight shots, even just to get to a Tube stop. During bump-and-grind rush hours (8:00–10:00 and 16:00–19:00), you'll go faster by Tube.

By Taxi

London is the best taxi town in Europe. Big, black, carefully regulated cabs are everywhere. (While historically known as "black cabs," some of London's official taxis are now covered with wildly colored ads.)

I've never met a crabby cabbie in London. They love to talk, and they know every nook and cranny in town. I ride in one each day just to get my London questions answered (drivers must pass a rigorous test about London geography to earn their license). Rides start at £2.20. Connecting downtown sights is quick and easy, and will cost you about £6 (for example, St. Paul's to the Tower of London). For a short ride, three people in a cab generally travel at Tube prices. Groups of four or five should taxi everywhere. While telephoning a cab will get you one in a few minutes (tel. 0871-871-8710; £2 surcharge, plus extra fee to book ahead by credit card), it's generally not necessary; hailing a cab is easy and costs less. If a cab's top light is on, just wave it down. Drivers flash lights when they see you wave. They have a tiny turning radius, so you can hail cabs going in either direction. If waving doesn't work, ask someone where you can find a taxi stand.

Don't worry about meter cheating. Licensed British cab meters come with a sealed computer chip and clock that ensures you'll get the regular tariff #1 most of the time (Mon–Fri 6:00–20:00), tariff #2 during "unsociable hours" (Mon–Fri 20:00–22:00 and Sat–Sun 6:00–22:00), and tariff #3 at night (daily 22:00–6:00) and on holidays. (Rates go up about 15–20 percent with each higher tariff.) All extra charges are explained in writing on the cab wall. The only way a cabbie can cheat you is by taking a needlessly long route. Another pitfall is taking a cab when traffic is bad to a destination efficiently served by the Tube. On a recent trip to London, I hopped in a taxi at South Kensington for Waterloo Station and hit bad traffic. Rather than spending 20 minutes and £2 on the Tube, I spent 40 minutes and £16 in a taxi.

Tip a cabbie by rounding up (maximum 10 percent). If you over-drink and ride in a taxi, be warned: Taxis charge £40 for "soiling" (a.k.a., pub puke).

TOURS

▲▲▲**Hop-on, Hop-off Double-Decker Bus Tours**—Two competitive companies (Original and Big Bus) offer essentially the same two tours of the city's sightseeing highlights, with nearly  30 stops on each route. One tour has buses with live (English-only) guides, and a second (sometimes slightly different route) comes with tape-recorded, dial-a-language narration. These two-hour, once-over-lightly bus tours drive by all the famous sights, providing a stress-free way to get your bearings and see the biggies. With a good guide and nice weather, sit back and enjoy the entire two hours. Narration is important—and each company has both entertaining and boring guides—so hop on and hop off to see the sights or to change guides.

Buses run about every 10–15 minutes in summer, every 20 minutes in winter, and operate daily (from about 9:00 until early evening in summer, until late afternoon in winter). It's an inexpensive form of transport, stopping at a core group of sights regardless of which overview tour you're on: Victoria Station, Marble Arch, Piccadilly Circus, Trafalgar Square, the Tower of London, and elsewhere.

In addition to the overview tours, both Original and Big Bus include a narrated Thames boat tour covered by the same ticket (buy ticket from driver, credit cards accepted at major stops such as Victoria Station, ticket good for 24 hours, bring a sweater and a camera). Big Bus tours are a little bit more expensive (£22), while Original tours are cheaper (£16 with this book) and nearly as good. Pick up a map from any flier rack or from one of the countless salespeople, and study the complex system. Note: If you start at Victoria Station at 9:00, you'll finish near Buckingham Palace in time to see the Changing of the Guard at 11:30; ask your driver for the best place to hop off. Sunday morning—when the traffic is

London

Daily Reminder

Sunday: The Tower of London and British Museum are both especially crowded today. Hyde Park Speakers' Corner rants from early afternoon until early evening. These places are closed: Banqueting House, Sir John Soane's Museum, and legal sights (Houses of Parliament, City Hall, and Old Bailey; the neighborhood called The City is dead). Westminster Abbey and St. Paul's are open during the day for worship and closed to sightseers, though Westminster Abbey offers a free organ recital at 17:45. Many stores are closed, and some minor sights don't open until noon. The Camden Lock, Spitalfields, Greenwich, and Petticoat Lane street markets flourish, but Portobello Road and Brixton are closed. There are few plays on Sunday.

Monday: Virtually all sights are open except for Apsley House, Sir John Soane's Museum, and a few others. At Somerset House, the Courtauld Gallery is free until 14:00. Vinopolis is open until 21:00. The Houses of Parliament are usually open until 22:30.

Tuesday: Virtually all sights are open, except for Vinopolis. The British Library is open until 20:00. On the first Tuesday of the month, Sir John Soane's Museum is also open 18:00–21:00. The Houses of Parliament are usually open until 22:30.

Wednesday: All sights are open, plus evening hours at Westminster Abbey (until 19:00, but no evensong) and the National Gallery (until 21:00).

light and many museums are closed—is a fine time for a tour. The last full loop leaves Victoria at 17:00. Unless you're using the bus tour mainly for hop-on, hop-off transportation, consider saving money by taking a night tour (described later in this chapter).

Original London Sightseeing Bus Tour: For a live guide on the city highlights tour, look for a yellow triangle on the front of the bus. A red triangle means a longer, tape-recorded multilingual tour that includes Madame Tussauds—avoid it, unless you have kids who'd enjoy the entertaining recorded kids' tour. A green triangle on the front denotes a short *Da Vinci Code* tour, while a blue triangle connects far-flung museums. All routes are covered by the same ticket. Keep it simple and just take the main, introductory tour (£19, £3 discount with this book, limit two discounts per book, they'll rip off the corner of this page—raise bloody hell if they don't honor this discount, also online deals, ticket good for 24 hours, tel. 020/8877-1722, www.theoriginaltour.com). Your ticket includes a 50-minute round-trip boat tour from Westminster Pier (departs hourly, tape-recorded narration) or a point-to-point boat

Thursday: All sights are open, plus evening hours at the British Museum (selected galleries until 20:30), National Portrait Gallery (until 21:00), and Vinopolis (until 21:00).

Friday: All sights are open, plus evening hours at the British Museum (selected galleries until 20:30), National Portrait Gallery (until 21:00), Vinopolis (until 21:00), Victoria and Albert Museum (until 22:00), and Tate Modern (until 22:00). The Houses of Parliament close early today (15:00). Best street market today: Spitalfields.

Saturday: Most sights are open except legal ones (Old Bailey, City Hall, Houses of Parliament; skip The City). Vinopolis is open until 21:00, and the Tate Modern until 22:00. Best street markets: Portobello, Camden Lock, Greenwich.

Notes: The St. Martin-in-the-Fields church offers lunchtime concerts (free, Mon, Tue, and Fri at 13:00) and evening concerts (£8–18, at 19:30 Thu–Sat, sometimes Tue and Wed). Evensong occurs daily at St. Paul's (Mon–Sat at 17:00 and Sun at 15:15) and daily except Wednesday at Westminster Abbey (Mon–Tue and Thu–Fri at 17:00, Sat–Sun at 15:00). London by Night Sightseeing Tour buses leave from Victoria Station every evening (19:30–21:30, only at 20:30 in winter). The London Eye spins nightly until 21:00, until 20:00 in winter (closed Christmas–mid-Jan). See also "London for Early Birds and Night Owls" on page 78.

London

trip from Embankment Pier to Greenwich, with stops in between (14 departures per day).

Big Bus Hop-on, Hop-off London Tours: For £22 (£20 if you book online), you get the same basic overview tours: Red buses come with a live guide, while the blue route has a recorded narration and a longer path around Hyde Park. Your ticket includes coupons for several silly one-hour London walks, as well as the scenic and usually entertainingly guided Thames boat ride between Westminster Pier and the Tower of London (normally £6). The pass and extras are valid for 24 hours. These pricier tours tend to have better, more dynamic guides than Original (daily 8:30–18:00, winter until 16:30, from Victoria Station, tel. 020/7233-9533, www.bigbus.co.uk).

At Night: The London by Night Sightseeing Tour operates two routes, but after hours, with none of the extras (e.g., walks, boat tours), and at a lower price. While the narration can be pretty lame, the views at twilight are grand (though note that it stays light out late on summer nights). Their West End Tour drives by more biggies than their City Tour. Each tour costs £13.50 and lasts

60 minutes. You can pay the driver when you board (at any of the stops on their route, such as the London Eye, where the two routes intersect); or buy tickets at the Victoria Station or Paddington Station TIs; or save £3.50 by booking on their website (April–Dec only, West End Tour normally departs 19:30, 20:30, and 21:30 from Victoria Station, only at 20:30 tour in winter; Taxi Road, at front of station near end of Wilton Road, tel. 020/8545-6109, www.london-by-night.net). For a memorable and economical evening, munch a scenic picnic dinner on the top deck. There are plenty of take-away options within the train stations and near the various stops.

▲▲**Walking Tours**—Several times a day, top-notch local guides lead (often big) groups through specific slices of London's past. Schedule fliers litter the desks of TIs, hotels, and pubs. *Time Out* lists many, but not all, scheduled walks. Simply show up at the announced location, pay £6, and enjoy two chatty hours of Dickens, the Plague, Shakespeare, Legal London, the Beatles, Jack the Ripper, or whatever is on the agenda. **The Original London Walks,** the dominant company, lists its extensive daily schedule in a beefy, plain, black-and-white *London Walks* brochure and on their website, where you can plan an itinerary online (walks offered year-round—even Christmas, private tours for groups-£100, tel. 020/7624-3978, for a recorded listing of today's walks call 020/7624-9255, www.walks.com). They also run **Explorer day trips,** a good option for those with limited time and transportation (different trip daily: Stonehenge/Salisbury, Oxford/Cotswolds, York, Bath, and so on).

The Beatles: Fans of the still–Fabulous Four can take one of two Beatles walks (Original London Walks, above, has 5/week; Big Bus, above, has a daily walk included with their bus tour). For a photo op, go to Abbey Road and walk the famous crosswalk (at intersection with Grove End, Tube: St. John's Wood). The Beatles Store is at 231 Baker Street (daily 10:00–18:30, next to Sherlock Holmes Museum, Tube: Baker Street, tel. 020/7935-4464, www .beatlesstorelondon.co.uk).

Private Guides—Standard rates for London's registered guides usually run about £120 for four hours, and £200 for eight hours (tel. 020/7780-4060, www.touristguides.org.uk, www.blue-badge .org.uk). Consider Sean Kelleher (£110/half-day, £170/day, tel. 020/8673-1624, mobile 07764-612-770, seankelleher@btinternet .com) or Britt Lonsdale (tel. 020/7386-9907, mobile 07812-278-077, brittl@ntlworld.com).

Drivers: Robina Brown leads tours of small groups in her Toyota Previa (£250/half-day, £350–540/day, prices vary by destination, tel. 020/7228-2238, www.driverguidetours.com, robina @driverguidetours.com). Janine Barton provides a similar driver-

and-guide tour and similar prices (£225–245/half-day for up to six people, £340–500/day, prices vary by destination, entrance fees extra, tel. 020/7402-4600, jbsiis@aol.com), and offers a 15 percent discount to readers of this book. Robina and Janine's services are particularly helpful for wheelchair-using travelers who want to see more of London.

London Duck Tours—A bright-yellow amphibious WWII-vintage vehicle (the model that landed troops on Normandy's beaches on D-Day) takes a gang of 30 tourists past some famous sights on land—Big Ben, Trafalgar Square, Piccadilly Circus—then splashes into the Thames for a cruise. All in all, it's good fun at a rather steep price; the live guide works hard, and it's kid-friendly to the point of goofiness (£18, 2/hr, daily 10:00–17:30, 75 min—45 min on land and 30 min in the river, £2.50 booking fee online, these book up in advance, departs from Chicheley Street—you'll see the big ugly vehicle parked 100 yards behind the London Eye Ferris Wheel, Tube: Waterloo or Westminster, tel. 020/7928-3132, www .londonducktours.co.uk).

Bike Tours—The **London Bicycle Tour Company** offers three tours covering London from their base at Gabriel's Wharf on the south bank of the Thames. Sunday is the best, as there is less car traffic (Central Tour—£14.95, daily at 10:30, 6 miles, 2.5 hrs, includes Westminster, Covent Garden, and St. Paul's; West Tour—£17.95, Sat–Sun at 12:00, 9 miles, 3.5 hrs, includes Waterloo and Victoria stations, Hyde Park, Buckingham Palace, and Covent Garden; East Tour—£17.95, Sat–Sun at 14:00, 9 miles, 3.5 hrs, includes south side of the river to Tower Bridge, then The City to the East End). They also rent bikes (office open daily 10:00–18:00, west of Blackfriars Bridge on the South Bank, 1a Gabriel's Wharf, tel. 020/7928-6838, www.londonbicycle.com).

▲▲**Cruises**—Boat tours with entertaining commentaries sail regularly from many points along the Thames. It's confusing, since there are several companies offering essentially the same thing. Your basic options are downstream (to the Tower and Greenwich), upstream (to Kew Gardens and Hampton Court), and round-trip scenic tour cruises. Most people depart from the Westminster Pier (at the base of Westminster Bridge, under Big Ben). You can catch many of the same boats (with less waiting) from Waterloo Pier at the London Eye Ferris Wheel across the river. For pleasure and efficiency, consider combining a one-way cruise (to Kew, Greenwich, or wherever) with a Tube ride back. While Tube and bus tickets don't work on the boats, an Oyster card or Travelcard can snare you a 33 percent discount on most cruises (just show the card when you pay for the cruise). Children and seniors get discounts. You can purchase drinks and small, pricey snacks on board. Buy boat tickets at the small ticket offices on the docks. Clever budget travelers

Thames Boat Piers

While Westminster Pier is the most popular, it's not the only dock in town. Consider all the options:

Westminster Pier, at the base of Big Ben, offers round-trip sightseeing cruises and lots of departures in both directions.

Waterloo Pier, at the base of London Eye Ferris Wheel, is a good, less-crowded alternative to Westminster, with many of the same cruise options.

Embankment Pier is near Covent Garden, Trafalgar Square, and Cleopatra's Needle (the obelisk on the Thames). You can take a round-trip cruise from here, or catch a boat to the Tower of London and Greenwich.

Tower Millennium Pier is at the Tower of London. Boats sail west to Westminster Pier or east to Greenwich.

Bankside Pier (near Tate Modern and Shakespeare's Globe) and **Millbank Pier** (near Tate Britain) are connected to each other by the Tate Boat ferry service.

pack a picnic and munch while they cruise.

Here are some of the most popular cruise options:

To the Tower of London: City Cruises boats sail 30 minutes to the Tower from Westminster Pier (£6.20 one-way, £7.40 round-trip, one-way included with Big Bus London tour; covered by £10 "River Red Rover" ticket that includes Greenwich—see next paragraph; daily April–Oct roughly 10:00–21:00, until 18:00 in winter, every 20 min).

To Greenwich: Two companies head to Greenwich from Westminster Pier. Choose between **City Cruises** (£7.20 one-way, £9.40 round-trip; or get their £10 all-day, hop-on, hop-off "River Red Rover" ticket to have option of getting off at the London Eye Ferris Wheel and Tower of London; daily April–Oct generally 10:00–17:00, less off-season, every 40 min, 70 min to Greenwich, usually narrated only downstream—to Greenwich, tel. 020/7740-0400, www.citycruises.com) and **Thames River Services** (£7.20 one-way, £9.40 round-trip, daily April–Oct 10:00–16:00, July–Aug until 17:00, has shorter hours and runs every 40 min rest of year, 2/hr, 60 min, usually narrated only to Greenwich, tel. 020/7930-4097, www.westminsterpier.co.uk).

To Kew Gardens: Westminster Passenger Services Association leaves for Kew Gardens from Westminster Pier (£11 one-way, £17 round-trip, 4/day, generally departing 10:30–14:00, 90 min, narrated for 45 min, tel. 020/7930-2062, www.wpsa.co.uk). Some boats continue on to **Hampton Court Palace** for an additional £3 (and 90 min). Because of the river current, you'll save 30 minutes cruising from Hampton Court back into town.

Round-Trip Cruises: Fifty-minute round-trip cruises of the Thames go hourly from Westminster Pier to the Tower of London (£7.40, included with Original London Sightseeing Bus tour—listed on page 58, tape-recorded narration, Catamaran Circular Cruises, tel. 020/7987-1185). The London Eye operates its own "River Cruise Experience," offering a similar 40-minute live-guided circular tour from Waterloo Pier (£10, £21 with London Eye, reservations recommended, departures generally :45 past each hour, tel. 0870-443-9185, www.ba-londoneye.com).

From Tate to Tate: The Tate Boat service for art-lovers connects the Tate Modern and Tate Britain in 18 scenic minutes, stopping at the London Eye Ferris Wheel en route (£4 one-way or £8 for a day ticket; with a Travelcard it's £2.60 one-way or £5.20 for day ticket; buy ticket at gallery desk or on board, departing every 40 min from 10:00–17:00, 18-min trip, tel. 020/7887-8008).

On Regent's Canal: Consider exploring London's canals by taking a cruise on historic Regent's Canal in north London. The good ship *Jenny Wren* offers 90-minute guided canal boat cruises from Walker's Quay in Camden Town through scenic Regent's Park to Little Venice (£7.50, March–Oct daily 12:30 and 14:30, Sat–Sun also at 16:30, Walker's Quay, 250 Camden High Street, 3-min walk from Tube: Camden Town, tel. 020/7485-4433, www.walkersquay.com). While in Camden Town, stop by the popular, punky Camden Lock Market to browse through trendy arts and crafts (daily 10:00–18:00, busiest on weekends, a block from Walker's Quay).

SELF-GUIDED WALK

Westminster Walk

Just about every visitor to London strolls the historic Whitehall Boulevard from Big Ben to Trafalgar Square. Under London's modern traffic and big-city bustle lie two thousand fascinating years of history. This three-quarter-mile, self-guided orientation walk (see map on page 64) gives you a whirlwind tour and connects

the sights listed in this section.

Start halfway across **Westminster Bridge** (❶) for that "Wow, I'm really in London!" feeling. Get a close-up view of the **Houses of Parliament** and **Big Ben** (floodlit at night). Downstream you'll see the **London Eye.** Down the stairs to Westminster Pier are boats to the

Westminster Walk

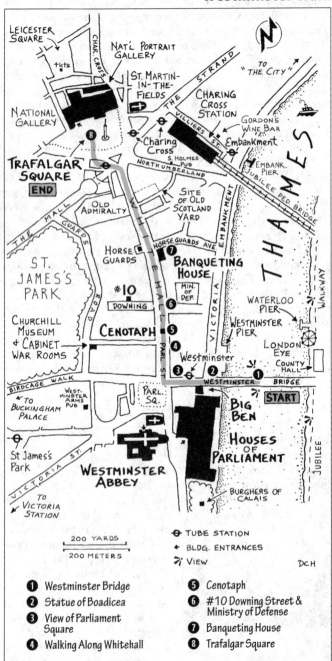

LEICESTER SQUARE

+tkts

NAT'L PORTRAIT GALLERY

CHAR. CROSS

ST. MARTIN-IN-THE-FIELDS

THE STRAND

"TO THE CITY"

NATIONAL GALLERY

CHARING CROSS STATION

VILLIERS ST.

GORDON'S WINE BAR

Charing Cross

EMBANKMENT

8

S. HOLMES PUB

THAMES

TRAFALGAR SQUARE

NORTHUMBERLAND

EMBANK. PIER

END

JUBILEE PED. BRIDGE

THE MALL

OLD ADMIRALTY

SITE OF OLD SCOTLAND YARD

WHITEHALL

GUARDS

EMBANKMENT

ST. JAMES'S PARK

HORSE GUARDS

HORSE GUARDS AVE.

7

BANQUETING HOUSE

WALKWAY

#10 DOWNING

6

MIN. OF DEF.

VICTORIA

WATERLOO PIER

CHURCHILL MUSEUM & CABINET WAR ROOMS

CENOTAPH

5

WESTMINSTER PIER

THAMES

4

PARL. ST.

Westminster

LONDON EYE

COUNTY HALL

3

2

1

BIRDCAGE WALK

WESTMINSTER BRIDGE

→ TO BUCKINGHAM PALACE

WEST-MINSTER ARMS PUB

PARL. SQ.

START

BIG BEN

St James's Park

VICTORIA ST.

HOUSES OF PARLIAMENT

JUBILEE

TO VICTORIA STATION

WESTMINSTER ABBEY

BURGHERS OF CALAIS

N

200 YARDS

200 METERS

⊖ TUBE STATION

← BLDG. ENTRANCES

👁 VIEW

DCH

1 Westminster Bridge
2 Statue of Boadicea
3 View of Parliament Square
4 Walking Along Whitehall

5 Cenotaph
6 #10 Downing Street & Ministry of Defense
7 Banqueting House
8 Trafalgar Square

London

Tower of London and Greenwich.

En route to Parliament Square, you'll pass a **statue of Boadicea (❷)**, the Celtic queen defeated by Roman invaders in A.D. 60.

To thrill your loved ones (or bug the envious), call home from a pay phone near Big Ben at about three minutes before the hour. You'll find a phone on Great George Street, across from **Parliament Square (❸)**. As Big Ben chimes, stick the receiver outside the booth and prove you're in London: Ding dong ding dong...dong ding ding dong.

Wave hello to Churchill in Parliament Square. To his right is **Westminster Abbey** with its two stubby, elegant towers.

Head north up Parliament Street, which turns into (❹) Whitehall, and walk toward Trafalgar Square. You'll see the thought-provoking **Cenotaph (❺)** in the middle of the street, reminding passersby of Britain's many war dead. To visit the Churchill Museum and Cabinet War Rooms (see page 70), take a left before the Cenotaph, on King Charles Street.

Continuing on Whitehall, stop at the barricaded and guarded **#10 Downing Street** to see the British "White House" (❻), home of the prime minister. Break the bobby's boredom and ask him a question.

Nearing Trafalgar Square, look for the **Horse Guards** behind the gated fence (Changing of the Horse Guards Mon–Sat 11:00, Sun at 10:00, dismounting ceremony daily at 16:00) and the 17th-century **Banqueting House** across the street (❼); described on page 71.

The column topped by Lord Nelson marks **Trafalgar Square (❽)**. The stately domed building on the far side of the square is the **National Gallery** (free), which has a classy café upstairs in the Sainsbury wing. To the right of the National Gallery is **St. Martin-in-the-Fields Church** and its Café in the Crypt.

To get to Piccadilly from Trafalgar Square, walk up Cockspur Street to Haymarket, then take a short left on Coventry Street to colorful **Piccadilly Circus.**

Near Piccadilly you'll find the **Britain and London Visitors Centre** (on Lower Regent Street) and piles of theaters. **Leicester Square** (with its half-price "tkts" booth for plays, see page 109) thrives just a few blocks away. Walk through seedy **Soho** (north of Shaftesbury Avenue) for its fun pubs (see page 135 for the "Food is

Fun" Dinner Crawl). From Piccadilly or Oxford Circus, you can take a taxi, bus, or the Tube home.

SIGHTS

▲▲▲Westminster Abbey

The greatest church in the English-speaking world, Westminster Abbey is the place where England's kings and queens have been crowned and buried since 1066. A thousand years of English history—3,000 tombs, the remains of 29 kings and queens, and hundreds of memorials to poets, politicians, and warriors—lie within its stained-glass splendor and under its stone slabs. Like a stony refugee camp huddled outside St. Peter's Pearly Gates, this place has a story to tell. You can take a tour (live or audioguide, see below), experience evensong or an organ concert (see below), visit several small museums, and even have coffee in the cloister...but you can't take photos.

Three tiny **museums** ring the cloisters: the Chapter House (where the monks held their daily meetings, notable for its fine architecture and well-described but faded medieval art), the Pyx Chamber (containing an exhibit on the King's Treasury), and the Abbey Museum (which tells of the abbey's history, royal coronations, and burials). Look into the impressively realistic eyes of Henry VII's funeral effigy (one of a fascinating series of wax-and-wood statues that, for three centuries, graced royal coffins during funeral processions).

The church hosts **evensong** performances every night but Wednesday (Mon–Tue and Thu–Fri at 17:00; Sat–Sun at 15:00) and a free 30-minute **organ recital** on Sunday (at 17:45).

Cost, Hours, Location: £10, £24 family ticket, includes cloisters and Abbey Museum, free for prayer, Mon–Sat 9:30-15:45, Wed until 19:00, last admission 60 min before closing, closed Sun to sightseers but open for services, Abbey Museum open daily 10:30–16:00, cloisters open daily 8:00–18:00, £5 guided tours—up to 6/day in summer, £4 audioguide tours, Tube: Westminster or St. James's Park, info desk tel. 020/7654-4900, www.westminster-abbey.org.

The main entrance, on the Parliament Square side, often has a sizable line; visit early or late to avoid tourist hordes. Midmornings are most crowded. On weekdays after 14:30 it's less crowded; come then and stay for the 17:00 evensong (except Wed). Since the church is often closed to the public for special services, it's wise to call first.

For a free peek inside (without seeing all the historic tombs) and a quiet moment in the nave, you can tell a marshal at the west end (where the tourists exit) that you'd like to pay your respects to Britain's Unknown Soldier, and he will let you slip in.

Between the Abbey and Trafalgar Square

▲▲Houses of Parliament (Palace of Westminster)—This Neo-Gothic icon of London, the royal residence from 1042 to 1547, is now the meeting place of the legislative branch of government. Tourists are welcome to view debates in either the bickering House of Commons or the genteel House of Lords (in session when a flag flies atop the Victoria Tower). While the actual debates are generally quite dull, it is a thrill to be inside and see the British government inaction (both Houses usually open Mon–Tue 14:30–22:30, Wed–Thu 11:30–17:50, Fri 9:30–15:00, closed Sat–Sun, generally less action and no lines after 18:00, Tube: Westminster, tel. 020/7219-4272; see www.parliament.uk for schedule). The House of Lords has more pageantry, shorter lines, and less interesting debates (tel. 020/7219-3107 for schedule, and visit www.parliamentlive.tv for a preview).

Houses of Parliament Tours: In August and September, you can get a behind-the-scenes peek at the royal chambers of both houses with a tour led by a Blue Badge guide (£7, 75 min, roughly Mon and Fri–Sat 9:15–16:30, Tue–Thu 1:15–16:30, confirm times when you book, first tours begin 15 min before the Houses open, to book a spot in advance—avoiding waits and guaranteeing a spot—use Keith Prowse ticket service, tel. 0870-906-3773, www.keithprowse.com, no booking fee).

Visiting the Houses of Parliament: In 2008, the Houses of Parliament will undergo major changes, including the addition of a new Visitors Centre. To enter the venerable HOP, look for the new entrance on the west side of the building (across from Westminster Abbey); it'll be slightly north of the St. Stephen's entrance, which was the previous entry for tourists. You'll likely see construction in process; follow the people and signs, or ask a guard. If there's only one line outside, it's for the House of Commons. Go to the gate and tell the guard you want the House of Lords (it just takes a few minutes and both Houses are worth seeing). You may pop right in—that is, after you've cleared the security gauntlet. Once you've seen the Lords (hide your HOL flier), you can often slip directly over to the House of Commons and join the gang waiting in the lobby. Inside the lobby, you'll find an announcement board with the day's lineup for both houses.

Just past security to the left, study the big dark **Westminster Hall,** which survived the 1834 fire. The hall was built in the 11th century, and its famous self-supporting hammer-beam roof was

London at a Glance

▲▲▲Westminster Abbey Britain's finest church and the site of royal coronations and burials since 1066. **Hours:** Mon–Sat 9:30–15:45, Wed until 19:00, closed Sun to sightseers but open for services. See page 66.

▲▲▲Churchill Museum and Cabinet War Rooms Underground WWII headquarters of Churchill's war effort. **Hours:** Daily 9:30–18:00. See page 70.

▲▲▲National Gallery Remarkable collection of European paintings (1250–1900), including Leonardo, Botticelli, Velázquez, Rembrandt, Turner, van Gogh, and the Impressionists. **Hours:** Daily 10:00–18:00, Wed until 21:00. See page 72.

▲▲▲British Museum The world's greatest collection of artifacts of Western civilization, including the Rosetta Stone and the Parthenon's Elgin Marbles. **Hours:** Daily 10:00–17:30, Thu–Fri until 20:30 but only a few galleries open after 17:30. See page 79.

▲▲▲British Library Impressive collection of the most important literary treasures of the Western world. **Hours:** Mon–Fri 9:30–18:00, Tue until 20:00, Sat 9:30–17:00, Sun 11:00–17:00. See page 82.

▲▲▲St. Paul's Cathedral The main cathedral of the Anglican Church, designed by Christopher Wren, with a climbable dome and daily evensong services. **Hours:** Mon–Sat 8:30–16:30, closed Sun except for worship. See page 92.

▲▲▲Tower of London Historic castle, palace, and prison, today housing the crown jewels and a witty band of Beefeaters. **Hours:** March–Oct Tue–Sat 9:00–18:00, Sun–Mon 10:00–18:00; Nov–Feb Tue–Sat 9:00–17:00, Sun–Mon 10:00–17:00. See page 94.

▲▲▲London Eye Enormous observation wheel, dominating—and offering commanding views over—London's skyline. **Hours:** Daily June–Sept 10:00–21:00, Oct–Christmas and mid-Jan–May 10:00–20:00, closed Christmas–mid-Jan. See page 96.

▲▲▲Tate Modern Works by Monet, Matisse, Dalí, Picasso, and Warhol displayed in a converted powerhouse. **Hours:** Daily 10:00–18:00, Fri–Sat until 22:00. See page 99.

▲▲Houses of Parliament London's famous Neo-Gothic landmark, topped by Big Ben and occupied by the Houses of

Lords and Commons. **Hours** (both Houses): Generally Mon–Tue 14:30–22:30, Wed–Thu 11:30–17:50, Fri 9:30–15:00, closed Sat–Sun. See page 67.

▲▲**National Portrait Gallery** *Who's Who* of British history, featuring portraits of this nation's most important historical figures. **Hours:** Daily 10:00–18:00, Thu–Fri until 21:00. See page 73.

▲▲**Somerset House** Grand 18th-century civic palace housing three fine-art museums: Courtauld Gallery (decent painting collection), Hermitage Rooms (rotating exhibits from famous St. Petersburg museum), and the Gilbert Collection (decorative arts). **Hours:** Daily 10:00–18:00. See page 77.

▲▲**Victoria and Albert Museum** The best collection of decorative arts anywhere. **Hours:** Daily 10:00–17:45, Fri until 22:00. See page 89.

▲▲**Imperial War Museum** Examines the military history of the bloody 20th century. **Hours:** Daily 10:00–18:00. See page 98.

▲▲**Shakespeare's Globe** Timbered, thatched-roofed reconstruction of the Bard's original wooden "O." **Hours:** Theater complex, exhibition, and actor-led tours generally daily 9:00–17:00; in summer, morning tours only. Plays are also held here. See page 100.

▲▲**Old Operating Theatre Museum** 19th-century hall where surgeons performed amputations for an audience of aspiring med students. **Hours:** Daily 10:30–17:00. See page 101.

▲▲**Vinopolis** Offers a breezy history of wine with plenty of tasting opportunities. **Hours:** Mon and Thu–Sat 12:00–21:00, Wed and Sun 12:00–18:00, closed Tue. See page 101.

▲▲**Tate Britain** Collection of British painting from the 16th century through modern times, including works by William Blake, the Pre-Raphaelites, and J. M. W. Turner. **Hours:** Daily 10:00–17:50. See page 103.

▲**Buckingham Palace** Britain's royal residence with the famous Changing of the Guard. **Hours:** Palace—Aug–Sept only, daily 9:45–18:00; Guard—almost daily in summer at 11:30, every other day all year long. See page 85.

London

added in 1397. The Houses of Parliament are located in what was once the Palace of Westminster, long the palace of England's medieval kings, until it was largely destroyed by fire in 1834. The palace was rebuilt in the Victorian Gothic style (a move away from Neoclassicism back to England's Christian and medieval heritage, true to the Romantic Age). It was completed in 1860.

The **Jewel Tower** is the only other part of the old Palace of Westminster to survive (besides Westminster Hall). It contains a fine little exhibit on Parliament (first floor—history, second floor—Parliament today) with a 25-minute video and lonely, picnic-friendly benches (£2.90, daily April–Oct 10:00–17:00, Nov–March 10:00–16:00, across street from St. Stephen's Gate, tel. 020/7222-2219).

Big Ben, the clock tower (315 feet high), is named for its 13-ton bell, Ben. The light above the clock is lit when the House of Commons is sitting. The face of the clock is huge—you can actually see the minute hand moving. For a good view of it, walk halfway over Westminster Bridge.

▲▲▲**Churchill Museum and Cabinet War Rooms**—This is a fascinating walk through the underground headquarters of the British

government's fight against the Nazis in the darkest days of the Battle for Britain. The 27-room nerve center of the British war effort was used from 1939 to 1945. Churchill's room, the map room, and other rooms are just as they were in 1945. For all the blood, sweat, toil, and tears details, pick up the excellent, essential, and included audioguide at the entry and follow the 60-minute tour; be patient—it's well worth it. Don't bypass the Churchill Museum (entrance is a half-dozen rooms into the exhibit), which shows the man behind the famous cigar, bowler hat, and V-for-victory sign—allow an hour for that museum alone. It shows his wit, irascibility, work ethic, American ties, writing talents, and drinking habits. A long touch-the-screen timeline lets you zero in on events in his life from birth (November 30, 1874) to his appointment as prime minister in 1940. It's all the more amazing considering that, in the 1930s, the man who would become my vote for greatest statesman of the 20th century was considered a washed-up loony ranting about the growing threat of fascism (£12, daily 9:30–18:00, last entry 60 min before closing, on King Charles Street, 200 yards off Whitehall, follow the signs, Tube: Westminster, tel. 020/7930-6961, www.iwm.org.uk). The museum's gift shop is great for anyone nostalgic for the 1940s.

If you're hungry, get your rations at the Switch Room café (in the museum, daily 10:00–17:00) or, for a nearby pub lunch, try the Westminster Arms (food served downstairs, on Storeys Gate, a couple of blocks south of War Rooms).

Horse Guards—The Horse Guards change daily at 11:00 (10:00 on Sun), and there's a colorful dismounting ceremony daily at 16:00. The rest of the day, they just stand there—terrible for video cameras (on Whitehall, between Trafalgar Square and #10 Downing Street, Tube: Westminster). While Buckingham Palace pageantry is canceled when it rains, the Horse Guards change regardless of the weather.

▲Banqueting House—England's first Renaissance building was designed by Inigo Jones around 1620. It's one of the few London

landmarks spared by the 1698 fire and the only surviving part of the original Palace of Whitehall. Don't miss its Rubens ceiling, which, at Charles I's request, drove home the doctrine of the legitimacy of the divine right of kings. In 1649—divine right ignored—Charles I was beheaded on the balcony of this building by a Cromwellian Parliament. Admission includes a restful 20-minute audiovisual history, which shows the place in banqueting action; a 30-minute audio tour—interesting only to history buffs; and a look at the exquisite banqueting hall (£4.50, Mon–Sat 10:00–17:00, closed Sun, last entry at 16:30, subject to closure for government functions, aristocratic WC, immediately across Whitehall from the Horse Guards, Tube: Westminster, tel. 020/3166-6154, www.hrp.org.uk). Just up the street is Trafalgar Square.

Trafalgar Square

▲▲Trafalgar Square—London's recently renovated central square, the destination of most marches and demonstrations, is a thrilling place to simply hang out. Lord Nelson stands atop

his 185-foot-tall fluted granite column, gazing out toward Trafalgar, where he lost his life but defeated the French fleet. Part of this 1842 memorial is made from his victims' melted-down cannons. He's surrounded by spraying fountains,

Trafalgar Square

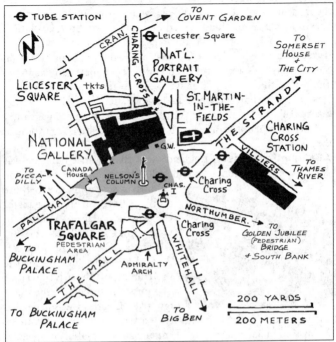

- TUBE STATION
- TO COVENT GARDEN
- Leicester Square
- CRAN.
- CHARING CROSS
- NAT'L. PORTRAIT GALLERY
- LEICESTER SQUARE
- tkts
- ST. MARTIN-IN-THE-FIELDS
- TO SOMERSET HOUSE & THE CITY
- THE STRAND
- CHARING CROSS STATION
- NATIONAL GALLERY
- G.W.
- VILLIERS
- TO PICCA-DILLY
- CANADA House
- NELSON'S COLUMN
- CHAS. I
- Charing Cross
- TO THAMES RIVER
- PALL MALL
- TRAFALGAR SQUARE
- PEDESTRIAN AREA
- Charing Cross
- NORTHUMBER.
- TO GOLDEN JUBILEE (PEDESTRIAN) BRIDGE & SOUTH BANK
- TO BUCKINGHAM PALACE
- ADMIRALTY ARCH
- THE MALL
- WHITEHALL
- TO BUCKINGHAM PALACE
- TO BIG BEN
- 200 YARDS
- 200 METERS

giant lions, hordes of people, and—until recently—even more pigeons. London's mayor, Ken Livingstone, nicknamed "Red Ken" for his passion for an activist government, decided that London's "flying rats" were a public nuisance and evicted the venerable seed salesmen (Tube: Charing Cross).

▲▲▲**National Gallery**—Displaying Britain's top collection of European paintings from 1250 to 1900—including works by Leonardo, Botticelli, Velázquez, Rembrandt, Turner, van Gogh,

and the Impressionists—this is one of Europe's great galleries. While the collection is huge, following the route suggested on the map on page 74 will give you my best quick visit. The audioguide tour (suggested £3 donation) is one of the finest I've used in Europe. The excellent-but-pricey café in the museum's restaurant, called the National Dining Rooms, is a good spot to share high tea (see page 142).

   Cost, Hours, Location: Free admission, daily 10:00–18:00, Wed until 21:00; free one-hour overview tours daily at 11:30 and 14:30. Photography is prohibited. It's on Trafalgar Square (Tube: Charing Cross or Leicester Square, recorded info tel. 020/7747-2885, switchboard tel. 020/7839-3321, www.nationalgallery.org.uk).

▲▲**National Portrait Gallery**—Put off by halls of 19th-century characters who meant nothing to me, I used to call this "as interesting as someone else's yearbook." But a selective walk through this 500-year-long *Who's Who* of British history is quick and free, and puts faces on the story of England. A bonus is the chance to admire some great art by painters such as Holbein, van Dyck, Hogarth, Reynolds, and Gainsborough. The collection is well-described, not huge, and in historical sequence, from the 16th century on the second floor to today's royal family on the ground floor.

Some highlights: Henry VIII and wives; several fascinating portraits of the "Virgin Queen" Elizabeth I, Sir Francis Drake, and Sir Walter Raleigh; the only real-life portrait of William Shakespeare; Oliver Cromwell and Charles I with his head on; self-portraits and other portraits by Gainsborough and Reynolds; the Romantics (Blake, Byron, Wordsworth, and company); Queen Victoria and her era; and the present royal family, including the late Princess Diana.

The excellent audioguide tours (free, but £2 donation requested) describe each room (or era in British history) and more than 300 paintings. You'll learn more about British history than art and actually hear interviews with 20th-century subjects as you stare at their faces.

Cost, Hours, Location: Free, daily 10:00–18:00, Thu–Fri until 21:00. It's 100 yards off Trafalgar Square (around corner from National Gallery, opposite Church of St. Martin-in-the-Fields, Tube: Charing Cross or Leicester Square, tel. 020/7306-0055, recorded info tel. 020/7312-2463, www.npg.org.uk). The elegant Portrait Restaurant on the top floor comes with views and high prices (reservations smart, tel. 020/7312-2490); the cheaper Portrait Café is in the basement. The eateries close 30 minutes before the museum closes.

▲**St. Martin-in-the-Fields**—This church, built in the 1720s with a Gothic spire atop a Greek-type temple, is an oasis of peace on wild and noisy Trafalgar Square (free, donations welcome, open daily, Tube: Charing Cross, www.smitf.com). St. Martin cared for the poor. "In the fields" was where the first church stood on this spot (in the 13th century), between Westminster and the City. Stepping inside, you still feel a compassion for the needs of the people in this community. A free flier provides a brief yet worthwhile self-guided tour. The church is famous for its concerts. Consider a free lunchtime concert (Mon, Tue, and Fri at 13:00) or an evening concert (£8–18, at 19:30 Thu–Sat and on some Tue and

National Gallery Highlights

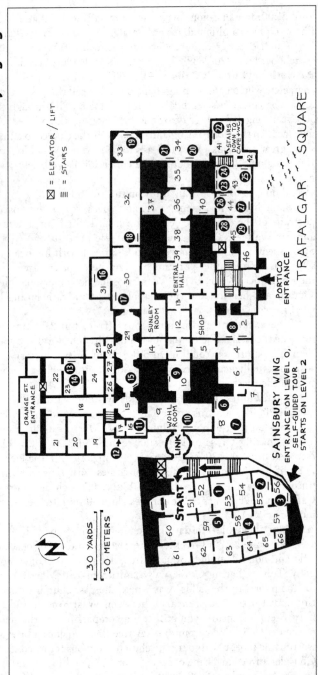

MEDIEVAL & EARLY RENAISSANCE

❶ ANONYMOUS – *The Wilton Diptych*
❷ UCCELLO – *Battle of San Romano*
❸ VAN EYCK – *The Arnolfini Marriage*

ITALIAN RENAISSANCE

❹ BOTTICELLI – *Venus and Mars*
❺ CRIVELLI – *The Annunciation with Saint Emidius*

HIGH RENAISSANCE

❻ MICHELANGELO – *Entombment*
❼ RAPHAEL – *Pope Julius II*
❽ LEONARDO DA VINCI – *The Virgin of the Rocks; Virgin and Child with St. John the Baptist and St. Anne*

VENETIAN RENAISSANCE

❾ TITIAN – *Bacchus and Ariadne*
❿ TINTORETTO – *The Origin of the Milky Way*

NORTHERN PROTESTANT ART

⓫ VERMEER – *A Young Woman*
⓬ "A Peepshow"
⓭ REMBRANDT – *Belshazzar's Feast*
⓮ REMBRANDT – *Self-Portrait*

BAROQUE & ROCOCO

⓯ RUBENS – *The Judgment of Paris*
⓰ VAN DYCK – *Charles I on Horseback*
⓱ VELÁZQUEZ – *The Rokeby Venus*
⓲ CARAVAGGIO – *The Supper at Emmaus*
⓳ BOUCHER – *Pan and Syrinx*

BRITISH

⓴ CONSTABLE – *The Hay Wain*
㉑ TURNER – *The Fighting Téméraire*
㉒ DELAROCHE – *The Execution of Lady Jane Grey*

IMPRESSIONISM & BEYOND

㉓ MONET – *Gare St. Lazare*
㉔ MONET – *The Water-Lily Pond*
㉕ MANET – *Corner of a Café-Concert (a.k.a. The Waitress)*
㉖ RENOIR – *Boating on the Seine*
㉗ SEURAT – *Bathers at Asnières*
㉘ VAN GOGH – *Sunflowers*
㉙ CÉZANNE – *Bathers*

London's Top Squares

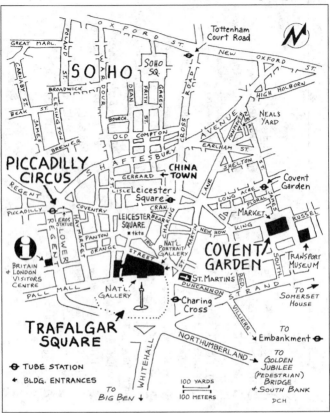

Wed, box office tel. 020/7839-8362, church tel. 020/7766-1100, www2.stmartin-in-the-fields.org). Downstairs, you'll find a ticket office for concerts, a newly renovated gift shop, a brass-rubbing center, and a fine support-the-church cafeteria (see page 131).

Piccadilly, Soho, and Covent Garden

For a "Food is Fun" dinner crawl from Covent Garden to Soho, see page 135.

▲▲**Piccadilly Circus**—London's most touristy square got its name from the fancy ruffled shirts—*picadils*—made in the neighborhood long ago. Today, the square, while pretty grotty, is surrounded by fascinating streets swimming with youth on the rampage. For overstimulation, drop by the extremely trashy **Trocadero Center** for its Funland virtual-reality games, nine-screen cinema, and 10-lane bowling alley (admission to Trocadero is free; individual attractions cost £2–10; located between Coventry and Shaftesbury, just off Piccadilly, Tube: Piccadilly Circus). Chinatown, to the east, has swollen since the British colony of Hong Kong gained its independence and was returned to China in 1997. Nearby Shaftesbury Avenue and Leicester Square teem with fun-seekers, theaters, Chinese restaurants, and street singers.

Soho—North of Piccadilly, seedy Soho has become seriously trendy and is well worth a gawk. But Soho is also London's red light district, where "friendly models" wait in tiny rooms up dreary stairways, and voluptuous con artists sell strip shows. While venturing up a stairway to check out a model is interesting, anyone who goes into any one of the shows will be ripped off. Every time. Even a £5 show in a "licensed bar" comes with a £100 cover or minimum (as it's printed on the drink menu) and a "security man." You may accidentally buy a £200 bottle of bubbly. And suddenly, the door has no handle.

Telephone sex ads are hard to avoid these days in London. Phone booths are littered with racy fliers of busty ladies "new in town." Some travelers gather six or eight phone booths' worth of fliers and take them home for kinky wallpaper.

▲▲**Covent Garden**—This boutique-ish shopping district is a people-watcher's delight, with cigarette eaters, Punch-and-Judy acts, food that's good for you (but not your wallet), trendy crafts, sweet whiffs of marijuana, two-tone hair (neither natural), and faces that could set off a metal detector (Tube: Covent Garden). For better Covent Garden lunch deals, walk a block or two away from the eye of this touristic hurricane (check out the places north of the Tube station along Endell and Neal Streets).

Museums near Covent Garden

▲▲**Somerset House**—This grand 18th-century civic palace offers a marvelous public space, three fine art collections, and a riverside terrace (between the Strand and the Thames). The palace once

housed the national registry that records Britain's births, marriages, and deaths: "...where they hatch 'em, match 'em, and dispatch 'em." Step into the courtyard to enjoy the fountain. Go ahead...walk through it. The 55 jets get playful twice an hour. (In the winter, this becomes a popular ice-skating rink with a toasty café for viewing.)

Surrounding you are three small and sumptuous sights: the Courtauld Gallery (paintings), the Gilbert Collection (fine arts), and the Hermitage Rooms (the art of czarist Russia). All three

London for Early Birds and Night Owls

Most sightseeing in London is restricted to the hours between 10:00 and 18:00. Here are a few exceptions:

Sights Open Early
Every day these sights open by 9:30 or earlier.

Churchill Museum and Cabinet War Rooms: Daily at 9:30.

Kew Gardens: Daily at 9:30.

Madame Tussauds Waxworks: Mid-July–Aug at 9:00, otherwise 9:30.

Westminster Cathedral: Daily at 9:30.

Shakespeare's Globe: May–Sept daily at 9:00.

Buckingham Palace: Aug–Sept daily at 9:45.

Southwark Cathedral: Mon–Fri at 8:00, Sat–Sun at 9:00.

St. Paul's Cathedral: Mon–Sat at 8:30.

Westminster Abbey: Mon–Sat at 9:30.

British Library: Mon–Sat at 9:30.

Tower of London: Tue–Sat at 9:00.

Houses of Parliament: Fri at 9:30.

Sights Open Late
Every night in London at least one sight is open late, in addition to the London Eye. Here's the scoop from Monday through Sunday:

London Eye: June–Sept daily until 21:00, off-season until 20:00.

Vinopolis: Mon until 21:00 (also Thu–Sat).

Houses of Parliament (when in session): Mon–Tue until 22:30.

British Library: Tue until 20:00.

Sir John Soane's Museum: First Tue of month until 21:00.

Westminster Abbey: Wed until 19:00.

National Gallery: Wed until 21:00.

Vinopolis: Thu–Sat until 21:00 (also on Mon).

British Museum (some galleries): Thu–Fri until 20:30.

National Portrait Gallery: Thu–Fri until 21:00.

Victoria and Albert Museum: Fri until 22:00.

Tate Modern: Fri–Sat until 22:00.

Clink Prison Museum: Sat–Sun until 21:00.

are open the same hours (daily 10:00–18:00, last entry 17:15, £5 per sight, £8 for any two sights, £12 for all three within 3 days; easy bus #6, #9, #11, #13, #15, or #23 from Trafalgar Square; Tube: Temple or Covent Garden, tel. 020/7845-4600, www.somerset-house.org .uk). The website lists a busy schedule of tours, kids' events, and concerts. The riverside terrace is picnic-friendly (deli inside lobby).

The **Courtauld Gallery** is less impressive than the National Gallery, but its wonderful collection of paintings is still a joy. The gallery is part of the Courtauld Institute of Art, and the thoughtful description of each piece of art reminds visitors that the gallery is still used for teaching. You'll see medieval European paintings and works by Rubens, the Impressionists (Manet, Monet, and Degas), Post-Impressionists (such as Cézanne), and more (£5, free Mon until 14:00, downstairs cafeteria, lockers, and WC).

The **Hermitage Rooms** offer a taste of Romanov imperial splendor. As Russia struggles and tourists are staying away, someone had the bright idea of sending the best of its art to London to raise some hard cash. These five rooms host a different collection every six months, with a standard intro to the czar's winter palace in St. Petersburg (£5, tel. 020/7420-9410). To see what's on, visit www.hermitagerooms.com.

The **Gilbert Collection** displays 800 pieces of the finest in European decorative arts, from diamond-studded gold snuffboxes to intricate Italian mosaics. Maybe you've seen Raphael paintings and Botticelli frescoes...but this lush collection is refreshingly different (£5, includes free audioguide with a highlights tour and a helpful loaner magnifying glass).

▲**London Transport Museum**—This wonderful museum—newly renovated—is a delight for kids. Whether you're cursing or marveling at the buses and Tube, the growth of Europe's biggest city has been made possible by its public transit system. Watch the growth of the Tube, then sit in the simulator to "drive" a train (likely daily 10:00–18:00, in southeast corner of Covent Garden courtyard, Tube: Covent Garden, tel. 020/7379-6344 or recorded info tel. 020/7565-7299, www.ltmuseum.co.uk).

North London

▲▲▲**British Museum**—Simply put, this is the greatest chronicle of civilization...anywhere. A visit here is like taking a long hike through Encyclopedia Britannica National Park. Entering on Great Russell Street, you'll step into the Great Court, the glass-domed hub of a two-acre cultural complex, containing restaurants, shops, and lecture halls plus the Reading Room.

The most popular sections of the museum fill the ground floor: Egyptian, Mesopotamian, and ancient Greek—with the famous Elgin Marbles from the Athenian Parthenon. Huge winged lions

North London

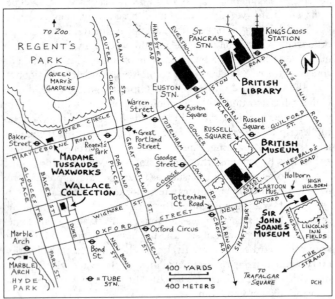

(which guarded Assyrian palaces 800 years before Christ) guard these great ancient galleries. For a brief tour, connect these ancient dots:

Start with the **Egyptian.** Wander from the Rosetta Stone past the many statues. At the end of the hall, climb the stairs to mummy land.

Back at the winged lions, explore the dark, violent, and mysterious **Assyrian** rooms. The Nimrud Gallery is lined with royal propaganda reliefs and wounded lions (from the ninth century B.C.).

The most modern of the ancient art fills the **Greek** section. Find Room 11, behind the winged lions, and start your walk through Greek art history with the simple and primitive Cycladic fertility figures. Later, painted vases show a culture really into partying. The finale is the Elgin Marbles. The much-wrangled-over bits of the Athenian Parthenon (from about 450 B.C.) are even more impressive than they look. To best appreciate these ancient carvings, take the audioguide tour (available in this gallery).

Be sure to venture upstairs to see artifacts from **Roman Britain** (Room 50) that surpass anything you'll see at Hadrian's Wall or elsewhere in Britain. Nearby, the Dark Age Britain exhibits offer a worthwhile peek at that bleak era; look for the Sutton Hoo Burial Ship artifacts from a seventh-century royal burial on the east coast of England (Room 41). A rare Michelangelo cartoon (preliminary sketch) is in Room 90.

British Museum Overview

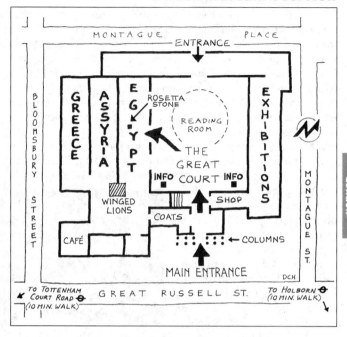

The **Great Court** is Europe's largest covered square—bigger than a football field. This people-friendly court—delightfully out of the London rain—was for 150 years one of London's great lost spaces...closed off and gathering dust. While the vast British Museum wraps around the court, its centerpiece is the stately **Reading Room,** famous as the place Karl Marx hung out while formulating his ideas on communism and writing *Das Kapital.* The Reading Room, which is normally free and open to the quiet public, will instead host special exhibitions (on China's Terracotta Warriors through early April and on Roman Emperor Hadrian July–Oct), requiring a separate entry fee.

Cost, Hours, Location: The British Museum is free (£3 donation requested, temporary exhibits extra, daily 10:00–17:30, plus Thu–Fri until 20:30—but only a few galleries open after 17:30, least crowded weekday late afternoons, Great Russell Street, Tube: Tottenham Court Road, tel. 020/7323-8000, recorded info tel. 020/7388-2227, www.thebritishmuseum.ac.uk).

The Great Court has longer opening hours than the museum

(daily 9:00–18:00, Thu–Sat until 23:00).

Tours: The various Eye-Opener tours are free (generally run every half hour 11:00–15:30, 50 min); each one is different, focusing on one particular subject within the museum. The Highlights tours are expensive but meaty (£8, 90 min, at 10:30, 13:00, and 15:00). There are also several different audioguide tours (£3.50, requires leaving photo ID), including Top 50 Highlights (90 min), the Parthenon Sculptures (60 min), and Family Tours (length varies; "Bodies, Beasts, and Boardgames," narrated by Stephen Fry, is particularly good).

▲▲▲**British Library**—Here, in just two rooms, are the literary treasures of Western civilization, from early Bibles to Shakespeare's *Hamlet* to Lewis Carroll's *Alice's Adventures in Wonderland*. You'll

see the Lindisfarne Gospels transcribed on an illuminated manuscript, as well as Beatles' lyrics scrawled on the back of a greeting card. The British Empire built its greatest monuments out of paper. And it's with literature that England made her lasting contribution to civilization and the arts (free, Mon–Fri 9:30–18:00, Tue until 20:00, Sat 9:30–17:00, Sun 11:00–17:00; 60-min tours for £8 are usually offered Mon, Wed, and Fri at 15:00; Sat at 10:30 and 15:00; Sun at 11:30 and 15:00; call 020/7412-7639 to confirm schedule and reserve; helpful free computers also give you extra info; Tube: King's Cross, from the station walk a block west to 96 Euston Road, library tel. 020/7412-7000, www.bl.uk). The ground-floor café is next to a vast and fun pull-out stamp collection, and the self-service café upstairs serves good hot meals.

▲**Wallace Collection**—Sir Richard Wallace's fine collection of 17th-century Dutch Masters, 18th-century French Rococo, medieval armor, and assorted aristocratic fancies fills the sumptuously furnished Hertford House on Manchester Square. From the rough and intimate Dutch life-scapes of Jan Steen to the pink-cheeked Rococo fantasies of François Boucher, a wander through this little-visited mansion makes you nostalgic for the days of empire (free, daily 10:00–17:00, audioguide-£3; guided tours available—but call to confirm times; just north of Oxford Street on Manchester Square, Tube: Bond Street, tel. 020/7563-9500, www.wallacecollection.org).

▲**Madame Tussauds Waxworks**—This is gimmicky and expensive but dang good. The original Madame Tussaud did wax casts of heads lopped off during the French Revolution (such as Marie-Antoinette's). She took her show on the road and ended up in

British Library Highlights

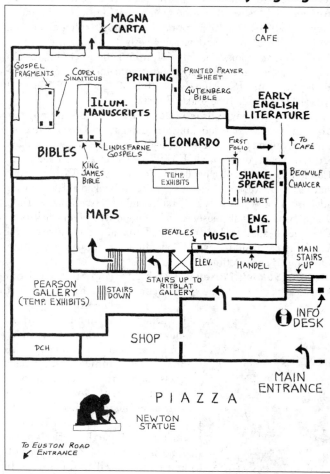

MAGNA CARTA

CAFE

GOSPEL FRAGMENTS

CODEX SINAITICUS

PRINTING

PRINTED PRAYER SHEET

GUTENBERG BIBLE

EARLY ENGLISH LITERATURE

ILLUM. MANUSCRIPTS

BIBLES

LINDISFARNE GOSPELS

LEONARDO

FIRST FOLIO

To CAFÉ

KING JAMES BIBLE

TEMP. EXHIBITS

SHAKE-SPEARE

BEOWULF

CHAUCER

HAMLET

MAPS

ENG. LIT

BEATLES

MUSIC

HANDEL

MAIN STAIRS UP

ELEV.

PEARSON GALLERY (TEMP. EXHIBITS)

STAIRS DOWN

STAIRS UP TO RITBLAT GALLERY

INFO DESK

DCH

SHOP

MAIN ENTRANCE

P I A Z Z A

NEWTON STATUE

To EUSTON ROAD ENTRANCE

London

London. And now it's much easier to be featured. The gallery is one big photo-op—a huge hit with the kind of travelers who skip the British Museum. After looking a hundred famous people in their glassy eyes and surviving a silly hall of horror, you'll board a Disney-type ride and cruise through a kid-pleasing "Spirit of London" time trip. Your last stop is the auditorium for a 12-minute stage show (runs every 15 min). They've dumped anything really historical (except for what they claim is the blade that beheaded Marie-Antoinette) because "there's no money in it and we're a business." Now, it's all about squeezing Brad Pitt's bum, wining and dining with George Clooney, and partying with Beyoncé, Kylie, Britney, and Posh (admission-£25, kids-£21; from 17:00 to closing it's £16, kids-£11; children under 5 always free; mid-July–Aug daily 9:00–18:00; Sept–mid-July Mon–Fri 9:30–17:30, Sat–Sun 9:30–18:00; Marylebone Road, Tube: Baker Street).

Saving Money and/or Time: The Waxworks are popular. You can avoid a wait by booking ahead to get a ticket with an entry time (by calling 0870-400-3000, booking online at www.madame-tussauds.com, or getting a Fast Track ticket at the Britain and London Visitors Centre or the TIs at Victoria and Waterloo train stations). The website offers better prices if booked a day or two in advance: adults-£20, kids-£16; adults and kids pay £10 after 17:00. The website also sells museum and London Eye combo-tickets for £29. The cheapest way to get in is to book online and arrive at the Waxworks at 17:00 to save £15 on admission and avoid any lines. One hour is enough time for the exhibit.

Sir John Soane's Museum—Architects and fans of eclectic knickknacks love this quirky place, as do Martha Stewarts and

lovers of Back Door sights. Tour this furnished home on a bird-chirping square and see 19th-century chairs, lamps, and carpets, wood-paneled nooks and crannies, and stained-glass skylights. The townhouse is cluttered with Soane's (and his wife's) collection of ancient relics, curios, and famous paintings, including Hogarth's series on *The Rake's Progress* (read the fun plot) and several excellent Canalettos. In 1833, just before his death, Soane established his house as a museum, stipulating that it be kept as nearly as possible in the state he left it. If he visited today, he'd be entirely satisfied. You'll leave wishing you'd known the man (free, Tue–Sat 10:00–17:00, first Tue of the month also 18:00–21:00, closed Sun–Mon, good £1 brochure, £3 guided tours Sat at 14:30, 13 Lincoln's Inn Fields, quarter-mile southeast of British Museum, Tube: Holborn, tel. 020/7405-2107).

Cartoon Museum—This humble but interesting museum is located in the shadow of the British Museum. While it's filled with British cartoons unknown to most Americans, the satire of famous bigwigs and politicians—from Napoleon to Margaret Thatcher, the Queen, and Tony Blair—shows the power of parody

Buckingham Palace Area

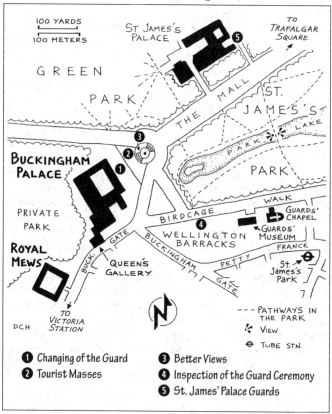

① Changing of the Guard
② Tourist Masses
③ Better Views
④ Inspection of the Guard Ceremony
⑤ St. James' Palace Guards

to deliver social commentary. Upstairs, you'll see pages spanning from *Tarzan* to *Tank Girl*—interesting only to comic-book die-hards (£3, Tue–Sat 10:30–17:30, Sun 12:00–17:30, closed Mon, 35 Little Russell Street—go one block south of the British Museum on Coptic Street and make a left, Tube: Tottenham Court Road, tel. 020/7580-8155, www.cartoonmuseum.org).

Buckingham Palace

▲**Buckingham Palace**—This lavish home has been Britain's royal residence since 1837. When the queen's at home, the royal standard flies (a red, yellow, and blue flag); otherwise the Union Jack flaps in the wind. Recently, the queen has opened her palace to the public—but only in August and September, when she's out of town (£15 for state apartments and throne room, Aug–Sept only, daily 9:45–18:00, last admission 15:45, only 8,000 visitors a day—to get an entry time, come early or for £1.25 extra you can book ahead by phone or online, Tube: Victoria, tel. 020/7766-7300, www .royalcollection.org.uk).

▲**Queen's Gallery at Buckingham Palace**—Queen Elizabeth's 7,000 paintings make up the finest private art collection in the world, rivaling Europe's biggest national art galleries. It's actually a collection of collections, built on by each successive monarch since the 16th century. She rotates her paintings, enjoying some privately in her many palatial residences while sharing others with her subjects in public galleries in Edinburgh and London. Small, thoughtfully presented, and always exquisite displays fill the handful of rooms open to the public in a wing of Buckingham Palace. As you're in "the most important building in London," security is tight. You'll see a temporary exhibit and the permanent "treasures"—which come with a room full of "antique and personal jewelry." Compared to the crown jewels at the Tower, it may be Her Majesty's bottom drawer—but it's still a dazzling pile of diamonds. Temporary exhibits change about twice a year, and are always lovingly described by the £2 audioguide. While the admissions come with an entry time, this is only enforced during rare days when crowds are a problem (£8, £12 with Royal Mews, daily 10:00–17:30, last entry 60 min before closing, Tube: Victoria, tel. 020/7766-7301 but Her Majesty rarely answers). Men shouldn't miss the mahogany-trimmed urinals.

Royal Mews—The queen's working stables, or "mews," are open to visitors. The visit is likely to be disappointing (you'll see four horses out of the queen's 30, a fancy car, and a bunch of old carriages) unless you follow the included guided tour, in which case it's thoroughly entertaining—especially if you're interested in horses and/or royalty. The 40-minute tours go twice an hour and finish with the Gold State Coach (c. 1760, 4 tons, 4 mph). Queen Victoria said absolutely no cars. When she died, in 1901, the mews got its first Daimler. Today, along with the hay-eating transport, the stable is home to five Rolls-Royce Phantoms, with one on display (£6.50, £12 with Queen's Gallery, Aug–Sept Sat–Thu 10:00–17:00, March–July and Oct Sat–Thu 11:00–16:00, closed Fri and Nov–Feb, Buckingham Palace Road, Tube: Victoria, tel. 020/7766-7302).

▲▲**Changing of the Guard at Buckingham Palace**—The guards change with much fanfare at around 11:30 almost daily in the summer and, at a minimum, every other day all year long (no band when wet). Each month it's either daily or on odd or even days. Call 020/7766-7300 for the day's plan, or check www .changing-the-guard.com. Then hop into a big black taxi and say, "Buck House, please" (a.k.a. Buckingham Palace).

Most tourists just mob the palace gates for a peek at the Changing of the Guard, but those who know the drill will enjoy the event more. Here's the lowdown on what goes down: It's just after 11:00, and the on-duty guards—actually working at nearby St. James's Palace—are ready to finish their shift. At 11:15, these tired guards, along with the band, head out to the Mall, and then take a right turn for Buckingham Palace. Meanwhile, their replacement guards—fresh for the day—gather at 11:00 at their Wellington Barracks, 500 yards east of the palace (on Birdcage Walk), for a review and inspection. At 11:30, they also head for

Buckingham Palace. As both the tired and fresh guards converge on the palace, the Horse Guard enters the fray, marching down the Mall from the Horse Guard Barracks on Whitehall. At 11:45, it's a perfect storm of Red Coat pageantry, as all three groups converge. Everyone parades around, the guard changes (passing the regimental flag, or "color") with much shouting, the band plays a happy little concert, and then they march out. A few minutes later, fresh guards set up at St. James's Palace, the tired ones dress down at the barracks, and the tourists disperse.

Stake out the high ground on the circular Victoria Monument for the best overall view. Or start early either at St. James's Palace or the Wellington Barracks (the inspection is in full view of the street) and stride in with the band. The marching troops and bands are colorful and even stirring, but the actual Changing of the Guard is a nonevent. It is interesting, however, to see nearly every tourist in London gathered in one place at the same time. Afterwards, stroll through nearby St. James's Park (Tube: Victoria, St. James's Park, or Green Park).

West London
▲**Hyde Park and Speakers' Corner**—London's "Central Park," originally Henry VIII's hunting grounds, has more than 600 acres of lush greenery, a huge man-made lake, the royal Kensington

Palace and Orangery, and the ornate neo-Gothic Albert Memorial across from the Royal Albert Hall. On Sundays from just after noon until early evening, Speakers' Corner offers soapbox oratory at its best (Tube: Marble Arch). "The grass roots of democracy" is actually a holdover from when the gallows

London

West London

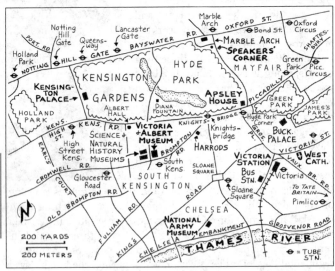

stood here and the criminal was allowed to say just about anything he wanted to before he swung. I dare you to raise your voice and gather a crowd—it's easy to do.

The **Princess Diana Memorial Fountain** honors the "People's Princess" who once lived in nearby Kensington Palace. The low-key circular stream is in the eastern part of the park, near the Serpentine Gallery. (Don't be confused by signs to the Diana Princess of Wales Children's Playground, also found within the park.)

▲**Apsley House (Wellington Museum)**— Having beaten Napoleon at Waterloo, the Duke of Wellington was once the most famous man in Europe. He was given London's ultimate address, #1 London. His newly refurbished mansion offers one of London's best palace experiences. An 11-foot-tall marble statue (by Canova) of Napoleon, clad only in a fig leaf, greets you. Downstairs is a small gallery of Wellington memorabilia (including a pair of Wellington boots). The lavish upstairs shows off the duke's fine collection of paintings, including works by Velázquez and Steen (£5.10, Tue–Sun 10:00–17:00 in summer, until 16:00 in winter, closed Mon, well-described by included audioguide, 20 yards from Hyde Park Corner Tube station, tel. 020/7499-5676, www.english-heritage.org.uk). Hyde Park's pleasant and picnic-wonderful rose garden is nearby.

▲▲**Victoria and Albert Museum**—The world's top collection of decorative arts (vases, stained glass, fine furniture, clothing, jewelry, carpets, and more) is a surprisingly interesting assortment of crafts from the West as well as Asian and Islamic cultures.

The V&A grew out of the Great Exhibition of 1851—that ultimate festival celebrating the greatness of Britain. After much support from Queen Victoria and Prince Albert, it was renamed after the royal couple.

Many visitors start with the **British Galleries** (upstairs)—a one-way tour stretching through 400 years of British lifestyles, almost a museum in itself.

In Room 46 are the plaster casts of **Trajan's Column,** a copy of Rome's 140-foot spiral relief telling the story of the conquest of Romania. (The V&A's casts are copies made for the benefit of

19th-century art students who couldn't afford a railpass.)

Room 46B, which has plaster casts of **Renaissance sculptures,** may be closed in 2008, but you may be able to peek down into the room from the upper mezzanine. Compare Michelangelo's monumental *David* with Donatello's girlish *David;* look also for Ghiberti's bronze Baptistery doors that inspired the Florentine Renaissance.

In Room 48A are **Raphael's "cartoons,"** seven huge watercolor designs by the Renaissance master for tapestries meant for the Sistine Chapel. The cartoons were sent to Brussels, cut into strips (see the lines), and placed on the looms. Notice that the scenes, the Acts of Peter and Paul, are the reverse of the final product (lots of left-handed saints).

Cost, Hours, Location: Free, £3 donation requested, possible pricey fee for special exhibits, daily 10:00–17:45, Fri until 22:00 (Tube: South Kensington, a long tunnel leads directly from the Tube station to the lower floor of the museum, tel. 020/7942-2000, www.vam.ac.uk).

The museum has 150 rooms and more than 12 miles of corridors. While just wandering works well here, consider catching one of the free 60-minute orientation **tours** (daily, usually on the half-hour from 10:30–15:30, also daily at 13:00, Fri at 16:30, and a half-hour version on Fri at 18:30) or buying the fine £5 *V&A Guide Book.* The V&A's helpful website lists its current exhibitions and offers interesting mix-and-match podcasts that allow you to create your own audiotour.

▲**Natural History Museum**—Across the street from Victoria and Albert, this mammoth museum is housed in a giant and wonderful Victorian, Neo-Romanesque building. Built in the 1870s specifically for the huge collection (50 million specimens), it has two halves: the Life Galleries (creepy-crawlies, human biology, "our place in evolution," and awesome dinosaurs) and the Earth Galleries (meteors, volcanoes, earthquakes, and so on). Exhibits are wonderfully explained, with lots of creative, interactive displays. Pop in, if only for the wild collection of dinosaurs and the roaring *Tyrannosaurus rex* (free, possible fee for special exhibits, daily 10:00–17:50, last entrance 17:30, a long tunnel leads directly from South Kensington Tube station to museum, tel. 020/7942-5000, exhibit info and reservations tel. 020/7942-5011, www.nhm .ac.uk). In 2008, parts of the museum may be closed for phase two of the Darwin Centre remodeling; the final goal is to display every insect specimen the museum has ever collected.

▲**Science Museum**—Next door to the Natural History Museum, this sprawling wonderland for curious minds is kid-perfect. It offers hands-on fun, from moonwalks to deep-sea exploration, with trendy technology exhibits, an IMAX theater (£7–10 tickets for grownups, kids less), cool rotating themed exhibits, and a revamped kids' zone on the third floor (free, daily 10:00–18:00, Exhibition Road, Tube: South Kensington, tel. 0870-870-4868, www.sciencemuseum.org.uk).

▲▲**Kensington Palace**—In 1689, King William and Queen Mary moved their primary residence from Whitehall in central London to the more pristine and peaceful village of Kensington (now engulfed by London). With a little renovation help from Sir Christopher Wren, they turned the existing house into Kensington Palace, which was the center of English court life until 1760, when the royal family moved into Buckingham Palace. Since then, lesser royals have bedded down in Kensington Palace (as Princess Diana did from her 1981 marriage to Prince Charles until her death in 1997). The palace, while still functioning as a royal residence, also welcomes visitors with an impressive string of historic royal apartments and a few rooms of queens' dresses and ceremonial clothing (late 19th and 20th centuries). Enjoy a re-created royal tailor and dressmaker's workshop, the 17th-century splendor of the apartments of William and Mary, and the bed where Queen Victoria was born (fully clothed). The displays are wonderfully described by the included audioguide. The empty, unfurnished Apartment 1A, the former home of Princess Margaret, is skippable (£12, daily 10:00–18:00, until 17:00 in winter, last entry 60 min before closing, a 10-min hike through Kensington Gardens from either Queensway or High Street Kensington Tube station, tel. 0870-751-5170, www.hrp.org.uk). Garden enthusiasts enjoy popping into the secluded Sunken Garden, 50 yards from the exit.

Consider high tea at the nearby Orangery (see page 142), built as a greenhouse for Queen Anne in 1704.

Victoria Station—From underneath this station's iron-and-glass canopy, trains depart for the south of England and Gatwick Airport. While Victoria Station is famous and a major Tube stop, few tourists actually take trains from here—most just come to take in the exciting bustle. It's a fun place to just be a "rock in a river" teeming with commuters and services. The station is surrounded by big red buses and taxis, travel agencies, and lousy eateries. It's next to the main bus station (National Express) and the best inexpensive B&Bs in town.

Westminster Cathedral—This largest Catholic church in England, just a block from Victoria Station, is striking but not very historic or important to visit. Opened in 1903, it has a brick Neo-Byzantine flavor (surrounded by glassy office blocks). While it's definitely not Westminster Abbey, half the tourists wandering around inside seem to think it is. The highlight is the lift to the viewing gallery atop its bell tower (fine view, £3 for the lift, tower open daily 9:30–12:30 & 13:00–17:00, cathedral sometimes open longer hours for Mass; 5-min walk from Victoria Station or take bus #11, #24, #148, #211, or #507 to museum's door; just off Victoria Street, Tube: Victoria).

National Army Museum—This museum is not as awe-inspiring as the Imperial War Museum, but it's still fun, especially for kids into soldiers, armor, and guns. And while the Imperial War Museum is limited to wars of the 20th century, this tells the story of the British Army from 1415 through the Bosnian conflict and Iraq, with lots of Red Coat lore and a good look at Waterloo. Kids enjoy trying on a Cromwellian helmet, seeing the skeleton of Napoleon's horse, and peering out from a WWI trench through a working periscope (free, daily 10:00–17:30, follow arrows in carpet to stay on track, bus #239 from Victoria Station stops at museum's door, Royal Hospital Road, Chelsea, Tube: Sloane Square, tel. 020-7730-0717, www.national-army-museum.ac.uk).

East London: The City

▲▲**The City of London**—When Londoners say "The City," they mean the one-square-mile center of business, banking, and journalism that 2,000 years ago was Roman Londinium. The outline of the Roman city walls can still be seen in the arc of roads from Blackfriars Bridge to Tower Bridge. Within the City are 23 churches designed by Sir Christopher Wren, mostly just ornamentation around St. Paul's Cathedral. Today, while home to only 5,000 residents, the City thrives with more than 500,000 office workers coming and going daily. It's a fascinating district to

East London: The City

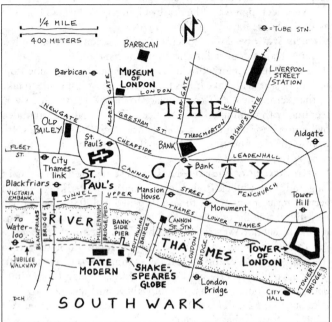

wander on weekdays, but since almost nobody actually lives there, it's dull in the evenings and on weekends.

▲**Old Bailey**—To view the British legal system in action—lawyers in little blond wigs speaking legalese with a British accent—spend a few minutes in the visitors' gallery at the Old Bailey, called the "Central Criminal Court." Don't enter under the dome; signs point you to the two visitors' entrances (free, generally Mon–Fri 10:30–13:00 & 14:00–16:30 depending on caseload, closed Sat–Sun, reduced hours in Aug; no kids under 14; no bags, mobile phones, or cameras, but small purses OK; Eddie at Bailey's Cafe across the street at #30 stores bags for £2; two blocks northwest of St. Paul's on Old Bailey Street, follow signs to public entrance, Tube: St. Paul's, tel. 020/7248-3277).

▲▲▲**St. Paul's Cathedral**—Wren's most famous church is the great St. Paul's, its elaborate interior capped by a 365-foot dome. The crypt (included with admission) is a world of historic bones and memorials, including Admiral Nelson's tomb and interesting cathedral models. Stroll down the

St. Paul's Cathedral

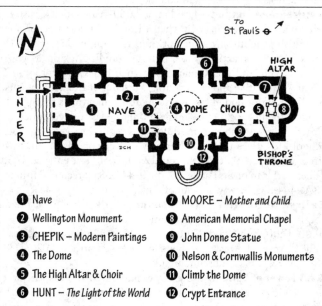

1 Nave

2 Wellington Monument

3 CHEPIK – Modern Paintings

4 The Dome

5 The High Altar & Choir

6 HUNT – The Light of the World

7 MOORE – Mother and Child

8 American Memorial Chapel

9 John Donne Statue

10 Nelson & Cornwallis Monuments

11 Climb the Dome

12 Crypt Entrance

same nave Prince Charles and Lady Diana walked on their 1981 wedding day. Imagine how they felt making the hike to the altar with the world watching. Sit under the second-largest dome in the world and eavesdrop on guided tours.

Since World War II, St. Paul's has been Britain's symbol of resistance. Despite 57 nights of bombing, the Nazis failed to destroy the cathedral, thanks to the St. Paul's volunteer fire watch, who stayed on the dome. Climb the dome for a great city view and some fun in the Whispering Gallery—where the precisely designed barrel of the dome lets sweet nothings circle audibly around to the opposite side.

The **evensong** services are free, but nonpaying visitors are not allowed to linger afterward (Mon–Sat at 17:00, Sun at 15:15, 40 min). The Sunday organ recital has been canceled while the organ is undergoing restoration (through 2009).

Cost, Hours, Location: £9.50, includes church entry and dome climb, Mon–Sat 8:30–16:30, last entry 16:00, last dome entry 15:30, closed Sun except for worship. No photography is allowed. Ninety-minute "super tours" of the cathedral and crypt cost £3 (Mon–Sat at 11:00, 11:30, 13:30, and 14:00—confirm schedule at church or call tel. 020/7236-4128; £3.50 for 60-min audioguide which covers 17 stops, available Mon–Sat 9:15–15:30). There's a cheery café in the crypt of the cathedral (Tube: St. Paul's, tel.

020/7236-4128, www.stpauls.co.uk).

▲**Museum of London**—London, a 2,000-year-old city, is so littered with Roman ruins that when a London builder finds Roman antiquities, he doesn't stop working. He simply documents the finds, moves the artifacts to a museum, and builds on. If you're asking, "Why did the Romans build their cities underground?" a trip to the creative and entertaining Museum of London is a must. Stroll through London history from pre-Roman times through the 1600s. (The lower galleries, representing the last few centuries, are closed for renovation until 2009.) This regular stop for the local school kids gives the best overview of London history in town (free, Mon–Sat 10:00–17:50, Sun 12:00–17:50, last entry at 17:30, Tube: Barbican or St. Paul's, tel. 0870-444-3852, recorded info tel. 0870-444-3851, www.museumoflondon.org.uk).

Geffrye Decorative Arts Museum—Walk through a dozen English front rooms dating from 1600 to 1990 (free, Tue–Sat 10:00–17:00, Sun 12:00–17:00, closed Mon, 136 Kingsland Road, Tube: Liverpool Street, then bus #149 or #242 north, tel. 020/7739-9893, www.geffrye-museum.org.uk).

▲▲▲**Tower of London**—The Tower has served as a castle in wartime, a king's residence in peacetime, and, most notoriously, as the

imprisonment and execution site of rebels. You can see the crown jewels, take a witty Beefeater tour, and ponder the executioner's block that dispensed with troublesome heirs to the throne and a couple of Henry VIII's wives (£16, family-£45; March–Oct Tue–Sat 9:00–18:00, Sun–Mon 10:00–18:00; Nov–Feb Tue–Sat 9:00–17:00, Sun–Mon 10:00–17:00; last entry 60 min before closing, the long but fast-moving ticket lines are worst on Sun, no photography allowed of jewels or in chapels, Tube: Tower Hill, tel. 0870-751-5177, recorded info tel. 0870-756-6060, booking tel. 0870-756-7070, www.hrp.org.uk). You can avoid the long lines by buying your ticket at any London TI, at the gift shop just below the Tower Hill Tube stop, or online. After your visit, consider taking the boat to Greenwich from here (see cruise info on page 62).

Ceremony of the Keys: Every night at precisely 21:30, with pageantry-filled ceremony, the Tower of London is locked up (as it has been for the last 700 years). To attend this free 30-minute event, you need to request an invitation at least two months before your visit. Write to Ceremony of the Keys, H.M. Tower of London, London EC3N 4AB. Include your name; the addresses, names, and ages of all people attending (up to 6 people, nontransferable, no kids under 8 allowed); requested date; alternative dates; and

Tower of London

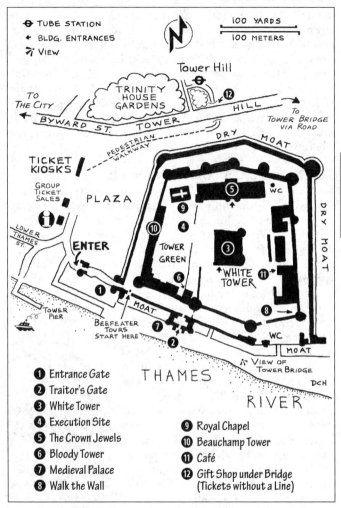

- TUBE STATION
- BLDG. ENTRANCES
- VIEW

100 YARDS
100 METERS

To The City

TRINITY HOUSE GARDENS

Tower Hill

BYWARD ST. TOWER HILL

To TOWER BRIDGE via ROAD

PEDESTRIAN WALKWAY

DRY MOAT

TICKET KIOSKS

GROUP TICKET SALES

PLAZA

LOWER THAMES ST.

ENTER

TOWER GREEN

Crown Jewels ⑤

WC

⑨

⑩

④

③

WHITE TOWER

DRY MOAT

⑥

⑪

TOWER PIER

MOAT

① ② ⑦

BEEFEATER TOURS START HERE

⑧

WC

MOAT

VIEW OF TOWER BRIDGE

DCH

THAMES

RIVER

1. Entrance Gate
2. Traitor's Gate
3. White Tower
4. Execution Site
5. The Crown Jewels
6. Bloody Tower
7. Medieval Palace
8. Walk the Wall
9. Royal Chapel
10. Beauchamp Tower
11. Café
12. Gift Shop under Bridge (Tickets without a Line)

two international reply coupons. International reply coupons cost $2 each and are available through any US post office (though few stock them, and some postal employees are unfamiliar with the form—direct your postal worker to section 372 of the International Mail Manual, at the post office or downloadable at http://pe.usps .gov/DMMdownload.asp). Your post office should be able to order international reply coupons for you just like they order stamps. Allow about a week's turnaround time.

More Sights near the Tower—The best remaining bit of London's **Roman Wall** is just north of the tower (at the Tower Hill Tube station). The impressive Tower Bridge is freshly painted and restored; for more information on this neo-Gothic maritime gateway to London, you can visit the **Tower Bridge Experience** for its 1894–1994 history exhibit and a peek at its Victorian engine room (£6, family-£10 and up, daily 10:00–18:30, last entry at 17:30, good view, poor value, enter at the northwest tower, tel. 020/7403-3761, www.towerbridge.org.uk). The chic **St. Katharine Dock,** just east of Tower Bridge, has mod shops and the classic old Dickens Inn, fun for a drink or pub lunch. Across the bridge is the South Bank, with the upscale Butlers Wharf area, City Hall, museums, and Jubilee Walkway.

South London, on the South Bank

The South Bank is a thriving arts and cultural center tied together by a riverside path. This popular, pub-crawling pedestrian promenade—called the Jubilee Walkway—stretches from Tower Bridge past Westminster Bridge, where it offers grand views of the Houses of Parliament. (The Walkway hugs the river except just east of London Bridge, where it cuts inland for a couple of blocks.)

City Hall—The glassy, egg-shaped building near the south end of Tower Bridge is London's City Hall, designed by Sir Norman Foster, the architect who worked on London's Millennium Bridge and Berlin's Reichstag. An interior spiral ramp allows visitors to watch and hear the action below in the Assembly Chamber; ride the lift to the second floor (the highest visitors can go) and spiral down. The Visitors Centre on the lower ground floor has a handy cafeteria. A top-floor observation deck known as "London's Living Room" is open for tours, usually on Monday morning (phone-in reservation required), and on occasional weekends from 10:00–16:30 (Visitors

Centre open Mon–Fri 8:00–20:00, generally closed Sat–Sun but open occasional weekends—check website, Tube: London Bridge station plus 10-min walk, or Tower Hill station plus 15-min walk; the Hall occasionally opens up for public tours—call or check website to confirm tour times and opening hours, tel. 020/7983-4100, www.london.gov.uk/gla/city_hall).

▲▲▲**London Eye**—Built by British Airways, this giant wheel towers above London opposite Big Ben. London's answer to the Eiffel Tower is the world's highest observational wheel, giving you a chance to fly British Airways without leaving London. Designed like a giant bicycle wheel, it's a pan-European undertaking: British steel and Dutch engineering, with Czech, German, French, and

London

The South Bank

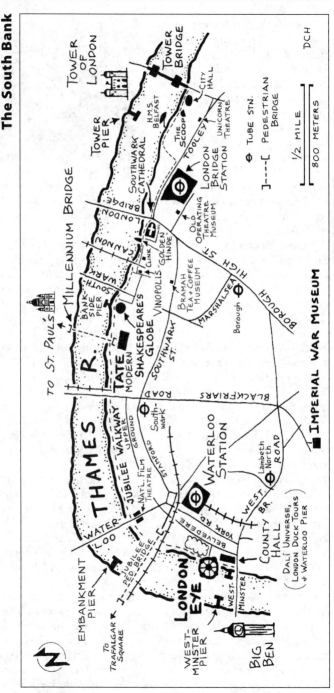

London

Italian mechanical parts. It's also very "green," running extremely efficiently and virtually silently. Twenty-five people ride in each of its 32 air-conditioned capsules for the 30-minute rotation (each capsule has a bench, but most people stand); you go around only once. From the top of this 450-foot-high wheel—the highest public viewpoint in the city—Big Ben looks small. The London Eye's original five-year lease has been extended to 25 years, and it looks like it will become a permanent fixture on the London skyline. Thames boats come and go from here using the Waterloo Pier at the foot of the wheel.

Cost, Hours, Location: £14.50, or buy the £29 combo-ticket with Madame Tussauds Waxworks—see page 82, daily June–Sept 10:00–21:00, Oct–Christmas and mid-Jan–May 10:00–20:00, closed Christmas–mid-Jan for annual maintenance, Tube: Waterloo or Westminster.

Crowd-Beating Tips: Visitors face two lines—one to get a ticket, and the other to board. You can generally just buy your ticket at the wheel (never more than a 30-min wait, worst on weekends and school holidays). If you want to book a ticket (with an assigned time) in advance, call 0870-500-0600, or save 10 percent by booking online at www.londoneye.com. Upon arrival, you either pick up your pre-booked ticket (if you've reserved ahead; use the ATM-type machines to save time—just type in your confirmation number) or wait in the line inside to buy tickets. Then you join the ticket-holders' line at the wheel (starting 10 min before your assigned half-hour time slot).

Dalí Universe—Cleverly located next to the hugely popular London Eye, this exhibit features 500 works of mind-bending art by Salvador Dalí. While pricey, it's entertaining if you like Surrealism and want to learn about Dalí (£12, audioguide-£2.50, daily 10:00–18:30, last entry 30 min before closing, Tube: Waterloo or Westminster, tel. 020/7620-2720, www.countyhallgallery.com). The Dalí Universe currently also has a secondary show, "Picasso: Art of a Genius."

▲▲**Imperial War Museum**—This impressive museum covers the wars of the last century, from heavy weaponry to love notes and Vargas Girls, from Monty's Africa campaign tank to Schwartzkopf's Desert Storm uniform. You can trace the development of the machine gun, watch footage of the first tank battles, see one of more than a thousand V2 rockets Hitler rained on Britain in 1944 (each with more than a ton of explosives), hold your breath through the gruesome WWI trench experience, and buy WWII-era toys in the fun museum shop. The "Secret War" section gives a fascinating peek into the intrigues of espionage in World Wars I and II. The section on the Holocaust is one of the best on the subject anywhere. Rather than glorify war, the museum does its best to shine a light on the powerful human side of one of mankind's most persistent traits (free, sometimes small fees for special exhibitions, daily 10:00–18:00, 2 hours is enough time for most visitors, often guided tours on weekends—ask at info desk, £3.50 audioguide, interesting bookshop, Tube: Lambeth North or bus #12 from Westminster, tel. 020/7416-5320 or 020/7416-5321, www.iwm.org.uk).

The museum is housed in what was the Royal Bethlam Hospital. Also known as "the Bedlam asylum," the place was so wild it gave the world a new word for chaos: "bedlam." Back in Victorian times, locals—without trash-talk shows and cable TV—came here for their entertainment. The asylum was actually open to the paying public on weekends.

▲▲▲**Tate Modern**—Dedicated in the spring of 2000, the striking museum across the river from St. Paul's opened the new century with art from the old one. Its powerhouse collection of Monet, Matisse, Dalí, Picasso, Warhol, and much more is displayed in a converted powerhouse. Each year, the main hall features a different monumental installation by a prominent artist (free but £3 donations appreciated, fee for special exhibitions, daily 10:00–18:00, Fri–Sat until 22:00—a good time to visit, audioguide-£2; free guided tours at 11:00, 12:00, 14:00, and 15:00—confirm at info desk; view restaurant on top floor; cross the Millennium Bridge from St. Paul's, or Tube: Southwark or Blackfriars plus a 10-min walk; or connect by Tate Boat ferry from Tate Britain for £4 one-way, discounted with Travelcard; switchboard tel. 020/7887-8888, recorded info tel. 020/7887-8008, www.tate.org.uk).

▲**Millennium Bridge**—The pedestrian bridge links St. Paul's Cathedral and the Tate Modern across the Thames. This is

London's first new bridge in a century. When it first opened, the $25 million bridge wiggled when people walked on it, so it promptly closed for a $7 million, 20-month stabilization; now it's stable and open again (free). Nicknamed "a blade of light" for its sleek minimalist design—370 yards long, four yards wide, stainless steel with teak planks—it includes clever aerodynamic handrails to deflect wind over the heads of pedestrians.

Crossing the Thames on Foot

You can cross the Thames on any of the bridges that carry car traffic over the river, but London's two pedestrian bridges are more fun. The Millennium Bridge connects the sedate St. Paul's Cathedral with the great Tate Modern. The Golden Jubilee Bridge (consisting of two walkways that flank a railway trestle) links bustling Trafalgar Square on the North Bank with the London Eye and Waterloo Station on the South Bank. Replacing the old, run-down  Hungerford Bridge, the Golden Jubilee Bridge—well-lit with a sleek, futuristic look—makes this busy route safer and more popular.

▲▲Shakespeare's Globe—The original Globe Theater has been rebuilt, half-timbered and thatched, as it was in Shakespeare's time. (This is the first thatched roof in London since they were outlawed after the Great Fire of 1666.) The Globe originally accommodated 2,000 seated and another 1,000 standing. Today, slightly smaller and leaving space for reasonable aisles, the theater holds 900 seated and 600 "groundlings"  (customers who pay very little to watch the play while standing). Its promoters brag that the theater melds "the three A's"—actors, audience, and architecture—with each contributing to the play.

Open as a museum and a working theater, it hosts authentic old-time performances of Shakespeare's plays (generally 14:00 and 19:30—but confirm). The Globe's exhibition on Shakespeare is the world's largest, with interactive displays and film presentations, a sound lab, a script factory, and costumes.

You can tour the theater when there are no plays going on—it's worth planning ahead for these excellent, actor-led guided tours (£9 includes exhibition and tour; theater complex open daily 9:00–17:00; exhibition and tours May–Sept daily 9:00–12:00 & 12:30–17:00—tours offered only in morning in summer due to afternoon matinees, Oct–April daily 10:00–17:00—tours run all day in winter; tours go every 15–30 min, on the South Bank directly across Thames over Southwark Bridge from St. Paul's, Tube: London Bridge plus a 10-min walk, tel. 020/7902-1400, www.shakespeares-globe.org). For details on seeing a play, see page 107.

The Globe Café is open daily (10:00–17:30, tel. 020/7902-1433).

Bramah Tea and Coffee Museum—Aficionados of tea or coffee will find this small museum fascinating. It tells the story of each drink almost passionately. The owner, Mr. Bramah, comes from a big tea family, and wants the world to know how the advent of commercial television, with breaks too short to brew a proper pot of tea, required a faster hot drink. In came the horrible English instant coffee. Tea countered with finely chopped leaves in tea bags, and it's gone downhill ever since (£4, daily 10:00–18:00, 40 Southwark Street, Tube: London Bridge plus 3-min walk, tel. 020/7403-5650, www.bramahmuseum.co.uk). Its café, which serves more kinds of coffees and teas than cakes, is open to the public (same hours as museum, £9 afternoon tea). Bus #RV1 zips you to the museum easily and scenically from Covent Garden.

▲▲Old Operating Theatre Museum and Herb Garret—Climb a tight and creaky wooden spiral staircase to a church attic where you'll find a garret used to dry medicinal herbs, a fascinating exhibit on Victorian surgery, cases of well-described 19th-century medical paraphernalia, and a special look at "anesthesia, the defeat of pain." Then you stumble upon Britain's oldest operating theater, where limbs were sawed off way back in 1821 (£5.25, daily 10:30–17:00, closed Dec 15–Jan 5, 9a St. Thomas Street, Tube: London Bridge, tel. 020/7188-2679, www.thegarret.org.uk).

▲▲Vinopolis: City of Wine—While it seems illogical to have a huge wine museum in London, Vinopolis makes a good case. Built over a Roman wine store and filling the massive vaults of an old wine warehouse, the museum offers an excellent audioguide with a light yet earnest history of wine. Sipping various reds and whites, ports, and champagnes—immersed in your headset as you stroll— you learn about the libation from its Georgian origins to Chile, including a Vespa ride through Chianti country in Tuscany. Allow some time, as the included audioguide takes 90 minutes—the sipping can slow things down wonderfully. This place is popular. Booking ahead for Friday and Saturday nights is a must ("Classic" ticket-£16 for five wine tastes; "Discovery" ticket-£21 for five wine tastes plus tastes of whiskey, beer, and absinthe; open Mon and Thu–Sat 12:00–21:00, Wed and Sun 12:00–18:00, closed Tue, last entry 2 hours before closing, between Shakespeare's Globe and Southwark Cathedral at 1 Bank End, Tube: London Bridge, tel. 0870-241-4040 or 020/7940-8322, www.vinopolis.co.uk).

Lesser Sights in Southwark, on the South Bank

These sights, while mediocre, are worth knowing about. The area stretching from the Tate Modern to London Bridge, known as Southwark (SUTH-uck), was for centuries the place Londoners would go to escape the rules and decency of the city and let their hair down. Bear-baiting, brothels, rollicking pubs, and theater—you name the dream, and it could be fulfilled just across the Thames. A run-down warehouse district through the 20th century, it's been gentrified with classy restaurants, office parks, pedestrian promenades, major sights (such as the Tate Modern and Shakespeare's Globe—described earlier in the chapter), and this colorful collection of lesser sights. The area is easy on foot and a scenic—though circuitous—way to connect the Tower of London with St. Paul's.

Southwark Cathedral—While made a cathedral only in 1905, it's been the neighborhood church since the 13th century, and comes with some interesting history. The enthusiastic docents give impromptu tours if you ask (admission free but £4 suggested donation, Mon–Fri 8:00–18:00, Sat–Sun 9:00–18:00, last entry 30 min before closing, £2.50 audioguide, £2.50 guidebook, no photos without permission, Tube: London Bridge, tel. 020/7367-6700, www.southwark.anglican.org/cathedral). The cathedral hosts **evensong** services almost daily (most weekdays at 17:30, Sat at 16:00, Sun at 15:00, not sung on Wed or alternate Mon).

The Clink Prison Museum—Proudly the "original clink," this was where law-abiding citizens threw Southwark troublemakers until 1780. Today, it's a low-tech torture museum filling grotty old rooms with papier-mâché gore. Unfortunately, there's little that seriously deals with the fascinating problem of law and order in Southwark, where 18th-century Londoners went for a good time (overpriced at £5, Mon–Fri 10:00–18:00, Sat–Sun until 21:00, 1 Clink Street, Tube: London Bridge, tel. 020/7403-0900, www.clink.co.uk).

***Golden Hinde* Replica**—This is a full-size replica of the 16th-century warship in which Sir Francis Drake circumnavigated the globe from 1577 to 1580. Commanding this ship, Drake earned the reputation as history's most successful pirate. The original is long gone, but this boat has logged more than 100,000 miles, including its own voyage around the world. While the ship is fun to see, its interior is not worth touring (£6, Mon–Fri 11:00–17:30, Sat–Sun 10:00–17:00, may be closed if rented out for pirate birthday parties, school groups, or weddings, Tube: London Bridge, tel. 0870-011-8700).

HMS *Belfast*—"The last big-gun armored warship of World War II" clogs the Thames just upstream from the Tower Bridge. This huge vessel—now manned with wax sailors—thrills kids who always dreamed of sitting in a turret shooting off their imaginary guns. If you're into WWII warships, this is the ultimate...otherwise, it's just lots of exercise with a nice view of Tower Bridge (£8, daily March–Oct 10:00–18:00, Nov–Feb 10:00–17:00, last entry 45 min before closing, Tube: London Bridge, tel. 020/7940-6300).

South London, on the North Bank

▲▲**Tate Britain**—One of Europe's great art houses, Tate Britain specializes in British painting from the 16th century through modern times. The museum has a good representation of William Blake's religious sketches, the Pre-Raphaelites' realistic art, and J. M. W. Turner's swirling works (free, £2 donation requested, daily 10:00–17:50, last entry 17:00, fine free and necessary audioguide; free tours: normally Mon–Fri at 11:00—on 16th, 17th, and 18th centuries; at noon—19th century; and at 15:00—20th century; Sat–Sun at 12:00 and 15:00—highlights; call to confirm schedule; kids' activities on weekends, no photography allowed, Tube: Pimlico, then 7-min walk; or arrive directly at museum by taking the Tate Boat ferry from Tate Modern—£4 one-way, discounted with Travelcard, or bus #88 from Oxford Circus or #77A from National Gallery, recorded info tel. 020/7887-8008, office tel. 020/7887-8888, www.tate.org.uk).

Greater London

▲**Kew Gardens**—For a fine riverside park and a palatial greenhouse jungle to swing through, take the Tube or the boat to every

botanist's favorite escape, Kew Gardens. While to most visitors the Royal Botanic Gardens of Kew are simply a delightful opportunity to wander among 33,000 different types of plants, to the hardworking organization that runs the gardens, it's a way to promote understanding and preservation of the botanical diversity of our planet. The Kew Tube station drops you in an herbal little business community, a two-block walk from Victoria Gate (the main garden entrance). Pick up a map brochure and check at the gate for a monthly listing of the best blooms.

Garden-lovers could spend days exploring Kew's 300 acres. For a quick visit, spend a fragrant hour wandering through three buildings: the Palm House, a humid Victorian world of iron, glass, and tropical plants built in 1844; a Waterlily House that Monet would swim for; and the Princess of Wales Conservatory, a modern greenhouse with many different climate zones growing countless cacti, bug-munching carnivorous plants,

Greater London

London

and more (£12.25, discounted to £10.25 one hour before closing, £5 for Kew Palace only; April–Aug Mon–Fri 9:30–18:30, Sat–Sun 9:30–19:30; until 18:00 Sept–Oct, until 16:15 Nov–Jan, until 17:00 Feb–March, last entry to gardens 30 min before closing, galleries and conservatories close at 17:30 in high season—earlier off-season, free tours daily at 11:00 and 14:00, a £3.50 narrated floral 35-min joyride on little train departs on the hour until 16:00 from Victoria Gate, Tube: Kew Gardens, boats run between Kew Gardens and Westminster Pier—see page 62, tel. 020/8332-5000, www.rbgkew .org.uk). For a sun-dappled lunch, walk 10 minutes from the Palm House to the Orangery (£6 hot meals, daily 10:00–17:30).

▲**Hampton Court Palace**—Fifteen miles up the Thames from downtown (£15 taxi ride from Kew Gardens) is the 500-year-old palace of Henry VIII. Actually, it was the palace of his minister, Cardinal Wolsey. When Wolsey, a clever man, realized Henry VIII was experiencing a little palace envy, he gave the mansion to his king. The Tudor palace was also home to Elizabeth I and Charles I.

Sections were updated by Christopher Wren for William and Mary. The stately palace stands overlooking the Thames and includes some impressive Tudor rooms, including a Great Hall with a magnificent hammer-beam ceiling. The industrial-strength Tudor kitchen was capable of keeping 600 schmoozing courtiers thoroughly—if not well—fed. The sculpted garden features a rare Tudor tennis court and a popular maze.

The palace, fully restored after a 1986 fire, tries hard to please, but it doesn't quite sparkle. From the information center in the main courtyard, visitors book times for tours with tired costumed guides or pick up audioguides for self-guided tours of various wings of the palace (all free). The Tudor Kitchens, Henry VIII's Apartments, and the King's Apartments are most interesting. The Georgian Rooms are pretty dull. The maze in the nearby garden is a curiosity some find fun (maze free with palace ticket, otherwise £4). The palace costs £13, or £36 for families (daily April–Oct 10:00–18:00, Nov–March 10:00–16:30, tel. 0870-751-5175, recorded info tel. 0870-752-7777, www.hrp.org.uk).

The train (2/hr, 30 min) from London's Waterloo station drops you just across the river from the palace (just walk across the bridge). Note that there are often discounts available for people riding the train from London to the palace. Check online or at the ticket office at Waterloo station for the latest offers.

Consider arriving at or departing from the palace by boat (connections with London's Westminster Pier, see page 62); it's a relaxing and scenic three-hour cruise past two locks and a fun new/old riverside mix.

Royal Air Force Museum London—A hit with aviation enthusiasts, this huge aerodrome and airfield contain planes from World War II's Battle of Britain up through the Gulf War. You can climb inside some of the planes, try your luck in a cockpit, and fly with the Red Arrows in a flight simulator (free, daily 10:30–18:30, café, shop, parking, Grahame Park Way, Tube: Colindale—top of Northern Line Edgware branch, tel. 020/8205-2266, www.rafmuseum.org.uk).

Disappointments of London

On the South Bank, the London Dungeon, a much-visited but amateurish attraction, is just a highly advertised, overpriced haunted house—certainly not worth the £20 admission, much less your valuable London time. It comes with long and rude lines. Wait for Halloween and see one in your hometown to support a better cause. "Winston Churchill's Britain at War Experience" (next to the London Dungeon) also wastes your time and money, especially considering the wonderful Churchill Museum in the Cabinet War Rooms (see page 70). The Jack the Ripper walking tours (by any of several companies) are big sellers, but don't offer much. Anything actually relating to the notorious serial killer was torn down a century ago, and all that's left are a few small sights and lots of bloody stories.

SHOPPING

Harrods—Harrods is London's most famous and touristy department store. With a million square feet of retail space on seven floors, it's a place where some shoppers could spend all day. (To me, it's still just a department store.) Big yet classy, Harrods has everything from elephants to toothbrushes (Mon–Sat 10:00–20:00, Sun 12:00–18:00, mandatory storage for big backpacks-£2.50, on Brompton Road, Tube: Knightsbridge, tel. 020/7730-1234, www.harrods.com).

Sightseers should pick up the free *Store Guide* at any info post. Here's what I enjoyed: On the ground and lower ground floors, find the Food Halls, with their Edwardian tiled walls, creative and exuberant displays, and staff in period costumes—not quite like your local supermarket back home.

Descend to the lower ground floor and follow signs to the Egyptian Escalator, where you'll find a memorial to Dodi Fayed and Princess Diana. The huge (and more than a little creepy) bronze statue was commissioned by Dodi Fayed's father, Mohamed al-Fayed, who owns Harrods. Photos and flowers honor the late Princess and her lover, who both died in a car crash in Paris in 1997. Sometimes other items are also on display, such as the wine glass still dirty from their last dinner, and the engagement ring that Dodi purchased the day before they died.

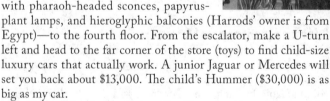

Ride the Egyptian Escalator—lined with pharaoh-headed sconces, papyrus-plant lamps, and hieroglyphic balconies (Harrods' owner is from Egypt)—to the fourth floor. From the escalator, make a U-turn left and head to the far corner of the store (toys) to find child-size luxury cars that actually work. A junior Jaguar or Mercedes will set you back about $13,000. The child's Hummer ($30,000) is as big as my car.

Also on the fourth floor is **The Georgian Restaurant,** where you can enjoy a fancy high tea (see listing in "Taking High Tea in London" sidebar on page 142). Many of my readers report that Harrods is overpriced, snooty, and teeming with American and Japanese tourists. Still, it's the palace of department stores. The nearby Beauchamp Place is lined with classy and fascinating shops.

Harvey Nichols—Once Princess Diana's favorite, "Harvey Nick's" remains the department store *du jour* (Mon–Sat 10:00–20:00, Sun 12:00–18:00, near Harrods, Tube: Knightsbridge, 109 Knightsbridge, www.harveynichols.com). Want to pick up a little £20 scarf for the wife? You won't do it here, where they're more like £200. The store's fifth floor is a veritable food fest, with a gourmet grocery store, a fancy restaurant, a Yo! Sushi bar, and a lively café. Consider a take-away tray of sushi to eat on a bench in the Hyde Park rose garden two blocks away.

Toys—The biggest toy store in Britain is **Hamleys,** with seven floors buzzing with 28,000 toys, managed by a staff of 200. At the "Bear Factory," kids can get a made-to-order teddy bear by picking out a "bear skin," and watch while it's stuffed and sewn (Mon–Fri 10:00–20:00, Thu until 21:00, Sat 9:00–20:00, Sun 12:00–18:00, 188 Regent Street, tel. 0870-333-2455, www.hamleys.com).

Street Markets—Antique buffs, people-watchers, and folks who brake for garage sales love to haggle at London's street markets. There's good early-morning market activity somewhere any day of the week. The best are **Portobello Road** (Mon–Wed and Fri–Sat 8:00–18:30, closes at 13:00 on Thu, closed Sun, Tube: Notting Hill Gate, near recommended B&Bs, tel. 020/7229-8354, www .portobelloroad.co.uk) and **Camden Lock Market** (daily 10:00–18:00, Tube: Camden Town, tel. 020/7284-2084, www .camdenlock.net). The TI has a complete, up-to-date list. Warning: Markets attract two kinds of people—tourists and pickpockets.

Famous Auctions—London's famous auctioneers welcome the curious public for viewing and bidding. You can preview estate catalogs or browse auction calendars online. For questions—or to set up a private appointment—contact **Sotheby's** (Mon–Fri 9:00–16:30, closed Sat–Sun, 34–35 New Bond Street, Tube: Oxford Circus, tel. 020/7293-5000, www.sothebys.com) or **Christie's** (Mon–Fri 9:00–16:30, Sun 14:00–17:00, closed Sat, 8 King Street, Tube: Green Park, tel. 020/7839-9060, www.christies.com).

ENTERTAINMENT

Theater (a.k.a. "Theatre")

London's theater rivals Broadway's in quality and beats it in price. Choose from Shakespeare, musicals, comedy, thrillers, sex farces, cutting-edge fringe, revivals starring movie celebs, and more. London does it all well. I prefer big, glitzy—even bombastic— musicals over serious chamber dramas, simply because London can deliver the lights, sound, dancers, and multimedia spectacle I rarely get back home.

London's Major Theaters

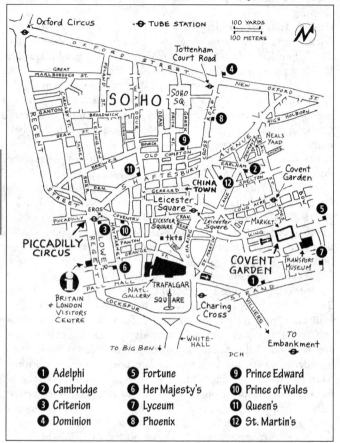

❶ Adelphi	❺ Fortune	❾ Prince Edward
❷ Cambridge	❻ Her Majesty's	❿ Prince of Wales
❸ Criterion	❼ Lyceum	⓫ Queen's
❹ Dominion	❽ Phoenix	⓬ St. Martin's

Most theaters, marked on tourist maps (also see map on this page), are found in the West End between Piccadilly and Covent Garden. Box offices, hotels, and TIs offer a handy free *London Theatre Guide* (also at www.londontheatre.co.uk) and *Entertainment Guide*. Performances are nightly except Sunday, usually with one or two matinees a week (Shakespeare's Globe is the rare theater that does offer performances on Sun, mid-May–Sept). Tickets range from about £11 to £55. Matinees are generally cheaper and rarely sell out.

To book a seat, simply call the theater box office directly, ask about seats and available dates, and buy a ticket with your credit card. You can call from the US as easily as from England (check www.officiallondontheatre.co.uk, the American magazine *Variety*, or photocopy your hometown library's London newspaper theater section). Arrive about 30 minutes before the show starts to pick up your ticket and to avoid lines.

For a booking fee, you can reserve online. Most theater websites link you to a preferred ticket vendor, usually www.ticketmaster.co.uk or www.seetickets.com. Keith Prowse Ticketing is also handy by phone or online (US tel. 800-223-6108, London tel. 020/7808-3871, www.keithprowse.com).

While booking through an agency is quick and easy, prices are inflated by a standard 25 percent fee. Ticket agencies (whether in the US, at London's TIs, or scattered throughout the city) are scalpers with an address. If you're buying from an agency, look at the ticket carefully (your price should be no more than 30 percent over the printed face value; the 17.5 percent VAT is already included in the face value), and understand where you're sitting according to the floor plan (if your view is restricted, it will state this on the ticket; for floor plans of the various theaters, see www.theatremonkey.com). Agencies are worthwhile only if a show you've just got to see is sold out at the box office. They scarf up hot tickets, planning to make a killing after the show is sold out. US booking agencies get their tickets from another agency, adding even more to your expense by involving yet another middleman. Many tickets sold on the street are forgeries. Although some theaters have booking agencies handle their advance sales, you'll stand a good chance of saving money and avoiding the middleman by simply calling the box office directly to book your tickets (international phone calls are cheap and credit cards make booking a snap).

Theater Lingo: Stalls (ground floor), dress circle (first balcony), upper circle (second balcony), balcony (sky-high third balcony), slips (cheap seats on the fringes). Many cheap seats have a restricted view (behind a pillar).

Cheap Theater Tricks: Most theaters offer cheap returned tickets, standing-room, matinee, and senior or student standby deals. These "concessions" are indicated with a "conc" or "s" in the listings. Picking up a late return can get you a great seat at a cheap-seat price. Even if a show is "sold out," you can usually get a seat. Call the theater box office and ask how.

If you don't care where you sit, the absolutely cheapest seats (obstructed view or nosebleed section) can be found at the box office, and generally cost less than £20 per ticket.

Many theaters are so small that there's hardly a bad seat. After the lights go down, scooting up is less than a capital offense. Shakespeare did it.

Half-Price "tkts" Booth: This famous ticket booth at **Leicester Square** sells discounted tickets for top-price seats to shows on the push list the day of the show only (£2.50 service charge per ticket, Mon–Sat 10:00–19:00, Sun 12:00–15:00, matinee

What's On in the West End

Here are some of the perennial favorites that you're likely to find among the West End's evening offerings. If spending the time and money for a London play, I like a full-fledged high-energy musical.

Generally you can book tickets for free at the box office or for a £2 fee by telephone or online. See the map on page 108 for locations.

Musicals

Billy Elliot—This adaptation of the popular British film is part family drama, part story of a boy who just has to dance, set to a score by Elton John (£17.50–60, Mon–Sat 19:30, matinees Thu and Sat 14:30, Victoria Palace Theatre, Victoria Street, Tube: Victoria, tel. 0870-895-5577, www.billyelliotthemusical.com).

Chicago—A chorus-girl-gone-bad forms a nightclub act with another murderess to bring in the bucks (£20–55, Mon–Sat 20:00, matinees Fri 16:30 and Sat 15:00, Cambridge Theatre, Earlham Street, Tube: Covent Garden or Leicester Square, booking tel. 0870-890-1102, www.chicagothemusical.com).

Mamma Mia!—This high-energy spandex-and-platform-boots musical weaves together 20 or 30 ABBA hits to tell the story of a bride in search of her real dad as her promiscuous mom plans her Greek Isle wedding. The production has the audience dancing by its happy ending (£27.50–55, Mon–Thu and Sat 19:30, Fri 20:30, matinees Fri 17:00 and Sat 15:00, Prince of Wales Theatre, Coventry Street, Tube: Piccadilly Circus, booking tel. 0870-850-0393, www.mamma-mia.com).

Mary Poppins—The beloved nanny, "practically perfect in every way," sings her way through this supercalifragilisticexpialidocious show (£15–55, Mon–Sat at 19:30, matinees Thu and Sat 14:30, Prince Edward Theatre, Old Compton Street, Tube: Leicester Square, tel. 0870-850-9191, www.marypoppins.co.uk).

Les Misérables—Claude-Michel Schönberg's musical adaptation of Victor Hugo's epic follows the life of Jean Valjean as he struggles with the social and political realities of 19th-century France. This inspiring mega-hit takes you back to the days of

tickets from noon, lines often form early, list of shows available online, www.tkts.co.uk). Most tickets are half-price; other shows are discounted 25 percent.

Here are some sample prices: A top-notch seat to *Chicago* costs £49 bought directly from the theater, but only £27 at Leicester (LESS-ter) Square. The cheapest balcony seat (bought from the theater) is £17.50. Half-price tickets can be a good deal, unless you want the cheapest seats or the hottest shows. But check the board;

France's struggle for a just and modern society (£12.50–50, Mon–Sat 19:30, matinees Wed and Sat 14:30, Queen's Theatre, Shaftesbury Avenue, Tube: Piccadilly Circus, box office tel. 0870-950-0930, www.lesmis.com).

The Lion King—In this Disney extravaganza, Simba the lion learns about the delicately balanced circle of life on the savanna (£20–42.50, Tue–Sat 19:30, matinees Wed and Sat 14:00, Sun 15:00, Lyceum Theatre, Wellington Street, Tube: Charing Cross or Covent Garden, booking tel. 0870-243-9000 or 020/7344-4444, theater info tel. 020/7420-8112, www.thelionking.co.uk).

Phantom of the Opera—A mysterious masked man falls in love with a singer in this haunting Andrew Lloyd Webber musical about life beneath the stage of the Paris Opera (£20–50, Mon–Sat 19:30, matinees Tue and Sat 14:30, Her Majesty's Theatre, Haymarket, Tube: Piccadilly Circus, booking tel. 0870-534-4444, www.thephantomoftheopera.com).

We Will Rock You—Whether or not you're a Queen fan, this musical tribute (more to the band than to Freddie Mercury) is an understandably popular celebration of their work (£27.50–55, Mon–Sat at 19:30, matinees Wed and Sat 14:30, Dominion Theatre, Tottenham Court Road, Tube: Tottenham Court Road, Ticketmaster tel. 0870-169-0116, www.queenonline.com /wewillrockyou).

Thrillers

The Mousetrap—Agatha Christie's whodunit about a murder in a country house continues to stump audiences after 55 years (£13.50–38, Mon–Sat 20:00, matinees Tue 14:45 and Sat 17:00, St. Martin's Theatre, West Street, Tube: Leicester Square, box office tel. 0870-162-8787, www.vpsmvaudsav.co.uk).

The Woman in Black—The chilling tale of a solicitor who is haunted by what he learns when he closes a reclusive woman's affairs (£12.50–32.50, Mon–Sat 20:00, matinees Tue 15:00 and Sat 16:00, Fortune Theatre, Russell Street, Tube: Covent Garden, box office tel. 020/7369-1717, www.thewomaninblack.com).

occasionally they sell cheap tickets to good shows. For example, a first-class seat to the long-running *Les Misérables* (which rarely sells out) costs £50 when bought from the theater ticket office, but you'll pay £27.50 at the tkts booth. Note that the real half-price booth (with its "tkts" name) is a freestanding kiosk at the edge of the garden in Leicester Square. Several dishonest outfits nearby advertise "official half-price tickets"; avoid these.

A second tkts booth is at the Canary Wharf Docklands Light

Railway (DLR) Station. The freestanding kiosk is located near platforms 4 and 5 above the DLR concourse (Mon–Sat 10:00–15:30, closed Sun, Tube: Canary Wharf).

West End Theaters: The commercial (non-subsidized) theaters cluster around Soho (especially along Shaftesbury Avenue) and Covent Garden. With a centuries-old tradition of pleasing the masses, these present London theater at its glitziest. See the "What's On in the West End" sidebar.

Royal Shakespeare Company: If you'll ever enjoy Shakespeare, it'll be in Britain. The RSC performs at various theaters around London and in Stratford year-round. To get a schedule, contact the RSC (Royal Shakespeare Theatre, Stratford-upon-Avon, tel. 01789/403-444, www.rsc.org.uk).

Shakespeare's Globe: To see Shakespeare in a replica of the theater for which he wrote his plays, attend a play at the Globe. This round, thatch-roofed, open-air theater performs the plays much as Shakespeare intended (with no amplification). The play's the thing from mid-May through October (usually Tue–Sat 14:00 and 19:30, Sun either 13:00 and 18:30 or 16:00 only, Mon 19:30, tickets can be sold out months in advance). You'll pay £5 to stand and £15–31 to sit (usually on a backless bench; only a few rows and the pricier Gentlemen's Rooms have seats with backs; £1 cushions and £3 add-on back rests are considered a good investment by many). The £5 "groundling" tickets—while open to rain—are most fun. Scurry in early to stake out a spot on the stage's edge leaning rail, where the most interaction with the actors occurs. You're a crude peasant. You can lean your elbows on the stage, munch a picnic dinner, or walk around. I've never enjoyed Shakespeare as much as here, performed as it was meant to be in the "wooden O." Plays can be long. Many groundlings leave before the end. If you like, hang out an hour before the finish and beg or buy a ticket from someone leaving early (groundlings are allowed to come and go).

For information on plays or £9 tours (see page 100), contact the theater at tel. 020/7902-1500 (or see www.shakespeares-globe.org). To reserve tickets for plays, call or drop by the box office (Mon–Sat 10:00–18:00, until 20:00 on day of show, at Shakespeare's Globe at New Globe Walk entrance, tel. 020/7401-9919). If you reserve online (www.seetickets.com/shakespeares-globe), be warned: Your ticket price will have an added booking fee (generally £1–2.20 per ticket).

The theater is on the South Bank, directly across the Thames over the Millennium Bridge from St. Paul's Cathedral (Tube: Mansion House or London Bridge). The Globe is inconvenient for public transport, but the courtesy phone in the lobby gets a minicab in minutes. (These minicabs have set fees—e.g., £8 to South Kensington—but generally cost less than a metered cab and provide fine and honest service.) During theater season, there's a regular supply of black cabs outside the main foyer on New Globe Walk.

Outdoor Theater in Summer: Enjoy Shakespearean drama and other plays under the stars at the **Open Air Theatre,** in leafy Regent's Park in north London. Bring your own picnic; pre-order an £11 picnic from the theater at least one week in advance; or order à la carte from a menu at the theater (tickets £10–33; season runs June–mid-Sept, box office open late-March–late-May Mon–Sat 10:00–18:00, closed Sun; late-May–mid-Sept Mon–Sat 10:00–20:00, Sun 12:00–20:00 on performance days only; order tickets online after mid-Jan or by phone at tel. 0870-060-1811, £1 booking fee by phone, no fee if ordering online or in person; grounds open 90 min prior to evening performances, 30 min prior for matinees; 10-min walk north of Baker Street Tube, near Queen Mary's Gardens within Regent's Park; detailed directions and more info at www.openairtheatre.org).

Fringe Theatre: London's rougher evening-entertainment scene is thriving, filling pages in *Time Out.* Choose from a wide range of fringe theater and comedy acts (generally £5).

Classical Music

Concerts at Churches
For easy, cheap, or free concerts in historic churches, check TI listings for **lunch concerts,** especially:
- St. Bride's Church, with free lunch concerts twice a week at 13:15 (generally Tue, Wed, or Fri—confirm by phone or online, church tel. 020/7427-0133, www.stbrides.com).
- St. James at Piccadilly, with 50-minute concerts on Monday, Wednesday, and Friday at 13:10 (suggested donation £3, info tel. 020/7381-0441, www.st-james-piccadilly.org).
- St. Martin-in-the-Fields, offering free concerts on Monday, Tuesday, and Friday at 13:00 (church tel. 020/7766-1100, www2.stmartin-in-the-fields.org).

St. Martin-in-the-Fields also hosts fine **evening concerts** by candlelight (£8–18, Thu–Sat at 19:30, sometimes also Tue or Wed, box office tel. 020/7839-8362).

Evensong and Organ Recitals at Churches
Evensong services are held at several churches, including:
- St. Paul's Cathedral (Mon–Sat at 17:00, Sun at 15:15).
- Westminster Abbey (Mon–Tue and Thu–Fri at 17:00, Sat–Sun at 15:00, no service on Wed).
- Southwark Cathedral (Mon–Tue and Thu–Fri at 17:30; Sat at 16:00, Sun at 15:00, no service on Wed or alternate Mon, tel. 020/7367-6700, www.southwark.anglican.org/cathedral).

- St. Bride's Church (Sun at 18:30, tel. 020/7427-0133, www.stbrides.com).

Free **organ recitals** are held on Sundays at 17:45 at Westminster Abbey (30 min, tel. 020/7222-7110). Many other churches have free concerts; ask for the *London Organ Concerts Guide* at the TI.

Prom Concerts and Opera

For a fun classical event (mid-July–early Sept), attend a **Prom Concert** (shortened from "Promenade Concert") during the annual festival at the Royal Albert Hall. Nightly concerts are offered at give-a-peasant-some-culture prices to "Promenaders"— those willing to stand throughout the performance (most seats £22–29 but depends on performance, £7 restricted-view seats, £4 standing-room spots sold at the door, Tube: South Kensington, tel. 020/7589-8212, www.royalalberthall.com).

Some of the world's best **opera** is belted out at the prestigious Royal Opera House, near Covent Garden (box office tel. 020/7304-4000, www.royalopera.org), and at the less-formal Sadler's Wells Theatre (Rosebery Avenue, Islington, Tube: Angel, info tel. 020/7863-8198, box office tel. 0870-737-7737, www.sadlerswells.com).

Walks, Bus Tours, and Cruises

Guided **walks** are offered several times a day. Original London Walks is the most established company (tel. 020/7624-3978, www.walks.com). Daytime walks vary: ancient London, museums, legal London, Dickens, Beatles, Jewish quarter, Christopher Wren, and so on. In the evening, expect a more limited choice: ghosts, Jack the Ripper, pubs, or a literary theme. Get the latest from a TI, fliers, or *Time Out*. Show up at the listed time and place, pay £6, and enjoy the two-hour tour.

To see the city illuminated at night, consider a **bus** tour. A one-hour London by Night Sightseeing Tour leaves every evening from Victoria Station and other points (see page 59).

During the summer, boats sail as late as 21:00 between Westminster Pier (near Big Ben) and the Tower of London. (For details, see page 61.)

A handful of outfits run Thames River evening **cruises** with four-course meals and dancing. London Showboat offers the best value (£62, April–Oct Wed–Sun, Nov–March Thu–Sat, 3 hours, departs at 19:00 from Westminster Pier and returns by 22:30, reservations necessary, tel. 020/7740-0400, www.citycruises.com). For more on cruising, get the *Thames River Services* brochure from a London TI.

Summer Evenings Along the South Bank

If you're visiting London in summer, consider the South Bank.

Take a trip around the **London Eye** while the sun sets over the city (Ferris wheel spins until 22:00). Then cap your night with an evening walk along the pedestrian-only **Jubilee Walkway,** which runs east–west along the river. It's where Londoners go to escape the heat. This pleasant stretch of the walkway—lined with pubs and casual eateries—goes from the London Eye past Shakespeare's Globe to London Bridge (you can walk in either direction, see www.jubileewalkway.com for maps and Tube stops).

If you're in the mood for a movie, take in a flick at the new **National Film Theatre,** located just across from Waterloo Bridge on the South Bank. Run by the British Film Institute, the state-of-the-art theater shows Hollywood films (both new and classic), as well as art cinema (£8.60, Tube: Waterloo or Embankment, box office tel. 020/7928-3232, check www.bfi.org.uk/incinemas/nft for schedules).

Farther east along the South Bank is **The Scoop**—an outdoor amphitheater next to City Hall. It's a good spot for outdoor movies, concerts, and theater productions throughout the summer—with Tower Bridge as a scenic backdrop. These events are free, nearly nightly, and family-friendly. The schedule usually includes movies three nights a week in June, twice-daily musical and dance performances in July, and nightly theater in August and September, with most events beginning at 19:00. For the latest event schedule, see www.morelondon.com/thescoop (next to City Hall, Riverside, The Queen's Walkway, Tube: London Bridge).

SLEEPING

London is expensive. Cheaper rooms are relatively dumpy. Don't expect £90 cheeriness in a £60 room. For £70 ($140), you'll get a double with breakfast in a safe, cramped, and dreary place with minimal service and the bathroom down the hall. For £90 ($180), you'll get a basic, clean, reasonably cheery double in a usually cramped, cracked-plaster building with a private bath, or a soulless but comfortable room without breakfast in a huge Motel 6–type place. My London splurges, at £150–255 ($300–510), are spacious, thoughtfully appointed places good for entertaining or romancing. Off-season, it's possible to save money by arriving late without a reservation and looking around. Competition softens prices, especially for multi-night stays. Check hotel websites for special deals. Remember that all of Britain's accommodations are now non-smoking. Street noise is a fact of life in London; if you're concerned, request a room in the back.

Hearty English or generous buffet breakfasts are included

unless otherwise noted, and TVs are standard in rooms, but may come with only the traditional four British channels (no cable).

Reserve your London room with an email or phone call as soon as you can commit to a date (see "Making Reservations" on page 22). To call a London hotel from the US or Canada, dial 011-44-20 (London's area code without the initial zero), then the local eight-digit number.

If you prefer to travel without reservations, be aware that some fancy £120 rooms rent for a third off if you arrive late on a slow day and ask for a deal.

Online Hotel Deals for London

Given the high hotel prices and relatively weak dollar, consider turning to the Internet to help score a hotel deal. Various websites list rooms in high-rise, three- and four-star business hotels. You'll give up the charm and warmth of a family-run establishment, and breakfast will probably not be included, but you might find the price is right.

Start by checking the websites of several big hotel chains to get an idea of typical rates and to check for online-only deals. Big London hotel chains include the following: Millennium/Copthorne (www.millenniumhotels.com), Thistle (www.thistlehotels.com), Intercontinental/Holiday Inn (www.ichotelsgroup.com), Radisson (www.radisson.com), and Red Carnation (www.redcarnationhotels.com). For information on the no-frills, more Motel 6–type chains, see page 24. For specific recommendations for London, see "London's Cheap Chain Hotels," below.

Favorite discount sites for London hotels that have been mentioned by my readers include www.londontown.com (an informative site with a discount booking service), www.londonbb.com, www.lastminute.com, www.visitlondon.com, http://roomsnet.com, and www.eurocheapo.com.

For a good overview on finding London hotel deals, go to www.smartertravel.com and click on "Travel Guides," then browse to "London."

London's Cheap Chain Hotels

These places are well-run and offer elevators and all the modern comforts in a no-nonsense package. With the notable exception of my second listing, they are often located on busy streets in dreary train-station neighborhoods, so use common sense after dark and wear your money belt. The doubles for £75–100 are a great value for London. Mid-week prices are generally higher than weekend rates. For more tips on chain hotels, see page 24.

$$$ **Jurys Inn Islington** rents 200 compact, comfy rooms near King's Cross station (Db/Tb-£110–120, some discounted

---

Sleep Code

(£1 = about $2, country code: 44, area code: 020)
S = Single, **D** = Double/Twin, **T** = Triple, **Q** = Quad, **b** = bathroom,
s = shower only. Unless otherwise noted, credit cards are
accepted and prices include a generous breakfast.

To help you easily sort through these listings, I've divided
the rooms into three categories, based on the price for a
double room with bath:

$$$ Higher Priced—Most rooms £100 or more.
$$ Moderately Priced—Most rooms between £70–100.
$ Lower Priced—Most rooms £70 or less.

rooms available online, 2 adults and 2 kids under age 12 can share
1 room, breakfast extra, 60 Pentonville Road, Tube: Angel, tel.
020/7282-5500, fax 020/7282-5511, www.jurysdoyle.com).

$$ Premier Travel Inn London County Hall, literally
down the hall from a $400-a-night Marriott Hotel, fills one end
of London's massive former County Hall building. This family-
friendly place is wonderfully located near the base of the London
Eye Ferris Wheel and across the Thames from Big Ben. Its 313
slick rooms come with all the necessary comforts (Db-£92 for 2
adults and up to 2 kids under age 16, big breakfast-£7.50, book
in advance, no-show rooms are released at 15:00, some easy-
access rooms, elevator, 500 yards from Westminster Tube stop
and Waterloo Station, Belvedere Road, central reservations tel.
0870-242-8000 or 0870-238-3300, you can fax 020/7902-1619
but you might not get a response, easiest to book online at www
.premiertravelinn.com).

$$ Premier Travel Inn London Southwark, with 59 rooms,
is near Shakespeare's Globe on the South Bank (Db for up to
2 adults and 2 kids-£85–92, breakfast extra, Bankside, 34 Park
Street, tel. 0870-990-6402, www.premiertravelinn.com).

$$ Premier Travel Inn King's Cross, with 276 rooms, is just
east of King's Cross station (Db-£82–94, breakfast extra, 24-hour
reception, elevator, 26–30 York Way, tel. 0870-990-6414, fax 0870-
990-6415, www.premiertravelinn.com).

Other **$$ Premier Travel Inns** charging £75–95 per room
include **London Euston** (big, blue, Lego-type building packed
with families on vacation on handy but noisy street, 141 Euston
Road, Tube: Euston, tel. 0870-238-3301), **London Kensington**
(11 Knaresboro Place, Tube: Earl's Court or Gloucester Road, tel.
0870-238-3304), and **London Putney Bridge** (farther out, 3 Putney Bridge Approach, Tube: Putney Bridge, tel. 0870-238-3302).

London's Hotel Neighborhoods

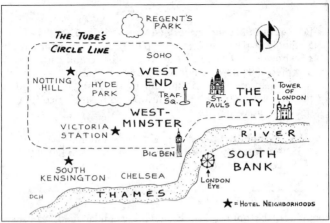

Avoid the **Tower Bridge** location, which is an inconvenient, 15-minute walk from the nearest Tube stop. For any of these, call 0870-242-8000, fax 0870-241-9000, or—the best option—book online at www.premiertravelinn.com.

$$ Hotel Ibis London Euston, which feels a bit classier than a Premier Travel Inn, rents 380 rooms on a quiet street a block behind and west of Euston Station (Db-£70–95, breakfast extra, no family rooms, 3 Cardington Street, tel. 020/7388-7777, fax 020/7388-0001, www.ibishotel.com, h0921@accor-hotels.com).

$ Travelodge London Kings Cross Royal Scot is another typical chain hotel with lots of cookie-cutter rooms just south of King's Cross Station (Db-£66–85, some £26 and £49 rooms available online only for scattered dates, breakfast extra, family rooms, 100 Kings Cross Road, tel. 0870-191-1773, fax 020/7833-8261, www.travelodge.co.uk). Other Travelodge London locations are at **Covent Garden, Liverpool Street,** and **Farringdon.** For all the details on each, see www.travelodge.co.uk.

Victoria Station Neighborhood (Belgravia)

The streets behind Victoria Station teem with budget B&Bs. It's a safe, surprisingly tidy, and decent area without a hint of the trashy, touristy glitz of the streets in front of the station. West of the tracks is Belgravia, where the prices are a bit higher and your neighbors include Andrew Lloyd Webber and Margaret Thatcher (her policeman stands outside 73 Chester

Victoria Station Neighborhood

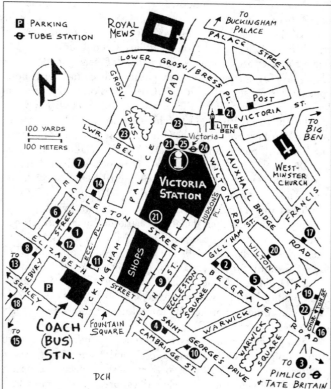

1. Lime Tree Hotel
2. Quality Hotel Westminster
3. To Holiday Inn Express
4. Elizabeth Hotel & Jubilee Hotel
5. Winchester Hotel
6. James House
7. Harcourt House
8. Morgan House
9. Cherry Court Hotel
10. Bakers Hotel
11. Goya Spanish Rest. & Tapas Bar
12. Ebury Wine Bar
13. To The Duke of Wellington Pub
14. Jenny Lo's Tea House
15. To La Poule au Pot Rest.
16. Grumbles Restaurant
17. The Jugged Hare Pub
18. The Belgravia Pub
19. Chimes English Rest. & Cider Bar
20. Seafresh Fish Rest.
21. Grocery Stores (3)
22. Launderette
23. Bus Tours - Day (2)
24. Bus Tours - Night
25. TI, Tube, Taxis, City Buses

Square). East of the tracks is Pimlico—cheaper and just as handy, but the rooms can be a bit dowdier. Decent eateries abound (see page 136).

All the recommended hotels are within a five-minute walk of the Victoria Tube, bus, and train stations. On hot summer nights, request a quiet back room. Nearby is the 400-space Semley Place NCP **parking garage** (£30/day, possible discounts with hotel voucher, just west of the Victoria Coach Station at Buckingham Palace Road and Semley Place, tel. 0870-242-7144, www.ncp .co.uk). The handy **Pimlico Launderette** is about five blocks south-west of Warwick Square (daily 8:00–20:00, self-service or full service, south of Sutherland Street at 3 Westmoreland Terrace, tel. 020/7821-8692). **Launderette Centre** is a block north of Warwick Square (Mon–Fri 8:00–22:00, Sat–Sun until 19:30, £7 wash and dry, £9 for full-service, 31 Churton Street, tel. 020/7828-6039).

$$$ Lime Tree Hotel, enthusiastically run by David and Marilyn Davies and their daughter Charlotte, comes with 28 spacious and thoughtfully decorated rooms and a fun-loving breakfast room (Sb-£80–85, Db-£110–140 depending on room size, Tb-£145–175, family room-£165–190, Internet access, Wi-Fi, quiet garden, David deals in slow times and is creative at helping travelers in a bind, 135 Ebury Street, tel. 020/7730-8191, fax 020/7730-7865, www.limetreehotel.co.uk, info@limetreehotel.co.uk, trusty Alan covers the night shift).

$$$ Quality Hotel Westminster is big, modern (but with chipped plaster), well-located, and a good bet for no-nonsense comfort (Db-£155–185, check for various Web specials, drop-ins can ask for "saver prices" on slow days, breakfast extra or bargained in, elevator, 82 Eccleston Square, tel. 020/7834-8042, fax 020/7630-8942, www.hotels-westminster.com, enquiries @hotels-westminster.com).

$$$ Holiday Inn Express fills an old building with 52 fresh, modern, and efficient rooms (Db-£120 rack rate, often £80—especially Sun or if booked online; up to 2 kids free, family rooms, elevator, 106 Belgrave Road, Tube: Pimlico, tel. 020/7630-8888, fax 020/7828-0441, www.hiexpressvictoria.co.uk, info @hiexpressvictoria.co.uk).

$$$ Elizabeth Hotel is a stately old place overlooking Eccleston Square, with fine public spaces and 37 well-worn, slightly overpriced, but spacious and decent rooms (S-£55, Sb-£85, D-£85, small Db-£103, big Db-£115, Tb-£130, Qb-£145, Quint/b-£150, air-con-£9, 37 Eccleston Square, tel. 020/7828-6812, fax 020/7828-6814, www.elizabethhotel.com, info@elizabethhotel .com). Elizabeth Hotel also rents apartments that sleep up to six (£230/night, includes breakfast).

$$ Winchester Hotel is a family-run place with 19 small rooms that are a fine value for the price (Db-£89, Tb-£115, Qb-£140, Internet access, 17 Belgrave Road, tel. 020/7828-2972, fax 020/7828-5191, www.londonwinchesterhotel.co.uk, info @londonwinchesterhotel.co.uk, commanded by no-nonsense Jimmy plus his crew: Juanita, Frank, and Shelina). The Winchester also rents apartments—with kitchenettes, sitting rooms, and beds on the quiet back side—around the corner (£125–230).

$$ James House is a basic, ramshackle 10-room place on quiet Ebury Street (S-£52, Sb-£62, D-£70, Db-£85, T-£95, Tb-£110, family bunk-bed Qb-£135, all rooms with fans, 108 Ebury Street, tel. 020/7730-5880, www.eburybedandbreakfast.co.uk, info @eburybedandbreakfast.co.uk, Carlo).

$$ Harcourt House rents 10 Neo-Victorian rooms (Sb-£65, Db-£90, Tb-£120, less off-season, 50 Ebury Street, tel. 020/7730-2722, www.harcourthousehotel.co.uk, harcourthouse@talk21.com, helpful David and Glesni Wood and cute dog Suki).

$$ Morgan House rents 11 good rooms and is entertainingly run, with lots of travel tips and friendly chat—especially about the local rich and famous—from owner Rachel Joplin and manager Fernanda (S-£52, D-£72, Db-£92, T-£92, family suites-£112–132 for 3–4 people, 120 Ebury Street, tel. 020/7730-2384, fax 020/7730-8442, www.morganhouse.co.uk, morganhouse@btclick .com).

$ Cherry Court Hotel, run by the friendly and industrious Patel family, rents 12 very small, basic, incense-scented rooms in a central location (Sb-£48, Db-£55, Tb-£80, Qb-£95, Quint/b-£110, prices promised with this book through 2008, paying with credit card costs 5 percent extra, fruit-basket breakfast in room, air-con, laundry, free Internet access with free disk burning, peaceful garden patio, 23 Hugh Street, tel. 020/7828-2840, fax 020/7828-0393, www.cherrycourthotel.co.uk, bookings@cherrycourthotel.co.uk).

$ Jubilee Hotel is a well-run slumber mill with 26 tiny rooms and many tiny beds—but good prices for London (S-£35, Sb-£50, tiny D-£50, tiny Db-£60, Db-£65, Tb-£75, Qb-£95, 5 percent discount with cash and this book through 2008 if you book direct, 31 Eccleston Square, tel. 020/7834-0845, www.jubileehotel.co.uk, stay@jubileehotel.co.uk, Bob Patel).

$ Bakers Hotel is a cheapie, with 10 small, neat-and-clean rooms, but it's well-located and offers youth hostel prices and a full breakfast (S-£30, D-£46, T-£55–60, family room-£65–70, 126 Warwick Way, tel. 020/7834-0729, www.bakershotel.co.uk, reservations@bakershotel.co.uk, Amin Jamani).

"South Kensington," She Said, Loosening His Cummerbund

To stay on a quiet street so classy it doesn't allow hotel signs, surrounded by trendy shops and colorful restaurants, call "South Ken" your London home. Shoppers like being a short walk from Harrods and the designer shops of King's Road and Chelsea. When I splurge, I splurge here. Sumner Place is just off Old Brompton Road, 200 yards from the handy South Kensington Tube station (on Circle Line, two stops from Victoria Station, direct Heathrow connection). There's a taxi stand in the median strip at the end of Harrington Road. The handy **Wash & Dry launderette** is on the corner of Queensberry Place and Harrington Road (Mon–Fri 7:30–21:00, Sat 9:00–20:00, Sun 10:00–19:00, bring 50p and £1 coins).

My first two recommendations are within easy walking distance of the Tube and are part of Firmdale's chain of small boutique hotels.

$$$ Number Sixteen, for well-heeled travelers, has over-the-top formality and class packed into its 42 rooms, plush lounges, and tranquil garden. It's in a labyrinthine building, with modern decor throughout—perfect for an urban honeymoon (Db-£185–265—but soft, ask for discounted "seasonal rates" especially in July–Aug, breakfast buffet in the garden-£14.50–16.50, elevator, 16 Sumner Place, tel. 020/7589-5232, fax 020/7584-8615, US tel. 800/553-6674, www.firmdalehotels.com, sixteen@firmdale.com).

$$$ The Pelham Hotel, a 52-room business-class hotel, shares the same easy elegance as its sister, above. It's genteel, with low lighting and a pleasant drawing room among the many perks (Sb-£170, Db-£190–260, breakfast extra, lower prices Aug and weekends, Web specials can include free breakfast, air-con, expensive Internet access and Wi-Fi, elevator, gym, 15 Cromwell Place, tel. 020/7589-8288, www.firmdalehotels.com, pelham@firmdale.com).

$$$ Aster House, run by friendly and accommodating Simon and Leonie Tan, has a sumptuous lobby, lounge, and breakfast room. Its rooms are comfy and quiet, with TV, phone, and air-conditioning. Enjoy breakfast or just lounging in the whisper-elegant Orangery, a Victorian greenhouse (Sb-£125, Db-£180, bigger Db-£225, 20 percent discount with this book through 2008 if you book three or more nights, additional 5 percent off for five or more nights with cash, VAT not included, fee for Internet access and Wi-Fi, 3 Sumner Place, tel. 020/7581-5888, fax 020/7584-4925, www.asterhouse.com, asterhouse@btinternet.com). Simon and Leonie offer free loaner mobile phones to their guests.

$$$ The Claverley, two blocks from Harrods, is on a quiet street similar to Sumner Place. The 30 fancy, dark-wood-and-

South Kensington Neighborhood

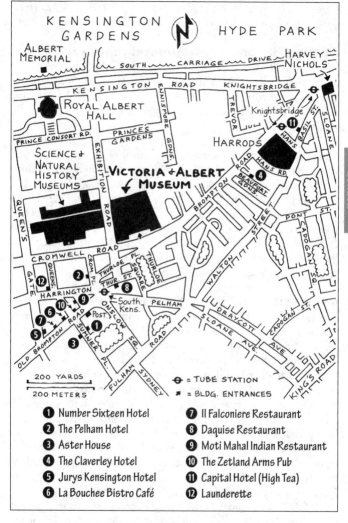

① Number Sixteen Hotel	⑦ Il Falconiere Restaurant
② The Pelham Hotel	⑧ Daquise Restaurant
③ Aster House	⑨ Moti Mahal Indian Restaurant
④ The Claverley Hotel	⑩ The Zetland Arms Pub
⑤ Jurys Kensington Hotel	⑪ Capital Hotel (High Tea)
⑥ La Bouchee Bistro Café	⑫ Launderette

marble rooms come with all the comforts (S-£85, Sb-£105, Db-£157, deluxe Db-£210, sofa-bed Tb-£230–251, ask for Rick Steves discount, air-con in some rooms, elevator, plush lounge, 13–14 Beaufort Gardens, Tube: Knightsbridge, tel. 020/7589-8541, fax 020/7584-3410, US tel. 800-747-0398, www.claverleyhotel.co.uk, reservations@claverleyhotel.co.uk).

$$$ Jurys Kensington Hotel is big, stately, and impersonal, with a greedy pricing scheme (Db-£140–190 depending on "availability," ask for a deal, drop-ins on slow nights sometimes luck into

£90 discount rates, breakfast-£8, elevator, piano lounge, 109–113 Queen's Gate, tel. 020/7589-6300, fax 020/7581-1492, www .jurysdoyle.com, kensington@jurysdoyle.com).

Notting Hill and Bayswater Neighborhoods

Residential Notting Hill has quick bus and Tube access to downtown, and, for London, is very "homely" (Brit-speak for cozy). It's also peppered with trendy bars and restaurants, and is home to the historic Coronet movie theater, as well as the famous Portobello Road Market.

Popular with young international travelers, Bayswater's Queensway street is a multicultural festival of commerce and eateries (see "Eating," on page 137). The neighborhood does its dirty clothes at **Galaxy Launderette** (£4 self-service, £8 full-service, daily 8:00–20:00, 65 Moscow Road, at corner of St. Petersburgh Place and Moscow Road, tel. 020/7229-7771). For **Internet access,** you'll find several stops along busy Queensway, and a self-serve bank of easyInternetcafé computer terminals at the food circus level of the Whiteleys Shopping Centre (daily 8:30–24:00, corner of Queensway and Porchester Gardens).

Near Kensington Gardens Square

Several big old hotels line the quiet Kensington Gardens Square (not to be confused with the much bigger Kensington Gardens), a block west of bustling Queensway, north of Bayswater Tube station. These hotels are quiet for central London.

$$$ Phoenix Hotel, a Best Western modernization of a 125-room hotel, offers American business-class comforts; spacious, plush public spaces; and big, fresh, modern-feeling rooms. Its prices—which range from fine value to rip-off—are determined by a greedy computer program, with huge variations according to expected demand. See their website and book online to save money (Db-£90–150, elevator, impersonal staff, 1–8 Kensington Gardens Square, tel. 020/7229-2494, fax 020/7727-1419, US tel. 800/528-1234, www.phoenixhotel.co.uk, info@phoenixhotel.co.uk).

$$$ Garden Court Hotel rents 32 comfortable rooms in what may be the best value for your hotel dollar in London. It's newly refurbished, with basic but bigger-than-average rooms, caring management, and a pleasant little garden out back (S-£48, Sb-£75, D-£76, Db-£115, Tb-£150, Qb-£170, 10 percent discount with this book through 2008, includes buffet breakfast, cooked breakfast extra, elevator, 30 Kensington Gardens Square, tel. 020/7229-2553, fax 020/7727-2749, www.gardencourthotel.co.uk, info @gardencourthotel.co.uk, well-run by Edward and his helpful staff).

$$$ Vancouver Studios offers 45 modern rooms with fully equipped kitchenettes (utensils, stove, microwave, and fridge)

Notting Hill and Bayswater Neighborhoods

1. Phoenix Hotel
2. Garden Court Hotel
3. Vancouver Studios
4. Kensington Gardens Hotel
5. London House Budget Hotel
6. Westland Hotel
7. Vicarage Private Hotel
8. To Norwegian YWCA
9. Maggie Jones Restaurant
10. The Churchill Arms Pub & Thai Kitchens
11. The Prince Edward Pub
12. Café Diana
13. Royal China Restaurant
14. The Orangery (High Tea)
15. Whiteleys Mall Food Court
16. Spar Market
17. Launderette

rather than breakfast (small Sb-£79, small Db-£110, big Db-£125, Tb-£155, extra bed-£10, 10 percent discount for week-long stay or more, call to confirm reservation a night or two before, welcoming lounge and garden, can be noisy, no elevator, near Kensington Gardens Square at 30 Prince's Square, tel. 020/7243-1270, fax 020/7221-8678, www.vancouverstudios.co.uk, info @vancouverstudios.co.uk). They also rent a six-person apartment nearby for £250/night.

$$ Kensington Gardens Hotel laces 16 pleasant rooms together in a tall, skinny building with lots of stairs and no elevator (S-£47–52, Sb-£52–57, Db-£77, Tb-£97, book by phone or email rather than through the pricier website, 9 Kensington Gardens Square, tel. 020/7221-7790, fax 020/7792-8612, www .kensingtongardenshotel.co.uk, info@kensingtongardenshotel .co.uk, Rowshanak).

$ London House Budget Hotel is a threadbare, chaotic, nose-ringed place renting more than 200 beds in about 80 stark rooms. While their rack rates are high (to hide Web booking commissions for those who don't go direct), their own website offers much better prices, such as Db-£43 (rack rates: S-£40–50, Sb-£45–56, twin-£54, Db-£48–60, dorm bed-£16, prices flex downward with demand, includes continental breakfast, Internet access, lots of school groups, 81 Kensington Gardens Square, tel. 020/7243-1810, fax 020/7243-1723, www.londonhousehotel.co.uk, londonhousehotel@yahoo.co.uk).

Near Kensington Gardens

$$$ Westland Hotel is comfortable, convenient (5-min walk from Notting Hill neighborhood), and feels like a wood-paneled hunting lodge, with a fine lounge. The rooms are spacious, recently refurbished, and quite plush. Their £105 doubles (less your 10 percent discount—see below) are the best value (Sb-£88–99, Db-£105, deluxe Db-£121, cavernous deluxe Db-£138, sprawling Tb-£132–154, gargantuan Qb-£150–175, Quint/b-£165–187, 10 percent discount with this book in 2008—claim upon arrival; elevator, garage-£8/day; between Notting Hill Gate and Queensway Tube stations, 154 Bayswater Road; tel. 020/7229-9191, fax 020/7727-1054, www.westlandhotel.co.uk, reservations@westlandhotel .co.uk, Nora ably staffs the front desk).

$$$ Vicarage Private Hotel is family-run, understandably popular, and elegantly British in a quiet, classy neighborhood. It has 17 rooms furnished with taste and quality, a TV lounge, and facilities on each floor. Mandy, Richard, and Francisca maintain a homey and caring atmosphere (S-£50, Sb-£85, D-£85, Db-£110, T-£105, Tb-£140, Q-£112, Qb-£155, 20 percent less in winter—check website, 6-min walk from Notting Hill Gate and

High Street Kensington Tube stations, near Kensington Palace at 10 Vicarage Gate, tel. 020/7229-4030, fax 020/7792-5989, www.londonvicaragehotel.com, reception@londonvicaragehotel.com).

Near Holland Park

$ Norwegian YWCA (Norsk K.F.U.K.)—where English is definitely a second language—is for women 30 and under only (and men 30 and under with Norwegian passports). Located on a quiet, stately street, it offers a study, TV room, piano lounge, and an open-face Norwegian ambience (goat cheese on Sundays!). They have mostly quads, so those willing to share with strangers are most likely to get a bed (July–Aug: Ss-£34, shared double-£33/bed, shared triple-£27/bed, shared quad-£24/bed, includes breakfast and sack lunch; includes dinner Sept–June; 52 Holland Park, tel. 020/7727-9346, fax 020/7727-8718, www.kfukhjemmet.org.uk, kontor@kfukhjemmet.org.uk). With each visit, I wonder which is easier to get—a sex change or a Norwegian passport?

Other Neighborhoods

North of Marble Arch: **$$$ The 22 York Street B&B** offers a casual alternative in the city center, renting 18 stark, hardwood, comfortable rooms (Sb-£89, Db-£100, Tb-£141, two-night minimum, social breakfast, inviting lounge; from Baker Street Tube station, walk 2 blocks down Baker Street and take a right, 22 York Street; tel. 020/7224-2990, fax 020/7224-1990, www.22yorkstreet.co.uk, mc@22yorkstreet.co.uk, energetically run by Liz and Michael Callis).

$$$ The Sumner Hotel, in a 19th-century Georgian townhouse, is located a few blocks north of Hyde Park and Oxford Street, a busy shopping destination. Decorated with fancy modern Italian furniture, this swanky place packs in all the extras (Db-£125–140, 20 percent discount with this book through 2008, extra bed-£30, includes breakfast, free Wi-Fi, 54 Upper Berkeley Street just off Edgware Road, Tube: Marble Arch, tel. 020/7723-2244, fax 0870-705-8767, www.thesumner.com, hotel@thesumner.com, manager Peter).

Near Covent Garden: **$$$ Fielding Hotel,** located on a charming, quiet pedestrian street just two blocks east of Covent Garden, offers 24 no-frills rooms, a fine location, and lots of stairs (Db-£105–125, Db with sitting room-£150, pricier rooms are bigger with better bathrooms, no breakfast, no kids under 13, 4 Broad Court, Bow Street, tel. 020/7836-8305, fax 020/7497-0064, www.the-fielding-hotel.co.uk, reservations@the-fielding-hotel.co.uk, manager Graham Chapman).

Near Buckingham Palace: **$$ Vandon House Hotel,** run by the Central College in Iowa, is packed with students most of the year, but its 32 rooms are rented to travelers from late May through August at great prices. The rooms, while institutional, are comfy, and the location is excellent (S-£44, D-£68, Db-£85, Tb-£99, Qb-£118, only twin beds, elevator, on a tiny road 3-min walk west of St. James's Park Tube station or 7-min walk from Victoria Station, near east end of Petty France Street at 1 Vandon Street, tel. 020/7799-6780, fax 020/7799-1464, www.vandonhouse.com, info@vandonhouse.com).

Near Euston Station and the British Library: The **$$$ Methodist International Centre,** a modern, youthful, Christian residence, fills its lower floors with international students and its top floor with travelers. Rooms are modern and simple yet comfortable, with fine bathrooms, phones, and desks. The atmosphere is friendly, safe, clean, and controlled; it also has a spacious lounge and game room (Db-£135, Db-£85 with £99 membership, 2-course buffet dinner-£14.50, elevator, on a quiet street a block west of Euston Station, 81–103 Euston Street—not Euston Road, Tube: Euston Station, tel. 020/7380-0001, fax 020/7387-5300, www .micentre.com, acc@micentre.com). In June, July, and August, when the students are gone, they also rent simpler rooms (S-£45, D-£68).

Hostels and Dorms

$ A cluster of three **St. Christopher's Inn** hostels, south of the Thames near London Bridge, have cheap dorm beds (£19–22, 161–165 Borough High Street, Tube: Borough or London Bridge, tel. 020/7407-1856, www.st-christophers.co.uk).

$ The **City of London Youth Hostel,** near St. Paul's, is clean, modern, friendly, and well-run. Most of the 152 beds are in shared, single-sex bunk rooms (bed-£24.60, drops to £17 off-season, twin D-£56, bunk-bed Q-£86, non-members pay £2 extra, includes breakfast, cheap meals, open 24 hours, 36 Carter Lane, Tube: St. Paul's, tel. 020/7236-4965, fax 020/7236-7681, www.yha.org.uk, city@yha.org.uk).

$ The **University of Westminster** opens up its dorm rooms to travelers during summer break, from mid-June through mid-September. Located in several high-rise buildings scattered around central London, the rooms—some with private bathrooms, others with shared bathrooms nearby—come with access to well-equipped kitchens and big lounges (S-£28–35, Sb-£28–37, "studio flat" Db-£60–65, tel. 020/7911-5181, www.wmin.ac.uk/comserv, comserv @wmin.ac.uk). **University College London** also has rooms for travelers from mid-June until mid-September; for details, see www .ucl.ac.uk/residences.

Near Heathrow and Gatwick Airports

At the Airports: The innovative **$ Yotel** has one branch in Gatwick and plans to open another in Heathrow in 2008. Based on Japanese capsule hotels, these small sleep dens offer a place to catch a quick nap (four hours for £25), or to stay overnight (tiny "standard cabin" starts at £40, "premium cabin" starts at £70), all with private bathrooms, free Internet and Wi-Fi, and rooms the size of a double bed (at Gatwick South Terminal and Heathrow Terminal 4, www.yotel.com).

Near Heathrow Airport: It's so easy to get to Heathrow from central London, I see no reason to sleep there. But for budget beds near the airport, consider **$ Heathrow Ibis** (Db-£70, Db-£45–50 on Fri–Sun, Web specials as low as £35, breakfast extra; £4 shuttle bus to/from terminals except T-4, look for "Hopabus" run by National Express; 112 Bath Road, tel. 020/8759-4888, fax 020/8564-7894, www.ibishotel.com, h0794@accor-hotels.com).

Near Gatwick Airport: **$$ Barn Cottage,** a converted 16th-century barn, sits in the peaceful countryside, with a tennis court, small swimming pool, and a good pub within walking distance. It has two wood-beamed rooms, antique furniture, and a large garden that makes you forget Gatwick is 10 minutes away (S-£55, D-£75, cash only, can drive you to airport or train station for £8, Church Road, Leigh, Reigate, Surrey, tel. 01306/611-347, warmly run by Pat and Mike Comer). Do not confuse this place with others of the same name; this Barn Cottage has no website.

$ London Gatwick Airport Premier Travel Inn rents cheap rooms at the airport (Db-£60, £2.50 shuttle bus from airport—must reserve in advance, tel. 0870-238-3305, www.premiertravelinn.com).

$ Gatwick Travelodge has budget rooms two miles from the airport (Db-£56, £3 shuttle from airport, breakfast extra, Church Road, Lowfield Heath, Crawley, tel. 0870-191-1531, www.travelodge.co.uk).

EATING

If you want to dine (as opposed to eat), drop by a London newsstand to get a weekly entertainment guide or an annual restaurant guide (both have extensive restaurant listings). Visit www.london-eating.co.uk or www.squaremeal.co.uk for more options.

The thought of a £40 meal in Britain generally ruins my appetite, so my London dining is limited mostly to easygoing, fun, inexpensive alternatives. I've listed places by neighborhood—handy to your sightseeing or hotel. Considering how expensive London can be, if there's any good place to cut corners to stretch your budget, it's by eating cheaply.

Central London Eateries

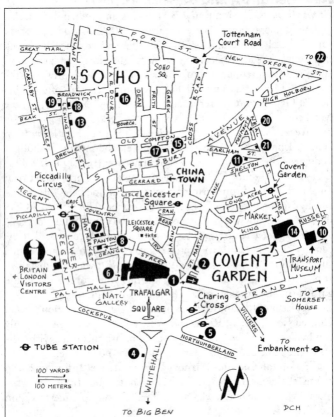

1. St. Martin-in-the-Fields Café in the Crypt
2. The Chandos Pub's Opera Room
3. Gordon's Wine Bar
4. The Lord Moon of the Mall Pub
5. The Sherlock Holmes Pub
6. The National Dining Rooms
7. Stockpot & Woodland South Indian Vegetarian Restaurant
8. West End Kitchen
9. Criterion Restaurant
10. To Food Balcony, PJ's Bar and Grill, Joe Allen & Livebait Restaurants

11. Belgo Centraal
12. Yo! Sushi
13. Wagamama Noodle Bar
14. Just Falafs
15. Kettners Restaurant
16. Soho Spice Indian & Busaba Eathai Thai Rest.
17. Y Ming Chinese Rest.
18. Andrew Edmunds Rest.
19. Mildred's Vegetarian Rest.
20. Neal's Yard Eateries
21. Food for Thought Café
22. To The Princess Louise Pub

Remember that London (and all of Britain) is now smoke-free, thanks to a recent smoking ban. Expect restaurants and pubs that sell food to be non-smoking indoors, with smokers occupying patios and doorways outside.

Pub grub is the most atmospheric budget option. Many of London's 7,000 pubs serve fresh, tasty buffets under ancient timbers, with hearty lunches and dinners priced at £6–8.

Ethnic restaurants—especially Indian and Chinese—are popular, plentiful, and cheap. Most large museums (and many churches) have inexpensive, cheery cafeterias. Of course, picnicking is the fastest and cheapest way to go. Good grocery stores and sandwich shops, fine park benches, and polite pigeons abound in Britain's most expensive city.

Near Trafalgar Square

Each of these places is within about 100 yards of Trafalgar Square. To locate the following restaurants, see the map on page 130.

St. Martin-in-the-Fields Café in the Crypt is just right for a tasty meal on a monk's budget, sitting on somebody's tomb in an ancient crypt. While their enticing buffet line is kept stocked all day, their cheap sandwich bar is generally sold out by 11:30 (£6–8 cafeteria plates, Mon–Wed 8:00–20:00, Thu–Sat 8:00–22:00, Sun 12:00–20:00, profits go to the church, underneath Church of St. Martin-in-the-Fields on Trafalgar Square, Tube: Charing Cross, tel. 020/7839-4342 or 020/7766-1100). The café was closed for renovation through late 2007, but should reopen by 2008. While here, check out the concert schedule for the busy church upstairs.

The Chandos Pub's Opera Room floats amazingly apart from the tacky crush of tourism around Trafalgar Square. Look for it opposite the National Portrait Gallery (corner of William IV Street and St. Martin's Lane) and climb the stairs to the Opera Room. This is a fine Trafalgar rendezvous point and wonderfully local pub. They serve traditional, plain-tasting £6–7 pub meals. The ground-floor pub is stuffed with regulars and offers serious beer along with some toasted sandwiches (kitchen open Mon–Thu and Sat 11:00–21:00, Fri and Sun 12:00–18:00, order and pay at the bar, tel. 020/7836-1401).

Gordon's Wine Bar, with a simple, steep staircase leading into a candlelit 15th-century wine cellar, is filled with dusty old bottles, faded British memorabilia, and local nine-to-fivers. At the buffet, choose a hot meal or a fine plate of cheeses and various cold cuts. Then step up to the wine bar and consider the many varieties of wine and port available by the glass. This place is passionate about port. The low, carbon-crusted vaulting deeper in the back seems to intensify the Hogarth-painting atmosphere. While it's crowded, you can normally corral two chairs and grab the corner of a table. On hot days, the crowd spills out into a leafy back patio (arrive before 17:30 to get a seat, Mon–Sat 11:00–23:00, Sun 12:00–22:00, 2 blocks from Trafalgar Square, bottom of Villiers Street at #47, Tube: Embankment, tel. 020/7930-1408, manager Gerard Menan).

The Lord Moon of the Mall pub has real ales on tap and good, cheap pub grub, including a two-meals-for-the-price-of-one deal (£8, offer valid Mon–Fri 14:00–22:00 and all day Sat–Sun). This kid-friendly pub fills a great old former Barclays Bank building a block down Whitehall from Trafalgar Square (daily 9:00–23:00, 18 Whitehall, tel. 020/7839-7701). Nearby are several cheap cafeterias and pizza joints.

The Sherlock Holmes pub has a casual ground-floor section serving cheap grub and a stodgier upstairs restaurant with a mediocre spy-theme menu (£10 main courses). Fans of the fictional detective will appreciate sitting next to a wonderful replica of Holmes' 221-B Baker Street home. The pub is located in the former Northumberland Hotel (featured in Holmes stories). The former Old Scotland Yard was just across the street (daily 11:00–22:00, 10 Northumberland Street, Tube: Charing Cross/Embankment, tel. 020/7930-2644).

The National Dining Rooms serves classy meals within the National Gallery, and is a good place to treat your palate to pricey cuisine (including high tea—see page 142). While tables in the main dining room are often reserved for dinner, you can usually grab a seat in the bistro-like café anytime (£15 lunches, daily 10:00–17:00, later on Wed—when the museum stays open late, Tube: Charing Cross or Leicester Square, tel. 020/7747-2525).

Cheap Eating near Piccadilly

Hungry and broke in the theater district? Head for Panton Street (off Haymarket, 2 blocks southeast of Piccadilly Circus) where several hardworking little places compete, all seeming to offer a three-course meal for about £7. Peruse the entire block (vegetarian, Japanese, Pizza Express, Moroccan, Thai, Chinese, and two famous eateries) before making your choice. **Stockpot** is a mushy-peas kind of place, famous and rightly popular for its edible, cheap meals (daily 7:00–23:00, 38 Panton Street, cash only). The **West End Kitchen** (across the street at #5, same hours and menu) is a direct competitor that's also well-known and just as good. Vegetarians prefer the **Woodland South Indian Vegetarian Restaurant.**

The palatial **Criterion** serves a special £15 two-course French fixed-price meal (or £18 for three courses) under gilded tiles and chandeliers in a dreamy Byzantine church setting from 1880. It's right on Piccadilly Circus but a world away from the punk junk. The house wine is great, as is the food. After 19:00, the menu

London

becomes really expensive. Anyone can drop in for coffee or a drink (Mon–Sat 12:00–14:30 & 17:30–23:30, Sun 12:00–15:30 & 17:30–22:30, tel. 020/7930-0488).

The Wolseley is the grand 1920s showroom of a long-defunct British car. While the last Wolseley drove out with the Great Depression, today this old-time bistro bustles with formal waiters serving traditional Austrian and French dishes in an elegant black-marble-and-chandeliers setting fit for its location next to the Ritz. While the food can be unexceptional, prices are reasonable, and the presentation and setting are grand. Reservations are a must (£16 plates, cheaper burger-and-sandwich menu available, Mon–Fri 7:00–24:00, Sat 8:00–24:00, Sun 8:00–23:00, 160 Piccadilly, tel. 020/7499-6996). They're popular for their fancy cream tea (£8, served 15:30–17:30).

Hip Eating from Covent Garden to Soho

London has a trendy, Generation X scene that most Beefeater-seekers miss entirely. These restaurants are scattered throughout the hipster, gay, and strip-club district, teeming each evening with fun-seekers and theater-goers. Even if you plan to have dinner elsewhere, it's a treat to just wander around this lively area.

Beware of the extremely welcoming women standing outside the strip clubs (especially on Great Windmill Street). Enjoy the sales pitch—but only fools fall for the "£5 drink and show" lure. They don't get back out without emptying their wallets.

Belgo Centraal serves hearty Belgian specialties in a vast, 400-seat underground lair. It's a seafood, chips, and beer emporium dressed up as a mod-monastic refectory—with noisy acoustics and waiters garbed as Trappist monks. The classy restaurant section is more comfortable and less rowdy, but usually requires reservations (the wait can be up to 2 hours Fri–Sat without a reservation). It's often more fun to just grab a spot in the boisterous beer hall, with its tight, communal benches (no reservations accepted). The same menu and specials work on both sides. Belgians claim they eat as well as the French and as heartily as the Germans. Specialties include mussels, great fries, and a stunning array of dark, blond, and fruity Belgian beers (even beer ice cream). Belgo actually makes Belgian things trendy—a formidable feat (£10–14 meals; Mon–Sat 12:00–23:30, Sun 12:00–22:30; Mon–Fri £5–6.30 "beat the clock" meal specials from 17:00–18:30—the time you order is the price you pay—including main dishes, fries, and beer; no meal-splitting after 18:30, and you must buy food with beer; daily £6.50 lunch special 12:00–17:00; 2 kids eat free for each parent ordering a regular entree; 1 block north of Covent Garden Tube station at intersection of Neal and Shelton streets, 50 Earlham Street, tel. 020/7813-2233).

London

Yo! Sushi is a futuristic Japanese-food-extravaganza experience. It's not cheap, but it's sure to be a memorable experience, complete with thumping rock, Japanese cable TV, a 195-foot-long conveyor belt—the world's longest sushi bar—and automated sushi machines. For £1 each you get unlimited tea or water (from spigot at bar, with or without gas). Snag a bar stool and grab dishes as they rattle by (priced by color of dish; check the chart: £1.50–5 per dish, £1.50 for miso soup, Mon–Sat 12:00–23:00, Sun 12:00–22:30, 2 blocks south of Oxford Street, where Lexington Street becomes Poland Street, 52 Poland Street, tel. 020/7287-0443). If you like Yo!, there are several locations around town, including a handy branch a block from the London Eye on Belvedere Road, as well as outlets within Selfridges, Harvey Nichols department stores, and Whiteleys Mall on Queensway—see later in this section.

Wagamama Noodle Bar is a noisy, pan-Asian, organic slurp-athon. As you enter, check out the kitchen and listen to the roar of the basement, where benches rock with happy eaters. Everybody sucks. Stand against the wall to feel the energy of all this "positive eating" (£7–12 meals, Mon–Sat 12:00–23:00, Sun 12:00–22:00, crowded after 20:00, 10A Lexington Street, tel. 020/7292-0990 but no reservations taken). If you like this place, handy branches are all over town, including one near the British Museum (Streatham Street), High Street Kensington (#26), in Harvey Nichols (109 Knightsbridge), Covent Garden (Tavistock Street), Leicester Square (Irving Street), Piccadilly Circus (Norris Street), Fleet Street (#109), and between St. Paul's and the Tower of London (22 Old Broad Street). Get two-for-one coupons in advance at www .wagamama.com (must register first).

Just Falafs is a healthy fast-food option in the chaos of Covent Garden. Located in the southeast corner, where rows of outdoor café tables line the tiny shop, they offer falafel sandwiches with yummy vegetarian-friendly extras (£6 sandwiches, Mon–Fri 8:00–21:00, Sat 10:00–21:00, Sun 10:00–18:00, closes earlier when it's raining, 27b Covent Gardens Square, tel. 020/7622-6262).

Soho Spice Indian is where modern Britain meets Indian tradition—fine cuisine in a trendy, jewel-tone ambience. Unlike many Indian restaurants, when you order an entrée here (£11), it comes with side dishes—naan, dal, rice, and vegetables (£7 lunch special, daily 12:00–23:00, 5 blocks north of Piccadilly Circus at 124 Wardour Street, tel. 020/7434-0808).

Busaba Eathai Thai Restaurant is a hit with locals for its snappy service, casual-yet-high-energy ambience, and good, inexpensive Thai cuisine. You'll sit communally around big, square 16-person hardwood tables or in two-person tables by the window—with everyone in the queue staring at your noodles. They don't take reservations, so arrive by 19:00 or line up (£10–14 meals, daily 12:00–23:00, 106 Wardour Street, tel. 020/7255-8686).

Y Ming Chinese Restaurant—across Shaftesbury Avenue from the ornate gates, clatter, and dim sum of Chinatown—has dressy European decor, serious but helpful service, and authentic Northern Chinese cooking (good £10 meal deal offered 12:00–18:00—last order at 18:00, open Mon–Sat 12:00–23:45, closed Sun, 35 Greek Street, tel. 020/7734-2721).

Andrew Edmunds Restaurant is a tiny, candlelit place where you'll want to hide your camera and guidebook and act as local as possible. This little place—with a jealous and loyal clientele—is the closest I've found to Parisian quality in a cozy restaurant in London. The modern European cooking and creative seasonal menu are worth the splurge (£25 meals, daily 12:30–15:00 & 18:00–22:45, come early or call ahead, request ground floor rather than basement, 46 Lexington Street in Soho, tel. 020/7437-5708).

Mildred's Vegetarian Restaurant, across from Andrew Edmunds, has cheap prices, an enjoyable menu, and a plain-yet-pleasant interior filled with happy eaters (£7 meals, Mon–Sat 12:00–23:00, closed Sun, vegan options, 45 Lexington Street, tel. 020/7494-1634).

Kettners is a grand, velvety old dining lounge serving affordable pizza, pasta, and burgers with a hint of 19th-century elegance (daily 12:00–24:00, across from Y Ming Chinese Restaurant at 29 Romilly Street, Soho, tel. 020/7734-6112).

Neal's Yard is *the* place for cheap, hip, and healthy eateries near Covent Garden. The neighborhood is a tabouli of fun, hippie-type cafés. One of the best is **Food for Thought,** packed with local health nuts (good £5 vegetarian meals, £7.50 dinner plates, Mon–Sat 12:00–20:30, Sun 12:00–17:00, 2 blocks north of Covent Garden Tube station, 31 Neal Street, near Neal's Yard, tel. 020/7836-0239).

The Soho "Food is Fun" Three-Course Dinner Crawl: For a multicultural, movable feast, consider eating (or splitting) one course and enjoying a drink at each of these places. Start around 18:00 to avoid lines, get in on early-bird specials, and find waiters willing to let you split a meal. Prices, while reasonable by London standards, add up. Servings are large enough to share. All are open nightly. Arrive before 18:00 at **Belgo Centraal** and split the early-bird dinner special: a kilo of mussels, fries, and dark Belgian beer. At **Yo! Sushi,** have beer or sake and a few dishes. Slurp your last course at **Wagamama Noodle Bar.** For dessert, people-watch at Leicester Square.

Near Recommended Victoria Station Accommodations

I've enjoyed eating at these places, a few blocks southwest of Victoria Station (see the map on page 119).

Ebury Wine Bar, filled with young professionals, provides a cut-above atmosphere, delicious £15–18 meals, and a £14.50 two-course special from 18:00–19:30. In the delightful back room, the fancy menu features modern European cuisine with a French accent; at the wine bar, find cheaper food that's better than pub grub. This is emphatically a "traditional wine bar" with only a few beers on tap (Mon–Fri 11:00–23:00, Sat 12:00–23:00, Sun 18:00–22:00, reserve after 20:00, at intersection of Ebury and Elizabeth Streets, near bus station, 139 Ebury Street, tel. 020/7730-5447).

Goya Spanish Restaurant and Tapas Bar is popular for its old-church-library ambience and tasty, reasonably priced food (£12–15 meals, good Spanish wine by the glass, daily 11:30–23:00, 2 Eccleston Place, tel. 020/7730-4299). Several cheap places are around the corner on Elizabeth Street (#23 for take-out or eat-in, super-absorbent fish-and-chips).

The Duke of Wellington pub is dominated by local drinkers. It's the neighborhood place for a good dinner, with woody sidewalk seating and an inviting interior (£6–7 meals, specials, Mon–Sat 11:00–15:00 & 18:00–21:00, closed Sun, 63 Eaton Terrace, at intersection with Chester Row, tel. 020/7730-1782).

The Belgravia Pub is a new, hardworking sports bar with less character than The Duke of Wellington, serving snacks and pub food under a set of big-screen TVs (£4–6 meals, beer garden seating or plush interior, daily 10:00–23:00, 11:00–23:00 in winter, corner of Ebury Street and South Eaton Place at 152 Ebury Street, tel. 020/7730-6040).

Jenny Lo's Tea House is a simple, budget place serving up reliably tasty £5–8 eclectic Chinese-style meals to locals in the know. While the menu is small, everything is high quality. Jenny clearly learned from her father, Ken Lo, one of the most famous Cantonese chefs in Britain, whose fancy place is just around the corner (Mon–Fri 12:00–15:00 & 18:00–22:00, Sat 18:00–22:00, closed Sun, cash only, 14 Eccleston Street, tel. 020/7259-0399).

La Poule au Pot, ideal for a romantic splurge, offers a classy, candlelit ambience with well-dressed patrons and expensive but fine country-style French cuisine (£18 lunch specials, £25 dinner plates, daily 12:30–14:30 & 18:45–23:00, Sun until 22:00, £50 for dinner with wine, leafy patio dining, reservations smart, end of Ebury Street at intersection with Pimlico Road, 231 Ebury Street, tel. 020/7730-7763).

Grumbles brags it's been serving "good food and wine at

London

non-scary prices since 1964." Offering a delicious mix of "modern eclectic French and traditional English," this hip and cozy little place with four nice sidewalk tables is *the* spot to eat well in this otherwise workaday neighborhood. While they have seating downstairs, I'd avoid it; call ahead to reserve a spot outside or on the appealing and cozy ground floor (£8–16 plates, £10 early-bird special, daily 12:00–14:30 & 18:00–23:00, reservations wise, half a block north of Belgrave Road at 35 Churton Street, tel. 020/7834-0149). Multitaskers take note: The self-service launderette across the street is open evenings.

Chimes English Restaurant and Cider Bar comes with a fresh, country farm ambience, serious ciders (rare in London), and very good, traditional English food. Experiment with the cider—it's legal here...just barely (£13 two-course meals, hearty salads, daily 12:00–15:00 & 17:30–22:15, 26 Churton Street, tel. 020/7821-7456).

The Jugged Hare, a 10-minute walk from Victoria Station, is a pub in a lavish old bank building, its vaults replaced by tankards of beer and a fine kitchen. They have a fun, traditional menu with more fresh veggies than fries, and a plush and vivid pub scene good for a meal or just a drink (£7 meals, daily 12:00–21:30, 172 Vauxhall Bridge Road, tel. 020/7828-1543).

Seafresh Fish Restaurant is the neighborhood place for plaice—either take-out on the cheap or eat-in, enjoying a chrome-and-wood mod ambience with classic and creative fish-and-chips cuisine. It feels like the chippie of the 21st century (meals-£5 to go, £8–13 to sit, Mon–Fri 12:00–15:00 & 17:00–22:30, Sat 12:00–22:30, closed Sun, 80 Wilton Road, tel. 020/7828-0747).

If you miss America, there's a mall-type **food court** at Victoria Place, upstairs in Victoria Station; **Café Rouge** seems to be the most popular here (£8–11 dinners, daily 9:30–22:30).

Groceries in and near Victoria Station: A handy **Marks & Spencer Simply Food** is inside Victoria Station (Mon–Sat 7:00–24:00, Sun 8:00–22:00, tel. 020/7828-9502), along with a small **Sainsbury's** (at rear entrance, on Eccleston Street) and a few other late-hours mini-markets. A large **Sainsbury's Market** is on Wilton Road, to the side of the station (daily 6:00–24:00).

Near Recommended Notting Hill B&Bs and Bayswater Hotels

The road called Queensway is a multi-ethnic food circus, lined with lively and inexpensive eateries. See the map on page 125.

Maggie Jones, a £30 splurge, is exuberantly rustic and very English. You'll get solid English cuisine, including huge plates of crunchy vegetables, by candlelight. Avoid the stuffy basement

Pub Appreciation

The pub is the heart of the people's Britain, where all manner of folks have, for generations, found their respite from work and a home-away-from-home. Britain's classic pubs are national treasures, with great cultural value and rich history, not to mention good beer and grub.

The Golden Age for pub building was in the late Victorian era (c. 1880–1905), when pubs were independently owned and land prices were high enough to make it worthwhile to invest in fixing up pubs. The politics were pro-pub as well: Conservatives, backed by Big Beer, were in, and temperance-minded liberals were out.

Especially in class-conscious Victorian times, traditional pubs were divided into sections by elaborate screens (now mostly gone), allowing the wealthy to drink in a more refined setting, while commoners congregated on the pub's rougher side. These were really "public houses," featuring nooks (snugs) for groups and clubs to meet, friends and lovers to rendezvous, and families to get out of the house at night. Since many pub-goers were illiterate, pubs were simply named for the picture hung outside (e.g., The Crooked Stick, The Queen's Arms—meaning her coat of arms).

Historic pubs still dot the London cityscape. The only place to see the very oldest-style tavern in the "domestic tradition" is at **Ye Olde Cheshire Cheese,** which was rebuilt in 1667 from a 16th-century tavern; open daily, 145 Fleet Street, Tube: Blackfriars, tel. 020/7353-6170). Imagine this place in the pre-Victorian era: With no bar, drinkers gathered around the fireplaces, while tap boys shuttled tankards up from the cellar. (This was long before barroom taps were connected to casks in the cellar. Oh, and don't say "keg"—that's a gassy modern thing.)

Late Victorian pubs, such as the 1897 **Princess Louise** (open daily, 208 High Holborn, see map on page 130, Tube: Holborn, tel. 020/7405-8816) are more common. These places are fancy, often coming with heavy embossed wallpaper ceilings, decorative tile work, fine-etched glass, ornate carved stillions (the big central hutch for storing bottles and glass), and even urinals equipped with a place to set your glass. London's best Art Nouveau pub is **The Black Friar** (c. 1900–1915), with fine carved capitals, lamp holders, and quirky phrases worked into the decor (open daily, across from Tube: Blackfriars at 174 Queen Victoria Street, tel. 020/7236-5474).

Historic Pubs

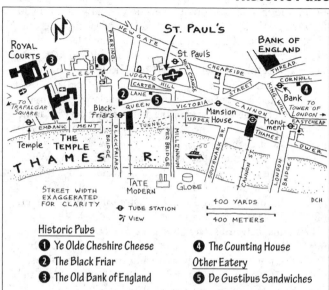

Historic Pubs
1. Ye Olde Cheshire Cheese
2. The Black Friar
3. The Old Bank of England
4. The Counting House

Other Eatery
5. De Gustibus Sandwiches

The "former-bank pubs" represent a more modern trend in pub building. As banks increasingly go electronic, they're moving out of lavish, high-rent old buildings. Many of these former banks are being refitted as pubs with elegant bars and free-standing

stillions, providing a fine center-piece. Three such pubs are **The Old Bank of England** (closed Sat–Sun, 194 Fleet Street, Tube: Temple, tel. 020/7430-2255), **The Jugged Hare** (open daily, 172 Vauxhall Bridge Road, see map on page 119, Tube: Victoria, tel. 020/7828-1543, also see listing on page 137), and **The Counting House** (closed Sat–Sun, 50 Cornhill, Tube: Bank, tel. 020/7283-7123, also see listing on page 141).

Go pubbing in the evening for a lively time, or drop by during the quiet late morning (from 11:00), when the pub is empty and filled with memories. For more information, see Bob Steel's website, www.aletrails.com. Bob also offers a historic pubs tour (about £50 for a leisurely half-day walk).

on hot summer nights, and request upstairs seating for the noisy but less-cramped section. If you eat well once in London, eat here—and do it quick, before it burns down (daily 12:30–14:30 & 18:30–23:00, less expensive lunch menu, reservations recommended, 6 Old Court Place, just east of Kensington Church Street, near High Street Kensington Tube stop, tel. 020/7937-6462).

The Churchill Arms pub and **Thai Kitchens** (same location) is a local hangout, with good beer and old-English ambience in front, and hearty £6 Thai plates in an enclosed patio in the back. You can eat the Thai food in the tropical hideaway or in the atmospheric pub section. The place is festooned with Churchill memorabilia and chamber pots (including one with Hitler's mug on it—sure to cure the constipation of any Brit during World War II). Arrive by 18:00 or after 21:00 to avoid a line. During busy times, diners are limited to an hour at the table (Mon–Sat 12:00–22:00, Sun 12:00–21:30, 119 Kensington Church Street, tel. 020/7792-1246).

The Prince Edward serves good grub in a quintessential pub setting (£7–10 meals, Mon–Sat 12:00–15:00 & 18:00–22:00, Sun 12:00–21:00, plush-pubby indoor seating or sidewalk tables, 2 blocks north of Bayswater Road at the corner of Dawson Place and Hereford Road, 73 Prince's Square, tel. 020/7727-2221).

Café Diana is a healthy little eatery serving sandwiches, salads, and Middle Eastern food. It's decorated—almost shrine-like—with photos of Princess Diana, who used to drop by for pita sandwiches (daily 8:00–22:30, 5 Wellington Terrace, on Bayswater Road, opposite Kensington Palace Garden Gates—where Di once lived, tel. 020/7792-9606).

Royal China Restaurant is filled with London's Chinese, who consider this one of the city's best eateries. It's dressy in black, white, and chrome, with candles, brisk waiters, and fine food (£7–11 dishes, Mon–Sat 12:00–23:00, Sun 11:00–22:00, dim sum until 16:45, 13 Queensway, tel. 020/7221-2535).

Whiteleys Mall Food Court offers a fun selection of ethnic and fast-food eateries among Corinthian columns in a delightful mall (Mon–Sat 10:00–20:00, Sun 12:00–18:00; options include Yo! Sushi, good salads at Café Rouge, pizza, Starbucks, and an Internet café; second floor, corner of Porchester Gardens and Queensway).

Supermarket: **Europa** is a half-block from the Notting Hill Gate Tube stop (Mon–Sat 8:00–23:00, Sun 12:00–18:00, near intersection with Pembridge Road, 112 Notting Hill Gate). The smaller **Spar Market** is at 18 Queensway (Mon–Sat 7:00–24:00, Sun 9:00–24:00), and **Marks & Spencer** can be found in Whiteleys Mall (Mon–Sat 10:00–20:00, Sun 12:00–18:00).

Near Recommended Accommodations in South Kensington

Popular eateries line Old Brompton Road and Thurloe Street (Tube: South Kensington). See the map on page 123. The **Tesco Express** grocery store is handy for picnics (daily 7:00–24:00, 54 Old Brompton Road).

La Bouchee Bistro Café is a classy, hole-in-the-wall touch of France—candlelit and woody—serving an early-bird, two-course £10 dinner weekdays from 17:30–19:00 and £15 *plats du jour* all *jour* (daily 12:00–15:00 & 17:30–23:00, 56 Old Brompton Road, tel. 020/7589-1929).

Il Falconiere Restaurant, just down the street, is popular for its Italian cuisine (£8 pastas, £10 plates, £19 three-course dinner special, closed Sun, 84 Old Brompton Road, tel. 020/7589-2401).

Daquise, an authentic-feeling 1930s Polish time warp, is ideal if you're in the mood for kielbasa and kraut. It's likeably dreary—fast, cheap, family-run—and a much-appreciated part of the neighborhood (£10 meals, £8 lunch special includes wine, daily 11:30–23:00, 20 Thurloe Street, tel. 020/7589-6117).

Moti Mahal Indian Restaurant is a new favorite for value, with minimalist-yet-classy mod ambience and attentive service (daily 12:00–23:00, 3 Glendower Place, tel. 020/7584-8428).

The Zetland Arms serves good pub meals in a classic pub atmosphere on the ground floor and a club-chair lounge upstairs (same menu throughout, £6–10 meals, food served Mon–Sat 12:00–21:00, Sun 12:00–20:30, 2 Bute Street, tel. 020/7589-3813).

Elsewhere in London

Between St. Paul's and the Tower: The **Counting House,** formerly an elegant old bank, offers great £7.50–8 meals, nice home-made meat pies, fish, and fresh vegetables (Mon–Fri 12:00–21:00, closed Sat–Sun, gets really busy with the buttoned-down 9-to-5 crowd after 12:15, near Mansion House in the City, 50 Cornhill, tel. 020/7283-7123).

Near St. Paul's: **De Gustibus Sandwiches** is where a top-notch artisan bakery meets the public, offering fresh, you-design-it sandwiches, salads, and soups with simple seating or take-out picnic sacks (great parks nearby), just a block below St. Paul's (Mon–Fri 7:00–17:00, closed Sat–Sun, from church steps follow signs to youth hostel a block downhill, 53–55 Carter Lane, tel. 020/7236-0056; another outlet is inside the Borough Market in Southwark).

Near the British Library: Drummond Street (running just west of Euston Station) is famous in London for very cheap and good Indian vegetarian food. Consider **Chutneys** (124 Drummond, tel. 020/7388-0604) and **Ravi Shankar** (133 Drummond, tel.

Taking High Tea in London

Once the sole province of genteel ladies in fancy hats, high tea has become more democratic in the 21st century. While some tearooms—such as the £34-a-head tea service at the Ritz and the recommended but finicky Fortnum & Mason—still require a jacket and tie (and a bigger bank account), most happily welcome tourists in jeans and sneakers.

The cheapest high tea on the menu is generally a "cream tea," while the most expensive is the "champagne tea." **Cream tea** is simply a pot of tea and a scone with jam and cream. **High tea** generally includes a pot of tea and a tier of three plates holding small finger foods (such as cucumber sandwiches), a small slice of cake, homemade scones, jam, and thick clotted cream. **Champagne tea** includes all of the goodies, plus a glass of champagne. For maximum pinkie-waving taste per calorie, slice your scone thin like a miniature loaf of bread.

Tearooms, which often also serve appealing light meals, are usually open for lunch and close about 17:00, just before dinner. At all the places listed below, it's perfectly acceptable to order one high tea and one regular tea (at about £3–4) and split the high-tea goodies. The fancier places, such as Harrods and The Capital Hotel, are happy to bring you seconds and thirds of your favorite goodies, making tea into an early dinner.

The Orangery at Kensington Palace serves a £12 "Orangery tea" and a £25 champagne tea in its bright white hall near Princess Di's former residence. The portions aren't huge, but who can argue with eating at a princess' house? (Tea served 15:00–18:00; located on map on page 125, a 10-min walk through Kensington Gardens from either Queensway or High Street Kensington Tube stations to the orange brick building, about 20 yards from Kensington Palace; tel. 020/7938-1406.)

The National Dining Rooms, a restaurant/café within the National Gallery on Trafalgar Square, is both classy and convenient. While the restaurant can book up in advance, you can generally waltz in for high tea at the café. To play it safe, arrive in the early afternoon to reserve a tea time, then take the self-guided National Gallery Tour (page 72) before or after your appointed time. (Spend any wait time touring the National Portrait Gallery, just a 5-minute walk away.) If you're really on vacation, consider adding a £4–8 "tipple"—a glass of champagne, a Bellini, or a similar drink—to your high-tea experience (£5 savory tarts, £12 high tea, £15 plates, high tea served 15:00–17:15, located in Sainsbury Wing of National Gallery, Tube: Charing Cross or Leicester Square, tel. 020/7747-2525, also see restaurant listing on page 132).

The Cafe at Sotheby's, located on the ground floor of the auction giant's headquarters, is manna for shoppers taking a break from fashionable New Bond Street. There are no windows—just a long leather bench, plenty of mirrors, and a dark-wood room where waiters serve sweet treats and the £5.50 mix-and-match Neal's Yard cheese plate to locals in the know (£3 cakes and creams, £5.25 "small tea," £12.50 high tea must be ordered 24 hours in advance—call 020/7293-5077, café open 9:30–11:30 & 12:00–16:45, high tea served after 15:00, located on color map on page iv, 34–35 New Bond Street, Tube: Bond Street or Oxford Circus).

For a classier experience with an attentive wait staff, try the **Capital Hotel,** a luxury hotel located a half-block from Harrods. The Capital caters to weary shoppers with its intimate, five-table, linen-tablecloth tearoom. It's where the ladies-who-lunch meet to decide whether to buy that Versace gown they've had their eye on. Even so, casual clothes, kids, and sharing plates—with a £3.50 split-tea service charge—are all OK (£18 high tea, daily 15:00–17:30, call to book ahead on weekends, see map on page 123, 22 Basil Street, Tube: Knightsbridge, tel. 020/7589-5171).

Two famous department stores—Harrods and Fortnum & Mason—serve high tea for sky-high prices. **Fortnum & Mason's St. James Restaurant,** on the fourth floor, offers plush seats under the elegant tearoom's chandeliers. You'll get the standard three-tiered silver tea tray: finger sandwiches on the bottom, fresh scones with jam and clotted cream on the first floor, and decadent pastries and "tartlets" on the top floor, with unlimited tea. Consider it dinner (about £24–32, Mon–Sat 15:00–19:00, Sun 14:00–17:00, dress up a bit for this—no shorts, "children must be behaved," see color map on page iv, 181 Piccadilly, tel. 020/7734-8040 ext. 2241, www.fortnumandmason.com).

At **Harrods' Georgian Restaurant,** you (along with 200 of your closest friends) can enjoy a fancy tea under a skylight as a pianist tickles the keys of a Bösendorfer, the world's most expensive piano (£19 high tea, includes finger sandwiches and pastries with free refills, served Mon–Fri 15:30–17:30, Sat 15:45–17:30, Sun 15:30–18:30, on Brompton Road, Tube: Knightsbridge, reservations tel. 020/7225-6800, store tel. 020/7730-1234, www.harrods.com). There's also Parisian-themed high tea in the store's new Ladurée tearoom (£21, ground floor), though it just doesn't seem right to eat croissants in London.

If you want the teatime experience but are put off by the price, most department stores on Oxford Street (including those between Oxford Circus and Bond Street Tube stations) offer an affordable high tea. **John Lewis** has a mod brasserie that serves a nice £10 high tea platter (on Oxford Street, one block west of Bond Street Tube station). **Selfridges'** high tea is pricier at £16.50. Near the Ritz, consider the £8 cream tea at Near the Ritz, or consider the £8 cream tea at **The Wolseley** (see page 133). Many museums and bookstores have cafés serving high tea goodies à la carte, where you can put together a spread for less than £10 (try Waterstone's fifth-floor café and the Victoria and Albert Museum café).

020/7388-6458) for a good *thali* (both generally open daily until 21:30, later Fri–Sat).

TRANSPORTATION CONNECTIONS

AIRPORTS

Phone numbers and websites for London's airports and major airlines are listed on page 641. For information on cheap flights, see page 657.

Heathrow Airport

Heathrow Airport is the world's third busiest, after Atlanta and Chicago O'Hare. Think about it: 68 million passengers a year on 470,000 flights from 185 destinations riding 90 airlines, like some kind of global maypole dance. While many complain about Heathrow, I think it's a great and user-friendly airport. Read signs, ask questions. For Heathrow's airport, flight, and transfers information, call the switchboard at 0870-000-0123 (www.baa.com). There are four terminals: T-1 (mostly domestic flights, with some European), T-2 (mainly European flights), T-3 (mostly flights from the US), T-4 (British Airways transatlantic flights and BA flights to Paris, Amsterdam, and Athens). A new, fifth terminal (T-5) is due to be completed in 2008. Taxis know which terminal you'll need.

Each terminal has an airport information desk, car-rental agencies, exchange bureaus, ATMs, a pharmacy, a **VAT refund desk** (tel. 020/8910-3682; you must present the VAT claim form from the retailer here to get your tax rebate on items purchased in Britain—see page 636 for details), and a **baggage-check desk** (£6.50/day, daily 6:00–23:00 at each terminal). Get online 24 hours a day at Heathrow's **Internet cafés** (T-4, mezzanine level) and with a laptop at pay-as-you-go wireless "hotspots"—including many hosted by T-Mobile—in its departure lounges (T-1, T-3, and T-4). There are **post offices** in T-2 and T-4. Each terminal has cheap **eateries** (such as the cheery Food Village self-service cafeteria in T-3). The **American Express** desk, in the Tube station at Terminal 4 (daily 7:00–19:00), has rates similar to the exchange bureaus upstairs, but doesn't charge a commission (typically 1.5 percent) for cashing any type of traveler's check.

Heathrow's small **TI** (tourist info shop), even though it's a for-profit business, is worth a visit to pick up free information: a simple map, the *London Planner,* and brochures (daily 8:30–18:00, 5-min walk from T-3 in Tube station, follow signs to Underground; bypass queue for transit info to reach window for London questions). Have your partner stay with the bags at the terminal while you head over to the TI. There's also an airport info desk in the arrivals concourse of each terminal (generally open daily 7:00–21:30).

If you're taking the Tube into London, buy a one-day Travelcard or Oyster card to cover the ride (see below).

Getting to London from Heathrow Airport

By Tube (Subway): For £4, the Tube takes you to downtown London in 50–60 minutes on the Piccadilly Line, with stops at

(among others) South Kensington, Leicester Square, and King's Cross Station (6/hr; depending on your destination, may require a transfer). Even better, buy a One-Day Travelcard that covers your trip into London and all your Tube travel for the day (£13.20 covers peak times, £6.70 "off-peak"

card starts at 9:30, less-expensive Travelcards cover the city center only). Or, if you're staying four or more days, consider an Oyster card. For information on both types of passes, see "Oyster Cards and Travelcards" on page 52. Buy tickets or cards at the Tube station ticket window. You can hop on the Tube at any terminal. If taking the Tube to the airport, note that Piccadilly Line subway cars post which airlines are served by which terminals.

By Bus: Most buses depart from the common area serving Terminals 1, 2, and 3 (a 5-min walk from any of these terminals), although some depart from T-4. National Express has regular service from Heathrow to Victoria Coach Station in downtown London, near several of my recommended hotels. While slow, the bus is affordable and convenient for those staying near Victoria Station (£4, 1–4/hr, 45–75 min, www.nationalexpress.com). For information on airport buses, call 0870-574-7777.

By Train: Two different rains run between Heathrow Airport and London's Paddington Station. At Paddington Station, you're in the thick of the Tube system, with easy access to any of my recommended neighborhoods—Notting Hill Gate is just two Tube stops away. The **Heathrow Connect** train is the slightly slower, much cheaper option (£6.90 one-way, 1–2/hr, 25 min, tel. 0845-850-0150, www.heathrowconnect.com). The **Heathrow Express** train is blazing fast (15 min to downtown from Terminals 1, 2, and 3; and 20 min from Terminal 4) and runs more frequently (4/hr), but it's pricey (£15.50 "express class" one-way, £29 round-trip, £1 cheaper if purchased online, ask about discount promos at ticket desk, kids under 16 ride half-price, under 5 ride free, buy ticket before you board or pay a £2 surcharge to buy it on the train, covered by BritRail pass, daily 5:10–23:30, tel. 0845-600-1515, www.heathrowexpress.co.uk). At the airport, you can use the Express as a free transfer between terminals.

By Taxi: Taxis from the airport cost about £45–55 to west and central London (one hour). For four people traveling together, this can be a deal. Hotels can often line up a cab back to the airport for about £30–40. For the cheapest taxi to the airport, don't order one from your hotel. Simply flag down a few and ask them for their best "off-meter" rate.

By Airport Shuttle Bus: Hotelink offers door-to-door service (Heathrow-£19 per person, Gatwick-£24 per person, book the day before departure, buy online and save £1–2, tel. 01293/532-244, www.hotelink.co.uk, reservations@hotelink.co.uk). The famous Airbus (which shuttled a generation of travelers between the airport and downtown) has gone extinct—replaced by the train link and minibus shuttles.

Getting to Bath from Heathrow Airport

By Bus: Direct buses run daily from Heathrow to Bath (£17, 10/day direct, 2–3 hours, more frequent but slower with transfer in London, tel. 0870-575-7747, www.nationalexpress.com). BritRail passholders may prefer the 2.5-hour Heathrow–Bath bus/train connection via Reading (£8.60 for bus with pass, rail portion free with pass, otherwise £33 total, payable at desk in terminal): first catch the twice-hourly RailAir Link shuttle bus to Reading (REDding), then hop on the hourly express train to Bath. Factoring in the connection in Reading—which can add at least an hour to the trip—the train is a less convenient option than the direct bus to Bath. For more bus information, see "By Bus," above.

Gatwick Airport

More and more flights, especially charters, land at Gatwick Airport, halfway between London and the South Coast (recorded airport info tel. 0870-000-2468).

Getting to London: Express trains—clearly the best way into London from here—shuttle conveniently between Gatwick and London's Victoria Station (£14.90, £26.80 round-trip, 4/hr during day, 1–2/hr at night, 30 min, runs 5:00–24:00 daily, can purchase tickets on train at no extra charge, tel. 0845-850-1530, www.gatwickexpress.co.uk). If you're traveling with three others, buy your tickets at the station before boarding, and you'll travel for the price of two. The only restriction on this impressive deal is that you have to travel together. So if you see another couple in line, get organized and save 50 percent.

You can save a few pounds by taking Southern rail line's slower and less frequent shuttle between Victoria Station and Gatwick (£9, 4/hr, hourly from midnight–4:00, 45 min, tel. 08451-272-920, www.southernrailway.com).

Getting to Bath: To get to Bath from Gatwick, you can catch a bus to Heathrow and take the bus to Bath from there (see above). By train, the best Gatwick–Bath connection involves a transfer in Reading (about hourly, 2.5 hrs; avoid transfer in London, where you'll likely have to change stations).

London's Other Airports

If you're flying into or out of **Stansted** (airport tel. 0870-000-0303), you can take the National Express bus between the airport and downtown London's Victoria Coach Station (£10, £16 round-trip, 2/hr, 1.5 hrs, runs 4:00–24:00, picks up and stops throughout London, tel. 0870-575-7747, www.nxairport.com), or take the Stansted Express train (£15.50 one-way, £25.50 round-trip, connects to London's Liverpool Station, 40 min, 2–4/hr, 5:00–23:00, tel. 0845-850-0150, www.stanstedexpress.com). Stansted is expensive by cab; figure £80 one-way from central London.

For **Luton** (airport tel. 01582/405-100, www.london-luton .com), there are three choices. Two different buses run between the airport and Buckingham Palace Road near Victoria Station (coach stop #6): a cheaper, faster bus operated by easyJet (£8 one-way walk-up price, £2–6 online, open to non-easyJet passengers if seats available, may have to pay for extra luggage, runs every 45 min 7:15–20:00, 40-min trip, www.easybus.co.uk), and the pricier Green Line bus #757 (£11 one-way, small discount for easyJet passengers, 2/hr, 1–1.25 hrs depending on time of day, runs 3:30–24:00, tel. 0870-608-7261, www.greenline.co.uk). Or you can connect by rail to London's King's Cross station (£12.10, runs 5:00–23:00, 25 min, tel. 0845-748-4950); catch the free five-minute shuttle from outside the terminal to the Luton Parkway train station.

There's a slim chance you might use **London City Airport** (tel. 020/7646-0088, www.londoncityairport.com). The Docklands Light Railway (DLR) connects the airport with Bank Tube station, one stop east of St. Paul's on the Central Line (£3.50 one-way, covered by Travelcard and Oyster card, 22 min, tel. 020/7363-9700, www.tfl.gov.uk/dlr).

Connecting London's Airports

The **National Express Airport** service offers direct Jetlink bus connections from **Heathrow** to **Gatwick Airport** (2/hr, 70 min or more, depending on traffic), departing just outside arrivals at all terminals (£19 one-way, £35.50 round-trip). To make a flight connection between Heathrow and Gatwick, allow three hours between flights.

More and more travelers are taking advantage of cheap flights out of London's smaller airports. A handy National Express bus runs between Heathrow, Gatwick, Stansted, and Luton airports—easier than having to cut through the center of London. Buses are frequent (less so between Stansted and Luton): Heathrow–Luton is 1.5 hours direct and costs £18 (£26 round-trip). Check schedules at www.nxairport.com.

TRAINS AND BUSES

London, Britain's major transportation hub, has a different train station for each region. The new St. Pancras International Station now handles the Eurostar to Paris or Brussels (see "Crossing the Channel" on page 150). King's Cross and Euston stations cover northeast England, North Wales, and Scotland. Paddington covers west and southwest England (including Bath) and South Wales. For information, call 0845-748-4950 (or visit www.nationalrail. co.uk or www.eurostar.com; £5 booking fee for telephone reservations). Also see the BritRail Routes map on page 648. Note that for security reasons, stations offer a left-luggage service (£6/day per bag) rather than lockers; because of long security lines, it can take a while to check or pick up your bag.

By Train

To Points West from Paddington Station

To Bath: Trains leave London's Paddington Station twice every hour between 7:00 and 19:00 (at :15 and :45 after each hour) for the 90-minute ride to Bath (about £47). Also consider a guided Evan Evans tour by bus (see below).

Other Destinations: Oxford (2–4/hr, 1 hr, possible transfer in Didcot or Reading), **Penzance** (about hourly, 5–7 hrs, possible change in Plymouth), **Cardiff** (2/hr, 2 hrs).

To Points North

From King's Cross Station: Trains run at least hourly, stopping in **York** (2 hrs), **Durham** (3 hrs), and **Edinburgh** (4.5 hrs). Trains to **Cambridge** also leave from here (2/hr, 50 min).

From Euston Station to: Conwy (1/hr, 3.5–4 hrs, transfer in Crewe), **Liverpool** (1–2/hr, 2.5–3 hrs direct; possible transfer in Birmingham, Crewe, and/or Manchester), **Blackpool** (2/hr, 3 hrs, possible transfer at Preston), **Keswick** (10/day, 4–5 hrs, transfer at Penrith), **Glasgow** (1–2/hr, 4.5–5 hrs direct).

From London's Other Stations

Trains run between London and **Canterbury,** leaving from Charing Cross Station and arriving in Canterbury West, as well as from London's Victoria Station and arriving in Canterbury East (2/hr, 1.5–2 hrs).

Direct trains leave for **Stratford-upon-Avon** from Marylebone Station, located near the southwest corner of Regents Park (every 2 hrs, 2–2.5 hrs).

Other Destinations: Dover (2/hr, 2 hrs, one direct from Victoria Station, one from Charing Cross Station—sometimes with transfer), **Portsmouth** (2/hr, 1.5–2 hrs, almost all Portsmouth-bound trains depart from Waterloo Station, and a few a day from Victoria Station).

By Bus

National Express' excellent bus service is considerably cheaper than the train, and a fine option for destinations within England (call 0870-575-7747, or visit www.nationalexpress.com or the bus station a block southwest of Victoria Station).

To Bath: The National Express bus leaves from Victoria Station nearly hourly (a little over 3 hrs, one-way-£17, round trip-£24).

To get to Bath via Stonehenge, consider taking a guided bus tour from London to Stonehenge and Bath, and abandoning the tour in Bath (confirm that Bath is the last stop). **Evan Evans'** tour is £65 and includes admissions. The tour leaves from the Victoria Coach station every morning at 8:30 (you can stow your bag under the bus), stops in Stonehenge (45 min), and then stops in Bath for lunch and a city tour before returning to London (offered year-round). You can book the tour at the Victoria Coach station, the Evan Evans office (258 Vauxhall Bridge Road, near Victoria Coach station, tel. 020/7950-1777, US tel. 866-382-6868, www.evanevans .co.uk, reservations@evanevanstours.co.uk), or at the Green Line Travel Office (4a Fountain Square, across from Victoria Coach station, tel. 0870-608-7261, www.greenline.co.uk). Golden Tours also runs a fully guided Stonehenge–Bath tour for the same price (departs from Fountain Square, located across from Victoria Coach Station, tel. 020/7233-7036, US tel. 800/548-7083, www .goldentours.co.uk, reservations@goldentours.co.uk). Another similarly priced day-trip hits Oxford, Stratford, and Warwick.

To Other Destinations: Oxford (2–4/hr, 1.75–2.25 hrs), **Cambridge** (hourly direct, 2 hrs), **Canterbury** (hourly, 2–2.5 hrs), **Dover** (hourly, about 3 hrs), **Penzance** (every 2 hrs direct, 9 hrs), **Cardiff** (every 2–3 hrs direct, 3 hrs), **Liverpool** (every 3 hrs direct, 4.5–6 hrs), **Blackpool** (2/day direct, 6–6.5 hrs), **York** (hourly, 6 hrs), **Durham** (5/day, 6–8 hrs, possible transfer in Leeds), **Glasgow** (2/day direct, 8.5 hrs, train is a much better option), **Edinburgh** (2/day direct, 8.5–9 hrs, go via train instead).

To Dublin, Ireland: The boat/bus journey takes between 9 and 10 hours and goes all day or all night (£48–57, 2/day, tel.

08705-143-219, www.nationalexpress.com or www.eurolines
.co.uk). Consider a cheap 70-minute Ryanair flight instead (see
page 658).

CROSSING THE CHANNEL

By Eurostar Train

The fastest and most convenient way to get from the Eiffel Tower
to Big Ben is by rail. Eurostar, a joint service of the Belgian,
British, and French railways, is the speedy passenger train that
zips you (and up to 800 others in 18 sleek cars) from downtown
London to downtown Paris (12–15/day, 2.5 hrs) faster and more
easily than flying. The actual tunnel crossing is a 20-minute, silent,
100-mile-per-hour non-event. Your ears won't even pop.

Eurostar Fares

Channel fares (essentially the same between London and Paris or
Brussels) are reasonable but complicated. Prices vary depending on
how early you reserve, whether you can live with restrictions, and
whether you're eligible for any discounts (children, youth, seniors,
railpass-holders, and round-trip travelers all qualify). The cheapest rates sell out first, especially for popular departure times. For
specifics, visit www.ricksteves
.com/eurostar.

As with airfares, the most
expensive and flexible option is
a full-fare one-way ticket with
no restrictions on refundability
(even refundable after the departure date; for a one-way trip,
figure about $380 in first class,
$280 in second class). A first-
class ticket comes with a meal (a
dinner departure nets you more
grub than breakfast)—but it's
not worth the extra expense.

Also like the airlines,

Eurostar Routes

cheaper tickets come with more restrictions—and are limited in
number (so they sell out more quickly; for second-class, one-way
tickets, figure $90–200). Non-full-fare tickets have severe restric-
tions on refundability (best-case scenario: you'll get 25 percent back,
but with the cheapest options you'll get nothing). But several do
allow you to change the specifics of your trip once before departure.

Those traveling with a railpass for Britain, France, or Belgium
should look first at the **passholder** fare, an especially good value
for one-way Eurostar trips (starting at $81).

Buying Eurostar Tickets

Refund and exchange restrictions are serious, so don't reserve until you're sure of your plans. If you're confident about the time and date of your crossing, order ahead from the US. Only the most expensive ticket (full fare) is fully refundable, so if you want to have more flexibility, hold off—keeping in mind that the longer you wait, the more likely the cheapest tickets will sell out. (You might end up having to pay for first class.) Only certain cars have outlets for plugging in a laptop; if you want this convenience, request it when you book.

You can check and book fares by phone or online in the US (order online at www.ricksteves.com/eurostar, prices listed in dollars; order by phone at US tel. 800-EUROSTAR) or in Britain (British tel. 0870-518-6186, www.eurostar.com, prices listed in pounds).

If you buy from a US company, you'll pay for ticket delivery in the US; if you book with the British company, you'll pick up your ticket at the train station.

In continental Europe, you can buy your Eurostar ticket at any major train station in any country or at any travel agency that handles train tickets (expect a booking fee). In Britain, tickets can be issued only at the Eurostar office in St. Pancras International Station or the American Express office in Victoria Station. Alternatively, you can order tickets online in the US; or you can order them by phone, then pick them up at the station.

Remember that Britain's time zone is one hour earlier than France's. Times listed on tickets are local times (departure from London is British time, arrival in Paris in French time).

Departing from London: At the end of 2007, Eurostar trains are scheduled to start using London's St. Pancras International Station (instead of the former terminal, Waterloo Station). Check in at least 30 minutes in advance for your Eurostar trip. It's very similar to an airport check-in: You pass through airport-like security, show your passport to customs officials, and find a TV monitor to locate your departure gate. There are a few airport-like shops, newsstands, horrible snack bars, and cafés (bring food for the trip from elsewhere), pay-Internet terminals, and a currency-exchange booth with rates about the same as you'll find on the other end.

Cheap Passage by Tour: A tour company called Britain Shrinkers sells one- or two-day "Eurostar Tours" to Paris or Brussels, enabling you to side-trip to these cities from London for less than most train tickets alone. For example, you'll pay £129 for a one-day Paris "tour" (unescorted day trip with Métro pass; tel. 0800-587-7660 or www.britainshrinkers.com). This can be a particularly good option if you need to get to Paris from London on short notice, when only the costliest fares are available.

Crossing the Channel Without Eurostar

The old-fashioned ways of crossing the Channel are cheaper than Eurostar. They're also twice as romantic, complicated, and time-consuming. You'll get better prices arranging your trip in London than you would in the US. Taking the bus is cheapest, and round-trips are a bargain.

By Train and Boat: You'll need to book your own train tickets to Dover; prices are for the ferry only. The **P&O Stena Line ferry** runs from Dover to Calais (£20 one-way or round-trip with 5-day return, £36 round-trip after 5 days, tel. 0870-520-2020, www.posl .com). For additional ferry info, visit www.aferry.to.

By Bus: You can take the bus direct to **Paris** (9.5–12 hrs, 6–7/day), **Brussels** (9 hrs, 6/day), or **Amsterdam** (10–13 hrs, 6/day) from Victoria Coach Station (via boat or Chunnel, day or overnight). Sample prices to Paris for economy fares booked at least two days in advance: £36 one-way, £64 round-trip (tel. 0870-514-3219; visit www.eurolines.co.uk and look for "fun fares").

By Plane: Check with budget airlines for cheap round-trip fares to Paris (see "Cheap Flights," page 657).

London

GREENWICH, WINDSOR, AND CAMBRIDGE

Three of the best day-trip possibilities near London are Greenwich, Windsor, and Cambridge (listed from nearest to farthest). Greenwich is England's maritime capital; Windsor has a very famous castle; and Cambridge is easily England's best university town.

Getting Around

By Train: The British rail system uses London as a hub and normally offers round-trip fares (after 9:30) that cost virtually the same as one-way fares. For day trips, "day return" tickets are best (and cheapest). You can save a little money if you purchase Super Advance tickets before 18:00 on the day before your trip.

By Train Tour: Original London Walks offers a variety of Explorer day trips year-round via train for about £12 plus transportation costs (pick up their walking-tour brochures at the TI or hotels, tel. 020/7624-3978, www.walks.com; see listing on page 60).

Greenwich

Tudor kings favored the palace at Greenwich. Henry VIII was born here. Later kings commissioned Inigo Jones and Christopher Wren to beautify the town and palace. In spite of Greenwich's architectural and royal treats, this is England's maritime capital, and visitors go for all things salty. While Greenwich's main attraction—the *Cutty Sark* clipper—is closed for restoration through

London Day Trips

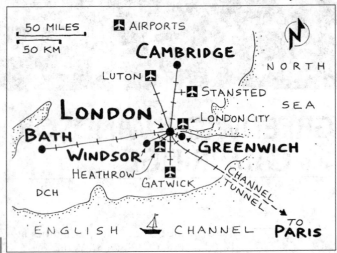

2010, the town is still worth a visit. It's got the world's most famous observatory, stunning Baroque architecture, appealing markets, a fleet of nautical shops, and hordes of tourists. And where else can you set your watch with such accuracy?

Planning Your Time

See the *Cutty Sark* temporary exhibit upon arrival. Then walk the shoreline promenade, with a possible lunch or drink in the venerable Trafalgar Tavern, before heading up to the National Maritime Museum and the Royal Observatory Greenwich.

Getting to Greenwich

It's a joy by boat or a snap by Tube.

By Boat: From central London (2/hr, 50–70 min), cruise down the Thames from the piers at Westminster, Waterloo, Embankment, or the Tower of London (see "Cruises" on page 61).

By Tube: Take the Tube to Bank and change to the Dockways Light Railway (DLR), which takes you right to the Cutty Sark station in Greenwich (one stop before the main Greenwich station, 20-min ride, all in Zone 2, included with Tube pass). Many DLR trains terminate at Canary Wharf, so make sure you get on one that continues to Lewisham or Greenwich.

By Train: Mainline trains also go from London (Charing Cross, Waterloo East, and London Bridge stations) several times an hour to the Greenwich station (10-min walk from the sights). While the train is fast and cheap, the Tube is probably easier.

Greenwich

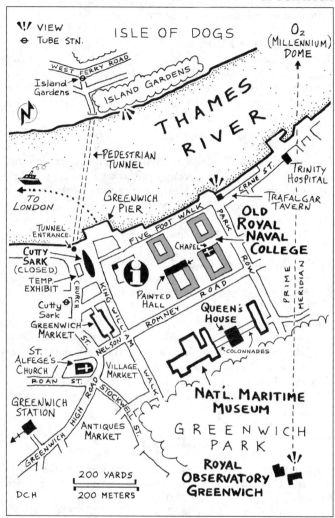

Greenwich

ORIENTATION

(area code: 020)

Covered markets and outdoor stalls make weekends lively. Save time to browse the town. Wander beyond the touristy Church Street and Greenwich High Road to where flower stands spill into the side streets, and antique shops sell brass nautical knick-knacks. King William Walk, College Approach, Nelson Road, and Turnpin Lane are all worth a look. If you need pub grub,

Greenwich has almost 100 pubs, with some boasting that they're mere milliseconds from the prime meridian.

Tourist Information

The TI faces the riverside square a few paces east of the *Cutty Sark* temporary exhibit (daily 10:00–17:00, Internet access-3p/min, 2 Cutty Sark Gardens, Pepys House, tel. 0870-608-2000, www .greenwich.gov.uk). Guided walks cover the big sights (£5, daily at 12:15 and 14:15, departs from TI).

Helpful Hints

Markets: The town throbs with day-trippers on weekends because of its markets. The **Greenwich Market** is an entertaining mini–Covent Garden, located between College Approach and Nelson Road (antiques on Thu only 9:00–17:00; arts and crafts Thu–Sun 9:30–17:30, biggest on Sun). The **Antiques Market** sells old odds and ends at high prices on Greenwich High Road, near the post office (Sat–Sun only 9:30–17:30). The **Village Market** has a little bit of everything—antiques, books, food, and flowers (Sat–Sun only 9:30–17:30, across Nelson Road from the Greenwich Market, enter from Stockwell Street or King William Walk).

Tourist Tram: A small tram (called the "Road Train") runs from in front of the National Maritime Museum to the Royal Observatory on top of the hill (free, erratic schedule but generally 11:00–16:30, 2/hr).

Supermarket: If you're picnicking, try the handy **Marks & Spencer Simply Food** on Church Street, across from the *Cutty Sark* exhibit.

SIGHTS

▲▲**Cutty Sark**—The Scottish-built *Cutty Sark* was the last of the great China tea clippers and was the queen of the seas when first launched in 1869. With 32,000 square feet of sail, she could blow with the wind 300 miles in a day. After the ship had already been closed for several months for renovation, a suspicious fire broke out in May 2007 and did considerable damage to the hull, likely delaying the reopening to early 2010. Nearby,  a spiky white tent houses a temporary exhibit that explains the painstaking £25 million restoration work (£2, daily 11:00–17:00, last entry 30 min before closing). You can also pay £6 to have your photo superimposed on a virtual backdrop of the ship. For the latest details, call 020/8858-2698 or visit www.cuttysark.org.uk.

Old Royal Naval College—Now that the Royal Navy has moved out, the public is invited in to see the college's elaborate Painted Hall and Chapel, grandly designed by Christopher Wren and completed by other architects in the 1700s (free, Mon–Sat 10:00–17:00, Sun 12:30–17:00, call ahead for £4 daily tours at 14:00, choral service Sun at 11:00 in chapel—all are welcome, in the two college buildings farthest from river).

Stroll the Thames to Trafalgar Tavern—From the *Cutty Sark,* pass the pier and wander east along the Thames on Five Foot Walk (named for the width of the path) for grand views in front of the Old Royal Naval College. Founded by William III as a naval hospital and designed by Wren, the college was split in two because Queen Mary didn't want the view from Queen's House blocked. The riverside view is good, too, with the twin-domed towers of the college (one giving the time, the other the direction of the wind) framing Queen's House, and the Royal Observatory Greenwich crowning the hill beyond.

Continuing downstream, just past the college, you'll see the

Trafalgar Tavern. Dickens knew the pub well, and used it as the setting for the wedding breakfast in *Our Mutual Friend.* Built in 1837 in the Regency style to attract Londoners downriver, the tavern is popular with Londoners (and tourists) for its fine lunches. The upstairs Nelson Room is still used for weddings. Its formal

moldings and elegant windows with balconies over the Thames are a step back in time (Mon–Sat 12:00–16:00 & 18:00–22:00, Sun lunch only 12:00–16:30, elegant ground-floor dining room as well as the more casual pub, Park Row, tel. 020/8858-2909).

From the pub, enjoy views of the former Millennium Dome a mile downstream. The dome languished for nearly a decade after its controversial construction and brief life as a millennial "world's fair" site. Plans for a casino and hotel project fell through, although it has come in handy as an emergency homeless shelter. It was finally bought by a developer in 2007 and rechristened "The O_2" in honor of the telecommunications company that paid for the naming rights. Currently, it hosts concerts and sporting events, and will likely see action during the 2012 Summer Olympics. No doubt locals will continue to call it the Millennium Dome, however, and grumble about its original cost.

From the Trafalgar Tavern, you can walk the two long blocks

up Park Row, and turn right into the park leading up to the Royal Observatory Greenwich.

Queen's House—This building, the first Palladian-style villa in Britain, was designed in 1616 by Inigo Jones for James I's wife, Anne of Denmark. All traces of the queen are long gone, and the Great Hall and Royal Apartments now serve as an art gallery for rotating exhibits from the National Maritime Museum. The Orangery is now home to the great J. M. W. Turner painting *Battle of Trafalgar*. His largest (so big that a wall had to be opened to get it in here) and only royal commission, it is surrounded by Christ-like paintings of Admiral Nelson's death (free, daily 10:00–17:00, last entry 30 min before closing, tel. 020/8312-6565, www.nmm .ac.uk).

▲▲National Maritime Museum—Great for anyone remotely interested in the sea, this museum holds everything from a *Titanic* ticket and Captain Scott's sun goggles (from his 1910 Antarctic expedition) to the uniform Admiral Nelson wore when he was killed at Trafalgar. Under a big glass roof—accompanied by the sound of creaking wooden ships and crashing waves—slick, modern displays depict lighthouse technology, a whaling cannon, and a Greenpeace "survival pod."

The new, permanent Nelson's Navy gallery, while taking up just a fraction of the floor space, deserves at least half of your time here. It offers an intimate look at Nelson's life, the Napoleonic threat, Nelson's rise to power, and his victory and death at Trafalgar.

Kids love the All Hands gallery, where they can send secret messages by Morse code and operate a miniature dockside crane (free, daily July–Aug 10:00–18:00, Sept–June 10:00–17:00, last entry 30 min before closing; look for events posted at entrance—singing, treasure hunts, storytelling—particularly on weekends; tel. 020/8858-4422, recorded info tel. 020/8312-6565, www .nmm.ac.uk).

▲▲Royal Observatory Greenwich—Located on the prime meridian (0° longitude), the observatory is the point from which all time is measured. However, the observatory's early work had nothing to do with coordinating the world's clocks to Greenwich Mean Time (GMT). The observatory was founded in 1675 by Charles II to find a way to determine longitude at sea. Today, the Greenwich time signal is linked with the BBC (which broadcasts the "pips" worldwide at the top of the hour).

Look above the observatory to see the orange Time Ball, also visible from the Thames, which drops daily at 13:00. (Nearby, outside the courtyard of the observatory, see how your foot measures up to the foot where the public standards of length are cast in bronze.)

In the courtyard, set your wristwatch to the digital clock showing GMT to a tenth of a second, and straddle the prime meridian.

Inside, check out the historic astronomical instruments and camera obscura. Listen to costumed actors tell stories about astronomers and historical observatory events (shows may require small fee, daily July–Sept). In the Time Galleries, see timepieces through the ages, including John Harrison's prize-winning marine chronometers that helped 18th-century sailors calculate longitude. In 2007, the observatory unveiled the state-of-the-art 120-seat Peter Harrison Planetarium, an education center, and the Weller Astronomy Galleries, where interactive displays allow you to guide a space mission and touch a 4.5-billion-year-old meteorite.

Cost and Hours: Free entry to observatory, planetarium shows–£6; observatory open daily 10:00–17:00, July–Aug until 18:00, last entry 30 min before closing; planetarium shows hourly Mon–Fri 13:00–16:00, Sat–Sun 11:00–16:00, book in advance at 020/8312-8565 or at planetarium before noon on day of visit; tel. 020/8858-4422, www.nmm.ac.uk. The observatory is crowded Sat–Sun afternoons—visit on a weekday or weekend morning if possible.

Before you leave the observatory grounds, enjoy the view from the overlook: the symmetrical royal buildings, the Thames, the Docklands and its busy cranes, the huge O_2 (Millennium) Dome, and the square-mile City of London, with its skyscrapers and the dome of St. Paul's Cathedral. At night (17:00–24:00), look for the green laser beam that the observatory projects into the sky (best viewed in winter), extending along the prime meridian for 15 miles.

Windsor

Windsor, a compact and easy walking town of about 30,000 people, originally grew up around the royal residence. In 1070, William the Conqueror continued his habit of kicking Saxons out of their various settlements, taking over what the locals called

"Windlesora" (meaning "riverbank with a hoisting crane")—later called "Windsor." William built the first fortified castle on a chalk hill above the Thames; later kings added on to William's early designs, rebuilding and expanding the castle and surrounding gardens.

By setting up primary residence here, modern monarchs increased Windsor's popularity and prosperity—most notably, Queen Victoria, whose stern statue glares at you as you approach the castle. After her death, Victoria rejoined her beloved husband Albert in the Royal Mausoleum at Frogmore House, a mile south of the castle in a private section of the Home Park (house and mausoleum rarely open; check www.royalcollection.org.uk). The current queen considers Windsor her primary residence, and the one where she feels most at home. You can tell if Her Majesty is in residence by checking to see which flag is flying above the round tower; if the royal standard (a red, yellow, and blue flag) is flying instead of the Union Jack, the queen is at home.

While 99 percent of visitors just come to see the castle and go, some enjoy spending the night. Windsor's charm is most evident when the tourists are gone. Consider overnighting here, since parking and access to Heathrow Airport are easy, day-tripping into London is feasible, and an evening at the horse races (on Mon) is hoof-pounding, heart-thumping fun.

Getting to Windsor

By Train: Windsor has two train stations: Windsor & Eton Central (5-min walk to palace, TI inside) and Windsor & Eton Riverside (5-min walk to palace and TI). First Great Western trains run between London's Paddington Station and Windsor & Eton Central (2/hr, 35 min, change at Slough). South West Trains run between London's Waterloo Station and the Windsor & Eton Riverside station (2/hr, 60 min, change at Slough; info tel. 0845-748-4950, www.nationalrail.co.uk). If you're day-tripping into London from Windsor, ask at the Windsor train station how you can combine a train ticket with a One-Day Travelcard (about £14–20, covers rail transportation to and from London with an all-day Tube and bus pass in town).

By Bus: Green Line buses #700, #701, and #702 run hourly between London's Victoria Colonnade (between the Victoria train and coach stations) and Windsor, where the bus stops in front of Legoland and near the castle; the castle stop is "Parish Church" (1.25 hours, info tel. 0870-608-2608, www.greenline.co.uk).

By Car: Windsor is 20 miles from London, and just off Heathrow Airport's landing path. The town (and then the castle and Legoland) is well-signposted from the M4 motorway. It's a convenient stop for anyone arriving at Heathrow, picking up a car,

Windsor

1 Castle Tickets & Entrance

2 Guildhall, The Crooked House Teahouse & Legoland Bus Stop

3 Boat Trips

4 To Royal Windsor Racecourse

5 Langton House B&B

6 Cornucopia Bistro

7 Blondes Café

and not going into London until the end of his or her trip.

From Heathrow Airport: Bus #77 makes the 30-minute trip between Windsor and the airport for £4 (2/hr), dropping you right below the castle on High Street. London black cabs can charge whatever they like from Heathrow to Windsor (and do); avoid them by calling a local Windsor cab (tel. 01753/677-677, £18 ride).

ORIENTATION

Windsor's pleasant pedestrian shopping zone litters the approach to its famous palace with fun temptations. You'll find most shops and restaurants around the castle on High and Thames Streets, and down the pedestrian Peascod Street (which runs perpendicular to High Street).

Tourist Information
The TI is in Windsor & Eton Central station, in the Old Booking Hall (May–Sept Mon–Sat 9:30–17:30, Sun 10:00–16:00; Oct–April Mon–Sat 10:00–17:30, Sun 10:00–16:00; tel. 01753/743-900, www .windsor.gov.uk). The TI sells discount tickets to Legoland.

Arrival in Windsor
The train to Windsor & Eton Central station from Paddington (via Slough) will spit you out in a shady shopping pavilion only a few minutes' walk from the castle and TI (see "Getting to Windsor," above). If you instead arrive at Windsor & Eton Riverside train station, you'll see the castle as you exit—just follow the wall to the castle entrance.

SIGHTS AND ACTIVITIES

In Windsor
▲▲**Windsor Castle**—Windsor Castle, the official home of England's royal family for 900 years, claims to be the largest and oldest occupied castle in the world. Thankfully, touring it is simple: You'll see immense grounds, lavish staterooms, a crowd-pleasing dollhouse, an art gallery, and the chapel.

Cost and Hours: £14.20, family pass-£36.50, daily March–Oct 9:45–17:15, Nov–Feb 9:45–16:15, last entry 1.25 hours before closing (Changing of the Guard alternate days at 11:00, nightly evensong in chapel at 17:15—free for worshippers).

Information: Tel. 020/7766-7304, www.royal.gov.uk. As you enter, ask about the warden's free 30-minute guided walks around the grounds (2/hr). They cover the grounds but not the castle, which is well-described by the included audioguide (skip the official guidebook).

◎ Self-Guided Tour: Immediately upon entering, you pass through a simple modern building housing a historical overview of the castle. This excellent intro is worth a close look, since you're basically on your own after this. Inside, you'll find the motte (artificial mound) and bailey (fortified stockade around it) of William the Conqueror's castle. Dating from 1080, this was his first castle in England.

Follow the signs to the staterooms/gallery/dollhouse. Queen Mary's Dollhouse—a palace in miniature (1:12 scale from 1923) and "the most famous dollhouse in the world"—comes with the longest wait. You can skip that line and go immediately into the lavish staterooms. Strewn with history and the art of a long line of kings and queens, they're the best I've seen in Britain—and well-restored after the devastating 1992 fire. Take advantage of the talkative docents in each room, who are happy to answer your questions.

The adjacent gallery is a changing exhibit featuring the royal art collection (and some big names, such as Michelangelo and Leonardo). Signs direct you (downhill) to St. George's Chapel. Housing 10 royal tombs, it's a fine example of Perpendicular Gothic, with classic fan vaulting spreading out from each pillar (dating from about 1500). The simple chapel housing the tombs of the current Queen's parents, King George VI and "Queen Mother" Elizabeth, and younger sister, Princess Margaret, is along the church's north aisle. Next door is the sumptuous 13th-century Albert Memorial Chapel, redecorated after the death of Prince Albert in 1861 and dedicated to his memory.

Legoland Windsor—Fun for Legomaniacs under 12, this huge, kid-pleasing park five miles from Windsor Castle has dozens of tame but fun rides (often with very long lines) scattered throughout its 150 acres. An impressive Mini-Land has 50 million Lego pieces glued together to create 800 tiny buildings and a mini-tour of Europe (adults-£33, or £28 with printable website coupon; children-£25, or £22 with coupon; under 3 free; late July–Aug daily 10:00–19:00; April and June–late July daily 10:00–17:00 or sometimes 18:00; May and Sept–Oct Wed–Mon 10:00–17:00 or 18:00, closed Tue–Wed; closed Nov–March except Dec 21–Jan 5 when it's open for the holidays; get discounted tickets from Windsor TI or by buying online at Legoland's website; £3.50 round-trip shuttle bus runs from near Windsor's St. John's Parish Church, 2/hr, clearly signposted, easy free parking, tel. 0870-504-0404, www.legoland.co.uk).

Boat Trips on the Thames—Boat trips leave every 30 minutes, ferrying you up and down the river for relaxing views of the castle, the village of Eton, Eton College, and the Royal Windsor Racecourse. Relax onboard and munch a picnic (£4.80, family pass-£12, 2/hr; April–Oct daily 10:00–17:00; Feb–March daily 11:00–16:00; Nov Sat–Sun 11:00–16:00 only, closed Mon–Fri; closed Dec–Jan; 40 min, longer trips available, tel. 01753/851-900, www.frenchbrothers.co.uk). There's also a longer two-hour circular trip (£7.60, 1/day).

Horse Racing—The horses race near Windsor every Monday evening at the Royal Windsor Racecourse (£12 entry, off A308 between Windsor and Maidenhead, info tel. 01753/498-400, www.windsor-racecourse.co.uk). The romantic way to get there is by a 10-minute shuttle boat (£5 round-trip, see "Boat Trips on the Thames," above). The famous Ascot Racecourse (see below) is also nearby.

Eton College—Across the bridge, you'll find many post-castle tourists filing towards the college, a "public" (our "private") school that has educated quite a few prime ministers, as well as members of the royal family. The college is sparse on sights (entry-£4, guided tour-£5, daily 14:00–18:00, longer hours when school's out).

Near Windsor

Ascot Racecourse—Located seven miles southwest of Windsor, Ascot—which is owned by the royal family—is one of the most famous horse-racing venues in the world. Originally opened in 1711, it reopened in June 2006 after an expensive renovation. The racecourse, which lies just north of the center of the town of Ascot, hosts races from late May through December (tickets generally £10–20, children under 16 free, parking-£5–7, 10–25 percent discount if you book online, tel. 0870-727-1234, www.ascot.co.uk).

SLEEPING

(£1 = about $2, country code: 44, area code: 01753)
Most visitors stay in London and do Windsor as a day trip. But here's a suggestion for those staying the night.

$$ **Langton House B&B** is a stately Victorian home with three well-appointed rooms lovingly maintained by Paul and Sonja Fogg (Sb-£65, Db-£80, Tb-£95, Qb-£110, prices soft in winter, family-friendly, guest kitchen, Internet access, 5 percent extra for credit card, 46 Alma Road, tel. & fax 01753/858-299, www.langtonhouse.co.uk, paul@langtonhouse.co.uk).

EATING

Cornucopia Bistro, a favorite with locals, is a welcoming little place two minutes from the TI and castle, just beyond the tourist crush. They serve tasty international dishes with everything made proudly from scratch. The hardwood floors add a rustic elegance (£9 two-course lunches, £10 three-course dinners, Tue–Sat 12:00–14:30 & 18:00–22:00, Sun 12:00–14:30 only, closed Mon, 6 High Street, tel. 01753/833-009, Mark Simmons).

The Crooked House, across from the TI, is a touristy 17th-century timber-framed teahouse, serving fresh, hearty £6–8 lunches and cream teas in a tipsy interior or outdoors on its cobbled lane (Mon–Sat 11:30–21:00, Sun 10:30–18:00, 51 High Street, tel. 01753/857-534). The important-looking building next door is the Guildhall, where Charles married Camilla Parker Bowles in April 2005. It's also the home of the town's public WC.

Blondes is a lively café that dishes up good food all day, including breakfast (until 15:00), fresh salads, and English dishes (Mon–Thu 8:00–15:00 & 18:30–23:00, Fri–Sat 8:00–15:00 & 18:00–24:00, Sun 9:00–15:00, 45 St. Leonard's Road, tel. 01753/470-079).

Cambridge

Cambridge, 60 miles north of London, is world-famous for its prestigious university. Wordsworth, Isaac Newton, Tennyson, Darwin, and Prince Charles are a few of its illustrious alumni. The university dominates—and owns—most of Cambridge, a historic town of 100,000 people that's more pleasant than its rival, Oxford. Cambridge is the epitome of a university town, with busy bikers, stately resi-

dence halls, plenty of bookshops, and proud locals who can point out where DNA was originally modeled, the first atom was split, and electrons were initially discovered.

In medieval Europe, higher education was the domain of the Church, and was limited to ecclesiastical schools. Scholars lived in "halls" on campus. This academic community of residential halls, chapels, and lecture halls connected by peaceful garden courtyards survives today in the colleges that make up the universities of Cambridge and Oxford. By 1350 (Oxford is roughly 100 years older), Cambridge had eight colleges, each with a monastic-type courtyard and lodgings. Today, Cambridge has 31 colleges. While a student's life revolves around his or her independent college, the university organizes lectures, presents degrees, and promotes research.

Planning Your Time

Cambridge is worth most of a day but not an overnight. Arrive in time for the 11:30 walking tour—an essential part of any visit—and spend the afternoon touring King's College Chapel and Fitzwilliam Museum (closed Mon) or simply enjoying the ambience of this stately old college town.

The university schedule has three terms: the Lent term from late January to late March, the Easter term from mid-April to mid-June, and the Michaelmas term from early October to early December. The colleges are closed to visitors during exams—in mid-April and late June—but King's College Chapel and the Trinity Library stay open, and the town is never sleepy.

Getting to Cambridge

By Train: It's an easy trip from London, 50 minutes away. Catch the train from London's King's Cross Station (2/hr, fast trains leaving at :15 and :45 past each hour run in each direction, 50 min, £16 one-way, cheap "day return" for £17.90 if you depart London after 9:30 weekdays or anytime Sat–Sun).

ORIENTATION

Cambridge is congested but small. Everything is within a pleasant walk. There are two main streets, separated from the river by the most interesting colleges. The town center, brimming with tearooms, has a TI and a colorful open-air market (daily 9:30–16:00, on Market Hill Square; arts and crafts Sun 10:30–16:30, clothes and produce rest of week).

Tourist Information

An info kiosk on the train station platform dispenses free city maps and sells fancier ones. The official TI is well signposted, just off Market Hill Square. They book rooms for £3.50, rent a £7 city audioguide, and sell bus tickets and a 30p mini-guide/map (Mon-Fri 10:00–17:30, Sat 10:00–17:00, Sun 11:00–15:00, closed Sun Oct–Easter, Wheeler Street, tel. 01223/464-732, room-booking tel. 01223/457-581, www.visitcambridge.org).

Arrival in Cambridge

To get to downtown Cambridge from the train station, take a 25-minute walk (the City Sightseeing map is fine for this), a £5 taxi ride, or bus #Citi1, #Citi3, or #Citi7 (£1.50 one-way, £2.50 round-

Cambridge

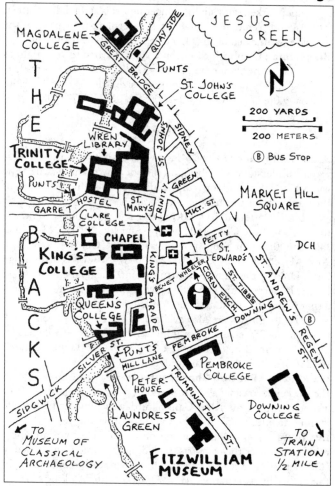

trip, every 5–10 min). Drivers can follow signs to any of the handy and central short-stay parking lots, or leave the car at one of five park-and-ride lots outside the city, and take the shuttle into town (free parking, £2 shuttle).

Helpful Hints

Festival: The Cambridge Folk Festival gets things humming and strumming in late July (July 31–Aug 3 in 2008, www .cambridgefolkfestival.co.uk).

Supermarkets: A Marks & Spencer Simply Food grocery is at the train station; a larger Marks & Spencer is at 3 Sidney Street

(Mon–Sat 9:00–19:00, Sun 11:00–17:00). The Sainsbury supermarket, with slightly longer hours, is at 44 Sidney Street. A good picnic spot is Laundress Green, a grassy park on the river, at the end of Mill Lane near the Silver Street punts.

Bike Rental: Cambridge Station Cycles, located to your right as you exit the station, rents bikes (£6/half-day) and stores luggage (£3–4 per bag depending on size, Mon–Fri 8:00–19:00, Sat 9:00–17:00, Sun 10:00–17:00, tel. 01223/307-125).

TOURS

▲▲Walking Tour of the Colleges—A walking tour is the best way to understand Cambridge's mix of "town and gown." The walks give a good rundown of the historic and scenic highlights of the university, as well as some fun local gossip.

The TI offers **daily walking tours** (£9, includes admission to King's College Chapel; daily July–Aug 10:30, 11:30, 13:30, and 14:30, no 10:30 tour Sun; April–June and Sept–Oct 11:30 and 13:30, Nov–March 13:30 only, tel. 01223/457-574, www.visitcambridge.org). Drop by the TI (the departure point) one hour early to snare a spot. If you're visiting on a Sunday, call the day before to reserve a spot with your credit card and confirm departure.

Private guides are also available through the TI (basic 60-min tour-£3.25/person, £47 minimum; 90-min tour-£3.75/person, £54 minimum; 2-hour city tour-£4.25/person, £60 minimum; tel. 01223/457-574, www.visitcambridge.org).

Walking and Punting Ghost Tour—If you're in Cambridge on the weekend, consider a £5 ghost walk Friday evenings at 18:00, or a spooky trip on the River Cam Saturday evenings at 19:00 (£15, 90 min, tel. 01223/457-574, www.visitcambridge.org).

Bus Tours—City Sightseeing hop-on, hop-off bus tours are informative and cover the outskirts, including the American Cemetery (£10, departing every 20 min, can use credit card to buy tickets in their office in train station, tel. 01708/866-000). Walking tours go where the buses can't—right into the center.

SIGHTS AND ACTIVITIES

▲▲King's College Chapel—Built from 1446 to 1515 by Henrys VI through VIII, England's best example of Perpendicular Gothic is the single most impressive building in town. Stand inside, look up, and marvel, as Christopher Wren did, at what was the largest single span of vaulted roof anywhere—2,000 tons of incredible fan vaulting. Wander through the Old Testament, with 25 stained-glass windows from the 16th century, the most Renaissance stained glass anywhere in one spot. The windows were removed to keep them safe during World War II, and then painstakingly replaced. Walk to the altar and admire Rubens' masterful *Adoration of the Magi* (£4.50, erratic hours depending on school schedule and events, but usually daily 9:30–15:30). During term, you're welcome to enjoy an evensong service (Mon–Sat at 17:30, Sun at 15:30, tel. 01223/331-447, www.kings.cam.ac.uk/chapel).

▲▲**Trinity College and Wren Library**—Half of Cambridge's 63 Nobel Prize winners have come from this richest and biggest of the town's colleges, founded in 1546 by Henry VIII. Don't miss the Wren-designed library, with its wonderful carving and fascinating original manuscripts. There's a small fee to visit the campus (£2.20), but if you just want to see Wren Library, enter the campus from the riverside entrance, located by the Garret Hostel Bridge (campus open daily 10:00–17:00; library open Mon–Fri 12:00–14:00, Sat 10:30–12:30 during term, always closed Sun and during exams; tel. 01223/338-400, www.trin.cam.ac.uk). Just outside the library entrance, Sir Isaac Newton, who spent 30 years at Trinity, clapped his hands and timed the echo to measure the speed of sound as it raced down the side of the cloister and back. In the library's display cases (covered with brown cloth that you flip back), you'll see handwritten works by Newton, Milton, Byron, Tennyson, and Housman, alongside Milne's original *Winnie the Pooh* (the real Christopher Robin attended Trinity College).

▲▲**Fitzwilliam Museum**—Britain's best museum of antiquities and art outside of London is the Fitzwilliam. Enjoy its wonderful paintings (Old Masters and a fine English section featuring Gainsborough, Reynolds, Hogarth, and others, plus works by all the famous Impressionists), old manuscripts, and Greek, Egyptian, and Mesopotamian collections (free, Tue–Sat 10:00–17:00, Sun 12:00–17:00, closed Mon, tel. 01223/332-900, www.fitzmuseum .cam.ac.uk).

Museum of Classical Archaeology—While this museum contains no originals, it offers a unique chance to see accurate copies (19th-century casts) of virtually every famous ancient Greek and Roman statue. More than 450 statues are on display (free, Mon–Fri 10:00–17:00, sometimes also Sat 10:00–13:00 during term, always closed Sun, Sidgwick Avenue, tel. 01223/335-153). The museum is a five-minute walk west of Silver Street Bridge; after crossing the bridge, continue straight until you reach a sign reading *Sidgwick Site*. The museum is in the long building on the corner to your right; the entrance is on the opposite side.

▲**Punting on the Cam**—For a little levity and probably more exercise than you really want, try hiring one of the traditional (and inexpensive) flat-bottom punts at the river and pole yourself up and down (around and around, more likely) the lazy Cam. Once you get the hang of it, it's a fine way to enjoy the scenic side of

Cambridge

Cambridge. After 17:00 it's less crowded (and less embarrassing).

Three places, one at each bridge, rent punts and offer £12, 45-minute punt tours. Trinity Punt, at Garrett Hostel Bridge near Trinity College, has the best prices (£8/hr rental, £30 deposit, ask for quick, free lesson, tel. 01223/338-483). Scudamore's runs two other locations: the central Silver Street Bridge and the less-convenient Quayside at Great Bridge, at the north end of town (£16–18/hr, £80 deposit required—can use credit card, tel. 01223/359-750, www.scudamores.com). Depending on the weather, punting season runs daily March through October, with Silver Street open all year.

TRANSPORTATION CONNECTIONS

From Cambridge by Train to: York (hourly, 2.5 hrs, transfer in Peterborough, about £57), **Oxford** (2/hr, 2.5 hrs), **London** (2/hr, 50 min). Train info: tel. 0845-748-4950, www.nationalrail.co.uk.

By Bus to: Heathrow Airport (1–2/hr, 2.25–2.75 hrs). Bus info: tel. 0870-575-7747, www.nationalexpress.co.uk.

Cambridge

BATH

The best city to visit within easy striking distance of London is Bath—just a 90-minute train ride away. Two hundred years ago, this city of 85,000 was the trendsetting Hollywood of Britain. If ever a city enjoyed looking in the mirror, Bath's the one. It has more "government-listed" or protected historic buildings per capita than any other town in England. The entire city, built of the creamy warm-tone limestone called "Bath stone," beams in its cover-girl complexion. An architectural chorus line, it's a triumph of the Georgian style. Proud locals remind visitors that the town is routinely banned from the "Britain in Bloom" contest to give other towns a chance to win. Bath's narcissism is justified. Even with its mobs of tourists (2 million per year), Bath is a joy to visit.

Long before the Romans arrived in the first century, Bath was known for its mineral hot springs. The importance of Bath has always been shaped by the healing allure of its 116°F hot springs. Romans called the popular spa town Aquae Sulis. The town's importance carried through Saxon times, when it had a huge church on the site of the present-day abbey and was considered the religious capital of Britain. Its influence peaked in 973 with King Edgar's sumptuous coronation in the abbey. Later, Bath prospered as a wool town.

Bath then declined until the mid-1600s, when it was just a huddle of huts around the abbey, with hot, smelly mud and 3,000 residents, oblivious to the Roman ruins 18 feet below their dirt floors. Then, in 1687, Queen Mary, fighting infertility, bathed here. Within 10 months she gave birth to a son...and a new age of popularity for Bath.

The revitalized town boomed as a spa resort. Ninety percent

Bath

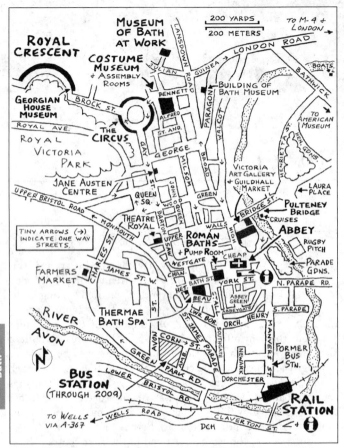

of the buildings you'll see today are from the 18th century. Local architect John Wood was inspired by the Italian architect Andrea Palladio to build a "new Rome." The town bloomed in the Neoclassical style, and streets were lined not with scrawny side-walks but with wide "parades," upon which the women in their stylishly wide dresses could spread their fashionable tails.

Beau Nash (1673–1762) was Bath's "master of ceremonies." He organized both the daily regimen of the aristocratic visitors and the city, lighting and improving street security, banning swords, and opening the Pump Room. Under his fashionable baton, Bath became a city of balls, gaming, and concerts—the place to see and be seen in England. This most civilized place became even more so with the great Neoclassical building spree that followed.

The buzz in the early 21st century is that the venerable baths are in the spotlight again. The new Thermae Bath Spa—finally open after years of delays—taps Bath's soothing hot springs, once again attracting visitors in need of a cure or a soak.

Planning Your Time

Bath deserves two nights even on a quick trip. On a three-week British trip, spend three nights in Bath, with one day for the city and one day for side-trips (see next chapter). Ideally, use Bath as your jet-lag recovery pillow, and do London at the end of your trip.

Consider starting a three-week British vacation this way:

Day 1: Land at Heathrow. Connect to Bath by National Express bus—the better option—or the less convenient bus/train combination (for details, see page 146). While you don't need or want a car in Bath, and some rental companies have an office there, those who land early and pick up their cars at the airport can visit Windsor Castle (near Heathrow) and/or Stonehenge on their way to Bath. (You can also consider flying into Bristol.) If you have the evening free in Bath, take a walking tour.

Day 2: 9:00–Tour the Roman Baths; 10:30–Catch the free city walking tour; 12:30–Picnic on the open deck of a Bath tour bus; 14:00–Free time in the shopping center of old Bath; 15:30–Tour the Costume Museum or Museum of Bath at Work. Take the evening walking tour (unless you did last night), consider seeing a play, or go for an evening soak in the new Thermae Bath Spa.

Day 3 (and possibly 4): By car, day-trip to nearby sights (see next chapter). Without a car, consider a one-day Avebury/Stonehenge/cute towns minibus tour from Bath (Mad Max tours are best; see "Tours," page 175).

ORIENTATION

(area code: 01225)

Bath's town square, three blocks in front of the bus and train station, is a bouquet of tourist landmarks, including the abbey, Roman and medieval baths, and the Pump Room.

Tourist Information

The TI is in the abbey churchyard (June–Sept Mon–Sat 9:30–18:00, Sun 10:00–16:00; Oct–May Mon–Sat 9:30–17:00, Sun 10:00–16:00; tel. 0870-420-1278, www.visitbath.co.uk). Pick up the £1 city map and—if you're interested in music, movies, and other nighttime listings—the free *This Month in Bath* booklet (be aware that its included map doesn't include sight information). Browse through scads of fliers, books, and maps. They also book rooms for £3.

Arrival in Bath

The Bath **train station** has a national and international tickets desk and a privately run tourism office masquerading as a TI. Immediately surrounding the train station is a sea of construction, as Bath gets a new mall and underground parking garage (due to be completed in 2011). To get to the TI from the train station, walk two blocks up Manvers Street and turn left at the triangular "square," following the small TI arrow on a signpost.

Because of the construction, Bath's **bus station** has been moved to a temporary location on Corn Street through 2009. It's at the southwest corner of town, a few blocks from the train station and town center.

My recommended B&Bs are all within a 10- to 15-minute walk or a £4–5 taxi ride from either station.

Helpful Hints

Festivals: The **Bath Literature Festival** is an open book February 23–March 2 in 2008 (www.bathlitfest.org.uk). The **Bath International Music Festival** bursts into song May 16–June 1 (classical, folk, jazz, contemporary; for the lineup, see www.bathmusicfest.org.uk), overlapped by the eclectic **Bath Fringe Festival** May 23–June 8 (theater, walks, talks, bus trips; www.bathfringe.co.uk). The **Jane Austen Festival** unfolds genteelly in late September (www.janeausten.co.uk/festival). Bath's festival box office sells tickets for most events, and can tell you exactly what's on tonight (2 Church Street, tel. 01225/463-362, www.bathfestivals.org.uk). Bath's local paper, the *Bath Chronicle*, publishes a "What's On" event listing on Fridays (www.thisisbath.com).

Internet Access: Try **@Internet** a block in front of the train station (£1/20 min, daily 9:00–22:00, 12 Manvers Street, tel. 01225/443-181).

Laundry: The **Spruce Goose Launderette** is around the corner from the recommended Brock's Guest House, on the pedestrian lane called Margaret's Buildings (self-service daily 8:00–21:00, full-service Mon–Fri 9:00–13:00—but book ahead, tel. 01225/483-309). Anywhere in town, **Speedy Wash** can pick up your laundry for same-day service (£10/bag, Mon–Fri 7:30–17:30, most hotels work with them, tel. 01225/427-616). East of Pulteney Bridge, the humble **Lovely Wash** is on Daniel Street (daily 9:00–21:00, self-service only).

Car Rental: **Enterprise** and **Thrifty** are each handy to central Bath, and have roughly the same rates: £40/day, £80/weekend, and £130–160/week. **Enterprise** provides a pick-up service for customers to and from their hotels, but doesn't do one-way rentals (at Lower Bristol Road in Bath, tel. 01225/443-311).

Thrifty is in the Bath train station, to the right as you exit (tel. 01225/442-911). **National/Alamo** is a £7 taxi ride from the train station, but will do one-way rentals (at Brass Mill Lane—go west on Upper Bristol Road, tel. 01225/481-898). **Europcar** advertises that it's in Bath, but it's relatively far outside of town. **Avis** is a mile from the Bristol train station; you'd need to rent a car to get there. Most offices close Saturday afternoon and all day Sunday, which complicates weekend pickups. Ideally, take the train or bus from downtown London to Bath, and rent a car as you leave Bath, rather than from within London.

TOURS

Of Bath

▲▲▲**Walking Tours**—Free two-hour tours are offered by **The Mayor's Corps of Honorary Guides,** led by volunteers who want to share their love of Bath with its many visitors. Their chatty, historical, and gossip-filled walks are essential for your understanding of this town's amazing Georgian social scene. How else will you learn that the old "chair ho" call for your sedan chair evolved into today's "cheerio" farewell? Tours leave from in front of the Pump Room (free, no tips, year-round Sun–Fri at 10:30 and 14:00, Sat at 10:30 only; evening walks offered May–Sept at 19:00 on Tue, Fri, and Sat). Advice for theatergoers: Guides stop to talk outside the Theatre Royal. You can skip out a moment, pop into the box office, and snare a great deal on a play for tonight (see "Nightlife" on page 185 for details).

For a **private tour,** call the local guides' bureau (£58/2 hrs, tel. 01225/337-111). For **Ghost Walks** and **Bizarre Bath** tours, see "Nightlife," page 185. Bath's Jane Austen Centre offers a **Jane Austen** tour on weekends (see listing on page 183).

▲▲**City Bus Tours**—City Sightseeing's hop-on, hop-off bus tours zip through Bath. Jump on a bus anytime at one of 17 signposted pick-up points, pay the driver, climb upstairs, and hear recorded commentary about Bath (£10, ticket valid for 24 hours, generally 4/hr daily from 9:30–19:00, 10:00–15:00 in winter). On a sunny day, this is a multitasking tourist's dream-come-true: You can munch a sandwich, work on a tan, snap great photos, and learn a lot all at the same time. Save money by doing the bus tour first—ticket stubs get you minor discounts at many sights. City Sightseeing has two routes: a 50-minute downtown tour, and a 45-minute "Skyline" route outside of town, handy for those wanting to visit the American Museum on the outskirts.

Taxi Tours—Local taxis, driven by good talkers, go where big buses can't. A group of up to four can rent a cab for an hour (about

Bath

Bath at a Glance

▲▲▲**Roman and Medieval Baths** Ancient baths that gave the city its name, tourable with good audioguide. **Hours:** Daily July–Aug 9:00–22:00, March–June and Sept–Oct 9:00–18:00, Nov–Feb 9:30–17:30.

▲▲▲**Costume Museum** 400 years of fashion under one roof, plus opulent Assembly Rooms. **Hours:** Daily March–Oct 11:00–18:00, Nov–Feb 11:00–17:00.

▲▲▲**Museum of Bath at Work** Gadget-ridden circa-1900 engineer's shop, foundry, factory, and office, best enjoyed with a live tour. **Hours:** April–Oct daily 10:30–17:00, Nov–March weekends only.

▲▲**Royal Crescent and the Circus** Stately Georgian (Neoclassical) buildings from Bath's late-18th-century glory days. **Hours:** Always viewable.

▲▲**Georgian House at No. 1 Royal Crescent** Best opportunity to explore the interior of one of Bath's high-rent Georgian beauties. **Hours:** Mid-Feb–Oct Tue–Sun 10:30–17:00, Nov Tue–Sun 10:30–16:00, closed Mon and Dec–mid-Feb.

▲**Pump Room** Swanky Georgian hall, ideal for a spot of tea or a taste of unforgettably "healthy" spa water. **Hours:** Daily 9:30–12:00 for coffee and breakfast, 12:00–14:30 for lunch, 14:30–16:30

£20) and enjoy a fine, informative, and—with the right cabbie—entertaining private joyride. It's probably cheaper to let the meter run than to pay for an hourly rate, but ask the cabbie for advice.

To Stonehenge, Avebury, and the Cotswolds

Bath is a good launch pad for visiting Wells, Avebury, Stonehenge, and more.

Mad Max Minibus Tours—Operating daily from Bath, Maddy and Paul offer thoughtfully organized, informative tours that run with a maximum group size of 16 people. Their **Stone Circles and Villages** full-day tour covers 110 miles and visits Stonehenge, the Avebury Stone Circles, and two cute villages: Lacock and Castle Combe. Photogenic Lacock is featured in parts of the BBC's *Pride and Prejudice* and the *Harry Potter* movies, and Castle Combe, the southernmost Cotswold village, is as sweet as they come (£27.50, does not include £6.30 Stonehenge entry, tours run daily 8:45–16:30, arrive 10 min early, leaves early to beat the Stonehenge

for high tea (open for dinner July–Aug only).

▲Thermae Bath Spa New relaxation center that puts the bath back in Bath. **Hours:** Baths-daily 9:00–22:00; visitors center-Mon–Sat 10:00–17:00, Sun 10:00–16:00.

▲Abbey 500-year-old Perpendicular Gothic church, graced with beautiful fan vaulting and stained glass. **Hours:** April–Oct Mon–Sat 9:00–18:00, Sun 13:00–14:30 & 16:30–17:30; Nov–March Mon–Sat 9:00–16:30, Sun 13:00–14:30.

▲Pulteney Bridge and Parade Gardens Shop-strewn bridge and relaxing riverside gardens. **Hours:** Bridge—always open; gardens—April–Sept daily 10:00–dusk, shorter hours off-season.

▲American Museum An insightful look primarily at colonial/early-American lifestyles, with 18 furnished rooms complete with guides eager to talk. **Hours:** April–Oct Tue–Sun 12:00–17:00, closed Mon and Nov–March.

Jane Austen Centre Exhibit on 19th-century Bath-based novelist, best for her fans. **Hours:** March–Oct daily 9:45–17:30, July–Aug Thu–Sat until 20:30; Nov–Feb Sun–Fri 11:00–16:30, Sat 9:45–17:30.

Building of Bath Museum Architecture buff's guide to Bath. **Hours:** Tue–Sun 10:30–17:00, closed Mon.

Bath

hordes). Their shorter tour of **Stonehenge and Lacock** leaves daily at 13:15 and returns at 17:15, and on some days, leaves at 8:45 and returns at 12:45 (£15 plus £6.30 Stonehenge entry).

Mad Max also offers a **Cotswold Discovery** full-day tour, a picturesque romp through the countryside with stops and a cream tea opportunity in the Cotswolds' quainter villages, including Stow-on-the-Wold, Bibury, Tetbury, the Coln Valley, The Slaughters (optional walk between the two villages), and others (£30; runs Sun, Tue, and Thu 8:45–17:15; arrive 10 min early). If you request it in advance, you can bring your luggage along and use the tour as transportation to get to Stow or, for £2.50 extra, Moreton-in-Marsh, with easy train connections to Oxford.

All tours depart from Bath at the Glass House shop on the corner of Orange Grove, a one-minute walk from the abbey. Remember to arrive 10 minutes before your departure time. Only cash is accepted as payment. It's better to book ahead—as far ahead as possible in summer—for these popular tours via email (maddy@madmax.abel.co.uk, www.madmaxtours.co.uk) rather than by phone (booking line open daily 8:00–21:00, tel. 07990/505-970). Please honor or cancel your seat reservation.

More Bus Tours—If Mad Max is booked up, don't fret. Plenty of companies in Bath offer tours of varying lengths, prices, and destinations. Note that the cost of admission to sites is usually not included with any tour.

Scarper Tours runs a minibus tour to Stonehenge (£12.50, departs daily Easter–Sept 9:30 and 13:30, Oct–Easter 13:30 only, tel. 07739/644-155, www.scarpertours.com).

Celtic Horizons, run by retired teacher Alan Price, offers tours from Bath to a variety of destinations, such as Stonehenge, Avebury, and Wells. He can provide a convenient transfer service (to or from London, Heathrow, Bristol airport, the Cotswolds, and so on) with a tour itinerary en route. Alan also does personalized genealogy tours. Allow about £25 per hour for a group (his comfortable minivan seats up to 8 people). It's best to make arrangements and get pricing information via email at alan@celtichorizons.com (tel. 01373/461-784, www.celtichorizons.com).

SIGHTS

In Bath's Town Center

▲▲▲**Roman and Medieval Baths**—In ancient Roman times, high society enjoyed the mineral springs at Bath. From Lon-

dinium, Romans traveled so often to Aquae Sulis, as the city was called, to "take a bath" that finally it became known simply as Bath. Today, a fine museum surrounds the ancient bath. It's a one-way system leading you past well-documented displays, Roman artifacts, mosaics, a temple pediment, and the actual mouth of the spring, piled high with Roman pennies. Enjoy some quality time looking into the eyes of Minerva, goddess of the hot springs. The included audioguide makes the visit easy and plenty informative. For those with a big appetite for Roman history, in-depth 40-minute tours leave from the end of the museum at the edge of the actual bath (included with ticket, on the hour, a poolside clock is set for the next departure time). The water is greenish because of algae—don't drink it. You can revisit the museum after the tour (£10.25, all prices increase £1 July–Aug to keep down the crowds, £13.50 combo-ticket includes Costume Museum—a £3.50 savings, family combo-£38, combo-tickets good for one week; daily July–

Aug 9:00–22:00, March–June and Sept–Oct 9:00–18:00, Nov–Feb 9:30–17:30, last entry 1 hour before closing, tel. 01225/477-784, www.romanbaths.co.uk). The museum and baths are fun to visit in the evening in summer—romantic, gas-lit, and all yours. After touring the Roman Baths, stop by the attached Pump Room for a spot of tea, or to gag on the water.

▲**Pump Room**—For centuries, Bath was forgotten as a spa. Then, in 1687, the previously barren Queen Mary bathed here, became pregnant, and bore a male heir to the throne. A few years later Queen Anne found the water eased her painful gout. Word of its wonder waters spread, and Bath earned its way back on the aristocratic map. High society soon turned the place into one big pleasure palace. The Pump Room, an elegant Georgian hall just above the Roman Baths, offers the visitor's best chance to raise a pinky in this Chippendale grandeur. Drop by to sip coffee or tea or to enjoy a light meal (daily 9:30–12:00 for coffee and £6–8 breakfast; 12:00–14:30 for £12 lunches; 14:30–16:30 for £15 traditional high tea; £7 tea/coffee and pastry available in the afternoons; open for dinner July–Aug only; live music daily—string trio 10:00–12:00, piano 12:45–14:30, string trio in high season or piano in winter 15:00–17:00; tel. 01225/444-477). Above the newspaper table and sedan chairs, a statue of Beau Nash himself sniffles down at you.

The Spa Water: This is your chance to eat a famous (but forgettable) "Bath bun" and split (and spit) a 50p drink of the awful curative water. The water is served from the King's Spring by appropriately attired Martin, who's ready to minuet (but refuses to gavotte). He explains that the water is 10,000 years old, pumped from nearly 100 yards deep, and marinated in wonderful minerals. Convenient public WCs are in the entry hallway that connects the Pump Room with the baths (but are not associated with the spa water).

▲**Thermae Bath Spa**—After simmering unused for a quarter-century, Bath's natural thermal springs once again offer R&R for

the masses. The state-of-the-art spa is housed in a complex of three buildings that combine historic structures with controversial new glass-and-steel architecture. (That's not the only controversy associated with the spa, which was delayed by years and went multiple millions over budget.)

The cheapest day pass, £20 for two hours, is a fine way to give it a try. With your pass, you'll get access to the large, ground-floor "Minerva Bath" (under a structure nicknamed the "big cube"); the small, circular "Cross Bath" (across from the main spa, with a hot-water fountain that shows the springs' real temperature straight from underground); the four steam rooms (including one with frankincense aromatherapy); and the view-filled, open-air, rooftop thermal pool.

The only natural thermal spa in the UK, the spa also has all the "pamper thyself" extras—massages, mud wraps, and various healing-type treatments and classes, including "wiatsu"—water shiatsu. These sessions are booked up to six months in advance on the weekends.

Bring your own swimsuit, come for a couple of hours (avoid the crowded Fri night and Sat afternoon scene), and consider an evening visit—when on a chilly day, Bath's twilight glows through the steam from the rooftop pool (£20/2 hrs, £30/4 hrs, £50/full day; towels-£3, robes-£4, slippers-£2; baths generally open daily 9:00–22:00, last entry at 19:45, visitors center open Mon–Sat 10:00–17:00, Sun 10:00–16:00; treatments, massage, and solarium cost £38–70 extra; salad-and-smoothies café for guests; 100 yards from Roman and medieval baths on Beau Street, tel. 01225/331-234, book treatments at www.thermaebathspa.com).

▲**Abbey**—The town of Bath wasn't much in the Middle Ages, but an important church has stood on this spot since Anglo-Saxon times. In 973, Edgar was crowned here.

Dominating the town center, the present church—the last great medieval church of England—is 500 years old and a fine example of Late Perpendicular Gothic, with breezy fan vaulting and enough stained glass to earn it the nickname "Lantern of the West." The glass, red-iron gas-powered lamps, and heating grates on the floor are all remnants of the 19th century. The window behind the altar shows 52 scenes from the life of Christ. A window to the left of the altar shows Edgar's coronation (worth the £2.50 donation; April–Oct Mon–Sat 9:00–18:00, Sun 13:00–14:30 & 16:30–17:30; Nov–March Mon–Sat 9:00–16:30, Sun 13:00–14:30; handy flyer narrates a self-guided 19-stop tour, www.bathabbey.org).

Posted on the door is the schedule for concerts, services, and **evensong** (Sun at 15:30 year-round, plus most Sat in Aug at 17:00). The facade (c. 1500, but mostly restored) is interesting for some of its carvings. Look for the angels going down the ladder. The statue of Peter (to the left of the door) lost his head to mean iconoclasts; it was re-carved out of his once super-sized beard. Take a moment to appreciate the abbey's architecture from the Abbey Green square.

A small but worthwhile exhibit, the abbey's **Heritage Vaults** tell the story of Christianity in Bath since Roman times (free, Mon–Sat 10:00–16:00, last entry 15:30, closed Sun, entrance just outside church, south side).

▲**Pulteney Bridge, Parade Gardens, and Cruises**—Bath is inclined to compare its shop-lined Pulteney Bridge to Florence's Ponte Vecchio. That's pushing it. But to best enjoy a sunny day, pay about £1 to enter the Parade Gardens below the bridge (April–Sept daily 10:00–dusk, shorter hours off-season, includes deck chairs, ask about concerts held some Sun at 15:00 in summer, tel. 01225/394-041). Taking a siesta to relax peacefully at the riverside provides a wonderful break (and memory).

Across the bridge at Pulteney Weir, tour boat companies run **cruises** (£7, £3.50 one-way, up to 7/day if the weather's good, 50–60 min to Bathampton and back, WCs on board). Just take whatever boat is running. Avon Cruisers actually stop in Bathampton (allowing you to hop off and walk back); Pulteney Cruisers come with a sundeck ideal for picnics.

Guildhall Market—The little shopping mall, located across from Pulteney Bridge, is a frumpy time warp in this affluent town, but it's fun for browsing and picnic shopping. Its cheap Market Café is recommended under "Eating," page 196.

Victoria Art Gallery—The one-room gallery, next to Guildhall Market, is filled with paintings from the 18th and 19th centuries (free, includes audioguide, Tue–Sat 10:00–17:00, Sun 13:30–17:00, closed Mon, WC, www.victoriagal.org.uk).

▲▲**Royal Crescent and the Circus**—If Bath is an architectural cancan, these are the knickers. These first Georgian "condos" by

John Wood (the Elder and the Younger) are well-explained in the city walking tours. "Georgian" is British for "Neoclassical," or dating from the 1770s. As you cruise the Crescent, pretend you're rich. Then pretend you're poor. Notice the "ha ha fence," a drop-off in the front yard that acted as a barrier, invisible from the windows, for keeping out sheep and peasants. The refined and stylish Royal Crescent Hotel sits unmarked in the center of the crescent. You're welcome to (politely) drop in to explore its fine ground-floor public spaces. A gracious and traditional tea is served in the garden out back (£11 cream tea, £16.50 high tea, daily 15:30–17:00, sharing is OK, reserve a day in advance in summer, tel. 01225/823-333).

Picture the round Circus as a coliseum turned inside out. Its Doric, Ionic, and Corinthian capital decorations pay homage to its Greco-Roman origin, and are a reminder that Bath (with its

Bath

seven hills) aspired to be "the Rome of England." The frieze above the first row of columns has hundreds of different panels, each representing the arts, sciences, and crafts. The first floor was high off the ground, to accommodate aristocrats on sedan chairs and women with sky-high hairdos. The tiny round windows on the top floors were the servants' quarters. While the building fronts are uniform, the backs are higgledy-piggledy, infamous for their "hanging loos." Stand in the middle of the Crescent among the grand plane trees, on the capped old well. Imagine the days when there was no indoor plumbing, and the servant girls gathered here to fetch water—this was gossip central. If you stand on the well, your clap echoes three times around the circle (try it).

▲▲Georgian House at No. 1 Royal Crescent—This museum (corner of Brock Street and Royal Crescent) offers your best look into a period house. It's worth the £5 admission to get behind one of those classy exteriors. The volunteers in each room are determined to fill you in on all the fascinating details of Georgian life... like how high-class women shaved their eyebrows and pasted on carefully trimmed strips of furry mouse skin in their place. On the bedroom dresser sits a bowl of black beauty marks and a head-scratcher from those pre-shampoo days. Fido spent his days in the kitchen treadmill powering the rotisserie (mid-Feb–Oct Tue–Sun 10:30–17:00, Nov Tue–Sun 10:30–16:00, last entry 30 min before closing, closed Mon and Dec–mid-Feb, £2 guidebook available, no photos, "no stiletto heels, please," tel. 01225/428-126, www.bath-preservation-trust.org.uk).

▲▲▲Costume Museum—One of Europe's great museums, it displays 400 years of fashion and is housed within Bath's Assembly Rooms. Follow the excellent included audioguide tour and allow two hours (£6.75, £13.50 combo-ticket covers Roman Baths—saving you £3.50, family combo-£38, daily March–Oct 11:00–18:00, Nov–Feb 11:00–17:00, last entry 1 hour before closing, on-site self-service café, tel. 01225/477-789, www.museumofcostume.co.uk).

The **Assembly Rooms,** which you can see for free en route to the museum, are big, grand, empty rooms. Card games, concerts, tea, and dances were held here in the 18th century, before the advent of fancy hotels with grand public spaces made them obsolete. Note the extreme symmetry (pleasing to the aristocratic eye) and the high windows (which assured their privacy). After the Allies bombed the historical and well-preserved German city of Lübeck, the Germans picked up a Baedeker guide and chose a similarly lovely city to bomb: Bath. The Assembly Rooms—gutted in this wartime tit-for-tat by WWII bombs—have since been restored to their original splendor. (Only the chandeliers predate the bombing.)

Below the Costume Museum (to the left as you leave, 20

yards away) is one of the few surviving sets of iron house hardware. "Link boys" carried torches through the dark streets, lighting the way for big shots in their sedan chairs as they traveled from one affair to the next. The link boys extinguished their torches in the black conical "snuffers." The lamp above was once gas-lit. The crank on the left was used to hoist bulky things to various windows (see the hooks). Few of these sets survived the dark days of the WWII Blitz, when most were collected, melted down, and turned into weapons to power the British war machine. (Not long ago, these well-meaning Brits found out that all this patriotic extra commitment to the national struggle was for naught, since the metal ended up on junk heaps.)

▲▲▲**Museum of Bath at Work**—This is the official title for Mr. Bowler's Business, a 1900s engineer's shop, brass foundry, and fizzy-drink factory with a Dickensian office. It's just a pile of meaningless old gadgets until a volunteer guide lovingly resurrects Mr. Bowler's creative genius. Also featured are various Bath creations through the years, including a 1914 car and the versatile plasticine (proto-Play-Doh, handy for claymation and more). Don't miss the fine "Story of Bath Stone" in the basement. While there are included audioguides, the live tours are the key (wonderful 45-min tours go regularly). If rushed, join one already in session (£4, April–Oct daily 10:30–17:00, Nov–March weekends only, last entry at 16:00, 2 steep blocks up Russell Street from Assembly Rooms, tel. 01225/318-348, www.bath-at-work.org.uk).

Jane Austen Centre—This exhibition focuses on Jane Austen's tumultuous, sometimes-troubled five years in Bath (circa 1800, during which time her father died), and the influence Bath had on her writing. While the exhibit is thoughtfully done and a hit with "Jane-ites," there is little of historic substance here. You'll walk through a Georgian townhouse that she didn't live in (one of her real addresses in Bath was a few houses up the road, at 25 Gay Street), and see mostly enlarged reproductions of things associated with her writing. The museum describes various places from two novels set in Bath (*Persuasion* and *Northanger Abbey*). After a live intro (15 min, 3/hr) explaining how this romantic but down-to-earth woman dealt with the silly, shallow, and arrogant aristocrats' world where "the doing of nothings all day prevents one from doing anything," you see a 15-minute video and wander through the rest of the exhibit (£6.50; March–Oct daily 9:45–17:30, July–Aug Thu–Sat until 20:30; Nov–Feb Sun–Fri 11:00–16:30, Sat 9:45–17:30; 40 Gay Street between Queen's Square and the Circus, tel. 01225/443-000, www.janeausten.co.uk). Jane Austen–themed walking tours of the city begin across from the Roman Baths and end at the Centre (£5, 90 min, Sat–Sun at 11:00, ask at the Centre for more information—no reservation necessary). Avid fans gather for the annual Jane Austen Festival (see "Festivals," page 174).

Recently, the Centre opened a Jane-themed **tearoom** on the top floor, where they offer so-so light lunches, snacks, and desserts with goofy names like Darcy's Chocolate Delight and Wetherby's Hot Cross Buns (same hours as Centre, above).

If you're male and feeling left out, head one door downhill from the museum and look through the window. You'll see a fine delftware-decorated powder bowl designed for men to touch up their wigs.

Outer Bath

Building of Bath Museum—This offers an intriguing look behind the scenes at how the Georgian city was actually built. Filling what was a Methodist church (erected in 1765), the museum is really just a series of exhibits, but those interested in construction—inside and out—find it worth the £4 (Tue–Sun 10:30–17:00, closed Mon, last entry 30 min before closing, north of the city center on a street called "The Paragon," tel. 01225/333-895, www.bath-preservation-trust.org.uk).

▲**American Museum**—I know, you need this in Bath like you need a Big Mac. The UK's only museum dedicated to American history, this may be the only place that combines Geronimo and Groucho Marx. While it has thoughtful exhibits on the history of Native Americans and the Civil War, the museum's heart is with the decorative arts and cultural artifacts that reveal how Americans lived from colonial times to the mid-19th century. Each of the 18 completely furnished rooms (from a plain 1600s Massachusetts dining/living room to a Rococo Revival explosion in a New Orleans bedroom) is hosted by an eager guide, waiting to fill you in on the everyday items that make domestic Yankee history surprisingly interesting. (In the Lee Room, look for the original mouse holes, lovingly backlit, in the floor boards.) One room is a quilter's nirvana. You can easily spend an afternoon here, enjoying the surrounding gardens, arboretum, and trails (£6.50, April–Oct Tue–Sun 12:00–17:00, last entry 1 hour before closing, closed Mon and Nov–March, at Claverton Manor, tel. 01225/460-503, www.americanmuseum.org). The museum is outside of town and a headache to reach if you don't have a car (10-min walk from bus #18).

ACTIVITIES

Walking—The Bath Skyline Walk is a six-mile wander around the hills surrounding Bath (leaflet at TI). Plenty of other scenic paths are described in the TI's literature. For additional options, get *Country Walks around Bath,* by Tim Mowls (£4.50 at TI or bookstores).

Hiking the Canal to Bathampton—An idyllic towpath leads from the Bath train station along an old canal to the sleepy village of Bathampton. Immediately behind the station, cross the footbridge and see where the canal hits the river. Turn left, noticing the series of Industrial Age locks, and walk along the towpath, giving thanks that you're not a horse pulling a barge. You'll be in Bathampton in less than an hour, where a classic pub awaits with a nice lunch and cellar-temp beer.

Boating—The Bath Boating Station, in an old Victorian boathouse, rents boats and punts (£7 per person/first hour, then £2/ additional hour, April–Sept daily 10:00–18:00, closed off-season, Forester Road, 1 mile northeast of center, tel. 01225/312-900, www.bathboating.co.uk).

Swimming and Kids' Activities—The Bath Sports and Leisure Centre has a fine pool for laps as well as lots of water slides. Kids have entertaining options in the mini-gym "Active Zone" area, which includes a rock wall (£3, daily 8:00–22:00 but kids' hours are limited, call for open swim times, just across North Parade Bridge, tel. 01225/462-565, www.aquaterra.org).

Shopping—There's great browsing between the abbey and the Assembly Rooms (Costume Museum). Shops close at 17:30, some have longer hours on Thursday, and many are open on Sunday (11:00–17:00). Explore the antique shops lining Bartlett Street just below the Assembly Rooms.

NIGHTLIFE

For an up-to-date list of events, pick up the local newspaper, the *Bath Chronicle,* on Fridays, when the "What's On" schedule appears (www.thisisbath.com). Younger travelers may enjoy the party-ready bar, club, and nightlife recommendations at www .itchybath.co.uk.

▲▲▲**Bizarre Bath Street Theater**—For an immensely entertaining walking-tour comedy act "with absolutely no history or culture," follow J. J. or Noel Britten on their creative and entertaining Bizarre Bath walk. This 90-minute "tour," which plays off local passersby as well as tour members, is a belly laugh a minute (£7, April–Sept nightly at 20:00, smaller groups Mon–Thu, heavy on magic, careful to insult all minorities and sensitivities, just racy enough but still good family fun, leaves from The Huntsman pub near the abbey, confirm at TI or call 01225/335-124, www .bizarrebath.co.uk).

▲**Plays**—The 18th-century, 800-seat Theatre Royal, newly restored and one of England's loveliest, offers a busy schedule of London West End–type plays, including many "pre-London" dress-rehearsal runs (£11–25, generally start at 19:30 or 20:00, box office open Mon–Sat 10:00–20:00, Sun 12:00–20:00, tel. 01225/448-844, www.theatreroyal.org.uk). Forty nosebleed spots on a bench (misnamed "standby seats") go on sale at noon on the day of each performance (£5, pay cash at box office or call and book with credit card, 2 tickets maximum). Or, you can snatch up any unsold seat in the house for £10–15 a half hour before "curtain up."

A handy cheap sightseers' tip: During the free Bath walking tour, your guide stops here. Pop into the box office, ask what's playing tonight, and see if there are many seats left. If the play sounds good and if enough seats remain unsold, you're fairly safe to come back 30 minutes before curtain time to buy a ticket at that £10 price. Oh...and if you smell jasmine, it's the ghost of Lady Grey, a mistress of Beau Nash.

Evening Walks—Take your choice: comedy (Bizarre Bath, described above), history, or ghost tour. The free city history walks (a daily standard described on page 175) are offered summer evenings (2 hours; May–Sept Tue, Fri, and Sat at 19:00; leave from Pump Room). Ghost Walks are a popular way to pass the after-dark hours (£6, 2 hours, unreliably April–Oct Mon–Sat at 20:00, Fri only in winter, leave from The Garrick's Head pub to the left and behind Theatre Royal as you face it, tel. 01225/350-512, www.ghostwalksofbath.co.uk). York and Edinburgh—which have houses thought to be actually haunted—are better for these walks.

Pubs—Most pubs in the center are very noisy, catering to a rowdy twentysomething crowd. But on the top end of town you can still find some classic old places with inviting ambience and live music. These are listed in order from closest to farthest away:

The Old Green Tree, the most convenient of all these pubs, is a rare traditional pub right in the town center (locally brewed real ales, no children, Green Street, tel. 01225/448-259; also recommended under "Eating," page 195, for lunch).

The Star Inn—not too far north from the Museum of Bath at Work—is smaller and more intimidating than the Old Green Tree, but it's much appreciated by local beer-lovers for its fine ale and "no machines or music to distract from the chat." It's called a "spit 'n' sawdust" place, and its long bench, nicknamed "death row," still comes with a complimentary pinch of snuff from tins on the ledge. Try the Bellringer Ale, made just up the road (Mon–Fri 12:00–15:00 & 17:30–24:00, Sat–Sun 12:00–24:00, no food served, 23 The Vineyards, top of The Paragon/A4 Roman Road, tel. 01225/425-072).

The Bell has a jazzy, pierced-and-tattooed, bohemian feel, but with a mellow older crowd. They serve pizza on the large concrete terrace out back in summer (Mon–Sat 11:00–23:00, Sun 12:00–10:30, live music Mon and Wed evenings and Sun lunch, sandwiches served all day, 103 Walcot Street, tel. 01225/460-426).

The Farmhouse, which was recently renovated, has a pleasant, grown-up environment. Its lunch and dinner specials change daily (£5 sandwiches, £10–15 dinner plates), and it fills its spacious and laid-back interior with live jazz on Tuesdays and Sundays from 21:00 (1 Landsdown Road, tel. 01225/316-162).

Summer Nights at the Baths—In July and August, you can stretch your sightseeing day at the Roman Baths, open nightly until 22:00 (last entry 21:00), when the gas lamps flame and the baths are far less crowded and more atmospheric. To take a dip yourself, consider popping in to the new Thermae Bath Spa (last entry at 19:45; see page 179).

SLEEPING

Bath is a busy tourist town. To get a good B&B, make a telephone reservation in advance. Competition is stiff, and it's worth asking any of these places for a weekday, three-nights-in-a-row, or off-season deal. Friday and Saturday nights are tightest, especially if you're staying only one night, since B&Bs favor those staying longer. If you're staying only Saturday night, you're very bad news to a B&B hostess. At B&Bs (and cheaper hotels), expect lots of stairs and no elevators.

For better availability and the lower end of the prices listed below, visit Bath mid-week. On the weekends, Londoners head here, driving up demand.

B&Bs near the Royal Crescent

These listings are all a 15-minute uphill walk or an easy £4–5 taxi ride from the train station. Or take any hop-on, hop-off bus tour from the station, get off at the stop nearest your B&B (hop off at Royal Avenue—confirm with driver), check in, then finish the

---

Sleep Code

(£1 = about $2, country code: 44, area code: 01225)
S = Single, **D** = Double/Twin, **T** = Triple, **Q** = Quad, **b** = bathroom, **s** = shower only. Unless otherwise noted, credit cards are accepted.

To help you sort easily through these listings, I've divided the rooms into three categories based on the price for a standard double room with bath:

$$$ **Higher Priced**—Most rooms £80 or more.
  $$ **Moderately Priced**—Most rooms between £60–80.
    $ **Lower Priced**—Most rooms £60 or less.

tour later in the day. The Marlborough Lane places have easier parking, but are less centrally located.

$$$ **The Town House,** overlooking the Assembly Rooms, is genteel, deluxe, and homey, with three fresh, mod rooms that have a hardwood stylishness. In true B&B style, you'll enjoy a gourmet breakfast at a big family table with the other guests (Db-£89–95, or £105–115 Fri–Sat, 2-night minimum, prices promised with this book through 2008, 7 Bennett Street, tel. & fax 01225/422-505, www.thetownhousebath.co.uk, stay@thetownhousebath.co.uk, Alan and Brenda Willey).

$$$ **Brock's Guest House** has six rooms in a Georgian town house built by John Wood in 1765. Located between the prestigious Royal Crescent and the courtly Circus, it was redone in a way that would make the great architect proud (Db-£87, deluxe Db-£99, Tb-£115, reserve with credit card far in advance, little top-floor library, 32 Brock Street, tel. 01225/338-374, fax 01225/334-245, www.brocksguesthouse.co.uk, brocks @brocksguesthouse.co.uk).

$$ **Parkside Guest House** has five thoughtfully appointed Edwardian rooms—tidy, clean, and homey, with nary a doily in sight—and a spacious back garden (Db-£72, 11 Marlborough Lane, tel. & fax 01225/429-444, www.parksidebandb.co.uk, post @parksidebandb.co.uk, Erica and Inge Lynall).

$$ **Prior House B&B,** with four well-kept rooms, is run by hardworking Lynn Shearn (D-£60, Db-£65, T-£80, serve-yourself breakfast at a common table, 3 Marlborough Lane, tel. 01225/313-587, www.greatplaces.co.uk/priorhouse, priorhouse@greatplaces .co.uk).

$$ **Elgin Villa** rents five comfy, well-maintained rooms (Ss-£38, Sb-£55, Ds-£58, Db-£80, Tb-£96, Qb-£120, more expensive for Sat-only stay, discount for 3 nights, special-diet breakfasts available, Wi-Fi, parking, 6 Marlborough Lane, tel. 01225/424-557, www.elginvilla.co.uk, stay@elginvilla.co.uk).

$ **Woodville House,** warmly run by Anne Toalster, is a grandmotherly little house with three tidy, charming rooms sharing two bathrooms and a TV lounge. Breakfast is served at a big, family-style table (D-£50, 2-night minimum, cash only, some parking, below the Royal Crescent at 4 Marlborough Lane, tel. 01225/319-335, annetoalster@btinternet.com).

B&Bs East of the River

These listings are a 10-minute walk from the city center. While generally a better value, they are less conveniently located.

$$$ **The Ayrlington,** next door to a lawn-bowling green, has 14 attractive rooms with Asian decor, and hints of a more genteel time. Though this well-maintained hotel fronts a busy street,

Bath Accommodations

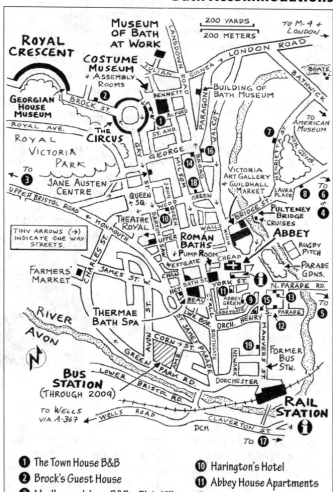

1. The Town House B&B
2. Brock's Guest House
3. Marlborough Lane B&Bs: Elgin Villa, Woodville House, Parkside Guest House & Prior House B&B
4. The Ayrlington
5. Holly Villa Guest House
6. 14 Raby Place
7. Villa Magdala
8. Edgar Townhouse
9. Three Abbey Green Guest House
10. Harington's Hotel
11. Abbey House Apartments
12. Pratt's Hotel
13. Parade Park Hotel
14. Royal York Travelodge
15. Henry Guest House
16. YMCA
17. White Hart Hostel
18. St. Christopher's Inn
19. Internet Café

it's quiet and tranquil. Rooms in the back have pleasant views of sports greens and Bath beyond. For the best value, request a standard double with a view of Bath (huge price range due to varying sizes of rooms and policy of charging 30 percent more on Fri–Sun, Db-£75–175—see website for specifics; fine garden, easy parking, 24–25 Pulteney Road, tel. 01225/425-495, fax 01225/469-029, www.ayrlington.com, mail@ayrlington.com).

$$ Holly Villa Guest House, with a cheery garden, six bright rooms, and a cozy TV lounge, is enthusiastically and thoughtfully run by chatty, friendly Jill and Keith McGarrigle (Ds-£60, small Db-£65, big Db-£70, Tb-£90, cash only, easy parking; 8-min walk from station and city center—walk over North Parade Bridge, take the first right, and then take the second left to 14 Pulteney Gardens; tel. 01225/310-331, www.hollyvilla.com, jill@hollyvilla.com).

$$ 14 Raby Place is another good value, mixing Georgian glamour with homey warmth and modern, artistic taste within its five rooms. Muriel Guy is a fun and endearing live wire who serves organic food for breakfast (S-£35, Db-£70, Tb-£75, cash only; go over bridge on North Parade Road, left on Pulteney Road, cross to church, Raby Place is first row of houses on hill; 14 Raby Place, tel. 01225/465-120).

B&Bs East of Pulteney Bridge
These B&Bs are a five-minute walk from the city center.

$$$ Villa Magdala rents 18 stately, hotelesque rooms in a freestanding Victorian town house opposite a park (Db-£95–160; price varies depending on day of week, size of room, view, and type of bed—less off-season; in quiet residential area, inviting lounge, Wi-Fi, parking, Henrietta Street, tel. 01225/466-329, fax 01225/483-207, www.villamagdala.co.uk, office@villamagdala.co.uk, Roy and Lois).

$$ Edgar Townhouse, with 18 simple rooms and lots of stairs, gives you a budget-hotel option in this smart Georgian neighborhood (Sb-£60, Db-£75–85 depending on room, Tb-£110, Qb-£140, less in winter, smaller rooms on top, avoid #18 on ground level, 2-night minimum on summer weekends; pleasant sitting room with old organ, gramophones, and free Wi-Fi; 64 Great Pulteney Street, tel. 01225/420-619, fax 01225/466-916, www.edgar-hotel.co.uk, edgar-hotel@btconnect.com).

In the City Center

$$$ Three Abbey Green Guest House, with seven rooms, is newly renovated, bright, fresh, and located in a quiet, traffic-free courtyard only 50 yards from the abbey and the Roman Baths. Its spacious rooms are a fine value (Sb-£77, Db-£85–125, four-poster Db-£145–175, family rooms-£135–165, families welcome, free Internet access and Wi-Fi, tel. 01225/428-558, www .threeabbeygreen.com, stay@threeabbeygreen.com, owners Sue and Derek and daughter Nici, pronounced "Nikki"). They also rent two self-catering apartments with two double beds each, good for families or couples traveling together (Qb-£160–195, higher prices are for Fri–Sat, 3-night minimum).

$$$ Harington's Hotel rents 13 fresh, modern, and newly refurbished rooms on a quiet street in the town center. This styl-ish place feels like a boutique hotel, but with a friendlier, laid-back vibe (Sb-£75–125, standard Db-£95–125, superior Db-£105–135, large Db-£118–145, family-room Qb-£115–165, higher prices are for Fri–Sat, lots of stairs, mini-fridges, attached restaurant-bar open all day, parking available, 10 Queen Street, tel. 01225/461-728, fax 01225/444-804, www.haringtonshotel.co.uk, post @haringtonshotel.co.uk). Melissa and Peter offer a 5 percent discount

with this book for three-night stays except on Fridays, Saturdays, and holidays. They also rent a self-catering apartment down the street that sleeps five (Db-£135–175/night).

$$$ Abbey House Apartments, run by a Goth rocker

named Laura, consists of three flats in a killer location. The apartments called Abbey View and Abbey Green (which comes with a washer and dryer) both have views of the abbey from their nicely equipped kitchens. The top-floor Abbey Flat is a part-time therapist's office, clut-tered but cozy (Sb-£90, Db-£100–125, higher prices are for Fri–Sat, rooms can sleep four with Murphy and sofa beds, Abbey Green, tel. 01225/464-238, www .laurastownhouseapartments.co.uk, laura@laurastownhouse apartments.co.uk). Laura will meet you to give you the keys. She has other less-central apartments around town.

$$$ Pratt's Hotel is as proper and olde-English as you'll find in Bath. Its creaks and frays are aristocratic. Even its public places make you want to sip a brandy, and its 46 rooms are bright and spacious. Since it's in the city center, occasionally it can get noisy—request a quiet room away from the street (Sb-£90, Db-£135, advance reservations get highest rate, drop-ins after 16:00 often snare Db for £90, dogs-£7.50 but children under 14 free, attached restaurant-bar, elevator, 4 blocks from station on South Parade, tel. 01225/460-441, fax 01225/448-807, www.forestdale.com, pratts@forestdale.com).

$$ Parade Park Hotel rents 35 modern, basic rooms in a very central location (S-£40, D-£55, small Db-£70, large Db-£90, Tb-£95, Qb-£120, lots of stairs, lively bar downstairs and noisy seagulls, 10 North Parade, tel. 01225/463-384, fax 01225/442-322, www.paradepark.co.uk, info@paradepark.co.uk).

$$ Royal York Travelodge—which offers 66 American-style, characterless yet comfortable rooms—worries B&Bs with its reasonable prices (Db-£70–80, Tb-same price, as low as £26 if you book online in advance, up to 2 kids sleep free, breakfast extra, 1 York Building, George Street, tel. 01225/442-061, central reservation tel. 08700-850-950, www.travelodge.co.uk). This is especially economical for families of four (who enjoy the Db price).

$$ Henry Guest House is a bare-bones, vertical place, offering eight clean rooms. It's in a central location with some street noise, two blocks in front of the train station (S-£40, D-£65, Db-£75, Tb-£85–105, family deals, lots of narrow stairs, 3 showers and 3 WCs for everybody, 6 Henry Street, tel. 01225/424-052, fax 01225/316-669, www.thehenry.com, stay@thehenry.com). Owners Steve and Liz also rent a self-catering apartment in the same area that sleeps four comfortably, and up to eight with cots and a sleeper couch (Db-£90).

Dorms

$ The YMCA, central on a leafy square, has 200 beds in industrial-strength rooms (S-£25–29, twin-£38–46, beds in big dorms-£13, £2 more per person on Fri and Sat, includes continental breakfast, cheap lunches, lockers, Internet access, dorms closed 10:00–14:00, down a tiny alley off Broad Street on Broad Street Place, tel. 01225/325-900, fax 01225/462-065, www.bathymca.co.uk, reservations@bathymca.co.uk).

$ White Hart Hostel is a simple place offering adults and families good, cheap beds in two- to six-bed dorms (£15/bed, D-£40, Db-£60, family rooms, kitchen, 5-min walk behind train station at Widcombe—where Widcombe Hill hits Claverton Street, tel. 01225/313-985, www.whitehartbath.co.uk, run by Jo).

$ St. Christopher's Inn, in a prime, central location, is part of a chain of low-priced, high-energy hubs for backpackers looking for beds and brews. Their beds are so cheap because they know you'll spend money on their beer (60 beds in 4- to 12-bed rooms-£14–22.50, D-£50, higher prices are for weekends, deals available online; lively and affordable pub and bar downstairs—20 percent off if you're a guest, Internet access, laundry, lounge with video, 9 Green Street, tel. 01225/481-444, www.st-christophers.co.uk).

EATING

Bath is bursting with quaint and stylish eateries. There's something for every appetite and budget—just stroll around the center of town. A picnic dinner of deli food or take-out fish-and-chips in the Royal Crescent Park is ideal for aristocratic hoboes. Reserve a table on Friday and Saturday evenings. Save money by eating before 19:00. Keep in mind that many restaurants in Bath are closed on Sunday nights, but the chain places remain open.

Near Abbey Green

The first two fine and popular places share North Parade Passage, a block south of the abbey.

Tilley's Bistro, popular with locals, serves healthy French, English, and vegetarian meals with candlelit ambience. Their fun menu lets you build your own meal, choosing from an interesting array of £7 starters (Mon–Sat 12:00–14:30 & 18:00–22:30, closed Sun, reservations smart, 3 North Parade Passage, tel. 01225/484-200).

Sally Lunn's House is a cutesy, touristy, quasi-historic place for traditional English meals, tea, pink pillows, and lots of lace (£15–20 meals, £10 early-bird 2-course special 17:00–19:00, open daily 10:00–21:30, until 22:00 Fri–Sat, 4 North Parade Passage, tel. 01225/461-634). They are famous for having a variety of cream teas and buns (£7, until 18:00). Lunch customers get a free peek at the basement Kitchen Museum (otherwise 30p).

The Garrick's Head, right around the corner from the Theatre Royal, reopened recently with a refurbished interior. The left side features a classy "gastro-pub" restaurant (with a fine cheese selection), while the other half offers a traditional-but-spruced-up bar. The dinner menu is a little pricey, but if you grab an outdoor table as the theater crowd rolls in, the people-watching can't be beat

Bath Restaurants

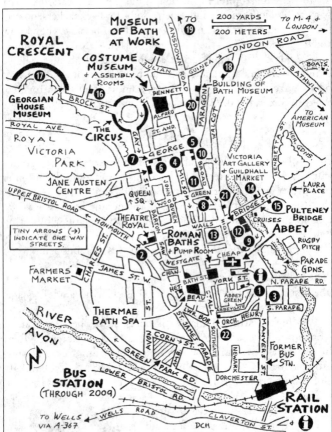

1. Tilley's Bistro & Sally Lunn's House
2. The Garrick's Head
3. Mai Thai Restaurant
4. Loch Fyne Restaurant
5. Wagamama
6. Martini Restaurant
7. Chandos Deli
8. The Old Green Tree
9. Browns Restaurant
10. Ask Restaurant
11. The Moon and Sixpence
12. Guildhall Market
13. Cornish Bakehouse
14. No. 5 Restaurant & Rajpoot Tandoori
15. Yak Yeti Yak & The Boater
16. Bistro Papillon
17. Royal Crescent Hotel (High Tea)
18. The Bell
19. To The Farmhouse
20. The Star Inn
21. Waitrose Supermarket
22. Marks & Spencer & Café Revive

(£12 plates, Mon–Sat 11:00–21:00, Sun 12:00–21:00, 8 St. John's Place, tel. 01225/318-368).

Near the Train Station

Mai Thai Restaurant is a favorite with locals. It's cheap and crowded, serves good curry, and also does take-out food (£6–7 meals, daily 12:00–14:00 & 18:00–22:30, 6 Pierrepont Street, 2 blocks up from the train station, tel. 01225/445-557).

Between the Abbey and the Circus

George Street is lined with cheery eateries: Thai, Italian, wine bars, and so on. Two good chains, listed first, are leaders of the pack.

Loch Fyne Restaurant, a Scottish fish place with a bright, airy, and youthful atmosphere, fills a former bank. The fish is fresh, prices are reasonable (£10–18 meals, £11 early-bird dinner until 19:00), the energy is high, and it doesn't feel like a chain (daily 12:00–22:00, until 22:45 Fri–Sat, until 21:45 Sun, 24 Milsom Street, tel. 01225/750-120).

Wagamama, a stylish, youthful, and modern chain of noodle shops, continues its quest for world domination. There's one in almost every mid-sized city in the UK, and after you've sampled their udon noodles, fried rice, or curry dishes, you'll know why (£7–9 meals, Mon–Sat 12:00–23:00, Sun 12:00–22:00, good vegetarian options, 1 York Buildings, George Street, tel. 01225/337-314).

Martini Restaurant, a hopping, purely Italian place, has class and jovial waiters (£12–16 entrées, £7–9 pizzas, daily 12:00–14:30 & 18:00–22:30, plenty of veggie options, daily fish specials, extensive wine list, reservations smart on weekends, 9 George Street, tel. 01225/460-818; Mauro, Nunzio, Franco, and chef Luigi).

Chandos Deli has good coffee and tasty £6–7 sandwiches made on artisan breads. This upscale but casual eight-table place serves breakfast and lunch to dedicated foodies who don't want to pay too much (Mon–Sat 9:00–17:00, closed Sun, 12 George Street, tel. 01225/314-418).

The Old Green Tree, in the old town center, serves good lunches to locals in a characteristic pub setting. As Bath is not a good pub-grub town, this is likely the best you'll do in the center (real ales on tap, lunch 12:00–15:00 only, no children, can be crowded on weekend nights, 12 Green Street, tel. 01225/448-259).

Two big, noisy chain restaurants offer decent, inexpensive food to a loyal local following: **Browns** fills an old police station just across from the abbey, serving English food throughout the day (£8–15 meals, daily 12:00–23:00, kid-friendly, nice terrace, half-block east of the abbey, Orange Grove, tel. 01225/461-199). Family-friendly **Ask** is a similar place up the street (pizza and pasta for £7, good salads, daily 12:00–23:00, George Street but entrance on Broad Street, tel. 01225/789-997).

The **Moon and Sixpence,** prized by locals for its quality international cuisine, is tucked away on a quiet lane. It's dressy, with well-presented food. Call first, as they may be closed for renovation in 2008 (£9 two-course lunch, £29 three-course dinner, daily 12:00–14:30 & 17:30–22:30, ground floor is preferable to upstairs, fine garden seating, 6a Broad Street, tel. 01225/460-962).

Guildhall Market, across from Pulteney Bridge, has produce stalls with food for picnickers. At its inexpensive **Market Café,** you can slurp a curry or sip a tea while surrounded by stacks of used books, bananas on the push list, and honest-to-goodness old-time locals (£4 meals, Mon–Sat 8:00–17:00, closed Sun, a block north of the abbey, on High Street).

The **Cornish Bakehouse,** near the Guildhall Market, has good take-away pasties (open until 17:30, off High Street at 11a The Corridor, tel. 01225/426-635).

Supermarkets: **Waitrose,** at the Podium shopping center, is great for picnics, with a good salad bar (Mon–Fri 8:30–20:00, Sat 8:30–19:00, Sun 11:00–17:00, just west of Pulteney Bridge and across from post office on High Street). **Marks & Spencer,** near the train station, has a grocery at the back of its department store, and the pleasant, inexpensive Café Revive on the top floor (Mon–Fri 8:30–19:00, Sat 8:30–18:00, Sun 11:00–17:00, Stall Street).

East of Pulteney Bridge

No. 5 Restaurant serves classic French and Mediterranean cuisine in a stylish setting (£16–20 main courses with vegetables, daily 12:00–14:30 & 18:30–22:00, later on Fri–Sat, Mon–Tue are "bring your own bottle of wine" nights—no corkage fee, reservations smart on weekends, just over Pulteney Bridge at 5 Argyle Street, tel. 01225/444-499).

Rajpoot Tandoori, next door to No. 5, serves—by all assessments—the best Indian food in Bath. You'll hike down deep into a cellar where the plush Indian atmosphere and award-winning cooking makes paying the extra pounds palatable. The seating is tight and the ceilings low, but it's air-conditioned (£8 three-course lunch special, £10 plates, £20 dinners, daily 12:00–14:30 & 18:00–23:00, 4 Argyle Street, tel. 01225/466-833, Ali).

Yak Yeti Yak Restaurant, a fun Nepali place way down in the basement, is run by a cheerful, hardworking Nepali family that cooks up great traditional food at prices a Sherpa could handle (£6–7 lunches, £15 fixed-price dinner for carnivores, £12 for vegetarians, daily 12:00–14:00 & 18:00–22:00, plenty of vegetarian plates, 12A Argyle Street, tel. 01225/442-299).

The Boater offers a £5 lunch in its huge, pleasant beer garden overlooking the river. It's popular with rowdy twentysomethings, who come together to watch soccer, drink, play pool, and enjoy its good ales and riverside perch. On tap is Bombardier Ale, made in nearby Wells (lunch served 12:00–15:00, otherwise drinks only, open Mon–Sat 11:00–23:00, Sun 12:00–20:30, 9 Argyle Street, tel. 01225/464-211).

Between the Circus and Royal Crescent

Bistro Papillon is small, fun, and unpretentious, dishing up "modern-rustic cuisine from the south of France." It has cozy indoor and outdoor seating on a fine pedestrian lane (£9 two-course lunch specials, £9–15 dinners, Tue–Sat 12:00–14:30 & 18:30–22:00, closed Sun–Mon, reservations smart, 2 Margaret's Buildings, tel. 01225/310-064).

TRANSPORTATION CONNECTIONS

Bath's train station is called Bath Spa (train info: tel. 08457-484-950). The National Express bus office is just west of the train station, in the area called South Gate (Mon–Sat 8:00–17:30, closed Sun, bus info tel. 08705-808-080, www.nationalexpress.com).

From London to Bath: To get from London to Bath and see Stonehenge to boot, consider an all-day organized **bus tour** from London (and skip out of the return trip; see page 149).

From Bath to London: You can catch a **train** to London's Paddington Station (2/hr, 90 min, £46 one-way after 9:30, www .firstgreatwestern.co.uk), or save money—but not time—by taking the National Express **bus** to Victoria Station (direct buses nearly hourly, a little over 3 hours, one-way-£17, round-trip-£24).

From Heathrow to Bath: See page 146. Also consider taking a minibus with Alan Price (see "Celtic Horizons" on page 178).

From Bath to London's Airports: You can reach **Heathrow** directly and easily by National Express bus (10/day, 2–3 hrs, £17 one-way, tel. 08705-757-747) or by a train-and-bus combination (take hourly train to Reading, catch twice-hourly airport shuttle bus from there, allow 2.5 hours total, £46, cheaper for BritRail passholders). Or take the Celtic Horizons minibus to Heathrow; see page 178.

You can get to **Gatwick** by train (about hourly, 2.5 hrs, £40 one-way, transfer in Reading) or by bus (hourly, 4.5 hrs, £25 one-way).

From Bristol Airport to Bath: Located about 20 miles west of Bath, this airport is closer than Heathrow, but they haven't worked out good connections to Bath yet. From Bristol Airport, your most convenient options are to take a taxi (£35) or call Alan Price (see "Celtic Horizons" on page 178). Otherwise, you can take the Bristol Airport Flyer (city bus #330 or #331), which takes you to the Temple Meads train station (£5, 2–4/hr, 30-min trip, buy bus ticket at airport info counter or from driver, tell driver you want the Temple Meads train station). At the Temple Meads station, check the departure boards for trains going to the Bath Spa station (3/hr, 15 min, £6). To get from Bath to Bristol Airport, just reverse these directions: Take the train to Temple Meads, then catch the Airport Flyer bus.

From Bath by Train to: Salisbury (2/hr, 1 hr), **Portsmouth** (hourly, 2–2.25 hrs), **Exeter** (2/hr, 1.5–2 hrs, 1 transfer), **Penzance** (1–3/hr, 4.5–5 hrs, 1–3 transfers), **Moreton-in-Marsh** (hourly, 2 hrs, 1–3 transfers), **York** (hourly, 4.5–5 hrs, 1–2 transfers), **Oxford** (hourly, 1.5 hrs, transfer in Didcot), **Cardiff** (hourly, 1 hr), **Birmingham** (hourly, 2–2.5 hrs, transfer in Bristol), and **points north** (from Birmingham, a major transportation hub, trains depart for Blackpool, Scotland, and North Wales; use a train/bus combination to reach Ironbridge Gorge and the Lake District).

From Bath by Bus to: Salisbury (hourly, 2.25 hrs on bus #X4, possible transfer in Warminster or Trowbridge), **Portsmouth** (1 direct bus/day, 3 hrs; more buses with transfer, 7–8 hrs), **Exeter** (4/day, change in Bristol, 3–4 hrs), **Penzance** (3/day, 8–12 hrs, transfer in Bristol), **Cheltenham** or **Gloucester** (1 direct bus/day, 2.5 hrs, more buses with transfer), **Stratford-upon-Avon** (1/day, 4 hrs, transfer in Bristol or Birmingham), and **Oxford** (1 direct bus/day, 2 hrs, more buses with transfer). Buses to **Wells** leave nearly hourly, but the last one back leaves before the evensong service is finished (75 min, last return 17:43).

Bath

NEAR BATH

Glastonbury, Wells, Avebury, Stonehenge, Salisbury, and South Wales

Ooooh, mystery, history. Glastonbury is the ancient home of Avalon, King Arthur, and the Holy Grail. Nearby, medieval Wells gathers around its grand cathedral, where you can enjoy an evensong service. Then get Neolithic at every Druid's favorite stone circles, Avebury and Stonehenge. Salisbury is known for its colorful markets and soaring cathedral.

An hour west of Bath, at St. Fagans National History Museum, you'll find South Wales' story vividly told in a park full of restored houses. Relish the romantic ruins and poetic wax of Tintern Abbey, the lush Wye River Valley, and the quirky Forest of Dean.

Planning Your Time

In England: Avebury, Glastonbury, and Wells make a wonderful day out from Bath. Splicing in Stonehenge is possible but stretching it. Everybody needs to see Stonehenge, but I'll tell you now, it looks just like it looks. You'll know what I mean when you pay to get in and rub up against the rope fence that keeps tourists at a distance. Avebury is the connoisseur's Neolithic circle: more subtle and welcoming.

Wells is simply a cute town, much smaller and more medieval than Bath, with a uniquely beautiful cathedral that's best experienced at the 17:15 evensong service (Sunday at 15:15). Glastonbury is normally done surgically, in two hours: See the abbey, climb the tor, ponder your hippie past (and where you are now), then scram. Just an hour from Bath, Salisbury makes a pleasant stop, particularly on a market day (Tue, Sat, and every other Wed), though its cathedral looks striking anytime.

In Wales: Think of the South Wales sights as a different grouping. Ideally, they fill the day you leave Bath for the

Sights near Bath

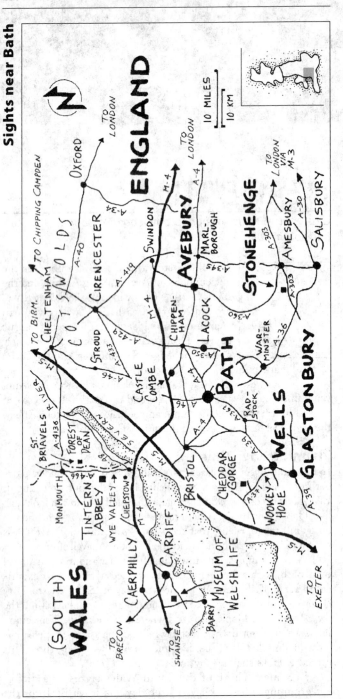

Cotswolds. Anyone interested in Welsh culture can spend four hours in St. Fagans National History Museum. Castle lovers and romantics will want to consider seeing Tintern Abbey, the Forest of Dean, and the castles of Cardiff, Caerphilly, and Chepstow.

For a great day in South Wales, consider this schedule: 9:00–Leave Bath for South Wales; 10:30–Tour St. Fagans; 15:00–Stop at Tintern Abbey and/or a castle of your choice, then drive to the Cotswolds; 18:00–Set up in your Cotswolds home base.

Getting Around

By Bus and Train: Wells and Glastonbury are both easily accessible by bus from Bath. These two towns are also connected with one another by a 9.5-mile foot and bike path.

You can reach Avebury from Bath by taking the #X72 bus to Devizes (hourly, 1 hr), then picking up the #49/X49 bus from Devizes to Avebury (hourly, 30 min, final destination is Swindon).

Various bus companies run these routes, including Stagecoach and the First Bus Company. Buses between Salisbury and Avebury are run by Wilts & Dorset. To find fare information, check with Traveline South West, which combines all the information from these companies into an easy-to-use website that covers all the southwest routes (tel. 0871-200-2233, www.travelinesw.com). Buses run much less frequently on Sundays.

Stonehenge is trickier. If you don't have a car, the most convenient and efficient way to see Avebury and Stonehenge from Bath is to take an all-day bus tour, or a half-day tour just to Stonehenge. Of the tours leaving from Bath, Mad Max is the liveliest (see page 176). Salisbury—with the best public transportation of all these towns—is a good jumping-off point for Stonehenge by tour bus or car.

To get to South Wales from Bath, take a train to Cardiff (transfer in Bristol), then connect by bus (or train) to the sights.

By Car: Drivers can do a 133-mile loop, from Bath to Avebury (25 miles) to Stonehenge (30 miles) to Glastonbury (50 miles) to Wells (6 miles) and back to Bath (22 miles).

A loop from Bath to South Wales is 100 miles, mostly on the 70-mph motorway. Each of the Welsh sights is just off the motorway.

Glastonbury

Marked by its hill, or "tor," and located on England's most powerful line of prehistoric sites (called a "ley" line), the town of Glastonbury gurgles with history and mystery.

In A.D. 37, Joseph of Arimathea—Jesus' wealthy disciple—

Glastonbury

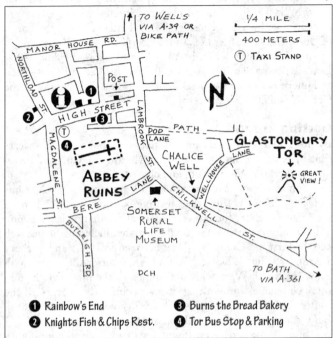

TO WELLS VIA A-39 OR BIKE PATH

¼ MILE

400 METERS

(T) TAXI STAND

MANOR HOUSE RD.

NORTHLOAD ST.

POST

HIGH STREET

LAMBROOK ST.

MAGDALENE ST.

(T)

POD LANE

PATH

DOD LANE

CHALICE WELL

WELLHOUSE LANE

GLASTONBURY TOR

GREAT VIEW!

ABBEY RUINS

LANE

BERE LANE

CHICKWELL

SOMERSET RURAL LIFE MUSEUM

BUTLEIGH RD.

DCH

TO BATH VIA A-361

❶ Rainbow's End
❷ Knights Fish & Chips Rest.
❸ Burns the Bread Bakery
❹ Tor Bus Stop & Parking

brought vessels containing the blood and sweat of Jesus to Glastonbury, and, with them, Christianity came to England. While this story is "proven" by fourth-century writings and accepted by the Church, the King-Arthur-and-the-Holy-Grail legends it inspired are not. (Another, even less-plausible legend claims that Jesus himself visited here with Joseph during his youth.)

The medieval tales of King Arthur came when England needed a morale-boosting folk hero for inspiration during a war with France. They pointed to the ancient Celtic fort at Glastonbury as proof enough of the greatness of the fifth-century warlord Arthur. His supposed remains (along with those of Queen Guinevere) were dug up from the abbey floor, and Glastonbury became woven into the Arthurian legends. Reburied in the abbey choir, their gravesite is a shrine today. Many think the Grail trail ends at the bottom of the Chalice Well (described below), a natural spring at the base of the Glastonbury Tor.

The Glastonbury Abbey was England's most powerful by the 10th century, and was part of a nationwide network of monasteries that by 1500 owned one-sixth of all English land and had four times the income of the crown. Then Henry VIII dissolved the abbeys in 1536. He was particularly harsh on Glastonbury—he not only destroyed the abbey but also hung and quartered the abbot, sending the parts of his body on four different national tours...at the same time.

But Glastonbury rebounded. In an 18th-century tourism campaign, thousands signed affidavits stating that they'd been healed by water from the Chalice Well, and once again Glastonbury was on the tourist map. Today, Glastonbury and its tor are a center for searchers, a little too creepy for mainstream churchgoers but just right for those looking for a place to recharge their crystals.

ORIENTATION

(area code: 01458)
Tourist Information: The TI is on High Street—as are many of the dreadlocked folks who walk it (April–Sept daily 10:00–17:00, until 17:30 Fri–Sat; Oct–March daily 10:00–16:00, until 16:30 Fri–Sat; tel. 01458/832-954, www.glastonbury.co.uk). The TI has several booklets about cycling and walking in the area. The 30p *Glastonbury Town Trail* brochure outlines a good tor-to-town walk (a brisk 10 min). The TI's *Glastonbury Millennium Trail* pamphlet (60p) sends visitors on a historical scavenger hunt, following 20 numbered, marble plaques embedded in the pavement throughout the town.

Located in the TI, the Lake Village Museum—featuring tools made of stones, bones, and antlers—is nothing special. Tuesday is market day for crafts, knickknacks, and produce behind the TI (same hours as TI).

Getting to the Tor: The **Tor Bus** shuttles visitors from the town center and abbey to the base of the tor. If you ask, the bus will stop at the Somerset Rural Life Museum and the Chalice Well (£2, 2/hr, daily Easter–Sept 9:30–19:30, Oct–Easter 10:00–15:30, bus does not run during lunchtime, catch bus at St. Dunstan's parking lot in the town center, pick up schedule at TI). It's £3 one-way by **taxi**—an easier and more economical choice if you're traveling in a group.

Glastonbury Festival: Every summer (June 20–22 in 2008), the gigantic Glastonbury Festival—billing itself as the "largest music and performing arts festival in the world"—brings all manner of postmodern flower children to its "Healing Fields." Music fans and London's beautiful people (such as supermodel Kate Moss) make the trek to see popular bands such as the Arctic

Monkeys and Radiohead. If you're near Glastonbury during the festival, anticipate increased traffic and crowds (especially on public transportation; over 100,000 tickets generally sell out), even though the actual music venue is six miles east of town (www .glastonburyfestivals.co.uk).

SIGHTS AND ACTIVITIES

▲▲**Glastonbury Abbey**—The evocative ruins of the first Christian sanctuary in the British Isles stand mysteriously alive in a lush, 36-acre park. Start your visit in

the good little museum, where a model shows the abbey in its pre–Henry VIII splendor, and exhibits tell the story of a place "grandly constructed to entice even the dullest minds to prayer." Today, the abbey attracts people who find God within. Tie-dyed, starry-eyed pilgrims seem to float through the grounds naturally high. Others lie on the grave of King Arthur, whose burial site is marked off in the center of the abbey ruins. The only surviving intact building is the abbot's conical kitchen. Here, you'll often find a monk demonstrating life in the abbey kitchen in a kind of medieval cooking show. If you'd like to see the demo, it's best to phone ahead for the schedule, especially off-season. They also offer earnest, costumed "Living History" reenactments (included with your ticket), generally daily March through October at 10:30, 12:00, 14:00, and 16:00—confirm times when you enter (£4.50, bring cash or pay 50p extra to use credit card, daily June–Aug 9:00–18:00, Sept–May 9:30 or 10:00 to dusk, closing times vary in the winter—call to check, last entry 30 min before closing, informative but long-winded 40-min audioguide-£2, check display clock or ask at entry for monk's "show" times, tel. 01458/832-267, www.glastonburyabbey.com).

Somerset Rural Life Museum—Exhibits include peat digging, cider making, and cheese making. The Abbey Farmhouse is now a collection of domestic and work mementos that illustrate the life of farmer John Hodges "from the cradle to the grave." The fine 14th-century barn, with its beautifully preserved wooden ceiling, is filled with Victorian farm tools and enthusiastic schoolchildren (free, Easter–Oct Tue–Fri 10:00–17:00, Sat–Sun 14:00–18:00, closed Mon; Nov–Easter Tue–Sat 10:00–17:00, closed Sun–Mon; last entry 30 min before closing, free parking, 8-min walk from abbey, at intersection of Bere Lane and Chilkwell Street, tel. 01458/831-197, www.somerset.gov.uk/museums).

Chalice Well—The well is surrounded by a peaceful garden. According to tradition, Joseph of Arimathea brought the chalice from the Last Supper to Glastonbury in A.D. 37. Even if the chalice is not in the bottom of the well and the water is red from iron ore and not Jesus' blood, the tranquil setting is one where nature's harmony is a joy to ponder. The stones of the well shaft date from the 12th century, and are believed to have come from the church in Glastonbury Abbey (which

was destroyed by fire). During the 18th century, pilgrims flocked to Glastonbury for the well's healing powers. Even today, there's a moment of silence at noon for world peace and healing. Have a drink or take some of the precious water home (£3, daily 10:00–18:00, less off-season, last entry 30 min before closing, £1–£1.50 bottles available, on Chilkwell Street; 4-min walk from Rural Life Museum, where drivers can park; tel. 01458/831-154, www.chalicewell.org.uk).

Glastonbury Tor—Seen by many as a kind of Mother Goddess symbol, the tor, a natural plug of sandstone on clay, has an undeniable geological charisma. The tower is the remnant of a 14th-century church of St. Michael. A fine Somerset view rewards those who hike to its 520-foot summit.

Back in the 1940s, Catherine Maltwood identified the signs of the zodiac in the ancient rock formations, hedgerows, and waterways surrounding Glastonbury. She saw the tor as the head of the phoenix, another symbol for Aquarius. If this sounds intriguing, you can buy her zodiac map at the TI (£3). The tor is a short bus ride or walk from the town center. Drivers should park at the nearby Rural Life Museum.

Path from Glastonbury Tor to Wells—A 9.5-mile cycling and foot path (a.k.a. Syrens Project) begins at the bottom of Glastonbury Tor and ends in Wells. It's marked by nine large Neolithic-looking sculptures along the way; designed by local artists, these funky stones are carved with willow leaves, swans, and other images of the journey. Note that you can rent a bike in Wells, but not in Glastonbury. For more on cycling from Wells to Glastonbury, see page 210.

Shopping—If you need spiritual guidance or just a rune reading, wander through the **Glastonbury Experience,** a New Age mall at the bottom of High Street.

EATING

Glastonbury has no shortage of healthy eateries. The vegetarian **Rainbow's End** is one of several fine lunch cafés for beans, salads, herbal teas, yummy homemade sweets, and New Age people-watching (£5–6 meals, daily 10:00–16:00, a few doors up from the TI, 17 High Street, tel. 01458/833-896). If you're looking for a midwife or a male-bonding tribal meeting, check their notice board.

Knights Fish and Chips Restaurant has been in business since 1909 because it serves good food (Mon 17:00–21:30, Tue–Sat 12:00–14:15 & 17:00–21:30, closed Sun, eat in or take away, 5 Northload Street, tel. 01458/831-882).

Burns the Bread makes hearty pasties (savory meat pies) as well as fresh pies, sandwiches, delicious cookies, and pastries. Ask about the Torsy Moorsy Cake, or try a gingerbread man made with real ginger. Grab a pasty and picnic with the ghosts of Arthur and Guinevere in the Abbey ruins (daily 6:00–17:00, 14 High Street, tel. 01458/831-532).

TRANSPORTATION CONNECTIONS

The nearest train station is in Bath. Local buses are run by First Bus Company (tel. 0845-606-4466, www.firstgroup.com).

From Glastonbury by Bus to: Wells (2/hr, 20 min, bus #375/376 runs frequently, bus #29 only 6/day), **Bath** (hourly, allow 2 hours, take bus #375/376 or #29 to Wells, transfer to bus #173 to Bath, 75 min between Wells and Bath). Buses are sparse on Sundays (generally one bus every two hours).

Wells

Because this wonderfully preserved little town has a cathedral, it can be called a city. While it's the biggest town in Somerset, it's England's smallest cathedral city (pop. 9,400), with one of its most interesting cathedrals and a wonderful evensong service. Wells has more medieval buildings still doing what they were originally built to do than any town you'll visit. Market day fills the town square on Wednesdays and Saturdays.

Tourist Information: The TI, on the main square, has information about the town's sights and nearby cheese factories (May–Sept Mon–Sat 9:00–17:00,

Wells

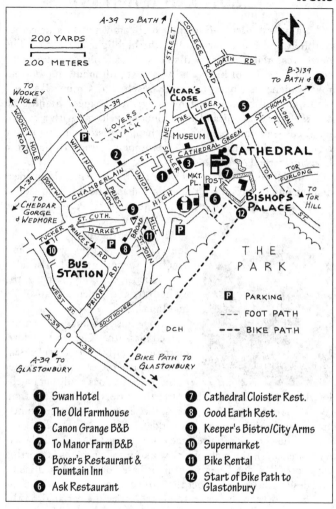

200 YARDS
200 METERS

A-39 TO BATH ↑

TO WOOKEY HOLE

WOOKEY HOLE ROAD

A-39

LOVERS WALK

WHITING

DORTWAY

A-39

TO CHEDDAR GORGE & WEDMORE

CHAMBERLAIN

PRIEST ROW

ST. CUTH.

MARKET

TUCKER

PRINCES RD.

PRIORY RD.

BUS STATION

WEST ST.

A-39

A-371

A-39 TO GLASTONBURY

COLLEGE ROAD

STREET

NORTH RD.

B-3139 TO BATH ↗

NEW ST.

SADLER

THE LIBERTY

VICAR'S CLOSE

MUSEUM

CATHEDRAL GREEN

UNION ST.

HIGH ST.

MKT. PL.

POST

BROAD ST.

ST. JOHN

MILL ST.

CATHEDRAL

ST. THOMAS

LORNE

ST. THOMAS PL.

TOR

TOR FURLONG

TO TOR HILL

BISHOP'S PALACE

THE PARK

SOUTHOVER

DCH

BIKE PATH TO GLASTONBURY

P PARKING
--- FOOT PATH
--- BIKE PATH

1 Swan Hotel
2 The Old Farmhouse
3 Canon Grange B&B
4 To Manor Farm B&B
5 Boxer's Restaurant & Fountain Inn
6 Ask Restaurant
7 Cathedral Cloister Rest.
8 Good Earth Rest.
9 Keeper's Bistro/City Arms
10 Supermarket
11 Bike Rental
12 Start of Bike Path to Glastonbury

Near Bath

Sun 10:00–16:00; April and Oct Mon–Sat 10:00–17:00, Sun 10:00–16:00; Nov–March Mon–Sat 10:00–15:00, closed Sun; tel. 01749/672-552, www.wells.gov.uk).

Local Guide: Edie Westmoreland offers 90-minute town walks in the summer by appointment (£15/group of two to five people, £3/person for six or more, tours usually start at Penniless Porch on town square, book three days in advance, tel. 01934/832-350, mobile 0789-983-6706, ebwestmoreland@btinternet.com).

SIGHTS AND ACTIVITIES

▲▲**Wells Cathedral**—England's first completely Gothic cathedral (dating from about 1200) is the highlight of the city. The newly restored west front displays almost 300 original 13th-century carvings of kings and the **Last Judgment.** The bottom row of niches is empty, too easily reached by Cromwell's men, who were hell-bent on destroying "graven images." Stand back and imagine it as a grand Palm Sunday welcome with a cast of hundreds—all gaily painted back then, choristers singing boldly from holes above the doors and trumpets tooting through the holes up by the 12 apostles.

Inside, you're immediately struck by the general lightness and the unique "scissors" or hourglass-shaped **double arch** (added  in 1338 to transfer weight from the west—where the foundations were sinking under the tower's weight—to the east, where they were firm). You'll be warmly greeted, reminded how expensive it is to maintain the cathedral, and given a map of its highlights.

Don't miss the fine 14th-century stained glass (the "Golden Window" on the east wall). The medieval **clock,** which depicts the earth at the center of the universe, does a silly but much-loved joust on the quarter hour (north transept, its face dates from 1390). The outer ring shows hours, the second ring shows minutes, and the inner ring shows the lunar dates.

In the **choir** (or "quire," the central zone where the daily services are sung), the embroidery work on the cushions is worth a close look. The floral roof painting is based on the original medieval design, discovered under the 17th-century whitewash.

Head over to the south transept. Notice the carvings on the pillars. The figures depict medieval life—a man with a toothache, another man with a thorn in his foot, and, around the top, a ticked-off farmer chasing fruit stealers. Look at the tombstones set in the floor. Notice there is no brass. After the Reformation in the 1530s, the church was short on cash, so they sold the brass to pay for roof repairs.

Walk the well-worn steps up to the grand, fan-vaulted **Chapter House**—an intimate place for the theological equivalent of a huddle among church officials. The cathedral **Reading Room** (£1, Fri–Sat 14:30–16:30 only), with a few old manuscripts, offers a peek into a real 15th-century library.

The requested £5.50 donation for the cathedral is not intended to keep you out (daily Easter–Sept 7:30–19:00 or dusk, Oct–Easter 7:30–18:00; 60-min tours Mon–Sat April–Oct at 10:00, 13:00, 14:00, and 15:00; pay £3 photography fee at info desk, no flash in choir, good shop and handy Cathedral Cloister Restaurant, tel. 01749/674-483, www.wellscathedral.org.uk).

The mediocre city museum is next door to the cathedral. For a fine cathedral-and-town view from your own leafy hilltop bench, hike 10 minutes from here up Tor Hill.

▲▲**Cathedral Evensong Service**—The cathedral choir takes full advantage of heavenly acoustics with a nightly 45-minute evensong service. You will sit right in the old choir as you listen to a great pipe organ and boys', girls', and men's voices (Mon–Sat at 17:15, Sun at 15:00, generally no service when school is out July–Aug unless a visiting choir performs, tel. 01749/674-483 to check). At 17:05 (Sun at 15:05) the verger ushers visitors to their seats. There's usually plenty of room.

On weekdays and Saturdays, if you need to catch the last bus to Bath at 17:43, request a seat on the north side of the presbytery, so you can slip out the side door without disturbing the service (10-min walk to station from cathedral).

The cathedral also hosts several evening **concerts** each month (£7–23, most around £16, generally Thu–Sat at 19:00 or 19:30, box office open Mon–Sat 14:00–16:30, closed Sun, tel. 01749/832-201). Concert tickets are also available at the TI.

Cathedral Green—In the Middle Ages, the cathedral was enclosed within the "Liberty," an area free from civil jurisdiction until the 1800s. The Liberty included the green on the west side of the cathedral, which, from the 13th to the 17th centuries, was a burial place for common folk, including 17th-century plague victims. During the Edwardian period, a local character known as Boney Foster used to dig up the human bones and sell them to tourists. The green later became a cricket pitch, then a field for grazing animals, and finally the perfect setting for an impressive cathedral.

Vicar's Close—Lined with perfectly pickled 14th-century houses, this is the oldest complete street in Europe (just a block north of the cathedral). It was built to house the vicar's choir, and it still houses church officials. Go into the chapel at the farthest end of the close and look out of the house on the left, which has been restored to its original state.

Bishop's Palace—Next to the cathedral stands the Bishop's Palace, built in the 13th century and still in use today as the residence of the Bishop of Bath and Wells. The interior offers a look at elegant furniture and clothing (£5; April–Oct Mon–Sat 10:30–18:00, Sun 12:00–18:00; closed Nov–March and some

Sat–Sun for events—call to confirm, guidebook-£2, tel. 01749/678-691, www.bishopspalacewells.co.uk).

The palace's spring-fed moat, built in the 14th century to protect the bishop during squabbles with the borough, now serves primarily as a pool for swans, which ring the bell to the left of the drawbridge for food. The bridge was last drawn in 1831. On the grounds (past the old-timers playing a proper game of croquet) is a fine garden with the idyllic springs that gave the city its name.

Bike Ride from Wells to Glastonbury Tor—The 9.5-mile cycling and foot path is ideal for cyclists and hikers. To find the trailhead, walk behind the cathedral, following along the moat, and look for the signs that lead you to Glastonbury (small blue metal signs say *byway*, with a red number 3). The trail is part of the West Country Way Cycle Route, which runs from Bristol to Padstow—including the small section from Wells to Glastonbury. This part of the trail is also marked by nine hulking stone sculptures. For more information or to buy the £6 *West Country Way Cycle Route* map, stop by the TI (see page 206). The path is also part of the National Cycle Route.

You can rent a bike in Wells at **Bike City** (£7.50/half-day, £15/day, Mon–Thu 9:00–17:30, Fri–Sat 9:00–17:00, closed Sun, helmets available, 31 Broad Street, tel. 01749/671-711, www.bikecity.biz). There is no bike rental in Glastonbury.

Near Wells

Near Bath

Cheddar Cheese—If you're in the mood for a picnic, drop by any local aromatic cheese shop for a great selection of tasty Somerset cheeses. Real farmhouse cheddar puts American cheddar to Velveeta shame. The **Cheddar Gorge Cheese Company,** eight miles west of Wells, welcomes and educates guests (£2, daily 10:00–16:00; take A39, then A371 to Cheddar Gorge; tel. 01934/742-810). For all things cheddar in Somerset, check out www.cheddarsomerset.co.uk.

▲Wookey Hole Caves—This lowbrow commercial venture, possibly worthwhile as family entertainment, is a real hodgepodge. It starts with a 35-minute wookey-guided tour of some big but mediocre caves, complete with history, geology lessons, and witch stories. Then you're free to wander through a traditional papermaking mill, with a demonstration, and into a 19th-century amusements room—a riot of color, funny mirrors, and old penny-arcade machines that visitors can actually play for as long as their pennies

last (pennies on sale there).
They even have old girlie
shows (£12.50 at the gate,
discounted tickets available
online and at TIs in Wells
and Bath, daily April–Oct
10:00–17:00, Nov–March
10:00–16:00, 2 miles east of
Wells, tel. 01749/672-243,
www.wookey.co.uk).

Scrumpy Farms—Scrumpy is the wonderfully dangerous hard
cider brewed in this part of England. You don't find it served in
many pubs because of the unruly crowd it attracts. Scrumpy, at 8
percent alcohol, will rot your socks. "Scrumpy Jack," carbonated
mass-produced cider, is not real scrumpy. The real stuff is "rough
farmhouse cider." This is potent stuff. It's said some farmers throw
a side of beef into the vat, and when fermentation is done only the
teeth remain.

TIs list local cider farms open to the public, such as
Mr. Wilkins' Land's End Cider Farm, a great Back Door travel
experience (free, Mon–Sat 10:00–20:00, Sun 10:00–13:00; west
of Wells in Mudgley, take B3139 from Wells to Wedmore, then
B3151 south for 2 miles, farm is a quarter mile off B3151—tough to
find, get close and ask locals; tel. 01934/712-385).

Glastonbury's **Somerset Rural Life Museum** has a cider
exhibit (see page 204). Apples are pressed from August through
December. Hard cider, while not quite scrumpy, is still typical of
the West Country, but more fashionable, decent, and accessible.
You can get a pint of hard cider at nearly any pub, drawn straight
from the barrel—dry, medium, or sweet.

SLEEPING

(area code: 01749)
Wells is a pleasant overnight stop with a handful of agreeable
B&Bs and eateries. The Swan Hotel and the Canon Grange B&B
(as well as the nearby Boxer's Restaurant at the Fountain Inn,
below) are all within a block of each other, behind (east of) the
cathedral. The Old Farmhouse is a short walk away. If you're coming in on B3139 from Bath, they're just before the cathedral.

In Wells

$$$ Swan Hotel, facing the cathedral, is a big, comfortable 50-
room hotel that's part of the Best Western chain. The price range
for these Tudor-style rooms varies based on whether you want
extras like a four-poster bed or a view of the cathedral (Sb-£90–105,

Sleep Code

(£1 = about $2, country code: 44)
S = Single, **D** = Double/Twin, **T** = Triple, **Q** = Quad, **b** = bathroom,
s = shower only. Unless otherwise indicated, you can assume
credit cards are accepted and breakfast is included.

To help you sort easily through these listings, I've divided
the rooms into three categories based on the price for a standard double room with bath:

$$$ Higher Priced—Most rooms £80 or more.
$$ Moderately Priced—Most rooms between £40–80.
$ Lower Priced—Most rooms £40 or less.

Db-£130–170, often cheaper if you just show up, ask about their weekend deals, full breakfast-£9.50, continental breakfast-£6.50, Sadler Street, tel. 01749/836-300, fax 01749/836-301, www .swanhotelwells.co.uk, info@swanhotelwells.co.uk).

$$ The Old Farmhouse, a five-minute walk from the town center, welcomes you with a secluded front garden and tastefully decorated rooms (Db-£70, two-night minimum, secured parking, 62 Chamberlain Street, tel. & fax 01749/675-058, www.plus44 .com/oldfarmhouse, charming owner Felicity Wilkes).

$$ Canon Grange B&B is a 15th-century, watch-your-head beamed house directly in front of the cathedral. It has five homey rooms and a cozy charm (Sb-£30–48, Db-£54–65, Db with cathedral view-£72, family room-£65 plus £10–15/child, on the cathedral green, tel. 01749/671-800, www.canongrange.co.uk, canongrange @email.com, Annette).

Near Wells

$$ At Manor Farm B&B, two miles northwest of Wells, Fiona Fridd and her family will welcome you to their restored 14th-century manor house. Come here for a taste of English country life, complete with billiards, open fires, and wood beams (Sb-£50–60, Db-£70–80, family room-£110–125, two-night minimum for peak season weekends, Old Frome Road in East Horrington, tel. 01749/679-832, fax 01749/679-849, www.somersetbed.co.uk, info@somersetbed.co.uk).

EATING

Boxer's Restaurant, in the Fountain Inn, serves restaurant-quality food in a cheery pub atmosphere. Their award-winning cheese plate lets you sample cheddar and its local cousins. For a good, traditional local dish, try their founders beef pie (£8–14 meals, Mon–Sat 12:00–14:00 & 18:00–22:00, Sun 12:00–14:00 & 19:00–21:30, creative cooking, veggie options, real ales, draft cider, reservations wise on weekends, behind cathedral on St. Thomas Street, tel. 01749/672-317).

Ask, a pasta chain, is a pleasant option on the main square (£7–8 meals, daily 12:00–23:00, Market Place, tel. 01749/677-681).

For a heavenly lunch, consider the **Cathedral Cloister Restaurant** in the cathedral, along a lovely stone corridor with lead-glass windows (£4–7.50 lunches, Mon–Sat 10:00–17:00, Sun 13:00–17:00; closes at 16:30 and occasional on Sun in winter).

Good Earth offers healthy quiches, pastas, and salads in their cheerful, yellow-walls-and-pine-tables interior. Follow signs through the multi-room labyrinth to "counter service" (£5 meals, Mon–Sat 9:00–17:00, closed Sun, 4 Priory Road at bottom of Broad Street, tel. 01749/678-600).

The **Keeper's Bistro/City Arms Pub and Restaurant,** run by friendly owner Jim, is a favorite with locals. A city jail in Tudor times and still circled by medieval walls, the restaurant serves a variety of regional specialties, including veggie alternatives. The adjacent pub (called Arches) has seven ales and three ciders on tap (£6–10 meals, Mon–Sat 9:00–22:00, Sun 9:00–21:00, terrace seating, 69 High Street, tel. 01749/673-916).

For picnickers, a Tesco **supermarket** is located west of the bus station on Tucker Street.

TRANSPORTATION CONNECTIONS

The nearest train station is in Bath. The bus station in Wells is actually a bus lot, at the intersection of Priory and Princes Roads. Local buses are run by First Bus Company (for Wells, tel. 0845-606-4446, www.firstgroup.com), while buses to and from London are run by National Express (tel. 08705-808-080, www.nationalexpress.com).

From Wells by Bus to: Bath (hourly, 75 min, last bus #173 leaves at 17:43), **Glastonbury** (2/hr, 20 min, bus #375/376 runs frequently, bus #29 only 6/day), **London**'s Victoria Coach Station (£26–28, hourly, 4 hrs, change in Bristol, buses run daily 6:20–17:45).

Avebury

The stone circle at Avebury is bigger (16 times the size), less touristy, and, for many, more interesting than Stonehenge. You're free to wander among 100 stones, ditches, mounds, and curious patterns from the past, as well as the village of Avebury, which grew up in the middle of this fascinating, 1,400-foot-wide Neolithic circle.

In the 14th century, in a kind of frenzy of religious paranoia, Avebury villagers buried many of these mysterious pagan stones. Their 18th-century descendants broke up the remaining stones and used them for building material. In modern times, the buried stones were dug up and re-erected. Concrete markers show where the missing broken-up stones once stood.

ORIENTATION

Avebury, just a little village with a big stone circle, is easier to reach by car than public transportation (see "Getting Around," page 201).

Tourist Information: The TI is located within the town chapel (June–Oct Tue–Sun 10:00–17:30, closed Mon; April–May Tue–Sun 10:00–17:00, closed Mon; Nov–March Thu–Sun 10:00–16:30, closed Mon–Wed; closes at 14:30 on the first and third Sunday year-round; Green Street, tel. 01672/539-425, www.visitkennet.co.uk/avebury).

Arrival by Car: You must pay to park in Avebury. Your most reliable bet is to follow signs to the public pay-and-display parking lot, which is a three-minute walk from the village (parking-£5 9:00–14:30, £3 after 14:30, lot closes at 18:00). The Red Lion (listed below) also has a pay lot available—when there's no barbeque or other event going on outside—and will refund your money if you eat in their restaurant (parking-£3–5, depending on how long you stay). No other public parking is available in the village.

SIGHTS

▲▲**Stone Circle**—Take the one-mile walk around the circle (free, always open).

Alexander Keiller Museum—This archaeology museum has an interactive exhibit in a 17th-century barn (£4.20, daily April–Oct 10:00–18:00, Nov–March 10:00–16:00, tel. 01672/539-250).

Silbury Hill—Notice the pyramid-shaped hill, a 130-foot-high, yet-to-be-explained mound of chalk just outside of Avebury. Almost 5,000 years old, this mound is the largest man-made object in prehistoric Europe (with the surface area of London's Trafalgar Square and the height of the Nelson Column). It's a reminder that you've just scratched the surface of England's mysterious ancient and religious landscape.

EATING AND SLEEPING

The pleasant **Circle Restaurant** serves healthy, hearty, à la carte meals, including at least one vegetarian soup, and cream teas on most days (daily April–Oct 10:00–16:00, Nov–March 11:00–16:00, next to National Trust store, tel. 01672/539-514).

The Red Lion has inexpensive, greasy pub grub; a creaky, well-worn, dart-throwing ambience; and a medieval well in its dining room (£6–12 meals, Mon–Sat 11:00–21:00, Sun 12:00–21:00, tel. 01672/539-266).

Sleeping in Avebury makes lots of sense, since the stones are lonely and wide open all night. **$$ Mrs. Dixon's B&B,** up the road from the public parking lot, rents three small, tidy rooms. Look for the green-and-white *Bed & Breakfast* sign from the main road (S-£40, D-£55, cash only, parking available, 6 Beckhampton Road, tel. 01672/539-588, run by earthy Mrs. Dixon and crew).

Stonehenge

Stonehenge—older than the pyramids, the Acropolis, and the Colosseum—amazed medieval Europeans, who figured it was built by a race of giants. And it still impresses visitors today. As one of Europe's most iconic sights, Stonehenge does a valiant job of retaining an air of mystery and majesty (partly because cordons, which keep hordes of tourists from trampling all over it, create the illusion that it stands alone in a field). While some people are underwhelmed by Stonehenge, most of its nearly one million annual visitors find that it's worth the trip.

Cost, Hours, Information: £6.30, daily June–Aug 9:00–19:00, mid-March–May and Sept–mid-Oct 9:30–18:00, mid-Oct–mid-March 9:30–16:00; shorter hours and possible closures June 20–22 due to huge, raucous solstice crowds; entry includes worthwhile hour-long audioguide—though they sometimes run out, £3 parking fee likely in summer—refundable with paid admission,

tel. 01980/623-108, www.english-heritage.org.uk/stonehenge). The plans for Stonehenge over the next several years are to divert nearby roads away from the ancient site and create a new visitors center, designed to blend in with the landscape and make the stone circle feel more pristine. Visitors will park farther away and ride a shuttle bus to the site.

Getting There: It's well-signed just off A303. It's about 15 minutes north of Salisbury, an hour east of Glastonbury, and 45 minutes south of Avebury. From Salisbury, head north on A345 (Castle Road) through Amesbury, then go west on A303 for 1.5 miles and watch for signs. For tours of Stonehenge from Bath, see page 176 (Mad Max is best); for tours from Salisbury, see "Helpful Hints" in Salisbury, page 220.

❍ Self-Guided Tour: The entrance fee includes a good audioguide, but this tour will help make your visit even more meaningful.

Walk in from the parking lot, buy your ticket, pick up your included audioguide, and head through the underpass beneath the road. On the way up the ramp, notice the artist's rendering of what Stonehenge once looked like.

As you approach the massive structure, walk right up to the knee-high cordon and let your fellow 21st-century tourists melt away. It's just you and the druids...

England has hundreds of stone circles, but Stonehenge—which literally means "hanging stones"—is unique. It's the only one that has horizontal crosspieces (called lintels) spanning the vertical monoliths, and the only one with stones that have been made smooth and uniform. What you see here is a bit more than half the original structure—the rest was quarried centuries ago for other buildings.

Now do a slow counterclockwise spin around the monument, and ponder the following points. As you walk, mentally flesh out the missing pieces and re-erect the rubble. Knowledgeable guides posted around the site are happy to answer your questions.

Built sometime between 3000 and 1000 B.C., Stonehenge still functions as a remarkably accurate celestial calendar. As the sun rises on the summer solstice (June 21), the "heel stone"—the one set apart from the rest, near the road—lines up with the sun and the altar at the center of the stone circle. A recent study of more than 300 similar circles in Britain found that each was designed to calculate the movement of the sun, moon, and stars, and to predict eclipses in order to help early societies know when to plant, harvest, and party. Even in modern times, as the summer solstice sun sets in just the right slot at Stonehenge, pagans boogie.

In addition to being a calendar, Stonehenge is built at the precise point where six ley lines intersect. While people today don't pay much attention to these lines of magnetic power criss-crossing the globe, they were paramount to prehistoric peoples. (Significantly, there are some 500 burial mounds within a three-mile radius of Stonehenge—most likely belonging to kings and chieftains.) Without realizing it, you follow these ley lines all the time: Many of England's modern highways are built on top of pre-historic paths, and many churches are built on the site of prehis-toric monuments where ley lines intersect. If you're a skeptic, ask one of the guides at Stonehenge to demonstrate the ley lines with a pair of L-shaped divining rods...creepy and convincing.

Notice that two of the stones (facing the entry passageway) are blemished. At the base of one monolith, it looks like someone has pulled back the stone to reveal a concrete skeleton. This is actually a clumsy repair job to fix damage done by souvenir-seekers long ago, who would actually rent a hammer and chisel to take home a piece of Stonehenge. On the stone to the right of the repaired one, notice that the back isn't covered with the same thin layer of protective lichen as the others. This lichen—and some of the stone itself—was sandblasted off to remove graffiti. (No wonder they've got Stonehenge roped off now.)

The builders of Stonehenge used two different types of stones. The tall, stout monoliths and lintels are made of sandstone blocks called sarsen stones. Most of the monoliths weigh about 25 tons (the largest is 45 tons), and the lintels are about seven tons apiece (the sarsen stones were brought from "only" 20 miles away). The shorter stones in the middle are called "bluestones" and came from the south coast of Wales—240 miles away. (Close if you're taking a train, but far if you're packing a megalith.) Imagine the logistical puzzle of floating six-ton stones up the River Avon, then rolling them on logs to this position...an impressive feat, even in our era of skyscrapers.

Why didn't the builders of Stonehenge use what seem like perfectly adequate stones nearby? This, like many other questions about Stonehenge, remains shrouded in mystery. Think again about the ley lines. Ponder the fact that many experts accept none of the explanations of how these giant stones were transported. Then imagine congregations gathering here 4,000 years ago, rais-ing thought levels, creating a powerful life force transmitted along the ley lines. Maybe a particular kind of stone was essential for maximum energy transmission. Maybe the stones were levitated here. Maybe psychics really do create powerful vibes. Maybe not. It's as unbelievable as electricity used to be.

Salisbury

The town of Salisbury, set in the middle of the expansive Salisbury Plain, is a favorite stop for its striking cathedral and intriguing

history. Salisbury was originally settled during the Bronze Age, possibly as early as 600 B.C., and later became a Roman town called Sarum. The modern city of Salisbury developed when the old settlement outgrew its boundaries, prompting the townspeople to move the city from a hill to the river valley below. Most of today's visitors come to marvel at the famous Salisbury Cathedral, featuring England's tallest spire and largest cathedral green. Collectors, bargain hunters, and foodies will savor the town's colorful market days. And archaeologists will dig the region around Salisbury, with England's highest concentration of ancient sites. The town itself is pleasant and walkable, and is a convenient base camp for visiting Stonehenge and Avebury, or for exploring the countryside.

ORIENTATION

(area code: 01722)

Salisbury (pop. 45,000) stretches along the River Avon in the shadow of its huge, landmark cathedral. The heart of the city clusters around Market Square, which is also a handy parking lot on non-market days. High Street, a block to the west, leads to the medieval North Gate of the Cathedral Close. Shoppers explore the streets south of the square. The area north of Market Square is generally residential, with a few shops and pubs.

Tourist Information

The TI, just off Market Square, hands out free city maps, books rooms for no fee, and sells a £1 city guide (May Mon–Sat 9:30–17:00, Sun 10:30–16:30; June–Sept Mon–Sat 9:30–18:00, Sun 10:30–16:30; Oct–April Mon–Sat 9:30–17:00, closed Sun; Fish Row, tel. 01722/334-956, www.visitsalisbury.com).

Ask the TI about 90-minute walking tours (£3.50, April–Oct daily at 11:00, Nov–March Sat–Sun only, depart from TI, other itineraries available, tel. 01722/320-349, www.salisburycityguides.co.uk).

Salisbury

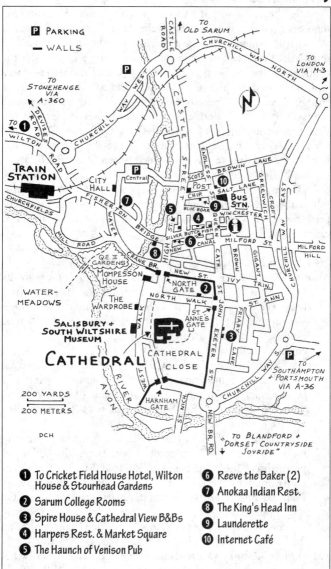

P PARKING
— WALLS

1 To Cricket Field House Hotel, Wilton House & Stourhead Gardens
2 Sarum College Rooms
3 Spire House & Cathedral View B&Bs
4 Harpers Rest. & Market Square
5 The Haunch of Venison Pub
6 Reeve the Baker (2)
7 Anokaa Indian Rest.
8 The King's Head Inn
9 Launderette
10 Internet Café

Arrival in Salisbury

From the **train** station, it's a 10–minute walk into the town center. Leave the station to the left, walk about 50 yards down South Western Road, and take the first right (at The Railway Tavern) onto Mill Road, following it around the bend and through the traffic roundabouts. Soon you'll see the Queen Elizabeth Gardens and the cathedral spire on your right. The road becomes Crane Bridge Road, then Crane Street, and finally New Street before intersecting with Catherine/St. John Street. Market Square and the TI are one long block north (left) on Catherine Street, and it's another two short blocks beyond that to the bus station. The Salisbury Cathedral and recommended Exeter Street B&Bs are to the south (right), on St. John Street.

Drivers will find several parking lots in Salisbury—simply follow the blue *P* signs. The "Central" lot, behind the giant red-brick Sainsbury's store, is within a 10-minute walk of the TI or cathedral.

Helpful Hints

Market Days: For centuries, Salisbury has been known for its lively markets. On Tuesdays and Saturdays, Market Square hosts the charter market, with general goods. Every other Wednesday is the farmers' market. There are also special markets, such as one with French products. Ask the TI for a current schedule.

Tours of Stonehenge: Catch a **City Sightseeing** tour bus from the Salisbury train station, or from Blue Boar Row near the TI (£17, includes £6.30 Stonehenge admission, 3/day mid-May–Sept, off-season only Sat–Sun, 2 hours, www.citysightseeing.co.uk).

   If you miss the City Sightseeing departure times or want to save a few pounds, you could take the Wilts & Dorset **public bus #3** to Stonehenge (£7.50 round-trip with an All-Day Explorer ticket, Stonehenge admission additional £6.30, 7/day in summer, 6/day off-season, departs train station on the hour from 10:00).

   For buses to Avebury's stone circle, see "Transportation Connections," page 225.

Internet: Salisbury Online has access a block from Market Square (£1/15 min, Mon–Sat 10:00–20:00, Sun 11:00–16:00, corner of Endless Street and Salt Lane).

Laundry: Washing Well has full-service (£6.50–12 per load depending on size, 2-hour service, Mon–Sat 8:30–17:30) as well as self-service (Mon–Sat 16:00–20:30, Sun 7:00–20:30, 28 Chipper Lane, tel. 01722/421-874).

SIGHTS

▲▲**Salisbury Cathedral**—This magnificent cathedral, visible for miles around because of its huge spire (the tallest in England at 404 feet), is a wonder to behold.

The surrounding enormous grassy field (called a "close" in Britain) makes the Gothic masterpiece look even larger. What's more impressive is that all this was built in a mere 38 years, while most medieval cathedrals took more than 200 years to complete. When the old hill town of Sarum was moved down to the valley, its cathedral had to be replaced in a hurry. So, in 1220, the townspeople began building, and in 1258 their sparkling-new cathedral was ready for ribbon-cutting. Since the structure was built in just a few decades, its style is uniform, rather than the patchwork of styles common in cathedrals of the time (which often took centuries to construct).

Cost and Hours: £5 suggested donation, mid-June–Aug Mon–Sat 7:15–19:15, Sun 7:15–18:15; Sept–mid-June daily 7:15–18:15; Chapter House usually opens at 9:30 and closes 45 min before the rest of the cathedral, and can be closed entirely for special events; choral evensong Mon–Sat at 17:30, Sun at 15:00; excellent cafeteria, tel. 01722/555-120, recorded info tel. 01722/555-113, www.salisburycathedral.org.uk. This working cathedral opens early for services—be respectful if you arrive when one is in session.

Tower Tours: Imagine building a cathedral on this scale before the invention of cranes, bulldozers, or modern scaffolding. An excellent 90-minute tower tour helps visitors understand how it was done. You'll climb in between the stone arches and the roof to inspect the vaulting and trussing; see a medieval winch that was used in the construction; and finish with the 330-step climb up the narrow tower for a sweeping view of the Wiltshire countryside. The £5.50 tower tour runs in summer Mon–Sat at 11:15, 14:15, 15:15, and 17:00; Sun at 16:30; fewer off-season.

❍ **Self-Guided Tour:** Entering the church, you'll instantly feel the architectural harmony. Volunteer guides posted at the entry are ready to answer your questions. (Free guided tours of the cathedral nave are offered—about twice hourly—when enough people assemble.)

As you look down the nave, notice how the stone columns march identically down the aisle, like a thick gray forest of tree trunks. The arches overhead soar to grand heights, helping church-goers appreciate the vast and amazing heavens.

From the entrance, head to the far wall (the back-left corner). You'll find a model showing how this cathedral was built so quickly in the 13th century. Next to that is the "oldest working clock in existence," dating from the 14th century (the hourly bell has been removed, so as not to interrupt worship services). On the wall by the clock is a bell from the decommissioned ship HMS *Salisbury*. Look closely inside the bell to see the engraved names of crew members' children who were baptized on the ship.

Wander down the aisle past monuments and knights' tombs. When you get to the transept, examine the columns where the arms of the church cross. These posts were supposed to support a more modest bell tower, but when a heavy tower was added 100 years later, the columns bent under the enormous weight, causing the tower to lean sideways. Although the posts were later reinforced, the tower still tilts about 2.5 feet.

Continue down the left side of the choir, and dip into the Morning Chapel. At the back of this chapel, find the spectacular glass prism engraved with images of Salisbury—donated to the church in memory of a soldier who died at the D-Day landing at Normandy.

The oldest part of the church is at the apse (far end), where construction began in 1220: the Trinity Chapel. The giant, modern stained-glass window ponders the theme "prisoners of conscience."

After you leave the nave, pace the cloister and follow signs to the medieval **Chapter House.** All English cathedrals have a chapter house, so-called because it's where the daily Bible verse or chapter is read. These spaces often served as gathering places for conducting church or town business. Here you can see a modest display of cathedral items plus one must-see display: one of the four original copies of the Magna Carta, a document as important to the English as the Constitution is to Americans. This "Great Charter," dating from 1215, settled a dispute between the slimy King John and some powerful barons. Revolutionary for limiting the king's power, the Magna Carta constitutionally guaranteed that the king was not above the law. This was one of the first major victories in the long battle between kings and nobles.

▲**Cathedral Close**—The enormous green surrounding the cathedral is the largest in England, and one of the loveliest. It's cradled in the elbow of the River Avon and ringed by row houses, cottages, and grand mansions. The church owns the houses on

the green and rents them to lucky people with holy connections. A former prime minister, Edward Heath, lived on the green, not because of his political influence, but because he was once the church organist.

The benches scattered around the green are an excellent place for having a romantic moonlit picnic or for gazing thoughtfully at the leaning spire. Although you may be tempted to linger until it's late, don't—this is still private church property...and the heavy medieval gates of the close shut at about 23:00.

A few houses are open to the public, such as the overpriced Mompesson House and the medieval Wardrobe. The most interesting attraction is the...

▲**Salisbury and South Wiltshire Museum**—Occupying the building just opposite the cathedral entry, this eclectic and sprawling collection was heralded by travel writer Bill Bryson as one of England's best. While that's a stretch, the museum does offer a little something for everyone, including exhibits on local archaeology and history, a costume gallery, the true-to-its-name "Salisbury Giant" puppet once used by the tailors' guilds during parades, some J. M. W. Turner paintings of the cathedral interior, and a collection of exquisite Wedgwood china and other ceramics. The highlight is the "Stonehenge Gallery," with informative and interactive exhibits explaining the ancient structure. Since there's not yet a good visitors center at the site itself, this makes for a good pre- or post-Stonehenge activity (£5, Mon–Sat 10:00–17:00, closed Sun, 65 The Close, tel. 01722/332-151, www.salisburymuseum .org.uk).

SLEEPING

(£1 = about $2, country code: 44, area code: 01722)
Salisbury's town center has very few affordable accommodations, and I've listed them below—plus the Cricket Field House, another good choice on the outskirts of town. The town gets particularly crowded during the art festival (late May through early June).

$$$ Cricket Field House, outside of town on A36 toward Milton, overlooks a cricket field, soccer pitch, and golf course. It has 19 clean, comfortable rooms, a gorgeous garden, and plenty of parking (Sb-£60–68, Db-£70–95, Tb-£105–120, depends on season, Wilton Road, tel. & fax 01722/322-595, www .cricketfieldhousehotel.co.uk, cricketfieldcottage@btinternet.com). While this place works best for drivers, it's just a 15-minute bus ride from the city center.

$$$ Sarum College is a theological college renting 48 rooms in its building right on the peaceful Cathedral Close. Much of the year, it houses visitors to the college, but about a third of the time it has rooms for tourists as well. The slightly institutional but clean rooms share hallways with libraries, bookstores, and offices, and the five attic rooms come with grand cathedral views (S-£45, Sb-£50, D-£75, Db-£80–90 depending on size, meals available at additional cost, elevator, 19 The Close, tel. 01722/424-800, fax 01722/338-508, www.sarum.ac.uk, hospitality@sarum.ac.uk).

$$ Spire House B&B, just off the Cathedral Close, is classy and cozy. The four bright, surprisingly quiet rooms come with busy wallpaper and canopied beds (Db-£70, cash only, 84 Exeter Street, tel. 01722/339-213, www.salisbury-bedandbreakfast.com, spire .enquiries@btinternet.com, friendly Lois).

$$ Cathedral View B&B, with four rooms next door at #83, is simpler, but still offers a good value in an outstanding location (Db-£70, cash only, 2-night minimum on weekends, free Wi-Fi, 83 Exeter Street, tel. 01722/502-254, www.cathedral-viewbandb .co.uk, enquiries@cathedral-viewbandb.co.uk, Wenda and Steve).

EATING

There are plenty of atmospheric pubs all over town. For the best variety of restaurants, head to the Market Square area. Many places offer great "early bird" specials before 20:00.

Harpers, an upstairs eatery overlooking Market Square, is beloved by locals for its "nice, proper food." The same chef has been preparing the three-course, £20 special for more than 20 years (£7–12 à la carte dishes, Mon–Sat 12:00–14:00 & 18:00–21:30, closed Sun, 6–7 Ox Row, tel. 01722/333-118).

The Haunch of Venison, possibly dating back to 1320, is a Salisbury institution with creaky, crooked floors. Downstairs, the "occasionally haunted" half-timbered pub serves nouvelle pub grub (£5–6 meals). The restaurant upstairs, while a little pretentious, has a good reputation for its traditional fare (£8–13 main dishes; pub open Mon–Sat 11:00–23:00, Sun 12:00–22:00, food served 12:00–14:30 & 18:00–21:30, reservations smart, look for discount coupons at TI, 1 Minster Street, tel. 01722/411-313).

Reeve the Baker, just up the street from the TI, crafts an array of high-calorie delights and handy pick-me-ups for a fast and affordable lunch. The long cases of pastries and savory treats will make you drool (Mon–Sat 8:00–17:30, closed Sun; one location is next to the TI at 2 Butcher Row, another is at the corner of Market and Bridge streets at 61 Silver Street, tel. 01722/320-367).

Anokaa is a splurge that's highly acclaimed for its updated Indian cuisine. You won't find the same old chicken *tikka* here, but clever newfangled variations on Indian themes, dished up in a dressy contemporary setting (£9–15 main dishes, £7.25 lunch buffet, daily 12:00–14:00 & 17:30–22:30, 60 Fisherton Street, tel.

Near Bath

01722/414-142).

The King's Head Inn is a youthful chain pub with a big, open, modern interior and fine outdoor seating overlooking pretty little River Avon. Its extensive menu has something for everyone (£3–4 sandwiches, £5–7 main dishes, Mon–Fri 7:00–23:00, Sat–Sun 8:00–23:00, kids welcome during the day but they must order meals by 21:00, 1 Bridge Street, tel. 01722/342-050).

TRANSPORTATION CONNECTIONS

From Salisbury by Train to: London's Waterloo Station (1–2/hr, 1.5 hrs), **Bath** (2/hr, 1 hr), **Oxford** (2/hr, 2 hrs, 1–2 transfers), **Portsmouth** (1–2/hr, 1.5 hrs), **Exeter** (1–2/hr, 2–3 hrs, some require transfers), **Penzance** (1–2/hr, 5–5.5 hrs, 1–2 transfers). Train info: tel. 08457-484-950, www.nationalrail.co.uk.

By Bus to: Bath (hourly, 2.25 hrs on bus #X4, possible transfer in Warminster or Trowbridge, £7.50), **Avebury** (6/day, 2 hrs). Many of Salisbury's long-distance buses are run by Wilts & Dorset (tel. 01722/336-855, www.wdbus.co.uk). National Express buses go once a day to Portsmouth (1.5 hrs).

Near Salisbury

Old Sarum

Right here, on a hill overlooking the plain below, is where the original town of Salisbury was founded many centuries ago. While little remains of the old town, the view of the valley is amazing...and a little imagination can transport you back to *very* olde England.

Human settlement in this area stretches back to the Bronze Age, and the Romans, Saxons, and Normans all called this hilltop home. From about 500 B.C. through A.D. 1220, Old Sarum flourished, giving rise to a motte-and-bailey castle, a cathedral, and scores of wooden homes along the town's outer ring. The town grew so quickly that by the Middle Ages, it had outgrown its spot on the hill. In 1220, the local bishop successfully petitioned to move the entire city to the valley below, where space and water was plentiful. So, stone by stone, Old Sarum was packed up and shipped to New Sarum, where builders used nearly all the rubble from the old city to create a brand-new town with a magnificent cathedral.

Old Sarum was eventually abandoned altogether, leaving only a few stone foundations. The grand views of Salisbury from here have "in-spired" painters for ages and provided countless picnickers with a scenic backdrop: Grab a sandwich or snacks from one of the grocery stores in Salisbury or at the excellent Waitrose supermarket on the road between Salisbury and Sarum (Old Sarum entry-£2.90, daily July–Aug 9:00–18:00, April–June and Sept 10:00–17:00, March and Oct 11:00–15:00, Nov–Feb 11:00–15:00, 2 miles north of Salisbury off A345; accessible by Wilts & Dorset buses #5, #6, #8, or #69a; tel. 01722/335-398).

Wilton House

This sprawling estate, with a grand mansion and lush gardens, has been owned by the Earls of Pembroke since King Henry VIII's time. Inside the mansion, you'll find a collection of paintings by Rembrandt and Brueghel, along with quirky odds-and-ends, such as a lock of Queen Elizabeth I's hair. The classic English gardens feature a river lazily winding its way through grasses and under Greek-inspired temples. Jane Austen fans will want to visit this stately home, where parts of 2005's Oscar-nominated *Pride and Prejudice* were filmed. But, alas, Mr. Darcy has checked out (house and garden-£12, garden only-£5; house open May–Aug Sun–Fri 10:30–17:30, closed Sat except holiday weekends; garden open April–Sept daily 10:30–17:30; last entry 1 hour before closing, closed Oct–March; 5 miles west of Salisbury via A36 to Wilton's Minster Street; or bus #60, #60A, or #61 from Salisbury to Wilton; tel. 01722/746-729, www.wiltonhouse.co.uk).

Stourhead Gardens

For a serious taste of traditional English landscape, don't miss this 2,650-acre delight. Stourhead, designed by prolific 18th-century master gardener Lancelot "Capability" Brown, is a wonderland of rolling hills, meandering paths, placid lakes, and colorful trees. It's what every other English estate aspires to be—like nature, but better (house and garden-£11, or £6.60 to see just one; house open mid-March–Oct Fri–Tue 11:30–16:30, closed Wed–Thu; garden open daily 9:00–19:00; closed Nov–mid-March, off B3092 in town of Stourton, 3 miles northwest of Mere, tel. 01747/841-152).

Dorset Countryside Joyride

The Dorset countryside southwest of Salisbury is full of rolling fields, winding country lanes, and quaint villages.

Starting in Salisbury, take A354 through Blandford to Winterborne Whitechurch. From here, follow signs and back roads to Bere Regis, with lovely 15th-century buildings. Follow A35 and B3075 to Wareham, where T. E. Lawrence (a.k.a. Lawrence of Arabia) is buried. Continue south on A351 to **Corfe Castle,** destroyed in a 17th-century siege (£5.30, daily April–Sept 10:00–18:00, March and Oct 10:00–17:00, Nov-Feb 10:00–16:00, tel. 01929/481-294). Retrace A351 to Wareham, then take A352 to Dorchester. Thomas Hardy was born and buried in nearby Stinsford. A35 connects to A37; then take A352 toward Sherborne.

A few miles down is **Cerne Abbas,** where the abbey well is reputed to have healing powers. Abbot's Tea Room has a nice cream tea and runs a B&B (7 Long St, tel. 01300/341-349). A large chalk figure, the **Cerne Abbas Giant,** is carved into a hillside outside town. The giant, possibly a fertility god, looks friendly...maybe a little too friendly. Legend says women having trouble conceiving can be cured by sleeping on the giant.

Leave Cerne Abbas toward Piddletrenthide and continue to **Milton Abbas.** (This area has some of the best town names in Britain, such as Droop, Plush, Pleck, and Folly.) In the 18th century, a wealthy man bought Milton Abbas' large abbey and estate and rebuilt the town a mile away, creating what is probably the first planned community, with identical houses, a pub, and a church. From Milton Abbas, A354 leads back to Winterborne Whitechurch, or Salisbury.

South Wales

▲Cardiff and Nearby

The Welsh capital of Cardiff (pop. 320,000) has a newly renovated waterfront area, with shops and entertainment.

Cardiff's helpful **TI** is located in the Old Library, a five-minute walk from Cardiff Castle and a 10-minute walk from the train station (Mon–Sat 9:30–18:00, Sun 10:00–16:00, The Hayes, tel. 08701-211-258, www.visitcardiff .com). They have Internet access (£1/30 min) and storage lockers (small-£3, large-£5, both require refundable £3 deposit, lockers open Mon–Sat 9:30–17:30, Sun 10:30–15:30).

Cardiff Castle (Castell Caerdydd)—A visit to Cardiff's castle is interesting only if you catch one of the entertaining tours of the interior. With its ornate clock tower, the castle is the latest in a series of fortresses erected on the site by Romans, Normans, and assorted British lords. The interior is a Victorian fantasy (£7.50 with 50-min tour, tours at least every 20 min, every 45 min in winter, £3.75 for grounds only without tour, daily March–Oct 9:30–18:00, Nov–Feb 9:30–17:00, last tour and entry 1 hour before closing, tel. 02920/878-100, www.cardiffcastle.com).

▲▲St. Fagans National History Museum/Amgueddfa Werin Cymru (Museum of Welsh Life)—This best look at traditional Welsh folk life has three sections: open-air folk museum, main museum (which you walk through as you enter), and castle/garden. Outside, in a 100-acre park that surrounds a castle, you'll find displays of more than 40 carefully reconstructed old houses from all corners of this little country. Each house is fully furnished and comes equipped with a local expert warming up beside a toasty fire, happy to tell you anything you want to know about life in this old cottage. Ask questions!

While everything is well-explained, the £2 museum guidebook (or 30p map)—available at the information desk as you enter—is a good investment. If you see construction in process, it's to build more storage for the museum's sizable collection of artifacts.

If the sky's dry, see the scattering of houses first. Otherwise, in the main museum building, head to Gallery One, a recently renovated multimedia gallery with artifacts from Welsh life—including elaborately carved "love spoons" as well as new memorabilia near and dear to local hearts (such as mementos from triumphant rugby teams). Don't miss the costume exhibit, hidden behind a gallery of farming equipment. Spend an hour in the large building's fascinating museum.

Head outside, where a small train trundles among the exhibits from Easter to October (five stops, 50p per stop, whole circuit takes 45 min). The castle interior is royal enough and surrounded by a fine garden.

The highlight of the open-air museum is the Rhyd-y-Car 1805 row house, which displays ironworker cottages as they might have looked in 1805, 1855, 1895, 1925, 1955, and 1985, offering a fascinating zip through Welsh domestic life from hearths to microwaves.

Step into an old schoolhouse, a chapel, or a blacksmith's shop to see traditional craft makers in action. Head over to the farm and wander among the livestock and funky old outbuildings. Then beam a few centuries forward to the House for the Future, an optimistic projection of domestic life in Wales 50 years from now. The timber house blends traditional building techniques with new technologies aimed at sustainability. The roof collects water and soaks up solar energy. The earth, which was removed to make way for the foundation, was made into bricks used in the structure.

Cost, Hours, Information: Free, parking-£2.50, daily 10:00–17:00, tel. 02920/573-500, www.museumwales.ac.uk/en/stfagans. While the coffee shop near the entrance and the restaurant upstairs are both handy, you'll eat light lunches better, cheaper, and with more atmosphere in the park at the Gwalia Tea Room. The Plymouth Arms pub just outside the museum serves the best food.

Near Bath

Getting There: To get from the Cardiff train station to the museum in the village of St. Fagans, catch bus #62 (£1.70 one-way, £2.90 round-trip, exact change required; departs Cardiff station Mon–Sat at :25 and :45 past the hour from 7:45 until late, and Sun at :05 past the hour between 10:05 and 17:05; Traveline bus info tel. 0870-608-2608). Drivers leave M4 at Junction 33 and follow the signs. Leaving the museum, jog left on the freeway, take the first exit, and circle back, following signs to M4.

▲**Caerphilly Castle**—The impressive but gutted old castle, spread over 30 acres, is the second largest in Europe after Windsor.

English Earl Gilbert de Clare erected this squat behemoth to try to establish a stronghold in Wales. With two concentric walls, it was considered to be a brilliant arrangement of defensive walls and moats. Attackers had to negotiate three drawbridges and four sets of doors and portcullises just to reach the main entrance. For the record, there were no known successful enemy forays beyond the current castle's inner walls.

The castle has its own leaning tower—the split and listing tower reportedly out-leans Pisa's—and, some say, a resident ghost. Legend has it that de Clare, after learning of his wife Alice's infidelity, exiled her back to France and had her lover killed. Upon learning of her paramour's fate, Alice died of a broken heart. Since then, the "Green Lady," named for her husband's jealousy, has reportedly roamed the ramparts.

Exhibits at the castle display clever catapults, castle-dwellers' tricks for harassing intruders, and a good dose of Welsh history.

Cost and Hours: £3.50, June–Sept daily 9:30–18:00, May and Oct daily 9:30–17:00; Nov–April Mon–Sat 9:30–16:00, Sun 11:00–16:00; last entry 30 min before closing, 45-min audioguide-£1, tel. 02920/883-143, www.cadw.wales.gov.uk.

Getting There: The town of Caerphilly—with its castle located right in the center—is nine miles north of Cardiff. To get there, take the train from Cardiff to Caerphilly (3/hr, 15–20 min 9:00–18:00, hourly otherwise) and walk five minutes. It's 20 minutes by car from St. Fagans (exit #32, following signs from M4).

Chepstow, Tintern, and Nearby

If you're seduced into spending the night in this charming area, you'll find plenty of B&Bs near the Tintern Abbey, or in the castle-crowned town of Chepstow, located just down the road (a one-hour drive from Bath).

The **Chepstow TI** is helpful (daily April–mid-Oct 10:00–17:30, mid-Oct–March 10:00–15:30, Bridge Street, tel. 01291/623-772, www.visitwyevalley.com) and sells the inexpensive *Chepstow Town Trail* guide to a 21-stop, 90-minute stroll around the village. The walk begins at the town gate, where, in medieval times, folks arriving to sell goods or livestock were hit up for tolls.

The **Tintern TI,** north of the abbey and the village of Tintern, is housed within a former railway station (daily April–Oct 10:30–17:30, closed Nov–March, café, railway exhibit, The Old Station, tel. 01291/689-566).

Chepstow Castle—Perched on a hill overlooking the pleasant village of Chepstow on one side and the Wye River on the other, this castle is worth a short stop for drivers heading for Tintern Abbey, or a 10-minute walk from the Chepstow train station (uphill going back).

The stone-built bastion dating to 1066 was among the first castles the British plunked down to secure their turf in Wales, and it remained in use through 1690. While many castles of the time were built first in wood, Chepstow, then a key foothold on the England–Wales border, was built from stone from the start for durability. As you clamber along the battlements, you'll find architectural evidence of military renovations through the centuries, from Norman to Tudor right up through Cromwellian additions. You can tell which parts date from Norman days—they're the ones made of yellow sandstone instead of the grayish limestone that makes up the rest of the castle (£3.50, daily June–Sept 9:30–18:00, April–May and Oct 9:30–17:00, Nov–March 9:30–16:00, last admission 30 min before closing, guidebook-£3.50, in Chepstow village a half-mile from train station, tel. 01291/624-065, www.cadw.wales.gov.uk).

▲▲**Tintern Abbey**—Inspiring monks to prayer, William Wordsworth to poetry, J. M. W. Turner to a famous painting, and rushed tourists to a thoughtful moment, this verse-worthy ruined-castle-of-an-abbey merits a five-mile detour off the motorway. Founded in 1131 on a site chosen by Norman monks for its tranquility, it functioned as an austere Cistercian abbey until its dissolution in 1536. The monks followed a strict schedule. They rose several hours after midnight for the first of eight daily prayer sessions, and spent the rest of their time studying, working the surrounding farmlands, and meditating. Dissolved under Henry VIII's Act of Suppression in 1536, the magnificent church moldered in relative obscurity until tourists in the Romantic era (mid 18th century) discovered the wooded Wye valley and abbey ruins. J. M. W. Turner made his first sketches in 1792, and William Wordsworth penned "Lines Composed a Few Miles Above Tintern Abbey..." in 1798.

Most of the external walls of the 250-foot-long, 150-foot-wide church still stand, along with the exquisite window tracery and outlines of the sacristy, chapter house, and dining hall. The daylight that floods through the roofless ruins highlights the Gothic decorated arches—in those days a bold departure from Cistercian simplicity (£3.50, June–Sept daily 9:30–18:00, April–May and Oct daily 9:30–17:00; Nov–March Mon–Sat 9:30–16:00, Sun 11:00–16:00; last entry 30 min before closing, 1-hour audioguide-£1, occasional summertime events in the cloisters—check website for schedule, tel. 01291/689-251, www.cadw.wales.gov.uk; from Cardiff catch a 90-min bus or train to Chepstow, then 20-min bus or taxi from Chepstow to abbey). It's flooded with tourists in the summer, so visit early or late to miss the biggest crowds. The abbey's shop sells Celtic jewelry and other gifts. Take an easy 15-minute walk up to St. Mary's Church for a view of England just over the River Wye.

▲**Wye River Valley and Forest of Dean**—This land is lush, mellow, and historic. Local tourist brochures explain the Forest of Dean's special dialect, its strange political autonomy, and its oaken ties to Trafalgar and Admiral Nelson.

Sleeping: **$$$ Florence Country House Hotel,** snuggled in the lower Wye Valley north of Tintern on the way to Monmouth,

is a good place for tea and scones—or a lunchtime salad—with a view. On a nice day, eat on the garden terrace in this 17th-century hotel and share the scenery with the cows lazing along the riverbanks. If you spend the night, request a room with a view of the river (Sb-£46, Db-£92, includes breakfast, tel. 01594/530-830, www.florencehotel .co.uk, enquiries@florencehotel.co.uk, kind owners Dennis and Kathy).

For a medieval night, check into the **$ St. Briavels Castle B&B/Youth Hostel** (70 beds, £17.50-24.50 beds in 4- to 12-bed dorms, non-members-£3 extra, includes breakfast, private 4- to 8-bed rooms available, reception daily 8:00–10:00 & 17:00–22:00, hostel closed to guests daily 10:00–17:00, curfew at 23:30, kitchen and lounge, brown-bag lunches and evening meals available, tel. 0870-770-6040, www.yha.org.uk, stbriavels@yha.org.uk).

The hostel hosts medieval banquets on Monday, Wednesday, and Saturday nights in August (£10, for hostel guests only, ask staff for schedule). An 800-year-old Norman castle used by King John in 1215 (the year he signed the Magna Carta), the hostel is comfortable (as castles go), friendly, and in the center of the quiet village of St. Briavels just north of Tintern Abbey. For dinner, eat at the hostel or walk "just down the path and up the snyket" to **The Crown Inn** (decent food and local pub atmosphere, tel. 01594/530-205).

TRANSPORTATION CONNECTIONS

From Cardiff by Train to: Caerphilly (3/hr, 15–20 min 9:00–18:00, hourly otherwise), **Bath** (hourly, 1 hr), **Birmingham** (2/hr, 2 hrs, change in Bristol, once an hour direct), **London** (2/hr, 2 hrs), **Chepstow** (hourly, 30 min; more with transfer, 2 hrs; 6 miles to Tintern by bus). Train info: tel. 08457-484-950.

Route Tips for Drivers
Bath to South Wales: Leave Bath following signs for A4, then M4. It's 10 miles north (on A46 past a village called Pennsylvania) to the M4 freeway. Zip westward, crossing a huge suspension bridge into Wales (£5.10 toll westbound only). Stay on M4 (not M48) past Cardiff, take exit 33, and follow the brown signs south to St. Fagans National History Museum/Amgueddfa Werin Cymru/Museum of Welsh Life. To get to Tintern Abbey, take M4 to exit 21 and get on M48. The abbey is six miles (up A466, follow signs to *Chepstow* then *Tintern*) off M48 at exit 2, right where the northern bridge across the Severn hits Wales.

Cardiff to the Cotswolds via Forest of Dean: On the Welsh side of the big suspension bridge, take the Chepstow exit and follow signs up A466 to *Tintern Abbey* and the *Wye River Valley*. Carry on to Monmouth, and follow A40 and M50 to the Tewkesbury exit, where small roads lead to the Cotswolds.

THE COTSWOLDS

The Cotswold Hills, a 25-by-90-mile chunk of Gloucestershire, are dotted with enchanting villages and graced with England's greatest countryside palace, Blenheim. As with many fairy-tale regions of Europe, the present-day beauty of the Cotswolds is the result of an economic disaster. Wool was a huge industry in medieval England, and Cotswold sheep grew the best wool. A 12th-century saying bragged, "In Europe the best wool is English. In England the best wool is Cotswold." The region prospered. Wool money built fine towns and houses. Local "wool" churches are called "cathedrals" for their scale and wealth. Stained-glass slogans say things like "I thank my God and ever shall, it is the sheep hath paid for all."

With the rise of cotton and the Industrial Revolution, the woolen industry collapsed. Ba-a-a-ad news. The wealthy Cotswold towns fell into a depressed time warp; the homes of impoverished nobility became gracefully dilapidated. Today, visitors enjoy a harmonious blend of man and nature—the most pristine of English countrysides decorated with time-passed villages, rich wool churches, tell-me-a-story stone fences, and "kissing gates" you wouldn't want to experience alone. Appreciated by throngs of 21st-century Romantics, the Cotswolds are enjoying new prosperity.

The north Cotswolds are best. Two of the region's coziest towns, Chipping Campden and Stow-on-the-Wold, are eight and four miles, respectively, from Moreton-in-Marsh, which has the best public transportation connections. Any of these three towns makes a fine home base for your exploration of the thatch-happiest of Cotswold villages and walks.

Planning Your Time

The Cotswolds are an absolute delight by car and, with patience, enjoyable even without a car. On a three-week British trip, I'd spend two nights and a day in the Cotswolds. The region's charm has a softening effect on many uptight itineraries. You could enjoy days of walking from a home base here.

Chipping Campden and Stow-on-the-Wold are quaint without being overrun, and both have good accommodations. Stow has a bit more character for an overnight stay, and offers the widest range of choices. The plain town of Moreton-in-Marsh is the only one of the three with a train station. With a car, consider really getting away from it all by staying in one of the smaller villages.

If you want to take in some Shakespeare, note that Stow, Chipping Campden, and Moreton are only a 30-minute drive from Stratford, which offers a great evening of world-class entertainment (see Stratford-upon-Avon chapter).

One-Day Driver's 100-Mile Cotswold Blitz, Including Blenheim: Use a good map and reshuffle to fit your home base: 9:00–Browse through Chipping Campden, following the self-guided walk; 10:00–Joyride through Snowshill, Stanway, Stanton, the Slaughters, and Bourton-on-the-Water; 13:00–Have lunch at Stow-on-the-Wold, then follow the self-guided walk; 15:00–Drive 30 miles to Blenheim Palace and take the hour-long tour (last tour departs at 16:45); 18:00–Drive home for just the right pub dinner. (If planning on a gourmet countryside pub dinner, reserve in advance by phone.)

Two-Day Plan by Public Transportation: This plan is best for weekdays, when buses run more frequently than on weekends. Make your home base Moreton-in-Marsh.

Day 1: Take the early bus to Chipping Campden, then bus to Stow (via Moreton). Rent a bike in Stow and explore the countryside, or take a bus to Bourton-on-the-Water and walk to the Slaughters. Have an early dinner in Stow, then return to Moreton at 19:15.

Day 2: Take a day trip to Blenheim Palace via Oxford (train to Oxford, bus to palace); or rent a bike and ride to Chastleton House; or take a day-long countryside walk.

Getting Around the Cotswolds
By Bus

The Cotswolds are so well-preserved, in part, because public transportation to and within this area has long been miserable.

To explore the towns, use the two bus routes that hop through the region nearly hourly, lacing together main stops and ending at rail stations. In each case, there are about eight buses per day; the entire trip takes about an hour; and you spend less than £2 per hop

(pay driver directly as you board). With the help of the TI, you can lace together a one-way or return trip by public transportation, making for a fine Cotswolds day. Ask the TI for their *Exploring the Cotswolds by Bus* booklet (and accompanying timetables), which summarize all of the bus routes in the area. If you're traveling one-way between two train stations, remember that the Cotswold villages—generally pretty clueless when it comes to the needs of travelers without a car—have no baggage-check services. You'll need to improvise. Note that service is poor on Saturdays and essentially non-existent on Sundays. For specifics, consult any TI or call the Cotswolds bus-travel info line at tel. 0870-608-2608, ext. 83.

While I've based this information on Moreton, you can derive Stow and Chipping Campden bus connections from this same write-up. Here are the bus lines that leave from Moreton:

From Moreton-in-Marsh to Chipping Campden: Buses #21, #22, and #522 run from Moreton-in-Marsh to Chipping Campden to the Stratford-upon-Avon train station. These are the only buses that go all the way through to Chipping Campden. (Bus #H3, which you may see on timetables, connects Stratford and Chipping Campden, but doesn't go all the way to Moreton.)

From Moreton-in-Marsh to Stow-on-the-Wold: Bus #855 goes from Moreton-in-Marsh to Stow-on-the-Wold to Bourton-on-the-Water to Northleach to Cirencester to the Kemble train station. Bus #801 goes from Moreton-in-Marsh to Stow-on-the-Wold to the Slaughters to Bourton-on-the-Water, and ends at Cheltenham.

By Bike

Despite narrow roads and high hedgerows (blocking some views), bikers enjoy the Cotswolds free from the constraints of bus schedules. For each area, TIs have fine route planners that indicate which peaceful, paved lanes are particularly scenic for biking. In summer, it's smart to book your bike a couple of days ahead.

In **Moreton-in-Marsh,** the nice folks at the Toy Shop rent mountain bikes. You can stop in the shop to rent a bike, or call ahead to pick up or drop off at other times—they're flexible (£14/day with route maps, bike locks, and helmets; shop open Mon and Wed–Sat 9:00–17:00, closed Sun and Tue, High Street, tel. 01608/650-756).

In **Chipping Campden,** try Cotswold Country Cycles (£15/day, tandems-£30/day, includes helmets and route maps, delivery for a fee, daily 9:30–dusk, tours available, 1.5 miles north of town at Longlands Farm Cottage, tel. 01386/438-706, mobile 077-4610-7728, www.cotswoldcountrycycles.com). In **Stow-on-the-Wold,** the youth hostel rents bikes (£9.50/day with lock and helmet, tel. 01451/830-497).

By Foot

Walking guidebooks abound, giving you a world of choices for each of my recommended stops (choose a book with clear maps). Villages are generally no more than three miles apart, and most have pubs that would love to feed and water you. For a list of guided walks, ask at any TI for the free *Cotswold Lion* newspaper. The walks are free, range from two to twelve miles, and often involve a stop at a pub or tearoom (April–Sept).

By Car

Distances here are wonderfully short (but only if you invest in the Ordnance Survey map of the Cotswolds, sold locally at TIs and newsstands). Here are distances from Moreton: Broadway (10 miles), Chipping Campden (8 miles), Stratford (17 miles), Warwick (23 miles), Stow (4 miles), Blenheim Palace (20 miles).

Robinson Goss Self Drive, six miles north of Moreton-in-Marsh, offers one-day rentals from £28, including everything but gas. They're in the middle of nowhere, but may pick you up for a charge of about £1/mile (Mon–Fri 8:30–17:00, Sat 8:30–12:30, closed Sun, tel. 01608/663-322, www.robgos.co.uk).

Car hiking is great. In this chapter, I cover the postcard-perfect (but discovered) villages. With a car and the local Ordnance Survey map (Tour #8, £5), you can easily ramble about and find your own gems. The problem with having a car is that you are less likely to walk. Consider taking a taxi or bus somewhere, so that you can walk back to your car and enjoy the scenery.

By Taxi

Two or three town-to-town taxi trips can make more sense than renting a car. While taking a cab cross-country seems extravagant at about £2 per mile, the distances are short (Stow to Moreton is 4 miles, Stow to Chipping Campden is 10), and one-way walks are lovely. If you call a cab, confirm that the meter will start only when you are actually picked up. Consider hiring a cab at the hourly "touring rate" (£25–30), rather than the meter rate (e.g., £20 Stow to Chipping Campden). For a few more quid, you can have a joy-ride peppered with commentary.

Note that the drivers listed below are not typical city taxi services (with many drivers on call), but are mostly individuals—it's smart to book ahead if you're arriving in high season, since they

The Cotswolds

TO WORCESTER
A-46
TO M-5
EVESHAM
TO STRATFORD-UPON-AVON
A-34
N
MICKLETON
B-4632
❹
ILMINGTON
CHIPPING CAMPDEN
SHIPSTON
B-4035
BROADWAY →
A-44
B-4081
BROAD CAMPDEN
STANTON
SNOWSHILL
❸ ❷
B-4479
BLOCKLEY
MORETON -IN-MARSH
TO TEWKESBURY
STANWAY
A-44
A-429
A-44
WINCHCOMBE
❶
UPPER SWELL
A-424
❻
B-4632
FORD
B-4077
❺
TO OXFORD & BLENHEIM PALACE
LOWER SWELL
A-436
STOW -ON-THE-WOLD
TO CHELTENHAM
B-4068
A-436
BOURTON-ON-THE-WATER
TO OXFORD
UPPER + LOWER SLAUGHTER
A-429
A-429
A-424
TO BURFORD & OXFORD
TO BIBURY, NORTHLEACH & CIRENCESTER

5 MILES
5 KM

❶ Stanway House
❷ Snowshill Lavender
❸ Sheepscombe House B&B
❹ Hidcote Manor Garden
❺ Cotswold Farm Park
❻ Chastleton House

— MAJOR ROAD
— MINOR ROAD
···· COTSWOLD WAY FOOTPATH

DCH

can book up in advance on weekends.

To scare up a driver in Moreton, call Richard at **Four Shires** (mobile 077-4780-2555) or **Iain's Taxis** (mobile 077-8989-7966, £20/hr); in Stow, call Iain (above) or **Tony Knight** (mobile 078-8771-4047, £25/hr); and in Chipping Campden, try **Marnic Cars & Taxis** (mobile 079-8085-7833, £30/hr) or **Cotswold Private Hire** (mobile 079-8085-7833, £25/hr). **Tim Harrison,** who

Cotswold Appreciation 101

Much history can be read into the names of the area. *Cotswold* could come from the Saxon phrase meaning "hills of sheep's coats." Or it could mean shelter ("cot" like cottage) on the open upland ("wold").

In the Cotswolds, a town's main street (called High Street) needed to be wide to accommodate the sheep and cattle being marched to market (and today, to park tour buses). Some of the most picturesque cottages were once humble row houses of weavers' cottages, usually located along a stream for their waterwheels (good examples in Bibury and Castle Combe). The towns run on slow clocks and yellowed calendars. An entire village might not have a phone booth.

Fields of yellow (rapeseed) and pale blue (linseed) separate pastures dotted with black and white sheep. In just about any B&B, when you open your window in the morning you'll hear sheep baaing. The decorative "toadstool" stones dotting front yards throughout the region are medieval staddle stones, which buildings were set upon to keep the rodents out.

Cotswold walls and roofs are made of the local limestone. The limestone roof tiles hang by pegs. To make the weight more bearable, smaller and lighter tiles are higher up. An extremely strict building code keeps towns looking what many locals call "overly quaint."

Towns are small, and everyone seems to know everyone. The area is provincial yet ever-so-polite, and people commonly rescue themselves from a gossipy tangent by saying, "It's all very...mmm...yyya."

This is walking country. The English love their walks and vigorously defend their age-old right to free passage. Once a year the Rambling Society organizes a "Mass Trespass," when each of the country's 50,000 miles of public footpaths is walked. By assuring each path is used at least once a year, they stop landlords from putting up fences. Any paths found blocked are unceremoniously unblocked.

Questions to ask locals: Do you think foxhunting should have been banned? Who are the Morris men? What's a kissing gate?

co-runs a recommended B&B in Snowshill (see page 249), is both a driver and a tour guide (mobile 077-7903-0820).

By Tour
Departing from Bath, **Mad Max Minibus Tours** offers a "Cotswold Discovery" full-day tour, and can drop you off in Stow with your luggage if you arrange it in advance (see specifics on page 176).

While none of the Cotswold towns offers regularly sched-uled walks, many have voluntary warden groups who love to meet visitors and give walks for just a small donation (£5 is plenty, £10 per group is great, specific contact information appears below for Chipping Campden and Stow).

Chipping Campden

Just touristy enough to be convenient, the north Cotswolds town of Chipping Campden (CAM-den) is a ▲▲ sight. This market town, once the home of the richest Cotswold wool merchants, has some incredibly beautiful thatched roofs. Both the great British historian G. M. Trevelyan and I call Chipping Campden's High Street the finest in England.

ORIENTATION

(area code: 01386)
Walk the full length of High Street; its width is characteristic

of market towns. Go around the block on both ends. On one end, you'll find impressively thatched homes (out Sheep Street, past the public WC and ugly gas station, and right on Westington Street). Walking north on High Street, you'll pass the Market Hall, the wavy roof of the first great wool mansion, a fine and free memorial garden, and, finally, the town's famous 15th-century Perpendicular Gothic "wool" church. (This route is the same as the self-guided town walk below.)

Tourist Information
Chipping Campden's TI is in the old police station on High Street. Get the 50p town guide, which includes a map (daily April–Oct

10:00–17:30, Nov–March 10:00–17:00, tel. 01386/841-206, www
.visitchippingcampden.com).

Helpful Hints:

Internet Access: Your best bet is to go back to London. Otherwise,
try the occasionally open library.

Bike Rental: Call **Cotswold Country Cycles;** see "Getting
Around the Cotswolds—By Bike" (above).

Taxi: Try **Marnic Cars & Taxis, Cotswold Private Hire,** or **Tim
Harrison** (see "Getting Around the Cotswolds—By Taxi,"
above).

Parking: Find a spot anywhere along High Street, and park for
free with no time limit. There's also a pay-and-display lot (90-
min maximum) on High Street (across from TI).

Local Tours: The local members of the **Cotswold Voluntary
Wardens** would be happy to show you around town for
a small donation to their conservation society (£10 for a
1-hour walk is more than enough, walks July–mid-Sept Wed
at 14:30, meet at Market Hall). Tour guide and coordinator
Ann Colcomb can help arrange for a walk on other days as
well (tel. 01386/832-131).

SELF-GUIDED WALK

Welcome to Chipping Campden

This 500-yard walk through "Campden" (as locals call their town)
takes you from the TI to the church in about 30 minutes.

If it's open, begin at the **Magistrate's Court** (can be closed for
meetings, events, and even weddings). This meeting room is in the
old police station, located above the TI (free, same hours as TI, ask
at TI to go up). Under the open-beamed courtroom, you'll find a
humble little exhibit on the town's history.

Campden's most famous monument, the **Market Hall,** stands

in front of the TI, marking the
town center. It was built in 1627
by the 17th-century Lord of the
Manor, Sir Baptist Hicks. (Look
for the Hicks family coat of arms
in the building's facade.) Back
then, it was an elegant—even
over-the-top—shopping hall for
the townsfolk who'd come here to
buy their produce. In the 1940s, it
was almost sold to an American, but the townspeople heroically
raised money to buy it first, then gave it to the National Trust for
preservation.

The Cotswolds

Chipping Campden

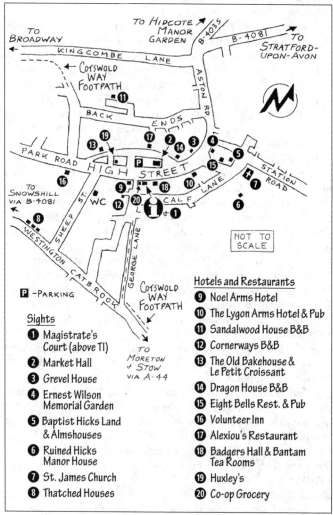

TO HIDCOTE MANOR GARDEN

TO BROADWAY

B-4035

B-4081

TO STRATFORD-UPON-AVON

KINGCOMBE LANE

COTSWOLD WAY FOOTPATH

BACK

ASTON RD.

ENDS

❶❶

PARK ROAD

⓭ ⓳

⓱ ❷ ❸ ❹

⓮

❺

HIGH STREET

P

⓯

STATION ROAD

TO SNOWSHILL VIA B-4081

⓰

❾

⓲

⓾

CALF LANE

✝

❼

SHEEP ST.

WC

⓬

⓴

ⓘ ✝ ❶

❻

❽

WESTINGTON

CATBROOK

GEORGE LANE

COTSWOLD WAY FOOTPATH

TO MORETON & STOW VIA A-44

NOT TO SCALE

P –Parking

Sights
❶ Magistrate's Court (above TI)
❷ Market Hall
❸ Grevel House
❹ Ernest Wilson Memorial Garden
❺ Baptist Hicks Land & Almshouses
❻ Ruined Hicks Manor House
❼ St. James Church
❽ Thatched Houses

Hotels and Restaurants
❾ Noel Arms Hotel
⓾ The Lygon Arms Hotel & Pub
⓫ Sandalwood House B&B
⓬ Cornerways B&B
⓭ The Old Bakehouse & Le Petit Croissant
⓮ Dragon House B&B
⓯ Eight Bells Rest. & Pub
⓰ Volunteer Inn
⓱ Alexiou's Restaurant
⓲ Badgers Hall & Bantam Tea Rooms
⓳ Huxley's
⓴ Co-op Grocery

The timbers inside are true to the original. Study the classic Cotswold stone roof, still held together with wooden pegs nailed in from underneath. (Tiles were cut and sold with peg holes, and stacked like waterproof scales.) Buildings all over the region still use these stone shingles. Today, the hall hosts local fairs.

Chipping Campden's **High Street** has changed little architecturally since 1840. (The town's street plan survives from the 12th century.) Notice the harmony of the long rows of buildings. While the street comprises different styles through the centuries, everything you see was made of the same Cotswold stone—the only stone allowed today.

To be level, High Street arcs with the contour of the hillside. Because it's so wide, you know this was a market town. In past centuries, livestock and packhorses laden with piles of freshly shorn fleece would fill the streets. Campden was a sales and distribution center for the wool industry, and merchants from as far as Italy would come here for the prized raw wool.

High Street has no house numbers—people know the houses by their names. In the distance, you see the town church (where this walk ends).

• *Hike up High Street to just before the first intersection.*

In 1367, William Grevel built what's considered Campden's first stone house: **Grevel House** (on the left). Sheep tycoons had big homes. Imagine back then, when this fine building was surrounded by humble wattle-and-daub huts. It had newfangled chimneys, rather than a crude hole in the roof. (No more rain inside!) Originally a "hall house" with just one big, tall room, it got its upper floor in the 16th century. The finely carved central bay window is a good early example of the Perpendicular Gothic style. The gargoyles scared away bad spirits—and served as rain spouts. The boot scrapers outside each door were a fixture in that muddy age—especially in market towns, where the streets were filled with animal dung.

• *Continue up High Street for about 100 yards. Go past Church Street (which we'll walk up later). Across the street, you'll find a small Gothic arch leading into a garden.*

The small and secluded **Ernest Wilson Memorial Garden,** once the church's vegetable patch, is a botanist's delight today. It's filled with well-labeled plants that the Victorian botanist Ernest Wilson brought back to England from his extensive travels in Asia. There's a complete history of the garden on the board to the left of the entry (free, open daily until dusk).

• *Backtrack to Church Street. Turn left, walk past the Eight Bells Inn, and head around the corner to the left.*

Sprawling adjacent the town church, the area known as **Baptist Hicks Land** holds Hicks' huge estate and manor house. This influential Lord of the Manor was from "a family of substance," who were merchants of silk and fine clothing as well as moneylenders. Beyond the ornate gate, only a few outbuildings and the charred corner of his mansion survive. The mansion was burned by Royalists in 1645 during the Civil War—notice how Cotswold stone turns red when burned. Hicks housed the poor, making a show of his generosity, adding a long row of almshouses (with his family coat of arms) for neighbors to see as they walked to church. These almshouses (lining Church Street on the left) are occupied by pensioners today, as they have been since the 17th century.

• *Walk between the almshouses and the wall that lines the Hicks estate to the church, where a scenic, tree-lined lane leads to the front door. On the way, notice the 12 lime trees, one for each of the apostles, that were planted in about 1760 (sorry, no limes).*

One of the finest churches in the Cotswolds, **St. James Church** graces one of its leading towns. Both the town and the church were built by wool wealth. The church is Perpendicular Gothic, with lots of light and strong verticality. Before you leave, notice the fine vestments and altar hangings behind protective blue curtains (near the back of the church). Tombstones pave the floor—memorializing great wool merchants through the ages.

At the altar is a brass relief of William Grevel, the first owner of the Grevel House (above), and his wife. In the way that Baptist Hicks dominated the town, Grevel dominates the church. His

huge, canopied tomb is the ornate final resting place for Grevel and his wife, Elizabeth. Study their faces, framed by fancy lace ruffs (trendy in the 1620s). Adjacent—as if in a closet—is a statue of their daughter, Lady Juliana, and her husband, Lutheran Yokels. Juliana commissioned the statue in 1642, when her husband died, but had it closed until *she* died in 1680. Then, the doors were opened, revealing these two people living happily ever after—at least in marble. The hinges were likely only ever used once.

SLEEPING

(area code: 01386)

In Chipping Campden—as in any town in the Cotswolds—B&Bs offer a better value than hotels. Rooms are generally tight on Saturdays (when many charge a bit more and are reluctant to rent to one-nighters) and in September, which is considered a peak month. Parking is never a problem. Always ask for a discount if staying longer than one or two nights.

$$$ Noel Arms Hotel, the characteristic old hotel on the main square, has welcomed guests for 600 years. Its lobby is decorated with armor, guns, and heraldry (insignias), and comes with a whiff of the medieval ages. Its 26 rooms are well-furnished with antiques (standard Db-£135, bigger Db-£160, fancier four-poster Db-£220, book direct for a 10 percent discount with this book in 2008, some ground-floor doubles, attached restaurant/bar, High Street, tel. 01386/840-317, fax 01386/841-136, www.noelarmshotel.com, reception@noelarmshotel.com).

The Cotswolds

Sleep Code

(£1 = about $2, country code: 44)
S = Single, **D** = Double/Twin, **T** = Triple, **Q** = Quad, **b** = bathroom,
s = shower only. Unless noted otherwise, you can assume credit cards are accepted.

To help you sort easily through these listings, I've divided the rooms into three categories based on the price for a standard double room with bath:

$$$ **Higher Priced**—Most rooms £90 or more.
$$ **Moderately Priced**—Most rooms between £60–90.
$ **Lower Priced**—Most rooms £60 or less.

$$ **The Lygon Arms Hotel,** attached to the popular pub of the same name, has small public areas and 10 cheery, open-beamed rooms (one small older Db-£65–75, huge "superior" Db-£95–110, lovely courtyard Db-£130–150, lower prices are for midweek or multi-night stays, family deals, High Street, tel. 01386/840-318, www.lygonarms.co.uk, Sandra@lygonarms.co.uk, Sandra Davenport).

$$ **Sandalwood House B&B** is a big, comfy, contemporary home with a pink, flowery lounge and a sprawling back garden. Just a five-minute walk from the center of town, it's in a quiet, woodsy, pastoral setting. Its two cheery pastel rooms are bright and spacious (D/Db-£65–67, T-£88, cheaper if you order a light breakfast instead of full, self-catering apartment sleeps four-£500–600/week, cash only, no kids under age 7, off-street parking, friendly Bobby the cat, tel. & fax 01386/840-091, Diana Bendall). To get to Sandalwood House, go west on High Street, and at the church and the Volunteer Inn, turn right and then right again; look for a sign in the hedge on the left, and head up the long driveway.

$$ **Cornerways B&B** is a fresh, bright, and comfy modern home (not "oldie worldie") a block off High Street. It's run by the delightful Carole Proctor, who can "look out the window and see the church where we were married." The huge, light, airy loft rooms are great for families (Db-£65, £5 off for 3 or more nights, Tb-£90, Qb-£110, children's discount, George Lane, just walk through the arch beside Noel Arms Hotel, tel. 01386/841-307, www.cornerways.info, carole@cornerways.info).

$$ **The Old Bakehouse** rents five small but pleasant rooms in a 600-year-old home with a plush fireplace lounge. Hardworking Sarah lives just up the road—phone ahead with an arrival time, or call her mobile phone if she's not there when you arrive (Sb-£45, Db-£65, family deals, £5 off for 2 or more nights, cash only, fun

The Cotswolds

attic room that sleeps up to 5 has beams running through it, Lower High Street, tel. & fax 01386/840-979, mobile 077-0235-9530, oldbakehouse@chippingcampden-cotswolds.co.uk).

$ Dragon House B&B rents tidy two-floor suites—with medieval beams—right on the center of High Street. They have laundry machines and a sumptuous, stay-awhile garden (Db-£58, £5 off for 3 or more nights, cash only, off-street parking available, near Market Hall, tel. & fax 01386/840-734, www.dragonhouse -chipping-campden.com, info@dragonhouse-chipping-campden .co.uk, Valerie and Graeme the potter). They also have an apartment that sleeps up to six (Sat to Sat only, £250–500/week depending on month).

EATING

This town—so filled with wealthy residents and tourists—comes with lots of choices. Here are some local favorites:

Eight Bells is a charming 14th-century inn on Leysbourne with a classy and woody restaurant and a more colorful pub (daily, £20 dinners, reservations recommended, tel. 01386/840-371).

Volunteer Inn does double duty, dishing up decent grub at lunchtime, and serving Indian dishes at dinner (£5–8 meals, daily 12:00–14:30 & 18:00–21:00, grassy courtyard out back, Park Road). The **Lygon Arms** pub also has good food (daily).

Alexiou's, a fun Greek restaurant on High Street, serves hearty portions and breaks plates at closing every Saturday night (closed Sun to clean up, tel. 01386/840-826).

Picnic: The **Co-op** grocery store is the town's small "supermarket" (daily 7:00–22:00, across from the market and next to TI on High Street). Munch lunch on the benches on the little green across the street.

Tearooms

To visit a cute tearoom, try one of these places, located in the town center.

Badgers Hall Tea Room is great for a wide selection of homemade cakes, crumbles, and scones. Along with light lunches, they serve an afternoon tea—a tall and ritualistic tray of dainty sandwiches, pastries, and scones with tea—for half the London price (£30 for 2 people, Wed–Mon 10:30–16:30, closed Tue, also rents rooms, High Street, tel. 01386/840-839).

Le Petit Croissant, a cheery little French deli with a tearoom in the back, serves pastries, quiche, cheese, and wine (Tue–Fri 9:00–17:00, Sat 8:30–17:00, closed Sun–Mon, Lower High Street, tel. 01386/841-861).

Two tearooms on High Street, near the Market Hall, are both

good values: **Bantam Tea Rooms** (daily until 17:00) and **Huxley's,** which serves tea, but is also a pleasant restaurant, serving light lunches and dinners (Wed–Sun 12:00–14:00 & 19:00–21:00, closed Mon–Tue, tel. 01386/840-520).

Near Chipping Campden

Located to the west of Chipping Campden, these are my nominations for the cutest Cotswold villages. Like marshmallows in hot chocolate, Stanway, Stanton, and Snowshill nestle side by side, awaiting your arrival. (Note the Stanway House's limited hours when planning your visit.) Other easy-to-access sights to the west and north of Chipping Campden are also included below.

▲▲Stanway House

Lord Neidpath, whose family tree charts relatives back to 1202, opens his melancholy home and grounds to visitors just two days a week in the summer. Walking through his house offers a unique glimpse into the lifestyles of England's eccentric and fading nobility.

Cost and Hours: £6, June–Aug Tue and Thu only 14:00–17:00, tel. 01386/584-469, www.stanwayfountain.co.uk. His lordship himself narrated the audioguide to his home (£2).

Getting There: By car, leave B4077 at a statue of (the Christian) George slaying the dragon (of pagan superstition); you'll round the corner and see the manor's fine 17th-century Jacobean gatehouse. There's no real public transportation to Stanway.

◗ Self-Guided Tour: Start with the grounds, then head into the house itself.

Lord Neidpath recently restored "the tallest fountain in Britain" on the grounds—300 feet tall, gravity-powered, and quite impressive (fountain spurts for 30 min at 14:45 and 16:00 on opening days).

The bitchin' Tithe Barn (near where you enter the grounds) dates to the 14th century, and predates the manor. It was originally where monks—in the days before money—would accept one-tenth of whatever the peasants produced. Peek inside: This is a great hall for village hoedowns. While the Tithe Barn is no longer used to greet motley peasants and collect their feudal "rents," the lord still gets rent from his vast landholdings, and hosts community fêtes in his barn.

Stepping into the obviously very lived-in palace, you're free to wander around pretty much as you like, but keep in mind that a family does live here. His lordship is often roaming about as well. The place feels like a time warp. Ask the ticket taker (inside) to demonstrate the spinning rent-collection table. In the great hall, marvel at the one-piece oak shuffleboard table and the 1780 Chippendale exercise chair (half an hour of bouncing on this was considered good for the liver).

The manor dogs have their own cutely painted "family tree," but Lord Neidpath admits that his last dog, C. J., was "all character and no breeding." Poke into the office. You can psychoanalyze the lord by the books that fill his library, the videos stacked in front of his bed (with the mink bedspread), and whatever's next to his toilet.

The place has a story to tell. And so do the docents stationed in each room—modern-day peasants who, even without family trees, probably have relatives going back just as far in this village. Really. Talk to these people. Probe. Learn what you can about this side of England.

From Stanway to Stanton: These towns are separated by a row of oak trees and grazing land, with parallel waves echoing the furrows plowed by medieval farmers. Centuries ago, farmers were allotted long strips of land called "furlongs." The idea was to dole out good and bad land equitably. (One square furlong equals an acre.) Over centuries of plowing, furrows were formed. Let someone else drive, so you can hang out the window under a canopy of oaks, passing stone walls and sheep. Leaving Stanway on the road to Stanton, the first building you'll see (on the left, just outside Stanway) is a thatched cricket pavilion overlooking the village cricket green. Dating only from 1930, it's raised up (as medieval buildings were) on rodent-resistant staddle stones. Stanton's just ahead; follow the signs.

▲Stanton

Pristine Cotswold charm cheers you as you head up the main street of the village of Stanton. Stanton's **Church of St. Michael** betrays a pagan past. It's safe to assume any church dedicated to St. Michael (the archangel who fought the devil) sits upon a sacred pagan site. Stanton is actually at the intersection of two ley lines (geographic lines along which many prehistoric sights are found). You'll see St. Michael's well-worn figure (with a sundial) above the door as you enter. Inside, above the capitals in the nave, find the pagan symbols for the sun and the moon. While the church probably dates back to the ninth century, today's building is mostly from the 15th century, with 13th-century transepts. On the north transept, medieval frescoes show faintly through the 17th-century whitewash. (Once upon a time, medieval frescoes were considered too "papist.") Imagine the church interior colorfully decorated throughout. Original medieval glass is behind the altar. The list of rectors (left side wall) goes back to 1269. Finger the grooves in the back pews, worn away by sheepdog leashes. (A man's sheepdog accompanied him everywhere.)

Horse Rides and Sleeping near Stanton: Anyone can enjoy the Cotswolds from the saddle. **Jill Carenza's Riding Centre,** set just outside Stanton village, is in the most scenic corner of the region. The facility has 50 horses, and takes rank beginners on an hour-long scenic "hack" through the village and into the high country (£25/person for a group hack, £35/person for a semi-private hack for 2 people, £45 for a private one-person hack; lessons, longer rides, rides for experts, and pub tours available; well-signposted in Stanton, tel. 01386/584-250, www.cotswoldsriding.co.uk).

Jill rents five rooms at her **$ Vine B&B,** but it takes a backseat to the horses. There's no greeting or check-in, and guests wander around wondering which room is theirs. Still, it's convenient if you want to ride all day (Ds/Db-£65, most rooms with four-poster beds, lots of stairs, tel. 01386/584-250, fax 01386/584-888, info @cotswoldsriding.co.uk).

Snowshill

Another nearly edible little bundle of cuteness, Snowshill (SNOWS-hill) has a photogenic triangular square with a characteristic pub at its base.

▲Snowshill Manor—Dark and mysterious, this old palace is filled with the lifetime collection of Charles Paget Wade. It's one big, musty celebration of craftsmanship, from finely carved spinning

wheels to frightening samurai armor to tiny elaborate figurines carved by prisoners from the bones of meat served at dinner. Taking seriously his family motto, "Let Nothing Perish," Wade dedicated his life and fortune to preserving things finely crafted. The house (whose management made me promise not to promote it as an eccentric collector's pile of curiosities) really shows off Mr. Wade's ability to recognize and acquire fine examples of craftsmanship. It's all very...mmm...yyya.

This popular sight only allows 22 people in every 10 minutes, and entry times are doled out at the ticket desk (no reservations taken). It can be up to an hour's wait—even more on busy days, especially weekends. A good strategy is to arrive close to the opening time (12:00), and if there's a wait, enjoy the surrounding gardens (it's a 15-min walk up to the manor itself).

Cost and Hours: £7.30, house open April–Oct Wed–Sun 12:00–17:00, closed Mon–Tue and Nov–March, restaurant, tel. 01386/852-410, www.nationaltrust.org.uk/snowshillmanor.

Getting There: The manor overlooks the town square, but there's no direct access from the square. Park at the shop and follow the walkway through the garden to get to the house. A golf-cart-type shuttle to the house is available for those who need assistance.

Snowshill Lavender—In 2000, farmer Charlie Byrd realized that tourists love lavender. He planted his farm with 250,000 plants,

and now visitors come to wander among his 53 acres, which burst with gorgeous lavender blossoms from mid-June through late August. His fragrant fantasy peaks late each July. Farmer Byrd produces lavender oil (an herbal product valued since ancient times for its healing, calming, and fragrant qualities), runs a fine little café (£5 lunches), and has a delightful shop. Lavender—so famous in France's Provence—is not indigenous to this region, but it fits the climate and soil just fine. A free flier in the shop explains the variations of flowers blooming.

Cost, Hours, Location: Mid-June–Christmas—£2.50 and open daily 10:00–17:00; Easter–mid-June (before the lavender blooms)—free and open Wed–Sun 11:00–17:00, closed Mon–Tue; closed Christmas–Easter; tel. 01386/854-821. It's a half-mile out of Snowshill on Chipping Campden Road (easy parking).

Sleeping near Snowshill: The pretty, one-pub village of Snowshill holds a gem of a B&B. **$$ Sheepscombe House B&B** is a clean and pristine home on a working sheep farm. It's immersed in the best of Cotswold scenery, with plenty of sheep in the nearby fields. Jacki and Tim Harrison rent three modern, spacious, and thoughtfully appointed rooms (Db-£80–85, Tb-£120, folding cots available, just a third of a mile south of Snowshill—look for signs, tel. 01386/853-769, www.broadway-cotswolds.co.uk/sheepscombe .html, reservations@snowshill-broadway.co.uk). Tim, who's happy to give you a local's perspective on this area, also runs a car service (see page 237).

More Sights near Chipping Campden

▲**Hidcote Manor Garden**—If you like gardens, the grounds around this manor house (which has only a few rooms open to the public) are worth a look. Located northeast of Chipping Campden, Hidcote is where garden designers pioneered the notion of creating a series of outdoor "rooms," each with a unique theme (e.g., maple room, red room, and so on) and separated by a yew-tree hedge. Follow your nose through a clever series of small gardens that lead delightfully from one to the next. Among the best in England, Hidcote gardens are at their fragrant peak in May, June, and July (£8, April–Oct Sat–Wed 10:30–18:00, closed Thu–Fri and Nov–March, last entry 1 hour before closing, tearoom, 4 miles northeast of Chipping Campden on B4035, tel. 01386/438-333, www.nationaltrust.org.uk).

▲**Cotswold Farm Park**—Here's a delight for young and old alike. This park is the private venture of the Henson family, who are pas-

sionate about preserving rare and endangered breeds of local animals. While it feels like a kids' zone (with all the family-friendly facilities you can imagine), it's actually a fascinating chance for anyone to get up close and (very) personal with piles of mostly cute animals, including the sheep that made this region famous—the big and woolly Cotswold Lion. A busy schedule of demonstrations gives you a look at local farm life. Take full advantage of the excellent (and included) audioguide, narrated by founder Joe Henson and filled with his passion for the farm's mission. Buy a bag of seed (50p) upon arrival, or have your map eaten by munchy goats as I did. Check the events board as you enter for times for the milking, shearing, or the well-done "sheep show." Tykes love the little tractor rides, maze, and zip line, but the "touch barn" is really where it's at for little kids (£5.75, kids-£4.75, daily mid-March–early-Sept 10:30–17:00, closed off-season, good £2 guidebook, decent cafeteria, tel. 01451/850-307, www.cotswoldfarmpark.co.uk, well-signposted 15 minutes from Stow just off the Tewkesbury road—B4077).

Broadway—This postcard-pretty town, a couple of miles west of Chipping Campden, is filled with inviting shops and fancy teahouses. Because most big bus tours stop here, I give Broadway a miss. But with a new road that allows traffic to skirt the town, Broadway has gotten cuter than ever. Broadway has good bus connections with Chipping Campden (bus #21).

Stow-on-the-Wold

Located 10 miles south of Chipping Campden, Stow-on-the-Wold—with a name that means "meeting place on the uplands"—is

the highest point of the Cotswolds. Despite its crowds, it retains its charm, and it merits ▲▲. Most of the tourists are day-trippers, so even summer nights are peaceful. Stow has no real sights other than the town itself, some good pubs, antique stores, and cute shops draped seductively around a big town square. Visit the church, with its evocative old door guarded by ancient yew trees and the tombs of wool tycoons. A visit to Stow is not complete until you've locked your partner in the stocks on the green.

ORIENTATION

Tourist Information

At the helpful TI on the main square, get the handy little 50p walking-tour brochure called *Town Trail* and the free *Cotswold Events* guide (March–Oct Mon–Sat 9:30–17:30, closed Sun, Nov–Feb closes at 16:30, tel. 01451/831-082). The TI also sells National Express Bus tickets; reserves tickets for events (Stratford plays, £2 fee); sells discounted tickets for Warwick Castle, Blenheim Palace, and other sights; and books rooms for a £2 fee (save money and book direct).

Helpful Hints

Internet Access: Try the erratically open library across from the TI, or at the youth hostel (17:00–23:00 nightly).

Taxi: See "Getting Around the Cotswolds—By Taxi" (page 236).

Parking: Park anywhere on Market Square free for two hours, or overnight between 16:00 and 11:00 (free from 18:00–9:00 plus any 2 hours—they note your license so you can't just move to another spot, £40 tickets for offenders). One "Long Stay" lot is 400 yards from the town square at the Tesco supermarket (free, follow the signs).

Local Tours: If you'd like to learn more about Stow, consider a walk with one of the **Cotswold Voluntary Wardens,** a group of guides who enjoy showing off their hometown to visitors. While no tours are regularly scheduled, they can be arranged through the TI—usually at very short notice. They only ask for a small donation for their club—£10 per group (£2 per person) for an hour-long walk is plenty.

SELF-GUIDED WALK

Welcome to Stow-on-the-Wold

This little four-stop walk covers about 500 yards and takes about 45 minutes.

Start at the **Stocks on the Market Square.** Imagine this village during the time when people were publicly ridiculed here as a punishment. Stow was born in pre-Roman times; it's where three trade routes crossed at a high point in the region (altitude: 800 feet). This main square hosted an international fair starting in 1107, and people came from as far away as Italy for the wool fleece. This grand square was a vast, grassy expanse. Picture it in the Middle

Ages (before the buildings in the center were added): a public commons and grazing ground, paths worn through the grass, and no well. Until 1867, Stow had no running water; women fetched water from the "Roman Well" a quarter-mile away.

A thin skin of topsoil covers the Cotswold limestone, from which these buildings were made. The **Stow Lodge** (next to the church) lies a little lower than the church; the lodge sits on the spot where locals quarried stones for the church. That building, originally the rectory, is now a hotel. The church (where we'll end this little walk) is made of Cotswold stone, and marks the summit of the hill upon which the town was built. The stocks are a great photo op (my kids locked me in for a photo our family used for a Christmas card).

• *Walk past the youth hostel to the market, and cross to the other side of the square. Notice how locals seem to belong to a tight little community.*

For 500 years, the **Market Cross** stood in the market reminding all Christian merchants to "trade fairly under the sight of God." Notice the stubs of the iron fence in the concrete base—a reminder of how countless wrought-iron fences were cut down and given to the government to be melted down during World War II. (Recently, it's been disclosed that all that iron ended up in junk heaps—frantic patriotism just wasted.)

Stow-on-the-Wold

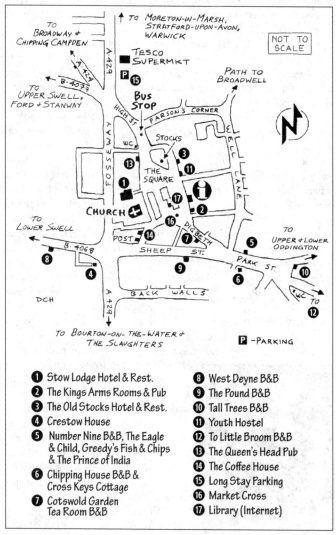

TO MORETON-IN-MARSH, STRATFORD-UPON-AVON, WARWICK

TO BROADWAY & CHIPPING CAMPDEN

A-429

B-4077

TO UPPER SWELL, FORD & STANWAY

NOT TO SCALE

TESCO SUPERMKT

PATH TO BROADWELL

BUS STOP

PARSON'S CORNER

HIGH ST.

FOSSEWAY

WC

STOCKS

THE SQUARE

CHURCH

TO LOWER SWELL

B-4068

POST

SHEEP ST.

DIGBETH

TO UPPER & LOWER ODDINGTON

PARK ST.

BACK WALLS

DCH

A-429

TO BOURTON-ON-THE-WATER & THE SLAUGHTERS

WC TO

P -PARKING

1. Stow Lodge Hotel & Rest.
2. The Kings Arms Rooms & Pub
3. The Old Stocks Hotel & Rest.
4. Crestow House
5. Number Nine B&B, The Eagle & Child, Greedy's Fish & Chips & The Prince of India
6. Chipping House B&B & Cross Keys Cottage
7. Cotswold Garden Tea Room B&B
8. West Deyne B&B
9. The Pound B&B
10. Tall Trees B&B
11. Youth Hostel
12. To Little Broom B&B
13. The Queen's Head Pub
14. The Coffee House
15. Long Stay Parking
16. Market Cross
17. Library (Internet)

The Cotswolds

The plaque on the cross honors the Lord of the Manor, who donated money back to his tenants, allowing the town to finally pay for running water in 1878. Scan the square for a tipsy shop locals call the "wonky house." Because it lists (tilts) so severely, it's a listed building—the facade is protected (but the interior is modern and level). The Kings Arms, with its great gables and scary chimney, was once where travelers parked their horses before spending the night. In the 1600s, this was considered the premium "posting house" between London and Birmingham. Today, the Kings Arms cooks up some of the best food in town, and rents rooms upstairs (see "Sleeping," below).

During the English Civil War, which pitted Parliamentarians against Royalists, Stow-on-the-Wold remained staunchly loyal to the king. (Charles I is said to have eaten at the Kings Arms before a great battle.) Because of its allegiance, the town has an abundance of pubs with royal names (King's This and Queen's That).

• *Walk past the Kings Arms down Digbeth Street to the little triangular park located in front of the Methodist Church and across from the Royalist Hotel. This hotel—along with about 20 others—claims to be the oldest in England, dating from 947.*

Just beyond the small grassy triangle with benches is the place where—twice a year, in May and October—the Gypsy Horse Fair attracts Roma (Gypsies) and Travelers (Irish Tinkers) from far and wide. They congregate down the street on the Maugersbury Road. Locals paint a colorful picture of the Roma, Travelers, and horses inundating the town. The young women dress up because the fair also functions as a marriage market.

• *Hike up Sheep Street. You'll pass a boutique-filled former brewery yard, Fleece Alley (just wide enough for a single file of sheep to walk on—easier to count them on market days), and a fine antique bookstore. Turn right on Church Street, which leads past the best coffee shop in town (The Coffee House), and find the church.*

Before entering the **church,** circle it. On the back side, a door is flanked by two ancient yew trees. While to many it looks like the Christian "Behold, I stand at the door and knock" door, J. R. R. Tolkien fans see something quite different. Tolkien hiked the Cotswolds, and had a passion for sketching evocative trees such as this. *Lord of the Rings* enthusiasts are convinced this must be the inspiration for the door into Moria.

While the church (open daily—apart from services—9:00–18:00) dates from Saxon times, today's structure is from the 15th century. Its history is played up in leaflets and plaques just inside the door. The floor is paved with the tombs of big shots who made their money from wool, and are still boastful in death. (Find the tombs crowned with bales of wool.)

During the English Civil War (1615), more than 1,000 soldiers were imprisoned here. The tombstone in front of the altar remembers the Royalist Captain Keyt. His long hair, lace, and sash indicate he was a "cavalier," and true blue to the king

(Cromwellians were called "round heads"—named for their short hair). Study the crude provincial art—child-like skulls and (in the upper corners) symbols of his service to the king (armor, weapons).

On the right wall, a monument remembers the many boys from this small town who were lost in World War I (50 out of a population of 2,000). There were far fewer in World War II. The biscuit-shaped plaque (to the left) remembers an admiral from Stow who lost four sons defending the realm. It's sliced from an ancient fluted column (which locals believe is from Ephesus, Turkey). While most of the windows are Victorian (19th-century), the two sets high up in the clerestory are from the dreamier Pre-Raphaelite school (c. 1920).

Finally, don't miss the kneelers, made by a committed band of women known as "the Kneeler Group." They meet most Tuesday mornings at 10:30 in the Church Room to needlepoint, sip coffee, and enjoy a good chat. (The vicar assured me that any tourist wanting to join them would be more than welcome. The help would be appreciated and the company would be excellent.)

SLEEPING

(£1 = about $2, country code: 44, area code: 01451)

In Stow

$$$ **Stow Lodge Hotel** fills the historic church rectory with lots of old English charm. Facing the town square, with its own sprawling and peaceful garden, this lavish old place offers 21 large, thoughtfully appointed rooms with soft beds, stately public spaces, and a cushy-chair lounge (Db-£105–134, closed Jan, The Square, tel. 01451/830-485, fax 01451/831-671, www.stowlodge.com, enquiries@stowlodge.com, helpful Hartley family).

$$$ **The Kings Arms,** with nine rooms, manages to keep its historic Cotswolds character while still feeling fresh and modern in all the right ways (Sb-£50–90, Db-£90–120, higher prices are for weekends, steep stairs, Market Square, tel. 01451/830-364, www .thekingsarmsstow.co.uk, info@thekingsarmsstow.co.uk). Jo, Peter, and Sam run the hotel while Peter's brother Thomas cooks—see "Eating," later in this chapter.

$$$ **The Old Stocks Hotel,** facing the town square, is a good value, even though the building itself is classier than its 18 big, simply furnished rooms. It's friendly and family-run, yet professional as can be. Beware the man-killer beams (Sb-£45, standard Db-£90, refurbished "superior" Db-£110, Tb-£120, these prices promised with this book through 2008, request this discount when you reserve, family deals, ground-floor rooms, attached

bar and restaurant, garden patio, The Square, tel. 01451/830-666, fax 01451/870-014, www.oldstockshotel.co.uk, rs@oldstockshotel .co.uk, Jason and Helen Allen).

$$ Crestow House, a grand manor house, dates predominantly from the Victorian era. It stands at the edge of town facing the wide-open countryside, keeping its back to the main road. With a gracious spaciousness and its four rooms holding antique furniture, this creaky place oozes with charm and character (Db-£80, 2-night minimum, 10 percent off for 3 nights, no children under 12, sunny-even-in-the-rain conservatory, 2 blocks from The Square at intersection of A429 and B4068, tel. 01451/830-969, fax 01451/832-129, www.crestow.co.uk, fsimonetti@btinternet.com, Frank). Frank also rents a six-person cottage (£550-650/week).

$$ Number Nine has three large, bright, recently refurbished, and tastefully decorated rooms. This 200-year-old home comes with watch-your-head beamed ceilings and old wooden doors (Db-£60-70, 9 Park Street, tel. 01451/870-333, www.number-nine.info, enquiries@number-nine.info, James and Carol Brown).

$$ Chipping House B&B is a fine, warm, old place with three rooms and a welcoming lounge—it feels like a visit to auntie's house (Db-£60-70, cash only, Park Street, tel. 01451/831-756, chippinghouse@tesco.net, dog-lovers Merv and Carolyne Oliver).

$$ Cotswold Garden Tea Room B&B rents two bright and comfy rooms in a charming if saggy 17th-century building. It has an inviting garden above a fun little tearoom (D-£60, £5 less for 2 nights or in off-season, family deals, cash only, Digbeth Street, tel. 01451/870-999).

$$ Cross Keys Cottage offers four smallish, outmoded rooms, complete with plenty of fringe and bright floral bedspreads. Kindly Margaret and Roger Welton take care of their guests in this 350-year-old beamed cottage (D-£60, Db-£65, Park Street, tel. & fax 01451/831-128, rogxmag@hotmail.com).

$ West Deyne B&B, with two cozy rooms, a peaceful garden, a fountain, and a small conservatory overlooking the countryside, has a comforting, grandmotherly charm. It offers plush privacy (D-£45-50, cash only, evening tea and biscuits, Lower Swell Road, tel. 01451/831-011, run by thoughtful Joan Cave).

$ The Pound is the quaint, 500-year-old, slanty, cozy, and low-beamed home of Patricia Whitehead. She offers two bright, inviting, twin-bedded rooms and a classic old fireplace lounge (D-£45-50, cash only, downtown on Sheep Street, tel. & fax 01451/830-229, brent.ford@zoom .co.uk).

$ **Tall Trees B&B,** on the Oddington Road 100 yards outside of Stow, is a rough and real farm, run by no-nonsense Jennifer, who rents six contemporary rooms in an old-style building (Db-£55–60, family room-£60–90, cash only, two ground-floor rooms, off-road parking available, tel. 01451/831-296, fax 01451/870-049, talltreestow@aol.com). She also rents a lovely cottage that sleeps eight (£500–800/week, kitchenette).

$ *Hostel:* The **Stow-on-the-Wold Youth Hostel,** on Stow's main square, is the only hostel in the Cotswolds, with 48 beds in nine rooms. It has a friendly atmosphere, good hot meals, and a members' kitchen (dorm bed-£16.30, non-members-£3 extra, includes sheets, some family rooms with private bathrooms, evening meals, reception closed 10:00–17:00, Internet-£1/15 min, laundry, lockers, rental bikes, reserve long in advance, tel. 01451/830-497, fax 01451/870-102, www.yha.org.uk, stow@yha.org.uk, manager Rob). Anyone can eat here: Breakfast is £4.50, and dinner is £9.

Near Stow

$ **Little Broom B&B** hides out in the neighboring hamlet of Maugersbury, which enjoys the peace Stow once had. It rents three cozy rooms that share a fine garden and a pool (S-£30, D-£50, Db-£55–65, apartment Db-£70 for two people plus £10–15 for each extra person, cash only, tel. & fax 01451/830-510, mobile 079-8983-2714). Brenda keeps racehorses just beyond her pool, which hides in a low-lying greenhouse to keep it warm throughout the summer (guests welcome). It's an easy eight-minute walk from Stow: Head east on Park Street, taking the right fork to Maugersbury, then turn right on the road marked *No Through Road.*

EATING

In Stow

These places are all within a five-minute walk of each other, either on the main square or downhill on Queen and Park streets.

Restaurants and Pubs

Stow Lodge is a formal but friendly bar serving fine £8 lunches and a popular £22 three-course dinner. This is the choice of the town's proper ladies (daily 12:00–14:00 & 19:00–20:45, smoke-free, veggie options, good wines, also has pricier restaurant, just off main square).

The Old Stocks Hotel Restaurant, which might at first glance seem like a tired and big hotel dining room, is actually a classy place to dine. With attentive service and an interesting menu, they provide tasty and well-presented food. If they're not too busy, you can order more economically from the bar menu, and sit in the fancy dining room enjoying views of the square. In good weather, the garden out back is a hit (£8–15 meals, nightly 18:30–20:30, tel. 01451/830-666).

The Kings Arms has two floors, both serving traditional English fare. Downstairs, you'll find pub food, while upstairs has an "English with a twist" menu in a once-medieval, now-classy ambience (£10–12 pub food, £15–20 meals, daily 12:30–14:30 & 19:00–21:30, sandwiches available all day, reserve for dinner, tel. 01451/830-364).

The Queen's Head faces the Market Square, next to the Stow Lodge. With a classic pub vibe, it's a great place to bring your dog, eat pub grub, and drink the local Cotswold brew, Donnington Ale (£8 plates, daily 12:00–14:30 & 18:30–20:30).

The Eagle and Child is more of a hotel restaurant than a pub, with delicious food and indifferent service (meals available daily 12:00–14:30 & 18:00–21:00, afternoon tea available Fri–Sun, Park Street, tel. 01451/830-670).

Eating Cheaply

Head to the grassy triangle where Digbeth hits Sheep Street; there, you'll find take-out fish-and-chips, Indian food, and Chinese. You can picnic at the triangle, or on the benches by the stocks on Market Street.

Greedy's Fish and Chips, on Park Street, is a favorite with locals for take-out (Mon–Sat 12:00–14:00 & 16:30–21:00, closed Sun).

The Prince of India offers good Indian food in a delightful setting, to take out or eat in (nightly 18:00–23:30, Park Street, tel. 01451/870-821).

The Coffee House provides a nice break from the horses-and-hounds traditional cuisine found elsewhere. Come here for £5–8 soup, salad, and good coffee (daily 10:00–16:00, Church Street, tel. 01451/870-802).

Even Cheaper: Small grocery stores face the main square, and a big Tesco supermarket is 200 yards north of town. The youth hostel (see above) welcomes non-hostelers for breakfast (£4.50) or its evening family-style meal (£9, drop by early to confirm time and book a spot).

Pub Dinner Hike from Stow

From Stow, consider taking a half-hour scenic countryside walk past the old Roman Well to the village of Broadwell. There, **The Fox Inn** serves good pub dinners and draws traditional ales (food served Mon–Fri 11:30–13:30 & 18:00–21:00, Sat 11:30–14:00 & 18:00–21:00, shorter hours Sun and no food Sun night, on the village green, tel. 01451/870-909).

Great Country Pubs near Stow

These three places—known for their great £10 meals and fine settings—are very popular. Arrive early or phone in a reservation. (If you show up at 20:00, it's unlikely that they'll be able to seat you for dinner if you haven't called first.) These pubs allow "well-behaved children," and are practical only for those with a car. The first two (in Oddington, two miles from Stow) are more trendy and fresh, yet still in a traditional pub setting. The Plough (in Ford, a few miles farther away) is your jolly olde dark pub.

The Horse and Groom Village Inn in Upper Oddington is a smart place with a sea-grass-green carpet in a 16th-century inn, serving modern English and Mediterranean food with a good wine list (28 wines by the glass) and serious beer (daily 12:00–14:00 & 18:30–21:00, tel. 01451/830-584).

The Fox Inn, a different Fox Inn than the one listed on the previous page, is old but fresh and famous among locals for its quality cooking (daily 12:00–14:00 & 18:30–22:00, in Lower Oddington, tel. 01451/870-555). They also rent three rooms.

The Plough Inn fills a fascinating old building, once an old coaching inn and later a courthouse. Ask the bar staff for some fun history—like what "you're barred" means. Eat from the same traditional English menu in the restaurant, bar, or garden. They are serious about both their beer and—judging by the extensive list of homemade temptations—their dessert (£10 meals, daily 12:00–21:00, 4 miles from Stow on Tewkesbury Road in hamlet of Ford, reservations smart, tel. 01386/584-215).

Near Stow-on-the-Wold

These sights are all south of Stow: Some are very close (Bourton-on-the-Water, the Slaughters, and Northleach), and one is 20 miles away (Cirencester).

▲Bourton-on-the-Water

I can't figure out whether they call this "the Venice of the Cotswolds" because of its quaint canals or its miserable crowds. Either way, it's very pretty. This town—four miles south of Stow and a mile from the Slaughters (see below)—gets overrun by midday and weekend hordes. Surrounding Bourton's green are sidewalks jammed with disoriented tourists wearing nametags. If you can avoid them, it's worth a drive-through, a few cynical comments, and maybe a short stop. While it's mobbed with Japanese tour groups during the day, it's pleasantly empty in the early evening and after dark.

Parking: Finding a spot here is predictably tough. Even during the busy business day, rather than park in the pay-and-display parking lot far from the center, drive right into town and wait for a spot on High Street just past the village green (there's a long row of free two-hour spots in front of the Edinburgh Woolen Mills Shop).

Tourist Information: The TI is just off Victoria Street (tel. 01451/820-211, www.bourtoninfo.com).

Sights: Bourton has three sights worth considering. All are on High Street in the town center. In addition to these, families also enjoy Bourton's new kid-perfect **leisure centre** (big pool and sauna, 5-min walk from town center, daily 8:00–18:00, tel. 01451/824-024).

▲**Motor Museum**—This excellent, jumbled museum shows off a lifetime's accumulation of vintage cars, old lacquered signs, threadbare toys, and prewar memorabilia. Wander the car-and-driver displays, from the automobile's early days to the stylish James Bond era. Talk to an elderly Brit who's touring the place for some personal memories (£3.60, Feb–Nov daily 10:00–18:00, closed Dec–Jan, in the mill facing the town center, tel. 01451/821-255, www.cotswold-motor-museum.co.uk).

Model Railway Exhibition—This exhibit of four model railway layouts is impressive only to train buffs (£2.25, June–Aug daily 11:00–17:00, Sept–May weekends only, limited hours Jan, located in the back of a hobby shop, tel. 01451/820-686, www.bourtonmodelrailway.co.uk).

Model Village—This light but fun display re-creates the town on a 1:9 scale in a tiny park, and has an attached room full of tiny models showing off various bits of British domestic life (£2.75 for the park, £1 more for the model room, daily 10:00–17:45, tel. 01451/820-467).

Upper and Lower Slaughter

Lower Slaughter is a classic village, with ducks, a working water mill, and usually an artist busy at her easel somewhere. Just behind the skippable Old Mill Museum, two kissing gates lead to the path that goes to nearby Upper Slaughter (a 10-minute walk or 2-minute drive away).

In **Upper Slaughter,** walk through the yew trees (sacred in pagan days) down a lane through the raised graveyard (a buildup of centuries of graves) to the peaceful church. In the back of the fine graveyard, the statue of a wistful woman looks over the tomb of an 18th-century rector (sculpted by the rector's son).

By the way, "Slaughter" has nothing to do with lamb chops. It comes from the sloe tree (the one used to make sloe gin). These towns are an easy two-hour round-trip walk from Bourton. You could also walk from Bourton through the Slaughters to Stow. The small roads from Upper Slaughter to Ford and Kineton are some of England's most scenic. Roll your window down and joyride slowly.

▲Northleach

One of the "untouched and untouristed" Cotswold villages, Northleach is worth a short stop. The town's impressive main square and church attest to its position as a major wool center in the Middle Ages. Park on the square to check out the TI (which has walking brochures), the mechanical music museum, and the church (both described below). Northleach is nine miles south of Stow, down A429. Bus #855 connects it to Stow and Moreton.

▲Keith Harding's World of Mechanical Music—In 1962, Keith Harding, tired of giving ad-lib "living room tours," opened this delightful little one-room place. It offers a unique opportunity to listen to 300 years of amazing self-playing musical instruments. It's run by people who are passionate about the restoration work they do on these musical marvels. The curators delight in demonstrating about 20 of the museum's machines with each tour. You'll hear Victorian music boxes and the earliest polyphones (record players) playing cylinders and then discs—all from an age when music was made mechanically, without the help of electricity. The admission fee includes an essential hour-long tour (£8, daily 10:00–18:00, last entry at 16:45, tours go constantly—join one in progress, High Street, Northleach, tel. 01451/860-181, www .mechanicalmusic.co.uk).

Church of Saints Peter and Paul—This fine Perpendicular Gothic church has been called the "cathedral of the Cotswolds." It's one of the Cotswolds' finest two "wool" churches (along with Chipping Campden's), paid for by 15th-century wool tycoons. Find the oldest tombstone. The brass plaques on the floor memorialize big shots, showing sheep and sacks of wool at their long-dead feet and inscriptions mixing Latin and the old English. You're welcome to do some brass rubbing if you get a permit from the post office (£2.50).

▲Bibury

Six miles northeast of Cirencester (described on next page), Bibury is a favorite with British picnickers fond of strolling and fishing. This village offers some relaxing sights, including a Cotswolds museum, a row of very old weavers' cottages, a trout farm, a stream teeming with fat fish and proud ducks, and a church surrounded by rosebushes, each tended by a volunteer of the parish. A protected wetlands area on the far side of the stream hosts newts and water voles—walk around to the old weavers' Arlington Row and back on the far side of the marsh, peeking into the rushes for wildlife.

Don't miss the scenic Coln Valley drive from A429 to Bibury

The Cotswolds

through the enigmatic villages of Coln St. Dennis, Coln Rogers, Coln Powell, and Winson.

▲▲Cirencester

Nearly 2,000 years ago, Cirencester (SIGH-ren-ses-ter) was the ancient Roman city of Corinium. It's 20 miles from Stow down A429, which was called Fosse Way in Roman times. In Cirencester, stop by the Corinium Museum to find out why they say, "If you scratch Gloucestershire, you'll find Rome" (£4, Mon–Sat 10:00–17:00, Sun 14:00–17:00). Cirencester's church is the largest of the Cotswolds "wool" churches. The cutesy Brewery Art crafts center entertains visitors with traditional weaving and potting, workshops, an interesting gallery, and a good coffee shop. Monday and Friday are general-market days, Friday features an antique market, and Saturday hosts a crafts market. The TI is in the Cornhill Marketplace (Mon–Sat 9:30–7:30, closed Sun, tel. 01285/654-180).

Moreton-in-Marsh

This workaday town—worth ▲—is like Stow or Chipping Campden without the touristy sugar. Rather than gift and antique shops, you'll find streets lined with real shops: ironmongers selling cottage nameplates and carpet shops strewn with the remarkable patterns that decorate B&B floors. A shin-kickin' traditional market of 260 stalls fills High Street each Tuesday, as it has for the last 400 years (8:00–16:00, handicrafts, farm produce, clothing, great people-watching, best if you go early). The Cotswolds has an economy aside from tourism, and you'll notice it here.

ORIENTATION

Moreton has a tiny, sleepy train station two blocks from High Street, lots of bus connections, and the best TI in the region (Mon 8:45–16:00, Tue–Thu 8:45–17:15, Fri 8:45–16:45, Sat 10:00–13:00, closed Sun, good public WC, 20p *Town Trail* leaflet for self-guided walk, rail and bus schedules, racks of fliers, tel. 01608/650-881).

Helpful Hints

Internet Access: It's free at the TI (see above) and at the library on High Street (Tue and Thu all day, Fri afternoon only, Sat morning only, closed Sun–Mon and Wed).

Laundry: The handy **Laundercentre** is a block in front of the train station on New Road (daily 7:30–18:00, £4.50 self-service,

The Cotswolds

Moreton-in-Marsh

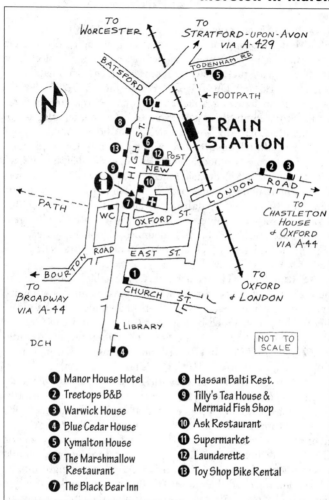

1. Manor House Hotel
2. Treetops B&B
3. Warwick House
4. Blue Cedar House
5. Kymalton House
6. The Marshmallow Restaurant
7. The Black Bear Inn
8. Hassan Balti Rest.
9. Tilly's Tea House & Mermaid Fish Shop
10. Ask Restaurant
11. Supermarket
12. Launderette
13. Toy Shop Bike Rental

or drop off Mon–Fri 9:00–10:30 for £1 extra and same-day service, tel. 01608/650-888).

Baggage Storage: While there is no formal baggage storage in town, the Black Bear Inn (next to the TI) might let you leave bags there if you buy a drink.

Parking: It's easy—anywhere on High Street is fine any time, as long as you want, for free.

Bike Rental, Taxis, and Car Rental: See "Getting Around the Cotswolds" (page 234).

SLEEPING

(£1 = about $2, country code: 44, area code: 01608)

$$$ Manor House Hotel is Moreton's big old hotel, dating from 1545 but sporting such modern amenities as toilets and electricity. Its 34 classy-for-the-Cotswolds rooms and its garden invite relaxation (Sb-£115–160, Db-£135–210, family suite-£175–220, elevator, Wi-Fi, log fire in winter, attached restaurant—no children under 8, on far end of High Street away from train station, tel. 01608/650-501, fax 01608/651-481, www.cotswold-inns-hotels.co.uk).

$ Kymalton House has two bright, tastefully decorated rooms in a gracious modern house. With a pleasant garden, it's set back off of a busy street just outside the town center (Db-£60, cheaper for 3 or more nights, double beds only, cash only, closed Dec–Jan, tel. 01608/650-487, kymalton@uwclub.net, Sylvia and Doug Gould). It's a seven-minute walk from town (walk past Budgens supermarket, turn right on Todenham Road, look for house on the right). They'll happily pick up and drop off train travelers at the station.

$ Blue Cedar House has four comfortable rooms and two bungalow apartments with an airy breakfast room full of plants. It's on a busy road but has double-paned windows and a pleasing setting, surrounded by a large garden. Sandra and Graham Billinger have been keeping travelers contented for decades (S-£28, D/Db-£56, Tb-£70, cash only, 5-min walk from center, Stow Road, tel. 01608/650-299, gandsib@dialstart.net).

$ Treetops B&B is plush, with six spacious, attractive rooms, a sun lounge, and a three-quarter-acre backyard. Liz and Ben (the family dog) will make you feel right at home—if you meet their two-night minimum (large Db-£55, gigantic Db-£60, ground-floor rooms have patios, set far back from the busy road, London Road, tel. & fax 01608/651-036, www.treetopscotswolds.co.uk, treetops1@talk21.com, Liz and Brian Dean). It's an eight-minute walk from town and the railway station (exit station, keep left, go left on bridge over train tracks, look for sign, then long driveway).

$ Warwick House, just down the road from Treetops, is where "half-American" Charlie Grant rents three rooms in a contemporary, casual house. It's on a noisy road, but the windows are triple-glazed. Charlie can do your laundry if you stay three or more nights (Sb-£35, Db-£50, Tb-£60, cash only, Wi-Fi, no kids under 12, will pick up from train station, access to nearby Fire Service College Leisure Club swimming pool, London Road, tel. 01608/650-773, www.snoozeandsizzle.com).

EATING

A stroll up and down High Street lets you survey your small-town options.

The Marshmallow is relatively upscale but affordable, with a menu that includes traditional English dishes as well as lasagna and salads (£8–12 entrées, 15 fancy teas, Tue 10:00–16:00, Wed–Sat 10:00–20:00, Sun 10:00–17:00, closed Mon, reservations advised, shady back garden for summer dining, tel. 01608/651-536).

The Black Bear Inn offers traditional English food. As you enter, choose between the dining room on the left, and the pub on the right (£5–8 meals and daily specials, daily 12:00–14:00 & 18:30–21:00, tel. 01608/652-992).

Hassan Balti, with tasty Bangladeshi food, is a fine value for sit-down or take-out (£7 meals, daily 12:00–14:00 & 18:00–23:30, tel. 01608/650-798).

Tilly's Tea House serves fresh soups, salads, sandwiches, and pastries for lunch in a cheerful spot on High Street across from the TI (£5 light meals, good cream tea-£5, daily 9:00–16:30, tel. 01608/650-000).

Ask, a chain restaurant across the street, has decent pastas, pizzas, and salads, and a breezy, family-friendly atmosphere (£7 pizzas, daily, take-out available, tel. 01608/651-119).

Mermaid fish shop is popular for its take-out fish and tasty selection of traditional pies (Mon–Sat 12:00–14:00 & 17:00–22:30, closed Sun).

Picnic: There's a small **Co-op** grocery in the town center (Mon–Sat 8:00–20:00, Sun 8:00–18:00), and the big **Budgens** supermarket is indeed super (Mon–Sat 8:00–22:00, Sun 10:00–16:00, far end of High Street). There are picnic tables across the busy street in pleasant Victoria Park.

TRANSPORTATION CONNECTIONS

Moreton, the only Cotswolds town with a train station, is also the best base to explore the region by bus (see "Getting Around the Cotswolds," page 234).

From Moreton by Train to: London's Paddington Station (one-way-£25, round-trip after 8:15-£28.50, 10/day, 1.5 hrs), **Heathrow** (10/day, 2.5 hrs, train to Reading, then RailAir Link shuttle bus to airport), **Bath** (hourly, 2 hrs, 1–3 transfers), **Oxford** (3/day direct, 10/day with transfers, 40 min), **Ironbridge Gorge** (hourly, 3.5 hrs, with transfers at Worcester Shrub Hill and Birmingham New Street, arrive Telford, then catch bus or cab 7 miles to Ironbridge Gorge). Train info: tel. 08457-484-950.

Near Moreton-in-Marsh

▲Chastleton House

This stately home, located about five miles southeast of Moreton-in-Marsh, was actually lived in by the same family from 1607 until 1991. It offers a rare peek into a Jacobean gentry house. (Jacobean, which comes from the Latin for "James," indicates the style from the time of King James I—the early 1600s.) Built, like most Cotswold palaces, with wool money, it gradually declined with the fortunes of its aristocratic family until, according to the last lady of the house, it

was "held together by cobwebs." It came to the National Trust on condition that they would maintain its musty Jacobean ambience. Wander on creaky floorboards, many of them original, and chat with volunteer guides stationed in each room. It's an uppity place that doesn't encourage spontaneity. The rules of croquet were formalized in this house in 1868, and docents are proud to be members of one of the best croquet teams in the region. Page through the early 20th-century family photo albums in the room just off the entry. Because only 175 visitors a day are allowed (25 people per half-hour), you're wise to call in advance to get a timed entry—though it's not possible on the same day (£7; April–Sept Wed–Sat 13:00–17:00, closed Sun–Tue; Oct Wed–Sat 13:00–16:00, closed Sun–Tue; last entry 1 hour before closing; closed Nov–March; well-signposted, 5-min hike to house from free parking lot, tel. 01494/755-560).

▲▲▲Blenheim Palace

Too many palaces can send you into a furniture-wax coma. But everyone should see Blenheim. The Duke of Marlborough's home—the largest in England—is still lived in, which is wonderfully obvious as you prowl through it. Note: Americans who pronounce the place "blen-HEIM" are the butt of jokes. It's "BLEN-em."

Cost, Hours, Information: £16, family deals, mid-Feb–Oct daily 10:30–17:30, last tour departs at 16:45, park open but palace closed Nov–mid-Dec Mon–Tue and mid-Dec–mid-Feb, tel. 01993/811-091, recorded info tel. 0870-060-2080, www.blenheimpalace.com.

Getting There: Blenheim Palace sits at the edge of the cute cobbled town of Woodstock, near the university town of Oxford.

The Cotswolds

The train station nearest the palace (Hanborough, 1.5 miles away) has no taxi or bus service. From the Cotswolds, your easiest train connection is from Moreton-in-Marsh to Oxford, then catch the bus to Blenheim (from the Oxford train station, it's a 5-min walk to Gloucester Green bus station, then catch bus #20a, #20b, or #20c to the palace gate; Mon–Sat 8:55–17:00, Sun 10:00–15:30, 2/hr, 30–40 min; bus tel. 01865/772-250).

Background: John Churchill, first duke of Marlborough, beat the French at the Battle of Blenheim in 1704. So the king built him this nice home, perhaps the finest Baroque building in England (designed by playwright-turned-architect John Vanbrugh). Ten dukes of Marlborough later, it's as impressive as ever. (The current, 11th duke considers the 12th more of an error than an heir, and what to do about him is quite an issue.) The 2,000-acre yard, well-designed by Lancelot "Capability" Brown, is as majestic to some as the palace itself. The view just past the outer gate as you enter is a classic.

➋ Self-Guided Tour: The well-organized palace tour begins with a fine **Churchill exhibit,** centered on the bed in which Sir Winston was born in 1874 (prematurely...begun while his mother was at a Blenheim Palace party). Take your time in the Churchill exhibit. Then catch the 45-minute guided tours (6/hr, included with ticket, last tour at 16:45). When the palace is really busy, they dispense with guided tours and go "free flow," allowing those with an appetite for learning to strike up conversations with docents in each room.

Recently, the palace added a modern, 45-minute, multimedia "visitors' experience"—a tour called the **Untold Story** (6/hr, included with ticket). You're guided through 300 years of history by a maid named Grace Ridley. (If you have limited time to spend at the palace, focus on Churchill instead.)

For a more extensive visit, follow up the general tour with a 30-minute guided walk through the actual **private apartments** of the duke. Tours leave at the top and bottom of each hour (£4, May–Sept daily 12:00–16:30, tickets are limited, tours don't run if the duke's home, buy from table in library or at Flagstaff info booth outside main gates, enter in corner of courtyard to left of grand palace entry).

Kids enjoy the **pleasure garden** (a tiny train takes you from the palace parking lot to the garden, but if you have a car, it's more efficient simply to drive there). A lush and humid greenhouse flutters with butterflies. A kid zone includes a few second-rate games and the "world's largest symbolic hedge maze." The maze is worth a look if you haven't seen one and could use some exercise.

Churchill fans can visit his **tomb,** a short walk away, in the Bladon town churchyard.

The Cotswolds

Sleeping near Blenheim Palace, in Woodstock: Blenheim nestles up against the two-road town of Woodstock, which offers walkable accommodations and a nice selection of eateries.

$$ Blenheim Guest House, charming and 200 years old, has six rooms in the town center. Literally next door to the palace's green gate, it's a five-minute walk from the palace (Db-£60–70 depending on size, 17 Park Street, tel. 01993/813-814, fax 01993/813-810, www.theblenheim.com, theblenheim@aol.com).

$$ The Townhouse is a refurbished 18th-century stone house with five plush rooms (Sb-£55, Db-£80, Tb-£100; includes breakfast, afternoon tea, and snacks on weekends; in town center at 15 High Street, tel. & fax 01993/810-843).

$$ Wishaw House B&B is grandmotherly and offers two rooms (D-£53, 2 Browns Lane, 5-min walk from palace, tel. 01993/811-343, Pat Hillier).

STRATFORD-UPON-AVON

Stratford is Shakespeare's hometown. To see or not to see? Stratford is a must for every big-bus tour in England, and probably the single most popular side-trip from London. Sure, it's touristy, but nobody back home would understand if you skipped Shakespeare's house. A walking tour with a play's the thing to bring the Bard to life. And the town's riverside charm, coupled with its hardworking tourist industry, makes it a fun stop.

While you're in the area, explore Warwick, England's finest medieval castle, and stop by Coventry, a blue-collar town with a spirit that the Nazis' bombs couldn't destroy.

Planning Your Time

Stratford, Warwick, and Coventry are a made-to-order day for drivers connecting the Cotswolds with points north (such as Ironbridge Gorge or North Wales). While connections from the Cotswolds to Ironbridge Gorge are tough, Stratford, Warwick, and Coventry are well served by public transportation.

If you're just passing through Stratford, it's worth a half-day, but to see a play, you'll need to spend the night, or drive in from the nearby Cotswolds (30 min to the south, see previous chapter).

Warwick is England's single most spectacular castle. It's very touristy, but it's also historic and fun (worth three hours of your time). Have lunch in Warwick town. Coventry, the least-important stop on a quick trip, is most interesting as a chance to see a real, struggling Midlands industrial city (with some decent sightseeing).

If you're speedy, hit all three sights on a one-day drive-through. If you're more relaxed, see a play and stay in Stratford, then stop by Warwick and Coventry the following morning en route to your next destination.

ORIENTATION

Stratford's old town is compact, with the TI and theater along the riverbank, and Shakespeare's birthplace a few blocks inland; you can walk easily to everything except Anne Hathaway's and Mary Arden's places. The river has an idyllic yet playful feel, with a park along both banks, paddleboats, hungry swans, and an old, crank-powered ferry.

Tourist Information
The TI is as central as can be, located where the main street hits the river. While the office has been swallowed whole by gimmicky knickknacks and fliers—and corrupted by a sales-pitch fervor—the people here can still provide a little help (April–Oct Mon–Sat 9:00–17:30, Sun 10:00–16:00; Nov–March Mon–Sat 9:00–17:00, Sun 10:00–15:00; room-finding service-£3, on Bridgefoot, tel. 0870-160-7930, www.shakespeare-country.co.uk). You can buy discount tickets to Warwick Castle here. Ask at the TI for other combo-ticket deals for local sights.

Helpful Hints
Name That Stratford: If you're coming by train or bus, be sure to request a ticket for "Stratford-upon-Avon," not just "Stratford." Located just outside London, Stratford—also known as Stratford Langthorne—is the location for the 2012 Olympics, and is nowhere near where you're trying to go.

Festival: Every year on the weekend following Shakespeare's birthday (traditionally considered to be April 23—also the day he died), Stratford celebrates. The town hosts free events, including activities for children. In 2008, expect tours and hotels to be booked up long in advance surrounding the weekend of April 26–27.

Internet Access: Get online at **Cyber Junction** (Mon–Fri 10:00–18:00, Sat 10:00–17:30, Sun 10:00–17:00, 28 Greenhill Street, tel. 01789/263-400) or the **library,** on Henley Street just a few doors down from Shakespeare's Birthplace (free, up to 1 hour, daily; if computers are all in use, reserve a time at the desk; tel. 01789/292-209).

Baggage Storage: Located directly behind the TI, the Old Barn Shop stores bags—but be back to pick them up before the store closes, or you're out of luck for the night (£2/bag, Mon–Sat 10:00–17:30, Sun 10:00–16:00, tel. 01789/269-567).

Stratford

Stratford Area

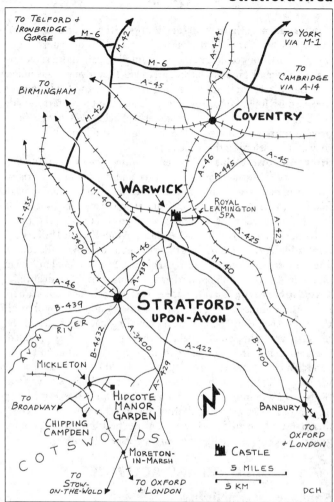

Laundry: Sparklean, a 10-minute walk from the city center, is near the Grove Road and Broad Walk B&Bs (daily 8:00–21:00, self-serve wash–£5–6, kindly washerwomen Sue and Jane will do it for you in a few hours if you drop it off before 15:00, 74 Bull Street, tel. 01789/269-075).

Taxis: Try **007 Taxis** (tel. 01789/414-007) or **Platinum Cars** (tel. 01789/264-626). A taxi stand is on Woodbridge, near the intersection with High Street.

TOURS

Shakespeare's Life in Stratford Walks—These Saturday-morning walks, the brainchild of a brilliant actor and writer named Jonathan Milton, offer an energetic, intellectual, and fascinating two-hour, small-group trek through town. They give you a wonderful insight into Stratford, the acting scene here, and Shakespeare's life. Led by Jonathan or his actor friends, the tours start outside the Swan Theatre on Waterside, described below (£8, Sat at 10:30, private tours available-£75 for small group, tel. 01789/412-617, thewalkinstratford@ntlworld.com).

Stratford Town Walks—These entertaining, award-winning 90-minute walks introduce you to the town and its famous playwright. Tours run daily year-round, rain or shine. Just show up at the Swan fountain (on the waterfront, opposite Sheep Street) in front of the Royal Shakespeare Theatre and pay the guide (£5, kids-£2, ticket stub offers good discount to some sights, Mon–Wed at 11:00, Thu–Sun at 14:00, tel. 01789/292-478, www.stratfordtownwalk.co.uk). They also run an evening ghost walk led by a professional magician (£5, kids-£3, Mon, Thu, and Fri at 19:30, must book in advance).

City Sightseeing Bus Tours—Open-top buses constantly make the rounds, allowing visitors to hop on and hop off at all the Shakespeare sights. Given the far-flung nature of two of the Shakespeare sights, and the value of the fun commentary provided, this tour makes the town more manageable. The full circuit takes about an hour, and comes with a steady and informative commentary (£10, buy tickets on bus or as you board, buses leave from the TI every 15 min in high season from 9:30–17:00, every 20 min off-season; buses basically alternate between tape-recorded commentary and live guides—if you want the best tour, wait for a live guide; tel. 01789/412-680, www.city-sightseeing.com).

SIGHTS AND ACTIVITIES

Shakespearean Sights

Fans of the Bard's work will want to visit at least a few of the following sights. Shakespeare's Exhibition and Birthplace has the best historical introduction to the playwright (as well as a disappointing house where he spent his early years). There are four other Shakespearean properties in and near Stratford, all run by the Shakespeare Birthplace Trust. Each has a garden and helpful docents who love to tell a story.

Pilgrims save money by buying one of the two Shakespeare sights combo-tickets: £11 gets you into the in-town sights (Birthplace, Hall's Croft, and Nash's House); £14 grants you entry to five sights (the same three, plus Anne Hathaway's Cottage and

The Look of Stratford

There's much more to Stratford than Shakespeare sights. Take time to appreciate the look of the town itself. While the main street goes back to Roman times, the key date for the city was 1196, when the king gave the town "market privileges." Stratford was shaped by its marketplace years. The market's many "departments" were located on logically named streets, whose names still remain: Sheep Street, Corn Street, and so on. Today's street plan—and even the 57' 9" width of the lots—survives from the 12th century. (The modern Woolworths store in the town center is the exact width.)

Starting about 1600, three great fires gutted the town, leaving very few buildings from before that era. Since those great fires, tinderbox thatch roofs were prohibited—the Old Thatch Tavern on Greenhill Street is the only remaining thatch roof in town, predating the law and grandfathered in.

The town's main drag, Bridge Street, is the oldest street in town, but looks the youngest. It was built in the Regency style—a result of a rough little middle row of wattle-and-daub houses being torn down in the 1820s to double the street's width. Today's Bridge Street buildings retain that early 19th-century style: Regency.

Throughout Stratford, you'll see striking black-and-white, half-timbered buildings, as well as half-timbered structures that were partially plastered over and covered up in the 19th century. During Victorian times, the half-timbered style was considered low-class, but in the 20th century—just as tourists came, preferring the ye olde style—timbers came back into vogue, and the plaster was removed on many old buildings. But any black and white you see is likely to be modern paint. The original coloring was "biscuit yellow" and brown.

Mary Arden's House). Shakespeare's grave isn't covered by any combo-ticket. If you've taken a walking tour with Stratford Town Walks (described earlier), your ticket stub will get you a five-sight pass for £11 (saving £3).

▲Shakespeare Exhibition and Birthplace—Touring this sight, you'll visit an excellent modern museum before seeing Shakespeare's place of birth (£7; June–Aug Mon–Sat 9:00–17:00, Sun 9:30–17:00; April–May and Sept–Oct daily 10:00–17:00; Nov–March Mon–Sat 10:00–16:00, Sun 10:30–16:00; these are last entry times, in town center on Henley Street, tel. 01789/204-016, www.shakespeare.org.uk).

The **Shakespeare exhibition** provides a fine historical background, with actual historic artifacts. Linger in the museum rather than rushing to the old house, since the meat of your visit is here.

Stratford-upon-Avon

1. Mercure Shakespeare Hotel
2. The Payton Hotel
3. Ambleside, Woodstock & Salamander Guest Houses
4. Emsley Guest House
5. To Hemmingford House Hostel
6. Russons Restaurant
7. The Coconut Lagoon, Lambs, The Oppo & Barnaby's Rests.
8. The Garrick Inn
9. Kingfisher Fish & Chips
10. Marks & Spencer Grocery
11. Somerfield Grocery
12. Morrison's Grocery
13. Internet Café
14. Launderette
15. City Bus Tours
16. Swan Fountain (Town Walks)
17. Falstaff Experience
18. Cox's Yard
19. Old Barn Shop (Bag Storage)

It's the best introduction to the life and work of Shakespeare in Stratford, with an original 1623 First Folio of Shakespeare's work. Of the 700 printed, about 150 survive. (Most are in America, but three are in Stratford.) Western literature owes much to this folio, which collects 36 of the 37 known Shakespeare plays (*Pericles* missed out). It came with an engraving of the only portrait from living memory of Shakespeare, and likely the most accurate depiction of the great playwright.

The **birthplace,** a half-timbered Elizabethan building furnished as it was when young William was growing up, is filled with

bits about his life and work. I found the old house disappointing—only the creaky floorboards feel authentic. After the Shakespeares moved out, the building was used as a pub and a butcher's shop. Since its restoration in the 1800s, it feels like millions of visitors have rubbed it clean of anything original. While the furnishings seem tacky and modern, they're supposed to be true to 1575, when William was 11. The house becomes interesting only if you talk up the attendants in each room.

While William Shakespeare was born in this house (in 1564), he spent most of his career in London. It was there that he taught the play-going public about human nature, with plots that entertained both the highest and the lowest minds. His tool was an unrivaled mastery of the English language. He retired—rich and famous—back in Stratford, spending his last five years at a house (now long gone) called New Place.

Little is known about Shakespeare the man. The scope of his brilliant work, his humble beginnings, and the fact that no original Shakespeare manuscripts survive raise a few scholarly eyebrows. While some wonder who penned all these plays, all serious scholars accept his authorship.

▲▲**Mary Arden's House and Shakespeare Countryside Museum**—Along with the birthplace museum, this is my favorite of the Shakespearean sights. Famous as the girlhood home of William's mom, this house is in Wilmcote (about three miles from town). Built around two historic farmhouses, it's an open-air folk museum depicting 16th-century farm life. It has many more domestic artifacts—and sees far fewer tourists—than the other Shakespeare sites (£6, daily June–Aug 9:30–17:00, April–May and Sept–Oct 10:00–17:00, Nov–March 10:00–16:00, these are last entry times).

The first building, **Palmer's farm** (mistaken for Mary Arden's home for hundreds of years, and correctly identified in 2000), is furnished as it would have been in Shakespeare's day.

Mary Arden actually lived in the neighboring **farmhouse**, less impressive and covered in brick facade. Dorothy Holmes, who lived here until 1979, left it as a 1920s time warp, and that's just what you'll see today. Ask the docent about how they discovered that Palmer's farm was actually built a few years too late to be from Shakespeare's time.

At both the farm and Dorothy Holmes' home, you'll see period interpreters in Tudor costumes. They'll likely be going through the day's chores as people back then would have done—activities like milking the sheep and cutting wood to do repairs on the house. They're there to answer questions and provide fun, gossipy insight into what life was like at the time.

The grounds also host a 19th-century farming exhibit, as

well as enjoyable and informative **falconry demonstrations** with lots of mean-footed birds. Chat with the falconers (either Steve or Becky) about their methods for earning the birds' trust. The birds' hunger sets them to flight (a round-trip earns the bird a bit of food; the birds fly when hungry—but don't have the energy if they're *too* hungry). Like Katherine, the wife described as "my falcon" in *The Taming of the Shrew*, these birds are tamed and trained with food as a reward. If things are slow, ask if you can feed one of the birds.

Getting to Mary Arden's House: The most convenient way to get here is by car or the hop-on, hop-off bus tour, but it's also possible to reach the site by train. The Wilmcote train station is directly across the street from Mary Arden's House (£1.70 round-trip fare, one stop from Stratford-upon-Avon on Birmingham-bound train, 10-min trip, train runs about every 90 min, call Traveline to confirm departure time—tel. 0870-608-2608).

▲**Anne Hathaway's Cottage**—Located a mile out of town (in Shottery), this home is a picturesque, thatched, 12-room farm-house where the Bard's wife grew up. William courted Anne here— she was 26, he was only 18—and his tactics proved successful. (Maybe a little too successful, as she was several months pregnant at their wedding.) They lived together for 34 years, until his death in 1616 at age 52.

Stop in the first room for a fun eight-minute intro talk. (If the place shakes, a tourist has thunked his or her head on the low beams.) The Hathaway family lived here for 400 years, until 1912, and much of the family's 92-acre farm remains part of the site. While the house has little to do with

Shakespeare, it offers an intimate peek at life in Shakespeare's day. Guides in each room do their best to lecture to the stampeding crowds. The garden comes with a prizewinning "traditional cottage garden," a yew maze (only planted in 2001, so not yet a challenge), a great photo-op statue of the British Isles, and a rotating exhibit, generally on a gardening theme (£5.50; June–Aug Mon–Sat 9:00–17:00, Sun 9:30–17:00; April–May and Sept–Oct Mon–Sat 9:30–17:00, Sun 10:00–17:00; Nov–March daily 10:00–16:00; these are last entry times, 1.5 miles from town—a 30-min walk; a stop on the hop-on, hop-off tour bus or a quick taxi ride; well-signposted for drivers entering Stratford from any direction, easy and free parking).

Hall's Croft—This former home of Shakespeare's daughter is in the Stratford town center. A fine old Jacobean house, it's the fanciest of the group (she married a doctor). It's worth a quick pop-in, especially if you already have one of the Shakespearean combo-tickets; to make the exhibits on 17th-century medicine interesting, ask the docent for the 15- to 20-minute introduction, which helps bring the plague—and some of the bizarre remedies of the time—to life (£3.75, daily June–Aug 9:30–17:00, April–May and

Sept–Oct 11:00–17:00, Nov–March 11:00–16:00, these are last entry times, on-site tea room).

Nash's House—Built beside New Place (the house where Shakespeare retired), this is the least impressive and least interesting of the Shakespeare-related prop-

erties. (Nash was the first husband of Shakespeare's granddaughter.) While Shakespeare's New Place is long gone (notice the foundation in the adjacent garden as you leave), Nash's house has survived. Your visit starts here with a five-minute guided intro in the parlor. The upper level hosts temporary exhibits (£3.75, same hours as Hall's Croft, above).

You can get into the neighboring gardens for free, and cheapskates can get a nice view of Nash's House's gardens (included in the entry price to the house) just by walking behind it along Chapel Street.

Shakespeare's Grave—To see his final resting place, head to the riverside Holy Trinity Church (£1.50, not covered by any

Stratford Thanks America

Residents of Stratford are thankful for the many contributions Americans have made to their city and its heritage. Along with pumping up the economy day in and day out with tourist visits, Americans paid for half the rebuilding of the Royal Shakespeare Theatre after it burned down in 1926. The Swan Theatre renovation was funded entirely by American aid. Harvard University inherited—you guessed it—the Harvard House, and it maintains the house today. London's much-loved theater, Shakespeare's Globe, was the dream (and gift) of an American. And there's even an odd but prominent "American Fountain" overlooking Stratford's market square on Rother Street, which was given in 1887 to celebrate the Golden Jubilee of the rule of Queen Victoria.

combo-ticket, free to view for churchgoers; 10-min walk past the theater—see its graceful spire as you gaze down the river). The church marks the ninth-century birthplace of the town, which was once a religious settlement.

Seeing a Shakespeare Play in Stratford

In 2008, the mighty Royal Shakespeare Company (RSC) will downsize, as its historic theater continues its multi-year renovation (estimated reopening date: 2010). Most performances will be in the new Courtyard Theatre, a testing ground for the lights, seats, and structure of the multi-million-dollar renovation of the main theater. (While you're in Stratford, you may also see ads for RSC productions scattered in other smaller theaters around town.)

For the most up-to-date show times, check with the TI or the Royal Shakespeare Company's box office or website (see below).

▲▲Royal Shakespeare Company

The RSC, undoubtedly the best Shakespeare company on earth and a memorable experience, performs year-round in Stratford and in London (see page 100). If you're a Shakespeare fan, see if the RSC schedule fits into your itinerary.

Tickets in Stratford range from £5 (standing) to £55 (Mon–Sat at 19:30, matinees vary, sporadic shows Sun; standing tickets available the day of performance only at the Royal Shakespeare Theatre). You'll probably need to buy your tickets ahead of time, although restricted-view and standing-room places are saved to be sold each morning in person at the box office (from 9:30, £5–16), and returned tickets can sometimes be picked up with cash the evening of an otherwise-sold-out show (box office window open

Mon–Sat 9:30–20:00, ticket hotline open 24/7, tel. 0870-609-1110, www.rsc.org.uk). Because the RSC website is so user-friendly, it makes absolutely no sense to pay extra to book tickets through any other source. If you're feeling bold, buy a £5 standing ticket and then slip into an open seat as the lights dim—if there's not something available during the play's first half, chances are there will be plenty of seats after intermission.

The Royal Shakespeare Theatre

The original theater was built in 1879 to honor the Bard, but burned down in 1926. The big replacement building you see under construction today (facing the riverside park) was erected in 1932. During the design phase, no actors were consulted; as a result, they built the stodgy Edwardian "picture frame"–style stage, even though the more dynamic "thrust"-style stage—which makes it easier for the audience to become engaged—is the actors' choice. (It would have also been closer in design to Shakespeare's Globe stage, which juts into the crowd.) This ill-conceived design is the reason for the three-year renovation described above. When the theater reopens in 2010, it will have an updated, thrust-style stage (the kind you'll see in the Courtyard Theater).

The Swan Theatre

Adjacent to the RSC Theatre is the smaller, Elizabethan-style Swan Theater, a galleried playhouse that opened in 1986. In the past, the Swan has hosted theater tours, but as part of the renovation of the main theater, the Swan has also shut its doors to visitors for the duration of the renovation project.

The Courtyard Theatre

This temporary theater, a two-minute walk down Southern Lane from the original Royal Shakespeare Theatre, seats 1,000 people, and is a prototype for the new Royal Shakespeare Theatre currently being built. If you plan to see a Shakespeare play during your visit, you may even be asked for your feedback about this interim theater.

Non-Shakespearean Sights

Falstaff Experience—While a bit gimmicky, this is about the best non-Shakespeare historical sight in the town center. (While it's named for one of his characters, the exhibit isn't about the Bard.) Filling Shrieve's House Barn with an informative and entertaining

Stratford, the Birthplace of...Teletubbies

Every three-year-old's favorite TV series, *Teletubbies* was first produced at a secret location somewhere around Stratford. Ragdoll, the local TV production company that made *Teletubbies*, became phenomenally successful, also creating the kids' series *Rosie and Jim*, *Brum*, and *Boohbah*. *Teletubbies*, comprising 365 episodes, is no longer in production, but its creator, Ann Wood, has had quite a ride. Sales of her little stuffed animals went through the roof in Britain, thanks in part to American televangelist Jerry Falwell. Falwell infamously declared that Tinky Winky, the purse-toting purple tubby with the triangle above his head, was gay; he issued an alert to parents that stated that the tubbies were sinisterly promoting deviant lifestyles among preschoolers. At first, Mrs. Wood—a proper and decent English woman—was crushed to hear about his claim. Then sales skyrocketed, and she went on to become Britain's fifth wealthiest woman, the beneficiary of Falwell's homophobic paranoia. Stratford's Ragdoll Productions, long a local fixture, has closed, but plans to move to a bigger location soon (www.ragdoll.co.uk).

exhibit, it sweeps through the town's history from the plague to the English Civil War. If you're into ghost-spotting, this may be your best shot (daily 10:30–17:30, Sheep Street).

Avon Riverfront—The River Avon is a playground of swans and canal boats. The swans have been the mascots of Stratford since 1623, when, seven years after the Bard's death, a poem in his First Folio nicknamed him "the sweet swan of Avon." Join in the bird-scene fun and buy **swan food** (50p) to feed swans and ducks; ask at the ice-cream boat for details. Don't feed the Canada geese, which locals disdain (according to them, the geese are vicious and have been messing up the eco-balance since they were imported by a king in 1665).

The **canal boats** saw their workhorse days during the short window of time between the start of the Industrial Revolution and the establishment of the railways. Today, they're mostly pleasure boats. The boats are long and narrow, so two can pass in the slim canals. There are 2,000 miles of canals in England's Midlands, built to connect centers of industry with seaports and provide vital transportation during the early days of the Industrial Revolution. Stratford was as far inland as you could sail on natural rivers from Bristol; it was the terminus of the man-made Birmingham Canal, built in 1816. Even today, you can motor your canal boat all the way to London from here.

For a little bit of mellow river action, rent a **rowboat** (£5 per

Stratford

couple per hour) or, for more of a challenge, pole yourself around on a Cambridge-style **punt** (canal is poleable—only 4 or 5 feet deep, same price and more memories/embarrassment if you do the punting; don't pay £10 per hour for a punter). Take a short stop on your lazy tour of the English countryside, and moor your canal boat at Stratford's Canal Basin. Try a sleepy half-hour **river cruise** (£4, no commentary), or jump on the only surviving **chain ferry** (c. 1930) in Britain (50p), which shuttles people across the river just beyond the theater.

Cox's Yard, a timber yard until the 1990s, is a rare physical remnant of the days when Stratford was an industrial port. Today, Cox's is a cheesy, touristic entertainment center with pubs that have live cover-band music most nights.

SLEEPING

If you want to spend the night after you catch a show, options abound. Ye olde timbered hotels are scattered through the city center. Most B&Bs are on the fringes of town, right on the busy ring roads that route traffic away from the center. (The recommended places below generally have double-paned windows for rooms in the front.) The weekend around Shakespeare's birthday (April 26–27 in 2008) is particularly tight, but Fridays and Saturdays are busy through the season. This town is so reliant upon the theater for its business that some B&Bs have secondary insurance covering their loss if the Royal Shakespeare Company stops performing in Stratford for any reason.

$$$ Mercure Shakespeare Hotel, located in a black-and-white building just up the street from Nash's House, has 74 central, spacious, and elegant rooms. Singles are cheaper on weekends, and doubles drop in price on Sunday and midweek—look for deals on the website (standard Db-£115–135, deluxe Db-£160–190,

---

Sleep Code

(£1 = about $2, country code: 44, area code: 01789)
S = Single, **D** = Double/Twin, **T** = Triple, **Q** = Quad, **b** = bathroom, **s** = shower only. Unless noted otherwise, you can assume credit cards are accepted and breakfast is included.

To help you sort easily through these listings, I've divided the rooms into three categories based on the price for a standard double room with bath:

$$$ Higher Priced—Most rooms £90 or more.
 $$ Moderately Priced—Most rooms between £60–90.
  $ Lower Priced—Most rooms £60 or less.

Stratford

prices soft depending on demand—can be as low as £90 for a double, Chapel Street, tel. 01789/294-997, fax 01789/415-411, www .mercure.com, h6630@accor.com).

$$ The Payton, tucked away on John Street, has a central and quiet location (rare for busy Stratford), as well as five tight but lovely rooms (Db-£70–75, 6 John Street, tel. & fax 01789/266-442, www.payton.co.uk, info@payton.co.uk, Peter).

$$ Ambleside Guest House is run with quiet efficiency and attentiveness by owners Peter and Ruth. Each of the seven rooms has been completely renovated, including the small but tidy bathrooms. The place has a homey, airy feel, with none of the typical B&B clutter (small S-£28–30, standard Db-£60–70, four-poster Db-£65–80, spacious top-floor Db-£80, Tb-£105, Qb-£120, secure parking available, 41 Grove Road, tel. 01789/297-239, fax 01789/295-670, www.ambleside guesthouse.com, ruth @amblesideguesthouse.com—include your phone number in your request, since they prefer to call you back to confirm).

$$ Emsley Guest House holds five bright rooms named after different counties in England. Hardworking, knowl-edgeable Val and Keith Barber create a homey and inviting atmosphere and are happy to offer local travel tips (Sb-£55–65, Db-£60–70, Tb-£90–96, Q-£120, 5-person family room-£150, families welcome, Wi-Fi, garage and off-street parking, 4 Arden Street, tel. 01789/299-557, www.theemsley.co.uk, val @theemsley.co.uk).

$$ Woodstock Guest House is a friendly, frilly, family-run, and flowery place with five comfortable rooms (Sb-£32–38, Db-£60–70, family room-£74–82, deals for 2 or more nights, parking, 30 Grove Road, tel. 01789/299-881, www.woodstock-house.co.uk, jackie@woodstock-house.co.uk, owners Denis and bubbly Jackie).

$ Salamander Guest House, run by gregarious Frenchman Pascal and his wife Anna, rents seven well-priced but basic rooms. They're on a busy street across from a small garden on the edge of town (S-£27.50–35, Db-£55–60, Tb-£80, Qb-£90–120, 40 Grove Road, tel. & fax 01789/205-728, www.salamanderguesthouse .co.uk, p.delin@btinternet.com).

$ *Hostel:* Hemmingford House, with 132 beds in 2- to 10-bed rooms, is a 10-minute bus ride from town (from £24.50 for non-members, includes breakfast; take bus #X18, #18, or #77 to Alveston; tel. 01789/297-093, stratford@yha.org.uk).

EATING

Stratford's numerous eateries vie for your pre- and post-theater business, with special hours and meal deals. (Most offer light two-and three-course menus from 17:30–19:00.) You'll find many hardworking places lined up along Sheep Street and Waterside.

Russons Restaurant, which specializes in fresh fish and sea-food, is probably the best place in town. It's cheery and chic, offering international cuisine in a woody and yellow candlelit ambience. Reserve in advance for evening meals (£10–15 plates, Tue–Sat 11:30–14:00 & 17:15–21:00, closed Sun–Mon, least central listing at 8 Church Street, tel. 01789/268-822). While they're primarily a restaurant, they also offer teas and pastries (Tue–Sat 8:00–14:00).

The Coconut Lagoon serves tasty, spicy nouveau–South Indian cuisine and offers pre-theater specials daily until 19:00: a £10 two-course deal or £13 for three courses (daily 12:30–14:30 & 17:00–23:00, 21 Sheep Street, tel. 01789/293-546).

Lambs is an intimate place serving meat, fish, and veggie dishes with panache (£15 two-course special, £20 three-course special, daily 12:00–14:00 & 17:00–22:00, closed for Sun dinner and Mon lunch, 12 Sheep Street, tel. 01789/292-554). The related **Oppo Restaurant,** next door, is similar but less formal (tel. 01789/269-980).

The Garrick Inn bills itself as the oldest pub in town, and comes with a cozy, dimly lit restaurant vibe. They serve pricey but above-average pub cuisine (£10 or less, daily 12:00–22:00, Sun until 21:00, 25 High Street, tel. 01789/292-186).

Barnaby's is a greasy fast-food fish-and-chips joint near the waterfront—but it's convenient if you want to get takeout for the riverside park just across the street (daily 11:30–19:30, at Sheep Street and Waterside). For a better set of fish-and-chips, queue up with the locals at **Kingfisher** (same hours as Barnaby's, a long block up at Ely Street).

Picnic: For groceries, you'll find **Marks & Spencer** on Bridge Street (daily, small coffee-and-sandwiches café upstairs), **Somerfield** in the Town Centre mall (daily), and a huge **Morrison's** next to the train station, a 10-minute walk from the city center (Mon–Sat 8:00–20:00, Sun 10:00–16:00, pharmacy, tel. 01789/267-106). To picnic, head to the canal and riverfront park between the Royal Shakespeare Theatre and the TI. Choose a bench with views of the river or of vacation houseboats, and munch your fish-and-chips while tossing a few fries into the river to attract swans. It's a fine way to spend a midsummer night's eve.

TRANSPORTATION CONNECTIONS

Remember—when buying tickets or checking schedules, ask for "Stratford-upon-Avon," not just "Stratford" (which is a different town).

From Stratford-upon-Avon to: London (every 2 hrs by train, 2–2.5 hrs, direct to Marylebone Station), **Chipping Campden**

(9 buses/day, 1 hr, on First Midland Red bus, tel. 01905-359-393), **Warwick** (every 1–2 hrs by train, 30 min; or hourly by Stagecoach bus, 20 min, tel. 01926/422-462, www.stagecoachbus.com), **Coventry** (hourly buses, 1 hr, tel. 01788/535-555; also hourly trains, 1–2 hrs with transfers). Train info: tel. 08457-484-950. Most intercity buses stop on Stratford's Bridge Street (a block up from the TI). For bus info that covers all the region's companies, call Traveline at 0871-200-2233 (www.travelinemidlands.co.uk).

By Car: Driving is easy and distances are brief: **Stow** (20 miles), **Warwick** (8 miles), **Coventry** (10 miles).

Near Stratford

Warwick

The pleasant town of Warwick—home to England's finest medieval castle—goes about its business almost oblivious to the busloads of tourists passing through. From the castle, a lane leads into the old-town center a block away, where you'll find the **TI** (daily 9:30–16:30, tel. 01926/492-212), plenty of eateries (including the recommended Ask restaurant chain), and several minor attractions. The TI can also sell same-day tickets to Warwick Castle—there's no discount, but it can save you time in line at the castle.

SIGHTS

▲▲Warwick Castle

Almost *too* groomed and organized, this theme park of a castle gives its crowds of visitors a decent value for the stiff £18.70 entry fee. The cash-poor but enterprising lord hired the folks at Madame Tussauds to wring maximum tourist dollars out of the castle. The greedy feel of the place is a little annoying, considering the already-steep admission. But there just isn't a better castle experience in England—especially for kids.

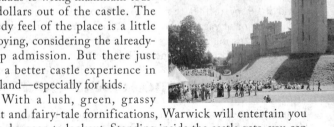

With a lush, green, grassy moat and fairy-tale fornications, Warwick will entertain you from dungeon to lookout. Standing inside the castle gate, you can see the mound where the original Norman castle of 1068 stood. Under this "motte," the wooden stockade (or "bailey") defined the courtyard in the way the castle walls do today. The castle is a 14th-

and 15th-century fortified shell, holding an 18th- and 19th-century royal residence, surrounded by another one of dandy "Capability" Brown's landscape jobs (like at Blenheim Palace).

Within the castle's mighty walls, there's something for every taste. The Great Hall and six lavish staterooms are the sumptuous highlights. You'll also find a Madame Tussauds–mastered re-creation of a royal weekend party—an 1898 game of statue-maker. You can ponder the weapons in the fine and educational armory, then line up to descend into a terrible torture chamber (the line here can be torturous by itself). The "King Maker" exhibit (set in 1471, when the townsfolk are getting ready for battle) is highly promoted, but not quite as good as a Disney ride. From the classic ramparts, the tower is a one-way, no-return, 250-step climb, offering a fun perch from which to fire your imaginary longbow. A recently restored mill and engine house come with an attendant who explains how the castle was electrified in 1894. (The "ghosts alive" experience costs extra.) And all around is a lush, peacock-patrolled, picnic-perfect park, complete with a Victorian rose garden. The castle grounds are often enlivened by a knight in shining armor on a horse that rotates with a merry band of musical jesters.

Cost, Hours, Location: Steep £18.70 entry fee, includes gardens and nearly all castle attractions, crazy pricing scheme varies based on anticipated crowds—may go down to £16 in slow periods, discounted tickets available at the Stratford TI, £3 parking. It's open daily April–Oct 10:00–18:00, Nov–March 10:00–17:00. It's a 15-minute walk from the Warwick train station to the castle (tel. 0870-442-2375, recorded info tel. 0870-442-2000, www.warwick-castle.co.uk).

Audioguide: The £3.50 audioguide provides 60 easy-listening minutes of number-coded descriptions of the individual rooms (rent from kiosk 20 yards after turnstile), while the £4 guidebook gives you nearly the same script in souvenir-booklet form. (Either is worthwhile if you want to understand the various rooms.) If you tour the castle without help, pick the brains of the earnest and talkative docents.

Events: During summer, special events (great for kids) are scheduled every half-hour throughout the day (jousting, giant catapult, longbow demo, sword fights, jester acts, and so on). Pick up the daily events flier (which also lists kiosks that sell snacks) and plan accordingly.

EATING

The castle has three main lunch options. **The Coach House** has cafeteria fare and grungy seating (located just before the turnstiles). **The Undercroft** offers the best on-site cooked food, and has a sandwich buffet line (located inside, in basement of palace); you can sit under medieval vaults or escape with your food and picnic outside. The **riverside pavilion** sells sandwiches and fish-and-chips, and has fine outdoor seating (in park just before the bridge, behind castle).

Literally a hundred yards from the castle turnstiles—through a tiny gate in the wall—is the workaday commercial district of the town of **Warwick,** with several much more elegant and competitive eateries that serve fine lunches at non-Tussauds prices. It's worth the walk.

TRANSPORTATION CONNECTIONS

From Warwick by Train to: London (2/hr, 1.75 hrs), **Stratford** (every 1–2 hrs, 30 min—buses are better, see below). Warwick's little train station is a 15-minute walk (or £2 taxi) from the castle. It has no official baggage check, but you can ask politely. The castle has a baggage-check facility.

By Bus to: Stratford (hourly, 20 min, bus #X16, also slower #18, www.stagecoachbus.com).

By Car: The main Stratford–Coventry road cuts right through Warwick. Coming from Stratford (8 miles to the south) you'll hit the castle parking lot first (£3; if it's full, lurk until a few cars leave and they'll let you in). The castle lot is expensive, and a 10-minute walk from the actual castle. Consider continuing into the town center (on main road). At the TI (near the big square church spire), grab any street-side parking (free for 2 hours). The castle is a block behind the TI.

Coventry

Coventry, a ▲ sight, was bombed to smithereens in 1940 by the Germans. From that point on, the German phrase for "to really blast the heck out of a place" was "to coventrate" it. But Coventry rose from its ashes, and its message to our world is one of forgiveness, reconciliation, and the importance of peace. Browse through Coventry, the closest thing to normal, everyday, urban

England you'll see. Get a map at the **TI** (Mon–Fri 9:30–17:00, Sat–Sun 10:00–16:30, shorter hours off-season, 4 Priory Row, tel. 02476/227-264, www.visitcoventry.co.uk, tic@cvone.co.uk).

The symbol of Coventry is the bombed-out hulk of its old **cathedral,** with the huge new one adjoining it. The inspirational complex welcomes visitors. Climb the tower (£2.50, 180 steps, daily 9:00–16:30, tel. 02476/521-200, www.coventrycathedral .org.uk).

Coventry's most famous hometown girl, Lady Godiva, rode bareback through the town in the 11th century to help lower taxes. You'll see her bronze statue a block from the cathedral (near Broadgate). Just beyond that is the **Coventry Transport Museum,** which features the first, fastest, and most famous cars and motorcycles that came from this "British Detroit" (free, daily 10:00–17:00, tel. 02476/234-270, www.transport-museum.com).

St. Mary's Guildhall has 14th-century tapestries, stained glass, and an ornate ceiling (free, Easter–Sept Sun–Thu 10:00– 16:00, closed Fri–Sat, during events, and off-season, www .coventry.gov.uk/stmarys).

TRANSPORTATION CONNECTIONS
Route Tips for Drivers
Stratford to Ironbridge Gorge via Warwick and Coventry

Entering Stratford from the Cotswolds, cross a bridge and pass the TI. Veer right (following *Through Traffic, P,* and *Wark* signs), go around the block—turning right and right and right—and enter the multistory Bridgefoot garage (80p/hr, £6/day, you'll find no place easier or cheaper). The TI and City Sightseeing bus stop are a block away. Leaving the garage, circle to the right around the same block, but stay on "the Wark" (Warwick Road, A439). Warwick is eight miles away. The castle is just south of town on the right. When you're trying to decide whether to stop in Coventry or not, factor in Birmingham's rush hour—try to avoid driving the section described below between 14:00–20:00, if you can (see next chapter for tips).

If You're Including Coventry: After touring the castle, carry on through the center of Warwick and follow signs to Coventry (still A439, then A46). If you're stopping in Coventry, follow signs painted on the road into the *city centre,* and then to *cathedral parking.* Grab a place in the high-rise parking lot. Leaving Coventry, follow signs to *Nuneaton* and *M6 North* through lots of sprawl, and you're on your way. (See below.)

If You're Skirting Coventry: Take M69 (direction: Leicester) and follow M6 as it threads through giant Birmingham.

Stratford

Once You're on M6: The highway divides into a free M6 and a toll M6 (designed to help drivers cut through the Birmingham traffic chaos). Take the toll road—£4 is a small price to pay to avoid all the nasty traffic.

When battling through sprawling Birmingham, keep your sights on M6. If you're heading for any points north—Ironbridge Gorge (Telford), North Wales, Liverpool, Blackpool, or the Lakes (Kendal for the South Lake District, Keswick for the North Lake District)—just stay relentlessly on M6 (direction: North West). Each destination is clearly signed directly from M6.

For Ironbridge Gorge, take the T8 exit (don't miss this exit, or you'll have to go all the way to T11 to turn around and backtrack). Follow M54 heading towards Telford. Keep an eye out for *Ironbridge* signs and do-si-do through a long series of roundabouts until you're there.

IRONBRIDGE GORGE

The Industrial Revolution was born in the Severn River Valley. In its glory days, this valley (blessed with abundant deposits of iron ore and coal and a river for transport) gave the world its first iron wheels, steam-powered locomotive, and cast-iron bridge (begun in 1779). The museums in Ironbridge Gorge, which capture the flavor of the Victorian Age, take you back into the days when Britain was racing into the modern era, and pulling the rest of the West with her.

Planning Your Time

Without a car, Ironbridge Gorge isn't worth the headache. Drivers can slip it in between the Cotswolds/Stratford/Warwick and points north (such as the Lake District or North Wales). Speed demons zip in for a midday tour of Blists Hill, a look at the bridge, and then speed out of town. For an overnight visit, arrive in the early evening to browse the town, and spend the morning and early afternoon touring the sights before driving on (10:00–Museum of the Gorge, which has a nice overview of the entire area; 11:00–Blists Hill Victorian Town for lunch and sightseeing; 15:30–Head to your next destination).

With more time—say, a full month in Britain—I'd spend two nights and a leisurely day: 9:30–Iron Bridge and the town; 10:30–Museum of the Gorge; 11:30–Coalbrookdale Museum of Iron; 14:30–Blists Hill, then dinner at Coalbrookdale Inn.

ORIENTATION

(area code: 01952)

The town is just a few blocks gathered around the Iron Bridge, which spans the peaceful, tree-lined Severn River. While the smoke-belching bustle is long gone, knowing that this wooded, sleepy river valley was the "Silicon Valley" of the 19th century makes wandering its brick streets almost a pilgrimage. The actual museum sites are scattered over three miles. The modern cooling towers (for coal, not nuclear energy) that loom ominously over these red-brick remnants seem strangely appropriate.

Tourist Information

The TI is in the tollhouse on the Iron Bridge (Mon–Fri 9:00–17:00, Sat–Sun 10:00–17:00, room-finding service, tel. 01952/884-391). The TI has lots of booklets for sale; hikers like the three booklets of nearby walks (£4–5).

Getting Around Ironbridge Gorge

On weekends March through October, the Gorge Connect buses link the museum sites (£2.60 day ticket, 1–2/hr, Sat–Sun 9:00–18:00 year-round, a couple mid-morning runs go all the way to the Telford rail station, tel. 01952/200-005).

SIGHTS

▲▲Iron Bridge

While England was at war with her American colonies, this first cast-iron bridge was built in 1779 to show off a wonderful new building material. Lacking experience with cast iron, the builders
erred on the side of sturdiness
and constructed it as if it were
made out of wood. Notice that
the original construction used
traditional timber-jointing techniques rather than rivets. (Any
rivets are from later repairs.) The
valley's centerpiece is free, open

all the time, and thought-provoking. Walk across the bridge to the tollhouse/TI/gift shop/museum (free, Mon–Fri 9:00–17:00, Sat–Sun 10:00–17:00). Read the fee schedule and notice the subtle slam against royalty. (England was not immune to the revolutionary sentiment brewing in the colonies at this time.) Pedestrians paid half a penny to cross; poor people crossed cheaper by coracle—a crude tub-like wood-and-canvas shuttle ferry (you'll see

Ironbridge Gorge

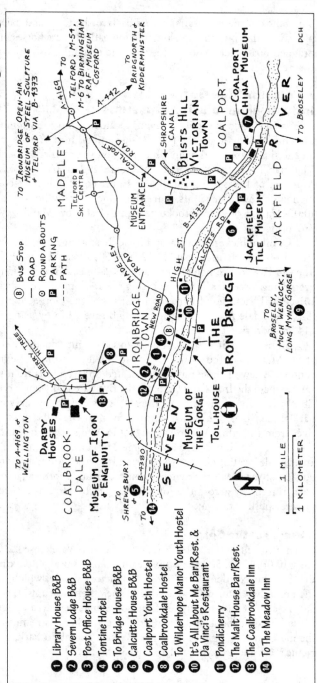

- **1** Library House B&B
- **2** Severn Lodge B&B
- **3** Post Office House B&B
- **4** Tontine Hotel
- **5** To Bridge House B&B
- **6** Calcutts House B&B
- **7** Coalport Youth Hostel
- **8** Coalbrookdale Hostel
- **9** To Wilderhope Manor Youth Hostel
- **10** It's All About Me Bar/Rest. & Da Vinci's Restaurant
- **11** Pondicherry
- **12** The Malt House Bar/Rest.
- **13** The Coalbrookdale Inn
- **14** To The Meadow Inn

old photos of these upstairs). Cross back to the town and enjoy a pleasant walk downstream along the towpath. Where horses once dragged boats laden with Industrial Age cargo, locals now walk their dogs.

▲▲▲Ironbridge Gorge Industrial Revolution Museums

Locals take pride in the 10 museums located within a few miles of each other, focused on the Iron Bridge and all it represents. Not all the sights are worth your time. Plan on seeing the Blists Hill Victorian Town, the Museum of the Gorge, and the Coalbrookdale Museum of Iron, using the £14 Passport combo-ticket recommended below. The sights share the same opening hours (daily 10:00–17:00, a few Coalbrookdale sights close Nov–March, www .ironbridge.org.uk).

Combo-Ticket: This group of widely scattered sites has varied admission charges (usually £2.50–5.50; Blists Hill is £9.50). The £14 Passport combo-ticket (families–£46) covers admission to everything for a year. If you're visiting the area's must-see sights— Blists Hill Victorian Town, the Museum of the Gorge, and the Coalbrookdale Museum of Iron—you'll save £4.75 by using the £14 Passport ticket.

Sightseeing Strategies: It helps to see the introductory movie at the Museum of the Gorge first, to help put everything else into context. A few of these museums, located up steep hills from the valley where the Iron Bridge crosses the river, are really only accessible by car. To see the most significant sights in a day by car, you'll park three times: Once either in the lot near the TI (across the river from the village) or in the pay lot located at the Museum of the Gorge (the Iron Bridge and Gorge Museum are connected by an easy, flat walk); once at the Blists Hill parking lot; and once outside of the Coalbrookdale Museum of Iron, a former factory, with Enginuity across the lot and the Darby Houses a three-minute uphill hike away.

Museum of the Gorge

Orient yourself to the valley here in the Severn Warehouse (£2.75, daily 10:00–17:00, 500 yards upstream from the bridge, parking-£1). See the excellent 11-minute introductory movie, which lays the groundwork for what you'll see in the other museums. Check out the exhibit and the model of the gorge in its heyday, and buy a Blists Hill guidebook and Passport ticket. Farther upstream from the museum parking lot is the fine riverside Dale End Park, with picnic areas and a playground.

Blists Hill Victorian Town

Save most of your time and energy for this wonderful town—an immersive, open-air folk museum. You'll wander through 50

acres of Victorian industry, factories, and a re-created community from the 1890s. The £2.25 Blists Hill guidebook gives a good step-by-step rundown (£9.50, daily 10:00–17:00, tel. 01952/601-010).

The board by the entry lists which exhibits are staffed with lively docents in Victorian dress. Pop in to say hello to the lonely bankers—when the schoolchildren visit, they lose the popularity contest to the "sweet shop" next door. It's fine to take photos.

Stop by the pharmacy and—after seeing the squirm-inducing setup of the dentist's chair from the time—appreciate the marvel of modern dental care. Down the street, kids like watching the candlemaker at work. Check the events in the barn across the path, where hands-on candle-making and other activities take place.

Just as it would've had in Victorian days, the village has a working pub, a greengrocer's shop, a fascinating squatter's cottage, and a snorty, slippery pigsty. Don't miss the explanation of the winding machine at the Blists Hill Mine (demos throughout the day, call for times). Located by the canal, a scale model made for a 2001 television program shows how the Iron Bridge was erected. Walk along the canal to the "inclined plane."

Grab lunch in the Victorian Pub or in the cafeteria near the squatter's cottage and children's old-time rides.

Coalbrookdale Museum of Iron

This does a fine job of explaining the original iron-smelting process. Compared to the fun and frolicking Blists Hill village, this museum is sleepy (£6.50, includes entry to the Darby Houses, listed below; £5.25 in winter—when Darby Houses are closed for lack of light; opposite Darby's furnace).

The Coalbrookdale neighborhood is the birthplace of the Industrial Revolution, where locals like to claim that mass production was invented. Abraham Darby's blast furnace sits like a shrine inside a big glass pyramid (free), surrounded by evocative Industrial Age ruins. It was here that, in 1709, Darby first smelted iron, using coke as fuel. If you're like me, "coke" is a drink, and "smelt" is the past tense of smell...nevertheless, this event kicked off the modern Industrial Age.

All the ingredients of the recipe for big industry were here in abundance—iron ore, top-grade coal, and water for power and shipping. Wander around Abraham Darby's furnace. Before this furnace was built, iron ore was laboriously melted by charcoal. With huge waterwheel-powered bellows, Darby burned top-grade coal at super-hot temperatures (burning off the impurities to make "coke"). Local iron ore was dumped into the furnace and melted. Impurities floated to the top, while the pure iron sank to the bottom of a clay tub in the bottom of the furnace. Twice a day, the plugs were knocked off, allowing the "slag" to drain away on the top and the molten iron to drain out on the bottom. The low-grade slag was used locally on walls and paths. The high-grade iron trickled into molds formed in the sand below the furnace. It cooled into pig iron (named because the molds look like piglets suckling their mother). The pig-iron "planks" were broken off by sledgehammers and shipped away. The Severn River became one of Europe's busiest, shipping pig iron to distant foundries, where it was re-melted and made into cast iron (for projects such as the Iron Bridge), or to forges, where it was worked like toffee into wrought iron.

Enginuity

Located across the parking lot from the Coalbrookdale Museum of Iron, Enginuity is a hands-on funfest for kids. Riffing on Ironbridge's engineering roots, this converted 1709 foundry is full of mesmerizing water contraptions, pumps, magnets, and laser games. Build a dam, try your hand at earthquake-proof construction, navigate a water maze, operate a remote-controlled robot, or power a turbine with your own steam (£5.50, daily 10:00–17:00).

Darby Houses

The Darby family, Quakers who were the area's richest neighbors by far, lived in these two homes located just above the Coalbrookdale Museum.

The 18th-century Darby mansion, **Rosehill House,** features a collection of fine china, furniture, and trinkets from various family members. It's decorated in the way the family home would have been in 1850. If the gilt-framed mirrors and fancy china seem a little ostentatious for the normally wealth-shunning Quakers, keep in mind that these folks were rich beyond reason. Docents assure visitors that, in another family's hands, Rosehill would have been completely over the top (included in Coalbrookdale Museum ticket, otherwise £3.75, April–Oct daily 10:00–17:00, closed Nov–March).

Skip the adjacent **Dale House.** Dating from the 1780s, it's older than Rosehill, but almost completely devoid of interior furniture and exhibits.

Coalport China Museum, Jackfield Tile Museum, and Broseley Pipeworks

Housed in their original factories, these showcase the region's porcelain, decorated tiles, and clay tobacco pipes. These industries were developed to pick up the slack when the iron industry shifted away from the Severn Valley. Each museum features finely decorated pieces, and the china and tile museums offer low-energy workshops.

Ironbridge Open-Air Museum of Steel Sculpture

This park is a striking tribute to the region's industrial heritage. Stroll the 10-acre grounds and spot works by Roy Kitchin and other sculptors stashed in the forest and perched in rolling grasslands (£3, March–Nov Tue–Sun 10:00–17:00, closed Mon except bank holidays, closed Dec–Feb, 2 miles from Iron Bridge, Moss House, Cherry Tree Hill, Coalbrookdale, Telford, tel. 01952/433-152, www.go2.co.uk/steelsculpture).

Near Ironbridge Gorge

Skiing, Swimming, and Fishing—There's a small, brush-covered ski slope with two Poma lifts at Telford Ski Centre in Madeley, two miles from Ironbridge Gorge; you'll see signs for it as you drive into Ironbridge Gorge (£10/hr including gear, less for kids, open practice times Mon and Thu 10:00–20:00, Tue and Fri 12:00–22:00, Wed 10:00–19:00, Sat 16:00–18:00, Sun 10:00–16:00, tel. 01952/382-688). A public swimming pool is next door. The Woodlands Farm, on Beech Road, runs a private business where only barbless hooks are used, and customers toss their catch back to hook again (a kind of fish hell).

Royal Air Force (RAF) Museum Cosford—This Red Baron magnet displays more than 80 aircraft, from warplanes to rockets. Get the background on ejection seats and a primer on the principles of propulsion (free, daily 10:00–18:00, last entry at 16:00, Shifnal, Shropshire, on A41 near junction with M54, tel. 01902/376-200, www.rafmuseum.org.uk).

More Sights—If you're looking for reasons to linger in Ironbridge Gorge, these sights are all within a short drive: the medieval town of Shrewsbury, the abbey village of Much Wenlock, the scenic Long Mynd gorge at Church Stretton, the castle at Ludlow, and the steam railway at the river town of Bridgnorth. Shoppers like Chester (en route to points north).

SLEEPING

In the Town Center

$$$ Library House is *Better Homes and Gardens* elegant. Located in the town center, a half-block downhill from the bridge, it's a classy, friendly gem. The Chaucer room, which includes a small garden, is a delight, but all of the house's four rooms are lovely. The complimentary drink upon arrival is a welcome touch (Sb-£70, Db-£75–85, DVD library, free parking just up the road, 11 Severn Bank, Ironbridge Gorge, tel. 01952/432-299, www.libraryhouse.com, info@libraryhouse.com). Lizzie Steel—who's joined by her husband and daughters most weekends—will pick you up from the Telford train station if you request it in advance.

$$$ Severn Lodge B&B is an elegant Georgian "captain of industry" house offering three fine, newly refurbished rooms (Sb-£65, Db-£87–89, two-night minimum stay, cash only, walled garden, easy parking; 200 yards above river, a block above town center on New Road, take Wharfage Steps off main road next to purple gate; tel. 01952/432-147, fax 01952/432-148, www.severnlodge.com, julia@severnlodge.com, Julia).

Two lesser places, right in the town center, overlook the bridge:

$$ Post Office House B&B is literally above the post office, where the postmaster's wife, Janet Hunter, rents three rooms. It's a shower-in-the-corner, old-fashioned, two-room place (Sb-£40–42, Db-£56–60, Tb-£66–90, family room available, discount for two or more nights, cash only, 6 The Square, tel. 01952/433-201, fax 01952/433-582, hunter@pohouse-ironbridge.fsnet.co.uk).

$$ Tontine Hotel is the town's big, 12-room, musty, Industrial Age hotel. Check out the historic photos in the bar (S-£25, D-£40, Db-£56, 10 percent discount with this book through 2008, The

---

Sleep Code

(£1 = about $2, country code: 44, area code: 01952)
S = Single, **D** = Double/Twin, **T** = Triple, **Q** = Quad, **b** = bathroom, **s** = shower only. You can assume credit cards are accepted unless noted otherwise.

To help you sort easily through these listings, I've divided the rooms into three categories based on the price for a standard double room with bath during high season:

$$$ Higher Priced—Most rooms £60 or more.
 $$ Moderately Priced—Most rooms between £40–60.
  $ Lower Priced—Most rooms £40 or less.

Square, tel. 01952/432-127, fax 01952/432-094, www.tontine-hotel
.com, tontinehotel@tiscali.co.uk).

Outside of Town

$$$ Bridge House rents four rooms in a 17th-century residence on
the banks of the Severn River, two miles from the town center on
B4380 (Sb-£55, Db-£75, family room-£95, Buildwas Road, tel. &
fax 01952/432-105, Mrs. Janet Hedges).

$$$ Calcutts House rents seven rooms in their 18th-century
ironmaster's home and adjacent coach house. Rooms in the main
house are elegant, while the coach-house rooms are simpler, but
still bright and tastefully done. Ask the owners, Colin and Sarah
Williams, how the rooms were named (Db-£50–75, price depends
on room size, located on Calcutts Road, Gorge Connect Jackfield
bus stop is across street, tel. 01952/882-631, www.calcuttshouse
.co.uk, enquiries@calcuttshouse.co.uk).

$ Coalport Youth Hostel, plush for a hostel, fills an old fac-
tory at the China Museum in Coalport (bunk-bed D/Db-£40,
most beds are in quads). The **Coakbrookdale Hostel,** built in 1859
as the grand Coalbrookdale Institute, is another fine hostel (a 20-
min walk from the Iron Bridge down A4169 toward Wellington,
4- to 6-bed rooms, cash only). Each hostel charges £17.50 per bed
with sheets, serves meals, has a self-service laundry, and uses the
same telephone number and email address (tel. 01952/588-755,
ironbridge@yha.org).

$ Wilderhope Manor Youth Hostel, a beautifully remote
and haunted 400-year-old manor house, is one of Europe's best
hostels. On Sundays, tourists actually pay to see what hostelers
sleep in (£17, under 18-£14.50, £3 less for members, single-sex
dorms, family rooms available, dinner served at 19:00, unreliable
hours throughout year, reservations recommended, tel. 01694/771-
363, wilderhope@yha.org.uk). It's six miles from Much Wenlock
down B4371 toward Church Stretton.

EATING

It's All About Me is an inviting café/bistro/bar in a prime location by the river. On a sunny day, sit on their inviting back patio,
with peek-a-boo views of the Iron Bridge. Inside, this two-story
place has the same menu upstairs or down: Mediterranean food,
including £4 tapas-style small meals called "nibbly bits" (£11 for
one course, £16 for two, Mon–Sat 12:00–14:30 & 18:00–21:00, Sun
12:00–16:00 & 18:00–21:00, plenty of indoor/outdoor seating, veggie options, on High Street, tel. 01952/432-716).

Pondicherry, in a renovated former police station, serves
delicious Indian curries and a few British dishes to keep the less

adventurous happy. The £11 mixed vegetarian sampler is popular even with meat-eaters (£10 plates, daily 17:00–22:00—starts to get hopping after 19:00, 57 Waterloo Street, tel. 01952/433-055, manager Arfon).

Da Vinci's serves good, though pricey, Italian food and has a dressy ambience (£16 main courses, Mon–Sat 19:00–22:00, closed Sun, 26 High Street, tel. 01952/432-250).

The Malt House, located in an 18th-century beer house, offers an English menu with a European accent. This is a very popular scene with the local twentysomething gang (£12–15 main courses, bar menu at Jazz Bar, daily 12:00–14:00 & 18:30–21:45, near Museum of the Gorge, 5-min walk from center, The Wharfage, tel. 01952/433-712). The Malt House is *the* vibrant nightspot in town, with live music and a fun crowd (generally Wed–Sat).

The Coalbrookdale Inn is filled with locals enjoying excellent ales and surprisingly good food. This former "best pub in Britain" has a tradition of offering free samples from a lineup of featured beers. Ask what real ales are available (Mon–Sat 12:00–15:00 & 18:00–21:00, Sun 12:00–15:00 only, no lunch served Mon, reservations unnecessary for the bar but a good idea for the fancier restaurant, lively ladies' loo, across street from Coalbrookdale Museum of Iron, 1 mile from Ironbridge Gorge, tel. 01952/433-953). Danny and Dawn Wood, the inn's owners, also rent a few rooms above the restaurant.

The Meadow Inn would have appealed to Lawrence Welk. This local favorite serves prizewinning pub grub, and has lovely riverside outdoor seating if the weather cooperates (£8 meals, daily 12:00–15:00 & 17:00–21:30, can get crowded, no reservations, a pleasant 15-min walk from the center; head upstream, at Dale End Park take the path along the river, the inn is just after railway bridge; tel. 01952/433-193).

TRANSPORTATION CONNECTIONS

Ironbridge Gorge is five miles from Telford, which has the nearest train station. To get between Ironbridge Gorge and Telford, take a bus (£3.30 "Day Saver" fare, 1–2/hr, 20 min, none on Sun) or taxi (£7.70). Although Telford's train and bus stations are an annoying 15-minute walk apart, you can connect on bus #44 (every 10 min, covered by "Day Saver") or #55 (every 20 min), or with a £2 cab ride. The Telford bus station is part of a large modern mall, an easy place to wait for the bus to Ironbridge Gorge. Buses are run by Arriva (www.arrivabus.co.uk), but you can also call Traveline for departure times and other information (tel. 0870-608-2608).

The Gorge Connect bus service, which runs among Ironbridge Gorge sights on weekends, makes a couple of morning runs between Ironbridge Gorge and the Telford train station. For schedule information on the Gorge Connect and other bus routes, call Telford Travelink at 0870-608-2608. If you need a **taxi** while in Ironbridge Gorge, call Central Taxis at tel. 01952/501-050.

By Train from Telford to: Birmingham (2/hr, 40 min), **Conwy** in North Wales (9/day, 3 hrs, 1–2 changes usually include Chester), **Blackpool** (1–2/hr, 3.5 hrs, usually 2 changes), **Keswick/ Lake District** (every 2 hrs, 3.5 hrs to Penrith with 2 changes, then catch a bus to Keswick, hourly except Sun 6/day, 40 min), **Edinburgh** (hourly, 5–6.5 hrs, 1–2 transfers). Train info: tel. 08457-484-950.

By Car to Telford: Driving in from the **Cotswolds** and **Stratford,** take M6 through Birmingham, then exit T8 to M54 to the Telford/Ironbridge exit. Follow the brown *Ironbridge* signs through lots of roundabouts to Ironbridge Gorge. The traffic north through Birmingham is miserable from 14:00 to 20:00, especially on Fridays. From **Warwick,** consider the M40/M42/Kidderminster alternative, coming into Ironbridge Gorge on A442 via Bridgnorth to avoid the Birmingham traffic. (Note: On maps, Ironbridge Gorge is often referred to as "Iron Bridge" or "Iron-Bridge.")

BLACKPOOL
AND LIVERPOOL

These two bustling cities—wedged between serene North Wales and the even-more-serene Lake District—provide an opportunity to sample the "real" England, both at work (Liverpool) and at play (Blackpool). Scream down roller coasters and eat "candy floss" until you're deliriously queasy in fun-loving Blackpool. In Liverpool, experience industrial England and relive the early mop-top days of some famous Liverpudlians...meet the Beatles.

Blackpool

Blackpool is Britain's fun puddle. It's one of England's most-visited attractions, the private domain of its working class, a faded and sticky mix of Coney Island, Las Vegas, and Woolworths. Juveniles of any age love it. My kids declared it better than Disneyland.

Blackpool grew up with the Industrial Revolution. In the mid-1800s, entire mill towns would close down and take a two-week break here. They came to drink in the fresh air (much needed after a hard year in the mills) and—literally—the seawater. Back then they figured it was healthy.

Blackpool's heyday is long past now, as more and more working people can afford the cheap charter flights to sunny Spain. Recently, the resort has become popular for "stag" and "hen" (bachelor and bachelorette) parties—basically a cheap boozy weekend for the twentysomething crowd. Consequently, there are two Blackpools: the daytime Blackpool of kids riding roller coasters and grannies getting early-bird specials; and the drunken, debauched, late-night Blackpool of glass-dance-floor clubs and bars.

Blackpool is hoping to reinvent itself and draw more visitors in the next few years. A large overhaul of the promenade has begun, as well as numerous renovations in the city center. No matter what, the town remains an accessible and affordable fun zone for the Flo and Andy Capps of northern England. People come year after year. They stay for a week, and they love it.

Most Americans don't even consider a stop in Blackpool. Many won't like it. It's an ears-pierced-while-you-wait, tipsy-toupee kind of place. Tacky, yes. Lowbrow, OK. But it's as English as can be, and that's what you're here for. An itinerary should feature as many facets of a culture as possible. Blackpool is as English as the queen—and considerably more fun.

Spend the day "muckin' about" the beach promenade of fortune-tellers, fish-and-chips joints, amusement piers, warped mirrors, and Englanders wearing hats with built-in ponytails. A million greedy doors try every trick to get you inside. Huge arcade halls advertise free toilets and broadcast bingo numbers into the streets; the wind machine under a wax Marilyn Monroe blows at a steady gale; and the smell of fries, tobacco, and sugar is everywhere. Milk comes in raspberry or banana in this land where people under incredibly bad wigs look normal. If you're bored in Blackpool, you're just too classy.

Planning Your Time

Ideally, get to Blackpool around lunchtime for a free afternoon and evening of making bubbles in this cultural mud puddle. For full effect, it's best to visit during peak season: June through early November.

Blackpool's Illuminations, when much of the waterfront is decorated with lights, draws crowds in fall, particularly on weekends (Aug 29–Nov 2 in 2008). The early-evening light is great with the sun setting over the sea. Walk out along the peaceful North Pier at twilight.

Blackpool is easy by car or train. Speed demons with a car can treat it as a midday break (it's just off M6 on M55) and continue north. If you have kids, they'll want more time here (hey, it's cheaper than Disneyland). If you're into nightlife, this town delivers. If you're pre- or post-kids and not into kitsch and greasy spoons, skip it. If the weather's great and you love nature, the lakes are just a few hours north. A visit to Blackpool sharpens the wonders of Windermere.

ORIENTATION

(area code: 01253)

Everything clusters along the six-mile-long beachfront promenade, a tacky, glittering good-time strip mall punctuated by three fun-filled piers reaching out into the sea. The Pleasure Beach rides are near the South Pier. Jutting up near the North Pier is Blackpool's stubby Eiffel-type tower. The most interesting shops, eateries, and theaters are inland from the North Pier. For a break from glitz, you can hike north along the waterfront path for 20 miles or so.

Tourist Information

There are two TIs near the tower. The main one is on Clifton Street (Mon–Sat 9:00–17:00, closed Sun, £1.50 fee to book shows, tel. 01253/478-222—the same number gives recorded entertainment info after hours, www.visitblackpool.com). The other TI is on The Promenade (June–early-Nov Mon–Sat 9:30–17:00, Sun 10:00–16:30, closed off-season).

At either TI, get the 50p city map, pick up brochures on the amusement centers, and ask about special shows. The *What's On* booklet listing local events costs £1.25. If you're doing the amusement blitz, buy your tickets for Sandcastle Waterpark and the Blackpool Tower at the TI to save a few pounds. Both TIs do same-day room bookings for a 10 percent fee (room-finding service closes at 16:30).

For a history fix, get the TI's £1 *Heritage Trail* booklet, which takes you on an hour's walk through downtown Blackpool. Saying much about little, it's endearing.

Arrival in Blackpool

The main (north) **train** station is three blocks from the town center (no maps given but one is posted, no ATM in station but many in town). The train station has no luggage storage, but if you're desperate, the Pleasure Beach has a few lockers big enough for a backpack.

If arriving by **car,** the motorway funnels you down Yeadon Way into a giant parking zone. If you're just spending the day, head for one of the huge £6/day garages. If you're spending the night, drive to the waterfront and head north. My top accommodations are north on The Promenade (easy parking). Leaving Blackpool, to go anywhere, follow signs to *M55,* which starts at Blackpool and zips you to M6 (for points north or south).

Helpful Hints

Markets: At the **Abingdon Street Market,** vendors sell fruit, bras, jewelry, eggs, and more (Mon–Sat 9:00–17:30, closed

Blackpool

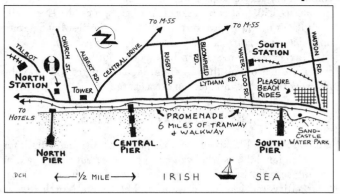

Sun, on Abingdon Street next to post office). The **Fleetwood Market,** eight miles north, is huge, with two buildings full of produce, clothes, and crafts spilling out onto the street (May–Oct Mon–Tue and Thu–Sat 9:30–16:30, closed Wed and Sun; Nov–April Tue, Fri, and Sat only; catch tram marked *Fleetwood*, 30 min, £2.50 one-way).

Tipping: The pubs of Blackpool have a unique tradition of "and your own, luv." Say that here and your barmaid will add 20p to your bill and drop it into her tip jar. (Say it anywhere else and they won't know what you mean.)

Internet Access: The public library, in the big domed building on Queen Street, lets visitors use its computers for 15 minutes (free, Mon and Fri 9:00–17:00, Tue and Thu 9:00–19:00, Wed and Sat 10:00–17:00, Sun 11:00–14:00, 24 computers, tel. 01253/478-111).

Post Office: The main P.O. is on Abingdon Street, a block inland from the TI (Mon–Sat 9:00–17:30, closed Sun).

Car Rental: In case you decide to tour the Lake District by car, you'll find plenty of rental agencies in Blackpool (closed Sat afternoon and Sun), including **Avis** (292 Waterloo Road, tel. 01253/408-003) and **Budget** (242 Waterloo Road, tel. 01253/691-632).

Getting Around Blackpool

Vintage and zippy bus-like **tram cars** run 13 miles up and down the waterfront, connecting all the sights. This electric tramway—the first in Europe—dates from 1885 (£1.60–2.90 depending on length of trip, £5.75 for all-day pass that also covers the bus, pay conductor, trams come every 5 min or so June–Oct, Nov–May every 10–20 min, runs 6:00–24:00).

A City Sightseeing **hop-on, hop-off bus tour** with a recorded commentary and 16 stops leaves the Blackpool Tower every 15–30 minutes (£6.50, first two weeks of April and June–early-Nov daily from 8:45 until last departure at 19:15, mid-April–May Sat–Sun only, doesn't run off-season, www.city-sightseeing.com).

Taxis are easy to snare in Blackpool, and three to five people travel cheaper by cab than by tram. Hotels can get you a taxi by phone within three minutes (no extra charge).

SIGHTS AND ACTIVITIES

▲▲**The Piers**—Blackpool's famous piers were originally built for Victorian landlubbers who wanted to go to sea but were afraid of getting seasick. Each of the three amusement piers has its own personality and is a joy to wander. The sedate **North Pier** is most traditional and refreshingly uncluttered (50p admission fee, refunded if you buy something). Dance down its empty planks at twilight to the early English rock playing on its speakers. Its Carousel Bar at the end is great for families—with a free kids' DJ nightly from 19:00 to 23:00 (parents drink good beer while the kids bunny-hop and boogie). The something-for-everyone **Central Pier** is lots of fun. Ride its great Ferris wheel for the best view in Blackpool (rich photography at twilight, get the operator to spin you as you bottom out). And check out the masochist running the adjacent Waltzer ride—just watch the miserably ecstatic people spinning. The rollicking **South Pier** is all rides. From the far end of any pier, you can see the natural-gas drilling platforms out in the Irish Sea lining the horizon.

▲**Blackpool Tower**—This mini-Eiffel Tower is a 100-year-old vertical fun center. You pay £13 to get in (£10 for kids, family tickets available, less on weekdays, tickets cheaper at TI every day); after that, the fun is free. Work your way up from the bottom through layer after layer of noisy entertainment: a circus (two to three acts a day, runs Aug-Oct), a 3-D cinema, an aquarium, and a wonderful old ballroom with barely live music and golden oldies dancing to golden oldies all day. Enjoy a break at the dance-floor-level pub or on a balcony perch. Kids love this place. With a little marijuana, adults would, too. Ride the glass elevator to the tip of the 500-foot-tall symbol of Blackpool for a smashing view,  especially at sunset (daily Easter–June 10:00–18:00, July–Oct 10:00–23:00, closed Nov–Easter, top of tower closed when windy, tel. 01253/292-029, www.theblackpooltower.co.uk). If you want to leave and return, request a hand stamp.

▲**Pleasure Beach**—These 42 acres attract seven million visitors annually, and are littered with more than 100 rides (including "the best selection of white-knuckle rides in Europe"), an ice show, circus and illusion shows, and varied amusements. Most of the rides are variations on the roller-coaster theme, but the top two are the Pepsi Max Big One (one of the world's fastest and highest roller coasters at 235 feet, 85 mph) and the Ice Blast (which rockets you straight up before letting you bungee down). Also memorable are the Pasaje del Terror and the Steeple Chase—carousel horses stampeding down a roller-coaster track. The Irn-Bru Revolution speeds you over a steep drop and upside-down in a loop, then does it again backwards. The Valhalla ride zips you on a Viking boat in watery darkness past scary Nordic things like lutefisk. With two 80-foot drops and lots of hype, first you're scared, then you're soaked, and—finally—you're just glad you survived. Pleasure Beach medics advise brittle senior travelers to avoid the old wooden-framed rides, which are much jerkier. Only the admission is free. You can pay individually for rides with your £1 tickets (2–9 tickets per ride), or get unlimited rides with a £30 armband (thrill seekers save with the armband, a few pounds cheaper if purchased in advance on their website, not available from TI; daily March–early-Nov, opens at about 10:30 and closes as early as 17:00 or as late as 24:00, depending on season, weather, and demand; tel. 0870-444-5566, www.blackpoolpleasurebeach.co.uk).

Sandcastle Waterpark—This popular attraction, across the street from Pleasure Beach, has a big pool, long slides, a wave machine, and a constant indoor temperature of 84 degrees. Newly renovated and featuring the longest tube waterslide in the world, this is a place where most kids could easily spend a day (£13.50, £11 for kids, TI sells discount tickets and £29 family pass, July–Aug daily 10:00–17:30, sometimes open later, last admission 1 hour before closing, shorter hours off-season, weekends only Nov–March, tel. 01253/343-602, www.sandcastlewaterpark.com).

▲▲▲**People-Watching**—Blackpool's top sight is its people. You'll see England here as nowhere else. Grab someone's hand and a big stick of rock (candy), and stroll. Grown men walk around with huge teddy bears looking for places to play "bowlingo," a short-lane version of bowling. Ponder the thought of actually retiring here and spending your last years, day after day, wearing plaid pants and a bad toupee, surrounded by Blackpool. This place puts people in a talkative mood. Ask someone to explain the difference between tea and supper. Back at your hotel, join in the chat sessions in the lounge.

▲**Illuminations**—Blackpool was the first town in England to "go electric" in 1879. Now, every fall (Aug 29–Nov 2 in 2008), Blackpool stretches its tourist season by illuminating its six miles of waterfront with countless lights, all blinking and twinkling. The American in me kept saying, "I've seen bigger, and I've seen better," but I filled his mouth with cotton candy and just had some simple fun like everyone else on my specially decorated tram. Look for the animated tableaux on North Shore.

St. Anne—Had enough greasy food and flashing lights? The seaside village of St. Anne is a short 20-minute bus ride away to the south, and offers a welcome break. The town's promenade and simple Victorian pier feel like a breath of sanity. The broad sand beach is perfect for flying a kite or building a sandcastle (bus #11 runs from the Blackpool tower every 10 minutes, covered by the all-day pass).

NIGHTLIFE

▲**Showtime**—Blackpool always has a few razzle-dazzle music, dancing-girl, racy-humor, magic, and tumbling shows. Box offices around town can give you a rundown on what's available (£7–15 tickets). Your hotel has the latest. For something more highbrow, try the Opera House for musicals (booking tel. 0870-380-1111, info tel. 01253/625-252) and the Grand Theatre for drama and ballet (£15–25, tel. 01253/290-190, www.blackpoolgrand.co.uk). Both are on Church Street, a couple of blocks behind the tower. For the latest in evening entertainment, see the window display at the tourist office on Clifton Street (www.blackpoollive.com).

▲▲**Funny Girls**—Blackpool's current hot bar is in a dazzling location a couple blocks from the train station. Most nights from 20:15 to 23:30, Funny Girls puts on a "glam bam thank you ma'am" burlesque-in-drag show that delights footballers and grannies alike.

Get your drinks at the bar...unless the transvestites are dancing on it. The show, while racy, is not raunchy. The music is very loud. The crowd is young, old, straight, gay, very down-to-earth, and fun-loving. Go on a weeknight; Friday and Saturday are too jammed. While the area up front can be a mosh pit, there are more sedate tables in back, where service comes with a vampish smile.

There are two tiers of seats: sitting and standing (Sun and Tue–Thu: £4.50 to stand, £11 to sit; Fri–Sat: £7 to stand, £17.50 to sit; no shows Mon). Getting dinner here before the show runs about £15 (dinner reservations required, must be 18 to enter, 5 Dickson Road, TI sells tickets, to reserve in advance call tel. 01253/624-901, www.funnygirlsshowbar.co.uk).

Other Nightspots—Blackpool's clubs and discos are cheap, with live bands and an interesting crowd (nightly 22:00–2:00 in the morning). With all the stag and hen parties, the late-night streets can be clotted with rude rowdies.

SLEEPING

(area code: 01253)
Blackpool's 140,000 people provide 120,000 beds in 3,500 mostly dumpy, cheap, nondescript hotels and B&Bs. Remember, this town's in the business of accommodating the people who can't afford to go to Spain. Most have the same design—minimal character, maximum number of springy beds—and charge £15–25 per person. Empty beds abound except from September through early November and summer weekends. It's only really tight on Illuminations weekends (when everyone bumps up prices). I've listed regular high-season prices. With the huge number of hotels in town, prices get really soft in the off-season. There's likely a launderette within a five-minute walk of your hotel; ask your host or hostess.

North of the Tower
These listings are on or near the waterfront in the quiet area they call "the posh end," a mile or two north of Blackpool Tower, with easy parking and easy access to the center by tram. The first two listings have classy extras you wouldn't expect in Blackpool. The last two are B&Bs with welcoming owners, lots of stairs, and house pets.

    $$$ Paramount Imperial Hotel is where the queen would stay in Blackpool. (They boast that every prime minister since they opened has visited their bar.) With dark-paneled Old World elegance, this splurge has all the comforts at its posh address

---

Sleep Code

(£1 = about $2, country code: 44)
S = Single, **D** = Double/Twin, **T** = Triple, **Q** = Quad, **b** = bathroom, **s** = shower only. You can assume credit cards are accepted unless otherwise noted.

    To help you sort easily through these listings, I've divided the rooms into three categories based on the price for a standard double room with bath:

  $$$ **Higher Priced**—Most rooms £90 or more.
    $$ **Moderately Priced**—Most rooms between £45–90.
      $ **Lower Priced**—Most rooms £45 or less.

Central Blackpool

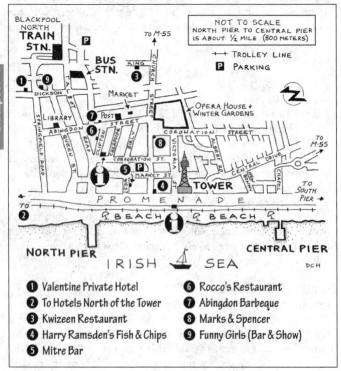

NOT TO SCALE
NORTH PIER TO CENTRAL PIER
IS ABOUT ½ MILE (800 METERS)

Trolley Line
P Parking

BLACKPOOL NORTH TRAIN STN.
BUS STN.
TO M-55
DICKSON
MARKET
LIBRARY
POST
CORONATION STREET
OPERA HOUSE + WINTER GARDENS
TO M-55
CORPORATION ST.
MARKET ST.
TOWER
TO SOUTH PIER
PROMENADE
BEACH
BEACH
NORTH PIER
IRISH SEA
CENTRAL PIER
DCH

1 Valentine Private Hotel
2 To Hotels North of the Tower
3 Kwizeen Restaurant
4 Harry Ramsden's Fish & Chips
5 Mitre Bar
6 Rocco's Restaurant
7 Abingdon Barbeque
8 Marks & Spencer
9 Funny Girls (Bar & Show)

(Db-£140–180, much lower in slow times, check website for deals, most rooms come with sea view, children stay free, tram stop: Warley Road, North Promenade, tel. 01253/623-971, fax 01253/751-784, www.paramount-hotels.co.uk/imperialblackpool).

$$$ I know, staying at the **Hilton Hotel** in Blackpool is like wearing a tux to eat falafel. But if you need a splurge, this is a grand place with lots of views, a pool, sauna, gym, and comfortable rooms (Db-£110–170, "club deal" Db with lots of extras-£20 more, ask if there are any "special rates" being advertised, check website for deals, request room with view for no extra charge, tram stop: Warley Road, North Promenade, tel. 01253/623-434, fax 01253/627-864, www.hilton.com).

$$$ **Carlton Hotel,** a Best Western, rents business-class rooms at rack rates too high for what you get—check for more reasonable rates online (Sb-£70–75, Db-from £110, can be a little higher during Illuminations, a long block closer to town from the Hilton, tram stop: Pleasant Street, North Promenade, tel. 01253/628-966, fax 01253/752-587, www.carltonhotelblackpool .co.uk, mail@carltonhotelblackpool.co.uk).

$$ Robin Hood Hotel is a cheery place with a big, welcoming living room, a family underfoot, and 10 spacious rooms with big beds and sea views (especially rooms 1, 5, and 9). Run by nutritionist and therapist Kathy, it also serves as a diet retreat center (Sb-£27–50, Db-£55, various facial and massage treatments available, tram stop: St. Stephen's Avenue and walk 1 block north; 1.5 miles north of tower across from a peaceful stretch of beach, 100 Queens Promenade, North Shore, tel. 01253/351-599, www.robinhoodhotel .co.uk, rhhblackpool@hotmail.com).

$$ Beechcliffe Private Hotel has seven clean rooms run by a friendly young couple, Ken and Carol Selman. The rooms are tight, but this place has a homey touch (Sb-£23, Db-£46–50, kids half-price, home-cooked dinner-£8, tram stop: Uncle Tom's Cabin; turn left from tram stop, then right at Shaftesbury Avenue, and walk a block away from beach; 16 Shaftesbury Avenue, North Shore, tel. 01253/353-075, www.beechcliffe.co.uk, info @beechcliffe.co.uk).

Near the Train Station

$ Valentine Private Hotel is a handy and friendly 13-room place in an otherwise grotty area. On-site owner Anthony Palmer is doing his best to keep the Blackpool spirit alive—complete with "dancers" from the Funny Girls bar, which is a block away, occasionally hanging out in the lounge downstairs (Db-from £44, bunk-bed family deals, one kid sleeps free; 2 blocks from station: with back to tracks, exit station far right, go up Springfield 2 blocks to Dickson, 35 Dickson Road; tel. 01253/622-775, www.valentinehotelblackpool .co.uk, info@valentinehotelblackpool.co.uk).

EATING

Your hotel may serve a cheap, early-evening meal. Generally, food in the tower and along the promenade is terrible. The following places are all between Blackpool Tower and the North Pier.

Kwizeen is a bistro that serves good Mediterranean and modern English "kwizeen" in a—refreshing for Blackpool—plain atmosphere. Popular with locals, it's recently been racking up awards for its food (£12 main dishes, Mon–Fri 12:00–13:30 & 18:00–21:00, Sat 18:00–21:00, closed Sun, 47 King Street, tel. 01253/290-045).

"World Famous" **Harry Ramsden's** will remind you of an English version of Denny's. This is *the* place for mushy peas, fish-and-chips, and a chance to get goofy with waiters—call the place *Henry* Ramsden's and see what happens (£6–10 meals, order a side of mushy peas, daily 11:30–22:00, off-season until 20:00, 60 The Promenade, tel. 01253/294-386).

The **Mitre Bar** serves light lunches and beers in a truly rare, old-time Blackpool ambience. Drop in anytime to survey the fun photos of old Blackpool and for the great people scene (daily 11:00–23:00, 3 West Street, tel. 01253/623-718).

Clifton Street is lined with decent ethnic-food eateries, including Indian and Chinese. For Italian, try **Rocco's** (£10 two-course early-bird special, daily 17:30–23:00, 36 Clifton Street, tel. 01253/627-440).

Abingdon Barbeque, with its expansive deli counter, is mobbed with hungry locals at lunch, munching on cheap roasted chicken and meat pies. Get a whole chicken and some sides, and you've got lunch for four for less than £10 (daily 7:00–18:00, take-away only, corner of Abingdon Street and Dean's Gate, tel. 01253/621-817).

Supermarket: **Marks & Spencer** has a big supermarket in its basement (Mon–Sat 9:00–18:00, Sun 10:30–16:30, near recommended eateries, on Coronation Street and Church Street). Go picnic at the beach.

TRANSPORTATION CONNECTIONS

If you're heading to (or from) Blackpool by train, you'll usually need to transfer at **Preston** (3/hr, 30 min). The following trains leave from Blackpool's main (north) station.

From Blackpool to: Keswick/Lake District (hourly, allow up to 4 hours total for journey: transfer in Preston—30 minutes away, then 1 hr to Penrith, then catch a bus to Keswick, 1/hr except Sun 6/day, 35 min), **Conwy** in North Wales (nearly hourly, 3–4 hrs, 1–2 transfers), **Edinburgh** (8/day, 3.5 hrs, transfer in Preston), **Glasgow** (hourly, 3.5 hrs, transfer in Preston), **Liverpool** (every 2 hrs, 1.5 hrs, direct), **York** (hourly, 3.25 hrs, direct), **Moreton-in-Marsh** in the Cotswolds (every 2 hrs, 5 hrs, 2 transfers), **Bath** (hourly, 5 hrs, 2 transfers), **London**'s Euston Station (nearly hourly, 3 hrs, usually 1 transfer). Train info: tel. 08457-484-950, www.nationalrail.co.uk.

Liverpool

Liverpool, a surprisingly friendly and enjoyable city, is a fascinating stop for Beatles fans and those who would like to look urban

England straight in the eye. The city is becoming a favorite holiday spot for Brits, who enjoy its lively atmosphere and cultural and historical sites. Banners, signs, and locals proudly announce that Liverpool has been named the European Capital of Culture 2008. Construction and architectural face-lifts abound—especially around the revitalized Albert Dock—as Liverpool preens for this event.

Planning Your Time

If you're a casual Beatles fan, make an afternoon pit-stop trip to Liverpool: Spend most of your time at the Albert Dock, popping in to see The Beatles Story, having lunch at the Tate's lunchtime café (and appreciating the art upstairs), and visiting the Maritime Museum. Consider getting a ticket to ride the ferry across the Mersey, which leaves from the docks north of the Albert Dock.

Beatles Blitz: If the Fab Four are what brought you to Liverpool, arrive the night before and follow this more ambitious, all-day sightseeing plan (which follows the Beatles' lives in roughly chronological order):

9:00—Visit the TI to book a seat on the 10:00 National Trust minibus tour to John and Paul's childhood homes, if you haven't pre-booked a time slot already (see reservations info on page 314).

9:50—Arrive at the Conservation Centre (near the TI) for the 2.5-hour minibus tour of John and Paul's childhood homes (departs at 10:00 sharp).

12:30—Return to the city center. Walk over to Mathew Street for a quick pop-in to the original (but unimpressive) Cavern Club.

13:00—Take the bus or a taxi, or walk 30 minutes, to the Albert Dock. Enjoy lunch in one of my recommended eateries (see page 319).

14:00—Choose between the bus and minivan tours (the "Magical Mystery" bus tour leaves the Albert Dock at 14:10) or The Beatles Story exhibit. Since the tours cover some of the same ground as the National Trust tour, an hour or two at The Beatles Story will satisfy all but the most die-hard fan.

Liverpool

M MERSEYLINK SUBWAY STOP

P PARKING

400 YARDS
400 METERS

DCH

1 Sir Thomas Hotel
2 Premier Travel Inn (2)
3 International Inn Hostel
4 Est Est Est Restaurant
5 Tate Café
6 The Slug and Lettuce Rest.

7 National Trust Beatles Tour Pick-Up Point (Mornings Only)
8 Yellow Duckmarine Tickets
9 Mathew Street & Site of Original Cavern Club
10 Departure Point for City Bus Tours

For those who just can't get enough, if it's summer, it's possible to do an afternoon "Magical Mystery" bus tour and also see The Beatles Story (the tour returns around 16:00, and The Beatles Story allows a last entry at 17:00).

ORIENTATION

Tourist Information

Liverpool's main TI is on Whitechapel Street, a six-minute walk downhill from the train station. Ignore the pavilion with the information symbol on it—the real TI is a glossy silver storefront on this main shopping street (Mon and Wed–Sat 9:00–18:00, Tue 10:00–18:00, Sun 11:00–16:00, tel. 0151/233-2008, www .liverpool08.com). Get the free, small map (also available at train station for £1). Walking tours are sometimes offered; the TI has the latest info.

Arrival in Liverpool

From the Lime Street **train** station to the Albert Dock, it's a 20-minute walk, a short ride on bus #1 (£1.50 one-way, £3 all-day ticket), or a £3 taxi trip. Liverpool, which still isn't really used to having many tourists, has no luggage storage available in the city center. For public-transportation information, call Merseytravel's Travel Line (tel. 0871-200-2233).

Drivers approaching Liverpool follow signs to *City Center* and *Albert Dock*, where you'll find a huge car park at the dock.

TOURS

Beatles Tours

▲**Lennon and McCartney Homes**—John and Paul's boyhood homes have both been restored to how they looked during their 1950s childhoods. This isn't Graceland—you won't find an over-the-top rock-and-roll extravaganza here. And if you don't know the difference between John and Paul, you'll likely be bored. But if you're a die-hard Beatles fan who wants to get a glimpse into the time and place that created these musical masterminds, this tour is worth ▲▲▲.

Because the houses are in residential neighborhoods—and in both cases, still share walls with neighbors—the National Trust runs only four tours per day with 14 Beatlemaniacs each, ending before 17:00. Just 7,000 people pass through these doors each year. While some Beatles bus tours stop here for photo ops, only the National Trust tour gets you inside the homes. And don't try to simply show up and stroll right in—you have to be on the tour to be allowed inside.

Tour Options: The National Trust runs four minibus tours per day. **Morning tours** (at 10:00 and 10:50) are better, as they follow a more scenic route that includes a quick pass by Penny Lane. They're also easier for non-drivers, as they depart from the Conservation Centre in downtown Liverpool, a few minutes' walk from the Lime Street train station and 100 yards from the TI. **Afternoon tours** (at 14:30 and 15:20) leave from Speke Hall, an out-of-the-way National Trust property located eight miles southeast of Liverpool. Allow 30 minutes to drive from the city center to Speke Hall—follow the brown *Speke Hall* signs through dozens of roundabouts, heading in the general direction of the airport (ample and free parking at the site).

Reservations: Because only 14 people are allowed on each tour, it's smart to make a reservation ahead of time, especially for the morning tours. You can reserve online (www.nationaltrust.org.uk/beatles), or by calling 0151/233-2457 (for the morning tours) or 0151/427-7231 (for the afternoon tours). If you haven't reserved ahead, you can try to book a same-day tour at the TI (arrive between 9:00–9:30 to get on the 10:00 or 10:50 city-center tours). The afternoon tours generally don't fill up, but remember that you'll need a car to reach the starting point at Speke Hall.

Cost, Hours, Information: £14, all tours run April–Oct Wed–Sun only, no tours Mon–Tue and off-season. Plan to arrive five to ten minutes before the tour departure time. Recorded info tel. 0870-900-0256, www.nationaltrust.org.uk/beatles.

Each home has a live-in caretaker who will act as your guide. These folks give an entertaining, insightful-for-fans 20- to 30-minute talk, and then leave you time (10–15 minutes) to wander through the house on your own. Ask lots of questions if their spiel peters out early—the docents are a wealth of information. You can take photos of the outside of the house after they give their talk, but not before. They ask you to turn off your mobile phones, and not to bring big bags.

Mendips (John Lennon's Home): Even though he sang about being a working-class hero, John grew up in the suburbs of Liverpool, surrounded by doctors, lawyers, and—beyond the back fence—Strawberry Field (he added the "s" for the song).

This was the home of John's Aunt Mimi, who raised him in this house from the time he was five years old. John moved out at age 23, but his first wife Cynthia bunked here for a while when John made his famous first trip to America. Yoko

Ono bought this house a few years ago, and gave it as a gift to the National Trust (which generated controversy among its members). The stewards, Colin and Sylvia, make this place come to life.

On the surface, it's just a 1930s house carefully restored to how it would have been in the past. But delve deeper. It's been lovingly cared for—restored to be the tidy, well-kept place Mimi would have recognized (down to her apron hanging in the kitchen). It's a lucky quirk of fate that the house's interior remained mostly unchanged after the Lennons left—the bachelor who owned it for the previous decades didn't upgrade much, so even the light switches are true to the time.

If you're a John Lennon fan, it's fun to picture him as a young boy drawing and imagining at his dining room table. It also makes for an interesting comparison to Paul's more-humble home, which is the second part of the tour.

20 Forthlin Road (Paul McCartney's Home): In comparison to Aunt Mimi's house, the home where Paul grew up is simpler,

much less "posh," and even a little ratty around the edges. Michael, Paul's brother, wanted it that way—their mother, Mary (famously mentioned in "Let It Be"), died when the boys were young, and it never had the tidiness of a woman's touch. It's been intentionally scuffed up around the edges to preserve a sense of historical accuracy. Notice the differences—Paul has said that John's house was vastly different and more clearly middle class; at Mendips, there were books on the bookshelves.

Over a hundred Beatles songs were written in this house (including "I Saw You Standing There") during days Paul and John spent skipping school. The photos from Michael, taken in this house, help make what's mostly a barren interior much more interesting.

There's no blue plaque identifying the house from the outside—those are only awarded once the person's been dead for 20 years, or when it's been 100 years since their birth, whichever comes first. In fact, Paul hasn't been back inside the house since it has been turned into a museum; he knocked on the door twice, but both times the custodian was out...an idea that might give you some comfort if you're not able to get inside yourself.

Beatles Tours—Beatles fans may want to invest a couple of hours taking the **"Magical Mystery" bus tour,** which hits the lads' homes (from the outside), Penny Lane, and so on (£13, 2 hours, departs from the Albert Dock daily at 14:10, from TI daily at 14:30,

Sat–Sun additional 11:40 Albert Dock departure). The TI has specifics.

For something more extensive, fun, and intimate, consider a four-hour minibus Beatles tour from **Phil Hughes.** It's longer because it includes information on historic Liverpool, as well as the Beatles stuff (£14/person, minimum £70/group of five, includes free beverages, can coordinate times with National Trust tour of Lennon and McCartney homes, 8-seat minibus, mobile 07961-511-223, tel. 0151/228-4565, www.tourliverpool.co.uk).

Jackie Spencer also hits the highlights and does private tours—just say when and where you want to go (five people in minivan-£140, four people in private taxi-£100, 2.5 hours, will pick you up at hotel or train station, mobile 0799-076-1478, www.liveapool.com, live@pooltours.com).

The "sights" each tour covers are basically houses where the Fab Four grew up (outside only), places they performed, and spots made famous by the lyrics of their hits ("Penny Lane," "Strawberry Fields," the Eleanor Rigby graveyard, and so on). While boring to anyone not into the Beatles, fans will enjoy the commentary and seeing the shelter on the roundabout, the fire station with the clean machine, and the barber who shaves another customer.

Other Tours

City Bus Tour—The City Sightseeing bus is a hop-on, hop-off bus tour with a canned soundtrack, but considering the size of the city center, it's a quick way to get an overview that links all the major sights in 55 breezy minutes (£6, buy ticket from driver, valid for 24 hours, £2 discount with Mersey Ferry ticket, daily April–Aug 10:00–17:00—every 30 min, Sept–Oct 10:00–17:00—hourly, Nov–March 10:00–16:00—every 90 min, tel. 0151/5242-2503, www.city-sightseeing.com).

Ferry Cruise—Mersey Ferries offers narrated cruises departing from Mersey Dock, an easy five-minute walk from the Albert Dock. The cruise makes two brief stops on the other side of the river; you can hop off and catch the next boat back (£6, year-round, Mon–Fri 10:00–15:00, Sat–Sun 10:00–18:00, leaves at top of hour, café, WCs on board, tel. 0151/330-1444, www.merseyferries.co.uk).

Harbor and City Tour—The Yellow Duckmarine runs wacky tours of Liverpool's waterfront, city, and docks by land and by sea in its amphibious tourist assault vehicles. Be prepared to quack (£12, or £10 midweek and off-peak, family deals, 1 hour, buy tickets at office on the Albert Dock near Beatles Story, departs from the Albert Dock every 75 min daily 10:30–17:00, more frequently with demand, tel. 0151/708-7799, www.theyellowduckmarine.co.uk).

SIGHTS

At the Albert Dock

All of these sights are at the Albert Dock. Opened in 1852 by Prince Albert, and enclosing seven acres of water, Albert Dock is surrounded by five-story brick warehouses. In its day, Liverpool was England's greatest seaport, but at the end of the 19th century, the port wasn't deep enough for the big new ships; trade declined after 1890, and by 1972 it was closed entirely.

Recently, like Liverpool itself, the docks have enjoyed a renaissance, and now contain the city's main attractions. A half-dozen trendy eateries are lined up here, out of the rain, and padded by lots of shopping mall–type distractions. There's plenty of parking. There's no TI at the Albert Dock, but the staff at the Maritime Museum's info desk can help in a pinch.

▲**Merseyside Maritime Museum**—This museum tells the story of Liverpool, once the second city of the British Empire. The port prospered in the 18th century as one corner of a commerce triangle with Africa and America. British shippers profited greatly through exploitation. From Liverpool, they exported manufactured goods to Africa in exchange for enslaved Africans; the slaves were then shipped to the Americas, where they were traded for raw material (cotton, sugar, and tobacco); and the goods were then brought back to Britain. While the merchants on all three sides made money, the big profit came home to England. As Britain's economy boomed, so did Liverpool's.

After participation in the slave trade was outlawed in Britain in the early 1800s, Liverpool kept its port busy as a transfer point for emigrants. If your ancestors came from Scandinavia, Ukraine, or Ireland, there's a good chance they left Europe from this port. Between 1830 and 1930, nine million emigrants sailed from Liverpool to find their dreams in the New World. Awe-inspiring steamers such as the *Lusitania* called this port home (free, daily 10:00–17:00, tel. 0151/478-4499).

Tate Gallery Liverpool—This prestigious gallery of modern art is next to the Maritime Museum. It won't entertain you as well

Liverpool

as its London sister, the Tate Modern, but if you're into modern art, any Tate's great (free, £5 for special exhibits; June–Aug daily 10:00–17:50; Sept–May Tue–Sun 10:00–17:50, closed Mon; tel. 0151/702-7400, www.tate.org.uk/liverpool). The Tate has a nice, inexpensive café (see "Eating," next page).

▲**The Beatles Story**—It's sad to think the Beatles are stuck in a museum (and their music turned into a Las Vegas show). Still,

while this exhibit is overpriced and not very creative, the story's a fascinating one, and even an avid fan will pick up some new information.

Listen to the included audioguide as you study the knickknacks. Cynthia Lennon, John's first wife, still marvels at the manic power of Beatlemania, while the narrator reminds listeners of all that made the group earth-shattering—and even a little edgy—at the time. For example, performing before the Queen Mother, John Lennon famously quips: "Will the people in the cheaper seats clap your hands? And the rest of you, if you'll just rattle your jewelry." The audioguide captures the Beatles' charm and cheekiness in the way the stuffy wax mannequins can't.

The last few rooms trace the members' solo careers (mostly John's and Paul's), and the last few steps are reserved for reverence about John's peace work, including a re-creation of the white room he used while writing *Imagine* (£10, includes audioguide, daily 10:00–18:00, last admission 1 hour before closing, tel. 0151/709-1963, www.beatlesstory.com). The shop has an impressive pile of Beatles buyables.

SLEEPING

(£1 = about $2, country code: 44, area code: 0151)

B&Bs are a rarity in urban Liverpool. Your best budget options are the boring, predictable, and central chain hotels.

$$$ Sir Thomas Hotel is a centrally located hotel that dearly wants to be chic. The 39 recently renovated rooms are comfortable (Db-£100, can jump to £150 on weekends, up to 2 adults and 2 kids OK, 5-min walk from station, 24 Sir Thomas Street and the corner of Victoria Street, tel. 0151/236-1366, fax 0151/227-1541, www.sirthomashotel.co.uk, reservations@sirthomashotel.co.uk).

$$ Premier Travel Inn, which has comfortable, American-style rooms and a friendly staff, is right on the Albert Dock (Db-£58, £60 Fri–Sat, mediocre breakfast costs extra—try good cafés nearby instead, best to book online, located next to The Beatles Story in East Britannia Building, Albert Dock, tel. 0870-990-6432, www.premiertravelinn.com). There's a second, downtown **$$ Premier Travel Inn** as well. While it's a much less desirable location than the Albert Dock branch, it's just a seven-minute walk from the Lime Street train station (same prices, Vernon Street, just off Dale Street, tel. 0870-238-3323).

$ International Inn Hostel, run by the daughter of the Beatles' first manager, is located in a former Victorian warehouse and has 100 budget beds (Db-£36–45, bed in 4- to 10-bed room-£15–20, includes sheets and towels, all rooms have bathrooms, free toast and tea/coffee, Internet access, laundry room-£2/load, games in lobby, TV lounge, video library, café, 4 South Hunter Street, bus #80A or #86A; if taking a taxi, tell them it's on the Hunter Street near Hardman Street; tel. & fax 0151/709-8135, www.internationalinn.co.uk, info@internationalinn.co.uk).

EATING

Your best bet is to dine at the Albert Dock (my first two listings, below). Here you'll find a slew of trendy restaurants that come alive with clubby energy at night, but are sedate and pleasant in the afternoon and early evening.

Est Est Est, a chain restaurant that doesn't seem like one, serves local businesspeople, travelers, and families alike in its cavernous but comfortable space (£9 pastas and pizzas, £13 fish dishes, children's menu available, Mon–Sat 12:00–23:00, Sun 12:00–22:30, Albert Dock, tel. 0870-401-2125).

Tate Café, in the Tate Gallery, serves soups, salads, and light lunches in a bright, light room that feels like one of its galleries (£5 sandwiches, £7 lunches, daily 11:45–15:30, Albert Dock, tel. 0151/702-7580).

The Slug and Lettuce, located in the city center, is another chain restaurant/bar. It mostly caters to the after-hours office crowd, who are more interested in drinking than eating, but it'll do in a pinch (£9 plates, daily 12:00–22:00, 16 North John Street, tel. 0151/236-8820).

TRANSPORTATION CONNECTIONS

By Train

From Liverpool by Train to: Blackpool (every 2 hrs direct, 1.5 hrs, more frequent with transfer at Preston), **York** (hourly, 3 hrs), **Edinburgh** (7/day, 4 hrs, some involve transfer), **Glasgow** (1–2/hr, 4 hrs Mon–Fri, 6–8 hrs Sat–Sun, requires 1–3 transfers), **London's** Euston Station (hourly, 2.5 hrs), **Crewe** (2/hr, 45 min), **Chester**

(2/hr, 45 min). Train info: tel. 08457-484-950, www.nationalrail
.co.uk.

By Ferry

By Ferry to Dublin, Republic of Ireland: It's an eight-hour
trip between Liverpool and Dublin by boat. Both ferry companies require you to check in one to two hours before the sailing
time—call to confirm the details. Ferries sail daily from both
companies at 22:00, with an extra trip at 10:00 Tue–Sat. You can
get to Dublin either from Liverpool on P&O Irish Sea Ferries
(Liverpool Freeport dock, tel. 0870-242-4777, www.poirishsea
.com) or from the nearby port of Birkenhead using Norfolkline Irish
Sea Ferry Services (Birkenhead Port, tel. 0870-600-4321, www
.norfolkline-ferries.co.uk). You can also take a ferry to Dublin via
the Isle of Man (www.steam-packet.com).

   By Ferry to Belfast, Northern Ireland: Norfolkline Irish Sea
Ferry Services sails most mornings (Tue–Sun) and every evening
year-round (8 hrs, tel. 0870-600-4321, www.norfolkline-ferries
.co.uk). You can also take a ferry to Belfast via the Isle of Man
(www.steam-packet.com).

Route Tips for Drivers

From Liverpool to Blackpool: Leaving Liverpool, drive north
along the waterfront, following signs to *M58* (Preston). Once
on M58 (and not before), follow signs to *M6*, and then *M55* into
Blackpool.

THE LAKE DISTRICT

In the pristine Lake District, Wordsworth's poems still shiver in trees and ripple on ponds. This is a land where nature rules, and humanity keeps a wide-eyed but low profile. Relax, recharge, take a cruise or a hike, and maybe even write a poem. Renew your poetic license at Wordsworth's famous Dove Cottage.

The Lake District, about 30 miles long and 30 miles wide, is nature's lush, green playground. Explore it by foot, bike, bus, or car. While not impressive in sheer height (Scafell Pike, the tallest peak in England, is only 3,206 feet), there's a walking-stick charm about the way nature and the culture mix. Locals are fond of declaring that their mountains are older than the Himalayas and were once as tall, but have been worn down by the ages. Walking along a windblown ridge or climbing over a rock fence to look into the eyes of a ragamuffin sheep, even tenderfeet get a chance to feel very outdoorsy. The tradition of staying close to the land remains true—albeit in an updated form—in the 21st century; you'll see restaurants serving organic foods as well as stickers advocating for environmental causes in the windows of local homes.

You'll probably have rain mixed with brilliant bright spells. Drizzly days can be followed by delightful evenings. Pubs offer atmospheric shelter at every turn.

Plan to spend the majority of your time in the unspoiled North Lake District. In this chapter, I focus on the town of Keswick, the lake called Derwentwater, and the vast, time-passed Newlands Valley. The North Lake District works great by car or by bus (with easy train access via Penrith), and is manna to nature-lovers—with good accommodations to boot.

The South Lake District—famous primarily for its Wordsworth and Beatrix Potter sights—is closer to London, and gets the promotion, the tour crowds, and the tackiness that comes with them. I strongly recommend that you skip the South Lake District, and enter the region from the north via Penrith. Make your home base in or near Keswick, and side-trip from here into the South Lake District only if you're interested in the Wordsworth and Beatrix Potter sights.

Planning Your Time

On a three-week trip to Great Britain, I'd spend two days and two nights in this area. Penrith is the nearest train station, just 35 minutes by bus or car from Keswick. Those without a car will use Keswick as a springboard: Cruise the lake and take one of the many hikes in the Cat Bells area. Non-hikers can hop on a mini-bus tour. If great scenery is commonplace in your life, the Lake District can be more soothing (and rainy) than exciting. If you're rushed, you could make this area a one-night stand—or even a quick drive-through.

Two-Day Driving Plan: Here's the most exciting way for drivers coming from the south—who'd like to visit South Lake District sights en route to the North Lake District—to pack their day of arrival: On **Day 1,** get an early start, aiming to leave the motorway at Kendal by 10:30; drive along Windermere and through Ambleside; 11:30–Tour Dove Cottage; 12:30–Backtrack to Ambleside, where a small road leads up and over the dramatic Kirkstone Pass (far more scenic northbound than southbound, get out and bite the wind) and down to Glenridding on Lake Ullswater. You could catch the 15:00 boat. Hike six miles (3–4 hours, roughly 15:30–19:00) from Howtown back to Glenridding. Drive to your farmhouse B&B near Keswick, with a stop as the sun sets at Castlerigg Stone Circle. On **Day 2,** make the circular drive from Keswick through the Newlands Valley, Buttermere, Honister Pass, and Borrowdale, and do the Cat Bells High Ridge Hike. Spend the evening at the same farmhouse B&B.

Getting Around the Lake District

With a Car

Nothing is very far from Keswick and Derwentwater. Pick up a good map, get off the big roads, and leave the car, at least occasionally, for some walking. In summer, the Keswick–Ambleside–Windermere–Bowness corridor (A591) suffers from congestion.

The Lake District

Keswick Motor Company rents cars in Keswick (from £32/day with insurance, Mon–Sat 8:30–17:15, closed Sun, only ages 25–70, must have an international license and passport, Lake Road, a block from Moot Hall in town center, tel. 017687/72064).

Parking is tight throughout the region. It's easiest to just park in the pay-and-display lots (gather small coins, as machines rarely make change). If you're parking free on the roadside, don't block the vital turnouts. Where there are double yellow lines, you must be beyond them.

Without a Car

Those based in Keswick without a car manage fine.

By Bus: Keswick has no real bus station; all buses stop at a turnout in front of the Booths Supermarket. Local buses take you quickly and easily (if not always frequently) to all nearby points of interest. The exhaustive *Cumbria & Lakes Rider* bus brochure (50 pages, free, at TI or on any bus) explains the schedules. You can purchase one-day passes on the bus (£9). For bus and rail info, call 0870-608-2608 or visit www.traveline.org.uk.

These buses connect Keswick with about everything of interest:

Buses **#X4, #X5,** and **#X50** connect Penrith train station to Keswick (hourly, 35 min).

Bus **#79,** the Borrowdale Rambler, goes topless in the summer, affording a wonderful sightseeing experience in and of itself (2/hr, hourly on Sun, 30 min each way, route: Keswick–Lodore Hotel–Grange Bridge–Rosthwaite–Seatoller at the base of Honister Pass).

Bus **#77/#77A,** the Honister Rambler, makes the gorgeous circle from Keswick around Derwentwater, over Honister Pass, past Buttermere, and through Whinlatter Valley (£6.25 Honister Dayrider all-day pass, 4/day clockwise, 4/day "anticlockwise," daily May–Oct, 2-hour loop).

Buses **#555** and **#556** connect Keswick with the south (hourly, 30 min to Grasmere and Windermere). From Grasmere, you can hop onto the Lakes Rider (#599, see below) for more breezy fun.

Bus **#599,** the open-top Lakes Rider, runs along the main Windermere corridor, connecting the big tourist attractions in the south (£6 Central Lakes Dayrider all-day pass, 3/hr daily April–Aug, 1 hour each way, route: Grasmere (Dove Cottage)–Rydal Mount–Ambleside–Brockhole–Windermere–Bowness Pier; see "Getting Around the South Lake District—By Bus," page 346).

By Bike: Several shops rent bikes in Keswick. **Keswick Mountain Bikes** has the largest selection (£17/day mountain bikes, includes helmet and toolkit, Mon–Sat 9:00–17:30, Sun 10:00–17:30, guided bike tours by request; several locations, including behind Pencil Museum; tel. 017687/75202, www.keswickbikes.co.uk). **Keswick Motor Company** in the town center also rents bikes (£15/day, includes helmet; for details, see "With a Car" on page 323). Keswick Mountain Bikes and the TI sell various cycling maps.

By Boat: A circular boat service glides you around Derwentwater, with several hiker-aiding stops along the way (for a cruise/hike option, see the Derwentwater listing, page 329).

By Foot: Hiking information is available everywhere. Consider buying a detailed map (good selection at Keswick TI, or borrow one from your B&B). For easy hikes, pick up the helpful fliers at TIs and B&Bs that describe routes. The Lake District's TIs advise hikers to check the weather before setting out (for an up-to-date weather report, ask at TI or call 0870-055-0575), wear suitable clothing, and bring a map.

By Tour: For organized bus tours that run the roads of the Lake District, see "Tours" on page 328.

Keswick and the North Lake District

As far as touristy Lake District towns go, Keswick (KEZ-ick, population 5,000) is far more enjoyable than Windermere, Bow-

ness, or Ambleside. An important mining center for slate, copper, and lead through the Middle Ages, Keswick became a resort in the 19th century. Its fine Victorian buildings recall those Romantic days when city slickers first learned about "communing with nature." Today, the compact town is lined with tearooms, pubs, gift

shops, and hiking-gear stores. Lake Derwentwater is a pleasant five-minute walk from the town center.

ORIENTATION

(area code: 017687)

Keswick is an ideal home base, with plenty of good B&Bs (see "Sleeping," page 337), an easy bus connection to the nearest train station at Penrith, and a prime location near the best lake in the area, Derwentwater. In Keswick, everything is within a five-minute walk of everything else: the pedestrian market square, the TI, recommended B&Bs, a grocery store, the municipal pitch-and-putt golf course, the bus stop, a lakeside boat dock, the post office (with Internet access), and a central parking lot. Saturday is market day, but the town square is lively throughout the summer.

Keswick town is a delight for wandering. Its centerpiece, Moot Hall (meaning "meeting hall"), was a 16th-century copper warehouse upstairs with an arcade below (closed after World War II). "Keswick" means "cheese market"—a legacy from the time when the town square was the spot to sell cheese. The market square recently went pedestrian-only, and locals are all abuzz about people tripping over the curbs. (The English are titillated by the ever-present dangers of "watch your head," "watch the step," and "mind the gap.")

Keswick and the Lake District are popular with British holi-daymakers who prefer to bring their dogs with them on vacation. If you are shy about connecting with local people, pal up to a British pooch (the main square in Keswick can look like the Westminster dog show), and you will often find they are happy to introduce you to their owners.

Tourist Information

The helpful TI is in Moot Hall, right in the middle of the main square (daily Easter–Oct 9:30–17:30, Nov–Easter 9:30–16:30, tel. 017687/72645, www.lake-district.gov.uk). The staff are pros at advising you about hiking routes. They'll also help you figure out public transportation to outlying sights, and book rooms (you'll leave a 10 percent deposit and pay a higher price for your room; it's cheaper to call B&Bs direct).

The TI sells bus passes, theater tickets, passes for various minibus tours, Keswick Launch tickets (discounted £1.20), and brochures and maps that outline nearby hikes (60p–£1.80, including a *Keswick Town Trail* for history buffs, and a very simple and driver-friendly £1.50 *Lap Map* featuring sights, walks, and a mileage chart). The TI bookstore has books and maps for hikers, cyclists, and drivers.

Check the "What's On" boards (inside the TI's foyer and on outside wall at post-office end) for information about walks, talks, and entertainment. The daily weather forecast is posted just outside the front door (or call 0870-055-0575). Pop upstairs for a series of short videos about the history of Keswick and the Lake District (free).

Walks of varying levels of difficulty depart from the Keswick TI daily at 10:00. They're led by local guides, leave regardless of the weather, and generally incorporate a bus ride into the outing (£10, Easter–Oct, wear suitable clothing and footwear, bring lunch and water, return by 17:00, TI tel. 017687/72645 or 017687/71292, www.keswickrambles.org.uk). TIs throughout the region also offer free walks by the "Voluntary Rangers" (generally from Keswick on Sun and Wed in summer, ask for schedule).

Helpful Hints

Book in Advance: Keswick hosts a variety of festivals and con-ventions, especially during the summer, so it's smart to book ahead. Please honor your bookings—the B&B proprietors here lose out on much-needed business if you don't show up.

A sampling of events for 2008: The Keswick Jazz Festival mellows out the town in mid-May, followed immediately by the new Mountain Festival, then a beer festival in early June. The Keswick Religious Convention packs the town with

Keswick

9 The Grove Rest.

10 Abraham Tea Room

11 The Lakeland Pedlar Vegetarian Rest.

12 Bryson's Bakery & Tea Room

13 Maysons Restaurant

14 Library

15 Post Office & Internet Café

16 Theatre by the Lake

17 Keswick Launch Cruises

18 Keswick Motor Co. (Bike & Car Rental)

19 Cricket Pitch

20 Lawn Bowling

21 Photo Fun with Sheep

1 Stanger Street B&Bs

2 Howe Keld Lakeland Hotel; Parkfield & West View Guest Houses

3 Berkeley & Brundholme Guest Houses

4 Keswick Youth Hostel

5 Denton House Hostel

6 Morrel's Restaurant

7 Pack Horse Inn

8 The Dog and Gun Pub

4,000 Evangelical Christians for the last three weeks in July. A music festival hums in September.

Several Bank Holiday Mondays in spring and summer (May 5, May 26, and August 25 in 2008) draw vacationers from all over the island for three-day weekends.

If you have trouble finding a room (or a B&B that accepts small children), try www.keswick.org to search for available rooms.

Internet Access: Located above the post office, **U-Compute** provides Internet access (£3/hr, daily 9:00–17:30, 14 terminals and Wi-Fi, corner of Main and Bank Streets, tel. 017687/75127). The **library** also has six terminals (£2/hr, 50p minimum charge, Mon and Wed 10:00–19:00, Tue and Fri 10:00–17:00, Thu and Sat 10:00–12:30, closed Sun, tel. 017687/72656).

Laundry: It's around the corner from the bus station on Main Street (self-service: daily 7:30–19:00, £5/load wash and dry, change machine and coin-op soap dispenser; full service: £7, you can drop off before 9:00—just leave clothes and a note inside by the office door closest to the front; tel. 017687/75448).

TOURS

Bus tours are great for people with money who'd like to wring maximum experience out of their limited time and see the area without lots of hiking or messing with public transport. For a cheaper alternative, take public bus #79 or #77 (see "Getting Around the Lake District—Without a Car," earlier in this chapter).

Lake District Tours—This company offers a variety of mostly half-day tours from Keswick (general schedule: Tue—North Lakes Explorer; Wed—Heart of the Lakes; Thu—full-day Best of the Lakes, departing at 10:00; Fri—Ullswater Treat). Their half-day "North Lakes Explorer" tour features the area around Keswick: Borrowdale, Buttermere, and Honister Pass. Guide Graham takes from 4 to 11 people in his minibus, and gives my readers who book direct and pay cash a 10 percent discount in 2008 (£19.50/half-day, £22 for Ullswater Treat, £29.50/full day, tours depart 13:00 April–Oct Mon–Fri, none Sat or Sun, book by phone or at 19 Church Street, private tours possible, tel. 017687/80732, www.laketours .co.uk).

Mountain Goat Tours—The region's dominant tour company runs a few minibus tours from Keswick (£20/half-day—afternoon tours £2.50 more and include lake cruise, £32.50/full day, year-round if there are sufficient sign-ups, minimum 4 to a maximum of 16 per hearty bus, book in advance with Keswick TI or by calling 015394/45161, www.mountain-goat.com). Note that most of their tours are Windermere-based. Confirm that the tour you're

Lake District

taking is actually a Keswick tour, so you won't be shuttled down to Windermere to catch the tour (adding an hour of needless driving to your day).

Touchstone Tours—Lucy Harrison takes small groups in her minibus for fascinating days out and about. Each tour has a theme (explained at www.touchstonetours.co.uk); the most popular are the Hadrian's Wall tour and the historical Lakeland Scenic Tour (£45/half-day, £75/full day; includes snacks, lunch, and photo disk of the day's events; 10 percent discount with this book in 2008, tours start at 9:30, 2–7 per group, tel. 017687/79599 to reserve). If you'd like to continue on from Hadrian's Wall, ask to be dropped at a convenient train station (see page 397 in the Durham and Northeast England chapter).

SIGHTS AND ACTIVITIES

In Keswick

▲**Derwentwater**—One of Cumbria's most photographed and popular lakes, Derwentwater has four islands, good circular boat service, plenty of trails, and the pleasant town of Keswick at its north end. The roadside views aren't much, so hike or cruise. You can walk around the lake (fine trail, floods in heavy rains, 9 miles, 4 hours) or cruise it (1 hour). I suggest a hike/cruise combo. The Lodore Walk and the Cat Bells High Ridge

Hike (both described later in "Hikes and Drives") start from Derwentwater docks.

Boating—Keswick Launch runs boats from mid-March to October (2/hr—alternating clockwise and "anticlockwise"—daily 10:00–17:30, Aug until 18:00, shoulder season until 16:30, in winter 5/day weekends only, at end of Lake Road, tel. 017687/72263, www.keswick-launch.co.uk). Boats make seven stops on each 60-minute round-trip. The boat trip costs £7.90 per circle (£6 if you book through TI) with free stopovers, or £1.60 per segment. Stand on the pier Gilligan-style, or the boat may not stop. Keswick Launch also rents **rowboats** for two (£6/30 min, £9/hr).

Keswick Launch's **evening cruise** is a delightful little trip that comes with a glass of wine and a mid-lake stop for a short commentary (60 min, 19:30 every evening late May–mid-Sept weather permitting and if enough people show up, £8, families for £18). You're welcome to bring a picnic dinner and munch scenically as you cruise.

▲**Pencil Museum**—Graphite was first discovered centuries ago in Keswick. A hunk of the stuff proved great for marking sheep in the 15th century. In 1832, the first crude Keswick pencil factory opened, and the rest is history (which is what you'll learn about here). While you can't actually tour the 150-year-old factory where the famous Derwent pencils are made, you can enjoy the smell of thousands of pencils getting sharpened for the first time. The adjacent, charming, and kid-friendly museum is a good way to pass a rainy hour. Take a look at the "war pencils" made for WWII bomber crews (filled with tiny maps and compasses) and relax for 10 minutes watching *The Humble Pencil* video in the theater, followed by a sleepy animated-snowman short (£3, daily 9:30–17:00, last entry at 16:00, humble café on-site, 3-min walk from the town center, signposted off Main Street, tel. 017687/73626, www.pencilmuseum.co.uk).

Fitz Park—An inviting, grassy park stretches alongside Keswick's tree-lined, duck-filled River Greta. There's plenty of room for kids to burn off energy. Consider an after-dinner stroll on the footpath. You may catch men in white (or frisky schoolboys in uniform) playing a game of cricket. There's the serious bowling green (where you're welcome to watch the experts play), and the public one where tourists are welcome to give lawn bowling a go (£2.50). You can try tennis on a grass court (£5/hr with rackets) or enjoy the putting green (£2).

▲**Golf**—A lush nine-hole pitch-and-putt golf course separates the town from the lake and offers a classy, cheap, and convenient chance to golf near the birthplace of the sport (£3 for 9 holes, £1.70 for putting, £1.90 for 18 tame holes of "obstacle golf," Easter–Oct daily 9:30–20:00 or dusk, closed Nov–Easter, tel. 017687/73445).

Swimming—While the Leisure Center doesn't have a serious adult pool, it does have an indoor pool kids love, with a huge water slide and wave machine (pool-£4.30, kids-£3.50, Mon 9:00–15:00, Tue 9:00–16:00, Wed–Thu 9:00–17:00, Fri 9:00–18:00, Sat–Sun 10:00–17:00, shorter hours off-season, longer during school break, no towels or suits for rent, lockers-50p deposit, a 10-min walk from town center, follow Station Road past Fitz Park and veer left, tel. 017687/72760).

Near Keswick

▲▲**Castlerigg Stone Circle**—For some reason, 70 percent of England's stone circles are here in Cumbria. This one's the best, and one of the oldest in Britain. The circle—90 feet across and 5,000 years old—has 38 stones mysteriously laid out on a line between the two tallest peaks on the horizon. They serve as a celestial calendar for ritual celebrations. Imagine the ambience here, as ancient people filled this clearing in spring to celebrate fertility, in late summer to commemorate the harvest, and in the winter to celebrate the solstice and the coming renewal of light. Festival dates were dictated by how the sun rose and set in relation to the stones. The more that modern academics study this circle, the more meaning they find in the placement of the stones. The two front stones face due north, toward a cut in the mountains. The rare-for-stone-circles "sanctuary" lines up with its center stone to mark where the sun rises on May Day. (Party!) For maximum "goose pimples" (as they say here), show up at sunset (free, open all the time, 3 miles east of Keswick—follow brown signs, 3 min off A66, easy parking).

▲**Lakeland Sheep and Wool Centre**—If you have a car, this is worth a stop to watch working sheepdogs in action. Catch a demonstration, see the twenty or so different breeds of sheep in Britain, and learn why each is bred. (Kneading the wool of the Merino sheep, you'll understand why it's so popular for sweaters.) You'll also see the quintessential sheepdog—the border collie—at work. At the end, you can pet whatever is still on stage: dogs, cows, sheep, sometimes a goose... if you can catch one. While the Visitors Centre and shop is free (daily 9:00–17:30), it's not really worth the trip unless you catch a sheep show (£4.50 for demo; March–Oct Sun–Thu at 10:30, 12:00, 14:00, and 15:30; no shows Fri–Sat or Nov–Feb, 13 miles west of Keswick on the A66 road A5086 roundabout in Cockermouth, tel. 01900-822-673, www.sheep-woolcentre.co.uk).

Rheged Centre and National Mountaineering Exhibition—This strange shopping and exhibition center, just off a highway roundabout (near Penrith, on A66 a mile west of the Keswick exit 40 off M6), is a good rainy-day option for anyone into mountain climbing—or adventures on Mount Everest. While it's mostly a modern shopping mall (showcasing and selling the best of Cumbria), it has a mountaineering exhibition with fascinating artifacts (such as the evolution of high-tech boots—and the amputated, frostbitten toes of a climber who could have used better ones).

An IMAX theater shows a rotating schedule of movies throughout the day, including the 60-minute *Rheged: The Lost*

Kingdom, which tells the story of the region's original Celtic inhabitants (£6 for the mountaineering exhibition, £6 more for any movie, £10 combo deals, daily 10:00–17:30, call ahead to check movie times, the #X4 and #X5 Keswick–Penrith buses stop here, tel. 017688/68000, www.rheged.com).

HIKES AND DRIVES

The first four hikes (Lodore, Cat Bells, Latrigg, and Walla Crag) originate in Keswick; the rest require a car or public transportation to get to the trailhead and/or views.

Lodore Walk—The best hour-long lakeside walk is the 1.5-mile path between the docks at High Brandelhow and Hawes End in Keswick. Continue on foot along the lake back into Keswick or—better yet—go on to Lodore.

Lodore is a good stop for two reasons: Lodore Falls is a 10-minute walk from the dock (behind Lodore Hotel), and Shepherds Crag (a cliff overlooking Lodore) was made famous by pioneering rock climbers. (Their descendants hang from little ridges on its face today.) This is serious climbing (with several fatalities a year).

For a great lunch, or tea and cakes, drop into the much-loved High Lodore Farm Café, where sheep farmer Martin is busy making hikers and day-trippers happy (daily 9:00–19:00; from the dock, walk up the road, turn right over bridge uphill to café; tel. 017687/77221).

▲▲**Cat Bells High Ridge Hike**—For a great (and moderately easy) "king of the mountain" feeling, sweeping views, and a close-up look at the weather blowing over the ridge, hike about two hours from Hawes End in Keswick up along the ridge to Cat Bells (1,480 feet) and down to High Brandelhow. From there, you can catch the boat or take the easy path along the shore of Derwentwater to your Hawes End starting point. (Extending the hike to Lodore takes you to a waterfall, rock climbers, a fine café, and another boat dock for a convenient return to Keswick—described above.) Cat Bells is probably the most dramatic family walk in the area (but wear sturdy shoes, bring a raincoat, and watch your footing). From Keswick, the lake, or your farmhouse B&B, you can see silhouetted stick figures hiking along this ridge. Drivers can park free at Hawes End. The Keswick TI sells a *Skiddaw and Cat Bells* brochure about the hike (60p).

Cat Bells is just the first of a series of peaks that are connected by a fine ridge trail. Hardier hikers continue up to nine miles along this same ridge, enjoying valley and lake views as they arc around the Newlands Valley toward (and even down to) Buttermere. After High Spy, you can descend an easy path into Newlands Valley. An ultimate, very full day-plan would be to bus to Buttermere, climb

Derwentwater and the Newlands Valley

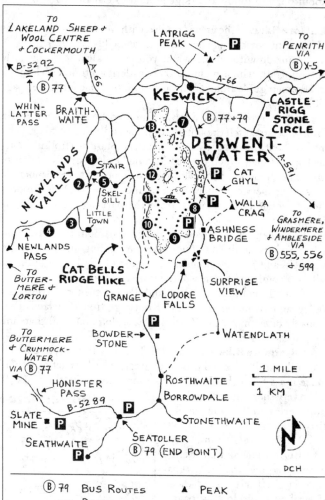

Legend:

B 79 BUS ROUTES
— ROAD
P PARKING
··· BOAT
- - - PATH

▲ PEAK
■ POINT OF INTEREST

Newlands Valley
1. Uzzicar Farm
2. Ellas Crag Guest House
3. Gill Brow Farm B&B
4. Keskadale Farm B&B
5. Swinside Inn Restaurant

Derwentwater
7. Keswick Launch Pier
8. Ashness Gate Pier
9. Lodore Pier
10. High Brandelhow Pier
11. Low Brandelhow Pier
12. Hawes End Pier
13. Nichol End Pier

Robinson, and follow the ridge around to Cat Bells and back to Keswick.

▲▲**More Hikes**—The area is riddled with wonderful hikes. B&Bs all have fine advice, but consider these as well:

From downtown Keswick, you can walk the seven-mile **Latrigg** trail, which includes the Castlerigg Stone Circle (pick up 60p map/guide from TI; for more on the stone circle, see page 330).

From your Keswick B&B, a fine two-hour walk to **Walla Crag** offers great fell (mountain) walking and a ridge-walk experience without the necessity of a bus or car. Start by strolling along the lake to Great Wood parking lot, and head up Cat Ghyl (where fell runners practice) to Walla Crag. You'll be treated to panoramic views over Derwentwater and surrounding peaks. You can do a shorter version of this walk from the parking lot at Ashness Bridge.

For a very short hike and the easiest mountain-climbing sensation around, drive to the Underscar parking lot just north of Keswick, and hike 20 minutes to the top of the 1,200-foot-high hill for a commanding view of the town and lake.

From the parking lot at Newlands Pass, at the top of Newlands Valley, an easy one-mile walk to **Knottrigg** from Newlands Pass probably offers more TPCB (thrills per calorie burned) than any walk in the region.

▲▲**Buttermere Hike**—The ideal little lake with a lovely, circular four-mile stroll offers nonstop, no-sweat Lake District beauty. If you're not a hiker (but kind of wish you were), take this walk. If you're very short on time, at least stop here and get your shoes dirty.

Buttermere is connected with Borrowdale and Derwentwater by a great road that runs over rugged Honister Pass (described on following page, under "Scenic Circle Drive South of Keswick"). From May through October, bus #77 makes a round-trip loop between Keswick and Buttermere over Honister Pass. The two-pub hamlet of Buttermere has a pay-and-display parking lot, but many drivers park free along the side of the road. You're welcome to leave your car at the Fish

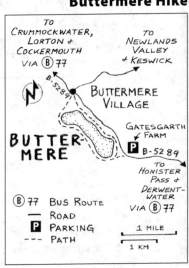

Buttermere Hike

Hotel if you eat in their pub (recommended). There's also a pay parking lot at the Honister Pass end of the lake (at Gatesgarth Farm, £3). The Syke Farm (in the hamlet of Buttermere) is popular for its homemade ice cream.

▲▲**Car Hiking from Keswick**— Distances are short, roads are narrow and have turnouts, and views are rewarding. Get a good map and ask your B&B host for advice. Two miles south of Keswick on the lakeside Borrowdale Valley Road (B5289), take the small road left (signposted *Ashness Bridge, Watendlath*) for a half-mile to the Ashness Packhorse Bridge (a quintessential Lake District scene, parking lot just above on right). A half-mile farther (parking lot on left) and you're startled by the "surprise view" of Derwentwater (great for a lakes photo op). Continuing from here, the road gets extremely narrow en route to the hamlet of Watendlath, which has a tiny lake and lazy farm animals. Return down to Borrowdale Valley Road and back to Keswick, or farther south to scenic Borrowdale and over dramatic Honister Pass to Buttermere.

▲▲**Scenic Circle Drive South of Keswick**—This hour-long drive, which includes Newlands Valley, Buttermere, Honister Pass, and Borrowdale, is demanding. But

it's also filled with the best scenery you'll find in the North Lake District. From Keswick, head west on the Cockermouth Road (A66). Take the second Newlands Valley exit (through Braithwaite), and follow signs up the majestic **Newlands Valley.** If the place had a lake, it would be packed with tourists. But it doesn't—and it isn't.

The valley is dotted with 500-year-old family-owned farms. Shearing day is reason to rush home from school. Sons get school out of the way ASAP, and follow their dads into the family business. Neighbor girls marry those sons and move in. Grandparents retire to the cottage next door. With the price of wool depressed, most of the wives supplement the family income by running B&Bs (virtually every farm in the valley rents rooms—see recommendations on page 340). The road has one lane, with turnouts for passing. From the Newlands Pass summit, notice the glacial-shaped wilds, once forested, now not. There's an easy hike from your car to a little waterfall (or a thrilling one to Knottrigg, described earlier).

After Newlands Pass, descend to **Buttermere** (scenic lake, tiny hamlet, see recommended hike, above, and pub), turn left and climb over rugged **Honister Pass,** strewn with glacial debris, remnants from old slate mines, and curious, shaggy Swaledale sheep (looking more like goats with their curly horns). The valleys you'll see are textbook examples of those carved out by glaciers. Look high on the hillsides for "hanging valleys"—small glacial-shaped scoops cut off by the huge flow of the biggest glacier, which swept down the main valley. An **old slate mine** at the summit of Honister Pass has reopened for tours (£9.75, 90-min tour; departures daily at 10:30, 12:30, and 15:30; tel. 017687/77230, book ahead, worthwhile slate-filled shop, www.honister-slate-mine.co.uk).

After stark and lonely Honister Pass, drop into sweet and homey **Borrowdale,** with a few lonely hamlets and fine hikes from Seathwaite (get specifics on walks here from your B&B or the TI). Circling back to Keswick past Borrowdale, you pass a number of popular local attractions (climb stairs to the top of the house-sized Bowder Stone—signposted, a few minutes walk off the main road), the postcard-pretty Ashness Bridge and "surprise view" (described earlier, turn-out signposted), and the rock climbers above Lodore. After that, you're home. A short detour before returning to Keswick takes you to the Castlerigg Stone Circle (see listing earlier in chapter).

NIGHTLIFE

▲▲**Theatre by the Lake**—Keswickians brag they enjoy "London theatre quality at Keswick prices." Their theater offers events year-round and a wonderful rotation of four to six plays through the summer (a different play each night, with music concerts on Sun). There are two stages: the main one seats 400, and the smaller "studio" theater seats 100 (and features more risqué plays, with rough language and nudity, £10–13). Attending a play here is a fine opportunity to do something completely local (£10–20, discounts for old and young, 20:00 shows in summer, 19:30 in spring and fall, 19:00 in winter, book ahead July–Aug, parking at the pay-and-display lot adjacent is free after 19:00, tel. 017687/74411, book at TI or www.theatrebythelake.com).

▲▲**Evenings in Keswick**—For a small and remote town, Keswick has lots of great things to do in the evening. Remember, at this latitude it's light until 22:00 in the midsummer. You can **golf** (fine course, pitch-and-putt, goofy golf, or just enjoy the putting green; see page 330), or **walk** among the grazing sheep as the sun gets ready to set (between the lake and the golf course, access from just above the beach, great photo ops on a balmy eve).

To socialize with locals, head to a pub for one of their special evenings: There's **folk music** at the Queens Hotel pub (£2, 20:30 Tue), and **quiz night** at the Pack Horse Pub (21:30 Wed) and the Dog and Gun (21:30 on some Thu—held when the crowds are fewer, £1, proceeds go to Keswick's Mountain Rescue team). At a quiz night, tourists are more than welcome. Drop in, say you want to join a team, and you're in. If you like trivia, it's a great way to get to know people here.

Other options: Join Bob, the Town Crier, when he does his routine many summer Tuesday evenings (see TI for details). Catch a **movie** at the Alhambra Cinema, a good, old-fashioned English theater. An **evening lake cruise** is perfect for an extremely scenic and relaxing picnic dinner (19:30 May–Sept, see page 329 for details).

SLEEPING

The Lake District abounds with attractive B&Bs, guest houses, and hostels. It needs them all when summer hordes threaten the serenity of this Romantic mecca. Reserve your room in advance.

From October through April, you should have no trouble finding a room. But to get a particular place (especially on Sat), call ahead. If you're using public transportation, you should stay in Keswick. For drivers, this town is your best chance for a remote farmhouse experience. Lakeland hostels offer £17 beds and come with an interesting crowd.

In Keswick, I've featured two streets, each within three blocks of the bus station and town square. Stanger Street, a bit humbler but quiet and handy, has smaller homes and more moderately priced rooms. "The Heads" is a classier area lined with proud Victorian houses, close to the lake and theater, overlooking a golf course.

Sleep Code

(£1 = about $2, country code: 44, area code: 017687)
S = Single, **D** = Double/Twin, **T** = Triple, **Q** = Quad, **b** = bathroom, **s** = shower only. You can assume credit cards are accepted unless otherwise noted, and all B&B stays include breakfast.

To help you sort easily through these listings, I've divided the rooms into three categories based on the price for a double room with bath:

$$$ **Higher Priced**—Most rooms £60 or more.
 $$ **Moderately Priced**—Most rooms between £30–60.
  $ **Lower Priced**—Most rooms £30 or less.

Many of my Keswick listings charge extra for a one-night stay. Most have a two-night minimum on weekends and don't welcome children under 12 (unless extremely well-behaved). Owners are enthusiastic about offering plenty of advice to get you on the right walking trail. These accommodations have inviting lounges with libraries of books on the region and loaner maps. Take advantage of these plush lounges to make your humble B&B room suddenly a suite.

This is still the countryside—expect huge breakfasts (with big selections including vegetarian options), no phones in the rooms, and shower systems that often need to be switched on to get hot water. Parking, while it may require you to hunt for a little while on a Saturday, is pretty easy overall (park either in congested little private lots or on the street).

On Stanger Street

This street, quiet but just a block from Keswick's town center, is lined with B&Bs. Each of these places is small, family-run, and accepts cash only. They are all good, offering comfortably sized rooms, with little to differentiate between them.

$$ Dunsford Guest House is an old Victorian slate town-house where they rent four color-coordinated rooms at a good price. Stained glass and wooden pews give the blue-and-cream breakfast room a country-chapel feel (Db-£58, prices promised in 2008 with this book, no kids under 16, non-smoking, parking, 16 Stanger Street, tel. 017687/75059, www.dunsford.net, enquiries @dunsford.net, Richard and Linda).

$$ Badgers Wood B&B, at the top of the street, has six bright, pastel, stocking-feet-comfortable view rooms, each named after a different tree. Their bathrooms were recently refurbished (Sb-£30, Db-£60, 2-night minimum, no children under 12, non-smoking, 30 Stanger Street, tel. 017687/72621, www.badgers-wood .co.uk, enquiries@badgers-wood.co.uk, Andrew and Anne).

$$ Abacourt House, with a daisy-fresh breakfast room, has five pleasant doubles (Db-£60, no children, 26 Stanger Street, tel. 017687/72967, www.abacourt.co.uk, abacourt@btinternet.com, friendly Judith and David Lewis).

$$ Ellergill Guest House has five spick-and-span rooms with an airy, contemporary feel. One has a super view (D-£54, Db-£60, 2-night minimum on weekends, 22 Stanger Street, tel. 017687/73347, www.ellergill.co.uk, stay@ellergill.co.uk, run by Clare and Robin Pinkney and dog Tess).

On The Heads

$$$ Howe Keld Lakeland Hotel, while the most formal of the accommodations I list in Keswick, is still warm, welcoming, and family-run, with 15 fine rooms and a wide variety of breakfast selections (Sb-£40, standard Db-£75–80, superior Db-£90–100, higher prices are for 1-night stays, cash preferred, 2 ground-floor rooms, family deals, Wi-Fi, 5 The Heads, tel. & fax 017687/72417, www.howekeld.co.uk, david@howekeld.co.uk, run with care by David and Valerie Fisher).

$$$ Berkeley Guest House, a big slate mansion enthusiastically run by Barbara Crompton, has a pleasant lounge, narrow hallways, and carefully appointed, comfortable rooms. The chirpy, skylight-bright £46 bathless double in the attic is a fine value if you don't mind the stairs (D-£50, Db-£66, family deals, great family room, cash only, The Heads, tel. 017687/74222, www.berkeley -keswick.com, berkeley@tesco.net).

$$$ Parkfield Guest House, thoughtfully run and decorated by John and Susan Berry, is another big Victorian house that has eight bright and pastel rooms with fine views (Db-£64 with this book through 2008, 2-night minimum stay, 1 ground-floor room available—but reserve in advance, no kids under 16, plenty of fruit at breakfast, off-street parking available, The Heads, tel. 017687/72328, www.parkfieldkeswick.co.uk, enquiries @parkfieldkeswick.co.uk).

$$$ West View Guest House, next to the Parkfield, has eight cheery rooms, a relaxing lounge, and a "borrow box" for those desperate for walking gear. Ask Paul about the cabinet in the lounge dedicated to pharmaceutical history (Sb-£32, Db-£64, The Heads, tel. 017687/73638, www.westviewkeswick.co.uk, info @westviewkeswick.co.uk).

$$ Brundholme Guest House, next door to the Berkeley, is run by friendly Barbara and Paul Motler. It has three bright and comfy rooms (two with grand views), and a friendly and welcoming atmosphere (Db-£58, cash only, The Heads, tel. 017687/73305, www.brundholme.co.uk, barbara@brundholme.co.uk).

Hostels in and near Keswick

The Lake District's inexpensive hostels, usually located in great old buildings, are handy sources of information and social fun. The free hostel-booking service (Easter–Oct daily 9:30–17:00, tel. 015394/31117) will tell you which of the area's 30 hostels have available beds, and can even book a place on your credit card (no more than seven days in advance). Since most hostels don't answer their phones during the day and many are full, this can be a helpful service, but don't consider this service the final word. (Since the service takes a commission from the hostels, hostels may have a space when they tell this service that they're full.) The first two hostels—both part of the Youth Hostels Association (www .yha.org.uk)—are former hotels, offering Internet access, laundry machines, and three cheap meals daily; at these, non-members pay about £3 extra a night, or buy a £15 membership.

$ Keswick Youth Hostel, with 85 beds in a converted old mill overlooking the river, has a great riverside balcony and plenty of handy facilities (£19 beds for members in high season, can drop to £13.50 in low, mostly 3- to 4-bed rooms, 23:30 curfew, restaurant, center of town just off Station Road before river, tel. 017687/72484, keswick@yha.org.uk).

$ Derwentwater Hostel, in a 200-year-old mansion on the shore of Derwentwater, is two miles south of Keswick and has 88 beds (£16 beds in 4- to 22-bed rooms, family rooms-£45, 23:00 curfew, follow B5289 from Keswick, look for sign 100 yards after Ashness exit, tel. 017687/77246, derwentwater@yha.org.uk).

$ Denton House is Keswick's *other* hostel—it's independent (not YHA), spartan, and grimly institutional, but provides good basic bunk beds in barracks (£12.50 beds in 4- to 14-bed dorm rooms, lockers-£1-2, breakfast extra, kitchen, on Penrith Road between the fire station and railway bridge at the east edge of town, tel. 017687/75351, www.vividevents.co.uk, sales@vividevents .co.uk).

West of Keswick, in the Newlands Valley

If you have a car, drive 10 minutes past Keswick down the majestic Newlands Valley (described in "Scenic Circle Drive South of Keswick" under "Hikes and Drives," page 335). This valley is studded with 500-year-old farms that have been in the same family for centuries, and now rent rooms to supplement the family income. The rooms are plainer than the B&Bs in town, and come with steep and gravelly roads, plenty of dogs, and an earthy charm. Traditionally, farmhouses lacked central heating, and while they are now heated, you can still request a hot-water bottle to warm up your bed.

Getting to the Newlands Valley: Leave Keswick heading west on the Cockermouth Road (A66). Take the second Newlands Valley exit through Braithwaite, and follow signs through Newlands Valley (drive toward Buttermere). All of my recommended B&Bs are on this road: Uzzicar Farm (under the shale field, which local boys love hiking up to glissade down), Ellas Crag Guest House, then (just after a curious—and haunted—purple house), Gill Brow Farm, and finally—the last house before the stark summit—Keskadale Farm (about four miles before Buttermere). The one-lane road has turnouts for passing. Each place offers easy parking, grand views, and perfect tranquility. These are listed in geographical order, the first being a five-minute drive from Keswick and the last being at the top of the valley (about a 15-min drive from Keswick).

$$ Uzzicar Farm is a big, rustic place with a comfy B&B in a low-ceilinged, circa-1550 farmhouse (£29 per person in S, D, or Db, family deals, cash only, tel. 017687/78200, http://uzzicar .bravehost.com, lynne@uzzicar.wanadoo.co.uk).

$$$ Ellas Crag Guest House, with four contemporary rooms, is more of a comfortable stone house than a farm. This homey place offers a good mix of modern and traditional decor (Ds-£58, Db-£62, these prices guaranteed with this book through 2008, cash only, 2-night minimum, packed lunches available, laundry-£10, Newlands Valley, tel. 017687/78217, www.ellascrag.co.uk, info @ellascrag.co.uk, Jane and Ed Ma and their children).

$$ Gill Brow Farm B&B is a rough, working farmhouse where Anne Wilson and her delightful teenage daughter Laura rent two simple but fine rooms (D or Db-£52, 10 percent discount with this book and 2-night stay in 2008, tel. 017687/78270, www .gillbrow-keswick.co.uk, wilson_gillbrow@hotmail.com).

$$ Keskadale Farm B&B is another good farmhouse experience, with ponderosa hospitality. One of the valley's oldest, the house is made from 500-year-old ship beams. This working farm has lots of curly-horned sheep and two rooms to rent. While her boys are now old enough to help dad in the fields, Margaret Harryman runs the B&B (Db-£57, £2 extra for one night, cash only, non-smoking, closed Dec–Feb, tel. 017687/78544, fax 017687/78150, www.keskadalefarm.co.uk, info@keskadalefarm .co.uk).

West and Southwest of Keswick, in Buttermere and Lorton

$$$ The **Bridge Hotel,** just beyond Newlands Valley at Buttermere, offers 21 rooms and a classic, Old World, countryside-hotel experience (standard Db-£100, superior Db-£130, suite-like Db-£190 with a fancy dinner, tel. 017687/70252, fax 017687/70215, www.bridge-hotel.com, enquiries@bridge-hotel.com). There are no shops within 10 miles—only peace and quiet a stone's throw from one of the region's most beautiful lakes. The hotel has a dark-wood pub/restaurant on the ground floor.

$$$ The Old Vicarage, with a lovely, genteel feeling, is in what once was the clergyman's house in this tiny village. It has six rooms in the main late-1800s house, and two more in the coach house. The owners, Jane and Peter Smith, offer an optional £26.50 four-course meal, with dishes like rack of lamb (Sb-£55, Db-£110, Church Lane, Lorton, tel. 01900/85656, www.oldvicarage.co.uk, enquiries@oldvicarage.co.uk).

$ The **Buttermere King George VI Memorial Hostel,** a quarter-mile south of Buttermere village on Honister Pass Road, has good food, 70 beds, family rooms, and a royal setting (£19/bed in 4- to 6-bed rooms, includes breakfast, inexpensive lunches and dinners, office open 7:00–10:00 & 17:00–23:00, 23:00 curfew, tel. 0870-770-5736, buttermere@yha.org.uk).

South of Keswick, near Borrowdale

$$$ **Seatoller Farm B&B** is a rustic old building in a five-building hamlet where Christine Simpson rents three rooms (Db-£64, less for 2 or more nights, tel. 017687/77232, www.seatollerfarm.co.uk, info@seatollerfarm.co.uk). Honister's Yew Tree pub is just across the street (with a museum of old-time photos decorating its walls, daily lunch and dinner Thu–Sun).

$ **Borrowdale Hostel,** in secluded Borrowdale Valley just south of Rosthwaite, is a well-run place surrounded by many ways to immerse yourself in nature (86 beds, £16.50 beds, Internet access, laundry machines, 23:00 curfew, 3 cheap meals daily, tel. 0870-770-5706, borrowdale@yha.org.uk).

EATING

In Keswick

Keswick has a huge variety of restaurants catering to its many visitors. Most restaurants stop serving by 21:00. Here's a selection of favorites:

Morrel's Restaurant is the Keswick favorite for a splurge—simple yet elegant, serving famously good and creative modern English cuisine (£12–18 meals, Tue–Sun 17:30–21:00, closed Mon, reservations recommended; tell them if you're going to the theater, otherwise expect a relaxed dinner; all meals cooked to order, 34 Lake Road, tel. 017687/72666).

Pack Horse Inn offers a great pub atmosphere, low exposed-beam ceilings, a fireplace, and what most locals consider the best pub food in town (£9–10 meals, daily 12:00–14:30 & 18:00–21:00, until 21:30 Fri-Sat, find alley off Market Street leading to Pack Horse courtyard, tel. 017687/71389).

The Dog and Gun serves good pub food, but mind your head—low ceilings and wooden beams (£7 meals, daily 12:00–20:30, goulash, no chips and proud of it, can get smoky, 2 Lake Road, tel. 017687/73463).

The Grove serves authentic Thai dishes in a dining room as tasteful as its food (£8 plates, daily 12:00–14:30 & 18:00–23:00, 89 Main Street, tel. 017687/71444).

Abraham Tea Room, popular with locals, may be the best lunch deal in town. It's tucked away on the first floor of the giant George Fisher outdoor store (£5 soups and sandwiches, daily 10:00–17:00ish, on the corner where Lake Road turns right).

The Lakeland Pedlar Vegetarian Restaurant, a wholesome, pleasant café (with a bike shop upstairs), serves freshly baked vegan and vegetarian fare, including soups, organic bread, and daily specials. Their interior is cute. Outside tables face a big parking lot (£7 meals, daily 9:00–17:00, Hendersons Yard, find the narrow walkway off Market Street between pink Johnson's sweet shop and Ye Olde Golden Lion Inn, tel. 017687/74492).

Bryson's Bakery and Tea Room has an enticing ground-floor bakery, with sandwiches and light lunches. The upstairs is a popular tearoom. Order lunch to go from the bakery, or for a few pence more, eat there, either sitting on stools or at a couple of sidewalk tables (£7 meals, Mon–Sat 8:30–17:30, Sun 9:30–17:00, 42 Main Street, tel. 017687/72257). Consider their £13 Farmhouse Tea, which is like high tea in London but cheaper, and made with local products. Sandwiches, scones, and little cakes are served on a three-tiered platter with tea (made for two people and perfectly splittable).

Maysons Restaurant, with Californian ambience, is fast and easy, with a buffet line of curry, Cajun, and vegetarian options. The food is cooked fresh on the premises, but it's nothing fancy: You point, they dish up and microwave (£7 plates; April–Oct daily 11:45–20:45; Nov–March Mon–Thu 11:45–17:00, Fri–Sun 11:45–20:30; family-friendly, also take-out—great for evening cruise picnic, 33 Lake Road, tel. 017687/74104).

Keswick Tea Room, in a big shopping center at the bus station, is popular with locals, and features cheap and cheery regional specialties (Mon–Sat 9:00–18:00, Sun 10:00–16:00).

Picnic: The fine **supermarket** faces the bus station (Mon–Sat 9:00–20:00, Sun 10:00–16:00, The Headslands). **Bryson's Bakery** (see above) does good sandwiches to go. **The Keswickian** serves up old-fashioned fish-and-chips to go (daily 11:00–23:30, on the main square). Just around the corner, **The Cornish Pasty** offers an enticing variety of fresh meat pies to go until they're sold out (£2.30 pies, daily 9:30–17:00, across from the Dog and Gun Pub on Borrowdale Road).

In the Newlands Valley

The farmhouse B&Bs of Newlands Valley don't serve dinner, so their guests have three options: Go into Keswick, walk to the **Swinside Inn** (daily 18:00–20:45, reservations required, tel. 017687/78253), or take the lovely 10-minute drive to Buttermere for your evening meal at the **Fish Hotel Pub,** which has fine indoor and outdoor seating, but takes no reservations (£7 meals, daily 12:00–14:00 & 18:00–21:00, family-friendly, good fish and daily specials with fresh vegetables). The neighboring **Bridge Hotel Pub** is a bit cozier, but less popular (£6–7 meals, daily 12:00–21:30).

TRANSPORTATION CONNECTIONS

The nearest train station to Keswick is in Penrith, with a ticket window (Mon–Sat 5:30–21:00, Sun 11:30–21:00) but no lockers. For train and bus info, check at a local TI, visit www.traveline .org.uk, or call 08457-484-950 (for train), or either tel. 0870-608-2608 or 01604/676-060 (for buses). Most routes run less frequently on Sundays.

From Keswick by Bus: For connections, see "Getting Around the Lake District: Without a Car,'" on page 323.

From Penrith by Bus to: Keswick (Mon–Sat roughly hourly 7:15–22:30, only 6 on Sun, 35 min, £4.25, pay driver, Stagecoach buses #X4, #X5, and #X50), **Ullswater** and **Glenridding** (6/day, 1 hr, direction: Patterdale). The Penrith bus stop is in the train station's parking lot (bus schedules posted inside and outside station).

From Penrith by Train to: Blackpool (hourly to Preston, 1 hr; then to Blackpool, 3/hr, 30 min), **Liverpool** (1/day, 2.5 hrs), **Birmingham**'s New Street Station (2/hr, 2 hrs), **London**'s Euston Station (hourly, 4 hrs), **Edinburgh** (6/day, fewer on Sun, 2 hrs), **Glasgow** (hourly, 2 hrs), **Oban** (hourly to Glasgow, 2 hrs; then to Oban, Mon–Sat 6/day, 3/day Sun, 3 hrs).

Route Tips for Drivers

Coming from (or Going to) the West: Only 1,300 feet above sea level, Hard Knott Pass is still a thriller, with a narrow, winding, steeply graded road. Just over the pass are the scant but evocative remains of the Hard Knott Roman fortress. There are great views but miserable rainstorms, and it can be very slow and frustrating when the one-lane road with turnouts is clogged by traffic. Avoid it on summer weekends.

From Points South (such as Blackpool, Liverpool, or North Wales) to the Lake District: The direct, easy way to Keswick is to leave M6 at Penrith, and take the A66 highway for 16 miles to Keswick. For the scenic sightseeing drive through the south lakes to Keswick, exit M6 on A590/A591 through the towns of Kendal and Windermere to reach Brockhole National Park Visitors Centre. From Brockhole, the A road to Keswick is fastest, but the high road—the tiny road over Kirkstone Pass to Glenridding and lovely Ullswater—is much more dramatic. See above for sightseeing details.

Near Keswick: Ullswater

▲▲**Ullswater Hike and Boat Ride**—Long, narrow Ullswater—which some consider the loveliest lake in the area—offers eight

miles of diverse and grand Lake District scenery. While you can drive it or cruise it, I'd ride the boat from the south tip halfway up (to Howtown—which is nothing more than a dock) and hike back. Boats leave **Glenridding** regularly for Howtown (4–9/day depending on the season, £5 one-way, £8 round-trip, daily 9:45–16:45, less off-season, 35-min one-way; safe pay-and-display parking lot costs £2/2 hrs, £4/12 hrs; café, free schedule shows walking route, tel. 017684/82229 for schedule, www.ullswater-steamers.co.uk). From Howtown, spend three to four hours hiking and dawdling along the well-marked path by the lake south to Patterdale, and then along the road back to Glenridding. This is a serious seven-mile walk with good views, varied terrain, and a few bridges and farms along the way. For a shorter hike from Howtown Pier, consider a three-mile loop around Hallin Fell.

Several **steamer trips** chug daily up and down Ullswater. A bad-weather plan is to ride the covered boat up and down the lake (to the furthest point—Pooley Bridge, £11 round-trip, 2 hours) or to Howtown and back (£8 round-trip, 1 hour).

Helvellyn—Often considered the best high-mountain hike in the Lake District, this breathtaking round-trip route from Glenridding includes the spectacular Striding Edge—about a half-mile along the ridge. Be careful; do this six-hour hike only in good weather since the wind can be fierce. While there are shorter routes, the Glenridding ascent is best. Get advice from the Keswick TI, which has a helpful *Helvellyn from Glenridding* leaflet on the hike (60p).

South Lake District

The South Lake District has a cheesiness similar to other popular British resort destinations, such as Blackpool. Here, piles of low-end vacationers eat ice cream and get candy floss caught in their hair. The area around Windermere is worth a drive-through if you're a fan of Wordsworth or Beatrix Potter; otherwise, spend the majority of your Lake District time (and book your accommodations) up north.

Lake District

Wordsworth at Dove Cottage

William Wordsworth (1770–1850) was a Lake District homeboy. Born in Cockermouth (in a house now open to the public), he was schooled in Hawkshead. In adulthood, he married a local girl, settled down in Grasmere and Ambleside, and was buried in Grasmere's St. Oswald's churchyard.

But the 30-year-old man who moved into Dove Cottage in 1779 was not the carefree lad who'd once roamed the district's lakes and fields. At Cambridge University, he'd been a C student, graduating with no job skills and no interest in a nine-to-five career. Instead, he and a buddy hiked through Europe, where Wordsworth had an epiphany of the "sublime" atop Switzerland's Alps. He lived a year in France, watching the Revolution rage. It stirred his soul. He fell in love with a Frenchwoman who bore his daughter, Caroline. But lack of money forced him to return to England, and the outbreak of war with France kept them apart.

Pining away in London, William hung out in the pubs and coffee houses with fellow radicals, where he met poet Samuel Taylor Coleridge. They inspired each other to write, they edited each other's work, and they jointly published a groundbreaking book of poetry.

In 1799, his head buzzing with words and ideas, William and his sister (and soulmate) Dorothy moved into the whitewashed, slate-tiled former inn now known as Dove Cottage. He came into

Getting Around the South Lake District

By Car: This is your best option to see the small towns and sights clustered in the South Lake District; consider combining your drive with the bus trip mentioned below.

If you're coming to or leaving the South Lake District from the west, you could take the Hard Knott Pass for a scenic introduction to the area (see page 344).

By Bus: As mentioned at the beginning of the chapter, the open-top "Lakes Rider" bus #599 stops at Bowness Pier (lake cruises), Windermere (train station), Brockhole (national park center), Ambleside, Rydal Mount, and Grasmere (Dove Cottage). It's a fine way to lace together this gauntlet of sights in the congested Lake Windermere neighborhood. Consider leaving your car at Grasmere and enjoying the breezy and extremely scenic ride, hopping off and on as you like (all-day pass-£6, buy from driver, daily April–Aug, 3/hr, 1 hour each way).

a small inheritance, and dedicated himself to poetry full time. In 1802, with the war over, William returned to France to finally meet his daughter. (He wrote of the rich experience: "It is a beauteous evening, calm and free.../Dear child! Dear Girl! that walkest with me here,/If thou appear untouched by solemn thought,/Thy nature is not therefore less divine.")

Having achieved closure, Wordsworth returned home to marry a former kindergarten classmate, Mary. She moved into Dove Cottage, along with an initially jealous Dorothy. Three of their five children were born here, and the cottage was also home to Mary's sister, the family dog Pepper (a gift from Sir Walter Scott; see Pepper's portrait), and frequent houseguests who bedded down in the pantry: Scott, Coleridge, and Thomas de Quincey, the Timothy Leary of opium.

After nearly nine years here, Wordsworth's family and social status were outgrowing the humble cottage. They moved first to a house in Grasmere before settling down in Rydal Hall. Wordsworth was changing. After the Dove years, he would write less, settle into a regular government job, quarrel with Coleridge, drift to the right politically, and endure criticism from old friends who branded him a sellout. Still, his poetry—most of it written at Dove—became increasingly famous, and he died honored as England's Poet Laureate.

SIGHTS

Wordsworth Sights

William Wordsworth was one of the first writers to reject fast-paced city life. During England's Industrial Age, hearts were muzzled and brains ruled. Science was in, machines were taming nature, and factory hours were taming humans. In reaction to the new obsession with progress and modernization, a rare few—dubbed Romantics—began to embrace untamed nature and undomesticated emotions.

Nobody back then climbed a mountain just because it was there, but Wordsworth did. He'd "wander lonely as a cloud" through the countryside, finding inspiration in "plain living and high thinking." He soon attracted a circle of like-minded creative friends.

The emotional highs the Romantics felt weren't all natural. Wordsworth and his poet friends Samuel Taylor Coleridge and Thomas de Quincey got stoned on opium and wrote poetry, combining their generation's standard painkiller drug with their tree-hugging passions. Today, opium is out of vogue, but the Romantic movement thrives as visitors continue to inundate the region.

▲▲Dove Cottage and Wordsworth Museum—The poet whose appreciation of nature and a back-to-basics lifestyle put this area on the map spent his most productive years (1799–1808) in this well-preserved stone cottage on the edge of Grasmere. After functioning as the Dove and Olive Bow pub for nearly 200 years, it was bought by his family. This is where he got married, had kids, and wrote much of his best poetry. The furniture, still owned by the Wordsworth family, was his, and the place comes with some amazing artifacts, including the poet's passport and suitcase (he packed light). Even during his lifetime, Wordsworth was famous, and Dove Cottage was turned into a museum in 1891—predating even the National Trust, which protects the house today.

Today, Dove Cottage is *the* obligatory sight for any Wordsworth admirer. Even if you're not a fan, Wordsworth's appreciation of nature, his Romanticism, and the ways his friends unleashed their creative talents with such abandon are appealing. The 30-minute cottage **tour** (departures on the hour and half-hour) and adjoining **museum**—with lots of actual manuscripts handwritten by Wordsworth and his illustrious friends—are both excellent. In dry weather, the garden where the poet often found inspiration is worth a wander. (Visit this before leaving the cottage, and pick up the description at the back door.) Allow at least an hour for this two-part attraction (£6.50, daily early Feb–mid-Jan 9:30–17:30, last entry at 17:00, last tour at 16:50, closed mid–Jan–early Feb, tel. 015394/35544, www.wordsworth.org.uk). Parking is free and easy in the Dove Cottage lot facing the main road (A591).

Poetry Readings: On Tuesday evenings in summer, the Wordsworth Trust puts on poetry readings, where national poets read their own works. They're hoping to continue the poetry tradition of the Lake District. Readings are held at the Waterfront Hotel (18:30 every other Tue, runs May–mid-Oct only, two 45-min sessions followed by an optional dinner, £7 at the door or £6 pre-booked, across the big road from Dove Cottage, tel. 015394/35544).

Rydal Mount—Wordsworth's final, higher-class home, with a lovely garden and view, lacks the charm of Dove Cottage. It feels like a B&B. He lived here for 37 years, and his family repurchased it in 1969 (after a 100-year gap). His great-great-great-granddaughter still calls it home on occasion, as shown by recent family photos sprinkled throughout some rooms. Located just down the road from Dove Cottage, it's worthwhile only for Wordsworth fans (£5;

Wordsworth's Poetry at Dove

At Dove Cottage, Wordsworth was immersed in the beauty of nature and the simple joy of his young, growing family. It was here that he reflected on both his idyllic childhood and his troubled twenties. The following are select lines from two well-known poems from this fertile time.

Ode: Intimations of Immortality

There was a time when meadow, grove, and stream,
The earth, and every common sight, to me did seem
Apparell'd in celestial light, the glory and the freshness
    of a dream.
It is not now as it hath been of yore; turn wheresoe'er I
    may, by night or day,
The things which I have seen I now can see no more.
Now while the birds thus sing a joyous song...
To me alone there came a thought of grief...
Whither is fled the visionary gleam?
Where is it now, the glory and the dream?
Our birth is but a sleep and a forgetting:
The Soul...cometh from afar...
Trailing clouds of glory do we come
From God, who is our home.

I Wandered Lonely as a Cloud

I wandered lonely as a cloud
That floats on high o'er vales and hills,
When all at once I saw a crowd,
A host, of golden daffodils;
Beside the lake, beneath the trees,
Fluttering and dancing in the breeze...
For oft, when on my couch I lie
In vacant or in pensive mood,
They flash upon that inward eye
Which is the bliss of solitude;
And then my heart with pleasure fills,
And dances with the daffodils.

March–Oct daily 9:30–17:00; Nov–Feb Wed–Mon 10:00–16:00, closed Tue; 1.5 miles north of Ambleside, well-signed, free and easy parking, tel. 015394/33002). If you're visiting Dove Cottage and Rydal Mount, a discount coupon saves you about £1.

Beatrix Potter Sights

Of the many Beatrix Potter commercial ventures in the Lake District, there are two serious Beatrix Potter sights: her farm (Hill Top Farm); and her husband's former office, which is now the Beatrix Potter Gallery, filled with her sketches and paintings. Both sights are in or near Hawkshead, a 20-minute drive south of Ambleside. If you're coming over from Windermere, catch the cute little 18-car ferry (£2.50, 10-min trip, runs constantly but not always on Thu–Fri). Note that both of these sights are closed on Thursday and Friday.

Hill Top Farm—A hit with Beatrix Potter fans, this farm was left just as it was when she died in 1943. While there's no information here (you'll need to buy the £3.50 guidebook for details on what you see), the dark and intimate cottage, swallowed up in the inspirational and rough nature around it, provides an enjoyable if quick experience (£5.40, April–Oct Sat–Wed 10:30–16:30—also open Thu June–Aug, closed Thu–Fri and Nov–March, last entry 30 min before closing, in Near Sawrey village, 2 miles south of Hawkshead, tel. 015394/36269, www.nationaltrust.org.uk /beatrixpotter). Park and buy your ticket 150 yards down the road, and walk back to tour the place.

▲▲**Beatrix Potter Gallery**—Located in the cute but extremely touristy town of Hawkshead (see below), this gallery fills her husband's former law office with the wonderful and intimate drawings and watercolors that Potter did to illustrate her books. The best of the Potter sights, the gallery has plenty of explanation about her life and work. Even non-Potter fans find her art surprisingly interesting. Of about 700 works in the gallery's possession, about 40 are shown at any one time (£3.80, tiny discount with Hill Top Farm, April–Oct Sat–Wed 10:30–16:30—also open Thu June–Aug, closed Thu–Fri and Nov–March, Main Street, use the nearby pay-and-display lot and walk 200 yards to the town center, tel. 015394/36355, www.nationaltrust.org.uk/beatrixpotter).

Hawkshead—The town of Hawkshead is engulfed in Potter tourism, and the extreme quaintness of it all is off-putting. If you must linger, use the pay-and-display lot. Just across from the parking lot is the interesting Hawkshead Grammar School, founded in 1585, where William Wordsworth studied from 1779 to 1787. It shows off old school benches and desks whittled with penknife graffiti (£1, daily 10:00–17:00).

Beatrix Potter
(1866–1943)

As a girl growing up in London, Beatrix Potter vacationed in the Lake District, where she became inspired to write her popular children's books. Unable to get a publisher, she self-published the first two editions of *The Tale of Peter Rabbit* in 1901 and 1902. When she finally landed a publisher, sales of her books were phenomenal. With the money she made, she bought Hill Top Farm, a 17th-century cottage; she fixed it up, living there from 1905 until she married in 1913. Potter was more than a children's book writer; she was a fine artist, an avid gardener, and a successful farmer. She married a lawyer and put her knack for business to use, amassing a 4,000-acre estate. An early conservationist, she used the garden-cradled cottage as a place to study nature. She willed it—along with the rest of her vast estate—to the National Trust, which she enthusiastically supported. The events of Potter's life were dramatized in the 2006 movie *Miss Potter*, starring Renée Zellweger as Beatrix.

The World of Beatrix Potter—This tour, a hit with children, is a gimmicky exhibit with all the history of a Disney ride. The 45-minute experience features a five-minute video trip into the world of Mrs. Tiggywinkle and company, a series of Lake District tableaux starring the same imaginary gang, and an all-about-Beatrix section, with an eight-minute video biography (£6, daily Easter–Sept 10:00–17:30, Oct–Easter 10:00–16:30, in Bowness near Windermere town, tel. 015394/88444, www.hop-skip-jump .com).

More Sights at Lake Windermere

▲**Brockhole National Park Visitors Centre**—Set in a nicely groomed lakeside park, the center offers a free 15-minute slide show on life in the Lake District (played upon request), an information desk, organized walks, exhibits, a bookshop (excellent selection of maps and guidebooks), a fine cafeteria, gardens, nature walks, and a large parking lot. Check the events board as you enter (free entry but steep £4 parking fee—coins only, or buy ticket at the Visitors Centre 100 yards away; Easter–Oct daily 10:00–17:00, shorter hours during shoulder season, closed Nov–Easter, tel.

015394/46601, www.lake-district.gov.uk). It's in a stately old lake-side mansion between Ambleside and the town of Windermere on A591. For a joyride around famous Windermere, catch the Brockhole cruise (40-min circle, 2/hr, £6, scant narration).

Aquarium of the Lakes—The aquarium gives a glimpse of the natural history of Cumbria. Exhibits describe the local wildlife living in lake and coastal environments, including otters, eels, pike, sharks, and the "much maligned brown rat." Experts give various talks throughout the day (£7.50, daily 9:00–18:00, until 17:00 in winter, last entry 1 hour before closing, in Lakeside, by Newby Bridge, at south end of Lake Windermere, tel. 015395/30153).

Hayes Garden World—This extensive gardening center, a popular weekend excursion for locals, offers garden supplies, a bookstore, a playground, and gorgeous grounds. Gardeners could wander this place all afternoon. Upstairs is a fine cafeteria-style restaurant (Mon–Sat 9:00–18:00, Sun 11:00–17:00, at south end of Ambleside on main drag, see *Garden Centre* signs, located at north end of Lake Windermere, tel. 015394/33434, www.hayesgardenworld.co.uk).

YORK

Historic York is loaded with world-class sights. Marvel at the York Minster, England's finest Gothic church. Ramble the Shambles, York's wonderfully preserved medieval quarter. Enjoy a walking tour led by an old Yorker. Hop a train at Europe's greatest railway museum, travel to the 1800s in the York Castle Museum, and head back a thousand years to Viking York at the Jorvik exhibit.

York has a rich history. In A.D. 71, it was Eboracum, a Roman provincial capital—the northernmost city in the Empire. Constantine was actually proclaimed emperor here in A.D. 306. In the fifth century, as Rome was toppling, a Roman emperor sent a letter telling England it was on its own, and York became Eoforwic, the capital of the Anglo-Saxon kingdom of Northumbria.

Locals built a church here in 627, and the town became an early Christian center of learning. The Vikings later took the town, and from the 9th through the 11th centuries, it was a Danish trading center called Jorvik. The invading and conquering Normans destroyed then rebuilt the city, fortifying it with a castle and the walls you see today.

Medieval York, with 9,000 inhabitants, grew rich on the wool trade and became England's second city. Henry VIII used the city's fine Minster as his Anglican Church's northern capital. (In the hierarchy of today's Anglican Church, the Archbishop of York is second only to the Archbishop of Canterbury.)

In the Industrial Age, York was the railway hub of North England. When it was built, York's train station was the world's largest. Today, York's leading industry is tourism.

Planning Your Time

York is the best sightseeing city in England after London. On even a 10-day trip through Britain, it deserves two nights and a day. For the best 36 hours, follow this plan: Catch the 18:45 city walking tour on the evening of your arrival (evening tours offered mid-June through Aug). The next morning, be at the Castle Museum at 9:30 when it opens—it's worth a good two hours. Then browse and sightsee through the day. Train buffs love the National Railway Museum, and scholars give the Yorkshire Museum an A. Tour the Minster at 16:00 before catching the 17:15 evensong service (16:00 on Sun). Finish your day with an early-evening stroll along the wall, and perhaps through the abbey gardens. This schedule assumes you're here in the summer (evening orientation walk) and that there's an evensong on. Confirm your plans with the TI.

ORIENTATION

(area code: 01904)

York has about 190,000 people; about one in ten is a student. But despite the city's size, the sightseer's York is small. Virtually everything is within a few minutes' walk: sights, train station, TI, and B&Bs. The longest walk a visitor might take (from a B&B across the old town to the Castle Museum) is 20 minutes.

Bootham Bar, a gate in the medieval town wall, is the hub of your York visit. (In York, a "bar" is a gate and a "gate" is a street. Go ahead—blame the Vikings.) At Bootham Bar and on Exhibition Square facing it, you'll find the TI, the starting points for most walking tours and bus tours, handy access to the medieval town wall, and Bootham Street, which leads to the recommended B&Bs. To find your way around York, use the Minster's towers as a navigational landmark, or follow the strategically located green signposts, which point out all places of interest to tourists.

Tourist Information

The TI at Bootham Bar sells a £1 *York Map and Guide*. Ask for the free monthly *What's On* guide and the *York MiniGuide,* which includes a map and some discounts (April–Sept Mon–Sat 9:00–18:00, Sun 10:00–17:00; Oct–March Mon–Sat 9:00–17:00, Sun 10:00–16:00; WCs next door, tel. 01904/550-099, www.visityork .org). The TI books rooms for a £4 fee. The train station TI is smaller but provides all the same information and services (same hours as main TI).

York Pass: The TI sells a pass that covers most York sights (but not Jorvik or the Yorkshire Wheel) and other major sights in the region, and gives you discounts on both City Sightseeing hop-on, hop-off bus tours. If you take the bus tour and are a busy sightseer, it can save money (£21/1 day, £27/2 days, £34/3 days, www.yorkpass.com).

Arrival in York

A five-minute walk from town, the train station offers luggage storage for day-trippers on platform 1 (£4, Mon–Sat 8:00–20:30, Sun 9:00–20:30). To walk downtown from the station, turn left down Station Road, and follow the crowd toward the Gothic towers of the Minster. After the bridge, a block before the Minster, signs to the TI send you left on St. Leonard's Place. Recommended B&Bs are a five-minute walk from there. For information on calling a taxi, see below.

For a shortcut to the B&B area from the train station, exit the station to the left on Station Road. When the road swings right and goes through the old gate, turn left onto the busy street (Leeman Road). Just before that street goes under the rail bridge, turn right and follow the walkway along the tracks. Cross the bridge over the river and continue into the big parking lot. From here, cross the lot to the right to reach B&Bs on St. Mary's Street, or duck through the pedestrian walkway under the tracks (on the left) to reach B&Bs on Sycamore and Queen Anne's Road.

Helpful Hints

Festivals: The Viking Festival features *lur* horn-blowing, warrior drills, and re-created battles (Feb 13–17 in 2008). The Late Music Festival is in early June...if it starts on time (www.latemusicfestival.org.uk). The Early Music Festival (medieval minstrels, Renaissance dance, and so on) zings its strings the first two weeks of July (July 3–12 in 2008, www.ncem.co.uk/yemf.shtml). And the York Festival of Food and Drink takes a bite out of the end of September (www.yorkfestivaloffoodanddrink.com). The town also fills up on horse-race weekends, especially the Ebor Races in mid-August (check schedules at www.yorkracecourse.co.uk). Book a room well in advance during festival times and on weekends any time of year. For a complete list of festivals, see www.yorkfestivals.com.

Internet Access: Get online at the creaky, hip, and funky **Evil Eye Lounge,** which has 10 terminals (Mon–Sat 10:00–23:00, Sun 11:00–23:00, upstairs at 42 Stonegate, tel. 01904/640-002), or at **Gateway Internet Café-Bar** (Tue–Sun 11:00–18:00, Mon 11:00–20:00, 9 terminals, in the basement of the City Screens Cinema, overlooking the river at 13 Coney Street, tel. 01904/612-940). Laptop users can pay £1 for unlimited Wi-Fi and sit upstairs in the sunny **Riverside Café-Bar** (pay for access code downstairs first, café open Mon–Sat 11:00–23:00, Sun 11:00–22:30).

Laundry: The nearest place is **Haxby Road Launderette,** a long 15-minute walk outside the town center (£4/load self-service or drop-off; start last loads Mon–Fri by 16:30, Sat by 16:00, Sun by 15:00; 124 Haxby Road, tel. 01904/623-379).

Bike Rental: Bob Trotter Cycles, just outside Monk Bar, rents bikes and has free cycling maps (£12/day, helmets-£2, Mon–Sat 9:00–17:30, Sun 10:00–16:00, 13–15 Lord Mayor's Walk, tel. 01904/622-868, www.bobtrottercycles.com). **Europcar** at platform 1 at the train station also rents bikes (£6/half-day, £9/full day, includes helmet, tel. 01904/656-161). The riverside path is pleasant.

Taxi: From the train station, taxis zip new arrivals to their B&Bs for £3–5. Queue up at the taxi stand, or call 01904/623-332 or 01904/638-833; cabbies don't start the meter until you get in.

Car Rental: If you're nearing the end of your trip, consider dropping your car upon arrival in York. The money saved by turning it in early almost pays for the train ticket that whisks you effortlessly to London. In York, you'll find these agencies: **Avis** (Mon–Fri 8:00–18:00, Sat 8:00–13:00, closed Sun, 3 Layerthorpe, tel. 01904/610-460); **Hertz** (April–Sept daily, Sat–Sun until 13:00, at train station, tel. 01904/612-586); **Budget** (Mon–Fri 8:00–18:00, Sat 8:00–13:00, Sun 9:00–11:00, a mile past recommended B&Bs at Clifton 82, tel. 01904/644-919); and **Europcar** (Mon–Fri 8:00–18:00, Sat until 16:00, closed Sun, train station platform 1, tel. 01904/656-181, central reservations tel. 0870-607-5000). Beware: Car-rental agencies close early on Saturday afternoon, and some close all day Sunday—when drop-offs are OK, but picking up is impossible.

TOURS

▲▲▲**Walking Tours**—Charming local **volunteer guides** give energetic, entertaining, and free two-hour walks through York (daily at 10:15 all year, plus 14:15 April–Oct, plus 18:45 mid-June–Aug, from Exhibition Square across from TI). These tours often go long because the guides love to teach and tell stories. You're welcome to cut out early—but say so or they'll worry, thinking they've lost you.

There are many other commercial York walking tours. **YorkWalk Tours,** for example, has reliable guides and many themes from which to choose, such as Roman York, Snickelways—small alleys—and a "Choccy & Sweetie" tour that describes York's historic association with the chocolate industry (£5; depart from Museum Street, just north of Lendal Bridge; tel. 01904/622-303, www.yorkwalk.co.uk, TI has schedule). The numerous ghost tours,

York

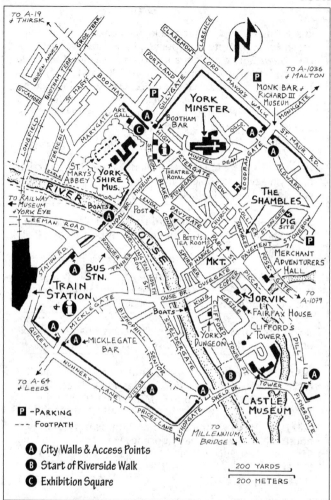

TO A-19 & THIRSK

CLAREMONT

PORTLAND

GILLYGATE

LORD MAYOR'S WALK

CLARENCE

TO A-1036 & MALTON

MONK BAR & RICHARD III MUSEUM

MONKGATE

QUEEN ANNE'S

GROS. TERR.

SYCAMORE

BOOTHAM TERR.

ST. MARY'S

BOOTHAM

ART. GALL.

MARYGATE

FREDERIC

LONGFIELD

EARLE

ST MARY'S ABBEY

YORK MINSTER

BOOTHAM BAR

HIGH ST. PETER

YORKSHIRE MUS.

OGLE

ST MAUR RD.

GOODRAMGATE

DEAN

MINSTER

LOW

ALDWARK

THE SHAMBLES

RIVER

LENDAL BR.

MUSEUM

THEATRE ROYAL

BLAKE

STONEGATE

CHURCH

COLLIER

DIG SITE

ST. SAV. GATE

STONEBOW

DAVYGATE

Post Office

CONEY

SHAMBLES

FOSS GATE

MERCHANT ADVENTURERS' HALL

TO RAILWAY MUSEUM & YORK EYE

Boats

LEEMAN ROAD

STATION RD.

WELLINGTON ROW

TANNER ROW

BETTYS TEA ROOMS

SPURRIERGATE

MARKET

MKT.

PAVEMENT

PICCA.

COPPERGATE

TO A-1079

BUS STN.

TRAIN STATION

MICKLEGATE

Boats

OUSE BR.

OUSEGATE

KING

JORVIK

FAIRFAX HOUSE

CLIFFORD'S TOWER

QUEEN ST.

BISHOPHILL JUNIOR

VICTOR ST.

SKELDERGATE

CASTLEGATE

CLIFFORD ST.

YORK DUNGEON

TOWER ST.

DILLY

MICKLEGATE BAR

NUNNERY LANE

TO A-64 & LEEDS

PRICES LANE

BISHOPGATE

SKELD. BR.

TO MILLENNIUM BRIDGE

TOWER

CASTLE MUSEUM

FISHERGATE

P —Parking

--- Footpath

Ⓐ City Walls & Access Points

Ⓑ Start of Riverside Walk

Ⓒ Exhibition Square

200 YARDS

200 METERS

York

all offered after dusk, are more fun than informative. **Haunted Walk** relies a bit more on storytelling and history than on masks and surprises (£4, April–Nov nightly at 20:00, 90 min, just show up, depart from Exhibition Square, across street from TI, end in the Shambles, tel. 01904/621-003).

▲**City Bus Tours**—Two companies run three different, color-coded, hop-on, hop-off bus tours circling York.

City Sightseeing—which also owns the Guide Friday bus company—sends two sets of buses along a similar route. Route A has red buses, lasts 45 minutes, and includes a recorded narration

York at a Glance

▲▲▲**Minster** York's pride and joy, and one of England's finest churches, with stunning stained-glass windows, textbook Decorated Gothic design, and glorious evensong services. **Hours:** Open for worship daily from 7:00 and for sightseeing Mon–Sat from 9:00, Sun from 12:30; flexible closing time (roughly May–Oct at 18:30, earlier off-season); shorter hours for tower and undercroft; evensong services Tue–Sat 17:15, Sun 16:00, occasionally on Mon, sometimes no services mid-July–Aug.

▲▲▲**York Castle Museum** Excellent, far-ranging collection displaying everyday objects from Victorian times to the present. **Hours:** Daily 9:30–17:00.

▲▲**National Railway Museum** Train buff's nirvana, tracing the history of all manner of rail-bound transport. **Hours:** Daily 10:00–18:00.

▲▲**Yorkshire Museum** Sophisticated archaeology museum with York's best Viking exhibit, plus Roman, Saxon, Norman, and Gothic artifacts. **Hours:** Daily 10:00–17:00.

▲**The Shambles** Atmospheric old butchers' quarter, with colorful, tipsy medieval buildings. **Hours:** Always open.

▲**Jorvik** Cheesy, crowded, but not-quite-Disney-quality exhibit/ride exploring Viking lifestyles and artifacts. **Hours:** Daily April–Oct 10:00–17:00, Nov–March 10:00–16:00.

▲**Fairfax House** Glimpse into an 18th-century Georgian house, with enjoyably chatty docents. **Hours:** Mon–Thu and Sat 11:00–16:30, Sun 13:30–16:30, Fri by tour only at 11:00 and 14:00.

(buses arrive every 10–15 min). Route B is covered by the green-and-cream buses, runs 60 minutes on a longer route, and comes with live guides in the summer (every 30 min). Both tours cover secondary York sights that the city walking tours skip—the mundane perimeter of town (£9, £12.50 combo-ticket with boat cruise—see below, pay driver cash, can also buy tickets from TI with credit card; departs from Exhibition Square daily in summer 9:45–16:45, in winter 10:00–15:00; both tours run April–Sept, limited departures in Oct, Route B only Nov–Feb, tel. 01708/866-000 or 01904/655-585, www.yorktourbuses.co.uk).

York Pullman Bus Tours, with burgundy-colored buses, are slightly less expensive than the others, but with fewer stops (£7.50, daily mid-June–Oct, fewer departures April–mid-June, no buses Nov–March, departs from Exhibition Square 9:20–17:15, 45 min, live guides, enclosed bus used when wet, tel. 01904/622-992, www .yorkpullmanbus.co.uk).

While you can hop on and off all day, the tours are of no real value from a transportation-to-the-sights point of view because York is so compact. I'd catch either tour at Exhibition Square (near the Bootham Bar TI) and ride it for an orientation all the way around, or get off at the National Railway Museum, skipping the last five minutes.

Boat Cruise—YorkBoat does a lazy, narrated 45-minute lap along the River Ouse (£7, £12.50 combo-ticket with City Sightseeing bus tours—see above, Feb–Nov 4/day starting at 10:30, every 30 min April–Oct, leaves from Lendal Bridge and King's Staith landing, near Skeldergate Bridge). They also offer themed evening cruises—ghost, dinner, floodlit, and so on (boat rentals possible, tel. 01904/628-324, www.yorkboat.co.uk).

SELF-GUIDED WALK

Wall Walk from the Minster

Start your time in York at its spectacular Minster (see sight listing on next page). After visiting the Minster, consider taking this stroll up along a segment of York's wall.

• *Head just across from the Minster to the...*

Roman Column: Erected in 1971, this column commemorates the 1,900th anniversary of the Roman founding of Eboracum (later called York). Across the street is a statue of Emperor Constantine, who was in York when his father died. The troops declared him emperor, and six years later, he went to Rome and claimed his throne. In 312, Constantine legalized Christianity, and in 314, York got its first bishop. Today's Minster stands upon the remains of a Roman fort.

Study the Minster. You're looking at the glory of Gothic. The main tower was intended to hold a towering spire—but it was too much. Even without all that extra weight, the church stands today only with the help of big, modern braces holding the foundation together.

• *Hike past the west portal of the Minster and down the street to...*

Bootham Bar: This is one of four gates on York's medieval walls (free, open until dusk). The 12th-century walls are three miles long. Norman kings built the walls to assert control over North England. This was a center for Romans, Normans, and

Henry VIII (for more on Henry, see "England's Anglican Church" sidebar on page 362). In the 19th century, York was a center of industry (and hub of the railway system).

• *Now climb up on...*

The Wall: Hike along the top of the wall behind the Minster to the first corner. Notice the pivots in the crenellations (square notches at the top of a medieval wall), which once held wooden hatches that provided cover for archers. At the corner, you can see the moat outside and enjoy a fine view of the Minster, with its truncated main tower and the pointy rooftop of its chapter house. The roofing—traditionally made of lead—melts during a fire and cascades to the ground.

Continue on to the next gate, **Monk Bar.** Keep an eye on the 12th-century guards, with their stones raised and primed to protect the town. Descend the wall at Monk Bar, and step past the portcullis and outside the city's protective wall. Lean against the last bollard and gaze up at the tower, imagining 10 archers behind the arrow slits.

Walking back into town from here, you'll find a number of good eateries on Goodramgate (see "Eating," page 377). At the first corner, College Street leads right to the east end of the Minster along St. Williams College (1461) and the home of bishops and priests.

SIGHTS

▲▲▲York Minster

The pride of York, this largest Gothic church north of the Alps (540 feet long, 200 feet tall) brilliantly shows that the High Middle Ages were far from dark. The word "minster" means a place from which people go out to minister, or spread the word of God. And because it's the seat of a bishop, it's also a cathedral. While Henry VIII destroyed England's great abbeys, this was not part of a monastery and was therefore left standing. It seats 2,000 comfortably; on Christmas and Easter, at least 4,000 worshippers pack the place. Today, more than 250 employees and 300 volunteers work to preserve its heritage and welcome the half-million visitors each year.

Cost, Hours, Tours: The cathedral opens for worship daily at 7:00 and for sightseeing Mon–Sat from 9:00 and Sunday from 12:30, when they begin charging £5.50 admission. The closing time flexes with the season (roughly May–Oct at 18:30, earlier off-

York Minster

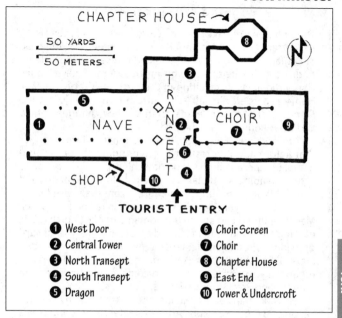

1 West Door
2 Central Tower
3 North Transept
4 South Transept
5 Dragon
6 Choir Screen
7 Choir
8 Chapter House
9 East End
10 Tower & Undercroft

season—call for details, tel. 01904/557-216). The tower and under-croft (£4 apiece) have shorter hours, typically opening a half-hour later and closing a half-hour earlier than the Minster. Two combo-ticket options save you money: £7.50 includes Minster entry and either the tower or the undercroft; £9 gets you all three.

When you enter, go directly to the welcome desk, pick up the worthwhile *Welcome to the York Minster* flier, and ask when the next free guided 60-minute **tour** departs (2/hr, Mon–Sat 9:30–15:00, they go even with just one or two people; you can join one in progress, or if none is scheduled, request a departure). The helpful Minster guides, wearing blue armbands, are happy to answer your questions.

Evensong and Church Bells: To experience the cathedral in musical and spiritual action, attend an evensong (Tue–Sat at 17:15, Sun at 16:00, visiting choirs occasionally perform on Mon, 45 min). When the choir is off on school break (mid-July–Aug), visiting choirs usually fill in (confirm at church or TI). Arrive 10 minutes early and wait just outside the choir in the center of the church. You'll be ushered in and can sit in one of the big wooden stalls. If you're a fan of church bells, you'll experience ding-dong ecstasy on Sunday morning (about 10:00) and during the Tuesday-evening practice (19:30–21:30). Stand in front of the church's west portal and imagine the gang pulling on a dozen ropes (halfway

England's Anglican Church

The Anglican Church came into existence in 1534 when Henry VIII declared that he, and not Pope Clement VII, was the head of England's Catholics. The Pope had refused to allow Henry to divorce his wife to marry his mistress Anne Boleyn (which Henry did anyway, resulting in the birth of Elizabeth I). Still, Henry regarded himself as a faithful Catholic—just not a *Roman* Catholic—and made relatively few changes to how and what Anglicans worshipped.

Henry's son, Edward VI, instituted many of the changes that Reformation Protestants were bringing about in continental Europe: an emphasis on preaching, people in the pews actually reading the Bible, clergy being allowed to marry, and a more "Protestant" liturgy in English from the revised Book of Common Prayer (1549). The next monarch, Edward's sister, Mary I, returned England to the Roman Catholic Church (1553), earning the nickname of "Bloody Mary" for her brutal suppression of Protestant elements. When Elizabeth I succeeded Mary (1558), she soon broke from Rome again. Today, many regard the Anglican Church as a compromise between the Catholic and Protestant traditions.

Is York's Minster the leading Anglican church in England? Yes and no (but mostly no). After a long feud, the archbishops of Canterbury and York agreed that York's bishop would have the title "Primate of England" and Canterbury's would be the "Primate of All England," directing Anglicans on the national level.

up the right tower—you can actually see the ropes through a little window).

◉ Self-Guided Tour: Upon entering, head left, to the back (west end) of the church. Stand in front of the grand **west door** (used only on Sundays) on the *Deo Gratias 627–1927* plaque—a place of worship for 1,300 years, thanks to God. On the door, the list of bishops goes unbroken back to the 600s. The statue of Peter with the key and Bible is a reminder that the church is dedicated to St. Peter, and the key to heaven is found through the word of God. While the Minster sits on the remains of a Romanesque church (c. 1100), today's church was begun in 1220 and took 250 years to complete.

Looking down the church, your first impression might be the spaciousness and brightness of the nave (built 1280–1360). The nave—from the middle period of Gothic, called "Decorated Gothic"—is one of the widest Gothic naves in Europe. Rather than risk a stone roof, builders spanned the space with wood. Colorful shields on the arcades are the coats of arms of nobles who helped tall and formidable Edward I, known as "Longshanks," fight the Scots in the 13th century.

The coats of arms in the clerestory (upper-level) glass represent the nobles who helped his son, Edward II, in the same fight. There's more medieval glass in this building than in the rest of England combined. This precious glass survived World War II—hidden in stately homes throughout Yorkshire.

Walk to the very center of the church, under the **central tower.** Look up. Look down. Read about how gifts and skill saved this tower from collapse. (The first tower collapsed in 1407.) While the tower is 197 feet tall, it was intended to be much taller. Use the neck-saving mirror to marvel at it.

From here, you can survey many impressive features of the church:

In the **north transept,** the grisaille windows—dubbed the "Five Sisters"—are dedicated to British women who died in all wars. Made in 1260 (before colored glass was produced in England), these contain more than 100,000 pieces of glass.

The **south transept** features the tourists' entry, where stairs lead down to the undercroft. The new "bosses" (carved medallions decorating the point where the ribs meet on the ceiling) are a reminder that the roof of this wing of the church was destroyed by fire in 1984. Some believe the fire was God's angry response to a new bishop, David Jenkins, who questioned the literal truth of Jesus' miracles. Others blame an electricity box hit by lightning. Regardless, the entire country came to York's aid. *Blue Peter* (England's top kids' show) conducted a competition among their young viewers to design new bosses. Out of 30,000 entries, there were six winners (the blue ones—e.g., man on the moon, feed the children, save the whales).

Look back at the west end to marvel at the **Great West Window,** especially the stone tracery. While its nickname is the "Heart of Yorkshire," it represents the sacred heart of Christ, meant to remind people of his love for the world.

Find the **dragon** on the right of the nave (two-thirds of the way up). While no one is sure of its purpose, it pivots and has a hole through its neck—so it was likely a mechanism designed to raise a lid on a baptismal font.

The **choir screen** is an ornate wall of carvings separating the nave from the choir. It's lined with all the English kings from William I (the Conqueror) to Henry VI (during whose reign it was carved, 1461). Numbers indicate the years each reigned. To say "it's slathered in gold leaf" sounds impressive, but the gold's very thin... a nugget the size of a sugar cube is pounded into a sheet the size of a driveway.

Step into the **choir** (or "quire"), where Mass is held daily. All the carving was redone after an 1829 fire, but its tradition of glorious evensong services (sung by choristers from the Minster School) goes all the way back to the eighth century.

The 18th-century astronomical clock in the **north transept** is dedicated to the 18,000 airmen who died in World War II, flying from bases here in northern England. The Book of Remembrance contains all of their names.

A corridor that functions as a small church museum leads to the Gothic, octagonal **Chapter House,** the traditional meeting place of the governing body (or chapter) of the Minster. Fighting the Scots in 1295, King Edward I (the "Longshanks" we met earlier) convened the "Model Parliament" here, rather than down south, in London. (The Model Parliament is the name for its early version, back before the legislature was split into the Houses of Commons and Lords.) The government met here through the 20-year reign of King Edward II, before moving to London during Edward III's rule in the 14th century.

The Chapter House is remarkable (almost frightening) for its breadth without an interior support. The fanciful carvings decorating the canopies above the stalls date from 1280 (80 percent are originals) and are some of the Minster's finest. Above the doorway, the Virgin holds Baby Jesus while standing on the devilish serpent. Grates still send hot air up robes of attendees on cold winter mornings. A model of the wooden construction illustrates the impressive 1285 engineering.

The **east end** is square, lacking a semicircular apse, typical of England's Perpendicular Gothic style (15th century). The window, the size of a tennis court, is a carefully designed ensemble of biblical symbolism with God the Father presiding over ranks of saints and angels on the top; nine rows of 117 panels telling Bible stories in the middle; and a row of bishops and kings on the bottom. A chart (on the right, with a tiny, more helpful chart within—locate panels with color-coded numbers) highlights the core Old Testament scenes in this hard-to-read masterpiece. Enjoy the art close up on the chart, then step back and find the real thing. Because of its immense size, there's an extra layer of supportive stonework, making parts of it wide enough to walk along. In fact, for special occasions, the choir sings from the walkway halfway up the window. Monuments (almost no graves) were once strewn throughout the church, but in the Victorian age, they were gathered into the east end, where you see them today.

Tower and Undercroft: There are two extra sights to consider, both accessed from the south transept. (Remember, if you're interested in these, consider the money-saving combo-tickets described above—£7.50 for the Minster plus one of these, or £9 for everything.) You can scale the 275-step **tower** for the panoramic

York

view (£4, not good for kids or acrophobes). The **undercroft** consists of the crypt, treasury, and foundations (£4, includes audioguide). The crypt is an actual bit of the Romanesque church, featuring 12th-century Romanesque art, excavated in modern times. The foundations give you a chance to climb down—archaeologically and physically—through the centuries to see the roots of the much smaller, but still huge, Norman (Romanesque) church from 1100 that stood on this spot and, below that, the Roman excavations. As you wander, ponder the fact that Constantine was proclaimed Roman emperor here in A.D. 306. Peek also at the modern concrete save-the-church foundations.

More Sights in York

▲**The Shambles**—This is the most colorful old street in the half-timbered, traffic-free core of town. Walk to the midway point,

at the intersection with Little Shambles. Ye olde downtown York abounds with window-shopping, street musicians, and people-watching. This 100-yard-long street was once the "street of the butchers" (the name is derived from *sham-mell*—a butcher's cutting block). In the 16th century, it was busy with red meat. On the hooks under the eaves once hung rabbit, pheasant, beef, lamb, and pigs' heads. Fresh slabs were displayed on the fat sills. People lived above—as they did even in Roman times. The soil here wasn't great for building. Notice how things settled in the absence of a good soil engineer.

Little Shambles leads to the frumpy Newgate Market (popular for cheap produce and clothing), created in the 1960s with the demolition of a bunch of lanes as colorful as the Shambles. Return to the Shambles a little farther along, through a covered lane (or "snickelway"). Study the 16th-century oak carpentry—mortar and tenon joints with wooden plugs rather than nails.

For a cheap lunch, consider the cute, tiny **St. Crux Parish Hall.**

This medieval church is now used by a medley of charities selling tea, homemade cakes, and light meals. They each book the church for a day, often a year in advance. Chat to the volunteers (Mon–Sat 10:00–16:00, closed Sun, on the left at bottom end of the Shambles, at intersection with Pavement).

▲▲▲**York Castle Museum**—Truly one of Europe's top museums, this is a Victorian home show, the closest thing to a time-tunnel experience England has to offer. Even a speedy museumgoer will

want a couple hours here. Stroll down the museum's two re-created streets: Kirkgate, from the Victorian era, with roaming live guides in period dress; and a new street (scheduled to open in early 2008) that re-creates the spirit of the swinging 1960s—"a time when the cultural changes were massive but the cars and skirts were mini."

The "From Cradle to Grave" clothing exhibit and fine costume collection are also impressive. The one-way plan assures you'll see

everything: re-created rooms from the 17th to 20th centuries, prison cells with related exhibits, the domestic side of World War II, giant dollhouses from 1715 and 1895, Victorian toys, and a century of swimsuit fashions. The museum's £3 guidebook isn't necessary, but it makes a fine souvenir. The museum proudly offers no audioguides, as its roaming, costumed guides are enthusiastic about talking—engage them (£6.50, ticket good for one year, daily 9:30–17:00, parking, cafeteria midway through museum, tel. 01904/687-687, www.yorkcastlemuseum.org.uk; at the bottom of the hop-on, hop-off bus route; museum can call you a taxi—worthwhile if you're hurrying to the National Railway Museum).

Clifford's Tower—Located across from the Castle Museum, this

ruin is all that's left of York's 13th-century castle, the site of an 1190 massacre of local Jews (read about this at base of hill). If you climb inside, there are fine city views from the top of the ramparts (not worth the £3, daily April–Sept 10:00–18:00, Oct 10:00–17:00, Nov–March 10:00–16:00).

▲**Jorvik**—Take the "Pirates of the Caribbean," sail them north and back 1,000 years, and you get Jorvik—more a ride than a museum. Innovative 20 years ago, the commercial success of Jorvik (YOR-vik) inspired copycat ride/

museums all over England. Some love this attraction, while others call it a gimmicky rip-off. If you're looking for a grown-up museum, the Viking exhibit at the Yorkshire Museum is far better. If you're thinking Disneyland with a splash of history, Jorvik's fun. To me, Jorvik is a commercial venture designed for kids, with nearly as much square footage devoted to its shop as to the museum. You'll ride a little Disney-type people-mover for 20 minutes through the re-created Viking street of Coppergate. It's the year 975, and you're in the village of Jorvik. Next, your little train takes you through the actual excavation site that inspired the reconstructed village. Everything is true to the dig—even the faces of the models are derived by computer from skulls dug up here. Finally, you'll browse through a small gallery of Viking shoes, combs, locks, and other intimate glimpses of that redheaded culture. The exhibit on bone archaeology is fascinating (£8, £11.20 combo-ticket with Dig—see below, daily April–Oct 10:00–17:00, Nov–March 10:00–16:00, tel. 01904/643-211, www.vikingjorvik.com).

Crowd-Beating Tips: Midday lines can be an hour long in the peak of summer. Avoid the line by going very early or very late in the day, or by pre-booking a particular time slot (call 01904/543-403, £1 booking fee, can also book tickets for Dig).

Dig—This archaeological site gives young visitors an idea of what York looked like during Roman, medieval, Viking, and Victorian eras. Sift through "dirt" (actually shredded tires), reconstruct Roman wall plaster, and have a look at what archaeologists have dug up recently (£5.50, £11.20 combo-ticket with Jorvik, daily 10:00–17:00, St. Saviour's Church, Saviourgate, tel. 01904/543-403, www.digyork.co.uk).

▲▲**National Railway Museum**—If you like model railways, this is train-car heaven. The thunderous museum shows 200 illustrious

years of British railroad history. Fanning out from a grand round-house is an array of historic cars and engines, including Queen Victoria's lavish royal car and the very first "stagecoaches on rails," with a crude steam engine from 1830. A working steam engine is sliced open, showing cylinders, driving wheels, and smoke box in action. You'll trace the evolution of steam-powered transportation to the era of the aerodynamic Mallard, famous as the first train to travel at a startling two miles per minute (a marvel back in 1938). There's much more, including exhibits on dining cars, post cars, sleeping cars, train posters, and videos. At the Works section, you can see live train switchboards. And don't miss the English Channel Tunnel video (showing the first handshake at the site of the breakthrough). Purple-shirted "explainers" are everywhere, eager to talk trains. This biggest and best railroad museum anywhere is interesting even to people who think "Pullman" means "don't push" (free, £2.50 audioguide with 60 bits of railroad lore is worthwhile for train buffs, daily 10:00–18:00, tel. 01904/621-261, www.nrm.org.uk).

Getting There: It's about a 15-minute walk from the Minster (southwest of town, behind the train station—look for the Ferris wheel). A cute little "street train" shuttles you more quickly between the Minster and the Railway Museum (£2 each way, runs daily Easter–Oct, leaves Railway Museum every 30 min from 11:00 to 16:00 at the top and bottom of the hour; leaves the town—from Duncombe Place, 100 yards in front of the Minster—every 30 min, :15 and :45 min after the hour).

Yorkshire Wheel—Located within the National Railway Museum, this familiar-looking, 198-foot-high Ferris wheel was nicknamed the "York Eye" by locals. Come here on a clear day for great views of the city and the river (£6 for a 15- to 20-min ride, daily 10:00–18:00, until 20:00 mid-July–Aug, last entry 45 min before closing, tel. 01904/621-261).

▲▲Yorkshire Museum—Located in a lush, picnic-perfect park next to the stately ruins of St. Mary's Abbey, Yorkshire Museum is the city's forgotten, serious "archaeology of York" museum. While the hordes line up at Jorvik, the best Viking artifacts are here—with no crowds and a better historical context.

Your museum stroll starts in ancient times. The Roman collection includes slice-of-life exhibits from Roman gods and goddesses and the skull of a man killed by a sword blow to the head. (The latter makes it graphically clear that the struggle between Romans and barbarians was a violent one.) A fine eighth-century Anglo-Saxon helmet shows a bit of barbarian refinement; you'll notice that the Vikings wore some pretty decent shoes, and actually combed their hair.

The Middleham Jewel, an exquisitely etched 15th-century pendant, is considered the finest piece of Gothic jewelry in Britain. The noble lady who wore this on a necklace believed that it helped her worship and protected her from illness. The back of the pendant, which rested near her heart, shows the nativity. The front shows the Holy Trinity crowned by a sapphire (which people believed put their prayers at the top of God's to-do list).

The 20-minute video about the creation of the abbey plays continuously, and is worth a look. Kids will enjoy the interactive "Fingerprints of Time" exhibit (museum entry-£5, ticket good for one year, daily 10:00–17:00, within Museum Gardens, tel. 01904/687-687, www.yorkshiremuseum.org.uk). Before leaving, enjoy the evocative ruins of the abbey in the park (destroyed by

Henry VIII in the 16th century).

▲**Fairfax House**—This well-furnished building is perfectly Georgian inside, with docents happy to talk with you. Built in 1762, it's compact and bursting with insights into aristocratic life in 18th-century England. Pianists may be allowed to actually pluck the harpsichord (£5, Mon–Thu and Sat 11:00–16:30, Sun 13:30–16:30, Fri by tour only at 11:00 and 14:00—the tours are worthwhile, on Castlegate, near Jorvik, tel. 01904/655-543).

Theatre Royal—A full variety of dramas, comedies, and works by Shakespeare is put on to entertain the locals in either the main theater or the little 100-seat theater-in-the-round (£9–20, almost nightly at 19:30, closed much of Aug, tickets easy to get, on St. Leonard's Place next to TI and a 5-min walk from recommended B&Bs, booking tel. 01904/623-568, www.yorktheatreroyal.co.uk). Those under 25 get tickets for only £5.

Traditional Tea—York is famous for its elegant teahouses. Drop into one around 16:00 for tea and cakes. Ladies love **Bettys Café Tea Rooms,** where you pay £7.25 for a Yorkshire Cream Tea (tea and scones with clotted Yorkshire cream and strawberry jam) or £14.50 for a full traditional English afternoon tea (tea, delicate sandwiches, scones, and sweets). Your table is so full of doily niceties that the food is served on a little three-tray tower. While you'll pay a little extra here (and the food's nothing special), the ambience and people-watching are hard to beat (daily 9:00–21:00, piano music nightly 18:00–21:00, tel. 01904/659-142, St. Helen's Square; fine view of street scene from a window seat on the main floor, downstairs near WC is a mirror signed by WWII bomber pilots—read the story). If there's a line, it moves quickly (except at dinnertime). Wait for a seat by the windows on the ground level rather than sit in the much bigger basement.

Riverside Walk—The New Walk is a mile-long, tree-lined, riverside lane created in the 1730s as a promenade for York's dandy class to stroll, see, and be seen. With the creation of York's Millennium Bridge, it's now possible to take this walk, cross over, and return to York passing through Rowntree Park (a great Edwardian park with lawn bowling for the public, plus family fun including a playground and adventure rides for kids). This hour-long walk is a great way to enjoy a dose of countryside from York. It's clearly described in the TI's *New Walk* flier (60p). You start from the riverside under Skeldergate Bridge (near the Castle Museum), walk away from town for a mile until you hit a modern bridge, cross the river, and walk home.

Honorable Mentions

York has a number of other sights and activities (described in TI brochures) that, while interesting, pale in comparison to the biggies.

Merchant Adventurers' Hall—Claiming to be the finest medieval guildhall in Europe (from 1361), it's basically a vast half-timbered building with marvelous exposed beams and 15 minutes' worth of interesting displays about life and commerce back in the days when York was England's second city (£2.50, Mon–Thu 9:00–17:00, Fri–Sat 9:00–15:30, Sun 12:00–16:00, shorter hours off-season, south of the Shambles off Piccadilly, tel. 01904/654-818, www.theyorkcompany.co.uk).

Richard III Museum—This is interesting only for Richard III enthusiasts (£2.50, daily March–Oct 9:00–17:00, Nov–Feb 9:30–16:00, longer hours possible in summer, Monk Bar, tel. 01904/634-191, www.richardiiimuseum.co.uk).

York Dungeon—It's gimmicky, but if you insist on papier-mâché gore, it's better than the London Dungeon (£12, daily 10:00–17:30, shorter hours off-season, 12 Clifford Street, tel. 01904/632-599, www.thedungeons.com).

Lawn Bowling Green—Visitors are welcome to watch the action—best in the evenings—at the green on Sycamore Place (near recommended B&Bs). Buy a pint of beer and tell them which B&B you're staying at. Another green is in front of the Coach House Hotel Pub on Marygate.

SHOPPING

With its medieval lanes lined with classy as well as tacky little shops, York is a hit with shoppers. I find the **antique malls** interesting. Three places within a few blocks of each other are filled with stalls and cases owned by antique dealers from the countryside. The malls sell the dealers' bygones on commission. Serious shoppers do better heading for the countryside, but York's shops are a fun browse: The **Antiques Centre York** (Mon–Sat 9:00–17:30, Sun 9:00–16:00, 41 Stonegate, tel. 01904/635-888, www.theantiquescentreyork.co.uk), the **York Antique Centre** (Mon–Sat 10:00–17:00, closed Sun, 2 Lendal, tel. 01904/641-445), and the **Red House Antiques Centre** (Mon–Sat 9:30–19:00, Sun 10:00–17:00, closes weekdays at 17:30 in winter, a block from Minster at Duncombe Place, tel. 01904/637-000, www.redhouseyork.co.uk).

SLEEPING

I've listed peak-season, book-direct prices. Don't use the TI. Outside of July and August, some prices go soft. B&Bs will sometimes turn away one-night bookings, particularly for peak-season Saturdays. (York is worth two nights anyway.) Remember to book ahead during festival times (mid-Feb, March, mid-May, early June,

Sleep Code

(£1 = about $2, country code: 44, area code: 01904)
S = Single, **D** = Double/Twin, **T** = Triple, **Q** = Quad, **b** = bathroom,
s = shower only. You can assume credit cards are accepted
unless otherwise noted.

To help you sort easily through these listings, I've divided
the rooms into three categories based on the price for a standard double room with bath (during high season):

$$$ **Higher Priced**—Most rooms £90 or more.
 $$ **Moderately Priced**—Most rooms between £60–90.
  $ **Lower Priced**—Most rooms £60 or less.

early July, mid-Aug, and late Sept—see "Helpful Hints," page 355)
and weekends year-round.

B&Bs and Small Hotels

These B&Bs are all small and family-run. They come with plenty
of steep stairs but no traffic noise. For a good selection, call well in
advance. B&B owners will generally hold a room with a phone call
and work hard to help their guests sightsee and eat intelligently.
Most have permits to lend for street parking.

Near Bootham

These recommendations are in the handiest B&B neighborhood,
a quiet residential area just outside the old-town wall's Bootham
gate, along the road called Bootham. All are within a five-minute
walk of the Minster and TI, and a 10-minute walk or taxi ride
(£3–5) from the station. If driving, head for the cathedral and follow the medieval wall to the gate called Bootham Bar. The street
called Bootham leads away from Bootham Bar.

$$$ The Hazelwood, my most hotelesque listing in this neigh-
borhood, is plush, and more formal than a B&B. This spacious
house has 14 beautifully decorated rooms with modern furnish-
ings and lots of thoughtful touches (Db-£80/90/110 depending on
room size, two ground-floor rooms, laundry service-£5, parking; a
fridge, ice, and great travel library in the pleasant basement lounge;
24 Portland Street, tel. 01904/626-548, fax 01904/628-032, www
.thehazelwoodyork.com, reservations@thehazelwoodyork.com,
Ian and Carolyn). Ask about the bright, top-floor, two-bedroom
apartment, great for families and those with strong legs.

$$ 23 St. Mary's is extravagantly decorated. Chris and Julie
Simpson have done everything just right and offer nine spa-
cious and comfy rooms, a classy lounge, and all the doily touches

York Accommodations

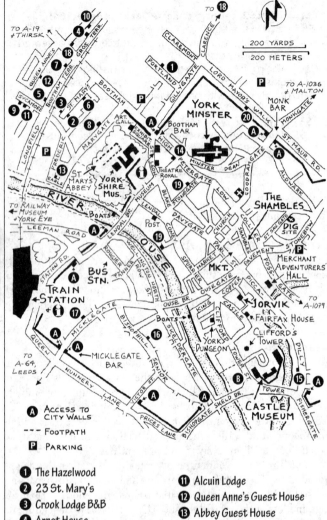

200 YARDS
200 METERS

Ⓐ ACCESS TO CITY WALLS
--- FOOTPATH
Ⓟ PARKING

❶ The Hazelwood
❷ 23 St. Mary's
❸ Crook Lodge B&B
❹ Arnot House
❺ Abbeyfields Guest House
❻ Airden House
❼ Hedley House Hotel
❽ The Coach House Hotel & Rest.
❾ The Sycamore
❿ Bootham Guest House & Number 34

⓫ Alcuin Lodge
⓬ Queen Anne's Guest House
⓭ Abbey Guest House
⓮ Best Western Dean Court Hotel
⓯ Travelodge York Central
⓰ York Youth Hotel
⓱ York Backpackers Hostel
⓲ To Launderette
⓳ Internet Cafés (2)
⓴ Bike Rental

(Sb-£45–50, Db-£75–95 depending on season and size, DVD library and some rooms with DVD players, free Wi-Fi, 23 St. Mary's, tel. 01904/622-738, fax 01904/628-802, www.23stmarys .co.uk, stmarys23@hotmail.com).

$$ Crook Lodge B&B, with seven charming but tight rooms, serves breakfast in an old Victorian kitchen (Db-£68–74, less on weekdays and off-season, free Wi-Fi, parking, quiet, 26 St. Mary's, tel. 01904/655-614, www.crooklodge.co.uk, crooklodge @hotmail.com, Brian and Louise Aiken).

$$ Arnot House, run by a hardworking daughter-and-mother team, is homey and lushly decorated with early-1900s memorabilia. The three well-furnished rooms have little libraries and DVD/VCRs (Db-£75, 2-night minimum stay, DVD/video library, 17 Grosvenor Terrace, tel. 01904/641-966, www.arnothouseyork.co.uk, kim .robbins@virgin.net, Kim and Ann Robbins and friendly cat Milly).

$$ Abbeyfields Guest House has eight comfortable, bright rooms and a quiet lounge. This doily-free place, which lacks the usual clutter, has been designed with care (Sb-£42, Db-£70, cash only, 19 Bootham Terrace, tel. 01904/636-471, www.abbeyfields .co.uk, enquire@abbeyfields.co.uk, Richard and Gwen Martin).

$$ Airden House, the most central of my Bootham-area listings, has nine spacious rooms (Db-£74–78, Db with sauna-£88, 10 percent discount with 2-night minimum and this book through 2008, ask for discount when booking, 1 St. Mary's, tel. 01904/638-915, www.airdenhouse.co.uk, info@airdenhouse.co.uk, Mark and Emma Turner).

$$ Hedley House Hotel has 16 simple, clean rooms on the same quiet street as the Abbeyfields (Sb-£45–70, Db-£70–100, less off-season, family rooms, daily breakfast specials, three-course evening meals for £15, parking, outdoor hot tub if you're willing to brave the weather, 3 Bootham Terrace, tel. 01904/637-404, www .hedleyhouse.com, greg@hedleyhouse.com, Greg Harrand and Cairn terrier Oscar).

$$ The Coach House Hotel is a labyrinthine, well-located, 17th-century coach house. Facing a bowling green and the abbey walls, it offers 12 beam-ceilinged rooms, some with views of the Minster (Sb-£39–45, Db-£77–81, free parking, 20 Marygate, Bootham, tel. 01904/652-780, www.coachhousehotel-york.com, info@coachhousehotel-york.com, Dawn Fielding and Macey the dog).

$$ The Sycamore is a fine value, with six homey rooms at the end of a dead-end street opposite a fun-to-watch bowling green (D-£46–52, Db-£60–68, family room-£70–75, less off-season, cash only, 19 Sycamore Place off Bootham Terrace, tel. 01904/624-712, www.thesycamore.co.uk, mail@thesycamore.co.uk, Elizabeth and Spiros).

$$ At **Bootham Guest House,** gregarious Emma welcomes you to her eight cheery green-toned rooms (D-£56–60, Db-£60–70, higher prices are for weekends, cheaper off-season, 56 Bootham Crescent, tel. 01904/672-123, www.boothamguesthouse .co.uk, boothamguesthouse1@hotmail.com).

$$ Alcuin Lodge has five fine rooms with comfy sofas and solid-wood furnishings (one small top-floor D-£55, Db-£64–66, family room-£70–90, Wi-Fi, 15 Sycamore Place, tel. 01904/632-222, www.alcuinlodge.com, info@alcuinlodge.com, Pete and Izzy).

$ Queen Anne's Guest House has seven clean, cheery rooms and is a fine value (April–Sept: D-£46, Db-£50; Oct–March: D-£40, Db-£44; prices good through 2008 with this book, family room, lounge, 24 Queen Anne's Road, tel. 01904/629-389, www .queen-annes-guesthouse.co.uk, queen.annes@btopenworld.com, John and Linda).

$ Number 34, run by hardworking Amy and Jason, has four light, airy rooms at fair prices (May–Oct: Sb-£45, Db-£56, Tb-£75; Nov–April: Sb-£35, Db-£50, Tb-£70, 34 Bootham Crescent, tel. 01904/645-818, www.number34york.co.uk, enquiries @number34york.co.uk).

Near the River

$$ Abbey Guest House is a peaceful refuge overlooking the River Ouse, with five recently renovated cheerful rooms (Db-£70–75, river-view four-poster Db-£78–80, family room-£80–90, ask about Rick Steves discount when booking, 13-14 Earlsborough Terrace, tel. 01904/627-782, www.abbeyghyork.co.uk, Gill—pronounced "Jill"—and Alec Saville).

Hotels in the Center

$$$ Dean Court Hotel, a Best Western facing the Minster, is a big, stately hotel with classy lounges and 37 comfortable rooms (small Db-£135, standard Db-£160, superior Db-£185, spacious deluxe Db-£205, elevator to most rooms, Wi-Fi, bistro, restaurant, Duncombe Place, tel. 01904/625-082, fax 01904/620-305, www .deancourt-york.co.uk).

$$ Travelodge York Central offers 90 identical, affordable rooms near the Castle Museum (Db-£70, Internet deals as low as £26, kids' bed free, 90 Piccadilly, central reservations tel. 0870-085-0950, www.travelodge.co.uk).

$ York Youth Hotel is a well-run hostel, with a kitchen, launderette, game room, and 120 beds (S-£30, bunk-bed D-£42, beds in 4- to 6-bed dorms-£18, beds in larger dorms-£14, less for multi-night stays, family rates, same-sex or coed rooms possible, no breakfast, 10-min walk from station at 11 Bishophill Senior Road, tel. 01904/625-904, fax 01904/612-494, www.yorkyouthhotel.com, info@yorkyouthhotel.com).

$ York Backpackers Hostel offers cheap beds a few minutes' walk from the train station. The jovial staff welcomes backpackers and budget travelers of any age, with 24-hour access, no lockouts, and a guests-only bar in the basement, complete with support beams made of reclaimed ship timbers (£14–15 beds in 18- to 20-bed dorms, D-£38, 88 Mickelgate, tel. 01904/627-720, www.yorkbackpackers.co.uk, mail@yorkbackpackers.co.uk).

EATING

York is bursting with inviting eateries. Picnic and light-meals-to-go options abound, and it's easy to find a churchyard, bench, or riverside perch upon which to munch cheaply. Perhaps the best picnic spot in town on a sunny day is under the evocative 12th-century ruins of St. Mary's Abbey in the Museum Gardens (near Bootham Bar).

There's a pub serving grub on every street. The best traditional chippie left in the center is **Petergate Fisheries** (good, cheap takeaway fish-and-chips, daily 11:00–18:00, 95 Low Petergate).

Near the Minster

Café Concerto, a casual bistro with a fun menu, has an understandably loyal following (soup, sandwich, and salad meals-£9–10; fancier dinners-£15; daily 10:00–22:00, smart to reserve for dinner, facing the Minster, 21 High Petergate, tel. 01904/610-478).

Plunkets Restaurant is a bit oxymoronic—serving Tex-Mex cuisine among B&W glamour photos with dark, hardwood, candlelit English ambience—but the food is fine (daily 12:00–23:00, £7–9 early-bird special before 18:00—main course and a beer or wine, no reservations and often a line on weekends, 9 High Petergate, tel. 01904/637-722).

St. Williams Restaurant is just behind the great east window of the Minster in a wonderful half-timbered, 15th-century building (read the history on the menu). This is where the priests use their meal card. It serves quick and tasty lunches and elegant candlelit dinners. Outside seating with a Minster view is fine when balmy (English and Mediterranean dishes; tea and pastries served daily 10:30–12:00 & 14:30–16:30; £7–8 lunches served daily 12:00–14:30; £12–16 dinners served only Fri–Sat 18:00–21:00, dinners also Wed–Thu in July–Aug; call ahead to confirm hours and reserve for dinner, College Street, tel. 01904/634-830).

Bettys Café Tea Rooms, a favorite among local ladies, is popular for its traditional English afternoon tea (which works as a meal—£14.50 for tea, delicate sandwiches, scones, and sweets; for details, see page 369).

York Restaurants

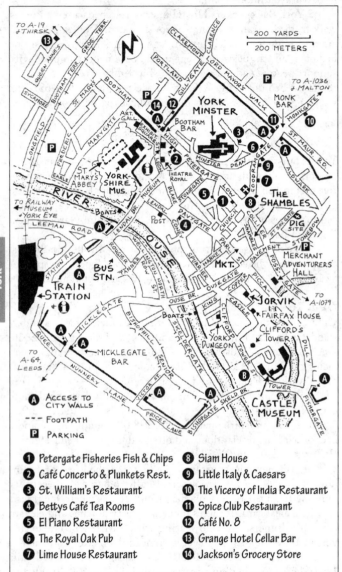

200 YARDS
200 METERS

TO A-19
& THIRSK

TO A-1036
& MALTON

YORK MINSTER

MONK BAR

BOOTHAM BAR

ST. MARY'S ABBEY

YORKSHIRE MUS.

THEATRE ROYAL

THE SHAMBLES

DIG SITE

MERCHANT ADVENTURERS' HALL

RIVER OUSE

POST

BUS STN.

MKT.

TRAIN STATION

JORVIK

TO A-1079

FAIRFAX HOUSE

CLIFFORD'S TOWER

YORK DUNGEON

MICKLEGATE BAR

TO A-64, LEEDS

CASTLE MUSEUM

A ACCESS TO CITY WALLS
– – – FOOTPATH
P PARKING

❶ Petergate Fisheries Fish & Chips
❷ Café Concerto & Plunkets Rest.
❸ St. William's Restaurant
❹ Bettys Café Tea Rooms
❺ El Piano Restaurant
❻ The Royal Oak Pub
❼ Lime House Restaurant
❽ Siam House
❾ Little Italy & Caesars
❿ The Viceroy of India Restaurant
⓫ Spice Club Restaurant
⓬ Café No. 8
⓭ Grange Hotel Cellar Bar
⓮ Jackson's Grocery Store

El Piano Restaurant, a few blocks from the Minster on charming Grape Lane, is a popular veggie option that serves vegan, gluten-free, and low-sodium dishes in tapas-style portions. Save money by getting it to go from their take-away window (Mon–Sat 10:00–24:00, Sun 12:00–17:00, between Low Petergate and Swinegate at 15–17 Grape Lane, tel. 01904/610-676).

On and near Goodramgate, in the Old Town Center

The Royal Oak, a traditional, mellow, 16th-century English pub, serves £6–8 meals throughout the day with hand-pulled ale. They happily swap out the peas and potatoes for more interesting vegetables—just ask (meals daily 12:00–20:00, three cozy rooms, hearty meat dishes, homemade desserts, Goodramgate, a block inside Monk Bar, tel. 01904/653-856).

Lime House Restaurant is a small, modern, candlelit place serving international dishes and always a good vegetarian plate. They offer a free glass of house wine to anyone with this book in 2008 (lunch plates-£7–10, dinner plates-£15–19, Tue–Fri 10 percent off orders before 19:15, open Tue–Sat 12:00–14:00 & 18:30–21:30, closed Sun–Mon, 55 Goodramgate, tel. 01904/632-734).

Siam House serves creative Thai food popular with locals (£8 lunches, £11–13 dinners, Mon 18:00–22:30, Tue–Sat 12:00–14:00 & 18:00–22:30, closed Sun, 63A Goodramgate, tel. 01904/624-677).

Two popular Italian places along Goodramgate offer pizzas and pastas for £7: **Little Italy** is a little more intimate (Mon–Fri 17:00–22:00, Sat–Sun 12:00–14:00 & 17:00–23:00, at #12, tel. 01904/623-539), while **Caesars** is bright and boisterous (Mon–Fri 12:00–14:30 & 17:30–23:00, Sat–Sun 12:00–23:00, at #27, tel. 01904/670-914).

The Viceroy of India, just outside Monk Bar (and therefore outside the tourist zone), serves decent, affordable Indian food (£7 plates, Mon–Sat 17:30–24:00, Sun 12:00–24:00, friendly staff, out Monk Bar to 26 Monkgate, tel. 01904/622-370). The same people own the **Spice Club** a block away, alongside Monk Bar (similar food and prices, Wed–Mon 17:30–24:00, closed Tue, 1 Monkgate, tel. 01904/468-202).

Near Bootham Bar and Your B&B

Café No. 8 is a local favorite and your best bistro choice on Gillygate, serving modern European comfort food and veggie options, with a shady little garden out back if the weather's good. Chef Pragnell lets what's fresh in the market shape his menu (£5–10 lunches, £12–15 dinners, Mon–Sat 10:00–22:00, Sun until 17:00, 8 Gillygate, tel. 01904/653-074).

The **Coach House** serves good-quality fresh food, with veggie options and homemade sweets, in a cozy atmosphere (£8–11, nightly 18:00–20:15, attached to a classic old guest house recommended above in "Sleeping," 20 Marygate, tel. 01904/652-780).

The **Grange Hotel Cellar Bar,** a couple of blocks from the B&Bs, is classier than a pub and serves a smattering of traditional European dishes. Eat downstairs rather than in the pricey mainfloor restaurant (£12–15 main dishes, Mon–Sat 11:00–23:00, Sun 19:00–21:30, 1 Clifton, tel. 01904/644-744).

Jackson's grocery store is open daily 7:00–23:00 (near B&Bs, 50 yards outside Bootham Bar, on Bootham).

TRANSPORTATION CONNECTIONS

From York by Train to: Durham (1–3/hr, 45–60 min), **London** (2/hr, 2 hrs), **Bath** (hourly, 4.5–5 hrs, 1–2 transfers), **Cambridge** (hourly, 2.5 hrs, change in Peterborough), **Birmingham** (2/hr, 2.5 hrs), **Keswick** (with transfers to Penrith then bus, 4.5 hrs), **Edinburgh** (2/hr, 2.5 hrs). Train info: tel. 08457-484-950.

Connections with London's Airports: Heathrow (hourly, allow 2.5–3 hrs, from airport take train to London's Paddington Station, tube to King's Cross, train to York—2/hr, 2 hrs), **Gatwick** (from Gatwick, catch low-profile Thameslink train to King's Cross–Thameslink station in London—from there, walk 100 yards to King's Cross Station; train to York: 2/hr, 2 hrs).

Route Tips for Drivers

As you near York (and your B&B), you'll hit the A1237 ring road. Follow this to the A19/Thirsk roundabout (next to river on northeast side of town). From the roundabout, follow signs for *York City*, traveling through Clifton into Bootham. All recommended B&Bs are four or five blocks before you hit the medieval city gate (see neighborhood map, page 372). If you're approaching York from the south, take M1 until it becomes A1M, exit at junction 45 onto A64, and follow it for 10 miles until you reach York's ring road (A1237), which allows you to avoid driving through the city center. If you have more time, A19 from Selby is a slower and more scenic route into York.

DURHAM
AND NORTHEAST ENGLAND

Northeast England harbors some of the country's best historical sights. Go for a Roman ramble at Hadrian's Wall, a reminder that Britain was an important Roman colony 2,000 years ago. Make a pilgrimage to Holy Island, where Christianity gained its first toehold in Britain. At Durham, marvel at England's greatest Norman church, and enjoy an evensong service. At the Beamish Open-Air Museum, travel back in time to the year 1913.

Planning Your Time

For train travelers, Durham is the most convenient overnight stop in this region. If you like Roman ruins, visit Hadrian's Wall (doable with transfers, easiest Easter–Sept). The Beamish Open-Air Museum is an easy day trip from Durham (hourly bus, 45 min). If you're traveling by train, note that it's problematic to visit Durham en route to another destination, since there's no luggage storage in Durham. Either stay overnight or do Durham as a day trip from York.

By car, you can easily visit Beamish Open-Air Museum, Hadrian's Wall, Bamburgh Castle, and Holy Island. Spend a night in Durham and a night near Hadrian's Wall.

For the best quick visit, arrive in Durham by mid-afternoon in time to tour the cathedral and enjoy the evensong service (Tue–Sat at 17:15, Sun at 15:30). Sleep in Durham. Visit Beamish (25 min north of Durham by car, or 45 min via bus) the next morning before continuing on to your next destination.

Durham

Without its cathedral, Durham would hardly be noticed. But this magnificently situated cathedral is hard to miss (even if you're zooming by on the train). Seemingly happy to go nowhere, Durham sits along its river, below its castle and famous cathedral. It has a medieval, cobbled atmosphere and a scraggly peasant's indoor market just off the main square. While Durham is the home to England's third-oldest university, the town feels working-class, surrounded by recently closed coal mines, and filled with tattooed and pierced people in search of job security and a good karaoke bar. Yet Durham has a youthful vibrancy and a small-town warmth that shines—especially on sunny days, when most everyone is licking an ice-cream cone.

ORIENTATION

(area code: 0191)
As it has for a thousand years, tidy little Durham clusters everything safely under its castle, within the protective hairpin bend of the River Wear. The longest walk you'll make will be a 20-minute jaunt from the train station to the cathedral.

Tourist Information

The TI books rooms and local theater tickets, and provides train times (Mon–Sat 9:30–17:30, Sun 11:00–16:00, WC, café; 1 block north of Market Place, past St. Nicholas Church, in Gala Theatre building; tel. 0191/384-3720, www.durhamtourism.co.uk).

Arrival in Durham

From the **train station,** follow the road downhill and take the second pedestrian turnoff (within sight of railway bridge), which leads almost immediately over a bridge above the busy road called Alexander Crescent. Then take North Road into town or to the first couple of B&Bs (take Alexander Crescent to the other B&Bs). Or you can just hop on the convenient Cathedral Bus (see "Getting Around Durham," next page).

Drivers simply surrender to the wonderful Prince Bishop's parking lot (at the roundabout at the base of the old town). It's perfectly safe and inexpensive, and an elevator deposits you right in the heart of Durham (a short block from Market Place).

Helpful Hints

Internet Access: The library, across from the TI, has about 40 terminals with free Internet access (Mon–Fri 9:30–19:00, Sat

9:00–17:00, Sun 10:30–16:30, bring ID, tel. 0191/386-4003).

Tours: The TI offers 90-minute city walking tours on summer weekends (£4, schedule varies often but usually June–Sept Sat–Sun at 14:00—confirm with TI). David Butler, the town historian, gives excellent private tours (reasonable prices, tel. 0191/386-1500, dhent@dhent.fsnet.co.uk).

Harry Potter Sights: Durham Cathedral was used in the films, as were other nearby sights. For details see page 634.

Getting Around Durham

While all listed hotels, eateries, and sights are easily walkable in Durham, taxis are available to zip tired tourists to their B&Bs or back to the station (£3, wait on Market Place or on west side of Framwellgate Bridge).

If you don't feel like walking Durham's hills, hop on the convenient **Cathedral Bus** (also called Service 40) that runs between the train station and the cathedral, with stops near the North Road bus station, Millburngate, and Market Place (50p for all-day ticket, 3/hr, leaves train station Mon–Fri 7:55–17:30, Sat 9:10–17:30, Sun 9:50–16:50; last bus leaves cathedral Mon–Sat at 17:40, Sun at 17:00; tel. 0871-200-2233).

SELF-GUIDED WALK

Welcome to Durham

• *Begin at Framwellgate Bridge (which connects the train station with the center).*

Framwellgate Bridge was a wonder when it was built in the 12th century—much longer than the river is wide, and higher than seems necessary. It was designed to connect stretches of solid high ground, and avoid steep descents to the marshy river. Note how elegantly today's Silver Street (which leads toward town) slopes into the Framwellgate Bridge. (Imagine that as late as the 1970s, this people-friendly lane was congested with traffic and buses.)

• *Follow Silver Street to the town's main square.*

Durham's **Market Place** retains the same platting the Prince Bishop gave it when he moved villagers here in about 1100. Each plot of land was the same width (about 8 yards). Find today's distinctly narrow buildings (Thomas Cook, Whittard, and the optician shop)—they still fit the 800-year-old plan. The rest of the buildings fronting the square are multiples of the width of that first shop. Plots were long and skinny, maximizing the number of shops that could have a piece of the Market Place action.

Examine the square's **statues.** Coal has long been the basis of this region's economy. The statue of Neptune was part of an ill-fated attempt by a coal baron to bribe the townsfolk into embracing

The History of Durham

Durham's location, tucked inside a tight bend in the River Wear, was ideal for easy fortifications. But it wasn't settled until A.D. 995, with the arrival of St. Cuthbert's body (buried in Durham Cathedral). Shortly after that, a small church and fortification were built upon the site of today's castle and church to house the relic. The castle was a classic "motte-and-bailey" design (with the "motte," or mound, providing a lookout tower for the stockade encircling the protected area, or "bailey"). By 1100, the Prince Bishop's bailey was filled with villagers—and he wanted everyone out. This was *his* place! He provided a wider protective wall, and had the town resettle below, around today's Market Place. But this displaced the townsfolk's cows, so the Prince Bishop constructed a fine stone bridge (today's Framwellgate) that connected the new town to the land he established as grazing land over the river. The bridge had a defensive gate, with a wall circling the peninsula and the river serving as a moat.

a canal project that would make the shipment of his coal more efficient. The statue of the fancy guy on the horse is Charles Stewart Vane, the Third Marquess of Londonderry. A general in Wellington's army, he was an Irish aristocrat who married a local coal heiress. A clever and aggressive businessman, he managed to create a vast commercial empire by controlling every link in the coal business chain—mines, railroads, boats, harbors, and so on.

In the 1850s, throughout England, towns were moving their markets off squares and into Industrial Age iron-and-glass market halls. Durham was no exception, and today its **indoor market** (which faces Market Place) is a funky 19th-century delight to explore.

Do you enjoy the sparse traffic in Durham's old town? It was the first city in England to institute a "congestion fee." Look where traffic enters the old town on the downhill side of the square. The bollard (series of short posts) is up, blocking traffic Monday through Friday from 10:00–16:00. Anyone can drive in...but it costs £2 to get out. This has cut downtown traffic by more than 50 percent. Locals brag that London (which now has a similar congestion fee) was inspired by their success.

• *Head up to the cathedral along Saddler Street. On the left, you'll see a bridge.*

Central Durham

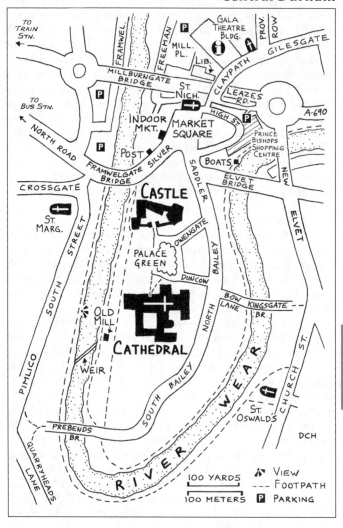

A 12th-century construction, **Elvet Bridge** led to a town market over the river. Like Framwellgate, it was very long (17 arches) to avoid river muck and steep inclines. Even today, Elvet Bridge leads to an unusually wide road—a reminder that it was once swollen to accommodate the market action. Shops lined the right-hand side of Elvet Bridge in the 12th century as they do today. An alley separated the bridge from the buildings on the left. When the bridge was widened, it met the upper stories of the buildings on the left, which became "street level."

The Scots were on the rampage in the 14th century. After their victory at Bannockburn in 1314, they pushed further south, and actually burned part of Durham. With this new threat, Durham's **city walls** were built. Since people settled within the walls, the population density soared. Soon open lanes were covered by residences, becoming tunnels (called "vennels"). A classic vennel leads to Saddlers Yard, a fine little 16th-century courtyard (immediately opposite Elvet Bridge). While these are cute today, centuries ago these were Dickensian nightmares...the filthiest of hovels.

• *Continue up Saddler Street. Between the two* Georgian Window *signs, go through the purple door to see a bit of the medieval wall incorporated into the brickwork of a newer building, and a turret from an earlier wall. Back on Saddler Street, you can see the ghost of the old wall. (It's exactly the width of the building now housing the Salvation Army.) Veer right at Owengate as you continue uphill, until you reach the Palace Green.*

The **Palace Green** was the site of the original 11th-century Saxon town, filling this green between the castle and an earlier church. Later the town made way for 12th-century Durham's defenses, which now enclose the green. With the threat presented by the Vikings, it's no wonder people found comfort in a spot like this.

The **castle** still stands—as it has for a thousand years—on its motte (man-made mound). The castle is now part of Durham University. Like Oxford and Cambridge, Durham U. is a collection of colleges scattered throughout the town. And, like Oxford and Cambridge, the town has a youthful liveliness because of its university. Look into the old courtyard from the castle gate. It traces the very first and smallest bailey. As future bishops expanded the castle, they left their coat of arms as a way of "signing" the wing they built. Because the Norman kings appointed the Prince Bishops here to rule this part of their realm, Durham was the seat of power for much of northern England. The bishops had their own army, and even minted their own coins (castle entrance by guided tour only, £5, 45 min, call ahead for schedule, tel. 0191/334-3800).

• *This walk ends at Durham's stunning **cathedral**, which is described below.*

SIGHTS AND ACTIVITIES

▲▲▲Durham's Cathedral

Built to house the much-venerated bones of St. Cuthbert from Lindisfarne, Durham's cathedral offers the best look at Norman architecture in England. ("Norman" is British for "Romanesque.") In addition to touring the cathedral and its attached sights, try to fit in an evensong service.

Cost and Hours: Entry to the cathedral itself is free, though a £4 donation is requested. You must pay to enter its several interior sights: the climbable tower (£3), relic-filled treasury (£2.50), Monk's Dormitory (£1), and boring AV show (£1). All are described next. It's open late-July–late-Aug daily 9:30–20:00; late-Aug–late-July Mon–Sat 9:30–18:00, Sun 12:30–17:30; opens daily at 7:30 for worship and prayer. Tel. 0191/386-4266, www.durhamcathedral .co.uk. A bookshop, cafeteria, and WC are tucked away in the cloisters. No photos or videos are allowed inside the cathedral.

Tours: The cathedral offers regular tours in summer. If one's already in session, you're welcome to join (£4; late-July–late-Sept Mon–Sat at 10:30, 11:00, and 14:30; also late-July–late-Aug Sat at 18:30, Sun at 17:00; call to confirm schedule, tel. 0191/386-4266).

Evensong: For a thousand years, this cradle of English Christianity has been praising God. To really experience the cathedral, go for an evensong service. Arrive early and ask to be seated in the choir. It's a spiritual Oz, as 40 boys sing psalms—a red-and-white-robed pillow of praise, raised up by the powerful pipe organ. If you're lucky and the service goes well, the organist will run a spiritual musical victory lap as the congregation breaks up (Tue–Sat at 17:15, Sun at 15:30, 1 hour, normally not sung on Mon; when choir is off on school break during mid-July–Aug, visiting choirs nearly always fill in; tel. 0191/386-4266).

◑ Self-Guided Tour: Begin your visit outside the cathedral. From the Palace Green, notice how this fortress of God stands boldly opposite the Norman keep of Durham's fortress of man.

The **exterior** of this awe-inspiring cathedral—if you look closely—has a serious skin problem. In the 1770s, as the stone was crumbling, they crudely peeled it back a few inches. The scrape marks give the cathedral a bad complexion to this day. For proof of this odd "restoration," study the masonry 10 yards to the right of the door. The L-shaped stones in the corner would normally never be found in a church like this—they only became L-shaped when the surface was cut back.

At the cathedral **door,** the big, bronze, lion-faced knocker (a replica of the 12th-century original—now in the treasury) was used by criminals seeking sanctuary (read the explanation).

Immediately inside, at the **information desk,** church attendants are standing by to happily answer questions. Ideally, follow a church tour (described above). The pamphlet, *A Short Guide to*

Durham

Durham Cathedral, is informative but dull.

Notice the **modern window** with the novel depiction of the Last Supper (above and to the left of the entry door). It was given to the church by a local department store in 1984. The shapes of the apostles represent worlds and persons of every kind, from the shadowy Judas to the brightness of Jesus. This window is a good reminder that the cathedral remains a living part of the community.

Near the info desk, the **black marble strip** on the floor was as close to the altar as women were allowed in the days when this was a Benedictine church (until 1540). Sit down (ignoring the black line) and let the fine proportions of England's best Norman—and arguably Europe's best Romanesque—nave stir you. Any frilly woodwork and stonework were added in later centuries.

The architecture of the **nave** is particularly harmonious because it was built in a mere 40 years (1093–1133). The round arches and zigzag carved decorations are textbook Norman. The church was also proto-Gothic, built by well-traveled French masons and architects who knew the latest innovations from Europe. Its stone and ribbed roof, pointed arches, and flying buttresses were revolutionary in England. Notice the clean lines and simplicity. It's not as cluttered as other churches for several reasons: Out of respect for St. Cuthbert, for centuries no one else was buried here. During Reformation times, sumptuous Catholic decor was cleaned out. And subsequent fires and wars destroyed what Protestants didn't.

Enter the **Galilee Chapel** (late Norman, from 1175) in the back of the nave. The paintings of St. Cuthbert and St. Oswald (seventh-century king of Northumbria) on the side walls of the side altar niche are rare examples of Romanesque (Norman) paintings. Facing this altar, look above to your right to see more faint paintings on the upper walls above the columns. Near the center of the chapel, the upraised tomb topped with a black slab contains the remains of the Venerable Bede, an eighth-century Christian scholar who wrote the first history of England. The Latin reads, "In this tomb are the bones of the Venerable Bede."

Back in the main church, stroll down the nave to the center, under the highest **bell tower** in Europe (218 feet). Gaze up. The ropes turn wheels upon which bells are mounted. If you're stirred by the cheery ringing of church bells, tune into the cathedral on Sunday (9:15–10:00 & 14:30–15:30) or Thursday (19:30 practice) when the resounding notes tumble merrily through the entire town.

Continuing east (all medieval churches faced east), you enter the **choir.** Monks worshipped many times a day, and the choir in the center of the church provided a cozy place to gather in this

Durham's Cathedral

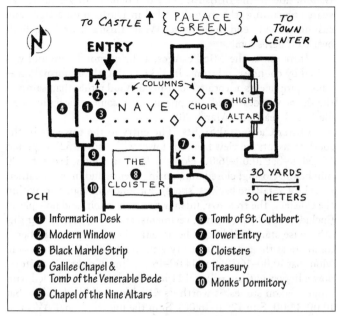

TO CASTLE ↑ { PALACE GREEN } TO TOWN CENTER

ENTRY

← COLUMNS →

2

4 **1** **3** NAVE CHOIR **6** HIGH ALTAR **5**

7

9

THE **8** CLOISTER

DCH **10**

30 YARDS
30 METERS

1 Information Desk
2 Modern Window
3 Black Marble Strip
4 Galilee Chapel &
    Tomb of the Venerable Bede
5 Chapel of the Nine Altars

6 Tomb of St. Cuthbert
7 Tower Entry
8 Cloisters
9 Treasury
10 Monks' Dormitory

vast, dark, and chilly building. Mass has been said daily here in the heart of the cathedral for 900 years. The fancy wooden chairs are from the 17th century. Behind the altar is the delicately carved stone Neville Screen from 1380 (made of Normandy stone in London, shipped to Newcastle by sea, then brought here by wagon). Until the Reformation, the niches contained statues of 107 saints. Exit the choir from the far right side (south). Look for the stained-glass window (to your right) commemorating the church's 1,000th anniversary in 1995. The colorful scenes depict England's history, from coal miners to cows to computers.

Step down behind the high altar into the east end of the church, which contains the 13th-century **Chapel of the Nine Altars.** Built later than the rest of the church, this is Gothic architecture—taller, lighter, and relatively more extravagant than the Norman nave.

Climb a few steps to the **tomb of St. Cuthbert.** An inspirational leader of the early Christian Church in north England, St. Cuthbert lived in the Lindisfarne monastery on Holy Island (100 miles north of Durham). He died in 687. Eleven years later, his body was exhumed and found to be miraculously preserved. This stoked the popularity of his shrine, and pilgrims came in growing numbers. When Vikings raided Lindisfarne in 875, the monks fled with his body (and the famous illuminated *Lindisfarne*

Durham

Gospels, now in the British Library in London). In 995, after 120 years of roaming, the monks settled in Durham on a tight and easy-to-defend bend in the River Wear. This cathedral was built over Cuthbert's tomb.

Throughout the Middle Ages, a shrine stood here and was visited by countless pilgrims. In 1539, during the Reformation—whose proponents advocated focusing on God rather than saints—the shrine was destroyed. But pilgrims still come, especially on St. Cuthbert's feast day (March 20).

Other Cathedral Sights: The entry to the **tower** is in the south transept; the view from the tower will cost you 325 steps and £3 (Mon–Sat 10:00–16:00, closes at 15:00 in winter, last entry 20 min before closing; closed Sun, during events, and in bad weather; must be 4'3" tall, no backless shoes). The following sights are within the cloisters: The **treasury,** filled with medieval bits and holy pieces (including Cuthbert's coffin, vestments, and cross), fleshes out this otherwise stark building. The actual relics from St. Cuthbert's tomb are at the far end (treasury well worth the £2.50 admission, Mon–Sat 10:00–16:30, Sun 14:00–16:30). The **Monks' Dormitory,** now a library with an original 14th-century timber roof filled with Anglo-Saxon stones, is worth its £1 admission (likely Mon–Sat 10:00–16:00, Sun 12:30–16:00). Skip the unexceptional **AV show** about St. Cuthbert in the unexceptional undercroft (£1, Mon–Sat 10:00–15:00, no showings Sun, off-season also no showings Fri, closed Dec–early-Jan).

Near the treasury, you'll find the **WCs, bookshop** (in the old kitchen), and fine **Undercroft** cafeteria (daily 10:00–16:30, tel. 0191/386-3721).

Activities

Riverside Path—For a 20-minute woodsy escape, walk Durham's riverside path from busy Framwellgate Bridge to sleepy Prebends Bridge.

Boat Cruise and Rental—Hop on the *Prince Bishop* for a relaxing one-hour narrated cruise of the river that nearly surrounds Durham (£5, Easter–Oct, for schedule call 0191/386-9525, check at TI, or go down to dock at Brown's Boat House at Elvet Bridge, just east of old town, www.princebishoprc.co.uk). Sailings vary based on weather and tides. For some exercise with the same scenery, you can rent a rowboat at the same pier (£3.50/hr per person, £10 deposit, Easter–Sept daily 10:00–18:00, last boat rental 1 hour before dusk, tel. 0191/386-3779).

Near Durham

Beamish Open-Air Museum—This huge museum, which re-creates the years 1825 and 1913 in northeast England, takes at least three hours to explore. Vintage trams and cool circa-1910 double-decker buses shuttle visitors to the four stations: Colliery Village, The Town, Pockerley Manor/Waggonway, and Home Farm. Tram routes are more plentiful than bus routes, but attendants on both are helpful and knowledgeable. Signs on the trams advertise a variety of 19th-century products, from "Borax, for washing everything" to "Murton's Reliable Travelling Trunks." This isn't a wax museum. If you touch the exhibits, they may smack you. Attendants at each stop happily explain everything. In fact, the place is only really interesting if you talk to the attendants.

Cost and Hours: £16, April–Oct daily 10:00–17:00; from Nov–March only The Town is open, Tue–Thu and Sat–Sun 10:00–16:00, closed Mon and Fri and most of Dec; check events schedule as you enter, last tickets sold 2 hours before closing, tel. 0191/370-4000, www.beamish.org.uk.

Getting There: The museum is five minutes off the A1/M1 motorway (one exit north of Durham at Chester-le-Street/Junction 63, well-signposted, 12 miles and a 25-min drive northwest of Durham). To get to Beamish from Durham, catch the #21, #X1, or #43 bus from the bus station (4–5/hr, 45 min, £4 round-trip, possible transfers at Stanley or Chester-le-Street, bus info tel. 0870-608-2608).

❍ **Self-Guided Tour:** Start with the **Colliery Village** (company town around a coal mine), with a school, a church, miners' homes, and a fascinating—if claustrophobic—20-minute tour into the Mahogany drift mine. Your guide will tell you about beams collapsing, gas exploding, and flooding; after that cheerful speech, you'll don a hard hat as you're led into the mine.

The Town is a bustling street featuring a 1913 candy shop (the chocolate room in back is worth a stop for chocolate fans), a dentist's office, a Masonic hall, a garage, a working pub (The Sun Inn, Mon–Sat 11:00–16:30, Sun 12:00–16:30), Barclays Bank, and a hardware store featuring a variety of "toilet sets" (not what you think). For lunch, try the Tea Rooms cafeteria (upstairs, daily 10:30–16:30). If the weather is good, picnic in the grassy pavilion next to the tram stop.

Pockerley Manor and the Waggonway has an 1820s manor house whose attendants have plenty to explain. Enjoy the lovely view from the gardens behind the manor, then enter through the kitchen, where they bake bread several times a week. Ask for a sample if you have a taste for tough rye. Adjacent is the re-created first-ever passenger train from 1825, which takes modern-day visitors for a spin on 1825 tracks—a hit with railway buffs. **Home Farm** is the least interesting section.

Durham

SLEEPING

B&Bs in Durham

$$$ Farnley Tower, a luxurious B&B, has 13 spacious rooms with all the comforts. The hotel is on a quiet street at the top of a hill, a 10-minute uphill hike from the town center (one Sb-£55, superior Sb-£70, Db-£80, superior Db-£90, family room-£110, some rooms have views, paying with credit card costs 2 percent extra, phones in rooms, easy parking, inviting yard, ask about evening meals at the wildly inventive Gourmet Spot restaurant, The Avenue, tel. 0191/375-0011, fax 0191/383-9694, www.farnley-tower.co.uk, enquiries@farnley-tower.co.uk, Raj and Roopal Naik).

$$ Castleview Guest House rents six airy, comfortable rooms in a classy, well-located house (Sb-£50–55, Db-£75–80, cash only, 4 Crossgate, tel. 0191/386-8852, www.castle-view.co.uk, castle_view@hotmail.com, Mike and Anne Williams).

$ The low-key **Bed & Breakfast at #12** has two simple rooms on a quiet dead-end street (small S-£25, D-£50, cash only, no sign on door, 12 The Avenue, tel. 0191/384-1020, janhanim@aol.com, Jan Metcalfe).

$ *Student Housing Open to Anyone:* **Durham Castle,** a student residence actually on the castle grounds facing the cathedral, rents rooms during the summer break (July–Sept only). Request a room in the classy old main building, or you may get one of the few bomb shelter–style modern dorm rooms (S-£29, Sb-£40, D-£51, Db-£70, fancier Db-£120–180, £30 non-refundable deposit required, elegant breakfast hall, parking-£5 on Palace Green, University College, The

Sleep Code

(£1 = about $2, country code: 44, area code: 0191)
S = Single, **D** = Double/Twin, **T** = Triple, **Q** = Quad, **b** = bathroom, **s** = shower only. You can assume credit cards are accepted unless otherwise noted.

To help you sort easily through these listings, I've divided the rooms into three categories based on the price for a standard double room with bath (during high season):

  $$$ **Higher Priced**—Most rooms £80 or more.
   $$ **Moderately Priced**—Most rooms between £50–80.
    $ **Lower Priced**—Most rooms £50 or less.

Durham Accommodations and Restaurants

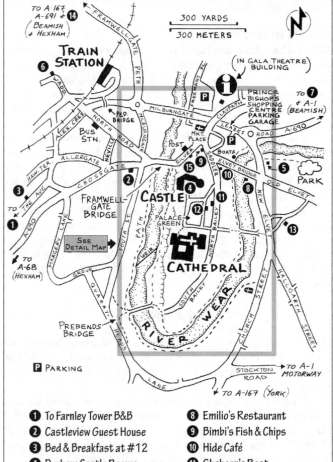

1. To Farnley Tower B&B
2. Castleview Guest House
3. Bed & Breakfast at #12
4. Durham Castle Rooms
5. Durham Marriott Hotel Royal County
6. Kingslodge Hotel & Rest.
7. To Travelodge Durham
8. Emilio's Restaurant
9. Bimbi's Fish & Chips
10. Hide Café
11. Shaheen's Rest.
12. The Almshouses
13. The Court Inn Pub
14. To Bistro 21
15. Marks & Spencer

Castle, Palace Green, tel. 0191/334-4108, fax 0191/374-7470, castle
.reception1@durham.ac.uk).

Hotels in Durham

$$$ **Durham Marriott Hotel Royal County** scatters its 150 posh,
four-star rooms among several buildings sprawling along the river
near the city center. The Leisure Club has a pool, sauna, Jacuzzi,
and fitness equipment (Db-£145, £30 less on weekends, 2 restau-
rants, bar, parking, Old Elvet, tel. 0191/386-6821, fax 0191/386-
0704, www.marriott.co.uk).

$$$ **Kingslodge Hotel & Restaurant,** a renovated lodge with
charming terraces, an attached restaurant, a pub, and a champagne
and oyster bar, is a cushy option convenient to the train station
(Sb-£80, Db-£110, includes breakfast, parking, Waddington
Street, Flass Vale, tel. 0191/370-9977, www.kingslodge.info).

$$ **Travelodge Durham**'s 57 simple rooms are in a converted
1844 train station, with the former waiting room now housing the
reception desk (Db-£55–65 but check website for £15 Supersaver
deals, breakfast-£4.50–7.50, half-mile northeast of cathedral, off
A690 at Station Lane, Gilesgate, tel. 0870-191-1636, fax 0191/386-
5461, www.travelodge.co.uk).

EATING

Durham is a university town with plenty of lively, inexpensive
eateries. Stroll down North Road, across Framwellgate Bridge,
through Market Place, and up Saddler Street, and consider these
places.

Emilio's, just over Elvet Bridge on the other side of town, is
perhaps the most popular Italian restaurant in Durham, with £8–9
pizzas and pastas in an inviting setting (Mon–Fri 11:30–14:30 &
17:30–22:30, Sat 11:30–22:30, Sun 11:30–21:00, even cheaper dur-
ing 17:30 happy hour, 96 Elvet Bridge, tel. 0191/384-0096).

Bimbi's, on Market Place, is a standby for fish-and-chips
(Mon–Sat 11:00–18:30, Sun 12:00–18:30).

Saddler Street, leading from Market Place up to the cathe-
dral, is lined with eateries. The hip **Hide Café,** with youthful,
jazz-filled ambience, serves the best modern continental cuisine in
the old town (£8–10 meals, £15 gourmet evening plates, good fish,
meals served daily 9:30–21:30, bar open until 24:00, reservations
smart, 39 Saddler Street, tel. 0191/384-1999).

Shaheen's is the place for good Indian cuisine (£6–10 meals,
Tue–Sun 18:00–23:30, closed Mon, 48 North Bailey Street, just
past turnoff to cathedral, tel. 0191/386-0960).

The Almshouses, on the Palace Green across from the cathe-
dral, serves tasty, light meals in a cheap cafeteria setting (£6 plates,

daily July–Sept 9:00–20:00, Oct–June 9:00–17:00, tel. 0191/386-1054).

The Court Inn, on the outskirts of town, is a local favorite for traditional pub grub (£7–10 bar meals, daily 11:00–22:30, 5-min walk east of old town over Elvet Bridge, Court Lane, tel. 0191/384-7350).

Bistro 21, with modern French/Mediterranean fare and good seafood, works well for drivers looking for a nontouristy splurge (£25–35 meals, Mon–Sat 12:00–14:00 & 19:00–22:00, closed Sun, 3 miles north of town, Aykley Heads, tel. 0191/384-4354).

Supermarket: **Marks & Spencer** is in the old town, just off the main square (Mon–Sat 9:00–18:00, Sun 11:00–17:00, on Silver Street, across from post office). You can **picnic** on the benches and grass outside the cathedral entrance (but not on the Palace Green, unless the park police have gone home).

TRANSPORTATION CONNECTIONS

From Durham by Train to: York (1–3/hr, 45–60 min), **London** (hourly, 3 hrs), **Hadrian's Wall** (take train to Newcastle—1–4/hr, 15 min, then a train/bus combination to Hadrian's Wall; see "Hadrian's Wall," below), **Edinburgh** (nearly hourly, 2 hrs, less frequent in winter), **Bristol** (near Bath, 9/day, 5 hrs). Train info: tel. 08457-484-950.

Hadrian's Wall

This is one of England's most thought-provoking sights. In about A.D. 130, during the reign of Emperor Hadrian, the Romans built this great stone wall. Its actual purpose is still debated. While Rome ruled Britain for 400 years, it never quite ruled its people. The wall may have been used for any number of reasons: to define the northern edge of the empire, to protect Roman Britain from invading Scottish clans (or at least cut down on pesky border raids), to monitor the movement of people, or to simply give an otherwise bored army something to do. (Emperors understood that nothing's more dangerous than a bored army.) Stretching

75 miles coast to coast across the narrowest stretch of northern England, it was built and defended by nearly 20,000 troops. The wall was flanked by ditches, and a military road lies on the south

Durham and Northeast England

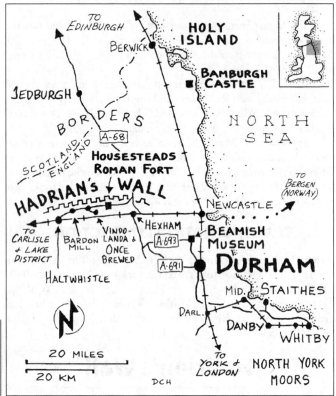

side. At every mile of the wall, a castle guards a gate, and two turrets stand between each castle. The mile castles are numbered. (Eighty of them cover the 75 miles, because a Roman mile was slightly shorter than our mile.)

Today, several chunks of the wall, ruined forts, and museums thrill history buffs. About a dozen Roman sites cling along the wall's route; the best are Housesteads Roman Fort and Vindolanda. Housesteads shows you where the Romans lived; Vindolanda's museum shows you how they lived. The Hadrian's Wall National Trail runs 84 miles, following the wall's route from coast to coast (for details, see www.nationaltrail.co.uk/HadriansWall).

SIGHTS AND ACTIVITIES

▲▲Housesteads Roman Fort—With its tiny museum, powerful scenery, and the best-preserved segment of the wall, this is your best single stop at Hadrian's Wall. All Roman forts were the same rectangular shape and design, containing a commander's headquarters, barracks, and latrines (lower end); this fort even has a hospital. The fort was built right up to the wall, which is on the far side (£4.10 for site and museum, daily April–Sept 10:00–18:00, Oct–March closes at 16:00 or dusk, parking-£2, tel. 01434/344-363, www.english-heritage.org.uk/housesteads). At the car park are WCs, a snack bar, and a gift shop. You can leave your luggage at the gift shop, but confirm its closing hours. From the car park, it's a half-mile, mostly uphill walk to the entrance of the minuscule museum and sprawling fort.

▲▲**Hiking the Wall**—From Housesteads, hike west along the wall speaking Latin. For a good, craggy, three-mile walk along the wall, hike between Housesteads and Steel Rigg. You'll pass a castle sitting in a nick in a crag (milecastle #39, called Castle Nick). There's a parking lot near Steel Rigg (take the little road up from Twice Brewed Pub).

▲**Vindolanda**—This larger Roman fort (which actually predates Hadrian's Wall by 40 years) and museum are just south of the wall. Although Housesteads has better ruins and the wall, Vindolanda has the better museum, revealing intimate details of Roman life. It's an active dig—April through September, you'll see the work in progress. Eight forts were built on this spot. The Romans, by carefully sealing the foundations from each successive fort, left modern-day archaeologists with seven yards of remarkably well-preserved artifacts to excavate: keys, coins, brooches, scales, pottery, glass, tools, leather shoes, bits of cloth, and even a wig. Impressive examples of early Roman writing were recently discovered here. While the actual letters—written on thin pieces of wood—are in London's British Museum, see the interesting video here and read the translations, including the first known example of a woman writing to a woman (an invitation to a birthday party). These varied letters, about parties held, money owed, and sympathy shared, bring Romans to life in a way that stones alone can't.

From the parking lot, you'll pay at the entrance, then walk 500 yards of grassy parkland decorated by the foundation stones of the Roman fort and a full-size replica chunk of the wall. At the far side of the site are the museum, gift shop, and cafeteria.

Cost and Hours: £5, £7.50 combo-ticket includes Roman Army Museum (see below), daily April–Sept 10:00–18:00, mid-Feb–March and Oct–Nov 10:00–17:00, last entry 45 min before closing, closed Dec–mid-Feb, can leave luggage at entrance, tel. 01434/344-277, www.vindolanda.com.

Roman Army Museum—This museum, a few miles farther west at Greenhead, is redundant if you've seen Vindolanda (£4, or buy £7.50 combo-ticket—see above, same hours as Vindolanda, tel. 016977/47485).

SLEEPING AND EATING

(£1 = about $2, country code: 44)

Between Haltwhistle and Hexham
(area code: 01434)

$$ **Montcoffer,** a restored country home in Bardon Mill, is decorated with statues, old enameled advertising signs, and other artifacts collected by owner John McGrellis and his wife, Dehlia, whose textile art is displayed in and around your room (Sb-£50, Db-£74, includes hearty breakfasts, 2 miles from Vindolanda, Bardon Mill, tel. 01434/344-138, fax 01434/344-730, www.montcoffer.co.uk, john-dehlia@talk21.com).

$$ **High Reins** offers three rooms in a stone house built by a shipping tycoon in the 1920s (Sb-£40, Db-£64, cash only, ground-floor bedrooms, lounge, 1 mile west of train station on the western outskirts of Hexham, Leazes Lane, tel. 01434/603-590, www.highreins.co.uk, pwalton@highreins.co.uk, Jan and Peter Walton).

$$ **The Twice Brewed Inn,** two miles west of Housesteads and a half-mile from the wall, rents rooms and serves real ales and decent pub grub all day (S-£28, D-£50, Db-£65–75, Internet access, tel. 01434/344-534, www.twicebrewedinn.co.uk, info@twicebrewedinn.co.uk).

$$ **West Wharmley Farm** rents two rooms in a friendly farmhouse about seven miles from the wall near Hexham (Sb-£40, Db-£60, cash only, family deals, lounge, off A69 between Hexham and Haydon Bridge, follow signs, tel. 01434/674-227, Ros Johnson).

$ **Craws Nest B&B** offers three rooms in a remodeled farmhouse a quarter-mile from the wall (D-£48, cash only, on B6318 road 500 yards from Once Brewed TI, Bardon Mill, tel. 01434/344-348). The nearby **Milecastle Inn** cooks up all sorts of exotic game and offers the best dinner around, according to hungry national park rangers (daily 12:00–20:30, North Road, tel. 01434/321-372).

$ **Once Brewed Youth Hostel** is a comfortable place near The Twice Brewed Inn (£15/bed with sheets in 4- to 8-bed room, £3 extra for non-members, breakfast-£4.50, packed lunch-£5, dinner-£9, reception open daily 8:00–10:00 & 14:00–22:00, Military Road, Bardon Mill, tel. 01434/344-360, fax 01434/344-045, www.yha.org.uk, oncebrewed@yha.org.uk). The Hadrian's Wall bus #AD 122 stops here several times a day.

In Haltwhistle
(area code: 01434)
$$ Ashcroft Guest House, a former vicarage, is 400 yards from the Haltwhistle train station. The family-run B&B has seven rooms, pleasant gardens, and views from the comfy lounge (Sb-£35, Db-£70, four-poster Db-£80, ask about family deals and two-bedroom suite, 1.5 miles from the wall, Lanty's Lonnen, tel. 01434/320-213, fax 01434/321-641, www.ashcroftguesthouse.co.uk, ashcroft.1 @btconnect.com, Geoff and Christine James).

Near Carlisle
(area code: 01228)
$$ Bessiestown Farm Country Guest House, located northwest of the Hadrian sights, is convenient for drivers connecting the Lake District and Scotland. It's a quiet and soothing stop in the middle of sheep pastures (Sb-£47.50, Db-£75, family room-£90, fancier suites-£120–140, discounts for 3-night stays; in Catlowdy, midway between Gretna Green and Hadrian's Wall just north of Carlisle; tel. 01228/577-219, fax 01228/577-019, www.bessiestown .co.uk, info@bessiestown.co.uk, Margaret Sisson).

TRANSPORTATION CONNECTIONS

By Car: Take B6318; it parallels the wall and passes several viewpoints, minor sights, and "severe dips." (If there's a certified nerd or bozo in the car, these road signs add a lot to a photo portrait.) Buy a good map locally to help you explore this interesting area more easily and thoroughly.

By Train and Bus: A train/bus combination (which operates with greatest frequency Easter–Sept) delivers you to the wall. Newcastle and Carlisle are the gateways to the **train** route that parallels the wall (Mon–Sat 8:20–18:20 every 30 min to Hexham, every hour to Haltwhistle, Sun hourly 9:00–18:30; from Newcastle, it's 30 min to Hexham, 20 more min to Haltwhistle; train info tel. 08457-484-950). But the train only gets you *near* the wall.

During peak season (generally Easter–Sept), take **Hadrian's Wall bus #AD 122** to get to the wall and all the Roman sights. Purists can take this bus for the entire length of the wall (4 hours and £6 if you make the entire journey in one trip). This bus leaves Newcastle Central Train Station daily at 9:00 and 14:00. It also runs with regularity from Carlisle (6 buses/day from 7:35–16:25), which has frequent train service from both the north and the south. If you're heading from Newcastle and miss the morning bus, get off the train at either Hexham or Haltwhistle to catch it (6 buses/day in each direction, late-May–late-Sept; Hexham–Housesteads 30 min, Housesteads–Vindolanda 10 min, Vindolanda–Haltwhistle 20 min). For those spending the night, this bus also stops at the Once Brewed Youth Hostel, which is less than a five-minute walk from the Craws Nest B&B and The Twice Brewed Inn.

At Newcastle's train station, ask about the Hadrian's Wall bus schedule at the info desk (the Newcastle TI is a 10-min walk from the station, but you can call them for info at tel. 0191-277-8000). You can store luggage at the station.

If you're coming into Carlisle, you can get the same schedule at the information racks next to the entrance. You can also call Haltwhistle's helpful **TI** for schedule information (Easter–Oct Mon–Sat 9:30–13:00 & 14:00–17:00, Sun 13:00–17:00; Nov–Easter Mon–Sat 9:30–12:00 & 13:00–15:30, closed Sun; tel. 01434/322-002, www.hadrians-wall.org).

To visit Housesteads off-season (Oct–Easter), take a train to Haltwhistle and catch a taxi (taxi services: Haltwhistle tel. 01434/322-556, Sprouls tel. 01434/321-064, Turnbull tel. 01434/320-105, one-way-£8; arrange for return pickup or have museum staff call a taxi; many taxis are contracted to pick up school kids between 8:00–9:00 and 15:00–16:00, confirm their availability if you need a cab during this time). If you're staying on the wall, your B&B host can arrange a taxi.

By Guided Tour: If you're coming from Keswick and you don't have a car, consider taking a Touchstone Tour; Lucy Harrison can motor you through the Lake District to Hadrian's Wall, then drop you off at a nearby train station (see page 329).

Holy Island and Bamburgh Castle

This area is only worthwhile for those with a car.

▲Holy Island

Twelve hundred years ago, this "Holy Island" was Christianity's toehold on England. It was the home of St. Cuthbert. We know it today for the *Lindisfarne Gospels*, decorated by monks in the seventh century with some of the finest art from Europe's "Dark Ages" (now in the British Museum). It's a pleasant visit—a quiet town with a striking castle (not worth touring) and an evocative priory.

Lindisfarne Priory: The museum in the priory is tiny but instructive. It's adjacent to the ruined abbey (£4; mid-March–Sept daily 9:30–17:00; Oct daily 9:30–16:00; Nov–Jan Mon and Sat–Sun 10:00–14:00, closed Tue–Fri; Feb–mid-March daily 10:00–16:00; tel. 01289/389-200, www.english-heritage.org.uk /LindisfarnePriory). You can wander the abbey grounds and graveyard, and pop into the church without paying.

Holy Island is reached by a two-mile causeway that's cut off daily by high tides. Tidal charts are posted, warning you when this holy place becomes Holy Island—and you become stranded.

For TI and tide information, call the **Berwick TI** at tel. 01289/330-733 (unpredictable hours but generally May–Sept Mon–Sat 10:00–17:00, Sun 11:00–15:00, off-season 10:00–16:00, call to confirm). Park at the pay-and-display lot and walk five minutes into the village.

▲▲Bamburgh Castle

About 10 miles south of Holy Island, this grand castle dominates the Northumbrian countryside and overlooks Britain's loveliest beach. The place was bought and passionately refurbished by Lord Armstrong, a Ted Turner–like industrialist and engineer in the 1890s. Its interior, lined with well-described history, feels lived-in because it still is—with Armstrong family portraits and aristocratic-yet-homey knickknacks hanging everywhere. Take advantage of the talkative guides posted throughout the castle. The included **Armstrong Museum** features the inventions of the industrialist family that has owned the castle through modern times (£6.50, daily 11:00–17:00, last entry at 16:30, closed Nov–mid-March, tel. 01668/214-515, www.bamburghcastle.com). Rolling dunes crisscrossed by walking paths lead to a vast sandy beach and lots of families on holiday.

Holy Island

WALES

WALES

Wales is not England—but its uniqueness, a crusty yet poetic vitality, makes it more than worth a visit. For the tourist, Wales is a land of stout castles, salty harbors, chummy community choirs, slate-roofed villages, and a landscape of mountains, moors, and lush green fields dotted with sheep. But the way you'll immediately know that you're not in England anymore is when you hear a local speak Welsh (or Cymraeg, pronounced kum-RAH-ig).

Despite centuries of English imperialism, the Welsh language remains alive and well, unlike Gaelic in Scotland or Cornish in Cornwall—which survive only on the fringe or on life-support. Today, the Welsh language and those who speak it are protected by law, the country is officially bilingual, and road signs always display both names (e.g., Cardiff/Caerdydd). Though everyone in Wales speaks English, one in five can also speak the native tongue. In schools, it's either the first or the required second language. In the northwest, well over half the population is fluent in Welsh, and uses it in everyday life. Listen in.

Welsh is a Celtic language (like Irish or Scotland's Gaelic) and most closely related to the Breton language in western France. Most certainly *not* a dialect of English, Welsh sounds to foreign ears like the Middle Earth languages from *The Lord of the Rings* films. One of Europe's oldest, Welsh has been a written language since about A.D. 600, and was spoken 300 years before French or German.

Though English has been the dominant language in Wales for many years (and most newspapers and media are in English), the Welsh people cherish their linguistic heritage as something that sets them apart. In fact, a line of the Welsh national anthem goes, "Oh, may the old language survive!"

Speaking Welsh

Welsh pronunciation is tricky. The common "ll" combination sounds roughly like "tl" (pronounced as if you were ready to make an "l" sound and then blew it out). As in Scotland, "ch" is a soft, guttural k, pronounced in the back of the throat. The Welsh "dd" sounds like the English "th," f = v, ff = f, w = the "u" in "push," y = i. Non-Welsh people often make the mistake of trying to say a long Welsh name too fast, and inevitably trip themselves up. A local tipped me off: Slow down and say each syllable separately, and it'll come out right. For example, Llangollen is tlang-GOT-hlen.

Although there's no need to learn any Welsh (since everyone also speaks English), make friends and impress the locals by learning a few polite phrases:

Hello	**Helo**	hee-LOH
Goodbye	**Hwyl**	hoo-il
Please	**Os gwelwch yn dda**	os GWELL-uck UN thah
Thank you	**Diolch**	dee-olkh
Wales	**Cymru**	KUM-ree
England	**Lloegr**	TLOY-ger

In a pub, toast the guy who just bought your drink with *Diolch* and *Yeach-hid dah* (YECH-id dah, "Good health to you").

The country of Wales is the size of Massachusetts. It's located on a peninsula on the west coast of the isle of Britain, facing the Irish Sea. Longer than it is wide (170 miles by 60 miles), it's shaped somewhat like a miniature Britain. The north is mountainous, rural, and sparsely populated. The south consists of plains and coastline, where two-thirds of the people live (including the capital, Cardiff, pop. 320,000). The country has 750 miles of scenic, windswept coastline and is capped by Mount Snowdon—at 3,560 feet, taller than any mountain in England.

Less urbanized than England, Wales consists of miles of green land where sheep graze (because the soil is too poor for crops). Wales, which has a weaker economy than England, is becoming a weekend destination for English drinkers who pour over the border to drink the cheap beer, before stumbling home on Sunday. This means Welsh towns can be surprisingly rowdy on Saturday nights.

Wales' three million people are mostly white and Christian (Presbyterian, Anglican, or Catholic). Like their UK counterparts, they enjoy "football" (soccer)—but rugby is the unofficial Welsh sport, more popular in Wales than in any country outside of New Zealand. Other sports are cricket and snooker (similar to billiards).

Culturally, Wales is "a land of poets and singers"—or so says the national anthem. From the myths of Merlin and King Arthur to the poetry of Dylan Thomas (1914–1953), Wales has a long literary tradition. In music, the country nourishes its traditional Celtic folk music (especially the harp), and exports popular singers such as Tom Jones, Charlotte Church, and Jem.

The Welsh love their choirs. Every town has a choir (men's or mixed) that practices weekly. Visitors are usually welcome to observe, and very often they follow the choir down to the pub afterwards for a good old-fashioned, beer-lubricated sing-along. Take in a weekly choir practice at one of the following towns in North Wales (note that some towns have more than one choir, and schedules are subject to change—confirm the schedule with a local TI or your B&B before making the trip): **Ruthin** (mixed choir at Tabernacle Church, Thu 20:00–21:30 except Aug), **Llangollen** (men's choir Fri at 19:30 at Hand Hotel, 21:00 pub singsong afterward, tel. 01978/860-303), **Denbigh** (men's choir Tue 19:30 and Thu 20:00), **Llandudno** (£4 concerts Tue 20:00 in summer, near Conwy), and **Caernarfon** (Tue 19:45–21:30 except Aug, at the Galeri convention center at Victoria Dock). Additionally, many of these groups regularly perform concerts—inquire locally for the latest schedule.

Wales has some traditional foods worth looking for, particularly lamb dishes and leek soup *(cawl)*. In fact, the national symbol is the leek, ever since medieval warriors—who wore the vegetable on their helmets in battle—saved the land from Saxon invaders. Cheese on toast is known as "Welsh rarebit." Cockles and seaweed bread were once common breakfast items—but don't expect your hotel to serve them.

The Welsh flag features a red dragon on a field of green and white. The dragon has been a symbol of Wales since at least the ninth century (maybe even from Roman days). According to legend, King Arthur's men carried the dragon flag into battle.

Welsh history stretches back into the mists of prehistoric Britain. The original Celtic tribes were conquered by the Romans, who built forts and cities, and (later) introduced Christianity. As Rome fell, Saxon tribes like the Angles from Germany conquered "Angle-land" (England) but failed to penetrate Wales. Brave Welsh warriors, mountainous terrain, and the 150-mile man-made ditch-and-wall known as Offa's Dyke helped preserve the

Wales

country's unique Celtic/Roman heritage. In 1216, Wales' medieval kingdoms unified under Llywelyn Fawr ("the Great").

This brief unification ended in 1282, however, when King Edward I of England invaded and conquered, forever ending  Wales' sovereignty. To solidify his hold on the country, Edward built a string of castles (at Caernarfon, Conwy, and many other places—see sidebar on page 420). He then named his son and successor the "Prince of Wales," starting the tradition (which continues to today's Prince Charles) of England's heir to the throne bearing that ceremonial title. Despite an unsuccessful rebellion in 1400, led by Owen Glendower (Owain Glyndwr), Wales has remained under English rule since 1282. In 1535, the annexation was formalized under Henry VIII.

By the 19th century, Welsh coal and iron stoked the engines of Britain's Industrial Revolution, and its slate was exported to shingle roofs throughout Europe. The stereotype of the Welsh as poor, grimy-faced miners continued into the 20th century. They began the slow transition from mining, factories, and sheep-farming to the service-and-software economy of the global world.

In recent decades, the Welsh have consciously tried to preserve their local traditions and language. In 1999, Wales was granted its own parliament, the National Assembly, with powers to distribute the national budget. Though still ruled by the UK government in London, Wales now has a measure of independence and self-rule.

I've focused my coverage of Wales on the north, which has the highest concentration of castles, natural beauty, and attractions. A few South Wales sights that are convenient to visit from Bath are covered in the Near Bath chapter, beginning on page 227.

Try to fit a rare bit of Welsh sights into your itinerary. Clamber over a castle, eat a leek, count sheep in a field, catch a rugby match, or share a pint of bitter with a baritone. Open your ears to the sound of words as old as the legendary King Arthur. "May the old language survive!"

NORTH WALES

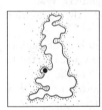

Wales' top historical, cultural, and natural wonders are found in the north part of the country. From towering Mount Snowdon to lush forests to desolate moor country, North Wales is a poem written in landscape. For sightseeing thrills and diversity, North Wales is Britain's most interesting slice of the Celtic crescent. But be careful not to be waylaid by the many gimmicky sights and bogus "best of" lists. The region's economy is poor, and they're wringing every possible pound out of the tourist trade. Sort carefully through your options.

Planning Your Time

On a three-week Britain trip, give North Wales two nights and a day. It'll give you mighty castles, a giant slate mine, and some of Britain's most beautiful scenery. Many visitors are charmed and decide to stay an extra day.

By Public Transportation: Use Conwy as a home base, and skip Ruthin. From Conwy, you can get around Snowdonia and Caernarfon by bus, train, or private driving tour (see "Getting Around North Wales," below).

By Car: Drivers interested in a medieval banquet should set up in Ruthin and do this ambitious loop: 9:00–Drive over Llanberis mountain pass to Caernarfon (with possible short stops in Trefriw Woolen Mills, Betws-y-Coed, Pen Y Gwryd Hotel Pub, and Llanberis); 12:00–Caernarfon Castle (catch the noon tour and 13:00 movie in Eagle Tower, and climb to the top for the view); 13:30-Browse through Caernarfon town and have lunch; 14:30–Drive the scenic road (A4085) to Blaenau Ffestiniog; 15:30–Tour Llechwedd Slate Mine; 17:30–Drive home to Ruthin;

North Wales

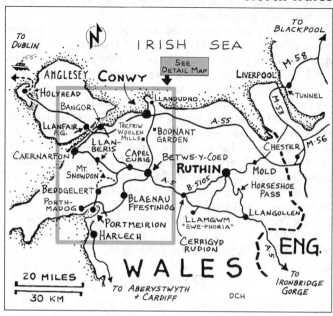

19:00—Arrive home; 19:45—Medieval banquet at castle (if you didn't already do it on the night of your arrival). For all the details, see "One-Day North Wales Blitz Tour from Ruthin" at the end of this chapter.

With a second day, slow down and take the train up Mount Snowdon. With more time and a desire to hike, consider using the mountain village of Beddgelert as your base.

If you have no interest in the castle banquet, skip Ruthin and shorten your drive time by spending two nights in Conwy or Beddgelert.

Getting Around North Wales

By Public Transportation: North Wales (except Ruthin) is surprisingly well-covered by a combination of buses and trains (though allow ample time if you want to visit several destinations).

A main **train** line runs along the north coast from Chester to Holyhead via Llandudno Junction, Conwy, and Bangor, with hourly departures. From Llandudno Junction, the Conwy Valley line goes scenically south to Conwy, Betws-y-Coed, and Blaenau Ffestiniog (5/day, 3/day on Sun).

Public **buses** (run by various companies) pick up where the trains leave off. Get the *Gwynedd Public Transport Guide* at any local TI. Certain bus lines—dubbed "Sherpa" routes (the bus numbers begin with #S)—circle Snowdonia National Park with the needs of hikers in mind.

Schedules get sparse on Sundays; plan ahead and confirm times carefully at local TIs and bus and train stations. For any questions about public transportation, call the Wales Travel Line at tel. 0870-608-2608, or check www.traveline-cymru.info.

Your choices for money-saving public-transportation **passes** are confusing. The Red Rover Ticket—the simplest and probably the best bet for most travelers—covers all buses west of Llandudno (£5.50/day, buy from driver). The £4 Snowdon Sherpa Day Ticket covers select buses that traverse the national park—but not connections between the park and Caernarfon or Conwy, so it's typically a worse deal than the Red Rover. The Tocyn Taith covers trains and certain buses within a complex zone system (£6-20/day, depending on how many zones you need; buy on bus or train).

By Private Tour: Mari Roberts does driving tours of the area out of Ruthin, but will happily pick you up in Conwy (£120/day, tel. 01824/702-713, mariroberts@yahoo.co.uk).

Ruthin

Ruthin (RITH-in; "Rhuthun" in Welsh) is a low-key market town whose charm is in its ordinary Welshness. The people are the sights, and admission is free if you start the conversation. The market square, castle, TI, bus station, and in-town accommodations are all within five blocks of each other. Ruthin is Welsh as can be, makes a handy base for drivers doing North Wales, and serves up an interesting medieval banquet.

ORIENTATION

Ruthin (pop. 5,000) is situated atop a gentle hill surrounded by undulating meadows. Simple streets branch out from the central roundabout (at the former medieval marketplace, St. Peter's Square) like spokes on a wheel.

Tourist Information

Ruthin's TI closed in 2007 to make way for the renovation of its former home, the crafts center on the northern edge of the town center (across from the Tesco megamarket). It may reopen there or

North Wales

Ruthin

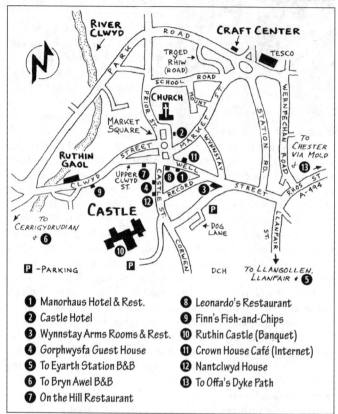

1. Manorhaus Hotel & Rest.
2. Castle Hotel
3. Wynnstay Arms Rooms & Rest.
4. Gorphwysfa Guest House
5. To Eyarth Station B&B
6. To Bryn Awel B&B
7. On the Hill Restaurant
8. Leonardo's Restaurant
9. Finn's Fish-and-Chips
10. Ruthin Castle (Banquet)
11. Crown House Café (Internet)
12. Nantclwyd House
13. To Offa's Dyke Path

somewhere else in 2008—inquire locally. If Ruthin lacks its own TI, the nearest TI is in Llangollen (see page 414).

Internet Access: You'll find it at Crown House Café, which also serves up drinks and thoughtfully prepared light lunches in an inviting indoor-or-out ambience (Internet-£3/hr, £3 sandwiches, Mon 9:00–16:00, Tue–Fri 9:00–17:00, Sat 9:30–16:00, closed Sun, Well Street, tel. 01824/704-516).

SIGHTS AND ACTIVITIES

▲▲**Ruthin Castle Welsh Medieval Banquet**—English, Scottish, Irish, and Welsh medieval banquets are all variations on the same touristy theme. This one, while growing more tired and tacky each year, remains fun and more culturally justifiable (if that's necessary) than most. The hefty £36-per-person price tag stings slightly less when you consider that you're paying both for a huge, good

meal and for an evening of entertainment.

You'll be greeted with a chunk of bread dipped in salt, which, the maiden explains, will "guarantee your safety." Your medieval master of ceremonies then seats you, and the candlelit evening of food, drink, and music rolls gaily on. You'll enjoy harp music, angelic singing, jokey stories and poems, and lots of other entertainment. With fanfare (and historical explanation), wenches serve mead, spiced wine, and four hearty traditional courses (pace yourself). Drink from a pewter goblet, wear a bib, and eat with your fingers and a dagger. Food and mead are unlimited—just ask for more. The hardworking actors—who go for it with gusto, and are really quite talented—kick up their energy even more if the audience reacts loudly. For the most entertaining experience, don't hesitate to clap, holler, stamp your feet, or pound the table. Yes, I know it's cheesy—but just enjoy it and go along for the ride (starts at 19:45, lasts about 2.5 hours, runs 2–5 nights per week year-round depending upon demand—most likely on weekends; vegetarian options, non-smoking, call for reservations; easy doorstep parking, down Castle Street from town square, tel. 01824/703-435 or, after hours, the hotel at tel. 01824/702-664). Ask to be seated with other readers of this book to avoid being stuck amidst a dreary tour group.

▲**Ruthin Gaol**—Get a glimpse into crime and punishment in 17th- to early 20th-century Wales in this 100-cell prison. Explore the "dark" and condemned cells, give the dreaded hand-crank a whirl, and learn about the men, women, and children who did time here before the prison closed in 1916. The included audioguide—partly narrated by a jovial "prisoner" named Will—is very good, informative, and engaging. You'll find out why prison kitchens came with a cat, why the bathtubs had a severe case of ring-around-the-tub, how they got prisoners to sit still for their mug shots (and why these photos often included the prisoners' hands), and why

the prison was renovated into the "panopticon" style in the late 19th century (£3.50, family-£10, mid-Feb–Oct daily 10:00–17:00, Nov–mid-Feb Sat–Sun and school holidays only 10:00–17:00, last entry 1 hour before closing, Clwyd Street, tel. 01824/708-281, www.ruthingaol.co.uk).

Nantclwyd House—This Elizabethan-era "oldest house in Ruthin"—a white-and-brown half-timbered house between the castle and the market square—has recently undergone a £600,000 renovation (funded partly by the EU) to convert it into a museum. It will likely be open in 2008, giving visitors a peek into 17th-century Wales. Inquire locally for the latest information.

Walks—For a scenic and interesting one-hour walk, try the Offa's Dyke Path to Moel Famau (the "Jubilee Tower," a 200-year-old war memorial on a peak overlooking stark moorlands). The trailhead is a 10-minute drive east of Ruthin on A494.

▲▲**Welsh Choir**—The mixed choir performs weekly at the Tabernacle Church Chapel (Thu 20:00–21:30 except Aug, tel. 01824/703-757).

SLEEPING

(area code: 01824)
For cheap sleeps, you'll have to stay at the youth hostels in Conwy or Caernarfon. Or, if you're driving, keep an eye out for rustic hostel-like "bunkhouses" that dot the North Wales countryside.

In Ruthin

$$$ Manorhaus rents the classiest rooms in Ruthin. The eight rooms are impeccably appointed with artsy-contemporary decor, and the halls serve as gallery space for local artists. Guests enjoy use of the sauna, steam room, fitness room, library, and mini-cinema in the cellar (Sb-£70–90, "compact" Db with lower ceilings-£95, standard Db-£105, superior Db-£125, pricier suites also available, free Wi-Fi, recommended restaurant—see listing on page 413, Well Street, tel. 01824/704-830, fax 01824/707-333, www.manorhaus.com, post@manorhaus.com).

$$$ The **Castle Hotel,** not to be confused with the hotel at Ruthin Castle, is a modern but faded 18-room hotel on the town square (Sb-£50, Db-£100, family suites-£120–129, deals on website, front rooms are larger and overlook the square, back rooms are quieter—especially on weekends, non-smoking rooms, 4 uneven funhouse floors with no elevator, St. Peter's Square, tel. 01824/702-479, fax 01824/703-488, www.castle-hotel-ruthin.co.uk, info@castle-hotel-ruthin.co.uk).

$$$ Wynnstay Arms is a pub renting six nicely updated rooms upstairs. As it's a dining pub rather than a rowdy drinking pub, noise isn't much of a problem (Sb-£45–50, Db-£65–75, Wall Street, tel. 01824/703-147, www.wynnstayarms.com, reservations@wynnstayarms.wanadoo.co.uk).

$$ Gorphwysfa Guest House ("Resting Place") is in a cozy 16th-century Tudor townhouse between the castle and the town

North Wales

Sleep Code

(£1 = about $2, country code: 44)
S = Single, **D** = Double/Twin, **T** = Triple, **Q** = Quad, **b** = bathroom,
s = shower only. You can assume credit cards are accepted
unless otherwise noted. Few of my accommodations in North
Wales have elevators.

To help you sort easily through these listings, I've divided
the rooms into three categories based on the price for a standard double room with bath:

$$$ **Higher Priced**—Most rooms £65 or more.
 $$ **Moderately Priced**—Most rooms between £45–65.
  $ **Lower Priced**—Most rooms £45 or less.

square, next door to Ruthin's oldest house. The three rooms are
huge, comfortable, and modern, while the public spaces are grand
and Old World—with wattle-and-daub construction, a library, a
grand piano, and a breakfast room with a gigantic fireplace (Db-
£55, Tb-£65, Qb-£75, cash only, 8a Castle Street, tel. 01824/707-
529, marg@gorphwysfa.fsnet.co.uk, Margaret O'Riain).

Near Ruthin

These places, just outside of town, are better for drivers.

$$$ Eyarth Station, an old railway station converted to a
country guest house, rents six rooms in the scenic Vale of Clwyd
about a mile outside Ruthin. Jan loves to dole out travel advice and
can suggest one-day driving routes for seeing North Wales (Sb-£45,
Db-£70, country supper-£16—request in advance, non-smoking,
closed for 2 months in winter, beautiful sunroom for breakfast and
dinner, swimming pool, Llanfair D.C., tel. 01824/703-643, www
.eyarthstation.co.uk, stay@eyarthstation.com).

$$ Bryn Awel, a traditional and charming farmhouse B&B
with two rooms and a paradise garden, is run by chatty Beryl and
John Jones in the hamlet of Bontuchel, just outside of Ruthin.
Beryl, a prizewinning quilter, is helpful with travel tips and key
Welsh words (Db-£52, 2-night minimum, use credit card for
deposit but must pay in cash, non-smoking, parking, Bontuchel,
tel. 01824/702-481, beryljjones@msn.com). From Ruthin, take
A494 (toward Bala) past the Ruthin Gaol, then the B5105/
Cerrigydrudion road. Turn right after the little white church, at
the *Bontuchel/Cyffylliog* sign. Look for the B&B sign on the right,
1.8 fragrant miles down a narrow road.

North Wales

EATING

On the Hill serves hearty £3–6 lunches and £10–15 dinners—mostly made with fresh local ingredients—to an enthusiastic crowd. The Old World decor complements the good cuisine (Tue–Sat 11:45–13:45 & 18:00–20:30, closed Sun–Mon, 1 Upper Clwyd Street, tel. 01824/707-736).

The **Wynnstay Arms** pub on Well Street, two blocks below the main square, has two different restaurants, both classy and new-feeling. **Fusion Brasserie** serves modern European cuisine (£14–20 main dishes, £17–22 fixed-price meals are an especially good deal on weeknights, when they include drinks; Tue–Sat 19:00–21:30, open Sun for brunch 12:00–14:30, closed Mon). **Bar W** serves pub food (£4–6 sandwiches, £7–12 main dishes, Mon–Sat 11:00–23:00, food served Mon–Sat 12:00–14:00 & 17:30–21:30, Sun 12:00–14:30, tel. for both: 01824/703-147).

Manorhaus is the town splurge, with updated Welsh and British dinners served in a mod, art-gallery space (£20 for two courses, £25 for three courses, Mon–Sat from 19:00, closed Sun, reservations recommended, also open as a café Fri–Sat 10:30–15:00, Well Street, tel. 01824/704-830).

Leonardo's is *the* place to buy a top-notch gourmet picnic, including £3 made-to-order sandwiches and a small salad bar (Mon–Sat 9:30–17:30, closed Sun, just off the main square, tel. 01824/707-161).

Finn's is the local favorite for take-away fish-and-chips (£3, daily 11:30–14:00 & 16:30–22:00, near Ruthin Gaol at the bottom of Clwyd Street, at #45A).

TRANSPORTATION CONNECTIONS

Ruthin has poor connections to just about everywhere. Skip it unless you have a car.

From Ruthin: The following bus connections are sparse and irregular—get local help figuring out the best trip for your itinerary. Note that bus frequency (including the Ruthin-Corwen bus crucial for the first two connections) dwindles to near nothing on Sundays: to **Llangollen** (hourly, 1–1.5 hrs, transfer in Corwen or Wrexham), **Betws-y-Coed** (1.5–2 hrs, transfer in Corwen), **Conwy** (1.75–2.5 hrs, take bus to Rhyl, then transfer to a Conwy-bound train), **Chester** in England (1.5–2.5 hrs, transfer in Corwen, Mold, Rhyl, or Wrexham; or take a 40-min taxi ride for around £30, set price up front).

North Wales

Near Ruthin

▲▲Ewe-Phoria Sheepdog Show

Despite the goofy name, this really is a fun and fascinating peek into the world of sheep farmers and their frantically loyal, well-trained border collies. Aled Owen's working farm has diversified, turning traditional farming methods into an enjoyable, educational show. Drop in for the 45-minute presentation at 13:00 on the days they're open. First, you'll head into the barn, where trained sheep enter one at a time to show the different breeds, followed by a sheep shearing demonstration. Then you'll head outside to see the dogs rounding up the sheep. The shepherd guides the dog with nothing but whistles (£4.50; Easter–Aug Wed–Fri and Sun 10:30–15:00; Sept–Oct Wed, Fri, and Sun 10:30–15:00; closed Nov–Easter; just off A5 midway between Betws-y-Coed and Llangollen in Llamgwm, tel. 01490/460-369, www.ewe-phoria.co.uk). They've just added "rally carting" (go-carts on a gravel track) and "quad biking" (ATV treks into the hills)—see website for details.

Llangollen

Worth a stop if you have a car, Llangollen (tlang-GOT-tlen) is a redbrick riverside town that's equal parts blue collar and touristy. The town is famous for its **International Musical Eisteddfod**, running July 8 through 13 in 2008 (tel. 01978/862-001, www.international -eisteddfod.co.uk), a very popular and crowded festival of folk songs and dance. Men's choir practice is held on Friday nights throughout the year (19:30 at the Hand Hotel, 21:00 pub singsong afterward, hotel tel. 01978/860-303).

The enthusiastic **TI** has the details on these events, the scenic steam-train trips, and other attractions (daily 9:30–17:30, until 17:00 Nov–March, tel. 01978/860-828, www.llangollen.org).

Llangollen's most interesting attraction is its **canal,** a narrow and shallow waterway up the hill and across the bridge from the town center. You can stroll along the canal, or take one of two different boat rides: a horse-drawn boat down to the Cistercian abbey (£5, Easter–Oct, 45 min, hourly in summer but less off-season, tel. 01978/860-702) or a longer motorized trip over the remarkable Pontcysyllte aqueduct (£10, 2 hrs, 2/day).

If you take a walk or the horse-drawn canal trip, you'll reach the lovely 13th-century Cistercian **Vale Crucis Abbey** (£2.50, daily 10:00–17:00, closes 1 hour earlier in winter) near the even older cross, **Eliseg's Pillar.**

Sleeping in Llangollen: **$$ Glasgwm B&B** rents four spacious rooms in a Victorian townhouse (Sb-£30, Db-£60, Abbey Road, tel. 01978/861-975, John and Heather).

Transportation Connections: Llangollen is a 30-minute drive from Ruthin. You can take the bus to **Ruthin,** but you have to transfer in Corwen or Wrexham (hourly, 1–1.5 hrs, no buses on Sun). Llangollen is connected by bus #X19 twice daily with **Betws-y-Coed** (1 hr) and **Conwy** (2.25 hrs). Llangollen is also connected by bus with train stations at **Ruabon** (4/hr, 15 min) and **Wrexham** (4/hr, 30 min).

Conwy

This garrison town was built along with the Conwy Castle in the 1280s to give Edward I an English toehold in Wales (see page 420).

What's left today are the best medieval walls in Britain surrounding a humble town, crowned by the bleak and barren hulk of a castle that was awesome in its day (and still is). Conwy's charming High Street leads down to a fishy harbor that permitted Edward to safely restock his castle. Since the highway was tunneled under the town, a strolling ambience has returned to Conwy. Beyond the castle, the mighty Telford suspension bridge is a 19th-century slice of English imperialism, built in 1826 to better connect (and control) the route to Ireland.

North Wales

ORIENTATION

Conwy is an enjoyably small community of 4,000 people. The walled old town center is compact and manageable. Lancaster Square marks the center, where you'll find the bus "station"

Conwy

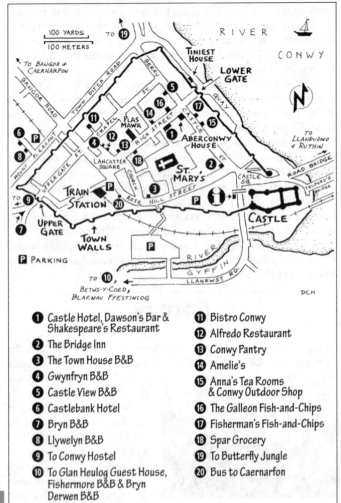

1 Castle Hotel, Dawson's Bar & Shakespeare's Restaurant
2 The Bridge Inn
3 The Town House B&B
4 Gwynfryn B&B
5 Castle View B&B
6 Castlebank Hotel
7 Bryn B&B
8 Llywelyn B&B
9 To Conwy Hostel
10 To Glan Heulog Guest House, Fishermore B&B & Bryn Derwen B&B

11 Bistro Conwy
12 Alfredo Restaurant
13 Conwy Pantry
14 Amelie's
15 Anna's Tea Rooms & Conwy Outdoor Shop
16 The Galleon Fish-and-Chips
17 Fisherman's Fish-and-Chips
18 Spar Grocery
19 To Butterfly Jungle
20 Bus to Caernarfon

(a blue-and-white shelter), the unstaffed train station (the little white hut at the end of a sunken parking lot), and the start of the main drag, High Street—and my self-guided walk.

Tourist Information

The TI shares a building with the castle's ticket office and gift shop (June–Sept daily 9:30–18:00; April–May and Oct daily 9:30–17:00; Nov–March Mon–Sat 9:30–16:00, Sun 11:00–16:00; tel. 01492/592-248). Since Conwy's train and bus stations are unstaffed, ask at the TI about train or bus schedules for your departure. The TI sells books and maps on the area, such as *The Ascent of Snowdon* (£3). The TI also reserves rooms for a £1 fee and makes theater bookings.

Don't confuse the TI with the tacky "Conwy Visitors Centre"—a big gift shop with a goofy little £1 video show—near the station.

Helpful Hints

Trains: Train schedules are posted outside the station (if your train is listed with an "x" or "stops on request," you'll need to flag it down and hope the conductor is paying attention; he may not see you if you're wearing neutral colors). The nearest "real" train station is in **Llandudno Junction,** visible a mile away beyond the bridges, and is a safer bet for more regular trains. Make sure to ask for trains that stop at Llandudno Junction, and not Llandudno proper, which is farther from Conwy.

Market: Every Tuesday and some Saturdays, a small market hums in the train station's parking lot (year-round, canceled if rainy).

Internet Access: Try the **library** at the bottom of High Street (free, Mon and Thu–Fri 10:00–17:30, Tue 10:00–19:00, Sat 10:00–13:00, closed Wed and Sun, tel. 01492/596-242) or the **O. J. Williams bakery** on High Street (1 terminal in back room, £2.20/hr, daily 8:30–17:30, at #29a).

Bike Rental: Conwy Outdoor, well-stocked with boots and jackets, also rents bikes for Snowdonia Bicycle Hire (£16/day, includes helmet, daily 9:00–18:00, packed lunches available from Anna's Tea Rooms upstairs, 9 Castle Street, tel. 01492/593-390, www.conwyoutdoor.co.uk).

Car Rental: A dozen car-rental agencies in the city of Llandudno (1.5 miles away, beyond Llandudno Junction) offer cars for about £40 per day and can generally deliver to you in Conwy; the Conwy TI has a list. The closest is **Avis,** a 10-minute walk from Conwy (tel. 01492/585-101).

SELF-GUIDED WALK

Welcome to Conwy

This brief orientation walk leads you through the heart of Conwy: Down its main street, then along its harborfront. It takes about 30 minutes. Begin at the top of High Street, at the center of the old town, on...

Lancaster Square: The square's centerpiece is a **column** honoring the town's founder, the Welsh prince Llywelyn the Great. Looking past the blue-and-white bus stop, find the cute pointed archway built into the medieval wall so the train could get through.

Side-trip up the lane called York Place (past Alfredo Restaurant) to a wall of **slate memorials** from the 1937 coronation of King George (his wife, the Queen Consort Elizabeth, was the late Queen Mum). Notice the Welsh-language lesson here: the counties (shires, or *sir*), months (only *mai* is recognizable), days, numbers, and alphabet with its different letters.

• *Go back out to the square and head down to the harborfront on Conwy's main drag...*

High Street: Wander downhill, enjoying the slice-of-Welsh-life scene: tearooms, bakery, butcher, newsstand, old-timers, and maybe even suds in the fountain. **Plas Mawr** (on the left), the first Welsh house built within the town walls, dates from the time of Henry VIII (well worth touring—see description on page 420). Opposite Castle Hotel, a lane leads to the **Carmel Church.** This is a fine example of stark Methodist "statement architecture": stern, with no frills, and typical of these churches built in the early 20th century.

Aberconwy House marks the bottom of High Street. One of the oldest houses in town, it's a museum (not worth touring). Conwy was once a garrison town filled with half-timbered buildings just like this one. From here, **Barry Street** leads left. Originally called "burial street," it was a big ditch for mass burials during a 17th-century plague.

• *Continue downhill, crossing under the wall to the harborfront.*

Harborfront: The stones date from the 13th century, when the harbor served Edward's castle and town. (Notice that the harborfront street is still called "King's Quay.") Conwy was once a busy slate port. Slate, barged downstream to here, was loaded onto big three-mast ships and transported to the Continent. Back when much of Europe was roofed with Welsh slate, Conwy was a boomtown. In 1900, it had 48 pubs. All the mud is new, as the modern bridge caused this part of the river to silt up.

Conwy's harbor is now a laid-back area locals treat like a town square. In fact, the town recently constructed a handy promenade to make this space even more inviting. On summer evenings, the action is on the quay. The scene is mellow, multigenerational, and perfectly Welsh. It's a small town and everyone is here: enjoying the local cuisine—"chips," ice cream, and beer—and savoring that great British pastime...torturing little crabs.

• *Let's join the Conwy people-parade by walking a little loop along the harbor. Start by strolling to the right—to the end of the harbor next to Conwy's top sight, its* castle *(described on page 419).*

Near the castle, the harbormaster's house fills the former customs building. The **lifeboat house** welcomes visitors. Each coastal town has a house like this one, outfitted with a rescue boat suited to the area—in the shallow waters around Conwy, inflatable boats work best. You'll see *Lifeboats* stickers around town, marking homes of people who donate to the valuable cause of the Royal National Lifeboat Institution (RNLI)—Britain's all-volunteer and totally donation-funded answer to the Coast Guard.

• *Head back toward the gate where you emerged onto this promenade.*

Mussels, historically a big "crop" for Conwy, are processed "in the months with an r" by the **Mussels Center.** In the other months, it's open to visitors (free, Easter–Aug daily 10:30–17:00). The benches are great for a picnic (two fish-and-chips shops are back through the gate—see "Eating," page 425) or a visit with the noisy gulls.

The **Liverpool Arms pub** was built by a captain who ran a ferry service to Liverpool in the 19th century, when the North Wales coast was discovered by English holiday-goers. Today it remains a salty and characteristic hangout. Nearby, the **Queen Victoria tour boat** departs from here (£5, lazy 30-min cruise, nearly hourly 11:00–17:00 depending on tides, pay on boat, tel. 07917/343-059).

It's easy to miss **The Smallest House in Great Britain,** but don't. It's red, 72 inches wide, 122 inches high, and worth £1 to pop in and listen to the short audioguide tour. (No WC—but it did have a bedpan.)

• *Our tour is finished. From this quay, there's a peaceful half-mile shoreline stroll along the harbor promenade (from the tiny house, walk through the wall gate and keep going).*

SIGHTS AND ACTIVITIES

In Conwy

▲**Conwy Castle**—Dramatically situated on a rock overlooking the sea with eight linebacker towers, this castle has an interesting story to tell. Built in just four years, it had a water gate that allowed safe entry for English boats in a land of hostile Welsh subjects (£4.50, or £7 Joint Ticket with Plas Mawr; June–Sept daily 9:30–18:00; April–May and Oct daily 9:30–17:00; Nov–March Mon–Sat 9:30–16:00,

King Edward's Castles

In the 13th century, the Welsh, unified by two great princes named Llywelyn, created a united and independent Wales. The English king Edward I fought hard to end this Welsh sovereignty. In 1282, Llywelyn was killed (and went to where everyone speaks Welsh). King Edward spent the next 20 years building or rebuilding 17 great castles to consolidate his English foothold in troublesome North Wales. The greatest of these (such as Conwy Castle) were masterpieces of medieval engineering, with round towers (tough to undermine by tunneling), castle-within-a-castle defenses (giving defenders a place to retreat and wreak havoc on the advancing enemy...or just wait for reinforcements), and sea access (safe to restock from England).

These castles were English islands in the middle of angry Wales. Most were built with a fortified grid-plan town attached, and were filled with English settlers. (With this blatant abuse of Wales, you have to wonder, where was Greenpeace 700 years ago?) Edward I was arguably England's best monarch. By establishing and consolidating the United Kingdom (adding Wales and Scotland to England), he made his kingdom big enough to compete with the other rising European powers.

Castle-lovers will want to tour each of Edward's five greatest

---

Sun 11:00–16:00; tel. 01492/592-358, www.cadw.wales.gov.uk). Guides wait inside to take you on a one-hour, £1 tour. They usually depart about once per hour (no set schedule). If the guide booth is empty, look for the group and join it, or check the clock to see when the next tour departs.

▲**City Wall**—Much of the wall, with its 22 towers and castle and harbor views, can be walked for free. Start at Upper Gate (the highest point) or Berry Street (the lowest), or do the small section at the castle entrance.

▲**Plas Mawr**—A rare Elizabethan house from 1580, this was constructed after the reign of Henry VIII. It was the first Welsh home to be built within Conwy's walls. (The Tudor family was Welsh—and therefore relations between Wales and England warmed.) Billed as "the oldest house in Wales," Plas Mawr offers a delightful look at 16th-century domestic life to anyone patient enough to spend an hour following the excellent included audio-

castles (see map on page 435). With a car and two days, this makes one of Europe's best castle tours. I'd rate them in this order:

Caernarfon is the most entertaining and best presented (page 431).

Conwy is attached to the cutest medieval town, and has the best public transport (see page 419).

Harlech is the most dramatically situated, on a hilltop (£3.50, June–Sept daily 9:30–18:00; April–May and Oct daily 9:30–17:00; Nov–March Mon–Sat 9:30–16:00, Sun 11:00–16:00; tel. 01766/780-552, TI is open Easter–Oct, tel. 01766/780-552).

Beaumaris, surrounded by a swan-filled moat, is the last, largest, and most romantic (£3.50, same hours as Harlech, tel. 01248/810-361).

Criccieth (KRICK-ith), built in 1230 by Llywelyn, is also dramatic and remote (£2.90; June–Sept daily 10:00–18:00; April–May and Oct daily 10:00–17:00; Nov–March Fri–Sat 9:30–16:00, Sun 11:00–16:00, closed Mon–Thu; tel. 01766/522-227).

CADW, the Welsh version of the National Trust, sells a three-day Explorer Pass that covers many sights in Wales. If you're planning to visit at least three of the above castles, the pass will probably save you money (three-day pass: £10.50 for 1 person, £17.50 for 2 people, £25 for a family; seven-day pass: £17 for 1 person, £28 for 2 people, £35 for a family; available at castle ticket desks). For photos and more information on the castles, as well as information on Welsh historic monuments in general, check www.cadw.wales.gov.uk.

guide. A display explains the long process involved in restoring historic buildings (this one was done in the 1990s). Docents, who are posted in some rooms, are happy to point out what's original and chat about how the restoration was done.

Visitors stepping into the house were wowed by the heraldry over the fireplace. This symbol, now repainted in its original bright colors, proclaimed the family's rich lineage and princely stock. The kitchen came with all the circa-1600 conveniences: hay on the floor to add a little warmth and soak up spills; a hanging bread cage to keep food away from wandering critters; and a good supply of fresh meat in the pantry. Upstairs, the bedroom of the lady of the house doubled as a sitting room—with a finely carved four-poster bed and a foot warmer by the chair. At night, the bedroom's curtains were drawn to keep in warmth. In the great chamber next door, hearty evening feasting was followed by boisterous gaming, dancing, and music. And fixed above all of

North Wales

this extravagant entertainment was...more heraldry, pronouncing those important—if unproven—family connections and leaving a powerful impact on impressed guests (£4.90, or £7 Joint Ticket with Conwy Castle; June–Aug Tue–Sun 9:30–18:00, closed Mon; April–May and Sept Tue–Sun 9:30–17:00, closed Mon; Oct Tue–Sun 9:30–16:00, closed Mon; closed Nov–March; last entry 45 min before closing, tel. 01492/580-167).

St. Mary's Parish Church—Sitting lonely in the town center, Conwy's church was the centerpiece of a Cistercian abbey that stood here a hundred years before the town. The Cistercians were French monks who built their abbeys in lonely places, "far from the haunts of man." Popular here because they were French and *not* English, the Cistercians taught locals farming and mussel-gathering techniques. Edward moved the monks 12 miles upstream but kept the church for his town. Notice the tombstone of a victim of the 1805 Battle of Trafalgar just left of the north transept. On the other side of the church, a tomb containing seven brothers and sisters is marked "We Are Seven." It inspired William Wordsworth to write his poem of the same name. The slate tombstones look new even though many are hundreds of years old; slate weathers better than marble (cemetery always open, church may be staffed June–Aug Mon–Fri 10:00–12:00 & 14:00–16:00).

Butterfly Jungle—Butterflies flutter in a steamy, lush greenhouse with tropical forest sounds. It's sweet, small, and too humid to linger long (£5, family deals, ticket valid all day so OK to return, ID chart not necessary because charts posted inside, late-March–Oct Wed–Mon 10:00–16:00, until 17:30 mid-May–Aug, closed Tue and Nov–late-March, follow signs from harbor, nice 5-min walk north, tel. 01492/593-149, www.conwy-butterfly.co.uk). If it's not busy, ask the owner why he started a butterfly house.

Near Conwy

Llandudno—This genteel Victorian beach resort, a few miles away, is bigger and better-known than Conwy. It was built after the advent of the railroads, which made the Welsh seacoast easily accessible to the English industrial heartland. In the 1800s, the notion that bathing in seawater was good for your health was trendy, and the bracing sea air was just what the doctor ordered. These days, Llandudno remains popular with the English, but you won't see many other foreigners strolling its long pier and line of old-time hotels.

Hill Climb—For lovely views across the bay to Llandudno, take a pleasant walk (40 min one way) along the footpath up Conwy Mount (follow Sychnant Pass Road past the Bryn B&B, look for fields on the right and a sign with a stick figure of a walker).

North Wales

SLEEPING

(£1 = about $2, country code: 44, area code: 01492)
Conwy's hotels are overpriced, but its B&Bs include some good-value gems. There's no launderette in town.

Inside Conwy's Walled Old Town

$$$ Castle Hotel in the town center rents 28 elegant rooms where Old World antique furnishings mingle with modern amenities. Owners Peter and Bobbi Lavin are eager to make your stay comfortable (Sb-£85–95, Db-£125–160, posh suites-£155–330, rates vary with season and room size, 10 percent discount if you show this book when checking in during 2008, High Street, tel. 01492/582-800, fax 01492/582-300, www.castlewales.co.uk, mail @castlewales.co.uk). The hotel has two restaurants: Shakespeare's is suitable for a splurge, while Dawson's is a bistro with lighter fare (see "Eating" on page 425).

$$$ The Bridge Inn rents five fine but forgettable (and forgotten) rooms above its pub. Check in at the bar. While the floor just above the pub can be noisy, particularly on weekend nights, the top floor is quieter (Db-£60–75 Sun–Thu and £65–80 Fri–Sat, discount for 2-night stay, some views, non-smoking, separate entrance from pub, intersection of Rosehill and Castle streets, tel. 01492/573-482).

$$ The Town House B&B is a colorful place renting six tidy, bright, updated rooms—some with views—between the train station and the castle (S-£35, D-£55, Db-£65, discount with this book in 2008 for 2-night stays, cash only, vegetarian breakfast available, free Wi-Fi, bike rental for guests-£10/day, parking, 18 Rosehill Street, tel. 01492/596-454, mobile 0797-465-0609, www.thetownhousebb.co.uk, thetownhousebb@aol.com, friendly Alan and Elaine Naughton).

$$ Gwynfryn B&B rents five recently renovated, bright airy rooms, each with eclectic decor, a DVD player, and access to a DVD library. The location is dead-center in Conwy, and out back there's a patio for pleasant breakfasts in good weather (D-£45–55, Db-£55–70, depends on season and room size, S/Sb possible for £5 less, cash only, free Internet access and Wi-Fi, 4 York Place, on the lane off Lancaster Square just past Alfredo Restaurant, tel. 01492/576-733, www.gwynfrynbandb.co.uk, info @gwynfrynbandb.co.uk, energetic Monica and Colin).

$ Castle View B&B, just inside the city wall near the waterfront, rents two cozy, pleasant rooms (sharing one bathroom) with warm wood furnishings (D-£45, T-£60, cash only, call ahead, 3 Berry Street, tel. 01492/596-888, elainepritchard156@hotmail .com, Elaine and Ernest Pritchard). Ernest, who's a huge *Lord of the Rings* fan, named his boat Sméagol.

Just Outside the Wall

The first three options are a two-minute walk from Conwy's old town wall; the hostel is about 10 minutes uphill beyond those.

$$$ Castlebank Hotel is a small hotel with nine spacious rooms, an inviting lounge, a small bar, and a restaurant (open for dinner nightly except Tue). Owners Jo and Henrique are doing a heroic job of rehabilitating a formerly dumpy hotel—and onetime Ministry of Agriculture building—into a dolled-up and comfortable home away from home (S with private b down the hall-£40, Sb-£55–80, Db-£80–95, depends on season, 10 percent discount with this book for 2 or more nights through 2008—except on Bank Holiday weekends, family rooms, easy parking, just outside town wall at Mount Pleasant, tel. 01492/593-888, www.castlebankhotel .co.uk, bookings@castlebankhotel.co.uk).

$$ Bryn B&B offers four large, clutter-free rooms in a big 19th-century house with the city wall right in the backyard. Owner Alison Archard is proud of her fresh, organic breakfasts and can cater to special diets. This popular place books up quickly—reserve early (Sb-£42, Db-£62, 1 ground-floor room, parking, immediately outside upper gate of wall, Sychnant Pass Road, tel. 01492/592-449, www.bryn.org.uk, stay@bryn.org.uk).

$$ Llywelyn B&B has seven faded rooms, but Alan Hughes' pleasant nature helps compensate (Sb-£30–35, D-£40–50, Db-£50–55, depends on season, 10 percent discount with this book in 2008, Internet access starting at £2, easy parking, ramp from parking lot allows access to first-floor rooms, next to Castlebank Hotel—see above, Mount Pleasant, tel. 01492/593-257).

$ The well-run Conwy Hostel, welcoming travelers of any age, has super views from all of its 24 rooms (including eight bunk-bed doubles) and a spacious garden. Each room is equipped with either two or four bunk beds and a shower; toilets are down the hall. The airy dining hall and glorious rooftop deck make you feel like you're in the majestic midst of Wales (Ds-£40–45, bed in Qs-£12–18 per person, depends on season and age—under 18 is cheaper, non-members pay £3 more, book in advance for doubles, Internet access, laundry, lockers, dinners, elevator, parking, no lock-out times but office closed 10:00–14:00, 10-min uphill walk from upper gate of Conwy's wall—go along the right side of Bryn B&B and follow *hostel* signs, Sychnant Pass Road, in Larkhill, tel. 01492/593-571, fax 01492/593-580, conwy@yha .org.uk).

Below the Old Town, on Llanrwst Road

These three options are along busy Llanrwst Road, which skirts the south side of Conwy's old town wall on its way to Bodnant Garden, Trefriw Woolen Mills, and Betws-y-Coed. They're a longer walk from town than the rest of my listings (except the hostel). To find them from the train station, exit the station from its farthest and lowest corner, go through the gate in the city wall to busy Llanrwst Road, and turn right. Glan Heulog and Bryn Derwen are about a six-minute walk from town, and the Fishermore is about eight minutes beyond that (each one is set back from the road up a hill—look for signs at road level).

$$ Glan Heulog Guest House offers seven fresh, bright rooms and a pleasant enclosed sun porch. Practice speaking Welsh with your host, Stanley (Sb-£30–35, Db-£50–60, depends on room size, ask about healthy breakfast option, will pick up from train station, tel. 01492/593-845, www.snowdoniabandb.co.uk, info@ snowdoniabandb.co.uk, Stanley and Vivien Watson-Jones).

$$ Fishermore B&B, my farthest listing from downtown Conwy, is good for drivers but also fine for anyone who doesn't mind the 15-minute walk into town. It's in a large house with a sprawling yard, a sweet garden patio, and three tidy rooms with flowery bedspreads (Db-£48, cash only, closed Oct–Easter, free Internet access, parking, 0.75-mile south of Conwy on Llanrwst Road, tel. 01492/592-891, www.northwalesbandb.co.uk, dyers @tesco.net, helpful Cath and Peter Dyer). After passing the first two B&Bs on Llanrwst Road, follow the road when it bends left (just after the school) and continue uphill, watching for the low-profile B&B sign on the right.

$$ Bryn Derwen rents six rooms next door to Glan Heulog Guest House, in a near-mansion atop a hill (Sb-£30–35, Db-£50–55, cash only, tel. 01492/596-134, www.conwybrynderwen.co.uk, info@conwybrynderwen.co.uk, Andrew and Gill).

EATING

All of these places are inside Conwy's walled old town. My first two listings are the town splurges; the rest are easier on the budget. For dinner, consider just strolling down High Street, comparing the cute teahouses and workaday pubs.

The busy **Bistro Conwy,** tucked away on Chapel Street, serves freshly prepared modern and traditional Welsh cuisine in a cozy wood-floor and candlelit setting. The menu (with tasty daily specials) is a delight and the food must be the best in town (£13–16 entrées with vegetables, potato, and salad; open for dinner Wed–Sat 18:30–21:00, brunch Sun 12:00–14:30, closed for dinner Sun and all day Mon–Tue, reservations a must, tel. 01492/596-326).

Shakespeare's Restaurant, with cuisine from award-winning chef Graham Tinsley, is a hit with locals and worth the splurge (£17–19 main dishes, nightly for dinner, lunch served Sun–Fri, reservations smart—especially weekends, at recom-

North Wales

mended Castle Hotel on High Street, tel. 01492/582-800). For lighter bistro-style meals from an eclectic menu with an emphasis on fish, try the adjoining hotel bar, **Dawson's** (£8–15 main dishes, daily 12:00–21:30).

Alfredo Restaurant, a family-friendly place right on Lancaster Square, serves good and reasonably priced Italian food (£7–8 pizzas, £7–10 pastas, £11–14 main dishes, nightly from 18:00, last orders at 22:00, reservations recommended, York Place, tel. 01492/592-381, Christine).

Conwy Pantry serves up cheap, hearty, daily lunch specials, salads, and homemade sweets in a cheery setting (£4–6 lunches, daily 9:00–17:00, until 16:30 in winter, 26 High Street, tel. 01492/592-445).

Amelie's, named for the French film, enjoys one of Conwy's most pleasant locations, in a relaxed loft space overlooking High Street (£5–8 lunches, £9–18 dinners, Tue–Sun 12:00–14:15 & 18:00–21:15, closed Mon, 8 High Street, tel. 01492/583-142).

Anna's Tea Rooms, a frilly, doily, very feminine-feeling eatery located upstairs in the masculine-feeling Conwy Outdoor Shop, is popular with locals (£4–7 main dishes and teas, also sells lunches to go, daily 10:00–17:00, near Fisherman's fish-and-chips, 9 Castle Street, tel. 01492/580-908).

Fish-and-Chips: At the bottom of High Street, on the intersecting Castle Street, are two fish-and-chips joints—**The Galleon** (daily) and **Fisherman's** (daily generally 11:30–18:30, later in summer, closed Mon off-season). Both brag that they're the best (Fisherman's probably is). Consider taking your fish-and-chips down to the harbor and sharing it with the noisy seagulls.

Pub Grub: The **Bridge Inn,** right near the castle at the intersection of Rosehill and Castle streets, is a great spot to rub elbows with chatty locals and dine on decent meals (food served daily 12:00–14:30 & 18:00–20:00, might not serve food Mon off-season, tel. 01492/573-482; also listed under "Sleeping" on page 423).

Picnic Fixings: The **Spar** grocery is conveniently located and well-stocked (daily 7:00–22:00, top of High Street). Several other shops on High Street—including the bakery and the butcher a few steps down—sell meat pies and other microwaveables that can quickly flesh out a sparse picnic.

TRANSPORTATION CONNECTIONS

Whether taking the bus or train, be proactive and let the driver or conductor know you want to stop at Conwy. Consider getting train times and connections for your onward journey at a bigger station before you come here. For train info in town, ask at the

TI, check www.traveline-cymru.info or call 08457-484-950. If you want to depart Conwy by train, flag it down; for more frequent trains, go to Llandudno Junction (catch the hourly bus, take a £3 taxi, or walk a mile). Remember, all of these connections are less frequent on Sundays.

From Conwy by Bus to: Llandudno Junction (2–4/hr, less Sat–Sun, 5 min), **Caernarfon** (express bus #9A—hourly, 1 hr; bus #5 or #X5—2/hr, 1.5 hrs), **Betws-y-Coed** (3/day, 50–60 min; or take bus #X1 from Llandudno; train more frequent—see below), **Blaenau Ffestiniog** (7/day, 1.25 hrs, transfer in Llandudno Junction to bus #X1, also stops in Betws-y-Coed; train is better—see below), **Beddgelert** (6/day with a transfer in Caernarfon, 1.75 hrs; a few more but longer with a transfer in Betws-y-Coed), **Llangollen** (2/day, 2.25 hrs, bus #X19, same bus stops at Trefriw and Betws-y-Coed).

From Conwy by Train: The Conwy Valley line conveniently connects Conwy with **Betws-y-Coed** and **Blaenau Ffestiniog** (must wave for stop in Conwy; 5/day, 3/day on Sun, 30 min to Betws-y-Coed, 1 hr to Blaenau Ffestiniog). Other destinations: **Llandudno Junction** (hourly, 5 min—consider walking or taking a £3 taxi instead), **Chester** (hourly, 1 hr), **Holyhead** (almost hourly, 1 hr), **London's Euston Station** (7/day, 3.25–4 hrs, with a transfer in Chester, Crewe, or Llandudno Junction).

From Llandudno Junction by Train to: Chester (2/hr, 1 hr), **Birmingham** (2/hr, 2.5 hrs, some with change in Crewe), **London's Euston Station** (hourly, 3.5 hrs, most with 1 change).

Near Conwy

These two attractions are south of Conwy, on the route to Betws-y-Coed and Snowdonia National Park. Note that Bodnant Garden is on the east side of the Conwy River, on A470, while Trefriw is on the west side, along B5106. To see them both, you'll have to cross the river (most convenient at Tal-y-Cafn).

▲Bodnant Garden

This sumptuous 80-acre display of floral color six miles south of Conwy is one of Britain's best gardens. Originally the private garden of the stately Bodnant Hall, this lush landscape was donated by the Bodnant family (who still live in the house) to the National Trust in 1948. The map you receive on entering suggests a handy walking route. The highlight for many is the "Laburnum Arch"—a 180-foot-long canopy made of bright-yellow laburnum, hanging like stalactites over the heads of garden-lovers who stroll beneath it (blooms mid-May through early June). The garden is also famous for its magnolias, rhododendrons, and camellias, and the way that the buildings of the estate complement the

carefully planned landscaping. The wild English-style gardens seem to spar playfully with the more formal, Italian-style gardens (£7, mid-March–Oct daily 10:00–17:00, closed Nov–mid-March, café, WCs in parking lot and inside garden, best in spring, phone message tells what's blooming, tel. 01492/650-460, www.bodnant -garden.co.uk).

Getting There: To reach it by public transportation from Conwy, first head to Llandudno Junction and catch the hourly bus #25 (toward Eglwysbach), which will take you right to the garden in about 20 minutes.

Trefriw Woolen Mills

The mill in Trefriw (TREV-roo), five miles north of Betws-y-Coed, lets you peek into a working woolen mill. It's surprisingly interesting and rated ▲ if the machines are running (weekdays Easter–Sept). Various parts of the mill show off different processes, and have different hours—but everything's free.

This mill buys wool from local farmers, and turns it into scarves, sweaters, bedspreads, caps, and more. You can peruse the finished products in the **shop** (daily June–Sept 9:30–17:30, Oct–May 10:00–17:00, attached café closes 1 hour before shop, tel. 01492/640-462). The whole complex creates its own hydroelectric power; the **"turbine house"** in the cellar lets you take a peek at the enormous, fiercely spinning turbines, dating from the 1930s and 1940s, powered by streams that flow down the hillside above the mill (same hours as shop). The **weaving looms,** with bobbin-loaded shuttles flying to and fro, allow you to watch a bedspread being created before your eyes (same hours as shop, but closed for lunch 13:00–14:00). But the highlight is the **"working museum,"** which follows the 11 stages of wool transformation: blending, carding, spinning, doubling, hanking, spanking, warping, weaving, and so on. Follow a matted glob of fleece on its journey to becoming a fashionable cap or scarf. It's impressive that this Rube Goldberg-type process could have been so ingeniously designed and coordinated in an age before computers (mostly the

Conwy or Caernarfon?

Trying to decide between these two walled towns, and their castles? Here are some comparisons:

The town of Conwy is more quaint, with a higgledy-piggledy medieval vibe and a modern workaday heart and soul—both of which feel diluted in busier Caernarfon. Conwy also has more accommodations and good eateries than Caernarfon. All of this makes it the better home base, which also means its castle is more convenient to see. Conwy's castle is a bit more ruined and less slickly presented than Caernarfon's—with fewer fancy exhibits—but some think that makes it more evocative.

Caernarfon's castle is the best in Wales—beautifully maintained, and with a more diverting set of attractions inside.

If I had to pick one, it'd be Conwy...but if you have a healthy appetite for castles, doing both is a great option.

1950s and 1960s)—each machine seems to "know" how to do its rattling, clattering duty with amazing precision (some but not all machines are likely running at any one time; Easter–Sept Mon–Fri 10:00–13:00 & 14:00–17:00, closed Oct–Easter since they don't heat it in winter). In the summer, the **hand-spinning house** (next to the WC) has a charming spinster and a petting cupboard filled with all the various kinds of raw wool that can be spun into cloth (June–Sept only, Tue–Thu 10:00–17:00, also Mon and Fri in Aug, closed Sat–Sun).

The grade school next door is rambunctious with Welsh-speaking kids—fun to listen to at recess. The woolen mill at Penmachno (also near Betws-y-Coed) is smaller and much less interesting.

Getting There: Bus #19 goes from Conwy right to Trefriw (2/hr, 30 min).

Caernarfon

The small and lively little town of Caernarfon (kah-NAR-von) is famous for its striking castle—the place where the Prince of Wales is "invested" (given his title). Like Conwy, it has an Edward I garrison town marching out from the castle; it still follows the original, medieval grid plan laid within its well-preserved ramparts. Caernarfon lacks Conwy's quaintness—but its polished castle is Wales' best.

North Wales

Caernarfon is mostly a 19th-century town. At that time, the most important thing in town wasn't the castle but the area—now a parking lot—that sprawls below the castle. This was once a booming slate port, shipping tidy bundles of slate from North Wales mining towns to roofs all over Europe.

The statue of local boy David Lloyd George looks over the town square. A member of Parliament from 1890 to 1945, he was the most important politician Wales ever sent to London, and ultimately became Britain's prime minister. Young George began his career as a noisy nonconformist liberal advocating Welsh rights. He ended up an eloquent spokesperson for the notion of Great Britain, convincing his slate-mining constituents that only as part of the Union would their industry boom.

Caernarfon bustles with shops, cafés, and people. Market-day activities fill its main square on Saturdays year-round; a smaller, sleepier market yawns on Monday from late May to September. The charming town is worth a wander.

ORIENTATION

The small, walled old town of Caernarfon spreads out from its waterfront castle, its outer flanks fringed with modern sprawl (pop. 10,000). The main square, called Castle Square (Y Maes), is fronted by the castle (with the TI across from its entry). Public WCs and bike rental are off the main square, on the road down to the harbor and parking lot.

Tourist Information
The TI, facing the castle entrance, has a wonderful free town map/guide (with a good self-guided town walk) and train and bus schedules. They dispense tips about all of the North Wales attractions, sell hiking books, and book rooms here and elsewhere for a £2 fee (daily April–Oct 9:30–16:30, Nov–March 10:00–13:00 & 14:00–16:30, tel. 01286/672-232).

Arrival in Caernarfon
If you arrive by **bus,** walk straight ahead a few steps to Bridge Street, turn left, and walk two short blocks until you hit the main square (with a post office) and the castle. **Drivers** can park in the £3 lot along the harbor below the castle.

Helpful Hints

Internet Access: Get wired at **Dylan Thomas Internet Café** (£3/hr, Wi-Fi-£2/hr, Mon–Sat 10:00–18:00, closed Sun, 4 Bangor Street, across from Turf Square, tel. 01286/678-777).

Laundry: Pete's Launderette hides at the end of Skinner Street, a narrow lane branching off the main square (same-day full-service-£6/load, self-service-£5/load, Mon–Sat 9:00–17:30, Sun 11:00–17:30, tel. 01286/678-395).

Bike Rental: Try **Cycle Hire** on the harbor, near the start of a handy bike path (£12/2 hrs, £14/4 hrs, £16/6 hrs, £19/8 hrs, includes helmet and map of suggested routes, daily 10:00–15:00, longer hours in good weather, 1 Slate Quay—across from the payment booth for the parking lot, tel. 01286/676-804).

A Taste of Welsh: For a store selling all things Welsh—books, movies, music, and more—check out **Na-Nog** on the main square (Mon–Sat 9:00–17:00, closed Sun, tel. 01286/676-946).

Local Guide: Donna Goodman leads historic walks almost nightly through the tourist season (£4.50, 1.5 hours), as well as private day trips of the area (£180/day—book in advance, tel. 01286/677-059 for her schedule, mobile 07946-163-906, www.turnstone-tours.co.uk, info@turnstone-tours.co.uk).

SIGHTS

▲▲**Caernarfon Castle**—Edward I built this impressive castle 700 years ago to establish English rule over North Wales (see sidebar on page 420). Rather than being purely defensive, it also had elements of a palace—where Edward and his family could stay on visits to Wales. Modeled after the striped and angular walls of ancient Constantinople, the castle, while impressive, was never finished and never really used. From the inner courtyard, you can see the notched walls ready for more walls—that were never built. Its fame derives from its physical grandeur and its association with the Prince of Wales. The English king got the angry Welsh to agree that if he presented them with "a prince, born in Wales, who spoke not a word of English," they would submit to the crown. In time, Edward had a son born in Wales (here in Caernarfon), who spoke not a word of English, Welsh, or any other language—as an infant. In modern times, as another political maneuver, the Prince of Wales has been "invested" (given his title) here. This "tradition" actually dates only from the 20th century, and only two of 21 Princes of Wales have taken part.

In spite of its disappointing history, it's a great castle to explore. An essential part of any visit is the guided tour (50-min tours for £2 leave on the hour—and occasionally, with demand, on the half-hour—from the courtyard steps just beyond the ticket booth; if you're late, ask to join one in progress).

In the huge **Eagle Tower** (on the seaward side, to the far right as you enter), see the ground-floor "Prospect of Caernarfon" history exhibit (look for the model of the original castle); watch the 23-minute movie ("The Eagle and the Dragon," a broad mix of Welsh legend and history enacted—or overacted—by an elfin narrator, shown upstairs on the hour and half-hour); and climb the tower for a great view. The nearby **Chamberlain's Tower** and **Queen's Tower** (ahead and to the right as you enter) house the mildly interesting "Museum of the Royal Welsh Fusiliers"—a military branch made entirely of Welshmen. The museum shows off medals, firearms, uniforms, and information about various British battles and military strategies. The **northeast tower,** at the opposite end of the castle (to the left as you enter), has a "Princes of Wales" exhibit highlighting the investiture of Prince Charles in 1969.

Cost and Hours: £4.90, June–Sept daily 9:30–18:00; April–May and Oct daily 9:30–17:00; Nov–March Mon–Sat 9:30–16:00, Sun 11:00–16:00; tel. 01286/677-617. Martin de Lewandowicz gives mind-bending tours of the castle (tel. 01286/674-369).

Distractions—A Welsh Highland **steam train** billows through the countryside to Rhyd Ddu and back (£9.60 round-trip to Waunfawr, 1.5 hours; £16.95 round-trip to Rhyd Ddu, 2 hours; March–Oct daily, 4/day, tel. 01766/516-000, www.festrail.co.uk). This line is being extended, and will eventually go through Beddgelert and on to Porthmadog.

Narrated **harbor cruises** on the *Queen of the Sea* run daily in summer (£5, May–Sept 11:30–18:00 or 19:00, depending on weather, tides, and demand, 40 min, castle views, tel. 01286/672-772).

The **Segontium Roman Fort,** dating from A.D. 77, is the westernmost Roman fort. It was manned for more than 300 years to keep the Welsh and the coast quiet. Little is left but foundations (free, Tue–Sun 12:00–16:30, closed Mon, a 20-min walk from town, tel. 01286/675-625).

For pony riding, try **Snowdonia Riding Stables** (£15/1 hr, longer times available, 3 miles from Caernarfon, off the road to Beddgelert, bus #S4 from Caernarfon, tel. 01286/650-342).

Welsh Choir—If spending a Tuesday night, drop by the local men's choir practice (Tue 19:45–21:30 except Aug, at the Galeri convention center at Victoria Dock).

SLEEPING

(£1 = about $2, country code: 44, area code: 01286)
$$$ Celtic Royal Hotel rents 110 comfortable rooms with a gym, pool, hot tub, and sauna. Its grand, old-fashioned look comes with

modern-day conveniences—but it's still overpriced (Db-£115, bar, restaurant; it's on Bangor Street, a 5-min walk from bus stop: go right on Bridge Street, which turns into Bangor Street; tel. 01286/674-477, fax 01286/674-139, www.celtic-royal.co.uk).

$$ Caer Menai B&B ("Fort of the Menai Strait") rents seven bright, attractive rooms one block from the harbor (Db-£60–65, family room-£75–80, ask for seaview room, cash only, 15 Church Street, tel. 01286/672-612, www.caermenai.co.uk, info @caermenai.co.uk, John and Sandy Price).

$$ Victoria House B&B, next door to the Caer Menai, rents four airy, fresh, large-for-Britain rooms (Db-£55–60, free Wi-Fi, 13 Church Street, tel. 01286/678-263, www.thevictoriahouse .co.uk, jan@thevictoriahouse.co.uk, friendly Jan Baker).

$ Totters Hostel is a creative little hostel well-run by Bob and Henriette (28 beds in 5 dorm rooms, £15 per bed with sheets, includes continental breakfast, cash only, couples can have their own twin room when available-£35, beautiful and large top-floor Db-£45, open all day, lockers, welcoming cellar game room/lounge, kitchen, a block from castle at 2 High Street, tel. 01286/672-963, mobile 07979-830-470, www.totters.co.uk, bob @totters.free-online.co.uk). Ask about a possible new annex across the street with more private rooms.

EATING

The streets near Caernarfon's castle teem with inviting eateries. Rather than recommending a particular one, I'll point you in the direction of several good streets. Just follow your nose.

"Hole-in-the-Wall Street" (between Castle Square and TI) is lined with several charming cafés and bistros.

Nearby **High Street** has plenty of cheap and cheery sandwich shops and tearooms.

The pedestrianized **Pool Street** offers several budget options, including the popular **J&C's** fish-and-chips joint (£4, Mon–Sat 11:00–21:00, Sun 12:00–19:00).

Picnic: For groceries, you'll find a small **Spar** supermarket on the main square, an **Iceland** supermarket near the bus stop, and a huge **Morrisons** supermarket a five-minute walk from the city center on Bangor Street (just past Celtic Royal Hotel; all of these are open long hours daily).

TRANSPORTATION CONNECTIONS

Caernarfon is a handy hub for buses into Snowdonia National Park (such as Llanberis, Beddgelert, and Betws-y-Coed).

From Caernarfon by Bus to: Conwy (express bus #9A—

North Wales

hourly, 1 hr; bus #5 or #X5—2/hr, 1.5 hrs), **Llanberis** (2/hr, 25 min, bus #88), **Beddgelert** (8/day, 30 min, bus #S4), **Betws-y-Coed** (1.5–2 hrs, transfer in Conwy or Beddgelert), **Blaenau Ffestiniog** (hourly, 1.5 hrs, bus #1).

Snowdonia National Park

This is Britain's second-largest national park, and its center-piece—the tallest mountain in Wales or England—is Mount Snowdon. Each year, half a mil-

lion people ascend one of seven different paths to the top of the 3,560-foot mountain. Hikes take from five to seven hours; if you're fit and the weather's good, it's an exciting day. Trail info abounds (local TIs sell the small £3 book *The Ascent of Snowdon,* by E. G. Bowland, which describes the routes). As you explore, notice the slate roofs—the local specialty.

Betws-y-Coed

The resort center of Snowdonia National Park, Betws-y-Coed (BET-oos-uh-coyd) bursts with tour buses and souvenir shops.

This picturesque town is cuddled by wooded hills, made cozy by generous trees, and situated along a striking, waterfall-rippled stretch of the Conwy River. And yet, it feels overly manicured, with uniform checkerboard-stone houses yawning at each other from across a broad central green. Once here, there's little to do except wander along the waterfalls (don't miss the old stone bridge—just up the river from the green—with the best waterfall views), have a snack or meal, or go for a walk in the woods.

Stop by Betws-y-Coed's good **national-park office/TI,** which books rooms for a £2 fee and sells the handy £2 *Forest Walks* map, outlining five different walks you can do from here (daily April–Oct 9:30–17:30, Nov–March 9:30–12:30 & 13:30–16:30, tel. 01690/710-426). Sometimes in summer there's live entertainment

North Wales

Snowdonia Area

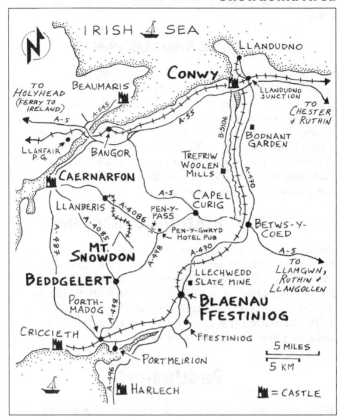

in the TI's courtyard. Robin Hamlett takes visitors on **guided walks** in the hills (£5/person, available Thu–Sun, call in advance to book, mobile 07790-851-333).

Arrival in Betws-y-Coed: Drivers can follow signs for *National Park* and *i* to find the main parking lot by the TI. **Trains** and **buses** arrive at the village green; with your back to the station, the TI is to the right of the green.

Nearby: If you drive west out of town on A5 (toward Beddgelert or Llanberis), after two miles you'll see the car park for scenic **Swallow Falls,** a pleasant five-minute walk from the road. A half-mile past the falls on the right, you'll see **The Ugly House,** built overnight to take advantage of a 15th-century law that let any quickie building avoid fees and taxes.

EATING AND SLEEPING

(£1 = about $2, country code: 44, area code: 01690)
$$ Bistro Betws-y-Coed—run by the owners of the popular Bistro Conwy (see page 425)—serves tasty Welsh cuisine just up the river from the TI on the main drag, with outdoor picnic-table seating (£5–8 lunches served daily from 11:00, £12–16 dinners served Wed-Sun from 18:30, closed for dinner Mon–Tue). They also rent two fine rooms upstairs (S-£33, Sb-£35, D-£45, Db-£50, Holyhead Road, tel. 01690/710-328, www.bistrobetws-y-coed .com, info@bistrobetws-y-coed.com).

TRANSPORTATION CONNECTIONS

Betws-y-Coed is connected to Conwy (north, 30 min) and Blaenau Ffestiniog (south, 30 min) by the Conwy Valley train line (5/day, 3/day on Sun). Buses connect Betws-y-Coed with **Conwy** (3/day, 50–60 min), **Llanberis** (6/day, 30 min, bus #S2), **Beddgelert** (4/day, 50 min, bus #S97), **Blaenau Ffestiniog** (7/day, 25 min, bus #X1), **Caernarfon** (1.5–2 hrs, transfer in Conwy or Beddgelert), and **Llangollen** (2/day, 1 hr, bus #X19).

Beddgelert

This is the quintessential Snowdon village, rated ▲▲ and packing a scenic mountain punch without the tourist crowds (17 miles from

Betws-y-Coed). Beddgelert (BETH-geh-lert) is a cluster of stone houses lining a babbling brook in the shadow of Mount Snowdon and her sisters. Cute as a hobbit, Beddgelert will have you looking for The Shire around the next bend. Thanks to the

fine variety of hikes from its doorstep and its decent bus service, Beddgelert makes a good stop for those wanting to experience the peace of Snowdonia.

There are no real "sights" here, but locals can recommend **walks.** You can follow the lane along the river (three miles round-trip), walk down the river and around the hill (3 hrs, 6 miles, 900-foot gain, via Cwm Bycham), hike along (or around) Llyn Gwynant

How Beddgelert Got Its Name

Prince Llywelyn, who had a dog named Gelert, went hunting one day, leaving his baby son with his dog. When the prince came home, he found the crib overturned and blood everywhere. The prince immediately drew his sword and killed the dog. In that instant, he heard a baby crying from under the crib. He turned the crib over and found the baby. Nearby, a dead wolf lay in the corner. The prince realized that his faithful dog Gelert had killed the preying wolf to protect the baby. He buried Gelert in a grave (*bedd* in Welsh).

Actually, the town is named for a sixth-century saint. Years ago, some clever entrepreneur invented the canine legend and set up a fake grave to attract visitors. To this day, local kids love to spy on gullible tourists mourning at the grave.

Lake and four miles back to Beddgelert (ride the bus to the lake), or try the dramatic ridge walks on Moel Hebog (Hawk Hill).

ORIENTATION

Beddgelert clusters around its triple-arch stone bridge. The five B&Bs line up single-file along one side of the brook, while the TI, hotels, and most eateries are on the other side. The **TI** can suggest tips for walks and hikes (April–Oct daily 9:30–17:30; Nov–March Fri–Sun 9:30–16:30—but closes for lunch, closed Mon–Thu; tel. 01766/890-615, www.beddgelerttourism.com). There's a small **Internet café** inside the TI (same hours). For **mountain-bike rental,** try Dawes Cycles (2 miles from Beddgelert, tel. 01766/890-434, www.beddgelertbikes.co.uk).

SLEEPING

(£1 = about $2, country code: 44, area code: 01766)

In Beddgelert

The five recommended B&Bs all line up in a row at the bridge. They're quite different from each other—each seems to fill its own niche. The larger inn (listed first) is across the river.

$$$ Tanronnen Inn has seven hotelesque rooms above a pub that's been beautifully renovated from the medieval timbers out (Sb-£55, Db-£100, cheaper for longer stays, tel. 01766/890-347, fax 01766/890-606, jilltan@12freeukisp.co.uk).

$$$ Plas Tan-y-Graig Guest House is the best value in town: seven thoughtfully updated, calming, uncluttered rooms run with care and contemporary style by Tony and Sharon (Db-£55–70 depending on season, fine lounge, beautiful breakfast terrace overlooking the village, tel. 01766/890-310, fax 01766/890-512, www .plastanygraig.co.uk, aklove@globalnet.co.uk).

$$ Plas Gwyn Guest House rents six rooms in a cozy, cheery, 19th-century town house with a comfy lounge. Friendly Brian Wheatley is happy to dispense travel tips (S-£30, Db-£60, 10 percent discount with this book in 2008, cash only, tel. 01766/890-215, mobile 07815-519-708, www.plas-gwyn.com, bandb@beddgelert .fsbusiness.co.uk).

$$ Colwyn Guest House has five tight but slick and new-feeling rooms (S-£25–30, D-£50–60, Db-£55–65, 10 percent discount with this book in 2008, cash only, free Internet access, tel. 01766/890-276, www.beddgelertguesthouse.co.uk, colwynguesthouse@tiscali.co.uk, Colleen).

$$ Plas Colwyn Guest House (not to be confused with "Colwyn Guest House," two doors down) is a lesser value, with six rooms run by Linda, Tony, and Puds the dog (S-£27, D-£54, Db-£60, free Wi-Fi, limited parking, tel. 01766/890-458, www.plascolwyn .co.uk, info@plascolwyn.co.uk). On peak-season evenings, the breakfast room becomes a restaurant with meals under £20.

$$ Beddgelert Antiques, Tea Rooms, and B&B is juggled by Sheila Johnson Porter with three rooms in a 300-year-old house that's cramped and creaky, but clean (Db-£50, snug bistro bar, tel. 01766/890-543).

Near Beddgelert

Mountaineers note that this area was used by Sir Edmund Hillary and his men as they practiced for the first ascent of Mount Everest. They slept at **$$$ Pen-y-Gwryd Hotel Pub,** at the base of the road leading up to the Pen-y-Pass by Mount Snowdon, and today the bar is strewn with fascinating memorabilia from Hillary's 1953 climb. The 17 rooms, with dingy old furnishings and crampon ambience, are a poor value—aside from the impressive history (S-£38, Sb-£45, D-£76, Db-£90, old-time-elegant public rooms, some D rooms share museum-piece Victorian tubs and showers, grand five-course dinners-£26, tel. 01286/870-211, www.pyg.co.uk).

EATING

In Beddgelert

Lyn's Café, just across the bridge from the B&Bs, serves nicely done home cookin' at good prices in a cozy one-room bistro (£3–5 lunches, £9 dinners, open daily for lunch and dinner but closes early off-season—don't wait too late; tel. 01766/890-374).

Many of Beddgelert's accommodations also serve food:

Tanronnen Inn serves up tasty food in an inviting pub setting, with several cozy and atmospheric rooms (£8-11 specials, cheaper snacks, tel. 01766/890-347). **Plas Colwyn Guest House** and **Beddgelert Antiques, Tea Rooms, and B&B** both run modest but good restaurants.

And for Dessert: The **Glaslyn Homemade Ice Cream** shop offers surprising quality and selection for this altitude.

TRANSPORTATION CONNECTIONS

Beddgelert is connected to **Caernarfon** by handy bus #S4 (8/day, 30 min), and to **Betws-y-Coed** by bus #S97 (4/day, 50 min). To reach **Conwy,** it's generally easiest to transfer in Caernarfon (6/day, 1.75 hrs); for **Blaenau Ffestiniog,** transfer in Betws-y-Coed (1–1.5 hrs).

Llanberis

A town of 2,000 people with as many tourists on a sunny day, Llanberis (TLAN-beh-ris) is a popular base for Snowdon activi-

ties. Most people prefer to take the train from here to the summit. But Llanberis is also loaded with hikers, as it's the launchpad for the longest (five miles) but least-strenuous hiking route to the Snowdon summit. (Routes from the nearby Pen-y-Pass, between here and Beddgelert, are steeper and even more scenic.)

ORIENTATION

Llanberis is a long, skinny, rugged, functional town that feels like a frontier village. **Drivers** approaching Llanberis will find several parking lots, including one right by the Snowdon Mountain Railway, and a lakeside lot (marked with an *i*) across the road from the town center and TI.

Tourist Information

The TI—right on the colorful main street (High Street) in the center of the village—sells maps and offers tips for ascending Snowdon (Easter–Sept daily 9:30–16:30; Oct–Easter Fri–Mon 10:30–16:30, closed Tue–Thu; 41B High Street, tel. 01286/870-765, www.visitsnowdonia.info).

SIGHTS

▲▲Snowdon Mountain Railway

This is the easiest and most popular ascent of Mount Snowdon. You'll travel 4.5 miles from Llanberis to the summit on a rack-and-pinion railway from 1896, climbing a total of 3,500 feet. On the way up, you'll hear a constant narration on legends, geology, and history. On the way down, there's only engine noise (£23 round-trip, 2.5 hrs, includes 30-min stop at top, train departs from station along the main road at the south end of Llanberis town center, tel. 0870-458-0033, www.snowdonrailway.co.uk).

The first departure is often at 9:00 (ask about possible discount if you book the day before). While the schedule flexes with weather and demand, they try to run several trips each day mid-March through October (up to 2/hr in peak season). On sunny summer days—especially in July and August—trains fill up fast. It's smart to reserve ahead by calling 0870-458-0033 (£2.50 fee per party). Otherwise, show up early—the office opens at 8:30, and on very busy days, tickets can be sold out by mid-morning; even if you get one, you may have to wait until afternoon for your scheduled departure time. Off-season trains often stop short of the summit (due to snow and high winds). A new visitors center is expected to be complete by mid-2008, but if it's not finished yet, the trains may not go all the way to the top even in summer. If for whatever reason you can't reach the summit, the ticket is discounted to £15.

Don't confuse this with the Llanberis Lake Railway, a different (and far less appealing) steam train that runs to the end of Padarn Lake and back.

Other Sights in Llanberis

▲Welsh Slate Museum—Across the lake from Llanberis yawns a giant slate quarry. To learn more, venture across to this fine and free museum. The well-presented exhibit, displayed around the workshop that was used until 1969 to support the giant slate mine above, explains various aspects of this local industry. In addition to a giant water wheel and the slate-splitting demo, the museum has a little row of modest quarrymen's houses from different eras, offering a thought-provoking glimpse into their hardy lifestyle. While not as in-depth (literally) as the Llechwedd Slate Mine in Blaenau Ffestiniog, this is interesting and convenient (free entry but £2 parking; Easter–Oct daily 10:00–17:00; Nov–Easter Sun–Fri 10:00–16:00, closed Sat; tel. 01286/870-630, www.museumwales.ac.uk/en/slate).

Electric Mountain—This attraction offers visits into a power plant burrowed into the mountain across the lake from town (£7, frequent tours June–Aug, otherwise call ahead, tel. 01286/870-636, www.electricmountain.co.uk).

SLEEPING

(£1 = about $2, country code: 44, area code: 01286)
$$ Dolafon Guest House ("River Meadows") is a beautiful 1860s Victorian building with seven traditionally furnished rooms (Db-£56–75, depends on size, garden, High Street, tel. & fax 01286/870-993, www.dolafon.com, sandra@dolafon.com).

TRANSPORTATION CONNECTIONS

Llanberis is easiest to reach from **Caernarfon** (2/hr, 25 min, bus #88) or **Betws-y-Coed** (6/day, 30 min, bus #S2); from **Conwy,** transfer in one of these towns (Caernarfon is generally best). While it's a quick 30-minute drive from Llanberis to **Beddgelert,** the bus connection is more complicated, requiring a transfer at Pen-y-Pass, on the high road around Mount Snowdon (transfer from bus #S1 or #S2 to bus #S97).

Blaenau Ffestiniog

Blaenau Ffestiniog (BLEH-nigh FES-tin-yog) is a quintessential Welsh slate-mining town, notable for its slate-mine tour and its old steam train. The town—a dark, poor place—seems to struggle on, oblivious to the tourists who nip in and out. Though it's tucked amidst a pastoral Welsh landscape, Blaenau Ffestiniog is surrounded by a gun-metal gray wasteland of "tips," huge mountain-like piles of excess slate.

Take a walk. The shops are right out of the 1950s. Long rows of humble "two-up and two-down" houses (four rooms) feel a bit grim.

The train station, bus stop, parking lot, and TI all cluster along a one-block stretch in the heart of town. The **TI** books rooms for a £2 fee (Easter–Oct daily 9:30–12:30 & 13:30–17:30, closed Nov–Easter, tel. 01766/830-360).

Getting There: Blaenau Ffestiniog is conveniently connected to **Betws-y-Coed** and **Conwy** both by the Conwy Valley train line (5/day, 3/day on Sun, 30 min to Betws-y-Coed, 1 hr to Conwy) and by bus #X1 (7/day, 25 min to Betws-y-Coed, 1 hr to Llandudno Junction near Conwy). To connect with **Beddgelert,** transfer in Betws-y-Coed (1–1.5 hrs).

North Wales

SIGHTS

▲▲Llechwedd Slate-Mine Tour

Slate mining played a blockbuster role in Welsh heritage, and

this mine on the northern edge of Blaenau Ffestiniog does a fine job of explaining the mining culture of Victorian Wales.

The Welsh mined and split most of the slate roofs of Europe. For every ton of usable slate found, 10 tons were mined. The exhibit has a free section and two expensive tours. It's free to enter the tiny Victorian mining town (with a miners' pub and a view from "The Top of the Tip," free and worthwhile but closed Oct–March). The cool slate-splitting demonstration, which is at the end of the tramway tour, is also free to the public but occurs only at certain times (likely at 12:00, 14:00, and 16:00—check the posted schedule and plan your visit around it).

For a more in-depth visit, you'll have to pay for one or both of two different tours (2-6/hr): The **"tramway"** tour is a level train ride with three stops, not much walking, and a live guide. It focuses on working life and traditional mining techniques. The **"deep mine"** tour descends deep into the mountain for an audiovisual dramatization of social life and a half-mile of walking with lots of uneven stairs. The tours overlap slightly, but the combo-ticket makes doing both worth considering (£9.25 for 1 tour, £14.75 for both tours, daily March–Sept 10:00–18:00, Oct–Feb 10:00–17:00, last tour starts 45 min before closing, cafeteria, tel. 01766/830-306, www.llechwedd-slate-caverns.co.uk). Dress warmly—I mean it. You'll freeze underground without a sweater. Lines are longer when rain drives in the hikers.

Getting There: The slate mine is about a mile from the town center. Each arriving train on the Ffestiniog Railway from Porthmadog (see below) is met by a bus that takes you directly to the mine (except on Saturdays). Unfortunately, buses don't meet the more useful Conwy Valley train line from Conwy and Betws-y-Coed, but you can walk to the mine or take a taxi (£5, tel. 01766/762-465 or 01766/831-781).

Near Blaenau Ffestiniog

▲**Ffestiniog Railway**—This 13-mile narrow-gauge train line was built in 1836 for small horse-drawn wagons to transport the slate from the Ffestiniog mines to the port of Porthmadog. In the 1860s, horses gave way to steam trains. Today, hikers and tourists enjoy these tiny titans (£17 round-trip, 2–8/day depending on season, 2.5 hours round-trip, first-class observation cars cost £8 extra, closed Nov–March, tel. 01766/516-000). This is a novel steam-train experience, but the full-size Llandudno–Blaenau Ffestiniog train is more scenic and works better for hikers (5/day, 3/day on Sun, 1 hr). **Portmeirion**—Ten miles southwest of Blaenau Ffestiniog, this "Italian Village" was the lifework of a rich local architect who began building it in 1925. Set idyllically on the coast just beyond the poverty of the slate-mine towns, this flower-filled fantasy is extravagant. Surrounded by lush Welsh greenery and a windswept mudflat at low tide, the village is an artistic glob of palazzo arches, fountains, gardens, and promenades filled with cafés, tacky shops, a hotel, and local tourists who always wanted to go to Italy (or who are fans of the cultish British 1960s TV series *The Prisoner*, which was filmed here).

TRANSPORTATION CONNECTIONS

North Wales

Two major transfer points out of (or into) North Wales are Crewe and Chester. Figure out your complete connection at www.nationalrail.co.uk.

From Crewe by Train to: London (2/hr, 2 hrs), **Bristol,** near Bath (hourly, 2.5 hrs), **Cardiff** (hourly, 2.5 hrs), **Holyhead** (nearly hourly, 2 hrs), **Blackpool** (4/day, 2.5 hrs, more frequent with transfer in Preston), **Keswick** in the Lake District (hourly, 1.75 hrs to Penrith, then catch a bus to Keswick, hourly except Sun 6/day, 40 min), **Glasgow** (nearly hourly, 3.5 hrs).

From Chester by Train to: London (hourly, 3.5 hrs), **Liverpool** (2/hr, 45 min), **Birmingham** (hourly, 2 hrs); points in North Wales including **Conwy** (hourly, 1 hr, some with transfer in Llandudno Junction).

Ferry Connections Between North Wales and Ireland

Two companies make the crossing between Holyhead (in North Wales, beyond Caernarfon) and Ireland. Some boats go to Dublin, while others head for Dublin's southern suburb of Dun Laoghaire (pronounced "Dun Leary"). **Stena Line** sails from Holyhead to Dublin (2/day, 3.25 hrs) and also to Dun Laoghaire (2/day, 1.75 hrs; one-way walk-on fare for either crossing-£23, cheaper if booked in advance, extra to use credit card, reserve by phone or online—they book up long in advance on summer weekends, Britain tel. 08705-707-070, or book online at www.stenaline.com). **Irish Ferries** sails to Dublin (4/day—2 slow, 2 fast; slow boat 3.25 hrs, fast boat 1.75

hrs; one-way walk-on fare for either crossing–£20; reserve online for best fares; Britain tel. 08705-171-717, for Irish number dial 00-353-818-300-400 from Britain, www.irishferries.co.uk).

Sleeping near Holyhead Dock: The fine **$$ Monravon B&B** has seven rooms a 15-minute uphill walk from the dock (Sb–£35, Db–£50, family deals, free Wi-Fi, Porth-Y-Felin Road, tel. & fax 01407/762-944, www.monravon.co.uk, monravon@yahoo.co.uk).

Route Tips for Drivers

One-Day North Wales Blitz Tour from Ruthin

Ruthin to Caernarfon (56 miles) to Blaenau Ffestiniog (34 miles) back to Ruthin (35 miles): This route connects the top sights with the most scenic routes. From Ruthin, take B5105 (steepest road off main square) and follow signs to *Cerrigydrudion*. Then follow A5 into Betws-y-Coed, with a possible quick detour to the Trefriw Woolen Mills (5 miles north on B5106, well-signposted). Climb west on A5 through Capel Curig, then take A4086 over the rugged Pass of Llanberis, under the summit of Mount Snowdon (to the south, behind those clouds), and on to Caernarfon. Park under the castle in the harborside car park.

Leaving Caernarfon, take lovely A4085 southeast through Beddgelert to Penrhyndeudraeth. (Make things even more beautiful by taking the little B4410 road from Garreg through Rhyd.) Then take A487 toward What Maentwrog and A496 to Blaenau Ffestiniog. Go through the dark and depressing mining town of Blaenau Ffestiniog on A470, continue over hills of slate, and turn right into the Llechwedd Slate Mine.

After the mine, continue uphill on A470, snapping photos north through Dolwyddelan (passing a fine old Welsh castle ruin) and back to A5. For a high and desolate detour, return to Ruthin via curvy A543. Go over the stark moors to the Sportsman's Arms Pub (the highest pub in Wales, good food), continue through Denbigh, and then go home.

Reaching and Departing North Wales
From Points South in England to North Wales

To Ruthin: Drive to Wales via A5 through Shrewsbury, crossing into Wales and following A5 to Llangollen. Cross the bridge in Llangollen, turn left, and follow A542 and A525 past the romantic Vale Crucis Abbey, over the scenic Horseshoe Pass, and into Ruthin.

To Conwy and the North Coast: Driving to Conwy is faster via Wrexham and then A55, but more scenic if you stay on A5 from Llangollen to Betws-y-Coed and then zip north to Conwy from there.

North Wales

From North Wales to Points North in England

From North Wales to Liverpool (40 miles): From Ruthin or A55, follow signs to the town of *Mold*, then *Queensferry*, then *Manchester M56*, then *Liverpool M53*, which tunnels under the Mersey River (£1.30).

From North Wales to Blackpool, Skipping Liverpool (100 miles): From A55, follow the blue signs to the motorway. (From Ruthin, you can reach A55 by taking A494 through the town of Mold). The M56 road zips you to M6, where you'll turn north toward Preston and Lancaster (don't miss your turnoff). A few minutes after Preston, take the not-very-clearly signed next exit (#32, M55) into Blackpool, and drive as close as you can to the stubby Eiffel-type tower in the town center. For parking tips, see page 302.

SCOTLAND

SCOTLAND

Rugged, feisty, colorful Scotland is the yin to England's yang. Whether it's the looser, less-organized nature of the people, the stone and sandstone architecture, the unmanicured landscape, or simply the haggis, you'll know you've left jolly olde England. The home of kilts, bagpipes, whisky, golf, lochs, and shortbread lives up to its clichéd image—and then some.

Scotland makes up about a third of Britain's geographical area (30,400 square miles), but has less than a tenth of its population (just over five million). This sparsely populated chunk of land stretches to Norwegian latitudes. Its Shetland Islands, at about 60°N (similar to Anchorage, Alaska), are the northernmost point in Britain.

The southern part of Scotland, called the Lowlands, is relatively flat and urbanized. The northern area—the Highlands—

features a wild, severely undulating terrain, punctuated by lochs (lakes) and fringed by sea lochs (inlets) and islands. The Highland Boundary Fault that divides Scotland geologically also divides it culturally. Historically, there was a big difference between grizzled, kilt-wearing Highlanders in the northern wilderness, and the more refined Lowlanders in the southern flatlands and cities. The Highlanders talk and act like "true Scots," while the Lowlanders often seem more British than Scottish. While this division has faded over time, some Scots still cling to it today—city slickers down south think that Highlanders are crude and unrefined...while those who live at high latitudes grumble about the soft, pampered urbanites in the Lowlands.

The Lowlands are dominated by a pair of rival cities: Edinburgh, the old royal capital, oozes with Scottish history and is the country's single best tourist attraction. Glasgow, once a gloomy industrial city, is becoming a hip, laid-back city of today, known

Scotland

FERRY ROUTES (NOT ALL SHOWN)

ATLANTIC OCEAN

ORKNEY

STROMNESS

KIRKWALL

50 MILES

30 KM

THURSO

JOHN O'GROATS

LEWIS

NORTH UIST

KYLE OF LOCHALSH

MORAY FIRTH

CULLODEN

SOUTH UIST

PORTREE

SKYE

INVERNESS

LOCH NESS

ABERDEEN

RUM

MALLAIG

BEN NEVIS

PITLOCHRY

NORTH SEA

COLL

TIREE

FT. WILLIAM

GLENCOE

DUNDEE

MULL

OBAN

PERTH

ST. ANDREWS

EAST NEUK

IONA

LOCH LOMOND

STIRLING

FIRTH OF FORTH

JURA

ISLAY

GLASGOW

EDINBURGH

CAMPBELTOWN

ARRAN

TROON

AYR

LOWLANDS

BERWICK-UPON-TWEED

NORTHERN IRELAND

CAIRNRYAN

STRANRAER

ENGLAND

CARLISLE

LARNE

BELFAST

HADRIAN'S WALL

NEW-CASTLE

IRISH SEA

TO DUBLIN

TO LAKE DISTRICT

TO YORK & LONDON

CALEDONIAN CANAL

HIGHLANDS

DCH

for its modern architecture. The university town and golf mecca of St. Andrews, the whisky village of Pitlochry, and the historic city of Stirling round out the Lowlands' top sights.

The Highlands provide your best look at traditional Scotland (though frankly, Ireland has more charm and North Wales has better sights). There are a lot of miles, but they're scenic, the roads are good, and the traffic is light. Generally, the Highlands are hungry for the tourist dollar, and everything overtly Scottish is exploited to the kilt. You'll need more than a quick visit to get away from that. But if two days is all you have, you can get a feel for the area with a quick drive to Oban, through Glencoe, then up the Caledonian Canal to Inverness. With more time, the islands of Iona and Mull (an easy day trip from Oban), the Isle of Skye, and

countless brooding countryside castles will flesh out your
Highlands experience.

The Highlands are more
rocky and harsh than other
parts of the British Isles. It's no
wonder that most of the scenes
around Hogwarts in the Harry
Potter movies were filmed in
this moody, even spooky landscape. While Scotland's "hills" are
technically too short to be called "mountains," they do a convincing imitation. Scotland has 284 hills over 3,000 feet. A list of
these was compiled in 1891 by Sir Hugh Munro, and to this day
the Scots still call their high hills "Munros." About 3,300 intrepid
hikers can brag that they've climbed all of the Munros.

In the summer, the Highlands swarm with tourists...and
midges. These miniscule mosquitoes—called "no-see-ums" in some
parts of the US—are bloodthirsty and determined. Depending on
the weather, you'll be covered with them between mid-June and late
August. Hot sun or a stiff breeze blows the tiny buggers away, but
they thrive in damp, shady areas. Locals suggest blowing or brushing
them off, rather than swatting them—since killing them only seems
to attract more (likely because of the smell of fresh blood). Locals
say, "If you kill one midge, a million will come to his funeral." Better
yet, even if you don't usually travel with bug spray, consider bringing
or buying some for a summer visit...or your most vivid memory of
your Scottish vacation might be itchy arms and legs.

Keep an eye out for another uniquely
Scottish animal: shaggy Highland
cattle, with their hair falling in their
eyes. Dubbed "hairy coos," these adorable beasts will melt your heart. With a
heavy coat to keep them insulated, hairy
coos graze on sparse vegetation that
other animals ignore.

In this northern climate, cold and
drizzly weather isn't uncommon—even
in midsummer. The blazing sun can
quickly be covered over by black clouds
and howling wind. Scots warn visitors
to prepare for "four seasons in one day." Because the Scots feel
personally responsible for bad weather, they tend to be overly optimistic about forecasts. Take any Scottish promise of "sun by the
afternoon" with a grain of salt...and bring your raincoat.

The major theme of Scottish history is the drive for independence, especially from England. (Scotland's rabble-rousing

national motto: "No one provokes me with impunity.") Like Wales, Scotland is a country of ragtag Celts sharing an island with wealthy and powerful Anglo-Saxons. Scotland's Celtic culture is a result of its remoteness—the invading Romans were never able to conquer this rough-and-tumble people, and even built Hadrian's Wall to lock off this distant corner of their empire (see page 393). The Anglo-Saxons, and their descendants the English, had no more luck than the Romans did. Even King Edward I—who so successfully dominated Wales—was unable to hold onto Scotland, largely thanks to the relentlessly rebellious William Wallace (a.k.a. "Braveheart"—see sidebar on page 465).

Failing to conquer Scotland by the blade, England eventually absorbed it politically. In 1603, England's Queen Elizabeth I died without an heir, so Scotland's King James VI took the throne, becoming King James I of England. It took another century or so of battles, both military and diplomatic, but the Act of Union in 1707 definitively unified the Kingdom of Great Britain. In 1745, Bonnie Prince Charlie attempted to reclaim the Scottish throne, but his army was trounced at the Battle of Culloden (see sidebar on page 602). This cemented English rule over Scotland, and is seen by many Scots as the last gasp of the traditional Highlands clan system.

Scotland has been joined—however unwillingly—to England ever since, and the Scots have often felt oppressed by their English countrymen (see "British, Scottish, and English" on page 468). During the Highland Clearances in the 18th century, landowners (mostly English) decided that vast tracks of land were more profitable as grazing land for sheep, than as farmland for people. Many Highlanders were forced to abandon their traditional homes and lifestyles and seek employment elsewhere. Large numbers ended up in North America, especially parts of eastern Canada, such as Prince Edward Island and Nova Scotia (literally, "New Scotland").

Today, Americans and Canadians of Scottish descent enjoy coming "home" to Scotland. If you're Scottish, your surname will tell you which clan your ancestors likely belonged to. "Mac" means "son of"—so "MacDonald" means the same thing as "Donaldson." ("Mc" is an abbreviation of "Mac," and can indicate Irish ancestry...or lazy immigration officials at Ellis Island.) Tourist shops everywhere are happy to help you track down your clan's tartan, or distinctive plaid pattern.

Is Scotland really a country? Increasingly, the answer is yes. Over the last several years, Scotland has enjoyed its greatest measure of independence in centuries—a trend called "devolution." In 1998, the Scottish Parliament opened its doors in Edinburgh for the first time in almost 300 years. While the Scottish Parliament's powers are limited (most major decisions are still made in London), the Scots are enjoying the refreshing breeze of freedom. Today's politicians are poised to ask the EU to recognize Scotland as a separate country.

Scotland even has its own currency. While they use the same coins as England, Scotland prints its own bills (with Scottish rather than British people and landmarks). Confusingly, three different banks print Scottish pound notes, each with a different design. In the Lowlands (around Edinburgh and Glasgow), you'll receive both Scottish and English pounds from ATMs and in change. But in the Highlands, you'll almost never see English pounds. In England, Scottish pounds are technically not legal tender—so, while some English vendors accept them, others (especially small businesses) don't.

The Scottish flag—a diagonal, X-shaped white cross on a blue field—represents the diagonal cross symbolizing Scotland's patron saint, the Apostle Andrew. You may not realize it, but you see the Scottish flag every time you look at the Union Jack: England's flag (a red cross) superimposed on Scotland's (a blue field with a white diagonal cross). The diagonal red cross over Scotland's white cross represents Ireland.

Scots are known for their inimitable burr, but they are also proud of their old Celtic language, called Gaelic (pronounced "gallic"; Ireland's language is spelled the same but pronounced "gaylic"). Gaelic thrives only in the remotest corners of Scotland, such as the Outer Hebrides islands. In the towns and cities, virtually nobody speaks Gaelic every day, but the language is kept on life-support by a Scottish population keen to remember their heritage. New Gaelic schools are opening all the time, and Scotland recently passed a law to replace road signs with new ones listing both English and Gaelic spellings (e.g., Edinburgh/Dùn Èideann).

Scottish cuisine is down-to-earth, often with an emphasis on local produce. Both seafood and "land food" (beef and chicken) are common. One Scottish mainstay—eaten more by tourists than by Scots these days—is the famous haggis, a rich assortment of oats and sheep organs stuffed into a chunk of sheep intestine, liberally seasoned and boiled. Usually served with "neeps and tatties" (turnips and potatoes), it's tastier than it sounds and worth trying... once.

The "Scottish Breakfast" is similar to the English version, but they add a potato scone (like a flavorless, soggy potato pancake) and occasionally haggis (which is hard enough to get down at dinnertime).

Scotland

Scottish Words

While **scotch** is the peaty drink the bartender serves you, the nationality of the bartender is **Scots** or **Scottish.** Here are some other Scottish words that may come in handy during your time in Edinburgh:

aye	yes
ben	mountain
blether	talk
bonnie	beautiful
brae	slope, hill
cairn	pile of stones
close	courtyard or square
craig	rock, cliff
inch, innis	island
inver	river, mouth
kyle	strait
loch	lake
neeps	turnips
ree	royal, king ("righ" in Gaelic)
tattie	potato
wee	small
wynd	tight, winding lane connecting major streets

A sharp intake of breath (like a little gasp), sometimes while saying "aye," means "yes."

Breakfast, lunch, or dinner, the Scots love their whisky—and touring one of the country's many distilleries is a sightseeing treat. The Scots are fiercely competitive with the Irish when it comes to this peaty spirit. Scottish "whisky" is distilled twice, while Irish "whiskey" adds a third distillation (and an extra *e*). Also note that what we call "scotch"—short for "scotch whisky"—is just "whisky" here. I've listed several of the most convenient and interesting distilleries to visit, but if you're a whisky connoisseur, make a point of tracking down and touring your favorite.

Another unique Scottish flavor to sample is the soft drink called Irn-Bru (pronounced "Iron Brew"). This bright-orange beverage tastes not like orange soda, but like bubblegum with a slightly bitter aftertaste. (The diet version is even more bitter.) While Irn-Bru's appeal eludes non-Scots, it's hugely popular here, even outselling Coke. Be cautious sipping it—as the label understates, "If spilt, this product may stain."

Whether toasting with beer, whisky, or Irn-Bru, enjoy meeting the Scottish people. Many travelers fall in love with the irrepressible spirit and beautiful landscape of this faraway corner of Britain.

EDINBURGH

Edinburgh is the historical and cultural capital of Scotland. Once a medieval powerhouse sitting on a lava flow, it grew into Europe's first great grid-planned modern city. The colorful hometown of Robert Louis Stevenson, Sir Walter Scott, and Robert Burns is Scotland's showpiece and one of Europe's most entertaining cities. Historic, monumental, fun, and well-organized, it's a tourist's delight—especially in August, when the Edinburgh Festival takes over the town.

Promenade down the Royal Mile through Old Town. Historic buildings pack the Royal Mile between the grand castle (on the top) and the Palace of Holyroodhouse (on the bottom). Medieval skyscrapers stand shoulder to shoulder, hiding peaceful courtyards connected to High Street by narrow lanes or even tunnels. This colorful jumble is the tourist's Edinburgh.

Edinburgh (ED'n-burah) was once the most crowded city in Europe—famed for its skyscrapers and filth. The rich and poor lived atop one another. In the Age of Enlightenment, a magnificent Georgian city (today's New Town) was laid out to the north, giving Edinburgh's upper class a respectable place to promenade. Georgian Edinburgh—like the city of Bath—shines with broad boulevards, straight streets, square squares, circular circuses, and elegant mansions decked out in colonnades, pediments, and sphinxes in the proud Neoclassical style of 200 years ago.

While the Georgian city celebrated the union of Scotland and England (with streets and squares named after English kings and emblems), "devolution" is the latest trend. For the past several centuries, Scotland was ruled from London, and Parliament had not met in Edinburgh since 1707. But in a 1998 election, the Scots

Greater Edinburgh

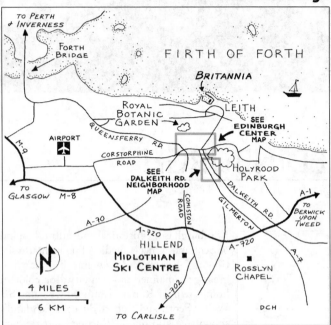

voted to gain more autonomy and bring their Parliament home. In 2000, Edinburgh resumed its position as home to the Scottish Parliament (although London still calls the strategic shots). A strikingly modern new Parliament building, which opened in 2004, is one more jewel in Edinburgh's crown. Today, you'll notice many references to the "nation" of Scotland.

Planning Your Time

While the major sights can be seen in a day, on a three-week tour of Britain, I'd give Edinburgh two days and three nights.

Day 1: Tour the castle. Then consider either catching an 11:00 walking tour (leaves from Mercat Cross on the Royal Mile) or one of the city bus tours (from a block below the castle at The Hub/ Tolbooth church) for a 60-minute loop, returning to the castle. Wander down the Royal Mile, have lunch, go to museums, and shop. (Note that in August, another walking tour leaves at 14:00 from Mercat Cross.) Finish your sightseeing day with a tour of the Palace of Holyroodhouse, at the bottom of the Mile.

Day 2: Tour the Museum of Scotland. After lunch, stroll through the Princes Street Gardens and the National Gallery of Scotland. Then tour the good ship *Britannia*.

Evenings: Options include various "haunted Edinburgh"

Edinburgh

walks, literary pub crawls, live music in pubs, or a touristy bagpipe-music evening. Sadly, traditional folk shows are just about extinct, surviving only in excruciatingly schmaltzy variety shows put on for tour-bus groups. Perhaps the most authentic local evening out is just settling down in a pub to sample the whisky and local beers while meeting the natives...and attempting to understand them through their thick Scottish accents.

ORIENTATION

(area code: 0131)
The center of Edinburgh holds the Princes Street Gardens park and Waverley Bridge, where you'll find the TI, Princes Mall, train station, bus info office (starting point for most city bus tours), National Gallery, and a covered dance-and-music pavilion. Weather blows in and out—bring your sweater and be prepared for rain. Locals say the bad weather is one of the disadvantages of living so close to England.

Tourist Information
The crowded TI is as central as can be atop the Princes Mall and train station (July–Aug Mon–Sat 9:00–20:00, Sun 10:00–20:00; May–June and Sept Mon–Sat 9:00–19:00, Sun 10:00–19:00; April and Oct Mon–Sat 9:00–18:00, Sun 10:00–18:00; Nov–March Mon–Wed 9:00–17:00, Thu–Sat 9:00–18:00, Sun 10:00–17:00; ATM outside entrance, tel. 0845-225-5121). The staff is knowledge-able and eager to help, but much of their information—including their assessment of museums and even which car-rental companies "exist"—is skewed by tourism payola.

Pick up a free map or buy the excellent £4 *Collins Illustrated Edinburgh* map (which comes with opinionated commentary and locates virtually every major shop and sight). If you're interested in late-night music, ask for the free monthly entertainment Gig Guide. The free Essential Guide to Edinburgh, while not truly essential, lists additional sights and services. The TI also sells the mediocre Edinburgh Pass, which provides unlimited bus travel (includes the airport) and entry to dozens of B-list sights (£24/1 day, £36/2 days, £48/3 days, doesn't include Edinburgh Castle, www.edinburghpass.org).

Book your room direct, using my listings, without the TI's help (as the TI takes 10 percent plus a £3 booking fee, and B&Bs charge more for rooms booked through the TI). Browse the racks—tucked away in the hallway at the back of the TI—for brochures on the various Scottish folk shows, walking tours, and regional bus tours.

Connect@edinburgh, a small Internet café, is beyond the

brochure racks (see "Helpful Hints," below). The best monthly entertainment listing, *The List,* sells for £2.20 at newsstands.

Arrival in Edinburgh

By Train: Arriving by train at Waverley Station puts you in the city center and below the TI. High-security luggage storage is near platform 1 (£5/24 hrs, daily 7:00–23:00). Taxis queue almost track-side; the ramp they come and go on leads to Waverley Bridge. If there's a long line for taxis, it's faster to hike the ramp and hail one on the street. From the station, *Way Out to Princes Street* signs lead up to the TI and the city bus stop (for bus directions from here to my recommended B&Bs, see page 493). For picnic supplies, there's a **Marks & Spencer Simply Food** near platform 1.

   By Bus: Both Scottish Citylink and National Express buses use the bus station (which has luggage lockers) two blocks north of the train station on St. Andrew Square in the New Town.

   By Plane: Edinburgh's slingshot-of-an-airport, located 10 miles northwest of the center, is well-connected by taxi (£20, 30 min to the center) and shuttle bus (LRT Airlink bus #100 to Waverley Bridge, £3 or £5 with all-day Airsaver city-bus pass, 6/ hr, 30 min, buses run all day and more sporadically through the night, tel. 0131/555-6363, www.flybybus.com). Flight info: tel. 0870-040-0007, www.edinburghairport.com.

Helpful Hints

Festivals: August is a crowded, popular month to visit Edinburgh because of the multiple festivals hosted here, including the official Edinburgh Festival (Aug 8–31 in 2008, see page 487). Book ahead if you'll be visiting during this month, and expect to pay significantly more for your accommodations.

Sunday Activities: Many minor sights close on Sunday, but the major sights are open (and most sights are open daily in Aug). Sunday is a good day for a Royal Mile walking tour or a city bus tour (which go faster in light traffic). Arthur's Seat is lively with locals on weekends (see "Arthur's Seat Hike," page 486).

Internet Access: Get online at **easyInternetcafé** (daily 7:00– 21:00, 400 terminals, bring change for machines, a block from National Gallery at 58 Rose Street, above Caffè Nero); **Connect@edinburgh** (in the TI, same hours as TI); or the atmospheric **Elephant House Café** (daily 9:00–22:00, 4 sta- tions, 24 George IV Bridge, off top of Royal Mile, see page 497).

Laundry: Sun Dial launderette is located near the recommended B&Bs on Dalkeith Road (Mon–Fri 8:00–20:00, Sat 9:00– 17:00, Sun 10:00–16:00, self-service or drop-off; along the bus route to the city center at 13 South Clerk Street, opposite

Queens Hall; tel. 0131/667-0549).

Car Rental: Except for Budget, these places have offices both in the town center and at the airport: **Avis** (5 West Park Place, tel. 0870-153-9103, airport tel. 0131/344-3900), **Europcar** (24 East London Street, tel. 0131/557-3456, airport tel. 0131/333-2588), **Hertz** (10 Picardy Place, tel. 0131/556-8311, airport tel. 0131/333-1019), and **Budget** (airport only, tel. 0131/333-1926). Some downtown offices are closed on Sunday, but the airport locations tend to be open daily—call ahead to confirm. If you're going to rent a car, pick it up on your way out of Edinburgh, since you won't need it in town.

Local Guide: Ken Hanley wears his kilt as if pants don't exist, and loves sharing his passion for Edinburgh and Scotland. A licensed Blue Badge guide, Ken comes equipped with a car and all the great stories (£65/half-day, £105/day, extra if he uses his car, tel. 0131/666-1944, mobile 07710-342-044, www.small-world-tours.co.uk, k.hanley@blueyonder.co.uk).

Getting Around Edinburgh

Nearly all of Edinburgh's sights are within walking distance of each other.

City **buses** are handy, and run from about 6:00 to 23:00 (£1/ride, buy tickets on bus, LRT transit office at Old Town end of Waverley Bridge has schedules and route maps, tel. 0131/555-6363). Tell the driver where you're going, have change handy (buses require exact change—you lose any excess), take your ticket as you board, and ping the bell as you near your stop. Double-deckers come with fine views upstairs. Two companies handle the city routes: LRT (or Lothian) does most, and First does the rest. (To get from the city center to the recommended B&Bs on Dalkeith Road, you can catch LRT buses #30 and #33, or First buses #14 and #86; for details, see page 493.) Day passes sold by each company are valid only on their buses (£2.30, buy from driver).

The 1,300 **taxis** cruising Edinburgh's streets are easy to flag down (a ride between downtown and B&B district costs about £5). As they can turn on a dime, hail them in either direction.

TOURS

In Edinburgh

For evening ghost walks and pub tours, see page 488.

Royal Mile Walking Tours—**Mercat Tours** offers 90-minute guided walks of the Mile—more entertaining than historic (£8.50, daily at 14:15, leaves from Mercat Cross on the Royal Mile, tel. 0131/225-5445, www.mercattours.com). The guides, who enjoy making a short story long, ignore the big sights and take you behind the scenes with piles of barely historic gossip, bully-pulpit Scottish pride, and fun but forgettable trivia. These tours can move quickly, scaling the steep hills and steps of Edinburgh—wear good shoes. They've recently expanded to offer several ghost tours, as well as a tour focused on Edinburgh's literary history.

In August only, the **Voluntary Guides Association** leads free two-hour tours of Edinburgh (generally departing daily at about 10:00 and 14:00, check at TI or call for a schedule, tel. 0131/664-7180 or 0131/669-8263).

Edinburgh Bus Tours—Four different 60-minute, hop-on, hop-off bus tours, all operated by LRT, circle the town center and stop along one route at the biggies: Waverley Bridge, the castle, Royal Mile, Georgian New Town, and Princes Street. You can hop on and off at any stop all day with one ticket (pick-ups about every 10–15 min). To compare your options, talk to the guides and drivers at the Waverley Bridge starting point. (Why four different tours, all owned by the same big company? It has to do with local anti-monopoly laws.)

The ride comes with informative narration. Two of the tours have live guides: **Mac Tours' City Tour** (live Mon–Fri with "vintage buses") and **Edinburgh Tour** (always live). Avoid the **City Sightseeing Tours,** which have a recorded narration (better for non-English speakers). The tours have virtually the same route, cost, and frequency, except the **Majestic Tour,** whose regular route is longer and includes a stop at the *Britannia* and the Royal Botanic Garden (£9, tickets give 10 percent discount off castle admission, valid 24 hours, buy on bus, tel. 0131/220-0770, www.edinburghtour.com). Buses run daily year-round; in peak season, they leave Waverley Bridge daily between around 9:15 and 19:00 (mid-June–early Sept; hours shrink off-season). On sunny days they go topless (the buses), but come with increased traffic noise and exhaust fumes.

Busy sightseers might want to get the **Royal Edinburgh Ticket** (for £34), which covers two days unlimited travel on all four tour buses, as well as admission to Edinburgh Castle (normally costs £11), the Palace of Holyroodhouse (£9.50), and the *Britannia* (£9.50). If you plan to visit all these sights and to use a tour bus both days, the ticket will save you a few pounds (and, in the summer, help you bypass any lines). You can buy these tickets from the staff at the pick-up point on Waverley Bridge. If your main interest is seeing the *Britannia*, you'll save money by taking a regular bus instead (see page 485).

Edinburgh

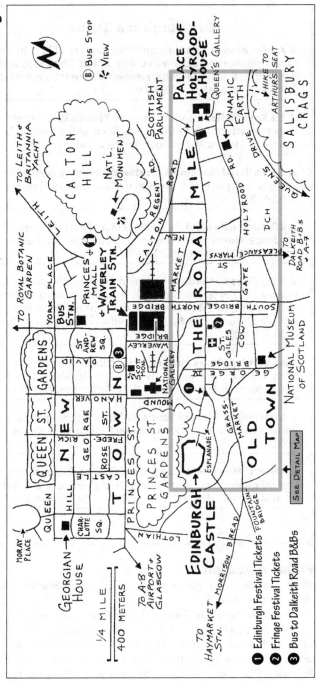

N

Ⓑ Bus Stop
☆ View

TO LEITH &
BRITANNIA
YACHT

TO ROYAL BOTANIC
GARDEN

CALTON HILL

NAT'L. MONUMENT

PALACE OF HOLYROOD-HOUSE

QUEEN'S GALLERY

SCOTTISH PARLIAMENT

DYNAMIC EARTH

HIKE TO ARTHUR'S SEAT

SALISBURY CRAGS

QUEEN'S DRIVE

HOLYROOD RD.

DCH

TO PLEASANCE B&BS

TO DALKEITH ROAD B&BS A-F

CALTON REGENT RD.

CALTON ROAD

LEITH

YORK PLACE

BUS STN.

PRINCES + MALL

WAVERLEY TRAIN STN.

NEW MARKET ST.

ST. MARY'S

NORTH BRIDGE

SOUTH BRIDGE

COWGATE

ST. ANDREW SQ.

OLD

VER

HANOVER ST.

GEORGE ST.

ROSE ST.

QUEEN ST. GARDENS

NEW TOWN

CASTLE

FREDE-RICK

SCOTT MON.

WAVERLEY BRIDGE

NATIONAL GALLERY

ST. GILES

THE ROYAL MILE

Ⓑ ❸

Ⓑ

❶

❷

BRIDGE ST.

GEORGE IV BRIDGE

NATIONAL MUSEUM OF SCOTLAND

SEE DETAIL MAP

MORAY PLACE

QUEEN

HILL

CHAR-LOTTE SQ.

PRINCES ST.

PRINCES ST. GARDENS

MOUND

GRASS-MARKET

OLD TOWN

GEORGIAN HOUSE

TO A-8 AIRPORT + GLASGOW

EDINBURGH CASTLE

ESPLANADE

LOTHIAN

FOUNTAIN-BRIDGE

MORRISON BREAD

TO HAYMARKET STN.

¼ MILE

400 METERS

❶ Edinburgh Festival Tickets
❷ Fringe Festival Tickets
❸ Bus to Dalkeith Road B&Bs

Edinburgh at a Glance

▲▲▲Edinburgh Castle Iconic 11th-century hilltop fort and royal residence complete with Crown Jewels, Romanesque chapel, memorial, and fine military museum. **Hours:** Daily April–Oct 9:30–18:00, Nov–March 9:30–17:00.

▲▲▲Royal Mile Historic road—good for walking—stretching from the castle down to the palace, lined with museums, pubs, and shops. **Hours:** Always open, but best during business hours.

▲▲▲National Museum of Scotland Intriguing, well-displayed artifacts from prehistoric times to the 20th century. **Hours:** Daily 10:00–17:00.

▲▲Gladstone's Land Sixteenth-century Royal Mile merchant's residence. **Hours:** Daily July–Aug 10:00–19:00, April–June and Sept–Oct 10:00–17:00, closed Nov–March.

▲▲St. Giles Cathedral Preaching grounds of Calvinist John Knox, with spectacular organ, Neo-Gothic chapel, and distinctive crown spire. **Hours:** May–Sept Mon–Fri 9:00–19:00, Sat 9:00–17:00, Sun 13:00–17:00; Oct–April Mon–Sat 9:00–17:00, Sun 13:00–17:00.

▲▲Georgian House Intimate peek at upper-crust life in the late 1700s. **Hours:** Daily April–June and Sept–Oct 10:00–17:00, July–Aug 10:00–19:00, March and Nov 11:00–15:00, closed Dec–Feb.

▲▲National Gallery of Scotland Choice sampling of European masters and Scotland's finest. **Hours:** Daily 10:00–17:00, Thu until 19:00.

▲Writers' Museum at Lady Stair's House Tribute to Scottish literary triumvirate: Robert Burns, Sir Walter Scott, and Robert Louis Stevenson. **Hours:** Mon–Sat 10:00–17:00, closed Sun.

From Edinburgh

Many companies run day trips to regional sights. Study the brochures at the TI's rack.

Heart of Scotland Tours offers various itineraries, but the best are the experience- and information-packed day trips of the Highlands and Loch Ness (£34, £3 discount with this book in 2008, departures daily 8:00–20:00, leaves from bus stand E on Waterloo Place near Waverley Station, fewer tours off-season,

▲**Museum of Childhood** Five stories of historic fun. **Hours:** Mon–Sat 10:00–17:00, Sun 12:00–17:00.

▲**John Knox House** Reputed 16th-century digs of the great reformer. **Hours:** Mon–Sat 10:00–18:00, closed Sun.

▲**People's Story** Proletarian life from the 18th to 20th centuries. **Hours:** Mon–Sat 10:00–17:00, closed Sun.

▲**Museum of Edinburgh** Historic mementos, from the original National Covenant inscribed on animal skin, to early golf balls. **Hours:** Mon–Sat 10:00–17:00, closed Sun.

▲**Scottish Parliament Building** Controversial new head-quarters for the recently returned Parliament. **Hours:** April–Oct Mon and Fri 10:00–18:00, Tue–Thu 9:00–19:00 or 10:00–18:00 if Parliament is in recess, Sat–Sun 10:00–16:00; Nov–March Mon and Fri–Sat 10:00–16:00, Tue–Thu 9:00–19:00 or 10:00–18:00 if Parliament is in recess.

▲**Palace of Holyroodhouse** The queen's splendid home-away-from-home, with lavish rooms, 12th-century abbey, and gallery with rotating exhibits. **Hours:** Daily April–Oct 9:30–18:00, Nov–March 9:30–16:30.

▲**Georgian New Town** Elegant 1776 subdivision spiced with trendy shops, bars, and eateries. **Hours:** Always open.

▲**Sir Walter Scott Monument** Climbable tribute to the famed novelist. **Hours:** April–Sept Mon–Sat 9:00–18:00, Sun 10:00–18:00, Oct–March Mon–Sat 9:00–15:00, Sun 10:00–15:00.

▲*Britannia* The royal yacht with a history of distinguished passengers, a 15-minute trip out of town. **Hours:** Daily April–Oct 9:30–16:30, Nov–March 10:00–15:30 (these are last entry times).

reserve at least a day ahead by phone or online, tel. 01828/627-799, www.heartofscotlandtours.co.uk, run by Nick Roche). The tour gives those with limited time a chance to experience the wonders of Scotland's wild and legend-soaked Highlands in a single long day (14- or 24-seat bus, talkative driver, good sound system). This Highlands joyride, named "Loch Ness and Legends," keeps a tight schedule, punctuated by several 30- to 90-minute stops. You'll see the vast and brutal Rannoch Moor; Glencoe, still evocative with memories of the clan massacre; views of Britain's highest mountain, Ben Nevis; Fort Augustus on Loch Ness (at the 90-min stop here, you can take the optional £9 boat ride or, if you're not into Nessie, enjoy free time in town); a scenic walk in the woods; and a 45-minute tea or pub break in the fine little village of Dunkeld. You'll learn a bit about Edinburgh to boot as you drive in and out.

Haggis Backpackers runs cheap tours on 22- to 35-seat buses with a very Scottish driver/guide. Their day trips (£39–45) include a distillery visit and the northern Highlands, or Loch Lomond and the southern Highlands. Their overnight trips are designed for young backpackers, but they welcome travelers of any age who want a quick look at the bonny countryside (£130/3 days, £259/6 days, office hours: Mon–Sat 9:00–18:00, summer Sun 13:00–18:00; 60 High Street, at Blackfriars Street, tel. 0131/557-9393, www.haggisadventures.com). They also offer an eight-day Island Adventure, visiting the Hebrides and the Orkney Islands.

Glasgow, Scotland's biggest city, is a happening cultural center and a mecca for those interested in architecture (particularly the Art Nouveau designs of Charles Rennie Mackintosh). Only 45 minutes away by train from Edinburgh (4/hr, £10–16 round-trip), it makes an interesting day trip (see Glasgow chapter).

SIGHTS

▲▲▲ Edinburgh Castle

The fortified birthplace of the city 1,300 years ago, this imposing symbol of Edinburgh sits proudly on a rock high above you. While the castle has been both a fort and a royal residence since the 11th century, most of the buildings today are from its more recent use as a military garrison. This fascinating and multifaceted sight deserves several hours of your time.

Cost and Hours: £11, daily April–Oct 9:30–18:00, Nov–March 9:30–17:00, last entrance 45 min before closing, tel. 0131/225-9846.

Tours: Twenty-minute guided introductory tours are free with admission (2–4/hr, depart from entry gate, see clock for next departure; fewer tours off-season). The excellent audioguide (£3) can be paid for at the ticket booth and picked up at the entry gate (4 hours of quick-dial digital descriptions of the sights, including the National War Museum of Scotland).

Services: The clean WC at the entry annually wins "British Loo of the Year" awards (marvel at the plaques near men's room;

William Wallace
(c. 1270–1305)

In 1286, Scotland's king died without an heir, plunging the prosperous country into a generation of chaos. As Scottish nobles bickered over a successor, the English king Edward I—nicknamed "Longshanks" because of his height—invaded and assumed power (1296). He placed a figurehead on the throne, forced Scottish nobles to sign a pledge of allegiance to England (the "Ragman's Roll"), moved the British Parliament north to York, and carried off the 336-pound, highly symbolic Stone of Scone to London, where it would remain for the next seven centuries.

A year later, the Scots rose up against Edward, led by William Wallace (nicknamed "Braveheart"). A mix of history and legend portrays Wallace as the son of a poor-but-knightly family that refused to sign the Ragman's Roll. Exceptionally tall and strong, he learned Latin and French from two uncles who were priests. In his teenage years, his father and older brother were killed by the English. Later, he killed an English sheriff to avenge the death of his wife, Marion. Wallace's rage inspired his fellow Scots to revolt.

In the summer of 1297, Wallace and his guerrillas scored a series of stunning victories over the English. On September 11, a large, well-equipped English army of 10,000 soldiers and 300 horsemen began crossing Stirling Bridge. Half of the army had made it across when Wallace's men attacked. In the chaos, the bridge collapsed, splitting the English ranks in two, and the ragtag Scots drove the confused English into the river. The Battle of Stirling Bridge was a rout, and Wallace was knighted and appointed Guardian of Scotland.

All through the winter, King Edward's men chased Wallace, continually frustrated by the Scots' hit-and-run tactics. Finally, at the Battle of Falkirk (1298), they drew Wallace's men out onto the open battlefield. The English with their horses and archers easily routed the spear-carrying Scots. Wallace resigned in disgrace and went on the lam, while his successors negotiated truces with the English, finally surrendering unconditionally in 1304. Wallace alone held out.

In 1305, he was tracked down and taken to London, convicted of treason, and mocked with a crown of oak leaves as the "King of Scotland." On August 23, they stripped him naked and dragged him to the execution site. There he was strangled to near death, castrated, and dismembered. His head was stuck on a stick atop London Bridge, while his body parts were sent on tour around the realm to spook future rebels. But Wallace's martyrdom only served to inspire his countrymen, and the torch of independence was picked up by Robert the Bruce (see sidebar on page 470).

the one-way mirrors peeking into the women's sink area are now shuttered—thanks in part to readers of this book complaining). For lunch here, you have the choice of the Red Coat Cafeteria and Jacobite Room (a handy cafeteria) or the Queen Anne Café (with table service), both located on the castle grounds (see "Eating," page 496).

Getting There: While regular city buses drop you far below (at the top of the Royal Mile, near the Camera Obscura), taxis take you right to the esplanade, in front of the gate. A castle bus does a circuit through central Edinburgh, beginning at George Street (near the train station) and leaving you at the castle's esplanade (£1, July–Aug only, daily 10:00–18:00, 4/hr in peak times, driver also sells £11 Fast Track Ticket for castle allowing you to bypass the line, though at 70p extra it's only worth considering in Aug, Edinburgh's busiest time).

● Self-Guided Tour: Start at the entry gate, where you can pick up your audioguide (pay at ticket booth) and take the wonderfully droll 20-minute introductory tour. The castle has five

essential stops: the Crown Jewels, Royal Palace, Scottish National War Memorial, St. Margaret's Chapel (with a city view), and the excellent National War Museum of Scotland. The first four are at the highest and most secure point—on or near the castle square, where your introductory guided tour ends (and the sights described below begin). Consider the National War Museum of Scotland (50 yards below the cafeteria and big shop) a separate sight and worth a serious look.

1. Crown Jewels: There are two ways to see the jewels. You can go in directly from the courtyard, but there's often a line. To avoid the line, enter the building around to the left as you're facing it (next to WC); you'll get to the jewels via the "Honors of Scotland" exhibition—a kid-friendly series of displays (which often moves at a very slow shuffle) telling the story of the Crown Jewels and how they survived the harrowing centuries.

Scotland's **Crown Jewels,** though not as impressive as England's, are older and treasured by the locals. While Oliver Cromwell destroyed England's jewels, the Scots managed to hide theirs. Longtime symbols of Scottish nationalism, they were made in Edinburgh—in 1540 for a 1543 coronation—out of Scottish diamonds, gems, and gold...some say the personal gold of King Robert the Bruce melted down (see Robert the Bruce sidebar, page 470). They were last used to crown Charles II in 1651. When the Act of

Union was forced upon the Scots in 1707—dissolving Scotland's Parliament into England's to create the United Kingdom—part of the deal was that the Scots could keep their jewels locked up in Edinburgh. The jewels remained hidden for more than 100 years. In 1818, Sir Walter Scott and a royal commission rediscovered them intact. In 1999, for the first time in nearly three centuries, the crown of Scotland was brought from the castle for the opening of the Scottish Parliament (see photos on the wall where the "Honors of Scotland" exhibit meets the Crown Jewels room; a smiling Queen Elizabeth II presides over the historic occasion).

The **Stone of Scone** (a.k.a. the "Stone of Destiny") sits plain and strong next to the jewels. This big gray chunk of rock is the coronation stone of Scotland's ancient kings (ninth century). Swiped by the English, it sat under the coronation chair at Westminster Abbey from 1296 until 1996. Queen Elizabeth finally agreed to let the stone go home—on one condition: that it be returned to Westminster Abbey in London for all future coronations. With major fanfare, Scotland's treasured Stone of Scone returned to Edinburgh on Saint Andrew's Day, November 30, 1996. Talk to the guard for more details.

2. The Royal Palace: Scottish royalty lived here only when safety or protocol required (preferring the Palace of Holyroodhouse at the bottom of the Royal Mile). The Royal Palace, facing castle square under the flagpole, has two historic yet unimpressive rooms (through door marked "1566") and the Great Hall (separate entrance from opposite side of square; see below). Enter the **Mary, Queen of Scots room,** where in 1566 the queen gave birth to James VI of Scotland, who later became King James I of England. The Presence Chamber leads into **Laich Hall** (Lower Hall), the dining room of the royal family.

The **Great Hall** was the castle's ceremonial meeting place in the 16th and 17th centuries. In later times, it was a barracks and a hospital. While most of what you see is Victorian, two medieval elements survive: the fine hammer-beam roof and the big iron-barred peephole (above fireplace on right). This allowed the king to spy on his subjects as they partied.

3. The Scottish National War Memorial: This commemorates the 149,000 Scottish soldiers lost in World War I, the 58,000 lost in World War II, and the 750 (and counting) lost in British battles since. Each bay is dedicated to a particular Scottish regiment. The main shrine, featuring a green Italian-marble memorial that contains the original WWI rolls of honor, sits—almost religiously—on an exposed chunk of the castle rock. Above you, the archangel Michael is busy slaying a dragon. The bronze frieze accurately shows the attire of various wings of Scotland's military. The stained glass starts with Cain and Abel on the left, and

British, Scottish, and English

Scotland and England have been tied together for 300 years, since the Act of Union in 1707. For a century and a half afterwards, Scottish nationalists rioted for independence in Edinburgh's streets, and led rebellions in the Highlands. In this controversial union, history is clearly seen through two very different filters.

If you tour a British-oriented sight, such as the National War Museum of Scotland, you'll find things told in a "happy union" way, which ignores the long history of Scottish resistance—from the ancient Picts through the time of Robert the Bruce (see sidebar on page 470). The official line: In 1706–1707, it was clear to England and some of Scotland (especially land-owners from the Lowlands) that it was in their mutual interest to dissolve the Scottish government and fold it into Britain, to be ruled from London.

But talk to a cabbie or your B&B host, and you may get a different spin. In a clever move by England to deflate the military power of its little sister, Scottish Highlanders were often sent to fight and die for Britain—in disproportionately higher numbers than their English counterparts. Poignant propaganda posters in the National War Museum of Scotland show a happy lad with the message: "Hey, look! Willie's off to Singapore with the Queen's own Highlanders."

Scottish independence is still a hot-button issue today. In 2007, the Scottish National Party (SNP) won a major election, and now has the largest majority in the fledgling Scottish Parliament. Alex Salmond, SNP leader and the First Minister of Scotland, is widely expected to push for Scotland to be recognized as an independent nation within the EU. (English leaders are obviously not in favor of breaking up the "united kingdom," though there's a like-minded independence movement in Wales, as well.)

The deep-seated rift shows itself in sports, too. While the English may refer to a British team in international competition as "English," the Scots are careful to call it "British." If a Scottish athlete does well, the English call him "British." If he screws up...he's a clumsy Scot.

finishes with a celebration of peace on the right. To appreciate how important this place is, consider that one out of every three adult Scottish men died in World War I.

4. St. Margaret's Chapel: The oldest building in Edinburgh is dedicated to Queen Margaret, who died here in 1093 and was sainted in 1250. Built in 1130 in the Romanesque style of the Norman invaders, it's wonderfully simple, with classic Norman zigzags decorating the round arch that separates the tiny nave from the sacristy. Used as a powder magazine for 400 years, very little survives. You'll see an 11th-century gospel book of St. Margaret's and small windows featuring St. Margaret, St. Columba (who brought Christianity to Scotland via Iona, see sidebar on page 558), and William Wallace (the brave-hearted defender of Scotland, see sidebar on page 465). The place is popular for weddings—and, since it seats only 20, it's particularly popular with brides' fathers.

Mons Meg, in front of the church, is a huge and once-upon-a-time frightening 15th-century siege cannon that fired 330-pound stones nearly two miles. It was a gift from the Belgians, who shared a common enemy with the Scots—England—and were eager to arm Scotland.

Belly up to the banister (outside the chapel, below the cannon) to enjoy the grand view. Below you are the guns—which fire the one o'clock salute—and a sweet little line of doggie tombstones, marking the soldiers' pet cemetery. Beyond stretches the Georgian New Town (read the informative plaque).

Crowds gather for the 13:00 gun blast, a tradition that gives ships in the bay something to set their navigational devices by. (The frugal Scots don't fire it at high noon, as that would cost 11 extra rounds a day.)

5. The National War Museum of Scotland: This museum is a pleasant surprise, thoughtfully covering four centuries of Scottish military history. Instead of the usual musty, dusty displays of endless armor, this museum has an interesting mix of short films, uniforms, weapons, medals, mementos, and eloquent excerpts from soldiers' letters. Just when you thought your castle visit was about over, this rivals any military museum you'll see in Europe.

Here, you'll learn the story of how the fierce and courageous Scottish warrior changed from being a symbol of resistance against Britain to being a champion of that same empire. Along the way, these military men received many decorations for valor, and did more than their share of dying in battle. But even when fighting for—rather than against—England, Scottish regiments still promoted their romantic, kilted-warrior image.

Queen Victoria fueled this ideal throughout the 19th century. (She was infatuated with the Scottish Highlands and the culture's untamed, rustic mystique.) Highland soldiers, especially officers, went to great personal expense to sport all their elaborate regalia, and the kilted men fought best to the tune of their beloved bagpipes. For centuries, the stirring drone of bagpipes accompanied Highland soldiers into battle—inspiring them, raising their spirits, and announcing to the enemy that they were about to meet a fierce and mighty foe.

This museum shows the human side of war, and the cleverness

Robert the Bruce
(1274–1329)

William Wallace's story (see sidebar on page 465) paints the Scottish fight for independence in black and white terms—the oppressive English versus the plucky Scots. But Scotland had to overcome its own divisiveness, and no one was more divided than Robert the Bruce. As Earl of Carrick, he was born with blood ties to England and a long-standing family claim to the Scottish throne.

When England's King Edward I ("Longshanks") conquered Scotland in 1296, the Bruce family welcomed it, hoping Edward would defeat their rivals and put Bruce's father on the throne. They dutifully signed the "Ragman's Roll" of allegiance...and then Edward chose someone else as king.

Twentysomething Robert the Bruce (the "the" comes from his original family name of "de Bruce") then joined William Wallace's revolt against the English. Legend has it that it was he who knighted Wallace after the victory at Stirling Bridge. When Wallace fell from favor, Bruce became co-Guardian of Scotland (caretaker ruler in the absence of a king), and continued fighting the English. But when Edward's armies again got the upper hand in 1302, Robert—along with Scotland's other nobles—diplomatically surrendered and again pledged loyalty.

In 1306, Robert the Bruce murdered his chief rival and boldly claimed to be King of Scotland. Few nobles supported him. Edward crushed the revolt and kidnapped Bruce's wife, the Church excommunicated him, and Bruce went into hiding on a distant North Sea island. He was now the king of nothing. Legend says he gained inspiration by watching a spider patiently build its web.

The following year, Bruce returned to Scotland and weaved alliances with both nobles and the Church, slowly gaining acceptance as Scotland's king by a populace chafing under English rule. On June 24, 1314, he decisively defeated the English (now led by Edward's weak son, Edward II) at the Battle of Bannockburn. After a generation of turmoil (1286–1314), England was finally driven from Scotland, and the country was united under Robert I, King of Scotland.

As king, Robert the Bruce's priority was to stabilize the monarchy and establish clear lines of succession. His descendants would rule Scotland for the next 400 years, and even today, Bruce blood runs through the veins of Queen Elizabeth II, Prince Charles, and princes William and Harry.

of government-sponsored ad campaigns that kept the lads enlisting. Two centuries of recruiting posters make the same pitch that still works today: a hefty signing bonus, steady pay, and job security with the promise of a manly and adventurous life—all spiked with a mix of pride and patriotism.

Leaving the castle, turn around and look back at the gate. There stand King Robert the Bruce (on the left, 1274–1329; see sidebar) and Sir William Wallace (Braveheart—on the right, 1270–1305; see page 465). Wallace—now well-known to Americans, thanks to Mel Gibson—fought long and hard against English domination before being executed in London. Bruce beat the English at Bannockburn in 1314. Bruce and Wallace still defend the spirit of Scotland. The Latin inscription above the gate between them reads, more or less, "What you do to us...we will do to you."

▲▲▲The Royal Mile

The Royal Mile is one of Europe's most interesting historic walks. Consisting of a series of four different streets—Castlehill, Lawnmarket, High Street, and Canongate (each with its own set

of street numbers), the Royal Mile is actually 200 yards longer than a mile. And every inch is packed with shops, cafés, and lanes leading to tiny squares.

Start at the top and amble down to the palace. These sights are listed in walking order. Bus #35 runs along the Mile, handy for going up after you've hit bottom.

Entertaining 90-minute guided walks bring the legends and lore of the Royal Mile alive (described under "Tours," above).

As you walk, remember that originally there were two settlements here, divided by a wall: Edinburgh lined the ridge from the castle at the top. The lower end, Canongate, was outside the wall until 1856. By poking down the many side alleys, you'll find a few surviving rough edges of an Old Town well on its way to becoming a touristic mall. See it now; in a few years it'll be all tartans and shortbread, with tourists slaloming through the postcard racks on bagpipe skateboards.

Royal Mile Terminology: A "close" is a tiny alley between two buildings (originally with a door that closed it at night). A close usually leads to a "court," or courtyard. A "land" is a tenement block of apartments. A "pend" is an arched gateway. A "wynd" is a narrow, winding lane. And "gate" is from an old Scandinavian word for street.

Edinburgh

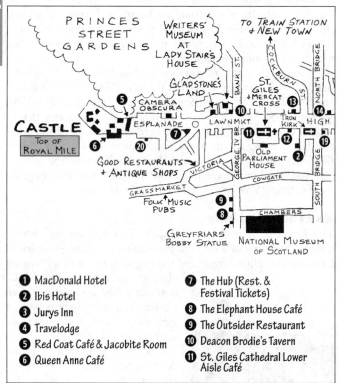

```
          P R I N C E S         WRITERS'        TO TRAIN STATION
           STREET              MUSEUM           & NEW TOWN
          G A R D E N S        AT
                               LADY STAIR'S
                               HOUSE
                          GLADSTONE'S           ST.
                    ❺  CAMERA  LAND              GILES
                       OBSCURA              ❿    & MERCAT      ⓭
 CASTLE                ESPLANADE  O    LAWN MKT.  CROSS            ⓮
  TOP OF          ❼                             TRON   HIGH
 ROYAL MILE   ❻                        ⓫        KIRK          ⓲
              ⓴                              ⓬        ❷
         GOOD RESTAURANTS→              OLD
         + ANTIQUE SHOPS               PARLIAMENT
                          VICTORIA     HOUSE
                      GRASSMARKET              COWGATE
                       FOLK MUSIC
                        PUBS           ❾
                                  ❽       CHAMBERS
                     GREYFRIARS
                     BOBBY STATUE   NATIONAL MUSEUM
                                    OF SCOTLAND
```

❶ MacDonald Hotel

❷ Ibis Hotel

❸ Jurys Inn

❹ Travelodge

❺ Red Coat Café & Jacobite Room

❻ Queen Anne Café

❼ The Hub (Rest. & Festival Tickets)

❽ The Elephant House Café

❾ The Outsider Restaurant

❿ Deacon Brodie's Tavern

⓫ St. Giles Cathedral Lower Aisle Café

Castle Esplanade—At the top of the Royal Mile, the big parking lot leading up to the castle was created as a military parade ground in 1816. It's often cluttered with bleachers for the Military Tattoo—a spectacular massing of the bands, filling the square nightly for most of August (see "Edinburgh Festival," page 487). At the bottom, on the left (where the square hits the road), a plaque above the tiny witch's fountain memorializes 300 women who were accused of witchcraft and burned here. Scotland burned more witches per capita than any other country—17,000 between 1479 and 1722. The plaque shows two witches: one good and one bad.

Camera Obscura—A big deal when it was built in 1853, this observatory topped with a mirror reflected images onto a disc before the wide eyes of people who had never seen a photograph or captured image. Today, you can climb 100 steps for an entertaining 15-minute demonstration (3/hr). At the top, enjoy the best view anywhere of the Royal Mile. Then work your way down through three floors of illusions, holograms, and early photos. This is a big hit with kids (£7.50, daily July–Aug 9:30–19:30, April–June and Sept–Oct

Edinburgh's Royal Mile

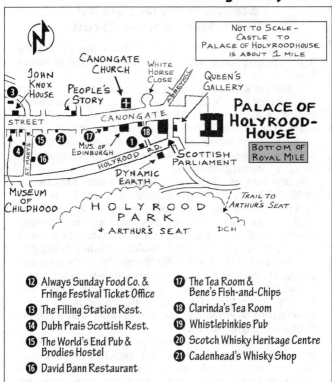

NOT TO SCALE –
CASTLE TO
PALACE OF HOLYROODHOUSE
IS ABOUT 1 MILE

- ⑫ Always Sunday Food Co. & Fringe Festival Ticket Office
- ⑬ The Filling Station Rest.
- ⑭ Dubh Prais Scottish Rest.
- ⑮ The World's End Pub & Brodies Hostel
- ⑯ David Bann Restaurant
- ⑰ The Tea Room & Bene's Fish-and-Chips
- ⑱ Clarinda's Tea Room
- ⑲ Whistlebinkies Pub
- ⑳ Scotch Whisky Heritage Centre
- ㉑ Cadenhead's Whisky Shop

9:30–18:00, Nov–March 10:00–17:00, tel. 0131/226-3709).
Scotch Whisky Heritage Centre (a.k.a. "Malt Disney")—This touristy ambush is designed only to distill £9.25 out of your pocket. You kick things off with a wee dram followed by a video history, a short talk, and a little whisky-keg train-car ride before finding yourself in the shop one hour later. Those in a hurry are offered the unadvertised quickie—a sample and a whisky-keg ride for £5. People do seem to enjoy it, but that might have something to do with the sample—which now comes at the start rather than the end of the experience (daily July–Sept 10:00–18:30, Oct–June 10:00–18:00, last tour 60 min before closing, tel. 0131/220-0441, www.whisky-heritage.co.uk). Serious connoisseurs of the Scottish firewater will want to pop into Cadenhead's Whisky Shop at the bottom of the Royal Mile (described on page 479).
The Hub (Tolbooth Church)—This Neo-Gothic church (1844), with the tallest spire in the city, is now The Hub, Edinburgh's Festival Ticket and Information Centre (for ticket information, see page 487).

Scotland's Literary Greats: Burns, Stevenson, and Scott

Edinburgh was home to Scotland's three greatest literary figures: Robert Burns, Robert Louis Stevenson, and Sir Walter Scott.

Robert Burns (1759–1796) was Scotland's bard. A poor farmer tuned into the social inequities of the late 1700s, he was an ardent supporter of the French Revolution. Even though Robby, as he's lovingly called even today, dared to speak up for the common man and attack social rank, he was a favorite of Edinburgh's high society, who'd gather in fine homes to hear the national poet recite his works.

One hundred years later, **Robert Louis Stevenson** (1850–1894) also stirred the Scottish soul with his pen. An avid traveler who always packed his notepad, Stevenson created settings that are vivid and filled with wonder. Traveling through Scotland, Europe, and around the world, he distilled his adventures into Romantic classics, including *Kidnapped* and *Treasure Island* (as well as *The Strange Case of Dr. Jekyll and Mr. Hyde*). Stevenson, who spent his last years in the South Pacific, wrote, "Youth is the time to travel—both in mind and in body—to try the manners of different nations." He said "I travel not to go anywhere...but to simply go." Travel was his inspiration and his success.

Sir Walter Scott (1771–1832) wrote the *Waverly* novels, including *Ivanhoe* and *Rob Roy*. He's considered the father of the Romantic historical novel. Through his writing, he generated a worldwide interest in Scotland, and re-awakened his fellow countrymen's pride in their inheritance. An avid patriot, he wrote "Every Scottish man has a pedigree. It is a national prerogative, as unalienable as his pride and his poverty." Scott is so revered in Edinburgh that his towering Neo-Gothic monument dominates the city center (see page 484). With his favorite hound by his side, Sir Walter Scott overlooks the city that he inspired, and that inspired him.

The best way to learn about and experience these literary greats is to visit the Writers' Museum at Lady Stair's House (see next page) and to take Edinburgh's Literary Pub Tour (see page 489).

▲▲**Gladstone's Land**—This is a typical 16th- to 17th-century merchant's house. "Land" means tenement, and these multi-story buildings—where merchants lived on the ground floor—were typ-
ical of the time. (For an interesting comparison of life in the Old Town versus the New Town, also visit the Georgian House, listed on page 483). Gladstone's Land comes complete with an almost-lived-in furnished interior and guides in each room who love to talk (£5, daily July–Aug 10:00–19:00, April–June and Sept–Oct 10:00–17:00, last entry 30 min before closing, closed Nov–March, no photos allowed).

For a good Royal Mile photo, simply climb the curved stairway outside the museum to the left of the entrance. Notice the snoozing pig outside the front door. Just like every house has a vacuum cleaner today, in the good old days a snorting rubbish collector was a standard feature of any well-equipped house.

▲**Writers' Museum at Lady Stair's House**—This aristocrat's house, built in 1622, is filled with well-described manuscripts and knickknacks of Scotland's three greatest literary figures: Robert Burns, Sir Walter Scott, and Robert Louis Stevenson. Edinburgh's high society would gather in homes like this in the 1780s to hear the great poet Robby Burns read his work. Burns' work is meant to be read aloud rather than in silence. In the Burns room, you can hear his poetry—worth a few minutes for anyone, and essential for fans (free, Mon–Sat 10:00–17:00, closed Sun).

Wander around the courtyard here. Edinburgh was a wonder in the 17th and 18th centuries. Tourists came here to see its skyscrapers, which towered 10 stories and higher. No city in Europe was so densely populated—or polluted—as "Auld Reekie."

Deacon Brodie's Tavern—Read the "Doctor Jekyll and Mister Hyde" story of this pub's notorious namesake on the wall facing Bank Street. Then, to see his spooky split personality, check out both sides of the hanging signpost.

Deacon Brodie's Tavern lies at the intersection of the Royal Mile and George IV Bridge. You can head across the bridge to reach some recommended eateries (The Elephant House and The Outsider, described on page 497), as well as the excellent National Museum of Scotland. Both are a five-minute walk from here.

Heart of Midlothian—Near the street in front of the cathedral, a heart-shaped outline in the brickwork marks the spot of a gallows and a prison (now long gone). Traditionally, locals stand on the rim of the heart and spit into it. Hitting the middle brings good luck. Go ahead...do as the locals do.

▲▲**St. Giles Cathedral**—This is Scotland's most important church. Its ornate spire—the Scottish crown steeple from 1495—is a proud part of Edinburgh's skyline. As the church functions as a kind of Westminster Abbey of Scotland, the interior is fascinating (May–Sept Mon–Fri 9:00–19:00, Sat 9:00–17:00, Sun 13:00–17:00; Oct–April Mon–Sat 9:00–17:00, Sun 13:00–17:00; ask about concerts or look for the *Music at St. Giles* pamphlet, some concerts are free, generally daily at 12:15; café and WC downstairs, see "Eating," page 498; tel. 0131/225-9442).

Just inside the entrance, turn around to see the modern stained-glass window hovering over the door. Then work your way clockwise around the church. Cathedral guides are strolling around waiting for you to engage them in conversation. You'll be glad you did.

Filling the west wall, the **Robert Burns window** celebrates Scotland's favorite poet. It was made in 1985 by an Icelandic artist (Leifur Breidfjord). The green of the lower level symbolizes the natural world—God's creation. The middle zone with the circle shows the brotherhood of man; Burns was a great internationalist. The top is a rosy red sunburst of creativity, reminding Scots of Burns' famous line, "My love is like a red, red rose"—part of a song near and dear to every Scottish heart. Why honor this "live fast and die young" Romantic here? This is Scotland's top church, and even this prodigal son has a place...a big place.

To the right of the Burns window is a fine Pre-Raphaelite window. Like most in the church, it's a memorial to an important patron (in this case, John Marshall). From here stretches a great swath of war memorials.

When you walk along the north wall, find **John Knox's statue.** Look into his eyes for 10 seconds from 10 inches away, and think of the Reformation struggles of the 16th century. Knox, the great reformer and founder of austere Scottish Presbyterianism, first preached here in 1559. His insistence that every person should be able to read the word of God gave Scotland an educational system 300 years ahead of the rest of Europe (for more on Knox, see "The

Scottish Reformation" on page 510). Thanks partly to Knox, it was Scottish minds that led the way in math, science, medicine, and engineering. Voltaire called Scotland "the intellectual capital of Europe."

Knox preached Calvinism. Consider that the Dutch and the Scots both embraced this creed of hard work, frugality, and strict ethics. This helps explain why Scots are so different from the English (and why the Dutch and the Scots—both famous for their thriftiness and industriousness—are so much alike).

The oldest parts of the cathedral—the **four massive central pillars**—date from 1120. After the English burned the cathedral in 1385, it was rebuilt bigger and better than ever, and in 1495, its famous crown spire was completed. During the Reformation—when Knox preached here (1559–1572)—the place was simplified and whitewashed. Before this, when the emphasis was on holy services provided by priests, there were lots of little niches. With the new focus on sermons rather than rituals, the grand pulpit took center stage. The **organ** (1992, Austrian-built, one of Europe's finest) comes with a glass panel in the back for peeking into the mechanism. Knox had the church's fancy medieval glass replaced with clear glass, and 19th-century Victorians had Knox's glass replaced with the brilliantly colored glass you see today.

The Neo-Gothic **Chapel of the Knights of the Thistle** (in the far right corner, from 1911), with its intricate wood-carving, was built in two years entirely with Scottish materials and labor. It is the private chapel of the Knights of the Thistle, the only Scottish chivalric order, and it's used about once a year to inaugurate new members. Scotland recognizes its leading citizens by bestowing upon them a membership. The queen presides over the ritual from her fancy stall, marked by her Scottish coat of arms—a heraldic zoo of symbolism. Are there bagpipes in heaven? Find the tooting angel above the door to the right.

John Knox is buried out back—with appropriate austerity—under the parking lot, at spot 23. The statue among the cars shows King Charles II riding to a toga party back in 1685. Near parking spot 15, enter the...

Old Parliament House—Step in to see the grand hall with its fine 1639 hammer-beam ceiling and stained glass. This hall housed the Scottish Parliament until the Act of Union in 1707 (explained in the history exhibition under the big stained-glass depiction of the initiation of the first Scottish High Court in 1532). It now holds the civil law courts and is busy with wigged and robed lawyers hard at work in the old library (peek through the door) or pacing the hall deep in discussion. The friendly doorman is helpful (free, public welcome Mon–Fri 9:00–16:30, closed Sat–Sun, best action midmornings Tue–Fri, open-to-the-public trials 10:00–16:00—

doorman has day's docket; enter behind St. Giles Cathedral).

Mercat Cross—This chunky pedestal, on the downhill side of St. Giles, holds a slender column topped with a white unicorn. Royal proclamations have been read here since the 14th century. In 1952, three days (traditionally the time it took for a horse to speed here from London) after the actual event, a town crier heralded the news that England had a new queen. Today, Mercat Cross is the meeting point of various walking tours—both historic and ghostly. A few doors downhill is the...

Police Information Center—This center provides a pleasant police presence (say that three times) and a little local law-and-order history to boot (free, daily May–Aug 10:00–21:30, until 18:00 in winter). Pick up *For the Record*, the police brag mag ("Thirteen murders in the last year...and all of them solved!"). Ask the officer on duty about the grave-robber William Burke's skin and creative poetic justice, Edinburgh-style.

Cockburn Street—This street was cut through High Street's dense wall of medieval skyscrapers in the 1860s to give easy access to the Georgian New Town and the train station. Notice how the sliced buildings were thoughtfully capped with facades in a faux-16th-century Scottish baronial style. In the Middle Ages, only tiny lanes (like the Fleshmarket Lane just uphill from Cockburn Street) interrupted the long line of Royal Mile buildings.

Tron Kirk—This fine old building across from Cockburn Street, used as a sales base for a local walking-tour company, sits over an old excavation site. It houses a free Old Town history display (daily 10:00–17:00). Perhaps even more important, just above Tron Kirk is a Starbucks with fine streetside tables and a spacious upstairs lounge. Continue downhill 100 yards to the...

▲Museum of Childhood—This five-story playground of historical toys and games is rich in nostalgia and history (free, Mon–Sat 10:00–17:00, Sun 12:00–17:00). Just downhill is a fragrant fudge shop offering delicious free samples.

▲John Knox House—Intriguing for Reformation buffs, this fine 16th-century house offers a well-explained look at the life of the great reformer (£3, Mon–Sat 10:00–18:00, closed Sun, 43 High Street, tel. 0131/556-9579). While some contend Knox never actually lived here, preservationists called it "his house" to save it from the wrecking ball in 1850. The museum has been undergoing periodic renovation and may be closed sporadically.

The World's End—For centuries, a wall halfway down the Royal Mile marked the end of Edinburgh and the beginning of Canongate, a community associated with Holyrood Abbey. Today, where the Mile hits St. Mary's and Jeffrey streets, High Street becomes Canongate. Just below the John Knox House (at #43), notice the hanging sign showing the old gate. At the intersection, find the brass bricks that trace the gate (demolished in 1764). Look down St. Mary's Street to see a surviving bit of that old wall. Then, entering Canongate, you leave what was Edinburgh and head for...

Cadenhead's Whisky Shop—The shop is not a tourist sight. It's a firm, founded in 1842, that prides itself on bottling good malt whisky from kegs straight from the best distilleries, without all the compromises that come with profitable mass production (coloring with sugar to fit the expected look, watering down to lessen the alcohol tax, and so on). Those drinking from Cadenhead-bottled whiskies will enjoy the distilleries' pure product as the owners of the distilleries themselves do, not as the sorry public does. If you want to learn about whisky—and perhaps pick up a bottle—Mark and Alan love to talk (Mon–Sat 10:30–17:30, Sun in Aug 12:30–17:30, call ahead to confirm additional sporadic Sun openings, check website for twice-monthly tastings, 172 Canongate, tel. 0131/556-5864, www.wmcadenhead.com, chws@wmcadenhead .com, friendly little dog Maggie). Keep in mind that customs laws won't allow you to ship home what you buy; unless you're buying it to drink on your trip, you'll have to carry it back in your checked luggage.

▲People's Story—This interesting exhibition traces the conditions of the working class through the 18th, 19th, and 20th centuries (free, Mon–Sat 10:00–17:00, closed Sun, tel. 0131/529-4057). Curiously, while this museum is dedicated to the proletariat, immediately around the back (embedded in the wall of the museum) is the tomb of Adam Smith—the author of *Wealth of Nations* and the father of modern free-market capitalism (1723–1790).

▲Museum of Edinburgh—Another old house full of old stuff, this one is worth a look for its early Edinburgh history and handy ground-floor WC. Don't miss the original copy of the National Covenant (written in 1638 on an animal skin), sketches of pre-Georgian Edinburgh (which show a lake, later filled in to become Princes Street Gardens when the New Town was built), and early golf balls. "Balls," said the queen, "If I had two, I'd be king." The king laughed—he had to. (Free, Mon–Sat 10:00–17:00, closed Sun, tel. 0131/529-4143.)

White Horse Close—Step into this 17th-century courtyard (bottom of Canongate, on the left, a block before the Palace of Holyroodhouse). It was from here that the Edinburgh stagecoach left for London. Eight days later, the horse-drawn carriage pulled into its destination: Scotland Yard. Across the street is the new...

▲Scottish Parliament Building—Scotland's Parliament originated in 1293, was dissolved by England in 1707, and was formally re-opened by the Queen in 1999. These extravagant, and therefore controversial, new digs opened in 2004. The Catalan architect Enric Miralles mixed wild angles, lots of light, bold windows, and local stone into a startling complex that would, as he envisioned, "arise from the sloping base of Arthur's Seat and arrive into the city almost surging out of the rock." For a conversation starter, ask a local what he or she thinks about the place.

For a peek at the new building and a lesson in how the Scottish Parliament works, drop in, pass through security, and find the visitors' desk (free, April–Oct Mon and Fri 10:00–18:00, Tue–Thu 9:00–19:00 or 10:00–18:00 if Parliament is in recess, Sat–Sun 10:00–16:00; Nov–March Mon and Fri–Sun 10:00–16:00, Tue–Thu 9:00–19:00 or 10:00–18:00 if Parliament is in recess; last entry 45 min before closing). You can sign up to witness the Scottish Parliament's debates (usually Wed 14:30–17:30, Thu 9:30–12:30 & 14:30–17:30, tel. 0131/348-5200). Guided one-hour tours are sometimes available (£5, July–Aug tours run daily every 20 min; Sept–June tours run Fri–Mon only, no tours Tue–Thu; call for times and details or check www.scottish.parliament.uk).

▲**Palace of Holyroodhouse**—Since the 14th century, this palace has marked the end of the Royal Mile. The queen spends a week in the palace each summer. The abbey—part of a 12th-century Augustinian monastery—originally stood in its place. It was named for a piece of the cross brought here as a relic by Queen (and later saint) Margaret. Because Scotland's royalty preferred living at Holyroodhouse to the blustery castle on the rock, the palace evolved over time.

Consider touring the interior (£9.50, £13 combo-ticket includes Queen's Gallery—listed below, daily April–Oct 9:30–18:00, Nov–March 9:30–16:30, last entry 1 hour before closing, tel. 0131/556-5100, www.royal.gov.uk). The palace is closed when the queen is at home—generally for a week around July 1—and whenever a prince or someone else important drops in. The building, rich in history and decor, is filled with elegantly furnished rooms and a few darker, older rooms with glass cases of historic bits and Scottish pieces that locals find fascinating.

Bring the palace to life with the included one-hour **audioguide.** You'll learn which of the kings featured in the 110 portraits lining the Great Gallery are real and which are fictional, what touches were added to the bedchambers to flatter King Charles II, and why the exiled Comte d'Artois took refuge in the palace. You'll also hear a goofy reenactment of the moment when conspirators—dispatched by Mary, Queen of Scots' jealous second husband—stormed into the queen's chambers and stabbed her male secretary. Royal diehards can pick up a palace guidebook for £4.50.

After exiting, you're free to stroll through the ruined abbey and the queen's gardens. Hikers: Note that the wonderful trail up Arthur's Seat starts just across the street from the gardens.

Queen's Gallery—This museum features rotating exhibits of drawings from the royal collection. For more than five centuries,

the royal family has amassed a wealth of art treasures. While the queen keeps most in her many private palaces, she shares an impressive load of it here, with exhibits changing about every six months. Though the gallery occupies just a few rooms, it can be exquisite, and generally comes with a well-done audioguide (£5, £13 combo-ticket includes Palace of Holyroodhouse, daily April–Oct 9:30–18:00, Nov–March until 16:30, last entry 1 hour before closing, on the palace grounds, to the right of the palace entrance).

Sights Just Off the Royal Mile

▲▲▲**National Museum of Scotland**—This huge museum has amassed more historic artifacts than everything else I've seen in

Scotland combined. It's all wonderfully displayed with fine descriptions offering a best-anywhere hike through the history of Scotland. Start in the basement and work your way through the story: prehistoric, Roman, Viking, the "birth of Scotland," Edinburgh's witch-

burning craze, clan massacres, all the way to life in the 20th century. Free audioguides offer a pleasant description of various rooms and exhibits, and even provide mood music for your wanderings.

The **Kingdom of the Scots** exhibit shows evidence of a vibrant young nation. While largely cut off from Europe by hostilities with England, Scotland connected with the Continent through trade, the church, and their monarch, Mary, Queen of Scots. Throughout Scotland's long, underdog struggle with England, its people found inspiration from romantic (and almost legendary) Scottish leaders, including Mary. Educated and raised in France during the Renaissance, Mary brought refinement to the Scottish throne. After she was imprisoned and then executed by the English, her countrymen rallied each other by invoking her memory. Pendants

and coins with her portrait stoked the irrepressible Scottish spirit. Near the replica of Mary's tomb are tiny cameos, pieces of jewelry, and coins with her image.

The industry exhibit explains how (eventually) the Scots were tamed, and the union with England brought stability and investment to Scotland. Powered by the Scottish work ethic and the new opportunities that came from the Industrial Revolution, the country came into relative prosperity. Education and medicine thrived. Cast iron and foundries were huge, and this became one of the most industrialized places in Europe. With the dawn of the modern age came leisure time, the concept of "healthful sports," and golf—a Scottish invention. The first golf balls, which date from about 1820, were leather stuffed with feathers (free, daily 10:00–17:00; free 30-min intro tours generally at 10:30, 12:30, and 15:30; additional and more in-depth tours available at other times—confirm tour schedule at info desk; 2 long blocks south of Royal Mile from St. Giles Cathedral, Chambers Street, off George IV Bridge, tel. 0131/247-4422, www.nms.ac.uk).

On the National Museum of Scotland's top floor, the upscale **Tower restaurant** serves fancy £15–25 meals (daily 12:00–23:00—open later than the museum itself, tel. 0131/225-3003).

The **Royal Museum,** next door, fills a fine iron-and-glass Industrial Age building (built to house the museum in 1851) with all the natural sciences as it "presents the world to Scotland." It's great for school kids, but of no special interest to foreign visitors (free, same hours and website as Museum of Scotland).

Greyfriars Bobby—The underwhelming yet famous statue of Greyfriars Bobby (Edinburgh's favorite dog—a terrier, immortalized by a 1960s Disney flick, who stood by his master's grave for 14 years) is across the street from the Museum of Scotland. Every business nearby is named for the pooch that put the fidelity into Fido.

Dynamic Earth—Located about a five-minute walk from the Palace of Holyroodhouse, this immense exhibit tells the story of our planet, filling several underground floors under a vast Gore-Tex tent. It's pitched, appropriately, at the base of the Salisbury Crags. The exhibit is designed for younger kids and does the same thing an American science exhibit would do—but with a charming Scottish accent. Standing in a time tunnel, you watch the years rewind

from Churchill to dinosaurs to the Big Bang. After several short films on stars, tectonic plates, and ice caps, you're free to wander past salty pools, a re-created rain forest, and various TV screens. End your visit with a 12-minute video finale (£9, family deals, April–Oct daily 10:00–17:00, July–Aug until 18:00; Nov–March Wed–Sun 10:00–17:00, closed Mon–Tue; last ticket sold 70 min before closing, on Holyrood Road, between the palace and mountain, tel. 0131/550-7800, www.dynamicearth .co.uk). Dynamic Earth is a stop on the hop-on-hop-off bus route.

Bonny Wee Sights in the New Town

Cross Waverley Bridge and walk through the Georgian New Town. According to the 1776 plan, the New Town was three streets (Princes, George, and Queen) flanked by two squares (St. Andrew and Charlotte), woven together by alleys (Thistle and Rose). George Street—20 feet wider than the others (so a four-horse carriage could make a U-turn)—was the main drag. And, while Princes Street has gone down-market, George Street still maintains its old grace. The entire elegantly planned New Town—laid out when George was king—celebrated the hard-to-sell notion that Scotland was an integral part of the United Kingdom. The streets and squares are named after the British royalty (Hanover was the royal family surname). Even Thistle and Rose streets are emblems of the two happily paired nations. Rose Street, mostly pedestrian-only, is famous for its rowdy pubs. Where it hits St. Andrew Square, Rose Street is flanked by the venerable Jenners department store and a Sainsbury's supermarket. Sprinkled with popular restaurants and bars, the stately New Town is turning trendy.

▲▲**Georgian House**—This refurbished Georgian house, set on Edinburgh's finest Georgian square, is a trip back to 1796. It recounts the era when a newly gentrified and well-educated Edinburgh was nicknamed the "Athens of the North." A volunteer guide in each of the five rooms shares stories and trivia—from the kitchen in the basement to the fully stocked medicine cabinet in the bedroom. Start your visit in the basement, viewing the interesting 16-minute video that shows the life of one family who owned this property, and touches on the architecture of the Georgian period (£5, daily April–June and Sept–Oct 10:00–17:00, July–Aug 10:00–19:00, March and Nov 11:00–15:00, last entry 40 min before closing, closed Dec–Feb, 7 Charlotte Square, tel. 0131/226-3318). A walk down George Street after your visit here can be fun for the imagination.

▲▲**National Gallery of Scotland**—The elegant Neoclassical building has a delightfully small but impressive collection of European masterpieces, from Raphael, Titian, and Peter Paul Rubens to Thomas Gainsborough, Claude Monet, and Vincent van Gogh. And it offers the best look you'll get at Scottish paintings (free, daily 10:00–17:00, Thu until 19:00, tel. 0131/624-6200). The skippable Royal Scottish Academy, next door, hosts temporary art exhibits and is connected to the National Gallery at the garden level (underneath the gallery) by the Weston Link building (same hours as the gallery, fine café and restaurant).

Two other museums are associated with the National Gallery, but are outside the downtown core: the Scottish National Gallery of Modern Art and the Scottish National Portrait Gallery. A free bus service links the museums (runs every 45 min, 15–20 min connections).

After your National Gallery visit, if the sun's out, enjoy a wander through Princes Street Gardens.

Princes Street Gardens—The grassy park, a former lakebed, separates Edinburgh's New and Old Towns and offers a wonderful escape from the city. Once the private domain of wealthy locals, it was opened to the public around 1870—not as a democratic gesture, but because it was thought that allowing the public into the park would increase sales for the Princes Street department stores. Join the local office workers for a picnic lunch break. There are also concerts in the park (prices vary—but can be as low as £2, Mon and Tue at 19:30 in June–July, at Ross Bandstand, tel. 0131/228-8616), plus the oldest floral clock in the world.

The big lake, Nord Loch, was drained around 1800 as part of the Georgian expansion of Edinburgh. Before that, the lake was the town's sewer, water reservoir, and handy place for drowning witches. Much was written about the town's infamous stink (a.k.a. the "flowers of Edinburgh"), and the town's nickname, "Auld Reekie," referred to both the smoke of its industry and the stench of its squalor.

While the Loch is now long gone, memories of the countless women drowned as witches remain. With their thumbs tied to their ankles, they'd be lashed to dunking stools. Those who survived the ordeal were considered "aided by the devil" and burned as witches. If they died, they were innocent and given a good Christian burial. Until 1720, Edinburgh was Europe's witch-burning mecca—as little a sign as a birthmark could condemn you.

▲**Sir Walter Scott Monument**—Built in 1840, this elaborate Neo-Gothic monument honors the great author, one of Edinburgh's many illustrious sons. Scott, who died in 1832, is considered the father of the Romantic historical novel. The 200-foot monument shelters a marble statue of Scott and his favorite dog, Maida, a deerhound who was one of the 30 canines this dog lover had during his lifetime. They're surrounded by busts of 16 great Scottish poets and 64 characters from his books. Climbing 287 steps earns you a fine city view (£3, April–Sept Mon–Sat 9:00–18:00, Sun 10:00–18:00; Oct–March Mon–Sat 9:00–15:00, Sun 10:00–15:00; tel. 0131/529-4098).

Near Edinburgh

▲**Britannia**—This much-revered vessel, which transported Britain's royal family for more than 40 years and 900 voyages before being retired in 1997, is permanently moored at the Ocean Terminal Shopping Mall in Edinburgh's Port of Leith. It's open to the public and worth the 15-minute bus or taxi ride from the center. Explore the museum, filled with engrossing royal-family-afloat history. Then, armed with your included audioguide, you're welcome aboard.

This was the last in a line of royal yachts that stretches back to 1660. With all its royal functions, the ship required a crew of more than 200. The captain's bridge feels like it's been preserved from the day it was launched in 1953. Queen Elizabeth II, who enjoyed the ship for 40 years, said, "This is the only place I can truly relax." This sunny lounge just off the back Veranda Deck was the Queen's favorite, with teak from Burma (now Myanmar, in Southeast Asia) and the same phone system she was used to in Buckingham Palace.

The back deck was the favorite place for outdoor entertainment. Ronald Reagan, Boris Yeltsin, Bill Clinton, and Nelson Mandela all sipped champagne here with the queen. When she wasn't entertaining, the queen liked it quiet. The crew wore sneakers, communicated in hand signals, and (at least near the queen's quarters) had to be finished with all their work by 8:00 in the morning.

The dining room, decorated with gifts given by the ship's many noteworthy guests, enabled the queen to entertain a good-size crowd. The silver pantry was just down the hall. The drawing room, while rather simple, is perfect for casual relaxing among royals. Princess Diana played the piano, which is bolted to the deck. Royal family photos evoke the fine times the Windsors enjoyed on the *Britannia* (£9.50, daily admission times April–Oct 9:30–16:30, Nov–March 10:00–15:30, these are last entry times, tel. 0131/555-5566, www.royalyachtbritannia.co.uk).

To get from Edinburgh to the *Britannia*, catch LRT bus #1, #11, #22, #34, or #35 at Waverley Bridge (£2 round-trip). If you're doing a city bus tour, consider the Majestic Tour, which includes transportation to the *Britannia* (see page 460).

Rosslyn Chapel—Founded in 1446 by the Knights Templar, this church became famous for its role in the final scenes of *The Da Vinci*

Code (£7, Mon–Sat 9:30–18:00, Sun 12:00–16:45, shorter hours off-season, last entry 30 min before closing, located in Roslin Village, www.rosslynchapel.org.uk). To get to the chapel by bus, take LRT bus #15 or First service #62A (no Sun service for either). By car, take A701 to Penicuik/Peebles, and follow signs for *Roslin*; once you're in the village, there are signs for the chapel.

Royal Botanic Garden—Britain's second-oldest botanical garden (after Oxford) was established in 1670 for medicinal herbs, and is now one of Europe's best (gardens free, glass house admission-£3.50, daily April–Sept 10:00–19:00, March and Oct 10:00–18:00, Nov–Feb 10:00–16:00, 90-min "rain forest to desert" tours April–Sept daily at 11:00 and 14:00 for £4, a mile north of center at Inverleith Row, Majestic Tour stops here—see page 460, tel. 0131/552-7171, www.rbge.org.uk).

ACTIVITIES

▲▲**Arthur's Seat Hike**—A 45-minute hike up the 822-foot remains of an extinct volcano (surrounded by a fine park overlook-

ing Edinburgh) starts from the Palace of Holyroodhouse. You can run up like they did in *Chariots of Fire,* or just stroll—at the summit you'll be rewarded with commanding views of the town and surroundings. On May Day, be on the summit at dawn and wash your face in the morning dew to commemorate the Celtic holiday of Beltaine, the celebration of spring. (Morning dew is supposedly very good for your complexion.)

From the parking lot below the Palace of Holyroodhouse, there are two trailheads. Take the wide path on the left (easier grade, through the abbey ruins and "Hunter's Bog"). After making the summit, you can return along the other path (to the right, with the steps), which skirts the base of the cliffs.

Those staying at my recommended B&Bs can enjoy a pre-breakfast or late-evening hike starting from the other side (in June, the sun comes up early, and it stays light until nearly midnight). From the Commonwealth Pool, take Holyrood Park Road, turn right on Queen's Drive, and continue to a small parking lot. From here, it's a 20-minute hike.

Drivers can drive up most of the way from behind (follow the one-way street from palace, park by the little lake, and hike up).

Brush Skiing—If you'd rather be skiing, the Midlothian Snowsports Centre in Hillend has a hill on the edge of town with a chairlift, two slopes, a jump slope, and rentable skis, boots, and poles. While you're actually skiing over what seems like a million toothbrushes, it feels like snow-skiing on a slushy day. Beware: Local doctors are used to treating an ailment called "Hillend Thumb"—thumbs dislocated when people fall here and get tangled in the brush (£8/first hour, then £3.30/hr, includes gear, beginners must take a lesson, Mon–Fri 9:30–21:00, Sat–Sun 9:30–19:00, closed last 2 weeks of June, LRT bus #4 from Princes Street—garden side, tel. 0131/445-4433, www.midlothian.gov.uk). It closes if it snows.

Royal Commonwealth Games Swimming Pool—When this complex reopens in 2009 after renovation, it will have a refurbished, well-equipped fitness center, sauna, and coffee shop overlooking the immense pool (tel. 0131/667-7211).

More Hikes—You can hike along the river (called Water of Leith) through Edinburgh. Locals favor the stretch between Roseburn and Dean Village, but the 1.5-mile walk from Dean Village to the Royal Botanic Garden is also good. This and other hikes are described in the TI's *Walks In and Around Edinburgh* (ask for the free one-page flier, not their £2 guide to walks).

Shopping—The streets to browse are Princes Street (the elegant old Jenners department store is nearby on Rose Street, at St. Andrew Square), Victoria Street (antiques galore), Nicolson Street (south of the Royal Mile for a line of interesting second-hand stores), and the Royal Mile (touristy but competitively priced). Shops are usually open from 9:00 to 17:30 (later on Thu, some closed Sun).

Edinburgh Festival

One of Europe's great cultural events, Edinburgh's annual festival turns the city into a carnival of the arts. There are enough music, dance, drama, and multicultural events to make even the most jaded traveler drool with excitement. Every day is jammed with formal and spontaneous fun. A riot of festivals—official, fringe, book, film, and jazz and blues—rage simultaneously for about three weeks each August, with the Military Tattoo starting a week earlier (the best overall website is www.edinburghfestivals.co.uk). Many city sights run on extended hours, and those along the Royal Mile that are normally closed on Sunday are open in the afternoon. It's a glorious time to be in Edinburgh.

The **official festival** (Aug 8–31 in 2008) is the original, more formal, and most likely to get booked up. Major events sell out well in advance. The ticket office is at **The Hub,** located in the former Tolbooth Church, near the top of the Royal Mile (tickets-£4–55, booking from mid-April, office open Mon–Sat 10:00–17:00 or longer, in Aug until 19:30 plus Sun 10:00–19:30, tel. 0131/473-2000, fax 0131/473-2003). You can also book online at www.eif.co.uk.

Call and order your ticket with your credit-card number (see The Hub contact info, above). Pick up your ticket at the office on the day of the show. Several publications—including the festival's official schedule, the *Edinburgh Festivals Guide Daily, The List,* the *Fringe Program,* and the *Daily Diary*—list and evaluate festival events.

The less-formal **Fringe Festival** features "on the edge" comedy and theater (Aug 3–25 in 2008, ticket/info office just below St. Giles Cathedral on the Royal Mile, 180 High Street, tel. 0131/226-0026, bookings tel. 0131/226-0000, can book online from mid-June on, www.edfringe.com). Tickets are usually available at the door, but popular shows can sell out.

The **Military Tattoo** is a massing of the bands, drums, and bagpipes with groups from all over the former British Empire. Displaying military finesse with a stirring lone-piper finale, this grand spectacle fills the castle esplanade nightly except Sunday, normally from a week before the festival starts until a week before it finishes (Aug 1–23 in 2008, Mon–Fri at 21:00, Sat at 19:30 and 22:30, £13–40, booking starts in Dec, Fri–Sat shows sell out first, all seats generally sold out many months ahead, some scattered same-day tickets may be available; office open Mon–Fri 10:00–16:30, during Tattoo open until show time and Sat 10:00–22:30, closed Sun; 32 Market Street, behind Waverley train station, tel. 0131/225-1188 or 0870-755-5118, www.edinburgh-tattoo.co.uk). If nothing else, it is a really big show.

Other summer festivals: jazz and blues (tel. 0131/553-4000, www.edinburghjazzfestival.co.uk), film (tel. 0131/228-4051, www.edfilmfest.org.uk), and books (tel. 0131/624-5050, www.edbookfest.co.uk).

If you do manage to hit Edinburgh during a festival, book a room far in advance and extend your stay by a day or two. Once you know your dates, reserve tickets to any show that you really want to see.

NIGHTLIFE

▲**Ghost Walks**—These walks are an entertaining and cheap night out (offered nightly, usually around 19:00 and 21:00, easy socializing for solo travelers). The theatrical and creatively staged **Witchery Tours,** the most established outfit, offers two different walks: "Ghosts and Gore" and "Murder and Mystery" (£7.50, 90 min, leave from top of Royal Mile near castle esplanade, reservations required, tel. 0131/225-6745, www.witcherytours.com).

Auld Reekie Tours offers a scary array of walks daily and nightly (£6–9, 90 min, leaves from front steps of Tron Kirk, pick up brochure or visit www.auldreekietours.co.uk). Auld Reekie is into the paranormal, witch covens, and pagan temples, taking groups into the "vaults" under the old bridges "where it was so dark, so crowded, and so squalid that the people there knew each other not by how they looked, but by how they sounded, felt, and smelt. If you had a candle, you weren't poor enough to live in the vaults. Then the great fire came. They crowded in, thinking that a brick refuge like this wouldn't burn...and they all roasted. To this day, creepy things happen in the haunted vaults of Edinburgh." If you want more, there's plenty of it (complete with screaming Gothic "jumpers").

▲▲**Literary Pub Tour**—This two-hour walk is interesting even if you think Sir Walter Scott was an arctic explorer. You'll follow the witty dialogue of two actors as they debate whether the great literature of Scotland was high art or the creative recreation of fun-loving louts fueled by a love of whisky. You'll wander from the Grassmarket, over the Old Town to the New Town, with stops in three pubs as your guides share their takes on Scotland's literary greats. The tour meets at The Beehive pub on Grassmarket (£10, book online and save £1, May–Sept nightly at 19:30, March–April and Oct Thu–Sun, Nov–Feb Fri only, call 0131/226-6665 to confirm, www.edinburghliterarypubtour.co.uk).

They also run a Literary Bus Tour, which leaves daily at 13:00 and 14:30 in July and August (£10, £15 combo-ticket with Pub Tour, 70 min, same phone and website).

Scottish Folk Evenings—These £35–40 dinner shows, generally for tour groups intent on photographing old cultural clichés, are held in the huge halls of expensive hotels. (Prices are bloated to include 20 percent commissions.) Your "traditional" meal is followed by a full slate of swirling kilts, blaring bagpipes, and Scottish folk dancing with an "old-time music hall" emcee. If you like Lawrence Welk, you're in for a treat. But for most travelers, these are painfully cheesy variety shows. You can sometimes see the show without dinner for about two-thirds the price. The TI has fliers on all the latest venues.

Prestonfield House offers its kitschy Scottish folk evening—a plaid fantasy of smiling performers accompanied by electric keyboards—with or without dinner Sunday to Friday. For £36, you get the show with two drinks and a wad of haggis (20:00–22:00); £47 buys you the same, plus a four-course meal and wine (be there at 18:45). It's in the stables of "the handsomest house in Edinburgh," which now houses the recommended Rhubarb Restaurant (Priestfield Road, a 10-min walk from Dalkeith Road B&Bs, tel. 0131/225-7800, www.scottishshow.com).

Theater—Even outside of festival time, Edinburgh is a fine place for lively and affordable theater. Pick up *The List* for a complete rundown of what's on (£2.20 at newsstands).

▲**Live Music in Pubs**—Edinburgh used to be a good place for traditional folk music, but in the last few years, pub owners—out of economic necessity—are catering to college-age customers more interested in beer-drinking. Pubs that were regular venues for folk music have gone pop. Rather than list places likely to change their format in a few months, I'll simply recommend the monthly *Gig Guide* (free at TI, accommodations, and various pubs, www.gigguide.co.uk). This simple little sheet lists eight or 10 places each night that have live music. Listings are divided by genre (pop, rock, world, and folk). Generally, several bars feature live folk music every night.

Pubs in the Old Town: The **Grassmarket** neighborhood (below the castle) is sloppy with live music and rowdy people spilling out of the pubs and into what was (once upon a time) a busy market square. It's fun to just wander through this area late at night and check out the scene at pubs such as Finnegans Wake, Biddy Mulligan, and White Hart Inn. By the music and crowds you'll know where to go...and where not to. Have a beer and follow your ear. On the Royal Mile, **Whistlebinkies** is famous for live music (South Bridge, tel. 0131/557-5114, www.whistlebinkies.com).

Pubs near Dalkeith Road B&Bs: Three fine and classic pubs (without a lot of noisy machines and rowdy twentysomethings) cluster within 100 yards of each other around the intersection of Duncan Street and Causewayside, near the Dalkeith Road B&B neighborhood (see "Sleeping," below). **Leslie's Pub,** sitting between a working-class and an upper-class neighborhood, has two sides. Originally, the gang would go in on the right to gather around the great hardwood bar, glittering with a century of *Cheers* ambience. Meanwhile, the more delicate folks would slip in on the left, with its discreet doors, plush snugs (cozy private booths), and ornate ordering windows. Since 1896, this Victorian classic has been appreciated for both its "real ales" and its huge selection of whiskies—the menu is six pages of fine scotch. (Leslie's is a block downhill from the others at 49 Ratcliffe Terrace.) **The Old Bell Inn,** with a nostalgic sports-bar vibe, serves only drinks after 19:00 (see "Scottish Grub and Pubs," page 501). **Swany's Pub,** perhaps a little less welcoming than the others, is a quintessential hangout for the working-class boys of the neighborhood—with some fun characters to get to know. **Bierex,** a much younger and noisier scene a few blocks away, is a favorite among young people for its cheap drinks (132 Causewayside, see "Scottish Grub and Pubs," page 501).

SLEEPING

The advent of big, cheap hotels has made life tough for B&Bs. Still, book ahead, especially in August, when the annual festival fills Edinburgh. Conventions, rugby matches, school holidays, and weekends can make finding a room tough at almost any time of year. For the best prices, book directly rather than through the TI, which charges a higher room fee and levies a £3 booking fee. "Standard" rooms, with toilets and showers a tissue-toss away, save you £10 a night.

B&Bs off Dalkeith Road

These B&Bs—south of town near the Royal Commonwealth Pool, just off Dalkeith Road—are all top-end, sporting three or four stars. While pricey, they come with uniformly friendly hosts and great cooked breakfasts, and are a good value for people with enough money. At these not-quite interchangeable places, character is provided by the personality quirks of the hosts.

All listings are on quiet streets, and within a two-minute walk of a bus stop (see "Getting There," page 493). While you won't find phones in the rooms, several offer Internet access. Most can provide triples or even quads for families.

The quality of all these B&Bs is more than adequate. Prices are a bit steep, but the cheaper places are often just as good as the more expensive ones. Prices listed are for most of peak season; if there's a range, prices slide up with summer demand. *Note: The highest prices in the range provided are for August, when B&Bs also do not accept bookings for one-night stays.* Conversely, in winter, when there's no demand, prices get really soft (less than what's listed here). These prices are for cash; expect a 3 to 5 percent fee for using your credit card.

Sleep Code

(£1 = about $2, country code: 44, area code: 0131)
S = Single, **D** = Double/Twin, **T** = Triple, **Q** = Quad, **b** = bathroom, **s** = shower only. You can assume credit cards are accepted unless otherwise noted.

To help you sort easily through these listings, I've divided the rooms into three categories based on the price for a standard double room with bath (during high season):

$$$ **Higher Priced**—Most rooms £110 or more.
$$ **Moderately Priced**—Most rooms between £50–110.
$ **Lower Priced**—Most rooms £50 or less.

Edinburgh's Dalkeith Road Neighborhood

1 Airdenair Guest House

2 Kenvie Guest House

3 Aonach Mór B&B; Turret & AmarAgua Guest Houses

4 Dunedin Guest House

5 Ard-Na-Said B&B

6 Hotel & Rest. Ceilidh-Donia

7 Priestville Guest House

8 Cherrytree Villa Guest House

9 Dorstan House

10 Gil Dun Guest House

11 Belford Guest House

12 Fenwicks Restaurant

13 Blonde Restaurant

14 The New Bell & The Old Bell Inn

15 Bierex Pub

16 To Prestonfield House & Rhubarb Restaurant

17 Pataka Indian Restaurant

18 Wild Elephant Thai & Chinatown Restaurants

19 Sambuca Italian Restaurant

20 Leslie's Pub

21 Swany's Pub

22 To Sainsbury's Supermarket

23 Tesco Express Supermarket

24 Launderette

Near the B&Bs, you'll find plenty of good eateries (see "Eating," page 500); several good, classic pubs (see "Nightlife," above); and easy, free parking. If you bring in take-out food, your host would probably prefer you eat it in the breakfast room rather than muck up your room—ask. The nearest launderette is **Sun Dial** (see page 458).

Getting There: This comfortable, safe neighborhood is a 10-minute bus ride from the Royal Mile. From the train station, TI, or Sir Walter Scott Monument, cross Princes Street and wait at the bus stop in front of the H&M store (check the signs). Buses also stop on the east side of the station (£1, use exact change; catch LRT buses #30 and #33, or First buses #14 and #86—these two go to and from North Bridge, a few minutes' walk from the TI—tell driver your destination is Dalkeith Road, ride 10 min to first or second stop—depending on B&B—after the pool, ping the bell, and hop out). These buses also stop at the corner of North Bridge and High Street on the Royal Mile. Buses run from 6:00 (9:00 on Sun) to 23:00. Taxi fare between the train station or Royal Mile and the B&Bs is about £5. Taxis are easy to hail on Dalkeith Road if it isn't raining.

$$ Airdenair Guest House, offering views and a friendly welcome, has five attractive rooms on the second floor with a lofty above-it-all feeling (Sb-£30–40, Db-£52–75, Tb-£75–90, Wi-Fi, 29 Kilmaurs Road, tel. 0131/668-2336, www.airdenair.com, jill @airdenair.com, Jill and Doug McLennan). Jill's parents provide guests with homemade treats such as scones and "tablet"—a Scottish delicacy that's sweet as can be.

$$ Kenvie Guest House, expertly run by Dorothy Vidler, comes with six pleasant rooms and lots of personal touches (one small twin-£50, D-£52–58, Db-£60–68, these prices with cash and this book through 2008—must claim when you reserve, family deals, Internet access and Wi-Fi, 16 Kilmaurs Road, tel. 0131/668-1964, fax 0131/668-1926, www.kenvie.co.uk, dorothy @kenvie.co.uk).

$$ Aonach Mór has seven lovingly maintained rooms decorated with both modern hipness and Victorian history in mind. In bad weather, they light a fire in their stay-a-while, leather-couch lounge. Leaf through the 19th-century books in your room or dawdle in the garden outside (S-£28–50, Db-£60–100, deluxe four-poster Db-£70–120, these prices and free stiff complimentary welcome drink promised with this book through 2008, family rooms, Internet access, 14 Kilmaurs Terrace, tel. 0131/667-8694, www.aonachmor.com, info@aonachmor.com, young go-getters Ross and Kathleen Birnie).

$$ Dunedin Guest House (dun-EE-din) is a fine value: bright, plush, and elegantly Scottish, with seven airy rooms

(S with private b on hall-£35–50, Db-£75–95, family rooms for up to five-£120–160, 8 Priestfield Road, tel. 0131/668-1949, fax 0131/668-3636, www.dunedinguesthouse.co.uk, reservations @dunedinguesthouse.co.uk, David and Irene Wright).

$$ Ard-Na-Said B&B is an elegant 1875 Victorian house with a comfy lounge and six classy rooms (Sb-£35–50, Db-£60–80, four-poster Db-£70–100, Tb-£110–120, family room, 5 Priestfield Road, tel. 0131/667-8754, www.ardnasaid.co.uk, jim@ardnasaid .co.uk, Jim and Olive Lyons).

$$ AmarAgua Guest House is an inviting Victorian home away from home—complete with a friendly Dalmatian, seven rooms, and Japanese garden. It's given a little extra sparkle by its energetic young proprietors, Dawn-Ann and Tony Costa (S with private b on hall-£35–42, Db-£64–84, fancy four-poster Db-£74–94, free Internet access, 10 Kilmaurs Terrace, tel. 0131/667-6775, www.amaragua.co.uk, reservations@amaragua.co.uk).

$$ Hotel Ceilidh-Donia rents 16 cheery, tricked-out rooms with a pleasant back deck, a bar, a DVD lending library, and the only restaurant—open to the public—in the immediate area (Sb-£50–60, Db-£80–100, less off-season, ask for discount with this book through 2008, free Internet access and Wi-Fi for guests and diners, 14 Marchhall Crescent, tel. 0131/667-2743, www .hotelceilidh-donia.co.uk, reservations@hotelceilidh-donia.co.uk, Max, Annette, Alan, and Struan).

$$ Priestville Guest House is homey, with a high, skylit ceiling and cozy charm. The six rooms have VCRs, Wi-Fi, and a free video library (D-£44–60, Db-£48–68, Q-£96–120, discount for 2 or more nights, free Internet access on downstairs computer with this book in 2008, 10 Priestfield Road, tel. 0131/667-2435, www.priestville.com, bookings@priestville.com, Trina and Colin Warwick and their dog Torrie).

$$ Cherrytree Villa Guest House is a good value; it's simple and clean, with lots of stairs and a unique breakfast room where you can chat with Denise while she cooks your breakfast (S-£22–30, Db-£48–80, less off-season, parking, 9 East Mayfield, tel. 0131/258-0009, www.cherrytreevilla.com, cherrytreevilla @blueyonder.co.uk, friendly Keith and Denise).

$$ Turret Guest House has seven teddy-on-the-beddy cozy rooms, with a vast, bay-windowed family room (S-£38–55, Db-£62–102, four-poster Db-£70–110, Qb-£96–160, £2/person discount with this book and cash through 2008, Wi-Fi, 8 Kilmaurs Terrace, tel. 0131/667-6704, www.turretguesthouse.co.uk, contact@turretguesthouse.co.uk, Jimmy and Fiona Mackie).

$$ Dorstan House is more hotelesque with a few extra comforts—but still friendly and relaxed. Several of its 14 thoughtfully decorated rooms are on the ground floor (S-£25–50,

Sb-£30–60, Ds-£40–80, Db-£50–90, Tb-£70–120, family rooms and suites available, Wi-Fi, laundry service, 7 Priestfield Road, tel. 0131/667-6721, www.dorstan-hotel.demon.co.uk, reservations @dorstan-hotel.demon.co.uk, Richard and Maki Stott).

$$ Gil Dun Guest House, eight rooms on a quiet cul-de-sac just off Dalkeith Road, is comfortable, pleasant, and managed with care by Gerald McDonald (S-£28–55, D/Db-£70–110, Tb-£90, family deals, 9 Spence Street, tel. 0131/667-1368, fax 0131/668-4989, www.gildun.co.uk, gildun.edin@btinternet.com).

$ Belford Guest House is a tidy, homey place offering seven good rooms and a warm welcome (D-£40, Db-£50, family deals, 13 Blacket Avenue, tel. 0131/667-2422, fax 0131/667-7508, www .belfordguesthouse.com, tom@belfordguesthouse.com, Tom Borthwick).

Big, Modern Hotels

The last three of these listings are cheap as hotels go and offer more comfort than character. The first one's a splurge. In each case I'd skip the institutional breakfast and eat out. To locate these hotels, see the map on page 472.

$$$ MacDonald Hotel, my only fancy listing, is an opulent four-star splurge, with 156 rooms up the street from the new Parliament building. With its classy marble-and-wood decor, fitness center, and pool, it's hard to leave. On a gray winter day in Edinburgh, this could be worth it. Prices can vary wildly (Db-£110–250, includes breakfast, near bottom of Royal Mile, across from Dynamic Earth, Holyrood Road, tel. 0131/550-4500, book online for better deals at www.macdonaldhotels.co.uk).

$$ Ibis Hotel, mid–Royal Mile behind Tron Kirk, is well-run and perfectly located. It has 98 soulless but clean and comfy rooms drenched in prefab American charm (Db in June–Sept-£70, discounted in off-season, lousy continental breakfast-£5, non-smoking rooms, elevator, Internet access in lobby, 6 Hunter Square, tel. 0131/240-7000, fax 0131/240-7007, www.ibishotels .com, h2039@accor.com).

$$ Jurys Inn, a cookie-cutter place with 186 dependably comfortable rooms, is capably run and well-located a short walk from the station (Sb, Db, and Tb-all £60–100, less on weekdays, much cheaper off-season and for online bookings, 2 kids sleep free, breakfast-£9, non-smoking rooms, some views, pub/restaurant, on quiet street just off Royal Mile, 43 Jeffrey Street, tel. 0131/200-3300, www.jurys.com).

$$ Travelodge has 193 no-nonsense rooms all decorated in dark blue and a great location. All rooms are the same, and suitable for two adults with two kids or three adults. While sleepable, it has a cheap feel with a quickly revolving staff (Sb, Db, and

Tb-all £60–70, weekend Db-£70–85, Aug Db-£130, cheaper off-season, breakfast-£7, 33 St. Mary's Street, a block off Royal Mile, tel. 08700-850-950, www.travelodge.co.uk). Travelodge's website offers a great £27–50-per-room "supersaver" deal for a limited number of midweek bookings.

Hostels

Edinburgh's cheap hostels are well-run and open to all, but they're scruffy and don't include breakfast. They do offer Internet access, laundry facilities, and £12–15 (unless otherwise noted) bunk beds in 8- to 16-bed single-sex dorms (about a £9–12 savings per person over B&Bs). Book a bed well in advance for July and August.

These three sister hostels are popular crash pads for young backpackers—youthful, hip, and beautifully located in the noisy center (www.scotlands-top-hostels.com): **High Street Hostel** (laundry-£2.50, kitchen, 8 Blackfriars Street, just off High Street/Royal Mile, tel. 0131/557-3984); **Royal Mile Backpackers** (105 High Street, tel. 0131/557-6120); and **Castle Rock Hostel** (just below the castle and above the pubs, 15 Johnston Terrace, tel. 0131/225-9666).

Brodies 2 Backpacker Hostel, spartan, clean, and beautifully located in the middle of the Royal Mile, rents 70 cheap beds in four- to eight-bed dorms (£13–20 per bed, less off-season, lockers, kitchen, Internet access-£1/20 min, laundry, 93 High Street, tel. 0131/556-2223, www.brodieshostels.co.uk). Older travelers feel more comfortable here than in the above hostels. To locate this hostel, see the map on page 473.

EATING

Reservations for restaurants are a good idea in August and on weekends. All restaurants in Scotland have been smoke-free since 2006. (England followed suit in 2007.)

Along the Royal Mile

Historic pubs and doily cafés with reasonable, unremarkable meals abound. While the eateries along this most-crowded stretch of the city are invariably touristy, the scene is fun and competition makes a well-chosen place a good value. Here are some handy, affordable options for a good bite to eat (listed in downhill order; for locations, see map on pages 472–473). Sprinkled in this list are some places a block or two off the main drag—and correspondingly filled with more locals than tourists.

The Red Coat Café and Jacobite Room—located within Edinburgh Castle—is a big, bright, efficient cafeteria (£6 quick, healthy meals). Punctuate the two parts of your castle visit (the castle itself and the impressive National War Museum of Scotland) with a smart break here. The **Queen Anne Café,** in a building right across from the Crown Jewels, serves sit-down meals in its small, tight space (last orders 30 min before castle complex closes).

The Hub, a classy place in the old Tolbooth Church at the top of the Mile, serves gourmet sandwiches and fine desserts. While it's a bit pricey, the food is delightfully presented, the service is smart, and you're supporting the Edinburgh Festival (which owns the restaurant, and also has its booking office here). Sit in the bright-yellow Gothic interior or outside, with a wonderful Royal Mile perch (£7 sandwiches, inexpensive lunch menu is stowed at 17:30, £15 dinners from 18:00, Mon–Sat 9:30–22:00, Sun 9:30–18:00, Castlehill, tel. 0131/473-2067).

The following two restaurants are in a cluster of pleasant eateries happily removed from the Royal Mile melee. Consider stopping at one of these on your way to the National Museum of Scotland, which is a half-block away.

The Elephant House, two blocks out of the touristy zone with an unmarked front door, is a comfy neighborhood coffee shop where locals browse newspapers in the stay-a-while back room, listen to soft rock, and sip coffee or munch a light meal. The friendly staff explains their enticing buffet line most of the day, then switches to table service after 18:00 (daily 9:00–22:00, 4 computers with cheap and fast Internet access, vegetarian options, 2 blocks south of Royal Mile near National Museum of Scotland at 21 George IV Bridge, tel.  0131/220-5355). It's easy to imagine J. K. Rowling annoying waiters with her baby pram while spending long afternoons here writing the first Harry Potter book.

The Outsider, also without a hint of Royal Mile tourism, is a sleek spot serving modern Mediterranean and Southeast Asian cuisine (good fish and stir-fry) in a minimalist maxi-chic setting. Cobble together a fun meal of £10–12 plates from their creative and trendy menu. As you'll be competing with local yuppies, reserve for dinner (daily 12:00–23:00, 30 yards up from Elephant House at 15 George IV Bridge, tel. 0131/226-3131).

Deacon Brodie's Tavern, at a dead-center location on the Royal Mile, is a sloppy pub. They serve soup, sandwiches, and snacks on the ground floor and basic £9 pub meals upstairs in the restaurant. While painfully touristy, it comes with a fun history (daily 12:00–22:00, kids welcome upstairs, tel. 0131/225-6531).

St. Giles Cathedral Lower Aisle, hiding under the landmark church, is *the* place for paupers to munch prayerfully. Stairs on the back side of the church lead into the basement, where you'll find simple, light lunches from 11:45 and coffee with cakes all day (Mon–Fri 9:00–16:30, Sun 10:00–13:30, closed Sat and early if crowds have petered out).

Always Sunday Food Company is a tiny place with a wonderful formula. It's a flexible fantasy of Scottish and Mediterranean hot dishes, fresh salads, smoked salmon, sharp cheese, homemade desserts, and so on. You're invited to mix and match at their user-friendly, create-a-lunch buffet line. They use healthy ingredients and are hip to any diet concerns. Sit inside or people-watch from Royal Mile tables outside (£6 lunches, Mon–Fri 8:00–18:00, Sat-Sun 9:00–18:00, 30 yards below St. Giles Cathedral at 170 High Street, tel. 0131/622-0667).

The Filling Station, a big, noisy eatery decorated with old car parts, has an American-type menu and rocks at night. Behind its youthful bar stretches a family-friendly dining hall where you'll get pizza, pasta, and burgers for £7–10, as well as breakfast (daily 9:30–23:30, 235 High Street, near North Bridge, tel. 0131/226-2488).

Dubh Prais Scottish Restaurant is a dressy nine-table place filling a cellar 10 steps and a world away from the High Street bustle. The owner-chef, James McWilliams, proudly serves Scottish "fayre" at its very best (including gourmet haggis). The daily specials are not printed, to guard against "zombie waiters." They like to get to know you a bit by explaining things (£27 dinners, Tue–Sat 17:00–22:30, closed Sun–Mon, reservations smart, opposite Radisson SAS Hotel at 123 High Street, tel. 0131/557-5732).

The World's End Pub, a colorful old place, dishes up hearty £7 meals from a creative menu in a fun, dark, and noisy space (daily 10:00–21:00, 4 High Street, tel. 0131/556-3628).

David Bann, just a three-minute walk from the Royal Mile, is a worthwhile pit stop for vegetarians in need of a break from the morning fry. Upscale (there's a cocktail bar) and organic, they serve polenta, tartlets, soups, and light meals (£5 starters, £7.50 lunches, £10 dinners, daily 11:00–midnight, vegan options, 56–58 St. Mary's Street, tel. 0131/556-5888).

The Tea Room, right on the Mile, is a fragile hole-in-the-wall serving light lunches, soups, scones, and fine tea in yellow elegance (daily 10:30–16:30, next to Museum of Edinburgh at 158 Canongate, tel. 07771/501-679). Next door, **Bene's** fries up good, greasy fish-and-chips to go (munch in graveyard across street).

Clarinda's Tea Room, near the bottom of the Royal Mile, is charming and girlish—a fine and tasty place to relax after touring the Mile or the Palace of Holyroodhouse. Stop in for a £5 quiche,

Edinburgh's New Town

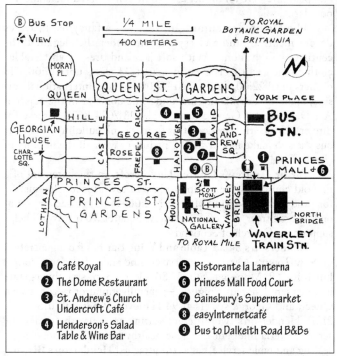

(B) BUS STOP   ¼ MILE   TO ROYAL
BOTANIC GARDEN
VIEW   400 METERS   & BRITANNIA

MORAY PL.

QUEEN   QUEEN ST. GARDENS   YORK PLACE

GEORGIAN HOUSE   HILL   CASTLE FREDERICK GEORGE HANOVER DAVID ST. AND-REW SQ.   ❹ ■ ❺ ■   BUS STN.

CHARLOTTE SQ.   ROSE   FREDE ❸ ■ ❷ ❼ ❶ ■ PRINCES MALL & ❻

❽ HANOVER ❾ (B) ❶

PRINCES   ST.

LOTHIAN   PRINCES ST. GARDENS   MOUND   SCOTT MON. WAVERLEY BRIDGE   NORTH BRIDGE

NATIONAL GALLERY   TO ROYAL MILE   WAVERLEY TRAIN STN.

❶ Café Royal
❷ The Dome Restaurant
❸ St. Andrew's Church Undercroft Café
❹ Henderson's Salad Table & Wine Bar
❺ Ristorante la Lanterna
❻ Princes Mall Food Court
❼ Sainsbury's Supermarket
❽ easyInternetcafé
❾ Bus to Dalkeith Road B&Bs

salad, and soup lunch (Mon–Sat 8:30–16:45, Sun 10:00–16:45, 69 Canongate, tel. 0131/557-1888). It's great for tea and cake anytime.

In the New Town

While most of your sightseeing will be along the Royal Mile, it's important that your Edinburgh experience stretches beyond this happy tourist gauntlet. Just a few minutes away, in the Georgian town, you'll find a bustling world of office workers, students, and pensioners doing their thing. At midday that includes eating. Simply hiking over to one of these places will give you a good helping of modern Edinburgh. All these places are within a few minutes' walk of the TI and main Waverley Bridge tour-bus depot.

Café Royal is a movie producer's dream pub—the perfect *fin de siècle* setting for a coffee, beer, or light meal. (In fact, parts of *Chariots of Fire* were filmed here.) Drop in, if only to admire the 1880 tiles featuring famous inventors (daily 12:00–14:30 & 18:00– late, bar food available during the afternoon, 2 blocks from Princes Mall on West Register Street, tel. 0131/556-1884). There are two eateries here: the pub (basic £8 meals) and the dressier restaurant, specializing in fish and game (two-course lunch with wine for £15,

£20 plates, reserve for dinner as it's quite small and understandably popular).

The Dome Restaurant, in what was a fancy bank, serves decent meals around a classy bar and under the elegant 19th-century skylight dome. With soft jazz and dressy, white-table-cloth ambience, it feels a world apart (£13 plates until 17:00, £18 dinners until 22:00, daily 10:00–22:00, modern international cuisine, open for a drink anytime under the dome or in the adjacent Art Deco bar, 14 George Street, tel. 0131/624-8624, reserve for dinner). Notice the facade of this former bank building—the various ways to make money fill the pediment with all the nobility of classical gods.

The St. Andrew's Church Undercroft, in the basement of a fine old church, is the cheapest place in town for lunch—just £2 for sandwich and soup (Mon–Fri 12:00–14:00, closed Sat–Sun, on George Street, just off St. Andrew Square). Your tiny bill helps support the Church of Scotland.

Henderson's Salad Table and Wine Bar has fed a generation of New Town vegetarians hearty cuisine and salads (two-course lunch for £9, Mon–Sat 7:30–22:30, closed Sun, strictly vegetarian; pleasant live music nightly—generally guitar or jazz; between Queen and George streets at 94 Hanover Street, tel. 0131/225-2131). Henderson's two different seating areas use the same self-serve cafeteria line. For the same healthy food with more elegant seating and table service, eat at the attached **Henderson's Bistro.**

Ristorante la Lanterna is packed with local office workers who enjoy good southern Italian cuisine with friendly service (£5 pastas, £12 plates, Mon–Sat 12:00–14:30 & 17:30–22:30, closed Sun, pricier at dinner, no pizza, dinner reservations wise, 83 Hanover Street, two blocks off Princes Street, tel. 0131/226-3090, attentive Antonietta oversees the action).

Princes Mall Food Court, below the TI and above the station, is a circus of sticky fast-food joints littered with paper plates and shoppers (Mon–Sat 9:00–18:00, Thu until 19:00, Sun 11:00–17:00). If you'd prefer pubs, browse nearby Rose Street.

Supermarket: The glorious **Sainsbury's** supermarket, with a tasty assortment of take-away food and specialty coffees, is just one block from the Sir Walter Scott Monument and the lovely picnic-perfect Princes Street Gardens (Mon–Sat 7:00–22:00, Sun 9:00–20:00, on corner of Rose Street on St. Andrew Square, across the street from Jenners, the classy department store).

The Dalkeith Road Area, near Your B&B

All these places are within a 10-minute walk of my recommended B&Bs. Most are on or near the intersection of Newington Road and East Preston Street. For locations, see map on page 492.

The nearest supermarket is the **Tesco Express;** it's small-ish, but has plenty of fresh produce and picnic supplies (daily 6:00–23:00, 158 Causewayside). **Sainsbury's** is a 10-minute walk or a quick bus ride down Dalkeith Road away from town in the Cameron Toll shopping complex (Mon–Sat 7:30–22:00, Sun 8:00–20:00, tel. 0131/666-5200).

Scottish/French Restaurants

These classy little eight-table places feature "Auld Alliance" cuisine—Scottish cooking with a French flair (seasoned with a joint historic disdain for England). Their small menus offer two- or three-course meals with three or four choices per course (about £10 for a two-course lunch, £20 for a three-course dinner). For a cozy drink after dinner, visit the recommended pubs in the area (see "Nightlife," page 490). Reserve on weekends and during the festival.

Fenwicks is cozy and reliable, with tasty Scottish and continental food, and no French fries. It's pricey, but this little linoleum, brown, and woody bistro is considered a good value by locals (main course-£13–16, three-course fixed-price meal-£22, daily 12:00–14:00 & 18:00–22:00, 15 Salisbury Place, tel. 0131/667-4265).

Blonde Restaurant, with a more eclectic and European menu, is less expensive, bigger, and more crowded than the others, with no set-price dinners. It's a bit out of the way, but a hit with locals (about £15–17 for two courses, Tue–Sun 12:00–14:30 & 18:00–22:00, open for dinner only on Mon, good vegetarian options, 75 St. Leonard's Street, tel. 0131/668-2917).

Hotel Ceilidh-Donia serves well-prepared fish, meat, and vegetarian dishes in a flagstone-floored, high-ceilinged space with a small, friendly adjoining pub. The decor is likeably kitschy with attitude, and the garden seating is a delight (£10 plates with good vegetables, Mon–Sat dinner from 18:00, open Sun June–Sept only, free Internet access for customers, 14 Marchhall Crescent, tel. 0131/667-2743). This is the only place in the immediate neighborhood of the recommended B&Bs.

Scottish Grub and Pubs

The New Bell serves up filling modern Scottish fare from steak and salmon to haggis in a Victorian living-room setting above the lovable Old Bell Inn. Along with wonderfully presented meals, you'll enjoy white tablecloths, oriental carpets on hardwood floors, and a relaxing spaciousness under open beams (two-course £13.50 special until 18:45, £15 plates, Mon–Thu 17:30–21:30, Fri–Sat 17:30–22:00, Sun 12:30–14:00 & 17:30–21:30, always a veggie option, 233 Causewayside, tel. 0131/668-2868).

The Old Bell Inn, with an old-time sports-bar ambience—

fishing, golf, horses—serves simpler £7 pub meals from the same fine kitchen on the ground floor. This is a classic snug pub, all dark woods and brass beer tapes, littered with evocative knickknacks. It comes with fine sidewalk seating and a mixed-age crowd (daily 12:00–14:30 & 17:30–19:00, then drinks only, 233 Causewayside, tel. 0131/668-1573).

Bierex, a youthful pub, is the neighborhood favorite for modern dishes (£6 plates), camaraderie, and cheap booze. It's a spacious, bright, mahogany-and-leather place popular for its long and varied happy hours (daily 10:00–24:00, food served 10:00–21:00, 132 Causewayside, tel. 0131/667-2335).

Rhubarb Restaurant is the hottest thing in Old World elegance. It's in "Edinburgh's most handsome house"—a riot of antiques, velvet, tassels, and fringes. The plush rhubarb color theme reminds visitors that this was the place where rhubarb was first grown in Britain. It's a 10-minute walk past the other recommended eateries behind Arthur's Seat, in a huge estate with big, shaggy Highland cows enjoying their salads *al fresco*. While most spend a wad here (plates about £20), smart budget travelers time their visit to take advantage of the great off-hours two-course meal for £17 (arrive during these windows of time to get the deal: Sun–Thu 12:00–14:00 & 18:30–19:00, Fri–Sat 12:00–14:00 & 18:00–19:00, reserve in advance and dress up if you can, in Prestonfield House, Priestfield Road, tel. 0131/225-1333). For details on the Scottish folk evening offered here, see "Nightlife," page 489.

Ethnic Options

Pataka Indian Restaurant is a tight little 12-table "Indian bistro" with attentive service and great food. Offering big portions and small prices (£8 dishes), it's understandably popular with locals (daily 12:00–14:00 & 17:30–23:30, also offers take-away, 190 Causewayside, tel. 0131/668-1167).

Wild Elephant Thai Restaurant is a small, hardworking eatery that locals consider the best around for Thai (daily 17:00–23:00, also does take-away, main dishes £6–10, £11 three-course meal until 20:00, 21 Newington Road, tel. 0131/662-8822).

Chinatown is an energetic little place that packs a lot of happy eating into its one small dining room (£6–9 meals, Tue–Fri 12:00–14:00 & 17:30–23:30, Sat–Sun dinner only, closed Mon, reservations smart on weekends, take-away food 25 percent cheaper, 13 Newington Road, tel. 0131/662-0555).

Sambuca Italian Restaurant dishes up good pizza and pasta in a lively bistro where the only decor is the food and the only music is the sound of contented eaters (£6 weekday lunch specials, £8–10 dishes, Mon–Sat 12:00–14:30 & 17:00–late, Sun 17:00–10:00, 103 Causewayside, tel. 0131/667-3307).

TRANSPORTATION CONNECTIONS

From Edinburgh by Train to: Glasgow (4/hr, 50 min, £9.20 one-way), **St. Andrews** (train to Leuchars, 1–2/hr, 1 hr, then 10-min bus into St. Andrews), **Stirling** (2/hr, 50 min), **Pitlochry** (6/day, 2 hrs), **Inverness** (8/day, 3.5 hrs, more with change in Perth), **Oban** (3/day, 4.5 hrs, change in Glasgow), **York** (2/hr, 2.5 hrs), **London** (hourly, 4.5 hrs), **Durham** (nearly hourly, 2 hrs, less frequent in winter), **Newcastle** (hourly, 1.5 hrs), **Keswick/Lake District** (south past Carlisle to Penrith, then catch bus to Keswick, 6/day, fewer Sun, 3 hrs including bus transfer in Penrith), **Birmingham** (6/day, 4.5 hrs), **Crewe** (6/day, 3.5 hrs), **Bristol/near Bath** (hourly, 6–7 hrs), **Blackpool** (8/day, 3.5 hrs, transfer in Preston). Train info: tel. 08457-484-950, www.thetrainline.com, or www.nationalrail.co.uk.

By Bus to: Glasgow (4/hr, 70 min), **Oban** (4/day Mon–Sat, 1/day Sun, 4.5 hrs, transfer in Glasgow; more with additional transfer in Tyndrum), **Fort William** (1/day direct, 4 hrs; 4/day with transfer in Glasgow, 5 hrs), **Portree** on the Isle of Skye (2/day, 8.75 hrs, transfer in Fort William or Glasgow), **Inverness** (hourly, 4 hrs), **Blackpool** (Fri, Sat, Mon only, requires change in Glasgow, 5 hrs), **York** (1/day at 9:45, 5 hrs). For bus info, call Scottish Citylink (tel. 08705-505-050, www.citylink.co.uk) or National Express (tel. 08705-808-080). You can get info and tickets at the bus desk inside the Princes Mall TI.

Route Tips for Drivers

Arriving in Edinburgh from the North: Rather than drive through downtown Edinburgh to the recommended B&Bs, circle the city on the A720 City Bypass road. Approaching Edinburgh on M9, take M8 (direction: Glasgow) and quickly get onto A720 City Bypass (direction: Edinburgh South). After four miles, you'll hit a roundabout. Ignore signs directing you into *Edinburgh North* and stay on A720 for 10 more miles to the next and last roundabout, named *Sheriffhall*. Exit the roundabout on the first left (A7 Edinburgh). From here it's four miles to the B&B neighborhood (see "Arriving from the South," below, and B&B neighborhood map, page 492).

Arriving from the South: Coming into town on A68 from the south, take the A7 Edinburgh exit off the roundabout. A7 becomes Dalkeith Road. If you see the huge swimming pool, you've gone a couple of blocks too far (avoid this by referring to B&B neighborhood map).

Leaving Edinburgh, Heading South: It's 100 miles from Edinburgh to Hadrian's Wall; to Durham it's another 50 miles. From Edinburgh, Dalkeith Road leads south and eventually becomes A68 (handy Cameron Toll supermarket with cheap gas is on the left as you leave Edinburgh Town, 10 min south of Edinburgh; gas and parking behind store). The A68 road takes you to Hadrian's Wall in two hours. You'll pass Jedburgh and its abbey after one hour. (For one last shot of Scotland shopping, there's a coach tour's delight just before Jedburgh, with kilt makers, woolens, and a sheepskin shop.) Across from Jedburgh's lovely abbey is a free parking lot, a good visitors center, and public toilets (20p to pee). The England/Scotland border is a fun, quick stop (great view, ice cream, and tea caravan). Just after the turn for Colwell, turn right onto A6079, and roller-coaster four miles down to Low Brunton. Then, turn right onto B6318, and stay on it by turning left at Chollerford, following the Roman wall westward. (For information on Hadrian's Wall, see page 393.)

ST. ANDREWS

For many, St. Andrews is synonymous with golf. But there's more to this charming town than its famous links. Dramatically situated at the edge of a sandy bay, St. Andrews is the home of Scotland's most important university—think of it as the Scottish Cambridge. And centuries ago, the town was the religious capital of the country.

In its long history, St. Andrews has seen two boom periods. First, in the early Middle Ages, the relics of St. Andrew made the town cathedral one of the most important pilgrimage sites in Christendom. The faithful flocked here from all over Europe, leaving the town with a medieval all-roads-lead-to-the-cathedral street plan that survives today. But after the Scottish Reformation, the cathedral rotted away and the town became a forgotten backwater. A new wave of visitors arrived in the mid-19th century, when a visionary mayor named (appropriately enough) Provost Playfair began to promote the town's connection with the newly-in-vogue game of golf. Most buildings in town date from this time (similar to Edinburgh's New Town).

Today St. Andrews remains a popular spot for both students and golf devotees (including professional golfers and celebrities such as Scotsman Sean Connery, often seen out on the links). With vast sandy beaches, golfing opportunities for pros and novices alike, a fun-loving student vibe, and a string of relaxing fishing villages nearby (the East Neuk), St. Andrews is the most appealing small town in Scotland—and a fine place to take a vacation from your busy vacation.

Planning Your Time

St. Andrews, hugging the east coast of Scotland, is a bit off the main tourist track. But it's well-connected by train to Edinburgh (via nearby Leuchars), making it a worthwhile day trip from the capital. Better yet, spend a night (or more, if you're a golfer) to enjoy this university town after dark.

If you're not here to golf, this is a good way to spend a day: Stroll up Market Street past the TI to the cathedral, then head back along the waterfront street called The Scores, visiting the castle and St. Salvator's College quad en route to the golf courses. Dip into the Golf Museum, watch the golfers on the Old Course, and play a round at "the Himalayas" putting green. With more time, walk along the West Sands beach, backtrack up Market Street to tour the cute St. Andrews Preservation Trust Museum (open only late May–late Sept daily 14:00–17:00), or take a spin by car or bus to the nearby East Neuk.

ORIENTATION

(area code: 01334)

St. Andrews (pop. 14,000), situated at the tip of a peninsula next to a broad bay, retains its old medieval street plan: Three main roads (North Street, Market Street, and South Street) converge at the cathedral, which overlooks the sea at the tip of town. The middle of these streets—Market Street—has the TI and many handy shops and eateries. North of North Street, the seafront street called The Scores connects the cathedral with the golf scene, which huddles along the West Sands beach at the base of the old town. It's an enjoyably compact town: You can stroll across town—from the cathedral to the historic golf course—in about 10 minutes.

Tourist Information

St. Andrews' helpful TI is right on the central Market Street, about two blocks in front of the cathedral. Pick up their stack of brochures on the town and region, consider renting a £6 audioguide for a town walk, and ask about other tours (such as ghost walks or witches walks). They also book rooms for a £3 fee (July–Aug Mon–Sat 9:15–19:00, Sun 10:00–17:00; April–June and Sept–mid-Oct Mon–Sat 9:15–17:00, Sun 11:00–16:00; mid-Oct–March Mon–Sat 9:30–17:00, closed Sun; 70 Market Street, tel. 01334/472-021).

Arrival in St. Andrews

By Train and Bus: The nearest train station is in the village of Leuchars, five miles away. From there, a handy 10-minute shuttle bus will bring you right into St. Andrews. The bus station is near the base of Market Street; to reach most B&Bs, turn left out of the

St. Andrews

St. Andrews

NORTH SEA

WEST SANDS

EAST SANDS

LONG PIER

ST. ANDREW'S CATHEDRAL

CASTLE

BRITISH GOLF MUSEUM

AQUARIUM

ST. SALVATOR'S COLLEGE

ST. MARY'S COLLEGE

THE OLD COURSE

ROYAL + ANCIENT GOLF CLUB

THE HIMALAYAS

ST. ANDREWS LINKS CLUBHOUSE

MORE GOLF

WEST SANDS RD.

BRUCE EMBT.

GOLF PLACE

THE LINKS

THE SCORES

NORTH STREET

MARKET STREET

SOUTH STREET

ABBEY ST.

CASTLE ST.

NORTH HAUGH

GUARDBRIDGE RD.

BRIDGE ST.

ARGYLE ST.

HEPBURN GDNS.

DOUBLE DYKES

QUEEN'S TERRACE

QUEEN'S GDNS.

W. BURN LANE

BELL ST.

GREY. GDNS.

HOPE ST.

CITY ROAD

LINKS CRES.

WINDMILL

MURRAY PK.

MURRAY PL.

PILMOUR PL.

BUTTS WYND

UNION ST.

CHURCH ST.

LIB.

POST

WEST PORT

ST. ANDREWS PRESERVATION TRUST MUSEUM

THE PENDS

ST. RULE'S TOWER

EXHIBIT

RUINS

ST. ANDREWS MUSEUM

BUS STN.

TO LEUCHARS (TRAIN STN.) & DUNDEE

TO EAST NEUK VILLAGES, A-917 & EDINBURGH

400 YARDS
400 METERS

P PARKING

1. Hoppity House
2. Cameron House
3. Lorimer House
4. Arran House
5. Doune House
6. St. Andrews Tourist Hostel
7. New Hall
8. McIntosh Hall
9. The Doll's House Rest.
10. The Seafood Rest.
11. Gregg's & Tesco (Groceries)
12. Aikmans Pub
13. Ma Bells Pub
14. Greyfriars Pub
15. PM's Fish-and-Chips
16. Fisher & Donaldson Pastries
17. B. Jannettas Ice Cream
18. Swilken Burn (Bridge)

station, then right at the roundabout, then look for Murray Park on the left. To reach the TI, turn right out of the station, then take the next left and head up Market Street.

By Car: For a short stay, drivers can simply head into the town center and park anywhere along the street. Shops sell parking vouchers, which you'll display in your window (read directions on voucher; 70p/1 hr, £1.40/2 hrs, monitored Mon–Sat 9:00–17:00). For longer stays, you can park free along certain streets near the center (such as along The Scores), or use one of the long-stay lots near the entrance to town.

Helpful Hints

Events: Every five years, St. Andrews is swamped with about 100,000 visitors when it hosts the British Open (called simply "The Open" around here; next in July 2010). The town also fills up the first week of October every year for the Alfred Dunhill Links Championship. Unless you're a golf pilgrim, avoid the town at these times.

School Term: The University of St. Andrews has two terms: spring semester ("Candlemas"), from mid-February through May; and fall semester ("Martinmas"), from late September until mid-January. St. Andrews feels downright sleepy in summer, when most students leave and golfers take over the town.

Internet Access: You can get online for free at the **public library,** behind the church on South Street (Mon and Fri–Sat 9:30–17:00, Tue–Thu 9:30–19:00, closed Sun, tel. 01334/412-685).

Walking Tour: June Riches does good walking tours that bring St. Andrews' history to life. There's no set schedule, so call or email ahead to join a tour or arrange for one of your own (£6 per person, £55 for a group, tel. 01334/850-638, june.riches @virgin.net).

SIGHTS AND ACTIVITIES

In the Medieval Town

▲▲**St. Andrew's Cathedral**—The walls and spires that were once the cathedral, although pecked away by centuries of scavengers, are among the most evocative ruins in Great Britain. Between the Great Schism and the Reformation (roughly the 14th–16th centuries), St. Andrews was the ecclesiastical capital of Scotland—and this was its showpiece church. Today the site features the remains of the cathedral and cloister (free to explore), a graveyard, and a small exhibit and climbable tower (both covered by one ticket).

It was the relics of the Apostle Andrew that first put this town on the map, and gave it its name. According to a (likely untrue) legend, in the fourth century, St. Rule was directed in a dream to bring the relics northward from Constantinople. When the ship wrecked offshore from here, it was clear that this was a sacred place. Andrew's bones (an arm, a knee, some fingers, and some teeth) were kept on this site, and starting in 1160, the cathedral was built and pilgrims began to arrive. Since St. Andrew had a direct connection to Jesus, his relics were believed to possess special properties, making them worthy of pilgrimages on par with St. James' relics in Santiago de Compostela, Spain (of Camino de Santiago fame). St. Andrew became Scotland's patron saint; in fact, the white "X" on the blue Scottish flag evokes the diagonal cross on which St. Andrew was crucified (he chose this type of cross because he felt unworthy to die as his master had).

You can stroll around the cathedral **ruins**—the best part of

the complex—for free. First walk between the two tall ends of the church, which used to be the apse (at the sea end) and the main entry (at the town end). Notice the gigantic footprint of the former church in the ground, including the bases of columns—like giant sawed-off tree trunks. Plaques identify where elements of the church once stood. Looking at the one wall that's still standing, you can see the architectural changes over the 150 years the cathedral was built—from the rounded, Romanesque windows at the front, to the more highly decorated, pointed Gothic arches near the back. Mentally rebuild the church, and try to imagine it in its former majesty, when it played host to pilgrims from all over Europe. The church wasn't destroyed all at once, like all those ruined abbeys in England (demolished in a huff by Henry VIII when he broke with the pope). Because the Scottish Reformation was more gradual (see sidebar), this church was slowly picked apart over time. First just the decorations were removed from inside the cathedral. Then the roof was removed to make use of its lead. Without a roof, the cathedral fell further and further into disrepair, and was quarried by locals for its handy pre-cut stones (which you'll still find in the walls of many old St. Andrews homes).

The surrounding **graveyard,** dating from the post-Reformation Protestant era, is much more recent than the cathedral. In this golf-obsessed town, the game even infiltrates the cemeteries: Many notable golfers from St. Andrews are buried here (such as

The Scottish Reformation

It's easy to forget that during the 16th-century English Reformation—when King Henry VIII split with the Vatican and formed the Anglican Church (so he could get a guilt-free divorce)—Scotland was still its own independent nation. Like much of northern Europe, Scotland eventually chose a Protestant path, but it was more gradual and grassroots than Henry VIII's top-down, destroy-the-abbeys approach. While the English Reformation resulted in the Church of England (a.k.a. the Anglican Church, called "Episcopal" outside of England), with the monarch at its head, the Scottish Reformation created the Church of Scotland, with elected leaders ("Presbyterian" in church jargon).

One of the leaders of the Scottish Reformation was John Knox (1514–1572), who learned at the foot of the great Swiss Reformer John Calvin. Returning to Scotland, Knox hopped from pulpit to pulpit, and his feverish sermons incited riots of "born-again" iconoclasts who dismantled or destroyed Catholic churches and abbeys (including St. Andrew's Cathedral). Knox's newly minted Church of Scotland gradually spread from the Lowlands to the Highlands. The southern and eastern part of Scotland, around St. Andrews—just across the North Sea from the Protestant countries of northern Europe—embraced the Church of Scotland long before the more remote and Catholic-oriented part of the country to the north and west. Today about 40 percent of Scots claim affiliation with the Church of Scotland, compared to 20 percent who are Catholic (still mostly in the western Highlands).

Young Tom—or "Tommy"—Morris, four-time British Open winner).

Go through the surviving wall into what was the former **cloister,** marked by a gigantic green square in the center. You can still see the cleats up on the wall, which once supported beams. Mentally re-construct the cloister, and imagine its passages filled with strolling monks.

At the end of the cloister is a small **exhibit.** You'll have to pay to enter this relatively dull collection of old tombs and other carved-stone relics that have been unearthed on this site (£4, included in £7 combo-ticket with castle, daily April–Sept 9:30–17:30, Oct–March 9:30–16:30, last entry 30 min before closing, tel. 01334/472-563). But the ticket also includes entry to the surviving **tower of St. Rule's Church** (the rectangular tower beyond the cathedral ruins). If you feel like hiking up the 156 very claustrophobic steps for the view over St. Andrews' rooftops, it's worth the price. Up top, you can also look out to sea to find the pier where students traditionally walk out in their robes (see "Student Life in St. Andrews" sidebar).

▲**Castle**—The remains of St. Andrews' castle sit overlooking the sea. Another casualty of the Scottish Reformation, they're basically an evocative empty shell. Built by a bishop to entertain visiting

diplomats in the late 12th century, the castle was home to the powerful bishops, archbishops, and cardinals of St. Andrews. In 1546, the cardinal burned a Protestant preacher at the stake in front of the castle. In retribution, Protestant Reformers took the castle and killed the cardinal.

In 1547, the French came to attack the castle on behalf of their Catholic ally, Mary Queen of Scots. During the ensuing siege, a young Protestant refugee named John Knox was captured and sent to France to row on a galley ship. Eventually he traveled to Switzerland and met the Swiss Protestant ringleader, John Calvin. Knox brought Calvin's ideas back home, and became Scotland's greatest reformer (see sidebar).

Today's castle is the ruined post-Reformation version. You'll first walk through a colorful and well-presented exhibit about the history of the castle, then you'll head outside to explore the ruins. The most interesting parts are underground: the "bottle dungeon," where prisoners were sent never to return (peer down into it in the Sea Tower); and, around under the main drawbridge, the tight "mine" and even tighter "counter-mine" tunnels (you'll have to crawl to reach it all; go in as far as your claustrophobia allows). This shows how the besieging French army dug a mine to take the castle—but were followed at every turn by the Protestant counter-miners (£5, or included in £7 combo-ticket with cathedral, daily April–Sept 9:30–17:30, Oct–March 9:30–16:30, last entry 30 min before closing, tel. 01334/477-196).

▲**The West Sands**—This broad sandy beach, stretching below the golf courses, is a wonderful place for a relaxing and invigorating walk. Or jog the beach, humming the theme to *Chariots of Fire* (which was partly filmed here). Thanks to the drizzly weather, you'll see rainbows over the sea almost every day in the spring.

▲**University Buildings**—Like Oxford and Cambridge, the University of St. Andrews is made up of several smaller colleges scattered around town. Many visitors (and even some students) don't realize how easy it is to visit some seemingly off-limits university buildings. Most are marked by blue doors and are open to the public. If the door's open, step in. There are two areas especially worth exploring:

Student Life in St. Andrews

While most people associate St. Andrews with golf, it's first and foremost a university town—the home of Scotland's first and most prestigious university. Founded in 1411, it's the third-oldest in the English-speaking world—only Oxford and Cambridge have been around longer.

The U. of St. A. has about 6,000 undergrads and 1,000 grad students. While Scots attend for free, others (including students from England) must pay tuition. Some Scots resent the high concentration of upper-class English students (disparagingly dubbed "Yahs" for the snooty way they say "yes"), who treat St. Andrews as a "safety school" if rejected by Cambridge or Oxford. The school has even been called "England's northernmost university," because it has as many English students as Scottish ones (about a quarter of the students come from overseas). Its most famous recent graduate is Prince William (class of '05). Soon after he started here, the number of female applicants to study art history—his major—skyrocketed. (He later switched to geography.)

As with any venerable university, St. Andrews has its share of quirky customs—as if the university, like the town's street plan, insists on clinging to the Middle Ages. Most students own traditional red woolen academic "gowns" (woolen robes). Today these are only for special occasions (such as graduation), but in medieval times, students were required to wear them always—supposedly so they could be easily identified in brothels and pubs. (In a leap of faith, divinity students—apparently beyond temptation—wear black.) The way the robe is worn indicates the student's progress toward graduation: first-year students (called "bejants") wear them normally, on the shoulders; second-years ("semi-bejants") wear them slightly off the shoulders; third-years

St. Salvator's College is accessible from The Scores, via the narrow lane called (no joke) Butts Wynd. (For some mysterious reason, the street sign is often missing.) Explore the green quad. Under the tall tower is a chapel dating from 1450 that supposedly contains the pulpit of reformer John Knox. Step inside to enjoy the Gothic interior, with its wooden ceiling and 19th-century stained glass.

St. Mary's College, home of the university's School of Divinity (theology), is at the other end of town on South Street. The peaceful quad has a gnarled tree purportedly planted by Mary Queen of Scots.

▲**St. Andrews' Preservation Trust Museum and Garden**—This adorable museum, on Market Street just before the cathedral, fills a 17th-century fishing family's house that was protected from developers. It's a time capsule of an earlier, simpler era. The ground

("tertians") wear them off one shoulder (right shoulder for "scientists" and left shoulder for "artists"); and fourth-years ("magistrands") wear them off both shoulders.

There's no better time to see these robes than during the Pier Walk on Sunday afternoons during the university term. After church services (around noon), students clad in their gowns parade out to the end of the lonesome pier beyond the cathedral ruins. The tradition dates back so far that no one's sure how it started (either to commemorate a student who died rescuing victims of a shipwreck, or to bid farewell to a visiting dignitary). Today students do it mostly because it's fun to be a part of the visual spectacle of a long line of red robes flapping in the North Sea wind.

St. Andrews also clings to an antiquated family system, where underclassmen choose an academic "mother" and "father." In mid-November comes Raisin Monday (named for the raisins traditionally given as treats to one's "parents"; today students usually give wine to their "dad" and lingerie to their "mum"), when the upperclassmen dress up their "children" in outrageous costumes and parade them through town. The dressed-up underclassmen are also obliged to carry around "receipts" for their gifts—often written on unlikely or unwieldy objects (e.g., plastic dinosaurs, microwave ovens, even refrigerators). Any upperclassmen they come across can demand a rendition of the school song (in Latin). The whole scene invariably turns into a free-for-all food fight in St. Salvator's quad (weapons include condiments, shaving cream, and, according to campus rumors, human entrails pilfered by med students).

floor features replicas of a grocer's shop and a chemist's, using original fittings from actual stores. Upstairs are temporary exhibits. And out back is a tranquil garden (dedicated to the memory of a beloved professor) with "great-grandma's washhouse," featuring an exhibit about the history of soap and washing. Lovingly presented, this humble and quaint house provides a nice contrast to the big-money scene around the golf course at the other end of town (free, late-May–late-Sept daily 14:00–17:00, closed off-season, 12 North Street, tel. 01334/477-629).

St. Andrews Museum—This small, modest museum, which traces St. Andrews' history from A to Z, is an enjoyable way to pass time on a rainy day. It's situated in an old mansion in Kinburn Park, a five-minute walk from the old town (free, daily April–Sept 10:00–17:00, Oct–March 10:30–16:00, café, Doubledykes Road, tel. 01334/659-380).

Golf Sights on the Links

St. Andrews is the Cooperstown and Mount Olympus of golf, a mecca for the plaid-knickers-and-funny-hats crowd. Even if you're not a golfer, consider going with the flow and becoming one for your visit. While St. Andrews lays claim to founding the sport, nobody actually knows exactly where and when golf was born. In the Middle Ages, St. Andrews traded with the Dutch, and some historians believe they picked up a golf-like Dutch game on ice, and translated it to the bonnie rolling hills of Scotland's east coast. Since the grassy beach-front strip just outside St. Andrews was too poor to support crops, it was used for playing the game—and, centuries later, it still is. Why do golf courses have 18 holes? Because that's how many fit at the Old Course in St. Andrews.

The Old Course and Other Golfing—The famous Old Course, golf's single most famous site, hosts the British Open every five years. At other times, it's open to the public for golfing. The course is watched over by the **Royal and Ancient Golf Club of St. Andrews** (or "R&A" for short), which is the world's governing body for golf (like the British version of the PGA). The R&A—the stately white building at the corner of the Old Course—is closed to the public, and only men can be members (which might be kind of quaint...if it wasn't the 21st century). In fact, women can enter the R&A building only during the Women's British Open on St. Andrew's Day (Nov 30). Anyone can enter the shop nearby, which is a great spot to buy a souvenir for the golf-lover back home. Even if you're not golfing, watch the action for a while. Consider walking around to the low-profile stone bridge called Swilken Burn, with golf's single most iconic view: back over the 18th hole, the R&A, and Hamilton Hall, the red-sandstone building next to R&A. Hamilton Hall was supposedly built to upstage the R&A by an American upset over being declined membership to the exclusive club. Once a hotel, then a university dorm, the Hall is now being converted into expensive timeshares.

Fortunately for women golfers, the R&A doesn't actually own the golf course, which is public and managed by the **St. Andrews Links Trust.** Drop by their clubhouse, overlooking the beach near the Old Course (hours change frequently with the season—figure May–July daily 6:00–22:00, progressively shorter until 7:30–16:00 in Dec, www.standrews.org.uk). To reserve a tee time (explained below), call 01334/466-666 or email reservations@standrews.org .uk. Note that no advance reservations are taken on Saturdays, and the courses are closed on Sundays—which is traditionally the day when townspeople can walk the course.

The Old Course is golf's pinnacle—accessible to the public, but pricey (£125 per person, less off-season). You can play the Old Course only if you have a handicap of 24 (men) or 36 (women). If you don't know your handicap—or don't know what "handicap" means—then you're not good enough to play here (they want to keep the game moving, rather than wait for novices to spend 10 strokes on each hole). If you play, you'll do nine holes out, then nine more back in—however, all but four share the same greens. To ensure a specific tee time, it's smart to reserve a full year ahead. Otherwise, about half of the tee times are determined each day by a lottery. Call or visit in person the day before by 14:00 to put your name in (2 players minimum, 4 players max)—then keep your fingers crossed when they post the results at 16:00.

The trust manages five **other courses** (including two—the New Course and the Jubilee Course—both right next to the Old Course) that are cheaper and much easier to get a tee time for (£65 for New and Jubilee, £12–35 for others). It's usually possible to get a tee time for the same day or next day (if you want a guaranteed reservation, you'll need to make it at least two weeks in advance). A seventh course, called the "Castle Course"—with great views overlooking the town (but even more wind to blow your ball around)—is scheduled to open in April 2008.

If you're not serious about golf, but catch golf fever while here, consider...

▲▲**The Himalayas**—For less than the cost of a Coke, you can pretend you're Tiger Woods, stuck in a sand trap on the Old

Course with the British Open title on the line. Technically the "Ladies' Putting Green," this cute little patch of undulating grass presents the perfect opportunity for a non-golfer (female or male) to say they've played the links at St. Andrews. So named for its dramatically hilly terrain, "The Himalayas" is basically a very classy (but still relaxed) game of mini-golf. It's remarkable how the contour of the land can present even more challenging obstacles than the tunnels, gates, and distractions of a corny putt-putt course back home. Flat shoes are required (no high heels). You'll see it on the left as you walk toward the clubhouse from the R&A.

Cost and Hours: £1.50 for 18 holes, £1 for 9 holes. Except for when it's open only to members (see below), the putting green is open to the public June–July Mon–Sat 10:30–19:30; May and Aug Mon–Sat 10:30–19:00; April and Sept Mon–Sat 10:30–18:30. It's closed to the public (because members are using it) Mon–Tue and Thu–Fri 17:00–17:30, Wed 12:30–16:00, and Thu 10:00–11:00, plus all day Sun and Oct–March (tel. 01334/475-196).

British Golf Museum—This exhibit, which started as a small collection in the R&A across the street, is the best place in Britain

St. Andrews

to learn about the Scots' favorite sport. It's a bit tedious for those of us who reach for the remote when we see a golfer, but a must (and worth at least ▲▲) for golf-lovers. The compact, one-way exhibit reverently presents a meticulous survey of the game's history—from the monarchs who loved and hated golf (including the king who outlawed it because it was distracting men from church and archery practice), right up to the "Golden Bear" and a certain Tiger. A constant two-and-a-quarter-hour loop film shows highlights of the British Open from 1923 to the present, and other video screens show scratchy black-and-white highlights from the days before corporate sponsorship. At the end, find items donated by the golfers of today, including Tiger Woods' shirt, hat, and glove (£5.25, ticket good for 2 days and includes informative book about the history of golf; April–Oct Mon–Sat 9:30–17:30, Sun 10:00–17:00; Nov–March daily 10:00–16:00; last entry 45 min before closing; Bruce Embankment, in the blocky modern building squatting behind the R&A by the Old Course, tel. 01334/460-046, www.britishgolfmuseum.co.uk).

Near St. Andrews: East Neuk

On the lazy coastline meandering south from St. Andrews, the cute-as-a-pin East Neuk (pronounced "nook") is a collection of tidy fishing villages. While hardly earth-shattering, the East Neuk is a pleasant detour if you've got the time. The villages of Crail and Pittenweem have their fans, but Anstruther (described below) is worth most of your

attention. The East Neuk works best as a half-day side-trip (by either car or bus) from St. Andrews, though drivers can use it as a scenic detour between Edinburgh and St. Andrews.

Getting There: It's an easy **drive** from St. Andrews. For the scenic route, follow A917 south of town along the coast, past Crail, on the way to Anstruther and Pittenweem. For a shortcut directly to Anstruther, take B9131 across the peninsula (or return that way after driving the longer coastal route there). **Buses** also connect St. Andrews to the East Neuk: Bus #95 goes hourly from St. Andrews to Crail and Anstruther (40 min total to Anstruther). The hourly bus #X26 goes directly to Anstruther, then on to Glasgow.

▲**Anstruther**—Stretched out along its harbor, colorful Anstruther (AN-stru-ther; pronounced ENT-ster by locals) is the centerpiece of the East Neuk. The main parking lot and bus stop are both right on the harbor, across from Anstruther's handy **TI**, which offers lots of useful information for the entire East Neuk area (April–Oct

Mon–Sat 10:00–17:00, Sun 11:00–16:00, closed Nov–March, tel. 01333/311-073). Stroll the harborfront to the end, detouring inland around the little cove (or crossing the causeway at low tide) to reach some colorful old houses, including one encrusted with seashells.

Anstruther's main sight is the **Scottish Fisheries Museum**—which, true to its slogan, is "bigger than you think." The endearingly hokey exhibit sprawls through several harborfront buildings, painstakingly tracing the history of Scottish seafaring from primitive dugout dinghies to modern vessels. You'll learn the story of Scotland's "Zulu" fishing boats, and walk through vast rooms filled with boats. For a glimpse at humble fishing lifestyles, don't miss the Fisherman's Cottage, hiding upstairs from the courtyard (£5; April–Sept Mon–Sat 10:00–17:30, Sun 11:00–17:00; Oct–March Mon–Sat 10:00–16:30, Sun 12:00–16:30; last entry 1 hour before closing, Harbourhead, tel. 01333/310-628, www.scotfishmuseum.org).

Eating in Anstruther: Anstruther's claim to fame is its fish-and-chips—considered by many to be Scotland's best. While there are several good chippies in town, the famous one is the **Anstruther Fish Bar**, facing the harbor just a block from the TI and Fisheries Museum. As you enter, choose whether you want to get take-out, or dine in for a few pounds more. While more expensive than most fish-and-chips, the food here is good (£5–7 take-out, £7–9 to dine in, dine-in prices include bread and a drink, daily 11:30–19:30, 42–44 Shore Street, tel. 01333/310-518).

SLEEPING

Owing partly to the high-roller golf tourists flowing through the town, St. Andrews' accommodations are the most expensive in Scotland. Solo travelers are at a disadvantage, as many B&Bs don't

---

Sleep Code

(£1 = about $2, country code: 44, area code: 01334)
S = Single, **D** = Double/Twin, **T** = Triple, **Q** = Quad, **b** = bathroom, **s** = shower only. Unless otherwise noted, you can assume credit cards are accepted and breakfast is included.

To help you sort easily through these listings, I've divided the rooms into two categories based on the price for a standard double room with bath (during high season):

$$$ **Higher Priced**—Most rooms £75 or more.
 $$ **Moderately Priced**—Most rooms between £60–75.
  $ **Lower Priced**—Most rooms £60 or less.

have singles—and charge close to the double price for one person (I've listed "S" or "Sb" below for those that actually have single rooms). But the quality at my recommendations is high, and budget alternatives—including a hostel and (in the summer) sleeping in the university's dorms—are workable. All of these, except the Hoppity House and the hostel, are on the streets called Murray Park and Murray Place, between North Street and The Scores in the old town. If you need to find a room on the fly, head for this same neighborhood, which has far more options than just the ones I've listed below.

$$$ Hoppity House is youthful and wonderfully located, just two blocks from the cathedral on Market Street. The three tight, modern rooms—all on the ground floor—each come with a small fridge and a do-it-yourself breakfast (Sb-£45, Db-£85; off-season: Sb-£35, Db-£70; cash only, free Wi-Fi, 38 Market Street, tel. 01334/461-192, www.hoppityhouse.co.uk, enquiries @hoppityhouse.co.uk, friendly Gordon and Heather Mitchell).

$$$ Cameron House has five old-fashioned, paisley, masculine-feeling rooms (including two singles that share one bathroom) around a beautiful stained-glass atrium (S-£38, Db-£76, prices soft Nov–March, free Wi-Fi, 11 Murray Park, tel. 01334/472-306, fax 01334/479-529, www.cameronhouse-sta.co.uk, elizabeth @cameronhouse-sta.co.uk, Elizabeth and Leonard Palompo).

$$$ Lorimer House has five comfortable, tastefully decorated rooms (Db-£62–92, more July–Aug, higher price is for deluxe top-floor rooms, free Internet access and Wi-Fi, 19 Murray Park, tel. 01334/476-599, fax 01334/478-463, www.lorimerhouse.com, info @lorimerhouse.com, Mick and Chris Cordner).

$$$ Arran House has six new-feeling, modern rooms, including a single with a private bathroom across the hall. Golf portraits line the otherwise stark staircase (S-£45, Db-£70–80, free Wi-Fi, 5 Murray Park, tel. 01334/474-724, mobile 07768-718-237, www .arranhousestandrews.co.uk, info@arranhousestandrews.co.uk, Anne and Jim McGrory).

$$$ Doune House is golfer-friendly with six straightforward, plaid-heavy rooms (S-£40, Db-£80, cheaper off-season, cash only, free Wi-Fi, 5 Murray Place, tel. 01334/475-195, www.dounehouse .com, info@dounehouse.com, Maria and Dell Roberts-Jones).

Hostel: **$ St. Andrews Tourist Hostel** has 44 beds in colorful rooms about a block from the base of Market Street (£14/bunk on weekends, £11.50/bunk during the week, no breakfast, self-service laundry, office open 8:00–15:00 & 18:00–22:00, open all day in summer, St. Mary's Place, tel. 01334/479-911, fax 01334/479-988, www.standrewshostel.com, info@standrewshostel.com).

University Accommodations

In the summer (early June–early Sept), two of the University of St. Andrews' student-housing buildings are tidied up and rented out to tourists (website for both: www.escapetotranquillity.com—that's "tranquillity" with two l's; £25 credit-card deposit due when you reserve). While institutional, the rooms are hotelesque and nicely maintained. (If it's good enough for Prince William...) You have two options: New Hall (more comfort, more expensive, less central) or McIntosh Hall (less comfort, less expensive, more central). Either place is a good deal for solo travelers, who could otherwise end up paying for a double at a B&B.

$$ New Hall, which has en-suite rooms (private bathrooms), is part of the modern "New Haugh" part of campus, about a 15-minute walk from the old town. Built in 1993 and featuring elevators, a big cafeteria, and lots of conferences, it feels like a modern college dorm in the US (Sb-£47, Db-£70, tel. 01334/467-000, new.hall@st-andrews.ac.uk).

$$ McIntosh Hall is more central (at the corner of the old town near the Old Course) and old-fashioned, with only shared bathrooms on the hall, and no TVs or air-conditioning. It's a fine budget alternative to the B&Bs (168 rooms, S-£31, D-£62, tel. 01334/467-035, mchall@st-andrews.ac.uk).

EATING

The Doll's House, part of a popular local chain, serves up reliably good international cuisine with a French flair. The two floors of indoor seating have a cozy, colorful, casual atmosphere; the sidewalk seating out front is across from Holy Trinity Church (£7–10 lunches, £9–15 dinners, £13 early-bird special 17:00–19:00, open daily 12:00–15:00 & 17:00–22:00, a block from the TI at 3 Church Square, tel. 01334/477-422). Also consider their sister restaurants, The Glass House (near the castle on North Street) and The Grill House (at St. Mary's Place).

The Seafood Restaurant is St. Andrews' favorite splurge. Situated in a modern glassy building overlooking the beach near the Old Course, it's like dining in an aquarium. The seafood is locally caught, the dining room wraps around the busy open kitchen, and dinner reservations are essential (two-course lunch-£22, three-course lunch-£26, three-course dinner-£45, daily 12:00–14:30 & 18:30–22:00, The Scores, tel. 01334/479-475).

On Market Street: In the area around the TI, you'll find a concentration of good restaurants—pubs, grill houses, coffee shops, Asian food, fish-and-chips (see below), and more...take your pick. A block down Market Street, you can stock up for a picnic at Gregg's and Tesco.

Pubs: There's no shortage in this college town. **Aikmans** features a cozy wood-table ambience and frequent live music (open-mic folk night once weekly, traditional Scottish music upstairs about twice per month, other live music generally Thu–Sat, £5–7 pub grub, open daily 11:00–24:00, 32 Bell Street, tel. 01334/477-425). **Ma Bells** is a bright, colorful, unpretentious college bar that clings to its status as one of Prince William's favorites (£6–9 pub grub, daily 11:00–24:00, a block from the Old Course and R&A at 40 The Scores, tel. 01334/472-622). **Greyfriars** is a classy, new, modern place near the Murray Park B&Bs (£5 light meals, £7–9 main dishes, daily 11:00–24:00, 129 North Street, tel. 01334/474-906).

Fish-and-Chips: **PM's** is a local favorite for take-away fish-and-chips, centrally located on Market Street near the TI (£4 fish-and-chips, £3 burgers, daily 11:00–23:00, at the corner of Union and Market). Brave souls will order a can of Irn-Bru with their fish (warning: it doesn't taste like orange soda—see page 453). For what's considered the country's best chippies, head for the famous place in the East Neuk (see page 517).

Dessert: **Fisher and Donaldson** is beloved for its rich and affordable pastries and chocolates. Try their Coffee Tower—like a giant cream puff filled with rich, lightly coffee-flavored cream (£1–2 pastries, Mon–Sat 6:00–17:15, closed Sun, just around the corner from the TI at 13 Church Street, tel. 01334/472-201). **B. Jannettas** features a wide and creative range of tasty ice cream flavors (£1 per scoop, daily 9:00–21:30, 31 South Street, tel. 01334/473-285).

TRANSPORTATION CONNECTIONS

Remember, trains don't go into St. Andrews itself—instead, use the Leuchars station (5 miles from St. Andrews, connected by a shuttle bus coordinated to meet trains—see "Arrival in St. Andrews," on page 506). The TI has useful train schedules, which also list shuttle-bus departure times from St. Andrews.

From Leuchars by Train: The southbound train runs once or twice per hour, and goes to **Edinburgh** (1 hr). For **Glasgow** or **Stirling**, transfer in Edinburgh (about 2 hrs total to either). The northbound train scenically follows the coast north to Aberdeen, where you can transfer to **Inverness** (1–2/hr, 1.5 hrs to Aberdeen, 3.5 hrs total to Inverness). Both trains run less frequently on Sundays (about hourly).

GLASGOW

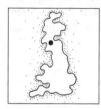
Glasgow (GLAS-goh), though bigger than Edinburgh, lives forever in the shadow of its more popular neighbor. Once a decrepit former port city, Glasgow—astride the River Clyde—has climbed out of its recession in recent years. Today, it's both a workaday Scottish city and a cosmopolitan destination with an energetic dining and nightlife scene. The city is also becoming a pilgrimage site of sorts for architecture buffs, thanks to a cityscape packed with Victorian architecture, early-20th-century touches, and modern flair (unfortunately, it also has some truly drab recent construction). Most beloved are the works by hometown boy Charles Rennie Mackintosh, the visionary turn-of-the-20th-century architect who left his mark all over Glasgow.

Edinburgh, a short train-trip away, may have the royal aura, but Glasgow has an unpretentious appeal. As my cab driver said, "The people of Glasgow have a better time at a funeral than the people of Edinburgh have at a wedding." In Glasgow, there's no upper-crust history, and no one puts on airs. Locals call sanded and polished concrete "Glasgow marble." You'll be hard-pressed to find a souvenir shop in Glasgow—and that's just how the locals like it. In this newly revitalized city, visitors are a novelty, and locals do their best to introduce you to the fun-loving, laid-back Glaswegian (rhymes with Norwegian) way of life.

Planning Your Time

For most visitors, a few hours are plenty to sample Glasgow. Focus on my self-guided walking tour in the city core, which includes Glasgow's two most interesting sights: Charles Rennie Mackintosh's Glasgow School of Art, and the time-warp Tenement

House. With more time, add some of the outlying sights, such as the cathedral area (to the
east), Kelvingrove Gallery and the West End
restaurant scene (to the west), and the Burrell
Collection (a few miles out of town).

Day Trip from Edinburgh: For a full day,
grab breakfast at your B&B in Edinburgh,
and catch the 9:30 train to Glasgow (morning
trains every 15 min); it arrives at Queen Street
Train Station at roughly 10:20. Call to reserve
tickets to tour the Glasgow School of Art (aim
for an early-afternoon time slot, which leaves
you time for lunch beforehand). On arrival
in Glasgow, take my self-guided walk to hit all the major sights,
making sure to reach the Tenement House by the last entry time
(16:30). For dinner, consider heading out to the thriving West
End restaurant scene, then hop the subway back to Queen Street
Station (use the Buchanan Street stop) and catch the 21:00 train
back to Edinburgh (evening trains every 30 min).

ORIENTATION

(area code: 0141)
With a grid street plan, a downtown business zone, and more than
its share of boxy office buildings, Glasgow feels more like a mid-
sized American city than a big Scottish one—like Cleveland or
Cincinnati with shorter skyscrapers and more sandstone. While
greater Glasgow is a sprawling city of 2.1 million people, the
tourist's Glasgow has three main parts: the city center, a cluster
of minor sights near the cathedral (in the east), and the West End
restaurant and shopping zone. The hilly but easily walkable city
center has two main drags, both lined with shops and crawling
with shoppers: Sauchiehall Street (pronounced "Sockyhall," running west to east) and Buchanan Street (running north to south).

Tourist Information

The TI is opposite Queen Street Station in the southwest corner
of George Square (at #11). They hand out an excellent free map,
informative *Essential Guide*, events listing, and other Glasgow brochures, and can book you a room for a £3 fee (Mon–Sat 9:00–18:00,
until 19:00 in June, until 20:00 in July–Aug; Sun 10:00–18:00;
tel. 0141/204-4400, www.seeglasgow.com or www.visitscotland
.com). Buses to the West End depart from in front of the TI (see
page 540), and the city bus tour leaves from across the square (see
below).

Mackintosh Trail Ticket: This ticket, sold by the TI and all

Mackintosh sights, covers entry to all "Charles Rennie Mac" sights and public transportation to those outside the city limits (£12/1 day, www.crmsociety.com).

Arrival in Glasgow

By Train: Glasgow, a major Scottish transportation hub, has two train stations, which are just a few blocks apart in the very heart of town: **Central Station** (with a grand, genteel interior) and **Queen Street Station** (more functional, with connections to Edinburgh, and closer to the TI—take the exit marked *George Square* and continue straight across the square). Both stations have pay WCs (20p) and left luggage (Central Station—at the head of track 1, £5.50; Queen Street Station—near the head of track 7, £5–7 based on size). Unless you're packing heavy, it's easier to walk the five minutes between the stations than to take the roundabout "RailLink" bus #398 between them (75p, or free if you have a ticket for a connecting train).

By Bus: Buchanan Street Bus Station is at Killermont Street, just two blocks behind Queen Street Train Station.

By Car: The M8, which slices through downtown Glasgow, is the easiest way in and out of the city. Ask your hotel for directions to and from the M8, and connect with other highways from there.

By Air: For information on Glasgow's two airports, see the end of this chapter.

Helpful Hints

Safety: The city center, which is packed with ambitious career types during the day, can feel deserted at night. Avoid the area near the River Clyde entirely (hookers and thugs), and confine yourself to the streets north of Argyle Street if you're in the downtown quarter. The West End and the Merchant City (east of the train stations) bustle with crowded restaurants well into the evening, and feel well-populated in the wee hours.

If you pick up a football (soccer) jersey or scarf as a souvenir, don't wear it in Glasgow; local passions run very high, and most drunken brawls in town are between supporters of Glasgow's two rival soccer clubs: Celtic (green and white) and Rangers (blue and red).

Sightseeing: Glasgow's city-owned museums—including the sights near the cathedral, but not biggies like the Glasgow School of Art or Tenement House—are free (www.glasgowmuseums.com).

Internet Access: You'll see signs advertising Internet cafés all around the city core (near Central Station and Buchanan Street). A big **easyInternetcafé** is between Central and Queen Street stations, at 57–61 St. Vincent Street (enter through Caffè Nero; Mon–Fri 7:00–21:00, Sat 8:00–21:00, Sun 9:00–19:00).

Sunday Travel: Bus and train schedules are dramatically reduced on Sundays—most routes have only half the departure times they normally have during the week (though Edinburgh is still easily accessible). If you plan to leave Glasgow for a remote destination on Sunday, check the schedules carefully when you arrive. All trains run less frequently in the off-season; if you want to get to the Highlands by bus on a Sunday in winter, forget it.

Local Guide: Joan Dobbie, a native Glaswegian and registered Scottish Tourist Guide, will give you the insider's take on Glasgow's sights (£72/half-day, tel. 01355/236-749, mobile 07773-555-151, joan.leo@lineone.net).

Getting Around Glasgow

By City Bus: Various companies run **Glasgow's buses,** but most city-center routes are operated by First Glasgow (price depends on journey, £2 for any two single journeys, £3 for all-day ticket, exact change required). Buses run every few minutes down Glasgow's main thoroughfares (such as Sauchiehall Street) to the downtown core (train stations). If you're waiting at a stop and a bus comes along, ask the driver if he's headed to Central Station; chances are he'll say yes. (For information on buses to the West End, see page 540.)

By Hop-on, Hop-off Bus Tour: This tour connects Glasgow's far-flung historic sights in an 80-minute loop (£9, daily 9:30–16:30; stops in front of Central Station, George Square, and major hotels; tel. 0141/204-0444, www.citysightseeingglasgow.co.uk). If there's a particular sight you want to see, confirm that it's on the route.

By Taxi: Taxis are affordable, plentiful, and often come with nice, chatty cabbies—all speaking in the impenetrable local accent. Just smile and nod. Most taxi rides in the downtown area will cost about £3; from the West End, a one-way trip is about £6. Use taxis or public transport to connect Glasgow's more remote sights; splurge for a taxi (for safety) any time you're traveling late at night.

By Subway: The claustrophobic, orange-line subway—nicknamed "clockwork orange"—runs in a loop around the edge of the city center. The "outer circle" runs clockwise, and the "inner circle" runs counterclockwise. (If you miss your stop, you can just wait it out—you'll come full circle in about 24 minutes. Or hop out and cross to the other side of the platform to go back the way you came.) While the subway is essentially useless for connecting city-center sightseeing (Buchanan Street is the only downtown stop), it's handy for reaching sights farther out, including the Kelvingrove Gallery (Kelvinhall stop) and West End restaurant neighborhood (Hillhead stop; £1 single trip, £1.90 Discovery Ticket lets you travel all day after 9:30; subway runs Mon–Sat 6:30–23:30, but Sun only 11:00–18:00; www.spt.co.uk/subway).

SELF-GUIDED WALK

Get to Know Glasgow

Glasgow isn't romantic, but it has an earthy charm, and architecture buffs love it. The trick to sightseeing here is to always look up—above the chain restaurants and mall stores, you'll see a wealth of imaginative facades, complete with ornate friezes and expressive sculptures. These buildings transport you to the heady days around the turn of the 20th century—when the rest of Great Britain was enthralled by Victorianism, but Glasgow set its own course, thanks largely to the artistic bravado of Charles Rennie Mackintosh and his friends (the "Glasgow Four"). This walking tour takes three to four hours, including one hour for Mackintosh's masterpiece, the Glasgow School of Art (in summer, consider calling ahead to reserve your tour there—see page 531).

• *Begin at Central Station. Exit the train station straight ahead from the tracks (to the north, onto Gordon Street), turn right, and cross busy Renfield/Union Street. Continue one block, then turn right down Mitchell Street, and look up on the left side of the street to see a multi-story brick water tower topped by a rounded cap. Turn left down a small alley (Mitchell Lane) just in front of the tower. Within about 25 yards, you'll see the entrance to...*

The Lighthouse: This facility, which houses the Scotland Center for Architecture and Design, is really made of two parts:

a water tower designed by Charles Rennie Mackintosh in the early 1900s, and a new, modern glass-and-metal museum built alongside it. The Lighthouse is mostly filled with design exhibitions, lonely floors of conference rooms, and funny icons directing desperate men and women to the bathrooms (£3, Mon and Wed–Sat 10:30– 17:00, Tue 11:30–17:00, Sun 12:00–17:00, 11 Mitchell Lane, tel. 0141/221-6362, www.thelighthouse.co.uk). This sight is skippable for most, but it does offer a fine view over the city. Before you head up, be sure to request the free *View from the Top* pamphlet, which indicates the buildings you'll see in the panorama. You have two options for scaling the heights: take the elevator to the sixth-floor

Charles Rennie Mackintosh
(1868–1928)

During his lifetime, Charles Rennie Mackintosh brought an exuberant Art Nouveau influence to the architecture of his hometown. His designs challenged the city planners of this otherwise practical, working-class port city to create beauty in the buildings they commissioned. A radical thinker, he freely shared credit with his artist wife, Margaret MacDonald.

When Mackintosh was a young student at the Glasgow School of Art, the Industrial Age dominated life here. Factories belched black soot into the city as they burned coal and forged steel. Mackintosh and his circle of artist friends drew their solace and inspiration from nature (just as the Romantics had before them), and created some of the original Art Nouveau buildings, paintings, drawings, and furniture.

As a student traveling abroad in Italy, Mackintosh ignored the famous Renaissance paintings inside the museum walls, and set up his easel to paint the exteriors of churches and buildings instead. He rejected the architectural traditions of ancient Greece and Rome. In Venice and Ravenna, he fell under the spell of Byzantine design, and in Siena, he saw a unified, medieval city design he would try to import—but with a Scottish flavor and Glaswegian palette—to his own hometown.

His first commission came in 1893, to design an extension to the Glasgow Herald building. More work soon followed, including the Glasgow School of Art and the Willow Tea Rooms 10 years later. Mackintosh envisioned a world without artistic borders, where an Islamic flourish could find its way onto a workaday building in a Scottish city. Inspired by the great buildings of the past and by his Art Nouveau peers, he in turn influenced others, such as painter Gustav Klimt and Bauhaus founder Walter Gropius. A century after Scotland's greatest architect set pencil to paper, his hometown is at last celebrating his unique vision.

windows; or (better) head to the third floor and climb the 135 spiral steps inside the water tower itself—at the top, you'll be able to walk out onto a wraparound balcony with 360-degree views. Also on the third floor of the Lighthouse, you'll find information about Mackintosh, with architectural plans and scale models. Linger here only if you're planning to skip the Glasgow School of Art.

• *Exiting the Lighthouse, turn right down the alley, then turn left onto the bustling pedestrian shopping drag called Buchanan Street—Glasgow's outdoor mall. Take the first right onto Exchange Place and pass through the arch, emerging onto the...*

Glasgow Walk

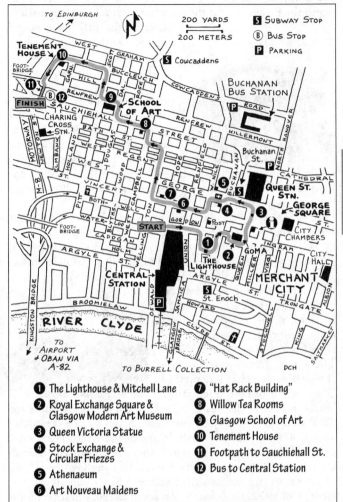

TO EDINBURGH

200 YARDS
200 METERS

S SUBWAY STOP
B BUS STOP
P PARKING

WEST GRAHAM

TENEMENT HOUSE

FOOT-BRIDGE

S Cowcaddens

COWCADDENS

BUCHANAN BUS STATION

HILL
BUCCLEUCH

RENFREW
GARN

B

FINISH

SAUCHIEHALL

CHARING CROSS STN.

BATH

WEST REGENT

VINCENT

BOTH-WELL

WATER-LOO

CADOGAN

HOLM

FOOT-BRIDGE

ARGYLE

BROOMIELAW

SCHOOL OF ART

RENFREW

STREET

GEORGE

GORDON

START

THE LIGHTHOUSE

CENTRAL STATION

P

ROAD

KILLERMONT

Buchanan St.

NORTH HANOVER

CATHEDRAL

QUEEN ST. STN.

GEORGE SQUARE

CITY CHAMBERS

GOMA

MERCHANT CITY

CITY HALL

ARGYLE ST.

St. Enoch **S**

HOWARD

CLYDE ST.

KINGSTON BRIDGE

RIVER CLYDE

TO AIRPORT & OBAN VIA A-82

TO BURRELL COLLECTION

JAMAICA

GLASGOW BRIDGE

ALBION

TRONGATE

KING

STOCKWELL

SALTMARKET

DCH

1 The Lighthouse & Mitchell Lane
2 Royal Exchange Square & Glasgow Modern Art Museum
3 Queen Victoria Statue
4 Stock Exchange & Circular Friezes
5 Athenaeum
6 Art Nouveau Maidens
7 "Hat Rack Building"
8 Willow Tea Rooms
9 Glasgow School of Art
10 Tenement House
11 Footpath to Sauchiehall St.
12 Bus to Central Station

Glasgow

Royal Exchange Square: This square—which marks the entrance to the shopping zone called Merchant City—is home to two interesting buildings. On your left as you enter the square is a stately Neoclassical bank-like building (today housing a Borders bookstore). This was once the **private mansion** of one of the tobacco lords, the super-rich businessmen who reigned here from the 1750s through the 1800s, stomping through the city with gold-tipped canes. During the port's heyday, these entrepreneurs made Glasgow Europe's sixth-biggest city.

In the middle of the square is the **Glasgow Modern Art**

Museum, nicknamed GoMA. Walk around the GoMA building to the main entry (at the equestrian statue), and step back to

take in the full Neoclassical facade. On the pediment (above the columns), notice the funky, mirrored mosaic—an example of how Glasgow refuses to take itself too seriously. The temporary exhibits inside GoMA are generally forgettable, but the museum does have an unusual charter: It displays only the work of living artists (free, Mon–Wed and Sat 10:00–17:00, Thu 10:00–20:00, Fri and Sun 11:00–17:00, tel. 0141/229-1996—in honor of the year it opened).

• *With the facade of GoMA behind you, turn left onto Queen Street. Within a block, you'll be at the southwest corner of...*

George Square: Here at the heart of the city, you'll find the TI (just to your right as you come to the square), Queen Street

Train Station, the Glasgow City Chambers (the big Neoclassical building to the east, not worth visiting), and—in front of that—a monument to Glaswegians killed fighting in the World Wars. The square is decorated with a *Who's Who* of statues depicting Glaswegians of note. Find James

Watt (inventor of the steam engine), as well as Robert Burns and Sir Walter Scott (Scotland's two most famous poets—see sidebar on page 474). As you head north along the edge of the square, you'll see an idealized, surprisingly skinny **statue of Queen Victoria** riding a horse. But you won't see a statue of King George III, for whom the square is named. The stubborn Scots are still angry at George for losing the colonies (a.k.a. us), and they never commissioned a statue of him.

• *Just past skinny Vic and Robert Peel, turn left onto West George Street and head for the tall church in the middle of the street. Cross Buchanan Street and go around the church on the left side, entering a little square called...*

Nelson Mandela Place: The area around this church features some interesting bits of architectural detail. First, as you stand along the left side of the church, look up and to the left (across from the church) to find the three circular friezes on the second floor of the former **Stock Exchange** (built in 1875). These idealized heads, which were recently cleaned and restored, represent the industries that made Glasgow prosperous during its heyday: building, engineering, and mining.

Continue around to the back of the church, and look to the right side of the street, for the **Athenaeum** (the sandy-colored building at #8; notice the low-profile label over the door). Now a law office, this was founded in 1847 as a school and city library during Glasgow's golden age. (Charles Dickens gave the building's inaugural address.) Like Edinburgh, Glasgow was at the forefront of the 17th-century Scottish Enlightenment, a celebration of education and intellectualism. The Scots were known for their extremely practical brand of humanism; all members of society, including the merchant and working classes, were expected to be well-educated. (Tobacco lords, for example, often knew Latin and Greek.) Look above the door to find the symbolic statue of a reader sharing books with young children, an embodiment of this ideal.

• *Continue beyond the church and turn left onto West Nile Street; then, one block later, turn right onto...*

St. Vincent Street: We'll enjoy more architectural Easter eggs as we continue along this street toward the Glasgow School of Art. After a block, on the left side of the street (at #115), look up to the second floor to see sculptures of **Art Nouveau maidens.** Their elongated, melancholy faces and downcast eyes seem to reflect Glasgow's difficult recent past, decades of economic decline and urban decay. (They mirror similar faces in Art Nouveau paintings in the Glasgow School of Art, particularly in the artwork of Margaret MacDonald, Charles Rennie Mackintosh's wife and artistic partner—see sidebar on page 526.)

Another block down on the right (at #144) is the building locals have nicknamed the **"Hat Rack Building."** Look up at the very top, and you'll see pointy spikes. Glasgow had roaring iron forges back in the day, and elaborate ironwork—like the kind that crowns this building—throughout the city. Much of it is reconstructed, since the decorative pieces were melted down during the height of World War II, when iron was in short supply. Above the left doorway as you face the building, notice the stained-glass ship in turbulent seas, another fitting icon for a city that's seen more than its share of ups and downs.

• *At the end of the block, turn right up...*

Wellington Street: Climb this street to the crest of the hill, where the two- and three-story buildings have a pleasing, uniform look. These sandstone structures were the homes of Glasgow's upper-middle class, the factory managers who worked for the city's barons (such as the titan who owned the mansion back on Royal Exchange Square). In the strict Victorian class structure, the people who lived here were distinctly higher on the social scale than the people who lived in the tenements (which we'll see at the end of this tour).

• *Turn left onto Bath Street, and then right onto West Campbell Street. It opens onto Sauchiehall, Glasgow's main commercial street. Turn left onto Sauchiehall. Half a block later at #217 (on the left), you'll see a black-and-white Art Nouveau building with a sign reading...*

Willow Tea Rooms: Charles Rennie Mackintosh made his living from design commissions, including multiple tearooms for businesswoman Kate Cranston. The Willow Tea Rooms, rated ▲▲, are the most intact, but others (on Ingram and Argyle streets) are in the process of being restored. (You might also see fake "Mockintosh" tearooms sprinkled throughout the city—ignore

them.) A well-known control freak, Mackintosh designed everything here—down to the furniture, lighting, and cutlery.

In the design of these tearooms, there was a meeting of the (very modern) minds. Cranston wanted a place for women to be able to gather while unescorted, in a time when traveling solo could give a woman a less-than-desirable reputation. An ardent women's rights supporter, Cranston requested that the rooms be bathed in white, the suffragists' signature color.

Enter the Willow Tea Rooms and make your way past the tacky jewelry and trinket store that now inhabits the bottom floor. On the open mezzanine level, you'll find 20 crowded tables run like a diner from a corner kitchen, serving bland meals to middle-class people—just as this place was originally intended to do (£2–3 teas, £4–5 sandwiches, £7 salads and main dishes). If you plan to have a spot of tea and a pastry here (as they did in 1903, the year it opened), request to sit upstairs, in the almost-hidden Room de Luxe. Head up the stairs (following signs for the toilet) to see this peaceful tearoom space. While some parts of the Room de Luxe are reproductions (such as the chairs and the doors, which were too fragile to survive), the rest is just as it was in Mackintosh's day (Mon–Sat 9:00–17:00, Sun 11:00–16:15, last orders 30 min before closing, 217 Sauchiehall Street, tel. 0141/332-0521, www.willowtearooms.co.uk).

• *From here, it's a five-minute, mostly uphill walk to the only must-see Mackintosh sight within the town center. Walk a block and a half west on Sauchiehall, and make a right onto Dalhousie Street; the big reddish-brown building on the left at the top of the hill is the Glasgow School of Art. If you have time to kill before your tour starts, consider heading across the street for a cheap lunch at the student café called **Where the Monkey Sleeps;** or go around the corner and one block downhill to the*

Glasgow

CCA Bar (both described on page 539). Or, if you have at least an hour before your tour, you can head to the Tenement Museum (listed on page 532, closed mornings and Nov–Feb), a preserved home from the early 1900s—right when Mackintosh was doing his most important work.

Glasgow School of Art: A pinnacle of artistic and architectural achievement (rated ▲▲), the Glasgow School of Art represented a unique opportunity for Charles

Rennie Mackintosh to design a massive project entirely to his own liking, down to every last detail. These details—from a fireplace that looks like a kimono to windows that soar for multiple stories—are the beauty of the Glasgow School of Art.

Mackintosh loved the hands-on ideology of the Arts and Crafts movement, but he was also a practical Scot. Study the outside of the building. Those protruding wrought-iron brackets that hover outside the multi-paned windows were a new invention during the time of the Industrial Revolution; they reinforce the big, fragile glass windows, allowing natural light to pour into the school. Mackintosh brought all the most recent technologies to this work, and added them to his artistic palate—which also merged clean Modernist lines, Asian influences, and Art Nouveau flourishes.

Because the Glasgow School of Art is still a working school, the interior can only be visited by one-hour **guided tour.** Walk up the stairs into the main vestibule, and buy your tour ticket at the shop (£6.50; April–Sept tours generally depart daily at the top of the hour 10:00–16:00; Oct–March tours Mon–Sat at 11:00 and 14:00, closed Sun; no tours for one week in early June during final exams; tip the starving students a pound or two if they give a good spiel). In the summer, tours are frequent, but they fill up quickly; it's smart to call the shop at 0141/353-4526 or email shop@gsa.ac.uk to confirm times and reserve a guided-tour ticket (shop open daily 9:45–17:00, leave call-back number if leaving a message, www.gsa .ac.uk). Several exhibition galleries in the school are free and open to the public, even if you don't go on a tour.

When the building first opened, it was modern and minimalist. Other elements were added later, such as the lobby's tile mosaics depicting the artistic greats, including mustachioed Mackintosh (who hovers over the gift shop). As you tour the building, you'll see how Mackintosh—who'd been a humble art student himself not too long before he designed this building—strove to create a space that was both artistically innovative and completely functional for students. The plaster replicas of classical sculptures lining the halls were part of Mackintosh's vision, to inspire students by the greats of the past. You'll likely see students and their canvases lining the halls. Do you smell oil paint?

Linking these useable spaces are clever artistic patterns and puzzles that Mackintosh embedded to spur creative thought. A resolute pagan in a very Protestant city, he romanticized the ideals of nature, and included an abstract icon of a spiral-within-a-circle rose design on many of his works. In some cases, he designed a little alcove just big enough for a fresh, single-stem rose and placed it next to one of his stained-glass roses—so students could compare reality with the artistic form. (You'll even find these roses on the swinging doors in the bathroom.)

Mackintosh cleverly arranged the school so that every one of the cellar studios is bathed in intense natural light. And yet, as you climb to the top of the building—which should be the brightest, most light-filled area—the space becomes dark and gloomy, and the stairwell is encumbered by a cage-like structure. Then, reaching the top floor, the professors' offices are again full of sunrays—a literal and metaphorical "enlightenment" for the students after slogging through a dark spell.

During the tour, you'll be able to linger a few minutes in the major rooms, such as the remarkable forest-like library and the furniture gallery (including some original tables and chairs from the Willow Tea Rooms). Walking through the GSA, remember that all of this work was the Art Nouveau original, and that Frank Lloyd Wright, the Art Deco Chrysler Building, and everything that resembles it came well after "Charles Rennie Mack's" time.

• *To finish this walk, we'll do a wee bit of urban "hillwalking" (a popular Scottish pastime). Head north from the Glasgow School of Art on Scott Street. Huff and puff your way over the crest of the hill, and make a left onto Buccleuch Street. The last house on the left is the...*

Tenement House: Packrats of the world, unite! A strange quirk of fate—the 10-year hospitalization of a woman who never redecorated—created this perfectly preserved middle-class residence, rated ▲. The Scottish Trust bought this otherwise ordinary row home, located in a residential neighborhood, because of the peculiar tendencies of Miss Toward. For five decades, she kept her home essentially unchanged. The kitchen calendar is still set for 1935, and an intact "feet shampoo" packet lies on the bathroom shelf. It's a time-warp experience, where Glaswegian old-timers enjoy coming to reminisce about how they grew up.

Buy your ticket on the main floor, and poke around the little museum. You'll learn that in Glasgow, a "tenement" isn't a slum—it's simply a stone apartment house. In fact, tenements like these were typical for every class except the richest. But with the city's economic decline, tenements went the way of the dodo bird as the city's population shrank.

Then head upstairs to the apartment, which is staffed by caring volunteers. Ask them to demonstrate how to make the bed in the kitchen or why the rooms still smell like natural gas. As you look through the rooms stuffed with lace and Victorian trinkets—such as the ceramic dogs on the living room's fireplace mantle—consider how different they are from Mackintosh's stark, minimalist designs from the same period (£5, £3.50 guidebook, daily March–Oct 13:00–17:00, last admission 16:30, closed Nov–Feb, 145 Buccleuch Street at the top of Garnethill, tel. 0141/333-0183, www.nts.org.uk).

• *To return to the Central Station, exit the Tenement House to the left, and take another left down the hill. Follow the leafy footpath that slopes downhill along the highway. After about three minutes, you'll come out the other side of the small park. Go straight ahead one more block (passing the pedestrian bridge on your right) until you arrive back at the far end of Sauchiehall Street. Turn left, walking to the first bus shelter, and take bus #16, #18, or #57 back to Central Station (every 10 min, other buses go the station—ask the driver if another bus pulls up while you're waiting). Taxis zip by on Sauchiehall; a ride to the station will cost you about £3.*

SIGHTS

Away from the Center

▲**Kelvingrove Art Gallery and Museum**—Reopened in 2006 after a three-year, £28-million renovation, this museum is like a

Scottish Smithsonian—with everything from a pair of stuffed elephants to fine artwork by the great masters. The well-described collection is impressively displayed in an impressive 100-year-old, Spanish Baroque-style building. It's divided into two sections. The "Life" section, in the West Court, features a menagerie of stuffed animals (including a giraffe, kangaroo, ostrich, and moose) with a WWII-era Spitfire fighter plane hovering overhead. Branching off are halls with exhibits ranging from Ancient Egypt to "Scotland's First Peoples" to weaponry ("Conflict and Consequence"), as well as several fine paintings (find Salvador Dalí's *Christ of St. John of the Cross*). The more serene "Expression" section, in the East Court, focuses on artwork, including Dutch, Flemish, French, and Italian paintings. It also has exhibits on "Scottish Identity in Art" and on Charles Rennie Mackintosh and the Glasgow School. The Kelvingrove claims to be one of the most-visited museums in Britain—presumably because of all the field-trip groups you'll see here. Watching all the excited Scottish kids—their imaginations ablaze—is as much fun as the collection itself (free, Mon–Thu and Sat 10:00–17:00, Fri and Sun 11:00–17:00, Argyle Street; subway to Kelvinhall stop, then 5-min walk; or buses #9, #16, #18, #42, and #62 all stop nearby; tel. 0141/276-9599).

▲**Burrell Collection**—This eclectic art collection of a wealthy local shipping magnate is one of Glasgow's top destinations, but

it's three miles outside the city center. If you'd like to visit, plan to make an afternoon of it, and leave time to walk around the surrounding park, where Highland cattle graze. The diverse contents of this museum include sculptures (from Roman to Rodin), stained glass, tapestries, furniture, Asian and Islamic works, and halls of paintings—starring Cézanne, Renoir, Degas, and a Rembrandt self-portrait (free, Mon–Thu and Sat 10:00–17:00, Fri and Sun 11:00–17:00, Pollok Country Park, 2060 Pollokshaws Road, tel. 0141/287-2550). To get here from Central Station, take bus #45, #47, or #57 to Pollokshaws Road, or take a train to the Pollokshaws West train station; the entrance is a 10-minute walk from the bus stop and the station. By car, take the M8 to exit at junction 22 onto M77 Ayr; exit junction 1 on M77 and follow signs.

Near the Cathedral, East of Downtown

To reach these sights from the TI on George Square, head up North Hanover Street, turn right on Cathedral Street, and walk about 10 minutes. All sights are free.

Glasgow Cathedral—This blackened, Gothic-to-the-extreme cathedral is a rare example of an intact, pre-Reformation Scottish cathedral. Look up to see the wooden barrel-vaulted ceiling, and notice the beautifully decorated section over the quire. Poke into the lower church, and don't miss the Blacader Aisle (stairs down to the right as you face the choir), where you can look up to see the "ceiling bosses"—colorful carved demons, dragons, skulls, and more (April–Sept Mon–Sat 9:30–17:30, Sun 13:00–17:00, Oct–March closes at 16:00, near junction of Castle and Cathedral Streets, tel. 0141/552-6891, www.glasgowcathedral.org.uk).

Provand's Lordship—With low beams and medieval decor, this creaky home—supposedly the "oldest house in Glasgow"—displays the *Lifestyles of the Rich and Famous*...circa 1471. The interior shows off a few pieces of furniture from the 16th, 17th, and 18th centuries. Out back, explore the St. Nicholas Garden, which was once part of a hospital that dispensed herbal remedies. The plaques in each section show the part of the body that the plants are used to treat (Mon–Thu and Sat 10:00–17:00, Fri and Sun 11:00–17:00, across the street from St. Mungo Museum at 3 Castle Street, tel. 0141/552-8819).

St. Mungo Museum of Religious Life and Art—This museum, next to the cathedral, aims to promote religious understanding. Taking an ecumenical approach, it provides a handy summary of major and minor world religions, showing how each faith handles various rites of passage through the human life span: birth, puberty, marriage, death, and everything in between (Mon–Thu and Sat 10:00–17:00, Fri and Sun 11:00–17:00, cheap ground-floor café, 2 Castle Street, tel. 0141/553-2557).

Necropolis—Built to resemble Paris' Père Lachaise cemetery, Glasgow's huge burial hill has a similarly wistful, ramshackle appeal, along with an occasional deer. Its gravestones seem poised to slide down the hill (open erratic hours at the caretaker's whim, mostly 10:00–16:00 year-round; if main black gates are closed, walk around to the side and see if you can get in and out through a side alleyway).

NIGHTLIFE

Glasgow is a young city, and its nightlife scene is renowned. Walking through the city center, you'll pass at least one club or bar on every block. For the latest, pick up a copy of *The List* (sold at newsstands).

In the West End: **Òran Mòr,** a converted 1862 church overlooking a busy intersection, is one of Glasgow's most popular hangouts. In addition to hosting an atmospheric bar, outdoor beer garden, and brasserie, the building's former nave (now decorated with funky murals) has a nightclub featuring everything from rock concerts to traditional Scottish music nights (brasserie serves £10–20 main dishes; pub with dressy conservatory or outdoor beer garden serves £5–10 pub grub; daily 11:00–2:00 in the morning, food served until 22:00, top of Byres Road at 731–735 Great Western Road, tel. 0141/357-6200, www.oran-mor.co.uk).

In the City Center: **The Pot Still** is an award-winning malt whisky bar from 1835 that boasts a formidable selection of more than 300 choices. You'll see locals of all ages sitting in its leathery interior, watching football (soccer) and discussing their drinks. They have whisky aged in sherry casks, whisky preferred by wine drinkers, and whisky from every region of Scotland. Give the friendly bartenders a little background on your beverage tastes, and they'll narrow down a good choice for you from their long list (whisky runs from £1.40 to £250 a glass, average price £4–5, no food served, Mon–Wed 11:00–23:00, Thu–Sat 11:00–24:00, Sun 18:00–23:00, 154 Hope Street, tel. 0141/333-0980, www.thepotstill.co.uk).

SLEEPING

On Renfrew Street

B&Bs line Renfrew Street, a block away from the Glasgow School of Art. From here, you can walk downhill into the downtown core in about 15 minutes (or take a £3–4 taxi). If approaching by car, you can't drive down one-way Renfrew Street from the city center. Instead, from the busy Sauchiehall Street, go up Scott Street or Rose Street, turn left onto Buccleuch Street, and circle around to Renfrew Street.

$$ Old Schoolhouse Hotel has 22 stylish rooms in a renovated Neoclassical schoolhouse (S-£32, Sb-£40, Db-£60, thin walls and noisy swinging doors can bother light sleepers, 194 Renfrew Street, tel. 0141/332-7600, fax 0141/332-8684, www.schoolhousehotelglasgow.co.uk, info@schoolhousehotelglasgow.co.uk, Mary).

$$ Rennie Mackintosh Hotel has 24 nice rooms decorated with knock-off "Mockintosh" decor inspired by Glasgow's favorite architect (slippery rates change with demand, but generally Sb-£33, Db-£55, 218–220 Renfrew Street, tel. 0141/333-9992, fax 0141/333-9995).

$$ Victorian House Hotel is a crank-'em-out guest house with 58 slightly worn but comfortable rooms sprawling through several old townhouses (S-£32, Sb-£39, Db-£60, lots of stairs with no elevator, 212 Renfrew Street, tel. 0141/332-0129, fax 0141/353-3155, www.thevictorian.co.uk, info@thevictorian.co.uk).

Sleep Code

(£1 = about $2, country code: 44, area code: 0141)
S = Single, **D** = Double/Twin, **T** = Triple, **Q** = Quad, **b** = bathroom, **s** = shower only. You can assume credit cards are accepted unless otherwise noted.

To help you sort easily through these listings, I've divided the rooms into two categories based on the price for a standard double room with bath (during high season):

$$ Higher Priced—Most rooms £50 or more.
$ Lower Priced—Most rooms less than £50.

Central Glasgow Hotels and Restaurants

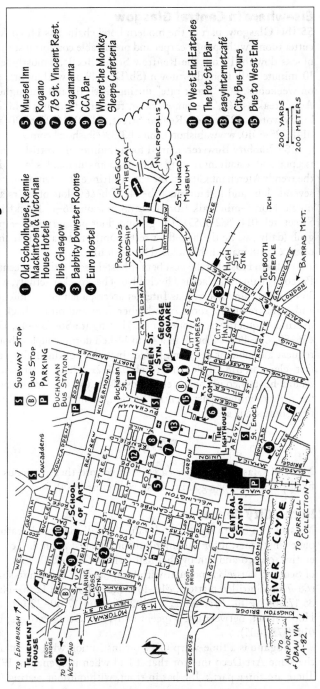

S Subway Stop
B Bus Stop
P Parking

1 Old Schoolhouse, Rennie Mackintosh & Victorian House Hotels
2 Ibis Glasgow
3 Babbity Bowster Rooms
4 Euro Hostel

5 Mussel Inn
6 Rogano
7 78 St. Vincent Rest.
8 Wagamama
9 CCA Bar
10 Where the Monkey Sleeps Cafeteria

11 To West End Eateries
12 The Pot Still Bar
13 easyInternetcafé
14 City Bus Tours
15 Bus to West End

200 YARDS
200 METERS

Glasgow

Elsewhere in Central Glasgow

$$ Ibis Glasgow, part of the modern hotel chain, has 141 cookie-cutter rooms with spongy carpet and predictable comfort just three blocks downhill from the Renfrew Street B&Bs, a mostly level 10-minute walk from downtown (Sb/Db-£49 on weeknights, £51 on weekends, £68 "event rate" during festivals and throughout Aug, breakfast-£6, air-con, elevator, restaurant, hiding behind a big Novotel at 220 West Regent Street, tel. 0141/225-6000, fax 0141/225-6010, www.ibishotel.com, h3139@ibishotel.com).

$$ Babbity Bowster, named for a traditional Scottish dance, is a pub and restaurant renting six basic rooms up top. It's located in the trendy Merchant City on the eastern fringe of downtown, near several clubs and restaurants (Sb-£45, Db-£60, lots of stairs and no elevator, 5-min walk from Central Station, 16–18 Blackfriars Street, tel. 0141/552-5055). The ground-floor pub serves £5–8 pub grub (daily), while the first-floor restaurant, run by a French chef, offers £15–18 main dishes (closed Sun–Mon).

$ Euro Hostel is the best bet for hostel beds in the city center. Part of a chain, this place is a lively hive of backpacker activity, with 364 beds on nine floors, plus Internet access, a laundry, a kitchen, and a bar (request a room on a higher floor and on the back for maximum quiet; very slippery rates, but figure Sb-£30–40, Db-£36–50, £13–19 for a bunk in a 4- to 14-bed dorm, couples should request a double or get a bunk-bed, includes continental breakfast, elevator, 318 Clyde Street, tel. 0141/222-2828, reservations @euro-hostels.co.uk, www.euro-hostels.co.uk). It's on the busy main thoroughfare past Central Station, along the Clyde River, near some seedy areas.

EATING

Many of Glasgow's fancier eateries serve "pre-theatre menus"—fixed-price meals at a good price served before 19:00.

In the City Center

Mussel Inn offers light, good-value fish dinners and seafood plates in an airy, informal environment. The restaurant is a cooperative, owned and run by shellfish farmers. Their £10 "kilo pot" of Scottish mussels is popular with locals and big enough to share (£6–7 small grilled platters, £10–16 meals, Mon–Thu 12:00–14:30 & 17:30–22:00, Fri–Sat 12:00–22:00, Sun 17:00–22:00, 157 Hope Street, between St. Vincent and West George streets, tel. 0141/572-1405).

Rogano is a time-warp Glasgow institution with essentially the same Art Deco interior that it had when it opened in 1935. There are three parts: The bar in front, with outdoor seating (£6 lunch sandwiches, £9–10 meals); the fancy dining room in the back part of the main floor, which is like dining on the officers' deck of the *Titanic* (£20–35 meals with a focus on seafood); and a more casual yet still dressy bistro in the cellar, with a 1930s-Hollywood glamour and £10–17 meals (daily 12:00–22:30, fancy restaurant closed 14:30–18:30, 11 Exchange Place—just before giant archway from Buchanan Street, reservations smart on weekends, tel. 0141/248-4055).

78 St. Vincent, offering modern British cuisine made with Scottish produce, has elegant tables and booths in a high-windowed former bank with frilly Art Nouveau touches. Their rotating gourmet menu specializes in meat and fish dishes, with local beef from nearby towns and salmon and cod caught off the west coast of Scotland (£8–16 lunches, £13–20 dinners, daily 8:30–22:00, 78 St. Vincent Street, tel. 0141/248-7878).

Wagamama is part of a reliably good UK chain that serves delicious Asian noodle dishes at a reasonable price (£6–10 main dishes, daily 12:00–23:00, 97–103 West George Street, tel. 0141/229-1468).

And More: Dozens of restaurants line the main commercial areas of town: Sauchiehall Street, Buchanan Street, and the Merchant City area. Most are very similar, with trendy interiors, Euro disco-pop soundtracks, and dinner for about £15–20 per person.

Budget Options near the Glasgow School of Art

CCA Bar, located in the first floor of Glasgow's edgy contemporary art museum, has delicious designer food at art-student prices. An 18th-century facade, discovered when the site was excavated to build the museum, looms over the courtyard restaurant (£5 salads, £7 main courses, same prices for lunch or dinner, Tue–Sat 10:30–23:00, closed Sun–Mon, 350 Sauchiehall Street, tel. 0141/332-7959).

Where the Monkey Sleeps is a cheap student cafeteria across the street from the entrance to the Glasgow School of Art. This is a good spot for a subsidized lunch (open to the public, choice of two hot meals a day for £2–3, soups for £2, and sandwiches for £1–2). Nothing is ever more than £3.50. It's your chance to mingle with the city's next generation of artists, and hear more of that lilting Glaswegian accent (Sept–June Mon–Sat 8:00–17:00, closed Sun, same hours outside of the school year but with fewer foods to choose from, entrance is on the left as you face the multi-colored windows, you'll pass through the teachers' lounge on the way to the food—no spitballs please, 167 Renfrew Street, tel. 0141/353-4728).

In the West End

The hip, lively residential neighborhood called the West End is worth exploring, particularly at dinnertime. A collection of fine and fun eateries line Ashton Lane, a small street just off bustling Byres Road (the scene continues north along Cresswell Lane). Before choosing a place, make a point of strolling the whole scene to comparison-shop.

Local favorites (all open long hours daily) include the landmark **Ubiquitous Chip** (with various pubs and restaurants sprawling through a deceptively large building; £5–7 pub grub, £8–20 restaurant meals, tel. 0141/334-5007) and **The Loft** (£7–9 pizzas and pastas in the lobby of a grand old movie theater; tel. 0141/341-1234). Up at Cresswell Lane, consider **Café Andaluz,** offering £3–6 tapas and sangria behind lacy wooden screens, as the waitstaff clicks past on the cool tiles (2 Cresswell Lane, tel. 0141/339-1111). Also note that the church-turned-pub **Òran Mòr** is a five-minute walk away (at the intersection of Byres and Great Western Road; see page 535).

Getting to the West End: It's easiest to take the subway to Hillhead, which is a two-minute walk from Ashton Lane (exit the station to the left, then take the first left to find the lane). From the city center, you can also take a £5–6 taxi, or catch bus #20 or #66 (stops just in front of the TI, runs every 10 min; get out when you reach Byres Road).

TRANSPORTATION CONNECTIONS

Traveline Scotland has a journey planner that's linked to all of Scotland's train and bus schedule info. Go online (www.travelinescotland.com); call them at 0870-608-2608; or use the individual websites listed below. If you're connecting with Edinburgh, note that the train is faster but the bus is cheaper.

From Glasgow's Central Station by Train to: Keswick in the Lake District (10/day, 2 hrs to Penrith, then catch a bus to Keswick, hourly except Sun 6/day, 35 min), **Stranraer** and ferry to Belfast (4/day direct, plus 3 more/day with change in Ayr, 2.5 hrs), **Troon** and ferry to Belfast (2/hr, 40 min), **Blackpool** (hourly, 3.5 hrs, transfer in Preston), **Liverpool** (1–2/hr, 4 hrs Mon–Fri, 6–8 hrs Sat–Sun, requires 1–3 transfers), **Durham** (2/hr, 3 hrs, may require change in Edinburgh), **York** (10/day, 3.5 hrs), **London** (1–2 hr, 4.5–5 hrs direct, check schedules to both Euston and King's Cross stations). Train info: tel. 0845-748-4950 or www.firstscotrail.com.

From Glasgow's Queen Street Station by Train to: Oban (Mon–Sat 6/day, Sun 3/day, 3 hrs), **Inverness** (2/day, 3.5 hrs, more frequent with change in Perth), **Edinburgh** (4/hr, 50 min),

Stirling (3/hr, 25–45 min), **Pitlochry** (8/day, 2 hrs, transfer in Perth).

From Glasgow by Bus to: Edinburgh (4/hr, 70 min), **Oban** (buses #976 and #977, 4/day Mon–Sat, 3/day Sun, 3 hrs, more with transfer in Tyndrum), **Fort William** (buses #914, #915, and #916; 7/day, 3 hrs), near Glencoe (buses #914, #915, and #916; 7/day, 2.5 hrs), **Inverness** (hourly, 4–4.5 hrs, transfer in Perth or Fort William), **Portree** on the Isle of Skye (buses #915 and #916, 3/day direct, 9.25 hrs), **Pitlochry** (8/day, 2 hrs, transfer in Perth). Bus info: tel. 08705-505-050 or www.citylink.co.uk.

Glasgow International Airport: Located eight miles west of the city, this airport has currency-exchange desks, an information center, and ATMs (tel. 0870-040-0008, www.glasgowairport.com). Taxis connect downtown to the airport for about £18–20. Bus #905 runs to central Glasgow (daily 5:00–24:30, Sun from 7:00, 3–6/hr, £4/one-way, £5.50/round-trip, 25 min, stops at both train stations en route to the bus station).

Prestwick Airport: A hub for Ryanair (as well as the US military, which refuels planes here), this airport is about 30 miles southwest of the city center (tel. 0871-223-0700, ext. 1006, www.gpia.co.uk). A train connects the airport and Central Station (Mon–Sat 2/hr, Sun 1/hr, 44 min). Buses run to and from Buchanan Street Station (£4–6, 1–3/hr, 50 min, daily 7:00–22:00, check schedules at airport TI or www.travelinescotland.com).

Glasgow

OBAN and the
SOUTHERN HIGHLANDS

Oban • Mull • Iona • Glencoe • Fort William

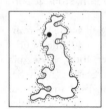

The area north of Glasgow offers a fun and easy dip into the southern part of the Scottish Highlands. Oban is a fruit crate of Scottish traditions, with a handy pair of wind-bitten Hebrides islands (Mull and Iona) just a hop, skip, and jump away. Nearby, the evocative "Weeping Glen" of Glencoe aches with both history and natural beauty. Beyond that, Fort William anchors the southern end of the Caledonian Canal, offering a springboard to more Highlands scenery—this is where Britain's highest peak, Ben Nevis, keeps its head in the clouds, and where you'll find a valley made famous by a steam train carrying a young wizard named Harry (for more on Harry Potter sights, see page 632 in the appendix).

Planning Your Time

Oban is a smart place to spend the night on a blitz tour of northern Scotland; with more time to linger (and an interest in a day trip to the islands), spend two nights—Iona is worthwhile but adds a day to your trip. Glencoe is worth considering as a very sleepy, rural overnight alternative to Oban, or if you have plenty of time and want a remote village experience on your way north.

Oban works well if you're coming from Glasgow, or even all the way from England's Lake District (for driving tips, see page 566). Assuming you're driving, here's an ambitious two-day plan for the Highlands:

Day 1: Morning: Drive up from the Lake District, or linger in Glasgow; 11:30–Depart Glasgow; 12:00–Rest stop on Loch Lomond, then joyride on; 13:00–Lunch in Inveraray; 16:00–Arrive in Oban, tour whisky distillery, and drop by the TI; 20:00–Dine in Oban.

Day 2: 9:00–Leave Oban; 10:00–Visit Glencoe museum and the valley's Visitors Centre; 12:00–Drive to Fort William and follow Caledonian Canal to Inverness, stopping at Fort Augustus to see the locks and along Loch Ness to search for monsters; 16:00–Visit the Culloden Battlefield (closes earlier off-season) near Inverness; 17:00–Drive south; 20:00–Arrive in Edinburgh.

With more time, head north from Fort William to the Isle of Skye, spend a night or two there, then head over to Inverness via Loch Ness.

Getting Around the Highlands

By Car: Drivers enjoy flexibility and plenty of tempting stopovers. Barring traffic, you'll make great time on good, mostly two-lane roads. Be careful, but if you're timid about passing, diesel fumes and large trucks might be your memory of driving in Scotland. For step-by-step instructions, don't miss the "Route Tips for Drivers" at the end of this chapter.

By Public Transportation: Glasgow is the gateway to this region (so you'll most likely have to transfer there if coming from Edinburgh). The **train** zips from Glasgow to Oban, but to most other destinations, the bus is better.

Buses are operated by Scottish Citylink (www.citylink.co.uk). Buy tickets at local TIs, pay the driver in cash as you board, or buy tickets in advance by calling 08705-505-050. The nondescript town of Fort William (described on page 563) serves as a hub for Highlands buses. Note that bus frequency is substantially reduced on Sundays and off-season—during these times, always carefully confirm schedules locally. Unless otherwise noted, I've listed bus information for summer weekdays.

These buses are particularly useful for connecting the sights in this book:

Buses **#976** and **#977** connect Glasgow with Oban (4/day Mon–Sat, 3/day Sun, 3 hrs).

Bus #913 is the only direct bus from Edinburgh to this region—stopping at Glasgow, Stirling, Oban, and Glencoe on the way to Fort William (1/day, 4 hrs total from Edinburgh to Fort William).

Bus **#914** goes from Glasgow to Fort William, stopping at Glencoe (4/day, 3 hrs).

Buses **#915** and **#916** follow the same route (Glasgow-Glencoe-Fort William), then continue all the way up to Portree on the Isle of Skye (3/day, 9.25 hrs for the full run).

Bus **#918** goes from Oban to Fort William, stopping en route at Ballachulish near Glencoe (4/day in summer, 2/day off-season, never on Sun; 1 hr to Ballachulish, 1.5 hrs total to Fort William).

Bus **#919** connects Fort William with Inverness (5/day, 2 hrs).

Oban

Oban

Oban (pronounced OH-bin) is called the "gateway to the isles."
Equal parts functional and scenic, this busy little ferry-and-train
terminal has no important sights.
It's a low-key resort, with a winding
promenade lined by gravel beaches,
ice-cream stands, fish-and-chip
take-away shops, and a surprising
diversity of fine restaurants. When
the rain clears, you'll see sun-
starved Scots sitting on benches
along The Esplanade, leaning

back to catch some rays. Wind, boats, gulls, layers of islands, and
the promise of a wide-open Atlantic beyond give Oban a rugged
charm.

ORIENTATION

(area code: 01631)
Oban's business action, just a couple of streets deep, stretches
along the harbor and its promenade. (The island just offshore is
Kerrera, with Mull looming behind it.) Everything in Oban is
close together, and the town seems eager to please its many visitors.
There's live, touristy music nightly in several bars and restaurants;
wool and tweed are perpetually on sale (tourist shops open until
20:00 in summer and on Sun); and posters announce a variety of
day tours to Scotland's wild and rabbit-strewn western islands.

Tourist Information

Oban's impressive TI, located in a former church, sells bus and
ferry tickets and has a fine bookshop. Stop by to get brochures
and information on everything from bike rental to golf courses
to horseback riding to rainy-day activities and more. They also
offer coin-operated Internet access and can book you a room for
a £3 fee (flexible hours, but generally July–Aug daily 9:00–19:00;
June and Sept Mon–Sat 9:00–18:00, Sun 10:00–17:00; April–May
and Oct Mon–Sat 9:00–17:30, Sun 10:00–16:00; Nov–March
Mon–Sat 10:00–17:00, Sun 12:00–17:00; on Argyll Square, just
off harbor a block from train station, tel. 01631/563-122, www
.visitscotland.com). Check the "What's On" board for the latest on
Oban's small-town evening scene (free live entertainment nearly
nightly year-round at the Great Western Hotel, Scottish Night
every Wed or Thu, call for details, tel. 01631/563-101). Wander
through their free exhibit on the area and pick up a few phones to

Oban

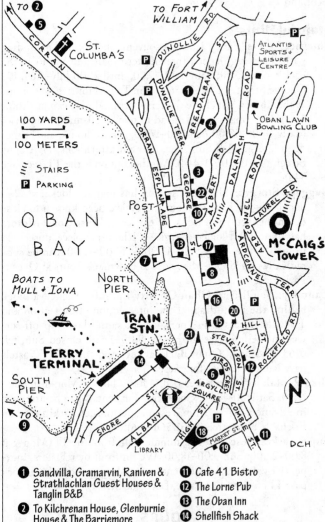

Oban

1. Sandvilla, Gramarvin, Raniven & Strathlachlan Guest Houses & Tanglin B&B
2. To Kilchrenan House, Glenburnie House & The Barriemore
3. The Town House
4. Oban Backpackers
5. IYHF Hostel
6. Jeremy Inglis' Hostel
7. Ee'usk & Piazza Restaurants
8. Cuan Mòr
9. To The Seafood Temple
10. Coast Restaurant
11. Cafe 41 Bistro
12. The Lorne Pub
13. The Oban Inn
14. Shellfish Shack
15. The Kitchen Garden Deli & Café
16. McTavish's Kitchens
17. Oban Whisky Distillery
18. Tesco Supermarket
19. Bike Rental
20. Laundry
21. Bowman's Tours
22. Fancy That Shop (Internet)

hear hardy locals talk about their life on the wild western edge of Scotland.

Helpful Hints

Internet Access: Fancy That is a souvenir shop on the main drag with seven high-speed Internet terminals and Wi-Fi in the back room (£3/hr, daily 9:30–17:00, until 21:00 July–Aug, 108 George Street, tel. 01631/562-996). To surf for free, get online at the **library** just above the ferry terminal; you can just show up, but it's smart to call ahead to book a 30-minute time slot (daily 10:00–13:00 & 14:00–17:00, erratic hours, sometimes open later, closed Sun, Tue, and Sat afternoons, 77 Albany Street, tel. 01631/571-444). Another option is the **TI** (see page 544).

Baggage Storage: The train station has luggage lockers (£2–4 depending on bag size), but these have been known to close down for security reasons. In this case, **West Coast Motors** has a pricey left-luggage service (£1/hour per piece, unsecured in main office, daily 9:00–13:00 & 14:00–17:00, can be sporadically closed Oct-May, next to Bowman's Tours at Queens Park Place).

Laundry: You'll find **Oban Quality Laundry** tucked a block behind the main drag, at the intersection of Stevenson and Tweedle streets (£6–9 per load for same-day drop-off service, no self-service, Mon–Sat 9:00–17:30, closed Sun, tel. 01631/563-554). **Oban Backpackers** and the **IYHF** hostels have laundry service for guests.

Bike Rental: Try **Evo Bikes** (£10/4 hrs, £14/day, Mon–Fri 9:00–17:30, Sat 9:00–17:00, closed Sun but rentals can be arranged in advance, across from Tesco supermarket parking lot on Lochside Street, tel. 01631/566-996).

Supermarket: Tesco is a five-minute walk from the TI (Mon–Sat 8:00–22:00, Sun 9:00–18:00, WC in front by registers, inexpensive cafeteria, look for entrance to large parking lot a block past TI on right-hand side, Lochside Street).

TOURS

Oban and Beyond

▲▲Nearby Islands—For the best day trip from Oban, tour the islands of Mull and Iona (offered daily May–Oct, fully described on page 554)—or consider staying overnight on remote and beautiful Iona (see page 557 for more details). With more time or other interests, consider one of many other options you'll see advertised. For example, those more interested in nature than church history will enjoy trips to the wildly scenic Isle of Staffa with Fingal's

Cave. The journey to Treshnish Island brims with puffins, seals, and other sea critters.

Open Top Bus Tours—If there's good weather and you don't have a car, take a spin out of Oban for views of nearby castles and islands, plus a stop at McCaig's Tower (£7, late May–Sept at 11:00 and 14:00, no tours Oct–late-May, 2.5 hours, departs from rail station, tel. 01586/555-887, www.westcoastmotors.co.uk).

SIGHTS AND ACTIVITIES

In Oban

▲**West Highland Malt Scotch Whisky Distillery Tours**—The 200-year-old Oban Whisky Distillery produces more than 16,000 liters a week. They offer serious and fragrant 45-minute, £6 tours explaining the process from start to finish, with a free, smooth sample and a discount coupon for the shop. The exhibition that precedes the tour gives a quick, whisky-centric history of Scotland. This is the handiest whisky tour you'll see, just a block off the harbor and better than anything in Edinburgh (July–Sept Mon–Fri 9:30–19:30, Sat 9:30–17:00, Sun 12:00–17:00; April–June and Oct Mon–Sat 9:30–17:00, closed Sun; March and Nov Mon–Fri 10:00–17:00, closed Sat–Sun; Dec and Feb Mon–Fri 12:30–16:00, closed Sat–Sun; closed Jan; last tour always 1 hour before closing—tel. 01631/572-004). In high season, these tours (which are limited to 15 people every 15 min) fill up quickly. Call or stop by early in the day to reserve your time slot.

McCaig's Tower—The unfinished "colosseum" on the hill overlooking town was an employ-the-workers-and-build-me-a-fine-memorial project undertaken by an early Oban tycoon in 1900. While the structure itself is nothing to see close-up, a 10-minute hike through a Victorian residential neighborhood gets you to a peaceful garden and a mediocre view.

Atlantis Sports and Leisure Centre—The industrial-type sports center is a good place to get some exercise on a rainy day or let the kids run wild for a few hours. There's an indoor swimming pool with a big water slide, a rock-climbing wall, tennis courts, and two playgrounds (Mon–Fri 7:00–22:00, Sat–Sun 8:30–18:30, pool hours vary by season, call or check online, pool entry: adults-£3.20, kids-£2, no rental towels or suits, lockers-20p, on the north end of Dalriach Road, tel. 01631/566-800, www.atlantisleisure.co.uk). The center's outdoor playground is free and open all the time; the indoor "soft play centre" for young children costs £1.65 per kid.

Oban Lawn Bowling Club—The club has welcomed visitors since 1869. This elegant green is the scene of a wonderfully British spectacle of old men tiptoeing wishfully after their balls. It's fun to watch, and—if there's no match and the weather's dry—for £3 each, anyone can rent shoes and balls and actually play (informal hours, but generally daily 10:00–16:00 & 17:00 to "however long the weather lasts," just south of sports center on Dalriach Road).

Near Oban

Kerrera—Just offshore from Oban, this stark but very green island offers a quick, easy opportunity to get that romantic island experience. While Kerrera (KEH-reh-rah) dominates Oban's sea view, you'll have to head two miles south of town to catch the boat there (ferry-£4 round-trip, 50p for bikes, 5-min trip, first ferry usually at 8:45, then about 15 ferries/day in summer, 6/day in winter—this changes with demand; at Gallanach's dock, tel. 01631/563-665, if no answer contact Oban TI for info—see above). If you want to spend the night on the island, your only option is the Bunkhouse, a converted 18th-century stable that has seven beds in dorm-like compartments (£14 per person, cheaper for 2 nights or more, £60 for whole bunkhouse, open year-round, kitchen, tel. 01631/570-223, ferry info at www.kerrerabunkhouse.co.uk, info @kerrerabunkhouse.co.uk, Andy and Jo). They also run a tea garden (Easter–Sept Wed–Sun 10:30–16:30, closed off-season).

Isle of Seil—Enjoy a drive, a walk, some solitude, and the sea. Drive 12 miles south of Oban on A816 to B844 to the Isle of Seil (pronounced "seal"), connected to the mainland by a bridge (which, locals like to brag, "crosses the Atlantic"...well, maybe a small part of it). Just over the bridge on the Isle of Seil is a pub called Tigh-an-Truish ("House of Trousers"). After a 1745 English law forbade the wearing of kilts on the mainland, Highlanders on the island used this pub to change from kilts to trousers before crossing the bridge. The pub serves great meals to those either in kilts or pants (pub open daily May–Aug 11:00–23:00—food served 12:30–17:00 & 18:00–21:00; Sept–April 11:00–14:30 & 17:00–23:00—food served 12:20–14:00 & 17:00–21:00; darts anytime, good seafood dishes, tel. 01852/300-242). Five miles across the island, on a tiny second island and facing the open Atlantic, is Easdale, a historic, touristy, windy little slate-mining town—with a slate-town museum and incredibly tacky egomaniac's "Highland Arts" shop (shuttle ferry goes the 300 yards).

Between Oban and Glasgow

If you're driving to Oban from Glasgow (or from England's Lake District via Glasgow), consider these stopovers, which are listed in order from Glasgow to Oban. (For specific tips on driving this route, see page 566.)

Loch Lomond—Twenty-four miles long and speckled with islands, Loch Lomond is second in size only to Loch Ness. It's well-known mostly because of its easy proximity to Glasgow (about 15 miles away)—and also because its bonnie, bonnie banks inspired a beloved folk song: *Ye'll take the high road, and I'll take the low road, and I'll be in Scotland afore ye...* (You'll be humming that one all day. You're welcome.)

Rest-and-Be-Thankful Pass—Offering a pleasant opportunity to stretch your legs and get your first taste of that rugged Scottish countryside, this low-profile pull-out is on A83 just west of A82. The colorful name comes from the 1880s, when second- and third-class coach passengers got out and pushed the coach and first-class passengers up the hill.

Inveraray—Nearly everybody stops at this lovely, seemingly made-for-tourists castle town on Loch Fyne. Park near the pier, and browse the wide selection of restaurants and tourist shops.

Inveraray's **TI** sells bus and ferry tickets, and offers a free mini-guide and an exhibit about the Argyll region (free Internet access, 20p WCs; April–Oct Mon–Sat 9:00–17:00, Sun 11:00–17:00, July–Aug until 18:00; Nov–March daily 10:00–15:00; tel. 01499/302-063.)

The town's main "sight" is the **Inveraray Jail,** a corny but mildly educational former jail that has been converted into a museum. This "living 19th-century prison" includes a courtroom where mannequins argue the fate of the accused. You'll have the opportunity to be locked up for a photo op by a playful guard (£6.50, daily Easter–Oct 9:30–18:00, Nov–Easter 10:00–17:00, last entry 1 hour before closing, Church Square, tel. 01499/302-381).

The dramatic **Inveraray Castle**—which you'll spot on the right as you cross the bridge coming from Glasgow—is striking from afar but dull inside; save your time for better Highlands castles elsewhere.

SLEEPING

(area code: 01631)
Oban's B&Bs offer a better value than its hotels.

B&Bs on Strathaven Terrace

The following B&Bs line up on a quiet, flowery street that's nicely located two blocks off the harbor, three blocks from the center, and a 10-minute walk from the train station. By car, as you enter town, turn left after King's Knoll Hotel, and take your first right onto Breadalbane Street. ("Strathaven Terrace" is actually just the name for this row of houses on Breadalbane Street.) The alley behind the buildings has parking for all of these places. Note that these B&Bs don't accept credit cards. The first three are more modern and pricey; the last two are simpler, more traditional, and less expensive.

Sleep Code

(£1 = about $2, country code: 44)
S = Single, **D** = Double/Twin, **T** = Triple, **Q** = Quad, **b** = bathroom,
s = shower only. Unless otherwise noted, you can assume credit cards are accepted at hotels and hostels—but not B&Bs—and breakfast is included.

To help you sort easily through these listings, I've divided the rooms into three categories based on the price for a standard double room with bath (during high season):

$$$ **Higher Priced**—Most rooms £65 or more.
$$ **Moderately Priced**—Most rooms between £30–65.
$ **Lower Priced**—Most rooms £30 or less.

$$ Sandvilla B&B rents five fine rooms—including one on the ground floor—with sleek contemporary decor (Db-£50, or £60 in July–Aug, at #4, tel. 01631/562-803, www.holidayoban.co.uk, sandvilla@holidayoban.co.uk, Joyce).

$$ Gramarvin Guest House has five fresh, cheery, and clean rooms (Db-£50, or £55 in July–Aug, family deals, at #5, tel. 01631/564-622, www.gramarvin.co.uk, mary@gramarvin.co.uk, Mary—but may be sold in 2008).

$$ Raniven Guest House has four tastefully decorated rooms (Sb-£25, Db-£50, cheaper off-season, at #1, tel. 01631/562-713, www.raniven.co.uk, info@raniven.co.uk, Moyra and Stuart).

$$ Tanglin B&B, with five ragtag but homey rooms, comes with lively, chatty hosts Liz and Jim Montgomery, who create an easygoing atmosphere (S-£22, tiny D-£40, Db-£44, flexible rates and family deals, at #3, tel. 01631/563-247, jimtanglin@aol.com).

$$ Strathlachlan Guest House, next door, is an old-fashioned good value, because the four comfortable rooms share three bathrooms on the hall. Enjoy the cozy TV lounge and the Scottish hospitality of Rena Anderson (S-£20, D-£40, family deals, closed Nov–Easter, at #2, tel. 01631/563-861).

Small Hotels

These options are a step up from the B&Bs—both in amenities and in price. The first three, which are along The Esplanade that stretches north of town (with beautiful bay views), are a five- to 10-minute walk from the center. The last one is on the main drag in town.

$$$ Kilchrenan House, the turreted former retreat of a textile magnate, has 10 tastefully renovated, large rooms, most with bay views (Sb-£40–45, Db-£64–90, 2-night minimum, higher prices are for seaview rooms in June–Aug, lower prices are for back-facing rooms and Sept–May, pleasant room #5 is worth the few extra pounds, welcome drink of whisky or sherry, different "breakfast special" every day, closed Dec–Jan, a few houses past the cathedral on The Esplanade, tel. 01631/562-663, www.kilchrenanhouse .co.uk, info@kilchrenanhouse.co.uk, oft-kilted Colin and his wife Frances).

$$$ Glenburnie House, a stately Victorian home, has an elegant breakfast room overlooking the bay. Its 12 spacious, comfortable older-feeling rooms are furnished like plush living rooms, but the bathrooms are an uninspired afterthought (Sb-£45–50, Db-£75–90, depends on size and view, cheaper off-season, free parking, closed mid-Nov–mid-March, The Esplanade, tel. & fax 01631/562-089, www.glenburnie.co.uk, graeme.strachan@btinternet.com, Graeme).

$$$ The Barriemore is the last place on Oban's grand waterfront esplanade. Its 11 woody, bright rooms are well-appointed (Sb-£40–60, Db-£70–90, depends on size and season, The Esplanade, tel. 01631/566-356, fax 01631/571-084, www.barriemore-hotel .co.uk, reception@barriemore-hotel.co.uk, Nic and Sarah Jones).

$$$ The Town House is a group-friendly place with a tacky British-holiday lobby, 24 cleanser-clean rooms reminiscent of a budget hotel in the US, and a central locale right on Oban's main drag (Sb-£50, Db-£75, £5 less Nov–April, prices soft for walk-ins, easy parking, George Street, tel. 01631/562-954, fax 01631/565-071, www.obanhotels.com). Light renovations planned for 2008 may increase prices.

Hostels

Oban offers plenty of cheap dorm beds. Your choice: easygoing, institutional, or spacey.

$ Oban Backpackers is the most central, laid-back, and fun, with a wonderful, sprawling public living room and 48 beds. The giant mural of nearby islands in the lobby is useful for orientation, and the staff is generous with travel tips (£13/bed, 50p more in July–Aug, 6–12 bunks per room, breakfast-£2, Internet terminal and £2.50 laundry service for guests only, 10-min walk from station, on Breadalbane Street, tel. 01631/562-107, www .scotlands-top-hostels.com, oban@scotlands-top-hostels.com).

$ The orderly **IYHF hostel,** on the scenic waterfront Esplanade, is in a grand building with 110 beds and smashing views of the harbor and islands. The smaller, private rooms—including several that can usually be rented as doubles—are in a separate newer building out back (£13–15/bed in 4- to 10-bed rooms, bunkbed Db-£35–45, price depends on demand, £1 cheaper for members, cheaper for youths under 18, breakfast-£3, great facilities and public rooms, Internet access, one laundry machine, tel. 01631/562-025, oban@syha.org.uk).

$ Jeremy Inglis' Hostel has 20 beds located two blocks from the TI and train station. This loosely run place feels more like a commune than a youth hostel...but it's cheap (£9–10/bed, cash only, breakfast comes with Jeremy's homemade jam, 21 Airds Crescent, tel. 01631/565-065).

EATING

Restaurants

Ee'usk (a phonetic rendering of *iasg*, Scots Gaelic for "fish") is a stylish, family-run place on the waterfront. It has tall tables, a casual-chic atmosphere, a bright and glassy interior, sweeping views, and fish dishes favored by both locals and tourists (£12–20 meals, daily 12:00–15:00 & 18:00–21:30, North Pier, tel. 01631/565-666, MacLeod family). Reservations are smart every day in summer and on weekends off-season; if you have to wait for a table, they have a loft bar with comfy sofas.

MacLeods' **Piazza,** next door, has similar decor but serves Italian cuisine and offers a more family-friendly ambience (£7–10 pizzas and pastas, daily 12:00–15:00 & 17:00–21:00, until 22:00 in summer, smart to reserve ahead July–Aug, tel. 01631/563-628).

Cuan Mòr is a new "gastro-pub" that combines traditional Scottish with modern flair—both in its tasty cuisine and in its furnishings, made entirely of wood, stone, and metal scavenged from the beaches of Scotland's west coast (£8–13 main dishes, food served daily 12:00–16:00 & 18:00–22:00, 60 George Street, tel. 01631/565-078).

The Seafood Temple is worth the 15-minute walk from the town center (follow the road past the ferry terminal, or take a £3 taxi ride). This small eatery is situated in a beautifully restored former public toilet building from the Victorian era (no joke), with sweeping views across the bay to the Isle of Kerrera. Owner/chef John—who also runs the shellfish shack at the ferry dock—prides himself on creating the best seafood dishes in town, listed on a limited, handwritten menu (£12–18 meals, Thu–Mon from 18:00, closed Tue–Wed, reservations smart, tel. 01631/566-000).

Coast proudly serves fresh local fish, meat, and veggies in a mod pine-and-candlelight atmosphere. As everything is prepared and presented with care by husband-and-wife team Richard and Nicola—who try to combine traditional Scottish elements in innovative new ways—come here only if you have time for a slow meal (£7–9 lunches, £12–17 dinners, daily 12:00–14:00 & 17:30–21:30, 104 George Street, tel. 01631/569-900).

Cafe 41 Bistro is a cozy, relaxed, local-feeling BYOB option with an emphasis on Scottish and French cuisine (£12–17 entrées, Sun and Wed–Thu 18:30–20:45, Fri–Sat until 21:30, closed Mon–Tue, 41 Combie Street, tel. 01631/564-117).

Pub Grub

The Lorne is a lively, high-ceilinged pub known for its good grub and friendly service. After hours, it becomes the most happening nightspot in town...which isn't saying much (£7–12, food served Sun–Fri 12:00–14:30 & 17:00–21:00, Sat 12:00–14:30 & 17:00–20:30 only—in order to get ready for live bands, tucked a couple of blocks off the main drag behind the stream at Stevenson Street, tel. 01631/570-020).

The Oban Inn, the oldest building in town, has a grungy local vibe in its hole-in-the-wall downstairs bar and a quiet lounge upstairs. Enjoy the "oldie-worldie" ambience, stained-glass coats-of-arms, and comfy booth seating (£5–6 meals, pub open "as late as the law allows," 1 Stafford Street, tel. 01631/562-484).

Lunch

The green **Shellfish** shack at the ferry dock is the best spot to pick up a seafood sandwich or snack (often free salmon samples, inexpensive coffee, meal-size £3 salmon sandwiches, picnic tables nearby, open daily from 9:00 until the boat unloads from Mull around 17:45). This is a good place to pick up a sandwich for your island day—or get a light, early dinner (or "appetizer") when you return from the isles. (For a full meal, check out the same folks' Seafood Temple restaurant, described above.)

The Kitchen Garden is fine for soup, salad, or sandwiches. It's a deli and gourmet-foods store with a charming café upstairs (£3–6 sandwiches to go, £5–11 dishes upstairs, Mon–Sat 8:30–17:00, Sun 11:00–17:30, closed Sun Jan–March, 14 George Street, tel. 01631/566-332).

Dinner and a Show

At **McTavish's Kitchens,** you can gum haggis while taking in a sappy folk show at a reasonable price. However, this place will change hands in 2008—so it's unclear whether the show will go on. If things stay the same, expect a huge, cafeteria-style eating hall that's popular with holiday-makers—not for its food (£6–8 dishes in the cafeteria), but for its live music upstairs each evening (generally nightly at 20:00 May–Sept; same food as cafeteria but a few pounds more, plus a £2.50 cover for the show). With the abundant other options in Oban, I'd skip this place's unremark-able food unless you're taking in the show (34 George Street, tel. 01631/563-064).

Oban

TRANSPORTATION CONNECTIONS

By Train from Oban: Trains link Oban to the nearest transportation hub in **Glasgow** (3/day, 4/day Sat in summer, just 1/day Sun in winter, 3 hrs); to get to **Edinburgh**, you'll have to transfer in Glasgow (3/day, 4.5 hrs). To reach **Fort William** (a transit hub for the Highlands—see page 563), you'll take the same Glasgow-bound train, but transfer in Crianlarich—the direct bus is easier (see below). Oban's small train station has limited hours (ticket window open Mon–Sat 7:15–18:10, Sun 11:00–18:00, same hours apply to lockers and free WC, train info tel. 08457-484-950).

By Bus: Scottish Citylink bus #918 passes through Ballachulish—a half-mile from **Glencoe**—on its way to **Fort William** (4/day in summer, 2/day off-season, never on Sun; 1 hr to Ballachulish, 1.5 hrs total to Fort William). Take this bus to Fort William, then transfer there, to reach **Inverness** (4 hrs total, with about a 20-min layover in Fort William) or **Portree** on the Isle of Skye (2/day, 5.5 hrs total, short layover in Fort William). A different bus (#976 or #977) connects Oban with **Glasgow** (4/day Mon–Sat, 3/day Sun, 3 hrs, more with transfer in Tyndrum), from where you can easily connect by bus or train to **Edinburgh** (figure 4/day Mon–Sat, 3/day Sun, 4.5 hrs total). Buses arrive and depart in front of the Caledonian Hotel, across from the train station (www.citylink.co.uk).

By Boat: Ferries fan out from Oban to the **southern Hebrides** (see information on the islands of Iona and Mull, below). Caledonian MacBrayne Ferry info: tel. 01631/566-688, www.calmac.co.uk.

Islands near Oban: Mull and Iona

For the easiest one-day look at two of the dramatic and historic Hebrides (HEB-rid-eez) Islands, take the Iona/Mull tour from Oban. (For a more in-depth look, head north to Skye—see next chapter).

Here's the game plan: You'll take a ferry from Oban to Mull (40 min), ride a Bowman's bus across Mull (1.25 hours), then board a quick ferry from Mull to Iona. The total round-trip travel time is 5.5 hours (all of it incredibly scenic), plus about two hours of free time on Iona. Buy your set of six tickets—one for each leg—at the Bowman's office in Oban (£32, £2 discount with this book in 2008 for Iona/Mull tour, no tours Nov–March, book one day ahead in July–Sept, bus tickets can sell out during busy summer weekends,

Oban and the Southern Highlands

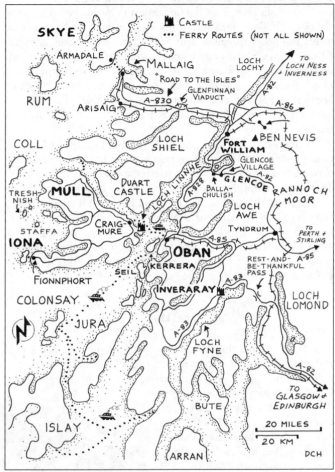

SKYE

ARMADALE

MALLAIG

"ROAD TO THE ISLES"

LOCH LOCHY

TO LOCH NESS + INVERNESS

GLENFINNAN VIADUCT

RUM

ARISAIG   A-830

A-82

A-86

COLL

LOCH SHIEL

FORT WILLIAM   ▲ BEN NEVIS

GLENCOE VILLAGE

TRESH-NISH

MULL

DUART CASTLE

LOCH LINNHE   A-828   GLENCOE   A-82   RANNOCH MOOR

BALLA-CHULISH

STAFFA

CRAIG-MURE

LOCH AWE

IONA

SEIL

TYNDRUM

TO PERTH + STIRLING

A-85

OBAN

KERRERA

REST-AND-BE-THANKFUL PASS   A-85

FIONNPHORT

A-83

INVERARAY

COLONSAY

LOCH LOMOND

N

JURA

LOCH FYNE

A-83

A-82

BUTE

TO GLASGOW + EDINBURGH

ISLAY

20 MILES

20 KM

ARRAN

DCH

🏰 CASTLE

••• FERRY ROUTES (NOT ALL SHOWN)

office open daily 8:00–18:00, 1 Queens Park Place, a block from train station, tel. 01631/566-809 or 01631/563-221, www.bowmanstours.co.uk).

You'll leave in the morning from the Oban pier on the huge Oban–Mull ferry run by Caledonian MacBrayne (boats depart Sun–Fri at 9:50, Sat at 9:30, you'll have to board at least 10 min before departure; boats return daily around 17:45). As the schedule can change slightly from year to year, confirm your departure time carefully in Oban. The best seats on the ferry—with the biggest windows—are in the sofa lounge on the uppermost deck on the back end of the boat. (Follow signs for the toilets, and look for big staircase to the top floor; this floor also has its own small snack bar with £3 sandwiches and £4 box lunches.) On board, if it's a clear day, ask a local or a crew member to point out Ben Nevis, the tallest mountain in Great Britain. The ferry has a fine cafeteria and a bookshop (though guidebooks are cheaper in Oban). Five minutes before landing on Mull, you'll see the striking Duart Castle on the left.

Upon arrival in Mull, find your tour company's bus for the entertaining and informative ride across the Isle of Mull. All drivers spend the entire ride chattering away about life on Mull. They are hardworking local boys who make historical trivia fascinating—or at least fun. Your destination is Mull's westernmost ferry terminal (Fionnphort), where you'll board a small, rocky ferry for the brief ride to Iona. Unless you stay overnight (see below), you'll have only about two hours to roam freely around the island, before taking the ferry–bus–ferry ride in reverse back to Oban.

Mull

The **Isle of Mull,** the third-largest in Scotland, has 300 scenic miles of coastline and castles and a 3,169-foot-high mountain. Called Ben More ("Big Hill" in Gaelic), it was once much bigger. The last active volcano in northern Europe, it was 10,000 feet tall—and was the entire island of Mull—before it blew. It's calmer now, and similarly, Mull has a notably laid-back population. My bus driver reported that there are  no deaths from stress, and only a few from boredom.

With steep, fog-covered hillsides topped by cairns (ancient stone circles, sometimes indicating graves), Mull has a gloomy, otherworldly charm. Bring plenty of rain protection and wear layers in case the sun peeks through the clouds. As my driver said, Mull is a place of cold, wet, windy winters and mild, wet, windy summers.

On the far side of Mull, the caravan of tour buses unloads at Fionnphort, a tiny ferry town. The ferry to the island of Iona takes about 200 walk-on passengers. Confirm the return time with your bus driver, then hustle to the dock to make the first trip over (otherwise, it's a 30-minute wait). There's a small ferry-passenger building/meager snack bar (and a pay WC). After the 10-minute ride, you wash ashore on sleepy Iona, and the ferry mobs that crowded your steps on the boat seem to disappear into Iona's back lanes.

Mull has a taxi service that can get you around Mull or Iona (tel. 01681/700-507 or mobile 0788-777-4550, www.mullionataxi .com).

Iona

The tiny island of **Iona,** just three miles by 1.5 miles, is famous as the birthplace of Christianity in Scotland. You'll have about two hours here on your own before you retrace your steps (your driver will tell you which return ferry to take back to Mull—don't miss this boat); you'll dock back in Oban about 17:45. While the day is spectacular when it's sunny, it's worthwhile in any weather.

A pristine quality of light and a thoughtful peace pervade the stark, car-free island and its tiny community. While the present

abbey, nunnery, and graveyard go back to the 13th century, much of what you'll see was rebuilt in the 19th century. It's free to see the ruins and the graveyard, but the abbey itself has a small fee (£4.50, not covered by tour, daily April–Sept 9:30–17:30, Oct–March 9:30–16:30, tel. 01681/700-512). It's worth the cost just to sit in the

stillness of its lovely, peaceful interior courtyard. With buoyant clouds bouncing playfully off distant bluffs, sparkling white sand crescents, and lone tourists camped thoughtfully atop huge rocks just looking out to sea, it's a place perfect for meditation. Climb a peak—nothing's higher than 300 feet above the sea.

The village, Baile Mòr, has shops, a restaurant/pub, enough beds, a meager heritage center, and no bank. The Finlay Ross Shop rents bikes (near ferry dock, £4.50/4 hrs, £8/day, £10 deposit per bike, tel. 01681/700-357). Iona's official website (www.isle-of-iona .com) has good information about the island.

Staying Overnight in Iona: For a chance to really experience peaceful, idyllic Iona, consider spending a night or two. Scots bring their kids and stay on this tiny island for a week. If you want to overnight in Iona, don't buy your tickets at Bowman's in Oban—they require a same-day return. Instead, buy each leg of the ferry–bus–ferry (and return) trip separately. Get your

Mull and Iona

History of Iona

St. Columba, an Irish scholar, soldier, priest, and founder of monasteries, got into a small war over the possession of an illegally copied psalm book. Victorious but sickened by the bloodshed, Columba left Ireland, vowing never to return. According to legend, the first bit of land out of sight of his homeland was Iona. He stopped here in 563, and established an abbey.

Columba's monastic community flourished, and Iona became the center of Celtic Christianity. Missionaries from Iona spread the gospel throughout Scotland and northern England, while scholarly monks established Iona as a center of art and learning. The *Book of Kells*—perhaps the finest piece of art from "Dark Ages" Europe—was probably made on Iona in the eighth century. The island was so important that it was the legendary burial place for ancient Scottish and even Scandinavian kings (including Shakespeare's Macbeth).

Slowly, the importance of Iona ebbed. Vikings massacred 68 monks in 806. Fearing more raids, the monks evacuated most of Iona's treasures to Ireland (including the *Book of Kells*, which is now in Dublin). Much later, with the Reformation, the abbey was abandoned, and most of its finely carved crosses were destroyed. In the 17th century, locals used the abbey only as a handy quarry for other building projects.

Iona's population peaked at about 500 in the 1830s. In the 1840s, a potato famine hit, and in the 1850s, a third of the islanders emigrated to Canada or Australia. By 1900, the population was down to 210, and today it's only around 100.

But in our generation, a new religious community has given the abbey fresh life. The Iona community is an ecumenical gathering of men and women who seek new ways of living the Gospel in today's world, with a focus on worship, peace and justice issues, and reconciliation.

Oban–Mull ferry ticket in the Oban ferry office (see above, one-way for walk-on passengers-£4.15, round-trip-£7.10). Once you arrive in Mull (Craignure), follow the crowds to the Bowman buses and buy a ticket directly from the driver (£10 round-trip). Once you arrive at the ferry terminal (Fionnphort), walk into the small trailer ferry office to buy a ticket to Iona (£3.85 round-trip, one-way tickets not available).

SLEEPING AND EATING

On Iona

(£1 = about $2, country code: 44, area code: 01681)

$$$ Argyll Hotel, built in 1867, sits proudly overlooking the waterfront, with 15 rooms and pleasingly creaky hallways lined with bookshelves (Sb-£69–137, Db-£98–158, depends on room size, cheaper off-season, extra bed for kids-£15, includes breakfast and dinner, Internet access, closed Dec–Jan, tel. 01681/700-334, fax 01681/700-510, www.argyllhoteliona.co.uk, reception @argyllhoteliona.co.uk, Daniel and Claire). Its restaurant is open to the public, and serves £20 dinners in an elegant, white-linen dining room.

$$$ St. Columba Hotel, situated in the middle of a peaceful garden with picnic tables, has 27 pleasant rooms and spacious, lodge-like common spaces (Sb-£73–83, Db-£136–154, higher prices are for sea view but windows are small, includes breakfast and dinner, extra bed for kids-£20, located next door to abbey on road up from dock, open Easter–Oct only, tel. 01681/700-304, fax 01681/700-688, www.stcolumba-hotel.co.uk, info@stcolumba -hotel.co.uk). Their fine 14-table restaurant, open to the public, overlooks the water (£10 lunches, £9–16 dinners, daily 12:00–15:30 & 18:30–20:00).

$$ Iona Cottage B&B, compact and comfortable, has four rooms with a woody, seabrushed feel in one of the oldest houses on Iona (S-£30, D-£60, located 50 feet directly up from ferry dock, book ahead for Aug, tel. 01681/700-579, iolaire@staffatrips.co.uk).

Glencoe

This valley is the essence of the wild, powerful, and stark beauty of the Highlands (and, I think, excuses the hurried tourist from needing to go north of Inverness). Along with its scenery, Glencoe offers a good dose of bloody clan history: In 1692, British Redcoats (led by a local Campbell commander) came to the valley, and were sheltered and fed for 12 days by the MacDonalds—whose leader had been late in swearing an oath to the British monarch. Then, the morning of February 13, the soldiers were ordered to rise up early and kill their sleeping hosts, violating the rules of Highland hospitality and earning the valley the name "The

Weeping Glen." It's fitting that such an epic, dramatic incident should be set in this equally epic and dramatic valley, where the cliffsides seem to weep (with running streams) when it rains.

ORIENTATION

(area code: 01855)

The valley of Glencoe is just off the main A828/A82 road between Oban and points north (such as Fort William and Inverness). The most appealing town here is the one-street Glencoe village, while the slightly larger and more modern town of Ballachulish (a half-mile away) has more services. While not quite quaint, the very sleepy village of Glencoe is worth a stop for its fine folk museum and its status as the gateway to the valley. The town's hub of activity is its **Spar** grocery store (daily 8:00–20:00).

Tourist Information

Your best source of information (especially for walks and hikes) is the **Glencoe Visitors Centre,** described below. The nearest **TI** is well-signed in Ballachulish (daily 9:00–17:00, until 17:30 July–Aug, bus timetables, free room-finding service, café, shop, tel. 01855/811-866, www.glencoetourism.co.uk).

SIGHTS AND ACTIVITIES

Glencoe Village

Glencoe village is just a line of houses. One is a tiny, thatched, early-18th-century croft house jammed with local history. The huggable **Glencoe and North Lorn Folk Museum** is filled with humble exhibits gleaned from the town's old closets and attics. When one house was being re-thatched, its owner found a cache of 200-year-old swords and pistols hidden there from the British Redcoats after the disastrous battle of Culloden. Don't miss the museum's little door that leads out back, where you'll find more exhibits: on the Glencoe Massacre, local slate, farm tools, and an infamous local murder that inspired Robert Louis Stevenson to write *Kidnapped* (£2, Mon–Sat 10:00–17:30, closed Sun, tel. 01855/811-664).

In Glencoe Valley

▲▲**Joyriding in Glencoe Valley**—If you have a car, spend an hour or so following A82 through the valley, past the Glencoe Visitors Centre (see below), into the desolate moor beyond, and back again. You'll enjoy grand views, flocks of "hairy coos" (shaggy Highland Cattle), and a chance to hear a bagpiper in the wind—

roadside Highland buskers (most often seen on good-weather summer weekends). If you play the recorder (and no other tourists are there), ask to finger a tune while the piper does the hard work. At the end of the valley, you hit the vast Rannoch Moor—500 desolate square miles with barely enough decent land to graze a sheep.

Glencoe Visitors Centre—This modern facility, a mile into the dramatic valley on A82, is designed to resemble a *clachan*, or traditional Highlands settlement. The information desk inside the shop is your single best resource for advice (and maps or guidebooks) about local walks and hikes, some of which are described below. At the back of the complex, you'll find a viewpoint with a handy 3-D model for orientation. There's also a pricey £5 exhibition about the surrounding landscape, local history, mountaineering, and conservation. It's worth the time to watch the more-interesting-than-it-sounds video on geology, and the 14-minute film on the Glencoe Massacre, which thoughtfully traces the events leading up to the tragedy rather than simply recycling romanticized legends (April–Aug daily 9:30–17:30; Sept–Oct daily 10:00–17:00; Nov–March Thu–Sun 10:00–16:00, closed Mon–Wed; tel. 01855/811-307).

Walks—For a steep one-mile hike, climb the Devil's Staircase (trailhead just off A82, 8 miles east of Glencoe). For a three-hour hike, ask at the Visitors Centre about the Lost Valley of the MacDonalds (trailhead just off A82, 3 miles east of Glencoe). For an easy walk above Glencoe, head to the mansion on the hill (over the bridge, turn left, fine loch views). This mansion was built in 1894 by Canadian Pacific Railway magnate Lord Strathcona for his wife, a Canadian with First Nations (Indian) ancestry. She was homesick for the Rockies, so he had the grounds landscaped to represent the lakes, trees, and mountains of her home country. It didn't work, and they eventually returned to British Columbia. The house originally had 365 windows to allow a different view each day.

Glencoe's Burial Island and Island of Discussion—In the loch just outside Glencoe (near Ballachulish), notice the burial island—where the souls of those who "take the low road" are piped home. (Ask a local about "Ye'll take the high road, and I'll take the low road.") The next island was the Island of Discussion—where those in dispute went until they found agreement.

SLEEPING

(£1 = about $2, country code: 44, area code: 01855)

Glencoe is an extremely low-key place to spend the night between Oban or Glasgow and the northern destinations. These places are accustomed to one-nighters just passing through, but some people stay here for several days to enjoy a variety of hikes. All of these B&Bs are along the main road through the middle of the village, and all are cash-only.

$$ Inchconnal B&B is a cute house with a bonnie wee garden out front, renting three bright, woody rooms (Sb-£22, Db-£44, tel. 01855/811-958, warm Caroline Macdonald).

$$ Heatherlea B&B, at the end of the village, has three pleasant, modern rooms and homey public spaces (Sb-£22, Db-£44, closed Nov–Easter, tel. 01855/811-799, ivan-thea.heatherlea @tiscali.co.uk, Ivan and Thea).

$$ Tulachgorm B&B has two spacious, comfortable rooms that share a bathroom in a modern house with fine mountain views (D-£34–40, soft prices off-season, on the village's main street, tel. 01855/811-391, mellow Ann Blake).

EATING

The choices in and near Glencoe are slim—this isn't the place for fine dining. But three options offer decent food a short walk or drive away. For evening fun, take a walk or ask your B&B host where to find music and dancing.

In Glencoe: The best choice in Glencoe village itself is **The Carnoch,** with happy diners tucked into a small modern house a few steps off the main street (£8–9 main dishes, daily in summer 11:00–21:00, closed for Sun dinner and all day Mon in winter, tel. 01855/811-140).

Near Glencoe: **Clachaig Inn** is a Highlands pub whose clientele is half locals and half tourists. This unpretentious place features billiards, jukeboxes, and pub grub (£7–10 main dishes, open daily for lunch and dinner, tel. 01855/811-252). Drive down the little road over the bridge at the end of Glencoe village, and follow it about five minutes until you reach the pub's big parking lot on the right.

In Ballachulish, near Glencoe: **Laroch Bar & Bistro,** in the next village over from Glencoe (towards Oban), is serene and family-friendly (£7–8 pub grub, tel. 01855/811-900). Drive into Ballachulish village, and you'll see it on the left.

TRANSPORTATION CONNECTIONS

Unfortunately, buses don't actually drive down the main road through Glencoe village. Some buses (most notably those going between Glasgow and Fort William) stop near Glencoe village at a place called **"Glencoe Crossroads"**—a short walk into the village center. Other buses (such as those between Oban and Fort William) stop at the nearby town of **Ballachulish,** which is just a half-mile away (or a £3 taxi ride). Let the driver know where you're going ("Glencoe village") and ask to be let off as close to there as possible.

From **Glencoe Crossroads,** you can catch bus #914, #915, or #916 (7/day) to **Fort William** (30 min) or **Glasgow** (2.5 hrs).

From **Ballachulish,** you can take bus #918 (4/day in summer, 2/day off-season, never on Sun) to **Fort William** (30 min) or **Oban** (1 hr).

To reach **Inverness** or **Portree** on the Isle of Skye, transfer in Fort William. To reach **Edinburgh,** transfer in Glasgow.

Near Glencoe: Fort William

Laying claim to the title of "outdoor capital," Fort William is well-positioned between Oban, Inverness, and the Isle of Skye. This crossroads town is a transportation hub and has a pleasant-enough, shop-studded, pedestrianized main drag, but few charms of its own. Most visitors just pass through...and should. But while you're here, consider buying lunch and stopping by the TI to get your questions answered.

Tourist Information: The TI is at the top of the town's main square, Cameron Square (Easter–Oct Mon–Sat 9:00–18:00, Sun 10:00–16:00; Nov–Easter Mon–Fri 9:00–17:00, Sat 10:00–16:00, closed Sun; Internet access, free public WCs behind building, tel. 01397/703-781).

SIGHTS

Fort William has no real sights, aside from a humble but well-presented **West Highland Museum,** with exhibits on local history, wildlife, dress, and more (£3, guidebook-£2.50; June–Sept Mon–Sat 10:00–17:00, July–Aug also Sun 14:00–17:00; Oct–May Mon–Sat 10:00–16:00, closed Sun; next to TI on Cameron Square, tel. 01397/702-169, www.westhighlandmuseum.org.uk). Two other appealing options lie just outside of town.

Glencoe

Ben Nevis

From Fort William, take a peek at Britain's highest peak, Ben Nevis (more than 4,408 feet). Thousands walk to its summit each year. On a clear day, you can admire it from a distance. Scotland's only mountain cable cars—at the **Nevis Range Mountain Experience**—can take you to a not-very-lofty 2,150-foot perch for a closer look (£8.50, daily July–Aug 9:30–18:00, Sept–June 10:00–17:00, 15-min ride, signposted on A82 north of Fort William, tel. 01397/705-825).

Toward the Isle of Skye: The Road to the Isles and the Jacobite Steam Train

The magical steam train that scenically transports Harry Potter to the wizard school of Hogwarts runs along a real-life train line. The West Highland Railway Line runs 42 miles from Fort William west to the ferry port at Mallaig. Along the way, it passes the iconic **Glenfinnan Viaduct,** with 416 yards of raised track over 21 supporting arches. This route is also graced with plenty of loch-and-mountain views, and near the end, passes along a beautiful stretch of coast with some fine sandy beaches. While many people take the Jacobite Steam Train to enjoy this stretch of Scotland, it can be more rewarding to drive the same route—especially if you're headed for the Isle of Skye.

By Train: The **Jacobite Steam Train** (they don't actually call it the "Hogwarts Express") offers a small taste of the Harry Potter experience...but many who take this trip are disappointed. Doing the round-trip from Fort William takes the better part of the day to show you the same scenery twice. Unfortunately for HP fans, the train company seems nearly oblivious to the Harry Potter connection—they make virtually no effort to tie the ride to the films...so don't expect a theme ride. Along the way, the train stops for 20 minutes at Glenfinnan station (just after the Glenfinnan Viaduct), and then gives you two hours (way too much time) to poke around the dull port town of Mallaig before heading back to Fort William (one-way—£20.50 adults, £12 kids; round-trip—£28 adults, £16 kids; 1/day Mon–Fri late-May–mid-Oct, also Sat–Sun July–Aug, departs Fort William at 10:20 and returns at 16:00, 3.75 hours each way; modern "Sprinter" trains follow the same line more frequently and off-season—consider taking the steam train one-way to Mallaig, then speeding back on a Sprinter to avoid the long Mallaig layover and slow return; book at least two days ahead July–Aug, www.steamtrain.info, tel. 01524/737-751). Note that you can use this train to reach the Isle of Skye: Take the train to Mallaig, walk onto the ferry to Armadale (on Skye), then catch a bus in Armadale to your destination on Skye.

Glencoe

By Car: While the train is time-consuming and expensive, driving the same **"Road to the Isles"** route (A830)—ideally on your way to Skye—can be a fun way to see the same famous scenery more affordably and efficiently. The key here is to be sure you leave enough time to make it to Mallaig before the Skye ferry departs—get timing advice from the Fort William TI. I'd allow at least an hour to get from Fort William to the ferry landing in Mallaig (if you keep moving, with no stops en route)—and note that vehicles are required to arrive 30 minutes before the boat departs. As you pace yourself, be warned that the road is well-paved and speedy most of the way to Mallaig, but becomes rough and narrow near the end (though they're working on improving this last stretch). As you leave Fort William on A830, a sign on the left tells you what time the next ferry will depart Mallaig. For more tips on the Mallaig-Armadale ferry, see "Getting to the Isle of Skye" on page 570.

SLEEPING

In Fort William, these two B&Bs are on Union Road, a five-minute walk up the hill above the main pedestrian street that runs through the heart of town. Each place has three rooms, one of which has a private bathroom on the hall.

$$ Glenmorven Guest House is a friendly, family-run place with views of Loch Linnhe (Db-£50, discounts for 2 or more nights, Union Road, Fort William, tel. 01397/703-236, www .glenmorven.co.uk, glenmorven@yahoo.com, Anne Jamieson).

$$ Gowan Brae B&B ("Hill of the Big Daisy") has three classy rooms in a hobbit-cute house (Db-£50, or £54 June–Aug, tel. 01397/704-399, www.gowanbrae.co.uk).

EATING

Fort William is a popular lunch stop. These two places are a few doors down from each other on the main walking street, near the start of town.

Hot Roast Company sells beef, turkey, ham, or pork sandwiches, topped with some tasty extras (£3 take-away, a bit more for sit-down service, Mon–Sat 9:30–15:30, closed Sun, 127 High Street, tel. 01397/700-606).

Café 115 features good food and modern decor (£5–7 sandwiches, £6–8 main dishes, daily 10:00–18:00, maybe also for dinner Fri–Sat, 115 High Street, tel. 01397/702-500).

Glencoe

TRANSPORTATION CONNECTIONS

Fort William is a major transit hub for the Highlands—so you'll likely change buses here at some point during your trip.

From Fort William by Bus to: Glencoe (all Glasgow-bound buses— #914, #915, and #916; 7/day, 30 min), **Ballachulish** near Glencoe (Oban-bound bus #918, 4/day in summer, 2/day off-season, never on Sun, 30 min), **Oban** (bus #918, 4/day in summer, 2/day off-season, never on Sun, 1.5 hrs), **Portree** on the Isle of Skye (buses #915 and #916, 3/day, 3 hrs), **Inverness** (bus #919 or #19, 7/day Mon–Fri, 6/day Sat, 5/day Sun, 2 hrs), **Glasgow** (buses #914, #915, and #916; 7/day, 3 hrs), **Edinburgh** (bus #913, 1/day direct, 4 hrs; more with a transfer in Glasgow).

Route Tips for Drivers

England's Lake District to Glasgow: From Keswick, take A66 for 18 miles to M6 and speed north nonstop (via Penrith and Carlisle), crossing Hadrian's Wall into Scotland. The road becomes M74 south of Glasgow. To slip quickly through Glasgow, leave M74 at Junction 4 onto M73, following signs to M8/Glasgow. Leave M73 at Junction 2, exiting onto M8. Stay on M8 west through Glasgow, exit on Junction 30, cross Erskine Bridge, and turn left on A82, following signs to *Crianlarich* and *Loch Lomond*. (For a scenic drive through Glasgow, take exit 17 off M8 and stay on A82 toward Dumbarton.)

Glasgow to Oban: Note that the best stopovers along this route are described in greater detail on page 548. Leaving Glasgow on A82, you'll soon be driving along scenic **Loch Lomond.** The first picnic turnout has the best lake views, benches, a park, and a playground. Halfway up the loch, at Tarbet, take the "tourist route" left onto A83, driving along Loch Long toward Inveraray via **Rest-and-Be-Thankful Pass. Inveraray** makes for an enjoyable break or lunch stop. Leaving Inveraray, drive through a gate (at the Woolen Mill) to A819, through Glen Aray, and along Loch Awe. A85 takes you into Oban.

Oban to Glencoe and Fort William: From Oban, follow coastal A828 toward Fort William. After about 20 miles, you'll see the photogenic Castle Staulker marooned on a lonely island. At North Ballachulish, you'll reach a bridge spanning Loch Leven; rather than crossing the bridge, turn off and follow A82 into Glencoe valley (see page 560). After exploring the valley, make a U-turn and return through Glencoe. To continue on to Fort William, backtrack to the bridge at North Ballachulish and cross it, following A82 north. (For a scenic shortcut directly back to Glasgow or Edinburgh, head north only as far as Glencoe, and then cut to Glasgow or Edinburgh on A82 via Rannoch Moor and Tyndrum.)

Fort William to Loch Ness and Inverness: Follow the Caledonian Canal north along A82, which goes through Fort Augustus (and its worthwhile Caledonian Canal Heritage Centre—see page 599) and then follows the west side of Loch Ness on its way to Inverness. Along the way, A82 passes Urquhart Castle and two Loch Ness Monster exhibits in Drumnadrochit (for more on Loch Ness sights, see page 597).

Fort William to the Isle of Skye: You have two options for this journey: Head west on A830 (the Road to the Isles), then catch the ferry from Mallaig to Armadale on the Isle of Skye (described on page 570); or head north on A82 to Invergarry, and turn left (west) on A87, which you'll follow (past Eilean Donan Castle—see page 580) to Kyle of Lochalsh and the Skye Bridge to the island. Consider using one route one way, and the other on the return trip—for example, follow the Road to the Isles from Fort William to Mallaig, take the ferry to Skye; later, leaving Skye, take A87 east from the Skye Bridge past Eilean Donan Castle to Loch Ness and Inverness.

Glencoe

ISLE OF SKYE

The rugged, remote-feeling Isle of Skye has a reputation for unpredictable weather ("Skye" means "cloudy" in Old Norse, and locals call it "The Misty Isle"). But it also offers some of Scotland's best scenery, and it rarely fails to charm its many visitors. Narrow, twisty roads wind around Skye in the shadows of craggy, black, bald mountains.

Skye seems to have a lot more sheep than people; 200 years ago, many human residents were forced to move off the island to make room for more livestock during the Highland Clearances. The people who remain are some of the most ardently Gaelic Scots in Scotland. The island's Sleat peninsula is home to a rustic but important Gaelic college. Half of all island residents speak Gaelic (which they pronounce "gallic") as their first language. A generation ago, it was illegal to teach Gaelic in schools; today, Skye offers its residents the opportunity to enroll in Gaelic-only education, from primary school to college. You may just meet one of the very few Gaelic-speaking teenagers on the planet.

Set up camp in one of the island's home-base towns, Portree or Kyleakin. Then dive into Skye's attractions. Drive around the appealing Trotternish Peninsula, enjoying stark vistas of jagged rock formations with the mysterious Outer Hebrides looming on the horizon. Explore a gaggle of old-fashioned stone homes, learn about Skye's ancient farming lifestyles, and pay homage at the grave of a brave woman who rescued a bonnie prince. Climb the dramatic Cuillin Hills, and drive to a lighthouse at the end of the world. Visit a pair of castles—run-down but thought-provoking Dunvegan, and nearby but not on Skye, the photo-perfect Eilean Donan.

Isle of Skye

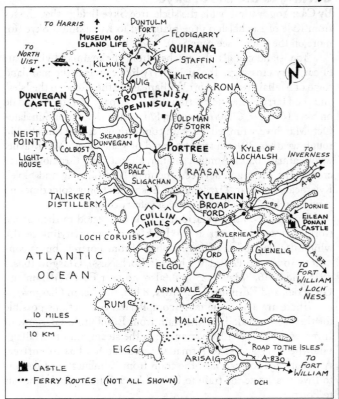

TO HARRIS
DUNTULM FORT
FLODIGARRY
TO NORTH UIST
MUSEUM OF ISLAND LIFE
QUIRANG
STAFFIN
KILMUIR
KILT ROCK
UIG
RONA
TROTTERNISH PENINSULA
DUNVEGAN CASTLE
OLD MAN OF STORR
NEIST POINT
SKEABOST
DUNVEGAN
PORTREE
KYLE OF LOCHALSH
TO INVERNESS
LIGHTHOUSE
COLBOST
RAASAY
A-890
BRACADALE
SLIGACHAN
TALISKER DISTILLERY
KYLEAKIN
BROAD-FORD
A-87
DORNIE
EILEAN DONAN CASTLE
CUILLIN HILLS
A-87
LOCH CORUISK
KYLERHEA
ATLANTIC
ORD
GLENELG
A-87
OCEAN
ELGOL
TO FORT WILLIAM & LOCH NESS
ARMADALE
10 MILES
10 KM
RUM
MALLAIG
Isle of Skye
EIGG
"ROAD TO THE ISLES"
ARISAIG
A-830
TO FORT WILLIAM
🏰 CASTLE
••• FERRY ROUTES (NOT ALL SHOWN)
DCH

Planning Your Time

With a week in Scotland, Skye merits two nights, with a full day to hit its highlights (Trotternish Peninsula, Dunvegan Castle, Cuillin Hills). Mountaineers enjoy extra time for hiking and hill-walking. Because it takes time to reach, Skye (the northernmost destination in this book) is skippable if you only have a few days in Scotland—instead, focus on Edinburgh and the more accessible Highlands sights near Oban.

Skye fits neatly into a Highlands itinerary between Oban/Glencoe and Loch Ness/Inverness. To avoid seeing the same scenery twice, it works well to drive the "Road to the Isles" from Fort William to Mallaig, then take the ferry to Skye (for details, see next page); leave Skye via the Skye Bridge and follow A87 east toward Loch Ness and Inverness, stopping at Eilean Donan Castle en route.

Getting to the Isle of Skye

By Car: Your easiest bet is the slick, free **Skye Bridge** that crosses from Kyle of Lochalsh on the mainland to Kyleakin on Skye (for more on the bridge, see page 579).

The island can also be reached from the mainland via a pair of **car ferry** crossings. The major ferry line connects the mainland town of Mallaig (west of Fort William along the "Road to the Isles" and the Harry Potter steam-train line—see page 564) to Armadale on Skye (£20/car, £3.50/passenger, 8/day each way, fewer Sun, late-Oct–March very limited Sat–Sun connections, can be cancelled in rough weather, 30-min trip, operated by Caledonian MacBrayne, www.calmac.co.uk). A much smaller, almost cute "turntable" ferry crosses the short gap between the mainland Glenelg and Skye's Kylerhea (£8.50/car, £1/passenger, Easter–Oct only, sometimes no service on Sun, Skye Ferry, www.skyeferry.co.uk).

By Public Transportation: Skye is connected to the outside world by a series of Scottish CityLink **buses** (www.citylink.co.uk), which use Portree as their Skye hub. From Portree, buses connect to **Inverness** (2–3/day, 3 hrs, via Loch Ness), **Glasgow** (buses #915 and #916, 3/day, 9.25 hrs), also stops at **Fort William** and **Glencoe**), and **Edinburgh** (2–3/day, 8 hrs, transfer in Glasgow).

There are also some more complicated connections possible for the determined: Take the train from Edinburgh, Glasgow, or Inverness to Fort William; transfer to the steam train to Mallaig; take the ferry across to Armadale; and catch a bus to Portree. Alternatively, you can take the train from Edinburgh or Glasgow to Inverness, take the train to Kyle of Lochalsh, then take the bus to Portree.

Getting Around the Isle of Skye

By Car: Once on Skye, a car is essential to enjoy the island. (Even if you're doing the rest of your trip by public transportation, a car rental is cheap and worthwhile to bypass the frustrating public-transportation options; I've listed some car-rental options in Portree, page 581). If you're driving, a good map is a must (look for a 1:130,000 map that covers the entire island with enough detail to point out side roads and attractions). You'll be surprised how long it takes to traverse this "small" island. Here are driving-time estimates for some likely trips: Kyleakin and Skye Bridge to Portree—45 min; Portree to Dunvegan—30 min; Portree to the tip of Trotternish Peninsula and back again—1.5–2 hours; Uig (on Trotternish Peninsula) to Dunvegan—45 min.

By Bus: Skye is frustrating by bus, especially on Sundays—when virtually no local buses run (except for a few long-distance buses to the ferry dock and mainland destinations). Portree is the hub for local bus traffic. Most Skye buses are operated by Highland

Country Buses (tel. 01463/710-555, www.rapsons.co.uk). If you'll be using local buses a lot, consider a Skye Roverbus ticket (£6/1 day, £15/3 days). From Portree, you can go around the **Trotternish Peninsula** (6/day in each direction—clockwise and counter-clockwise), to **Dunvegan** (4–5/day, goes right to the castle, use the 10:00 or 12:00 to get to the castle in time to tour it), and to **Kyleakin** (at least hourly Mon–Fri, fewer Sat–Sun, possible transfer in Broadford). Remember, none of these buses runs on Sunday.

By Tour: If you're without a car, consider taking a tour. Several operations on the island take visitors to hard-to-reach spots on a half-day or full-day tour. Some are more educational, while others are loose and informal. Look for brochures around the island, or ask locals for tips. For example, the Aros Center near Portree does three-hour tours twice daily (£12, can pick you up in Portree, reserve ahead by calling 01478/613-649).

ORIENTATION

The Isle of Skye is big (over 600 square miles), with lots of ins and outs—but you're never more than five miles from the sea. The island is punctuated by peninsulas and inlets (called "sea lochs"). The island is covered with hills, but the most striking are the mountain-like Cuillin Hills in the south-central part of the island.

There are only about 11,000 people on the entire island, roughly a quarter of whom live in the main village, Portree. Other population centers include Kyleakin (near the bridge connecting Skye with the mainland) and Broadford (a ho-hum string of houses on the road between Portree and the bridge).

A few of the villages—including Broadford and Dunvegan—have TIs, but the most useful is in Portree (see page 581).

The Trotternish Peninsula

This inviting peninsula north of Portree is packed with windswept castaway scenery, unique geological formations, and some offbeat sights. In good weather, a spin around Trotternish is the single best Skye activity (and you'll still have time to visit Dunvegan Castle or the Cuillin Hills later on).

SELF-GUIDED DRIVING TOUR

The following loop tour starts and ends in Portree, circling the peninsula counterclockwise. If you did it without stopping, you'd make it back to Portree within two hours—but it deserves the better part of a day.

Isle of Skye

Begin in the island's main town, Portree. (If you're heading up from Kyleakin, you'll enjoy some grand views of the Cuillin Hills on your way up—especially around the crossroads of Sligachan, described on page 576.) For sightseeing information on Portree—and the nearby Aros visitors center—see page 582.

• *Head north of Portree on A855, following signs for Staffin. About three miles out of town, you'll begin to enjoy some impressive views of the Trotternish Ridge. As you pass the small loch on your right, straight ahead is the distinctive feature called the...*

Old Man of Storr: This 160-foot-tall tapered volcanic plug stands proudly apart from the rest of the Storr. The lochs on your right have been linked together to spin the turbines at a nearby hydroelectric plant that once provided all of Skye's electricity.

• *After passing the Old Man, enjoy the scenery on your right, overlooking...*

Nearby Islands and the Mainland: Some of Skye's most appealing scenery isn't of the island itself, but of the surrounding terrain. In the distance, craggy mountains recede into the horizon. The long island in the foreground, a bit to the north, is called Rona. This military-owned island, and the channel behind it, were used to develop and test one of Margaret Thatcher's pet projects, the Sting Ray remote-control torpedo.

• *After about five miles, keep an eye out on the right for a large parking lot near a wee loch. Park and walk to the viewpoint to see...*

Kilt Rock: So named because of its resemblance to a Scotsman's tartan kilt, this 200-foot-tall sea cliff has a layer of volcanic rock with vertical lava columns that resemble pleats, sitting atop a layer of horizontal sedimentary rock.

• *After continuing through the village of Staffin (whose name means "the pinnacle place"), you'll begin to see interesting rock formations high on the hill to your left. When you get to the crossroads, head left toward Quiraing (a rock formation). This crossroads is a handy pit stop—the Pieces of Ate snack bar sells hot or cold sandwiches for £2–3 (Sun 11:00–15:00, Tue–Thu 10:30–16:30, Fri–Sat 10:30–20:00, closed Mon, tel. 01470/562-787), and there's a public WC in the little white building behind the red phone box just up the main road.*

Now twist your way up the road to...

Quiraing: As you drive up, notice (on your left) a couple of modern cemeteries high in the hills, far above the village. It seems like a strange spot to bury the dead, in the middle of nowhere, but the earth here is less valuable for development, and (since it's not clay, like down by the water) it provides better drainage.

You'll enjoy fine views on the right of the jagged, dramatic northern end of the Trotternish Ridge, called the Quiraing—rated ▲▲. Each rock formation has a name, such as "The Needle" or "The Prison." As you approach the summit of this road, you'll reach a parking area on the left. This marks a popular trailhead for hik-

ing out to get a closer look at the formations. If you've got the time, energy, and weather for a sturdy 30-minute uphill hike, here's your chance. You can either follow the trail along the base of the rock formations, or hike up to the top of the plateau and follow it to the end (both paths are faintly visible from the parking area). Once up top, your reward is a view of the secluded green plateau called "The Table," which isn't visible from the road.

• *You could continue on this road all the way to Uig, at the other end of the peninsula. But it's worth backtracking, then turning left onto the main road (A855), to see the...*

Tip of Trotternish: A few miles north, you'll pass a hotel called **Flodigarry,** with a cottage on the premises that was once home to Bonnie Prince Charlie's rescuer, Flora MacDonald (see page 574; cottage not open to the public or worth visiting).

Soon after, at the top of the ridge at the tip of the peninsula, you'll see the remains of an old **fort**—not from the Middle Ages or the days of Bonnie Prince Charlie, but from World War II, when the Atlantic was monitored for U-boats from this position.

Then you'll pass (on the right) the remains of another fort, this one much older: **Duntulm Castle,** which was the first stronghold on Skye of the influential MacDonald clan. In the distance beyond, you can see the **Outer Hebrides**—the most rugged, remote, and Gaelic part of Scotland. (Skye, a bit closer to the mainland, belongs to the Inner Hebrides.)

• *A mile after the castle, you'll come to a place called Kilmuir. Watch for the turn-off on the left to the excellent...*

Museum of Island Life: This fine little stand of seven thatched stone huts, organized into a family-run museum and worth ▲▲, explains how a typical Skye family lived a century and a half ago (£2.50, Easter–Oct Mon–Sat 9:30–17:00, until 16:00 in

Oct or when slow, closed Sun and Nov–Easter, tel. 01470/552-206). While there are ample posted explanations, the £1.25 guidebook is worthwhile.

The three huts closest to the sea are original (more than 200 years old). Most interesting is the one called The Old Croft House, which was the residence of the Graham family until 1957. Inside you'll find three rooms: kitchen (with peat-burning fire) on the right; parents' bedroom in the middle; and a bedroom for the 12 kids on the left. Nearby, The Old Barn displays farm implements, and the Ceilidh House contains some dense but very informative displays about crofting (the traditional tenant-farmer lifestyle on Skye—explained below), Gaelic, and other topics.

The four other huts were reconstructed here from elsewhere on the island, and now house exhibits about weaving and the village smithy (which was actually a gathering place for villagers). As you explore, admire the smart architecture of these humble but deceptively well-planned structures. Rocks hanging from the roof keep the thatch from blowing away, and the streamlined shape of the structure embedded in the ground encourages strong winds to deflect around the hut rather than hit it head-on.

• *After touring the museum, drive out to the very end of the small road that leads past the parking lot, to a lonesome cemetery. The tallest Celtic cross at the far end of the cemetery (you can enter the gate to reach it) is the...*

Monument to Flora MacDonald: This local heroine supposedly rescued beloved Scottish hero Bonnie Prince Charlie at his darkest hour. After his loss at Culloden, and with a hefty price on his head, Charlie retreated to the Outer Hebrides—but the Hanover dynasty, who controlled the islands, was closing in. Flora

MacDonald rescued him, disguised him as her Irish maid, Betty Burke, and sailed him to safety on Skye. (Charlie pulled off the ruse thanks to his soft, feminine features—hence the nickname "Bonnie," which means "beautiful.") The flight inspired a popular Scottish folk song: *Speed bonnie boat like a bird on the wing, / Onward, the sailors cry. / Carry the lad that's born to be king / Over the sea to Skye.* For more on Bonnie Prince Charlie, see page 602.

• *Return to the main road, and proceed*

about six miles around the peninsula. On the right, notice the big depression.

The Missing Loch: This was once a large loch, but was drained in the mid-20th century to create more grazing land for sheep. If you look closely, you may see a scattering of stones in the middle of the field. Once an island, this is the site of a former monastery...now left as high, dry, and forgotten as the loch. Beyond the missing loch is Prince Charlie's Point, where the bonnie prince supposedly came ashore on Skye with Flora MacDonald.

• *Soon after the loch, you'll drop down over the town of...*

Uig: Pronounced "OO-eeg," this village is the departure point for ferries to the Outer Hebrides (North Uist and Harris islands, 3/day). It's otherwise unremarkable, but does have a café with good £3 sandwiches (follow *Uig Pier* signs into town, blue building with white *café* sign, next to ferry terminal at entrance to town).

• *Continue past Uig, climbing the hill across the bay. Near the top is a large parking strip on the right. Pull over here and look back to Uig for a lesson about Skye's traditional farming system.*

Crofting: You'll hear a lot about crofts during your time on Skye. Traditionally, arable land on the island was divided into plots. If you look across to the hills above Uig, you can see strips of demarcated land running up from the water—these are crofts.

Crofts were generally owned by landlords (mostly English aristocrats or Scottish clan chiefs, and later the Scottish government) and rented to tenant farmers. The crofters lived and worked under very difficult conditions, and were lucky if they could produce enough potatoes, corn, and livestock to feed their family. Rights to farm the croft were passed down from father to son over generations, but always under the auspices of a wealthy landlord.

Finally, in 1976, new legislation kicked off a process of privatization called "decrofting." Suddenly a crofter could have their land decrofted, then buy it for an affordable price (£130 per quarter-hectare, or about £8,000 for one of the crofts you see here). Many decroftees would quickly turn around and sell their old family home for a huge profit, but hang on to most of their land and build a new house at the other end. In the crofts you see here, notice that some have a house at the top of a strip of land, and another house at the bottom. Many crofts (like most of these) are no longer cultivated, but a new law might require crofters to farm their land... or lose it. In many cases, families who have other jobs still hang on to their traditional croft, which they use to grow produce for themselves or to supplement their income.

• *Our tour is finished. From here, you can continue along the main road south toward Portree (and possibly continue from there on to the Cuillin Hills). Or, take the shortcut road just after Kensaleyre (B8036), and head west on A850 to Dunvegan and its castle (both options described below).*

More Sights on the Isle of Skye

▲▲Cuillin Hills

These dramatic, rocky "hills" (which look more like mountains to me) stretch along the southern coast of the island, dominating Skye's landscape. More craggy and alpine than anything else you'll see in Scotland, the Cuillin seem to rise directly from the deep. You'll see them from just about anywhere on the southern two-thirds of the island, but no roads actually take you through the heart of the Cuillin—that's reserved for hikers and climbers (who love this area). To get the best views with a car, consider these options:

Near Sligachan: The road from the Skye Bridge to Portree is the easiest way to appreciate the Cuillin (you'll almost certainly drive along here at some point during your visit). As you approach, you'll clearly see that there are three separate ranges (from right to left): red, gray, and black. (The steep and challenging Black Cuillin are the most popular for serious climbers.) The crossroads of Sligachan, with an old triple-arched bridge and a landmark hotel (see page 583), is nestled at the foothills of the Cuillin, and is a popular launchpad for mountain fun. The 2,500-foot-tall, cone-shaped hill looming over Sligachan, named Glamaig ("Greedy Lady"), is the site of an annual competition (July 13 in 2008): speed hikers begin at the door of the Sligachan Hotel, race to the summit, run around a bagpiper, and scramble back down to the hotel. The record: 46 minutes (30 minutes up, 15 minutes down, 1 minute dancing a jig up top).

Elgol: For the best view of the Cuillin, locals swear by the drive from Bradford (on the Portree-Kyleakin road) to Elgol, at the tip of a small peninsula that faces the Black Cuillin head-on. While it's just 12 miles as the crow flies from Sligachan, give it a half-hour each way to drive into Elgol from Broadford. To get an even better Cuillin experience, take a boat excursion from Elgol into Loch Coruisk, a "sea loch" (fjord) surrounded by the Cuillin (various companies do the trip several times a day, few or no trips on Sun and off-season, generally 3 hours round-trip including 1.5

hours free time on the shore of the loch, figure £13 round-trip).

▲Dunvegan Castle

Perched on a rock overlooking a sea loch, this past-its-prime castle is a strange and intriguing artifact of Scotland's antiquated, nearly extinct clan system. Dunvegan Castle is the residence of the MacLeod (pronounced "McCloud") clan—along with the

MacDonalds, one of Skye's preeminent clans. Worth ▲▲▲ to people named MacLeod, and mildly interesting to anyone else, this is a good way to pass the time on a rainy day.

Cost and Hours: £7.50. Consider picking up the £2 guidebook by the late chief. Daily mid-March–Oct 10:00–17:00, Nov–mid-March 11:00–16:00, tel. 01470/521-206, www.dunvegancastle .com.

Getting There: It's near the small town of Dunvegan in the northwestern part of the island, well-signposted from A850. You can also get there by bus (the 10:00 or 12:00 departures from Portree get you there in time to tour the castle). As you approach Dunvegan on A850, the two flat-topped plateaus you'll see are nicknamed "MacLeod's Tables."

Background: In Gaelic, *clann* means "children," and the clan system was the traditional Scottish way of passing along power—similar to England's dukes, barons, and counts. Each clan traces its roots to an ancestral castle, like Dunvegan. The MacLeods (or, as they prefer, "MacLeod of MacLeod") have fallen on hard times. Having run out of male heirs in 1935, Dame Flora MacLeod of MacLeod became the 28th clan chief. Her grandson, John MacLeod of MacLeod became the 29th chief after her death in 1976. Their castle is rough around the edges, and to raise money to fix the leaky roof, John MacL of MacL actually pondered selling the Black Cuillin ridge of hills (which technically belong to him) to an American tycoon for £10 million a few years back. The deal fell through, and the chief passed away in early 2007. Now his son Hugh Magnus MacLeod of MacLeod, in his mid-thirties, has become clan chief of the MacLeods.

○ **Self-Guided Tour:** The interior feels a bit shoddy and run-down, but the MacLeods proudly display their family heritage—old photographs and portraits of former chiefs. You'll wander through halls, the dining room, the library, and past the dungeon's deep pit. In the **Drawing Room,** look for the tattered remains of the Fairy Flag, a mysterious swatch with about a dozen different

Isle of Skye

legends attached to it (most say that it was a gift from a fairy, and somehow related to the Crusades). It's said that the clan chief can invoke the power of the flag three times, in the clan's darkest moments. It's worked twice before on the battlefield—which means there's just one use left.

The most interesting tidbits are in the **North Room.** The family's coat of arms (in the middle of the carpet) has a confused-looking bull and the clan motto, "Hold Fast"—recalling an incident where a MacLeod saved a man from being gored by a bull when he grabbed its horns and forced it to stop. In the case nearby, find the Dunvegan Cup and the Horn of Rory Mor. Traditionally, this horn would be filled with a half-gallon of claret (Bordeaux wine), which a potential heir had to drink without falling down to prove himself fit for the role. (The late chief, John MacLeod of MacLeod, bragged that he did it in less than two minutes...but you have to wonder if Dame Flora chug-a-lugged.) Other artifacts in the North Room include bagpipes and several relics related to Bonnie Prince Charlie (including a lock of his hair and several items belonging to Flora MacDonald).

At the end of the tour, you can wander out onto the **terrace** (overlooking a sea loch) and, in the cellar, watch a stuffy **video** about the clan. Between the castle and the parking lot are some enjoyable **gardens** to stroll through while pondering the fading clan system.

The flaunting of inherited wealth and influence in some English castles rubs me the wrong way. But here, seeing the rough edges of a Scottish clan chief's castle, I had the opposite feeling: sympathy and compassion for a proud way of life that's slipping into the sunset of history. You have to admire the way that they "hold fast" to this antiquated system (in the same way the Gaelic tongue is kept on life support). Paying admission here feels more like donating to charity than padding the pockets of a wealthy family. By the way, if the Scottish fixation on clans and chiefs seems odd to you, consider that it's kept alive in part by us Americans: watered-down McClouds and McDonalds in the US eager to reconnect with their Scottish roots.

▲Neist Point and Lighthouse

To get a truly edge-of-the-world feeling, consider an adventure on the back lanes of the Duirinish Peninsula, west of Dunvegan. This trip is best for hardy drivers looking to explore the most remote corner of Skye and undertake a strenuous hike to a lighthouse. (The lighthouse itself is a letdown, so do this only if you believe a journey is its own reward.) While it looks close on the map, give this trip 30 minutes each way from Dunvegan, plus 30 minutes or more for the lighthouse hike.

Head west from Dunvegan, following signs for *Glendale.* You'll cross a moor, then twist around the Dunvegan sea loch, before heading overland and passing through rugged and desolate hamlets that seem like the setting for a BBC sitcom about backwater Britain. After passing through Glendale, carefully track *Neist Point* signs until you reach an end-of-the-road parking lot. The owner of this private property has signs on his padlocked gate stating that you enter at your own risk—which many walkers happily do. (It's laughably easy to walk around the pitiful "wall.") From here, you enjoy sheep and cliff views, but can't see the lighthouse itself unless you do the sturdy 30-minute hike (with a steep uphill return). After hiking around the cliff, the lighthouse springs into view, with the Outer Hebrides beyond.

It's efficient and fun to combine this trek with lunch or dinner at the **Three Chimneys Restaurant,** on the road to Neist Point at Colbost (reservations essential; see page 584).

Talisker Distillery

If you have time to kill, and aren't visiting a whisky distillery elsewhere in Scotland, consider a tour of this one in Carbost (£5, Easter–Oct Mon–Sat 9:30–17:00, last tour at 16:00, closed Sun except in July–Aug when it's open 12:30–17:00, last tour at 16:00; Nov–Easter by appointment only, call ahead; tel. 01478/614-308).

Skye Bridge

While it's not really a "sight," the Skye Bridge—which you'll almost certainly cross on your visit—comes with an interesting history for such a recent construction. Connecting Kyleakin on Skye with Kyle of Lochalsh on the mainland, the new bridge severely damaged B&B business in the towns it connects. And environmentalists worry about the bridge disrupting the habitat for otters—keep an eye out for these furry native residents. But it's been a boon for Skye tourism—making a quick visit to the island possible without having to wait for a ferry.

The bridge, which was Europe's most expensive toll bridge when it opened in 1995, has stirred up a remarkable amount of controversy among island-dwellers. Here's the Skye natives' take on things: A generation ago, Lowlanders (city folk) began selling their urban homes and buying cheap property on Skye. Natives had grown to enjoy the slow-paced lifestyle that came with living life according to the whim of the ferry, but these new transplants found their commute into civilization too frustrating by boat. They demanded a new bridge be built. Finally a deal was struck to privately fund the bridge, but the toll wasn't established before construction began. So when the bridge opened—and the ferry line it replaced closed—locals were shocked to be charged upwards of £5 per car each way to go to the mainland. A few years ago, the bridge was bought by the Scottish Executive, the fare was abolished, and the Skye natives were appeased...for now.

▲▲Near the Isle of Skye: Eilean Donan Castle

This postcard castle, watching over a sea loch from its island perch, is conveniently and scenically situated on the road between the Isle of Skye and Loch Ness. Famous from such films as Sean Connery's *Highlander* (1986) and the James Bond movie *The World Is Not Enough* (1999), Eilean Donan might be Scotland's most photogenic countryside castle. Though it looks ancient, the castle is actually less than a century old. The original castle on this site (dating from 800 years ago) was destroyed in battle in 1719, then rebuilt between 1912 and 1932 by the MacRae family as their residence.

Even if you're not going inside, the castle warrants a five-minute photo stop. But the interior—with cozy rooms—is worth a peek if you have time. Walk across the bridge and into the castle complex, and make your way into the big, blocky keep. First you'll see the claustrophobic, vaulted Billeting Room (where soldiers had their barracks), then head upstairs to the inviting Banqueting Room. Docents posted in these rooms can tell you more. Another flight of stairs takes you to the circa-1930, non-en-suite bedrooms. Downstairs is the cute kitchen exhibit, with mannequins preparing a meal (read the recipes posted throughout). Finally you'll head through a few more assorted exhibits to the exit.

Cost and Hours: £5, good £3 guidebook, mid-March–mid-Nov daily 10:00–18:00, opens at 9:00 July–Aug, last entry 1 hour before closing, closed mid-Nov–mid-March, tel. 01599/555-202, www.eileandonancastle.com).

Getting There: It's not actually on the Isle of Skye, but it's quite close, in the mainland town of Donrie. Follow A87 about 15 minutes east of Skye Bridge, through Kyle of Lochalsh and toward Loch Ness and Inverness. The castle is on the right side of this road, just after a long bridge.

Portree

Skye's main attraction is its natural beauty, not its villages. But among them, Portree (Port Righ, literally, "Royal Port") is the best home base. This village (with 3,000 people, too small to be considered a "town") is Skye's largest settlement and the hub of activity and transportation.

ORIENTATION

(area code: 01478)

This functional village has a small harbor and, on the hill above it, a tidy main square (from which buses fan out across the island, and to the mainland—see "Getting to the Isle of Skye" and "Getting Around the Isle of Skye" on page 570). Surrounding the central square are just a few streets. Homes, shops, and B&Bs line the roads to other settlements on the island.

Tourist Information

Portree's helpful TI is a block off the main square, along the Bridge Road. They can help you sort through bus schedules, have Internet access, and can book you a room for a £3 fee (March–Sept Mon–Sat 9:00–18:00, Sun 10:00–16:00; Oct–Feb Mon–Fri 9:00–17:00, Sat 10:00–16:00, closed Sun; just south of Bridge Street, tel. 01478/612-137).

Helpful Hints

Internet Access: You can get online at the **TI** (£3/hr, see hours above), or for free at the **library** right in the heart of town (Mon and Wed 13:00–20:00, Thu–Fri 10:00–15:00, Sat 10:00–13:00, closed Sun and Tue).

Laundry: The **Independent Hostel,** just off of the main square, has a self-service launderette down below (about £4 self-service, £8 full-service, sporadic hours, last load starts at 20:00).

Bike Rental: Island Cycles rents bikes at the lower parking lot, along the water (£7.50/half-day, £14/day, closed Sun, tel. 01478/613-121).

Car Rental: You can rent a car for the day at the **MacRea Volkswagen Dealership**, a 10-minute walk from downtown Portree on the road toward Dunvegan (about £40/day, Mon–Fri 8:30–17:30, Sat 9:00–12:00, closed Sun, call one week in advance in summer, tel. 01478/612-554). Farther along the same road are two more options: **Jansvans** (tel. 01478/612-087) and **Portree Coachworks** (tel. 01478/612-688). Figure on paying about £40 per day.

SIGHTS

Harbor—There's little to see in Portree itself, other than to wander along the colorful harbor, where boat captains sell £10, 90-minute excursions out to the sea-eagle nests and around the bay.

Aros Centre—This visitors center, a mile outside of town on the road to Kyleakin and Skye Bridge, offers a humble but earnest exhibit about the island's history and wildlife. Enjoy the movie with aerial photos of otherwise-hard-to-reach parts of Skye, and chat with the ranger. The exhibit also explains about the sea eagles that have been reintroduced to the Skye ecosystem, with a live webcam showing their nests nearby—or, if there are no active nests, a "greatest hits" video show of past fledglings (£4, daily 9:00–18:00, Nov–Easter until 17:00, last entry 30 min before closing, a mile south of town center on Viewfield Road, tel. 01478/613-649, www.aros.co.uk).

SLEEPING

In Portree

$$$ The Pink Guest House has 11 nicely decorated rooms scenically situated right along the harbor (Sb-£35, Db-£70, family rooms, request a view for no extra charge, closed Oct–March, 1 Quay Street, tel. 01478/612-263, fax 01478/612-181, www.pinkguesthouse.co.uk, info@pinkguesthouse.co.uk, David).

$$$ Almondbank Guest House, on the road into town from Kyleakin, works well for drivers. It has four tidy, homey rooms (two with sea views for no extra charge) run by friendly Effie Nicolson (D-£60, Db-£68, Viewfield Road, tel. 01478/612-696, fax 01478/612-947, j.n.almondbank@btconnect.com).

$$ Braeside B&B has three rooms at the top of town, next to the big Bosville Hotel (Db-£50, cash only, closed Nov–Feb, steep stairs, Stormyhill, tel. 01478/612-613, www.braesideportree.co.uk, mail@braesideportree.co.uk, Judith and Philip Maughan and their dog Midge).

$$ Bayview House may be the best deal in town. While the seven new-feeling rooms are small, sterile, and basic, they're a good value and well-located on the main road just below the square (Db-£40–45, some street noise, tel. 01478/613-340, www.bayviewhouse.co.uk, info@bayviewhouse.co.uk, Murdo and Alison). If there's no answer, walk down the stairs to Bayfield Backpackers, described below.

Isle of Skye

Sleep Code

(£1 = about $2, country code: 44)
S = Single, **D** = Double/Twin, **T** = Triple, **Q** = Quad, **b** = bathroom,
s = shower only. Unless otherwise noted, you can assume
credit cards are accepted at hotels and hostels—but not
B&Bs—and breakfast is included.

     To help you sort easily through these listings, I've divided
the rooms into three categories based on the price for a standard double room with bath (during high season):

  $$$ **Higher Priced**—Most rooms £60 or more.
   $$ **Moderately Priced**—Most rooms between £40–60.
    $ **Lower Priced**—Most rooms £40 or less.

    $$ Marine House, run by sweet Fiona Stephenson, has two
simple rooms (one with a private bathroom on the hall) right at
the harbor (D or Db-£50, cash only, 2 Beaumont Crescent, tel.
01478/611-557).

    Hostel: **$ Bayfield Backpackers**—run by Murdo and Alison
from the Bayview House, above—is a new-feeling, institutional,
cinderblock-and-metal hostel with 24 beds in four- to eight-bed
rooms (£13 per bunk, kitchen, tel. 01478/612-231, www.skyehostel
.co.uk, info@skyehostel.co.uk).

Elsewhere on the Isle of Skye, in Sligachan

$$$Sligachan Hotel—actually a compound of related sleeping
and eating options (see also "Eating," below)—is a local institu-
tion and a haven for hikers. It's been in the Campbell family since
1913. The hotel's 21 recently renovated rooms are comfortable, if a
bit simple for the price, while the nearby campground and bunk-
house offer a budget alternative. The setting—surrounded by the
mighty Cuillin Hills—is remarkably scenic (Db-£108 May–Sept,
£88 Easter–April and Oct, closed Nov–Easter, campground-£4
per person, bunkhouse-£12 per person, on A87 between Kyleakin
and Portree in Sligachan, tel. 01478/650-204, fax 01478/650-207,
www.sligachan.co.uk, reservations@sligachan.co.uk).

EATING

In Portree

On the Waterfront: A pair of good eateries vie for your attention along
Portree's little harbor. **Lower Deck** feels like a salty sailor's restau-
rant, decorated with the names of local ships (£5–9 lunches, £12–
18 dinners, daily 12:00–16:00 & 17:30–22:00, tel. 01478/613-611).

Isle of Skye

Sea Breezes, with a more contemporary flair, serves tasty cuisine with an emphasis on seafood (£6–8 lunches, £12–18 dinners, Thu–Tue 12:00–14:30 & 17:30–22:00, closed Wed except July–Aug, reserve ahead for dinner, tel. 01478/612-016).

Café Arriba tries hard to offer eclectic flavors in this provincial Scottish small town. With an ambitious menu that includes local specialties, Mexican, Italian, and more, this youthful, colorful, easygoing eatery's hit-or-miss cuisine is worth trying. Drop in to see what's on the blackboard menu that day (£4–6 lunches, £8–15 dinners, lots of vegetarian options, daily 7:00–17:00 & 18:00–22:00, Quay Brae, tel. 01478/611-830).

The Café, a few steps off the main square, is a busy, popular hometown diner serving good crank-'em-out food to an appreciative local crowd. The homemade ice-cream stand in the corner is a nice way to finish your meal (£6–9 lunches and burgers, £9–11 dinners, daily 8:30–15:30 & 17:30–21:00, tel. 01478/612-553).

The Bosville Hotel has, according to locals, the best of Portree's many hotel restaurants. There are two parts: the inexpensive, casual bistro (£5 lunch sandwiches, £9–16 lunches and dinners, daily 12:00–22:00), and the well-regarded, formal Chandlery Restaurant (£32 two-course meal, £40 three-course meal, nightly 18:30–21:00). While pricey, it's a suitable splurge (just up from the main square, 9–11 Bosville Terrace, tel. 01478/612-846). Their 19 rooms, also expensive, are worth considering (Db-£118, www .bosvillehotel.co.uk).

Elsewhere on the Isle of Skye

In Sligachan

Sligachan Hotel—described under "Sleeping," above—has a restaurant and a microbrew pub serving up mountaineer-pleasing grub in an extremely scenic setting nestled in the Cuillin Hills (traditional dinners in restaurant—£25 for three courses, served nightly 18:30–21:00; pub grub served long hours daily—£7–11; closed Nov–Easter, on A87 between Kyleakin and Portree in Sligachan, tel. 01478/650-204).

In Colbost, near Dunvegan

Three Chimneys Restaurant is your big-splurge-on-a-small-island. The high-quality Scottish cuisine, using local ingredients, earns rave reviews. Its 11 tables fill an old three-chimney croft house, with a stone-and-timbers decor that artfully melds old and new. It's cozy, classy, and candlelit, but not stuffy. Because of its remote location—and the fact that it's almost always booked up—reservations are absolutely essential, ideally several days ahead (lunch: £21 for two courses, £28 for three courses; dinner: £48 for three courses, £55 for four courses; dinner served nightly from 18:30, lunch March–Oct Mon–Sat 12:30–14:00, no lunch Sun or Nov–Feb, closed for 3 weeks in January, tel. 01470/511-258, Eddie and Shirley Spear). They also rent six swanky, pricey suites next door (Db-£255, www.threechimneys.co.uk).

Getting There: It's in the village of Colbost, about a 15-minute drive west of Dunvegan on the Duirinish Peninsula (that's about 45 min each way from Portree). To get there, first head for Dunvegan, then follow signs toward *Glendale*. This road twists you through the countryside, over a moor, and past several dozen sheep before passing through Colbost. You can combine this with a visit to the Neist Point Lighthouse, which is at the end of the same road (see page 578).

Kyleakin

Kyleakin (kih-LAH-kin), the last town in Skye before the bridge, used to be a big tourist hub...until the bridge connecting it to the mainland made it much easier for people to get to Portree and other areas deeper in the island. Today this unassuming little village with a ruined castle (Castle Moil), a cluster of lonesome fishing boats, and a forgotten ferry slip still works well as a home base.

Isle of Skye

SLEEPING

In or near Kyleakin
(£1 = about $2, country code: 44, area code: 01599)

$$$ MacKinnon Country House Hotel is my favorite country-side home base on Skye. It sits quietly in the middle of five acres of gardens just off the bustling Skye Bridge. Ian and the Tongs family have lovingly restored this old country home with 20 clan-themed rooms, an inviting overstuffed-sofa lounge, and a restaurant with garden views in nearly every direction (Sb-£50, Db-£100–135 depending on room size and amenities, about 20 percent cheaper Oct–Easter, tel. 01599/534-180, www.mackinnonhotel.co.uk, info@mackinnonhotel.co.uk, a 10-minute walk from Kyleakin, at the turnoff for the bridge). Ian also serves a delicious dinner to guests and non-guests alike (see "Eating," below).

$$$ White Heather Hotel, run by friendly Gillian and Craig Glenwright, has nine small but nicely decorated rooms right along the waterfront across from the castle ruins (Sb-£45, Db-£66, cheaper for stays longer than 1 night, closed Nov–Easter,

The Harbour, tel. 01599/534-577, fax 01599/534-427, www .whiteheatherhotel.co.uk, info@whiteheatherhotel.co.uk).

$$ Cliffe House B&B rents three rooms in a white house perched at the end of town. All of the rooms, and the breakfast room, enjoy wonderful views over the strait and the bridge (Db-£50, or £60 in July–Aug, cash only, tel. 01599/534-019, i.sikorski @btinternet.com, Ian and Mary Sikorski).

Hostel: **$ Dun-Caan Hostel,** named for a dormant volcano on a nearby island, is mellow and friendly. With woody ambience and 16 beds in three rooms, it's quieter and cozier than most hostels—enjoying a genuine camaraderie without an obnoxious party atmosphere (£13–14/bed, pleasant kitchen and lounge, laundry service, The Pier Road, tel. 01599/534-087, www.skyerover.co.uk, info@skyerover.co.uk, Terry and Laila).

EATING

In or near Kyleakin

A few hotels and pubs in little Kyleakin serve decent food—ask your B&B host for advice. For a nice dinner, head up to **MacKinnon Country House Hotel** (listed under "Sleeping," above; £25 three-course dinner, cheaper in winter, nightly 19:00–21:00, just outside Kyleakin at roundabout for bridge, tel. 01599/534-180). Or dine in **Portree**—with more appealing options than Kyleakin—or at the **Sligachan Hotel** on your way back from a busy sightseeing day (see recommendations on page 584).

Isle of Skye

INVERNESS
and the NORTHERN HIGHLANDS

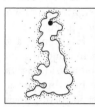

Filled with more natural and historical mystique than people, the northern Highlands are where Scottish dreams are set. Legends of Bonnie Prince Charlie linger around crumbling castles as tunes played by pipers in kilts swirl around tourists. Explore the locks and lochs of the Caledonian Canal while the Loch Ness monster plays hide-and-seek. Hear the music of the Highlands in Inverness, and the echo of muskets in Culloden, where the English drove Bonnie Prince Charlie into exile and conquered the clans of the Highlands.

I've focused my coverage on the handy hub of Inverness, with several day-trip options into the surrounding countryside. For Highlands sights to the south and west, see the Oban and the Southern Highlands chapter; for the Isle of Skye off Scotland's west coast, see the previous chapter.

Planning Your Time

Inverness doesn't merit much time on its own, but works well as an overnight en route between other Highlands destinations. One night here gives you enough time to take in some nearby sights. With two nights, you can find a full day's worth of sightseeing nearby.

Note that Loch Ness is on the way toward Oban or the Isle of Skye. If you're heading to one of those places, it makes sense to see Loch Ness en route, rather than as a side trip from Inverness.

For a speedy itinerary through the Highlands that includes Inverness and Loch Ness, see page 542.

Getting Around the Highlands

With a car, the day trips around Inverness are easy. Without a car, you can get to Inverness by train (better from Edinburgh or Pitlochry) or by bus (better from Skye, Oban, and Glencoe), then side-trip to Loch Ness, Culloden, and other nearby attractions by public bus or with a package tour.

Inverness

The only sizable town in the north of Scotland, with 42,000 people, Inverness is pleasantly situated on the River Ness at the base of a castle (now a court-house, not a tourist attraction). Inverness' charm is its normal-ity—it's a nice, mid-size Scottish city with few sights of its own, but it gives you a palatable taste of the "urban" Highlands, and is well-located for enjoying the surrounding countryside sights. Check out the bustling pedes-trian downtown or stroll the picnic-friendly riverside paths, where after dark, couples hold hands and stroll along the water and over the many footbridges.

ORIENTATION

(area code: 01463)

Inverness, marked by its castle, clusters along the River Ness. Where the main road crosses the river at Ness Bridge, you'll find the TI; within a few blocks (away from the river) are the train and bus stations and an appealing pedestrian shopping zone. The best B&Bs huddle atop a gentle hill behind the castle (a 10-minute mostly uphill walk, or a £3 taxi ride, from the city center).

Tourist Information

At the centrally located TI, you can pick up activity and day-trip brochures, the self-guided *Historic Trail* walking tour brochure, and the *What's On* events list for the latest local showings in theater, music, and film (June–Aug Mon–Sat 9:00–18:00, Sun 10:00–16:00, shorter hours off-season, may be closed Sun in winter, Internet access, free WCs behind TI, Castle Wynd, tel. 01463/234-353, www.visithighlands.com).

Inverness

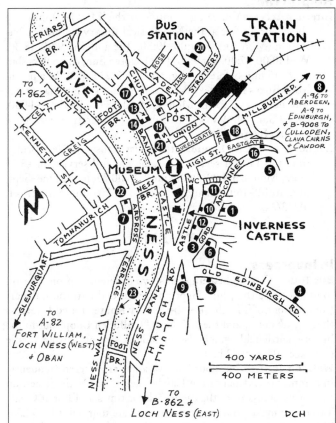

TRAIN STATION

BUS STATION

RIVER

TO A-862

TO A-96 TO ABERDEEN, A-9 TO EDINBURGH, & B-9008 TO CULLODEN, CLAVA CAIRNS & CAWDOR

MILLBURN RD.

POST

UNION ST.

QUEENSGATE

HIGH ST.

EASTGATE

MUSEUM

WC

NESS

ARDCONNEL

INVERNESS CASTLE

CASTLE

GOD

OLD EDINBURGH RD.

TO A-82 FORT WILLIAM, LOCH NESS (WEST) & OBAN

NESS WALK

HAUGH RD.

BANK RD.

FOOT BR.

400 YARDS

400 METERS

TO B-862 & LOCH NESS (EAST)

DCH

Inverness

1. Ardconnel House & Crown Hotel Guest House
2. Melness Guest House
3. Craigside Lodge B&B
4. Dionard Guest House
5. Ryeford Guest House
6. The Redcliffe Hotel & Rest.
7. Inverness Palace Hotel & Spa
8. To Premier Travel Inn Inverness Centre
9. Inverness Student Hotel & Bazpackers Hostel
10. Café 1
11. Number 27 Restaurant
12. La Tortilla Asesina Rest.
13. Hootananny Café/Bar
14. The Mustard Seed Rest.
15. Rajah Indian Restaurant
16. Girvans Café
17. Leakey's Bookshop & Café
18. Marks & Spencer
19. Scottish Showtime Experience (in Ramada Hotel)
20. Library (Internet)
21. Mail Boxes Etc. (Internet)
22. Launderette
23. Riverside Paths

Helpful Hints

Internet Access: You can get online at the **TI** (£1/20 min, see above), or for free at the Neoclassical **library** behind the bus station (Mon and Fri 9:00–19:30, Tue and Thu 9:00–18:30, Wed 10:00–17:00, Sat 9:00–17:00, closed Sun, computers shut down 15 min before closing, tel. 01463/236-463). In a pinch, **Mail Boxes Etc.,** next door to the train station, has pricey Internet access (£5/hr, Mon–Fri 8:30–18:00, Sat 9:00–14:00, closed Sun, tel. 01463/234-700). The launderette listed below also has Internet access.

Laundry: **New City Launderette** is just across the Ness Bridge from the TI (self-service–£8, same-day full-service for £3.50 more, Mon–Sat 8:00–18:00, until 20:00 Mon–Fri June–Sept, Sun 10:00–16:00, Internet access, 17 Young Street, tel. 01463/242-507).

TOURS

In Inverness

Bus Tour—**City Sightseeing** runs two different hop-on, hop-off tours (£6 for either, June-Sept only, recorded narration, depart from in front of TI): the 45-minute **City Route** around Inverness (hourly, 13 stops); and the 1.75-hour **"Culloden Loop"** out to the historic battlefield, which also includes a stop at Cawdor Castle (see page 604; every 2 hrs).

Walking Tour—One-hour "Storywalks" are offered frequently in summer (£7; depart from Castle Tavern up Castle Street, on the corner across from the castle; ask for times at TI or at Castle Tavern, or make arrangements for a private tour, tel. 01463/233-729, www.telliesperie.co.uk, greg@telliesperie.co.uk).

From Inverness

While thin on sights of its own, Inverness is a great home base for day trips. The biggest attraction is Loch Ness, a 20-minute drive southwest. All tours depart from and sell tickets at the TI. It's smart to book ahead for any of these, especially in peak season.

Jacobite Tours—Their tours come in a variety of options, from a one-hour basic boat ride to a six-hour extravaganza (£9.50–31, most tours run daily April–Sept). Their 3.5-hour "Sensation" tour is their most popular, and includes a guided bus tour with live narration, a cruise of Loch Ness with recorded commentary, and an hour each at the Urquhart Castle and the interesting Loch Ness exhibit (£21, includes admissions to both sights, departs from TI at 10:30—buy your tickets there, tel. 01463/233-999, www.jacobite.co.uk). If you'd like to see the Culloden Battlefield, their "Jacobite Rebellion" tour heads to that iconic sight (£12.50, 2 hours, leaves from TI).

Tattoos and the Painted People

In Inverness, as in other Scottish cities such as Glasgow and Edinburgh, hip pubs are filled with tattooed kids. In parts of Scotland, however, tattoos aren't a recent phenomenon...this form of body art has been around longer than the buildings and sights. Some of the area's earliest known settlers of the Highlands were called the Picts, dubbed the "Painted People" by their enemies, the Romans. The Picts, who conquered the northeast corner of Scotland (including Inverness), were believed to have ruled from the first century A.D. to approximately the ninth century, when they united with the Scots and were lost to written history.

Picts were known for their elaborate, full-body tattoos. The local plant they used for their ink, called *woad*, had built-in healing properties, helping to coagulate blood (a property particularly handy in battle). The elaborate, tattooed designs gave rise to a truly remarkable fighting technique: going to war naked. The Picts saw their tattoos as a kind of psychological armor, a combination of symbols and magical signs that would protect them more than any metal could. Imagine a Scottish hillside teeming with screaming, head-to-toe dyed-blue warriors, most with elaborate tattooed designs—and all of them buck naked.

Puffin Express—They offer daylong "Over the Sea to Skye" tours. The tour goes along Loch Ness, visits the scenic Eilean Donan Castle, and gives you a few hours on Skye; unfortunately, it goes only as far as the Sleat Peninsula at the island's southern end, rather than the more scenic Trotternish Peninsula (£29, includes entry to Armadale Castle Gardens, departs from Inverness TI at 9:15, returns at 19:45, convoluted schedule runs Sun, Mon, Wed, and Fri April–mid-Oct; plus Tue, Thu, and Sat June–Sept; reservations recommended, tel. 01463/717-181, www.puffinexpress.co.uk). For more on the Isle of Skye, see page 568.

More Options—Several other companies host daily excursions to Culloden Battlefield, whisky distilleries, Cawdor Castle, and the nearby bay for dolphin-watching (ask at TI).

SIGHTS

"Imaginverness" Museum and Art Gallery—This free, likeable town museum is worth poking around on a rainy day to get a taste of Inverness and the Highlands. The ground-floor exhibits on geology and archaeology peel back the layers of Highland history: Bronze and Iron ages, Picts (including some carved stones), Scots,

Vikings, and Normans. Upstairs you'll find the "social history" exhibit (everything from Scottish nationalism to hunting and fishing) and temporary art exhibits (free, Mon–Sat 10:00–17:00, closed Sun except may be open Sun 12:30–17:00 in July–Aug, cheap café, in the modern building behind the TI on the way up to the castle, tel. 01463/237-114).

Inverness Castle—Inverness' biggest non-sight has nice views from its front lawn, but the building itself isn't worth visiting. The statue outside depicts Flora MacDonald, who helped Bonnie Prince Charlie escape from the English (see sidebar on page 602). The castle is used as a courthouse, and when trials are in session, loutish-looking men hang out here, waiting for their bewigged barristers to arrive.

Folk Show—The **Scottish Showtime Experience** evening is a fun-loving, hardworking, Lawrence Welk-ish show giving you all the clichés in a clap-along two-hour package. I prefer it to the big hotel spectacles in Edinburgh (usually June–Sept Mon–Thu at 20:30, no meals, £12.50, kids-£7.50, in Ramada Hotel at 33 Church Street, tel. 0800-015-8001 or 01463/235-181, www.nessie.org.uk).

SLEEPING

B&Bs on and near Ardconnel Street and Old Edinburgh Road

These B&Bs are popular; book ahead for July and August, and be aware that some require a two-night minimum during busy times. The rooms are all a 10-minute walk from the train station and town center. To get to the B&Bs, either catch a taxi (£3) or walk: From the station, go left on Academy Street. At the first stoplight (the second if you're coming from the bus station), veer right onto Inglis Street in the pedestrian zone. Go up the Market Brae steps. At the top, turn right onto Ardconnel Street toward the B&Bs and hostels.

$$$ Ardconnel House has six tasteful, spacious, and comfy rooms with lots of extra touches (Sb-£35, Db-£65, less off-season, £80 family room, family deals but no children under 10, free Wi-Fi, 21 Ardconnel Street, tel. 01463/240-455, www.ardconnel -inverness.co.uk, ardconnel@gmail.com).

$$$ Melness Guest House has two lovely rooms, a comfy lounge, and a matching pair of West Highland Terriers—one jumpy and one mellow (Db-£70 in July–Aug and £60 Sept–June, 2-night minimum in summer, free Wi-Fi, 8 Old Edinburgh Road, tel. 01463/220-963, www.melnessie.co.uk, joy@melnessie.co.uk, Joy Joyce).

$$ Craigside Lodge B&B has four large, cheery rooms
recently remodeled with modern flair. The rooms share an inviting
conservatory and a cozy lounge with a great city view (Sb-£30,
Db-£60, some street noise, just above Castle Street at 4 Gordon
Terrace, tel. 01463/231-576, www.craigsideguesthouse.co.uk,
enquiries@craigsideguesthouse.co.uk, Janette).

$$ Crown Hotel Guest House has six clean, bright rooms
and an enjoyable breakfast room (Sb-£33, Db-£55, family room-
£80, 19 Ardconnel Street, tel. 01463/231-135, www.crownhotel
-inverness.co.uk, gordon@crownhotel-inverness.co.uk, friendly
and hardworking Gordon and Catriona—pronounced Katrina—
Barbour).

$$ Dionard Guest House, just up Old Edinburgh Road from
Ardconnel Street, has cheerful, blue-toned common spaces and
four pleasant rooms, with two on the ground floor (Sb-£35, Db-
£60, Wi-Fi, 39 Old Edinburgh Road, tel. 01463/233-557, www
.dionardguesthouse.co.uk, enquiries@dionardguesthouse.co.uk,
welcoming Val and John).

$$ Ryeford Guest House has six flowery rooms and plenty of
teddy bears (Db-£54, Tb-£81, family deals, vegetarian breakfast
available, small room #1 in back has fine garden view, above Market
Brae steps, go left on Ardconnel Terrace to #21, tel. 01463/242-871,
www.scotland-inverness.co.uk/ryeford, joananderson@uwclub.net,
Joan and brusque George Anderson).

Hotels

The following hotels may have rooms when the above B&Bs are
full.

$$$ The Redcliffe Hotel, which is actually in the midst of
all the B&Bs described above, has recently renovated its 13 rooms

Inverness

with smooth contemporary style. While a lesser value than the B&Bs, it's fairly priced for a small hotel (Sb-£45–60, Db-£80–100, depends on season, 1 Gordon Terrace, tel. & fax 01463/232-767, www.redcliffe-hotel.co.uk, enquiry@redcliffe-hotel.co.uk). They also have a good restaurant (see "Eating," below).

$$$ Inverness Palace Hotel & Spa, a Best Western, is a fancy splurge with a pool, a gym, and 88 overpriced rooms. It's located right on the River Ness, across from the castle (Db-£199, but you can generally get a better rate—even half-price—if you book a package deal on their website, especially on weekends; breakfast extra, elevator, free Wi-Fi, free parking, 8 Ness Walk, tel. 01463/223-243, fax 01463/236-865, www.bw-invernesspalace .co.uk, palace@miltonhotels.com).

$$ Premier Travel Inn Inverness Centre, a half-mile east of the train station along busy and dreary Millburn Road, offers 55 modern, identical rooms in a converted distillery. While it feels like a freeway rest-stop hotel (better for drivers), it's affordable, especially for families. The appealing on-site restaurant, Slice, offers steaks, salads, and more in a bright, contemporary atmosphere (Db for up to two adults and two kids-£65, £10 cheaper in winter, continental breakfast-£5.25, full cooked breakfast-£7.50, smoking rooms, B865/Millburn Road, just west of the A9 and A96 interchange, tel. 08701-977-141, fax 01463/717-826, www .premiertravelinn.com).

Hostels on Culduthel Road

For inexpensive dorm beds near the center and the recommended Castle Street restaurants, consider these friendly, side-by-side hostels (a 12-min walk from the train station). Both offer Internet access and laundry service.

$ Inverness Student Hotel has 57 beds in nine rooms and a cozy, inviting, laid-back lounge with a bay window overlooking the River Ness. The friendly staff accommodates groups doing the hop-on, hop-off bus circuit, but any traveler over 18 is welcome (£13–14 beds in 6- to 10-bed rooms, price depends on season, breakfast-£1.90, full-service laundry for £2.50, kitchen, free tea and coffee, cheap Internet access, 8 Culduthel Road, tel. 01463/236-556, www.scotlands-top-hostels.com, inverness @scotlands-top-hostels.com).

$ Bazpackers Hostel, a stone's throw from the castle, has a pleasant common room and 34 beds (beds-£13, D-£32, cheaper Oct–May, linens provided, reception open 7:30–24:00, 4 Culduthel Road, tel. 01463/717-663).

EATING

You'll find a lot of traditional Highland fare—game, fish, lamb, and beef. Reservations are smart at most of these places, especially on summer weekends.

Near the B&Bs, on or near Castle Street

The first three eateries line Castle Street, facing the back of the castle. The last one is right in the middle of the B&B scene.

Café 1 serves up high-quality modern Scottish and international cuisine with a trendy, elegant bistro flair (£9–16 entrées, lunch and early-bird dinner specials 17:30–18:45, Mon–Sat 12:00–14:00 & 17:30–21:30, closed Sun, 75 Castle Street, tel. 01463/226-200).

Number 27, a bit more lowbrow and a local favorite, is the Scottish version of T.G.I. Friday's. The straightforward, crowd-pleasing menu offers something for everyone—salads, burgers, seafood, and more (£7–15 entrées, Sun–Fri 12:00–14:45 & 17:00–21:45, Sat 12:00–21:30, until 21:00 off-season, generous portions, noisy adjacent bar up front, quieter restaurant in back, 27 Castle Street, tel. 01463/241-999).

La Tortilla Asesina has lively Spanish tapas such as spicy king prawns (the house specialty). It's an appealing and vivacious dining option (cold and hot tapas-£2–6, a few make a meal, Sun–Thu 12:00–22:00, Fri–Sat 12:00–23:00, 99 Castle Street, tel. 01463/709-809).

The Redcliffe Hotel's restaurant is conveniently located (right on the B&B street) and serves up good food in three areas: a bright and leafy sunroom, a pub, or an outdoor patio (£9–16 dinners, daily 12:00–14:30 & 17:00–21:30, 1 Gordon Terrace, tel. 01463/232-767). For information on the hotel's rooms, see the listing under "Sleeping," above.

In the Town Center

Hootananny is a cross-cultural experience, combining a lively pub atmosphere, nightly live music (rock, blues, and "bar music"), and Thai cuisine. It's got a great, join-in-the-fun vibe at night (£5-7 Thai dishes, food served 12:00–15:00 & 17:00–21:30, music begins every night at 21:30, 67 Church Street, tel. 01463/233-651, www.hootananny.co.uk). Upstairs is the Mad Hatter's nightclub, complete with a "chill-out room."

The Mustard Seed serves Scottish food with a modern twist and a view of the river in a lively-at-lunch, mellow-at-dinner atmosphere. It's pricey, pretentious, and (many locals grouse) overrated, but worth considering for a nice meal. Ask for a seat on the balcony if the weather cooperates (£10–14 meals, daily 12:00–15:00

Inverness

& 17:30–22:00, reservations smart on weekends, on the corner of Bank and Fraser Streets, 16 Fraser Street, tel. 01463/220-220).

Rajah Indian Restaurant provides a tasty break from meat and potatoes, with vegetarian options served in a classy red-velvet and white-linen atmosphere (£7–13 meals, 10 percent less for take-out, Mon–Sat 12:00–23:00, Sun 15:00–23:00, just off Church Street at 2 Post Office Avenue, tel. 01463/237-190).

Girvans serves sandwiches and tempting pastries in an easy-going atmosphere (£5–9 meals, daily 9:00–21:00, shorter hours off-season, 2 Stephens Brae, at the end of the pedestrian zone nearest the train station, tel. 01463/711-900).

Leakey's Bookshop and Café, located in a 1649 converted church, has the best lunch deal in town. Browse through stacks of old (and overpriced) books and vintage maps, warm up by the wood-burning stove, and climb the spiral staircase to the loft for hearty homemade soups, sandwiches, and sweets (£3–4 light lunches, Mon–Sat 10:30–16:30, bookstore stays open until 17:30, closed Sun, in Greyfriar's Hall on Church Street, tel. 01463/239-947, Charles Leakey).

Picnic: The **Marks & Spencer** food hall is best (can't miss it on the main pedestrian mall, near the Market Brae steps at the corner of the big Eastgate Shopping Centre; Mon–Wed and Fri–Sat 9:00–18:00, Thu 9:00–20:00, Sun 11:00–17:00, tel. 01463/224-844).

TRANSPORTATION CONNECTIONS

From Inverness by Train to: Pitlochry (9/day, 1.5 hrs), **Stirling** (every 2 hrs, 2.5–3 hrs, most transfer in Perth), **Kyle of Lochalsh** near Isle of Skye (4/day, 2.25 hrs), **Edinburgh** (8/day, 3.5 hrs, more with change in Perth), **Glasgow** (2/day direct, 3.5 hrs, more with change in Perth). ScotRail does a great sleeper service to **London** (generally around £150 first class or £119 standard class for a private compartment with breakfast, not available Sat night, www.firstscotrail.com). Consider dropping your car in Inverness and riding to London by train. Train info: tel. 08457-484-950.

By Bus: To reach most destinations in western Scotland, you'll first head for **Fort William** (7/day Mon–Fri, 6/day Sat, 5/day Sun, 2 hrs). For connections onward to **Oban** (figure 4 hrs total) or **Glencoe** (3 hrs total), see the "Transportation Connections" for Fort William on page 566. To reach **Portree** on the Isle of Skye, you can either take the direct bus (3/day in summer, 2/day in winter, 3.25–4 hrs direct), or transfer in Fort William. These buses are run by Scottish Citylink; for schedules, see www.citylink.co.uk. You can buy tickets in advance by calling Citylink at tel. 08705-505-050 or stopping by the Inverness bus station (Mon–Sat

8:30–17:30, Sun 9:00–17:30, 50p extra for credit cards, daily luggage storage-£4–5/bag, 2 blocks from train station on Margaret Street, tel. 01463/233-371). For bus travel to England, check www .nationalexpress.com.

Route Tips for Drivers

Inverness to Edinburgh (150 miles, 3 hours minimum): Leaving Inverness, follow signs to *A9* (south, toward Perth). If you haven't seen the Culloden Battlefield yet (described below), it's an easy detour: Just as you leave Inverness, detour four miles east off A9 on B9006. Back on A9, it's a wonderfully speedy, scenic highway (A9, M90, A90) all the way to Edinburgh. If you have time, consider stopping en route in Pitlochry (just off A9; see page 607). For directions to B&Bs, see the Edinburgh chapter.

To Oban, Glencoe, or Isle of Skye: See the "Route Tips for Drivers" at the end of the Oban and the Southern Highlands chapter.

Near Inverness

Inverness puts you in the heart of the Highlands, within easy striking distance of a gaggle of famous and worthwhile sights: Squint across Loch Ness looking for Nessie—or if you're a skeptic, just appreciate the majesty of Britain's biggest lake. Commune with the Scottish soul at the historic Culloden Battlefield, where Scottish, British, and world history reached a turning point. Ponder three mysterious piles of rocks, reminding visitors that Scotland's history goes back even before Braveheart. And enjoy a homey country castle at Cawdor.

Loch Ness

I'll admit it: I had my zoom lens out and my eyes on the water. The local tourist industry thrives on the legend of the Loch Ness Monster. It's a thrilling thought, and there have been several seemingly reliable "sightings" (monks, police officers, and sonar images). But even if you ignore the monster stories, the loch is impressive: 24 miles long, less than a mile wide, the third-deepest in Europe, and containing more water than in all the freshwater bodies of England and Wales combined.

Getting There: The Loch Ness sights are a quick drive southwest of Inverness. Various buses go from Inverness to Urquhart Castle in about a half-hour (8/day, various companies, ask at Inverness bus station or TI).

Inverness and the Northern Highlands

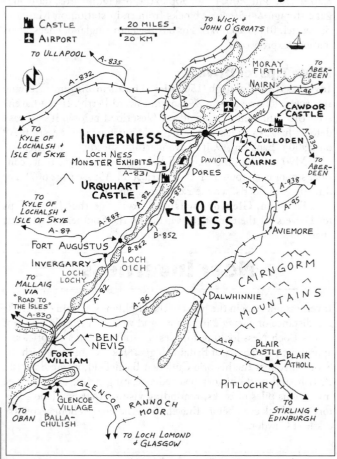

- ♜ CASTLE
- ✈ AIRPORT

20 MILES
20 KM

TO WICK &
JOHN O'GROATS

TO ULLAPOOL — A-835

A-832

A-9

MORAY
FIRTH

NAIRN

TO
ABERDEEN

A-96

CAWDOR
CASTLE

B-9006

CAWDOR

A-939

TO
KYLE OF
LOCHALSH +
ISLE OF SKYE

INVERNESS

LOCH NESS
MONSTER EXHIBITS

A-831

**URQUHART
CASTLE**

A-82

B-851

DAVIOT

DORES

CULLODEN

CLAVA
CAIRNS

TO
ABERDEEN

A-9

A-938

A-95

TO
KYLE OF
LOCHALSH +
ISLE OF SKYE

A-87

A-887

**LOCH
NESS**

B-862

B-852

AVIEMORE

FORT AUGUSTUS

INVERGARRY

LOCH
OICH

LOCH
LOCHY

TO
MALLAIG
VIA
"ROAD TO
THE ISLES"

A-830

A-82

A-86

DALWHINNIE

CAIRNGORM

MOUNTAINS

**BEN
NEVIS**

RANNOCH
MOOR

**FORT
WILLIAM**

GLENCOE

A-9

BLAIR
CASTLE

BLAIR
ATHOLL

PITLOCHRY

TO
OBAN

GLENCOE
VILLAGE

BALLA-
CHULISH

TO LOCH LOMOND
& GLASGOW

TO
STIRLING &
EDINBURGH

Near Inverness

Loch Ness Monster Exhibits—In July of 1933, a couple swore that
they saw a giant sea monster shimmy
across the road in front of their car by
Loch Ness. Within days, ancient legends
about giant monsters in the lake were
revived—and suddenly everyone was
spotting "Nessie" poke its head above the
waters of Loch Ness. For the last three-
quarters of a century, further sightings
and photographic "evidence" have bol-
stered the claim that there's something
mysterious living in this unthinkably
deep and murky lake. (Most sightings

The Caledonian Canal

The Highlands are cut in two by the impressive Caledonian Canal, which connects lakes (lochs) that lie in the huge depression created by the Great Glen Fault. The town of Fort William (see page 563) is located at the southwest end of the canal, and Inverness sits at its northeast end. The major sights—including the famous Loch Ness—cluster along the scenic 120-mile stretch between these two towns.

Three lochs and a series of canals trace the Great Glen Fault, which cuts Scotland in two. Oich, Lochy, and Ness were connected in the early 1800s by the great British engineer Thomas Telford. Traveling between Fort William and Inverness (60 miles), you'll follow Telford's work—20 miles of canals and locks between 40 miles of lakes, raising ships from sea level to 51 feet (Ness), to 93 feet (Lochy), and to 106 feet (Oich).

While "Neptune's Staircase," a series of locks near Fort William, is cleverly named, the best lock stop is midway, at Fort Augustus, where the canal hits the south end of Loch Ness. In Fort Augustus, the **Caledonian Canal Heritage Centre,** three locks above the main road, gives a good rundown on Telford's work (free, April–Oct daily 9:30–17:30, closed 1 hour midday for lunch). Stroll past several shops and eateries to the top of the locks for a fine view.

take place in the deepest part of the loch, near Urquhart Castle—see below.) Most witnesses describe a waterbound dinosaur (resembling the real, but extinct, plesiosaur). Others cling to the slightly more plausible theory of a gigantic eel. And skeptics figure the sightings can be explained by a combination of reflections, boat wakes, mass hysteria...and the chance to grab 15 minutes of fame. The most famous photo of the beast (dubbed the "Surgeon's Photo") was later discredited—the "monster's" head was actually attached to a toy submarine. But that hasn't stopped other cryptozoologists from seeking photographic, sonar, and other proof.

And that suits the thriving local tourist industry just fine. The Nessie commercialization is so tacky that there are two different monster exhibits within 100 yards of each other, both in the town of Drumnadrochit. Each has a tour-bus parking lot and more square footage devoted to their kitschy shop than to the exhibit. The overpriced exhibitions are actually quite interesting—even though they're tourist traps, they'll appease that small part of you that knows the *real* reason you wanted to see Loch Ness.

The better option—worth ▲—is the **Loch Ness Centre,** headed by a marine biologist who has spent more than 15 years researching lake ecology and scientific phenomena. With a 30-minute series of video bits and special effects, this exhibit explains the geological and historical environment that bred the monster story, and the various searches that have been conducted. Refreshingly, it retains an air of healthy skepticism instead of breathless monster-chasing (£6, daily July–Aug 9:00–20:00, June and Sept 9:00–18:00, April–May and Oct 9:30–17:00, Nov–March 10:00–16:00, last admission 30 min before closing, in the big stone mansion right on the main road to Inverness, tel. 01456/450-573, www.loch-ness-scotland.com).

The other exhibit, called the **Loch Ness Visitor Centre** (up a side road closer to the town center, affiliated with a hotel), is less serious. It's basically a tacky high school–quality photo report and a 30-minute *We Believe in the Loch Ness Monster* movie, which features credible-sounding locals explaining what they saw and a review of modern Nessie searches. (The most convincing reason for locals to believe: Look at the hordes of tourists around you.) There are also small exhibits on local history and on other "monsters" and hoaxes around the world (£5, daily April–June 9:00–19:30, July–Aug 9:00–21:00, Sept–March 9:00–17:00, tel. 01456/450-342).

Urquhart Castle—These ruins, just up the loch from the Nessie exhibits, are gloriously situated with a view of virtually the entire lake. Although its Visitors Centre has a museum with castle artifacts and an eight-minute film, the castle itself is an overpriced empty shell swarming with tourists (£6.50, guidebook-£4, daily April–Oct 9:30–18:30, Nov–March 9:30–16:30, last entry 45 min before closing, tel. 01456/450-551).

Culloden Battlefield

Jacobite troops under Bonnie Prince Charlie were defeated at Culloden (kuh-LAW-dehn) by supporters of the Hanover dynasty in 1746. This last land battle fought on British soil spelled the end of Jacobite resistance and the fall of the clans. Wandering the battlefield, you feel that something terrible occurred here. Locals still bring flowers and speak of "the '45" (as Bonnie Prince Charlie's entire campaign is called) as if it just happened.

The site is explained by an excellent **Visitors Centre,** a state-of-the-art, £10 million facility scheduled to open here in late 2007. The center traces the events leading up to the fateful battle, giving each side's perspective. The exhibit plunges the visitor into the middle of the action—including being immersed in a high-budget reenactment of the battle, where you're surrounded on all sides by attacking soldiers (on 360-degree

movie screens). It ends with a timeline tracing the aftermath of the battle (likely status for 2008: £8, daily April–Oct 9:00–18:00, Nov–March 10:00–16:00, possibly closed in Jan, tel. 01463/790-607, www.culloden.org.uk).

From the roof of the Visitors Centre, you can look out over the **battlefield.** In the foreground is a cottage used as a makeshift hospital during the battle (it's decorated as it would have been then). Then head out to the battlefield itself. To bring more meaning to your visit, ask at the Visitors Centre about a handheld computer guide (with GPS to pinpoint specific battlefield events) or guided tours. Once you get out there, a lonesome cairn marks the center of the fighting, and smaller graves around it show where various clans fell. Entire clans fought, died, and were buried together, in mass graves. The Mackintosh grave alone was 77 yards long. (If you're here after-hours, you can access the battlefield for free.)

While this hallowed site packs a punch-to-the-gut for patriotic Scots—who see this as the place where their cherished clan system gasped its last breath—it can be difficult for American visitors to appreciate. If you're having trouble grasping the significance of these events, play a game of "What if?": Had Bonnie Prince Charlie persevered on this battlefield and taken the throne, he likely wouldn't have plunged his nation into the Sixty Years' War with France (his ally). And increased taxes on either side of that war led directly to the French and American revolutions. So if the Jacobites had won...the American colonies might still be part of the British Empire today.

Getting There: It's a 15-minute drive east of Inverness: Follow signs to *Aberdeen*, then *Culloden Moor*, and B9006 takes you right there (well-signed on the right-hand side). Public buses from Inverness get you to the Culloden Moor Inn, a 200-yard walk from the battlefield. Better yet, to get the whole story, take a guided tour from Inverness (see page 590).

Bonnie Prince Charlie
(1720–1788)

The Battle of Culloden (April 16, 1746) marks the end of the Scottish Highland clans and the start of years of repression of Scottish culture by the English. It was the culmination of a year's worth of battles, known collectively as "the '45." At the center of it all was the charismatic, enigmatic Bonnie Prince Charlie.

Charles Edward Stuart, from his first breath, was raised with a single purpose—to restore his family to the British throne. His grandfather was King James II, deposed in 1688 by Parliament for his tyranny and pro-Catholic bias. In 1745, young Charlie crossed the Channel from exile in France to seize the throne for his father. He landed on the west coast of Scotland, and rallied support for the "Jacobite" cause (from the Latin for "James"). Though Charles was not Scottish-born, many Scots joined the Stuart family's rebellion out of resentment at English domination.

Bagpipes droned, and "Bonnie" (handsome) Charlie led an army of 2,000 tartan-wearing, Gaelic-speaking Highlanders across Scotland, seizing Edinburgh. Now 6,000 strong, they marched south toward London, and King George II made plans to flee the country. But the anticipated support for the Jacobites failed to materialize (both in England and from France), and Charles reluctantly retreated to the Scottish Highlands, with the English government troops on his heels.

They faced off at Culloden Moor on flat, barren terrain that was unsuited to the Highlanders' guerrilla tactics. The Scots— many of them brandishing only broadswords and spears—were mowed down by English cannons and horsemen. In less than an hour, the government forces routed the Jacobite army, but that was just the start. They spent the next weeks methodically

Clava Cairns

Scotland is littered with reminders of prehistoric peoples, but the Clava Cairns (or "Balnauran of Clava") are among the most interesting and easiest to reach. Forgotten in the spooky countryside just beyond Culloden Battlefield, the Clava Cairns are Bronze Age burial chambers dating from  3,000 to 4,000 years ago. While they simply look like giant piles of

hunting down ringleaders and sympathizers, ruthlessly killing, imprisoning, and banishing thousands.

Charles fled with a £30,000 price on his head. He escaped to the Isle of Skye, hidden by a woman named **Flora MacDonald** (her grave is on the Isle of Skye, and her statue is outside Inverness Castle). Flora dressed Charles in women's clothes and passed him off as her maid; legends persist that the two had a romantic fling during their week together on the run. Flora was arrested and thrown in the Tower of London before being released and treated like a celebrity.

Charles escaped to France. He spent the rest of his life wandering Europe trying to drum up support to retake the throne. He drifted into short-lived romantic affairs and alcohol, and died in obscurity in Rome.

While usually depicted as a battle of the Scottish versus the English, in truth Culloden was a civil war between two opposing dynasties: Stuart (Charlie) and Hanover (George). In fact, about one-fifth of the government's troops were Scottish, and several redcoat deserters fought along with the Jacobites. However, as the history has faded into lore, the battle has come to be remembered as a Scottish-versus-English standoff—or, in the parlance of the Scots, the Highlanders versus the Strangers.

The Battle of Culloden was the end of 60 years of Jacobite rebellions, the last battle fought on British soil, and the last stand of the Highlanders. From then on, clan chiefs were deposed; kilts, tartans, and bagpipes became illegal paraphernalia; and farmers were cleared off their ancestral land, replaced by more-profitable sheep. Scottish culture would never recover from the events of the campaign called "the '45."

rocks in a sparsely forested clearing, take a closer look to appreciate the prehistoric logic behind them. (The site is well-explained by informative plaques.) There are three structures: a central "ring cairn" with an open space in the center but no access to it, flanked by two "passage cairns," which were once covered. The entrance shaft in each passage cairn lines up with the setting sun at the winter solstice. Each cairn is surrounded by a stone circle, injecting this site with even more mystery.

Cost and Hours: Free, always open.

Getting There: Just after passing Culloden Battlefield on B9006 (coming from Inverness), signs on the right point to *Clava Cairns.* Follow this twisty road to the free parking lot by the stones. Skip it unless you have a car.

Cawdor Castle

Homey and intimate, this castle is still the residence of the Dowager (read: widow) Countess of Cawdor, a local aristocratic family. The castle's claim to fame is its connection to Shakespeare's *Macbeth*, in which the three witches correctly predict that the protagonist will be granted the title "Thane of Cawdor." The castle is not used as a setting in the play—which takes place in Inverness, 300 years before this

castle was built—but the play's dozen or so references to "Cawdor" are enough for the marketing machine to kick in. Today, virtually nothing tangibly ties Cawdor to the Bard or to the real-life Macbeth. But even if you ignore the Shakespeare lore, the castle is worth a visit.

The chatty, friendly docents (including Jean at the front desk, who can say "mind your head" in 42 different languages) give the castle an air of intimacy—most are residents of the neighboring village of Cawdor, and act as though they're old friends with the Dowager Countess (many probably are). Entertaining posted explanations—written by the countess' late husband, the sixth Earl of Cawdor—bring the castle to life. While many of today's castles are still residences for the aristocracy, Cawdor feels even more lived-in than the norm—you can imagine the Dowager Countess stretching out in front of the fireplace with a good book. Rooms on the tour include a tapestry-laden bedroom and a "tartan passage" speckled with modern paintings. In another bedroom (just before the stairs back down) is a tiny pencil sketch by Salvador Dalí. Inside the base of the tower, near the end of the tour, is the castle's proud symbol: a thorn tree dating from 1372. According to the beloved legend, a donkey leaned against this tree to mark the spot where the castle was to be built—which it was, around the tree. (The tree is no longer alive, but its withered trunk is still propped up in the same position. No word on the donkey.)

The **gardens,** included in the ticket, are also worth exploring, with some 18th-century linden trees, a hedge maze (not open to the public), and several surprising species (including sequoia and redwood).

The nearby, remote-feeling **village of Cawdor**—with a few houses, a village shop, and a tavern—is also worth a look if you've got time to kill.

Cost and Hours: £7.30, good £4.50 guidebook explains the family and the rooms, May–mid-Oct daily 10:00–17:30, last entry at 17:00, closed mid-Oct–April, tel. 01667/404-401, www .cawdorcastle.com.

Getting There: It's on B9090, just off A96, about 10 miles east of Inverness (just beyond Culloden and the Clava Cairns). Without a car, it's easiest to reach on the City Sightseeing "Culloden Loop" bus tour (see page 590).

BETWEEN INVERNESS AND EDINBURGH

Pitlochry and Stirling

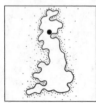

To break up the trip between Inverness and Edinburgh (3 hours by car, 3.5 hours by train), consider stopping over at one of these two worthwhile destinations. The town of Pitlochry, right on the train route, mixes whisky and hillwalking with a dash of countryside charm. Farther south, the historic city of Stirling (easier for drivers to reach) has one of Scotland's top castles and a monument to a Scottish hero.

Planning Your Time

Visiting both Pitlochry and Stirling on a one-day drive from Inverness to Edinburgh is doable but busy (especially since part of Pitlochry's allure is slowing down to taste the whisky).

Pleasant Pitlochry is well-located, a quick detour off of the main A9 highway from Inverness to Edinburgh (via Perth) or an easy stop for train travelers. The town deserves an overnight for whisky-lovers, or for those who really want to relax in small-town Scotland. In fact, many find the town of Pitlochry itself even more appealing than Oban or Glencoe...but it lacks the rugged Highlands scenery and easy access to other major sights found in those towns.

Stirling, off the busy A9/M9 motorway between Perth and Edinburgh, is worth a quick sightseeing stop, but not an overnight. (If skipping Stirling, notice that you can take M90 due south over the Firth of Forth to connect Perth and Edinburgh.) Also notice that Stirling is doable on a trip between Edinburgh and points west (such as Glasgow or Oban)—just take the northern M9/A80 route instead of more direct M8.

For my money, St. Andrews is the best stop between Inverness and Edinburgh (see St. Andrews chapter)—but it's farther out of the way than Pitlochry or Stirling.

Pitlochry

This likable tourist town, famous for its whisky and its hillwalking (both beloved by Scots), makes an enjoyable overnight stop on the way between Inverness and Edinburgh. Just outside the craggy Highlands, Pitlochry is set amid pastoral rolling hills that offer plenty of forest hikes (brochures at TI). A salmon ladder climbs alongside the lazy river (free viewing area—best in May, 10-min walk from town).

ORIENTATION

(area code: 01796)
Plucky little Pitlochry (pop. 2,500) lines up along its tidy and tourist-minded main road, where you'll find the train station, bus stops, TI, and bike rental. The River Tummel runs parallel to the main road, a few steps away. Most distilleries are a short drive out of town, but you can walk to the two best; see my self-guided hillwalk, below. Navigate easily by following the black directional signs to Pitlochry's handful of sights.

Tourist Information
The helpful TI provides train schedules, books rooms for a £3 fee, and sells good maps for walks and scenic drives (Mon–Sat 9:30–17:30, Sun 10:00–16:00; mid-July–Aug Mon–Sat 9:00–19:00, Sun 9:00–18:00; shorter hours off-season, no luggage storage—but if you ask politely, they might keep it for you; exit from station and follow small road to the right with trains behind you, turn right on Atholl Road, and walk 5 min to TI on left, at #22; tel. 01796/472-215).

Helpful Hints
Bike Rental: Escape Route Bikes, located across the street and a block from the TI (away from town), rents mountain bikes for adults and kids (£10/4 hours, £18/24 hours, price includes helmets and lock if you ask, Mon–Sat 9:00–17:30, Sun 10:00–17:00, shorter hours in winter, 3 Atholl Road, tel. 01796/473-859).

SELF-GUIDED HILLWALK

Pitlochry Whisky Walk

If you were a hobbit in a previous life, spend an afternoon hillwalking from downtown Pitlochry to both distilleries (listed below). The entire loop trip takes two to three hours, depending on how long you linger in the distilleries (at least 45 min–1 hour of walking each way). It's a good way to see some green rolling hills, especially if you've only experienced urban Scotland. The walk is largely uphill on the way to the Edradour Distillery; wear good shoes, bring a rain jacket just in case, and be happy that you'll stroll easily downhill *after* you've had your whisky samples.

At the TI, pick up the *Pitlochry Walks* brochure (50p). You'll be taking the **Edradour Walk** (marked on directional signs with the yellow hiker icons; on the map, it's a series of yellow dots). Leave the TI and head left along busy A924. While the walk can be done by going either direction, I'll describe it counterclockwise.

Within 10 minutes, you'll come to **Bell's Blair Athol Distillery.** If you're a whisky buff, stop in here. Otherwise, hold out for the much more atmospheric Edradour. After passing a few B&Bs and suburban homes, you'll see a sign (marked *Edradour Walk*) on the left side of the road, leading you up and off the highway. You'll come to a clearing, and as the road gets steeper, you'll see signs directing you 50 yards off the main path to see the "Black Spout"—a wonderful waterfall well worth a few extra steps.

At the top of the hill, you'll come to a clearing, where a narrow path leads along a field. Low rolling hills surround you in all directions. It seems like there's not another person around for miles, with just thistles to keep you company. It's an easy 20 minutes to the distillery from here.

Stop into the **Edradour Distillery** (described below). After the tour, leave the distillery heading right, following the paved road (Old North Road). In about five minutes, there's a sign that seems to point right into the field. Take the small footpath that runs along the left side of the road. (If you see the driveway with stone lions on both sides, you've gone a few steps too far.) You'll walk parallel to the route you took getting to the distillery, then you'll head back into the forest. Cross the footbridge and make a left (as the map indicates), staying on the wide road. You'll pass a B&B, and hear traffic noises as you emerge out of the forest. The trail leads back to the highway, with the TI a few blocks ahead on the right.

SIGHTS AND ACTIVITIES

Distillery Tours—The cute **Edradour Scotch Distillery** (ED-rah-dower), the smallest in Scotland, takes pride in making its whisky with a minimum of machinery. Small white-and-red buildings are nestled in an impossibly green Scottish hillside. Wander through the buildings and take the free one-hour guided tour (3/hr in summer, 2/hr in winter). They offer a 10-minute audiovisual show, and, of course, a free sample dram. Unlike the bigger distilleries, they allow you to take photos of the equipment (March–Oct Mon–Sat 9:30–18:00, Sun 12:00–17:00; Nov–Feb Mon–Sat 10:00–16:00, Sun 12:00–16:00; last tour departs 1 hour before closing, tel. 01796/472-095, www.edradour.co.uk). Most come to the distillery by car (fol-

low signs from the main road, 2.5 miles into the countryside), but you can also get there by a peaceful hiking trail that you'll have all to yourself (see above).

The big, ivy-covered **Bell's Blair Athol Distillery** is more conveniently located (about a half-mile from the town center) and more corporate-feeling, offering £5 hour-long tours with a wee taste at the end (Easter–Oct tours depart 2/hr Mon–Sat 9:30–17:00, June–Oct also Sun 12:00–17:00, last tour departs 1 hour before closing; Nov–Easter tours depart Mon–Fri at 11:00, 13:00, and 15:00, closed Sat–Sun; tel. 01796/482-003).

Pitlochry Power Station—The station, adjacent to the salmon ladder, offers a mildly entertaining exhibit about hydroelectric power in the region (£3, April–Oct Mon–Fri 10:30–17:30, closed Sat–Sun, July–Aug also open weekends, closed Nov–March, tel. 01796/473-152). While walkers can reach this easily by crossing the footbridge from the town center (about a 15-min walk), drivers will head east out of town (toward Bell's Blair Athol Distillery), then turn right on Bridge Road, cross the river, and backtrack to the power station.

Theater—From May through October, the Pitlochry Festival Theatre presents a different play every night and concerts on some Sundays (both £12–22.50 Sun–Thu, £16.50–23.50 Fri–Sat, purchase tickets at TI or theater—same price, tel. 01796/484-626). The Scottish Plant Collector's Garden adjacent to the theater is available for visits (£3, Mon–Sat 10:00–17:00, Sun 11:00–17:00).

Sleep Code

(£1 = about $2, country code: 44, area code: 01796)
S = Single, **D** = Double/Twin, **T** = Triple, **Q** = Quad, **b** = bathroom,
s = shower only.

To help you sort easily through these listings, I've divided the rooms into two categories based on the price for a standard double room with bath (during high season):

$$ Higher Priced—Most rooms £50 or more.
 $ Lower Priced—Most rooms less than £50.

SLEEPING

$$ Craigroyston House is a quaint, large Victorian country house with eight Laura Ashley–style bedrooms run by charming Gretta and Douglas Maxwell (Db-£50–70 depending on season, family room, cash only, above and behind the TI—small gate at back of parking lot—and next to the church at 2 Lower Oakfield, tel. & fax 01796/472-053, www.craigroyston.co.uk, reservations@craigroyston .co.uk). Gretta can find you another B&B if her place is full.

$ Pitlochry's fine **hostel** has 62 beds in 12 rooms, including some family rooms. It's on Knockard Road, well-signed from the town center, about a five-minute walk above the main drag (£13 bunks in 3- to 8-bed rooms, £15 July–Aug; Db-£39, £42 July–Aug; £1–1.50 more for non-members, Internet access, self-service laundry, office open 7:00–23:00, tel. 01796/472-308, pitlochry@syha .org.uk).

EATING

Plenty of options line the main drag, including several bakeries selling picnic supplies. For a heartier meal, try **Victoria's** restaurant and coffee shop, located midway between the train station and the TI (lunch: £5–8 sandwiches, £9–11 mains; dinner: £9 pizzas, £11–20 mains; daily 10:00–21:00, patio seating, at corner of memorial garden at 45 Atholl Road, tel. 01796/472-670).

TRANSPORTATION CONNECTIONS

The train station is open daily 8:00–18:00 (maybe less in winter).
From Pitlochry by Train to: Inverness (9/day, 1.5 hrs), **Stirling** (every 2 hrs, 1.25 hrs, most transfer in Perth), **Edinburgh** (6/day, 2 hrs), **Glasgow** (8/day, 2 hrs, transfer in Perth). Train info: tel. 08457-484-950.

Stirling

Once the Scottish capital, the quaint city of Stirling (pop. 41,000) is a mini-Edinburgh with a pair of attractions: its famous castle, dripping with history and boasting sweeping views; and, nearby, the William Wallace Monument honoring the real-life Braveheart.

ORIENTATION

Stirling's old town is situated along a long, narrow, steep hill, with the castle at its apex. The **TI** is near the base of the old town (July–Aug Mon–Sat 9:00–19:00, Sun 9:30–18:00, shorter hours off-season, 41 Dumbarton Road, tel. 01786/475-019).

Stirling's two main sights (Stirling Castle and the Wallace Monument) are difficult to reach by foot. If you lack a car, the **City Sightseeing** hop-on, hop-off bus tour is a must. From the train station (bus station nearby), it takes visitors to the Wallace Monument, TI, and up to Stirling Castle (£7.50, ticket good for 2 days, departs every 45 min April–Sept 9:30–16:20, 16 stops total, full route lasts 80 min). If you're headed only to the castle, ask about the route before you buy the ticket—it might go to the Wallace Monument first, causing you a long wait to get to the castle.

SIGHTS

▲Stirling Castle

"He who holds Stirling, holds Scotland." These fateful words have proven, more often than not, to be true. Stirling Castle's strategic position—perched on a volcanic crag overlooking a bridge over the River Forth, the primary passage between the Lowlands and the Highlands—has long been the key to Scotland. This castle of the Stuart kings is one of Scotland's most historic and popular. Offering spectacular views over a gentle countryside, and a mildly interesting but steadily improving exhibit inside, Stirling is worth a look.

Cost and Hours: £8.50, daily April–Sept 9:30–18:00, Oct–March 9:30–17:00, last entry 45 min before closing, tel. 01786/450-000, www.historic-scotland.gov.uk.

Getting There: Similar to Edinburgh's castle, Stirling Castle sits at the very tip of a steep old town. If you enter Stirling by car, follow the *Stirling Castle* signs, twist up the mazelike roads to the esplanade, and park at the £2 lot just outside the castle gate. Without a car, it's a bit more complicated: From the train or bus station, you can either hike the 20-minute uphill route to the

Stirling

castle, or you can take the convenient City Sightseeing bus up to the top (see above).

Tours: Posted information is skimpy, so a tour or audioguide is important for bringing the site to life. You can take the included 45-minute guided tour (1/hr April–June, 2/hr July–Sept, 4/day Oct–March, depart from the Castle Close just inside the entry) or rent the very good £2 audioguide from the kiosk near the ticket window. Knowledgeable docents posted throughout can tell you more.

Background: Stirling marks the site of two epic medieval battles where famous Scotsmen defeated huge English armies despite impossible odds: In 1297, William Wallace (a.k.a. "Braveheart") fended off an invading English army at the Battle of Stirling Bridge. And in 1314, Robert the Bruce won the battle of nearby Bannockburn. Soon after, the castle became the primary residence of the Stuart monarchs, who turned it into a showpiece of Scotland (and a symbol of one-upmanship against England). But when the crown moved to London, Stirling's prominence waned. The military, which took over the castle during the Jacobite Wars of the 18th century, bulked it up and converted it into a garrison—damaging much of its delicate beauty. Since 1966, the fortress has been undergoing an extensive and costly restoration to bring it back to its glory days and make it, once again, one of Britain's premier castles.

❷ Self-Guided Tour: From the parking lot at the esplanade, go through the gate to buy your ticket (ask about tour times, and consider renting the audioguide), then head up into the castle through another gate. If you have time to kill before the tour, dip into the grassy courtyard on the left to reach an introductory **castle exhibition** about the history of the town and its fortress. Historians at Stirling are proud of the work they've done to rebuild the castle—and they're not shy about saying so.

Then head up through the main gateway into the **Outer Close.** Tours depart from just to your right, near the Grand Battery, which boasts cannon-and-rampart views. Down the hill along this wall is the Great Kitchens exhibit (where mannequin cooks oversee medieval recipes), and below that, the North Gate leads to the Nether Bailey (dating from the castle's later days as a military base). Back in the Outer Close, at the top of the courtyard (to your left as you enter), is a narrow passageway lined with exhibits about Stirling's various medieval craftspeople.

Hike up into the **Inner Close,** where you're surrounded by Scottish history. Each of the very different buildings in this complex was built by a different monarch. Facing downhill, you'll see the Great Hall straight ahead. This grand structure was built by the great Renaissance king James IV. Step inside the grand, empty-feeling space to appreciate its fine flourishes. The Chapel Royal, where Mary Queen of Scots was crowned in 1543, is to your left, and also worth a visit. To your right is the Palace (likely closed for restoration in 2008). And behind you is the King's Old Building, with a regimental (military) museum.

▲William Wallace Monument

Commemorating the Scottish hero better known as "Braveheart," this sandstone tower—built during a wave of Scottish national-ism in the mid-19th century—marks the Abbey Craig hill on the outskirts of Stirling. From the parking lot and Visitors Pavilion, you can hike (a very steep 10 min) or take a shuttle bus up the hill to the monument itself. From the base of the monument, you can see the Stirling Bridge—a stone version that replaced the original wooden one—and imagine how Wallace's famous battle here played out (explained inside the monument). As you climb the 246 tight, narrow steps inside the tower for grand views, you'll dip into other parts of the exhibit: Learn about Wallace and his defiant stand against King Edward I, ogle his five-and-a-half-foot-long broadsword, and take a spin through a hall of other Scottish heroes (£6.50, daily March–May 10:00–17:00, June 10:00–18:00, July–Aug 9:00–18:00, Sept 9:30–17:30, Oct 10:00–17:00, Nov–Feb 10:30–16:00, last entry 45 min before closing, tel. 01786/472-140, www.nationalwallacemonument.com). To learn more about Wallace, read the sidebar on page 465.

Getting There: It's two miles northeast of Stirling on A8, signposted from the city center. From the Stirling train or bus sta-tion, you can take the City Sightseeing bus described on page 611.

TRANSPORTATION CONNECTIONS

From Stirling by Train to: Edinburgh (2/hr, 50 min), **Glasgow** (3/hr, 25–45 min), **Pitlochry** (every 2 hrs, 1.25 hrs, most transfer in Perth), **Inverness** (every 2 hrs, 2.5–3 hrs, most transfer in Perth).

Stirling

BRITISH HISTORY AND CULTURE

Britain was created by force and held together by force. It's really a nation of the 19th century, when this rich Victorian-era empire reached its financial peak. Its traditional industry, buildings, and the popularity of the notion of "Great" Britain are a product of its past wealth.

To best understand the many fascinating guides you'll encounter in your travels, have a basic handle on the sweeping story of this land. (Generally, the wonderful and terrible stories are made up...and the boring ones are true.)

What's So Great About Britain?

Regardless of the revolution we had 200-some years ago, many American travelers feel that they "go home" to Britain. This most popular tourist destination has a strange influence and power over us. The more you know of Britain's roots, the better you'll get in touch with your own.

Geographically, the Isle of Britain is small (about the size of Uganda or Idaho)—600 miles long and 300 miles at its widest point. Britain's highest mountain (Scotland's Ben Nevis) is 4,400 feet, a foothill by our standards. The population is a fifth that of the United States. At its peak in the mid-1800s, Britain owned one-fifth of the world and accounted for more than half the planet's industrial output. Today, the Empire has been reduced to the Isle of Britain itself and a few token, troublesome scraps, such as the Falklands, Gibraltar, and Northern Ireland.

Economically, Great Britain's industrial production is about five percent of the world's total. For the first time in history, Ireland has a higher per-capita income than Britain. Still, the economy is booming, and inflation, unemployment, and interest rates are all low.

Culturally, Britain is still a world leader. Her heritage, culture, and people cannot be measured in traditional units of power. London is a major exporter of actors, movies, and theater, of rock and classical music, and of writers, painters, and sculptors.

Ethnically, the British Isles are a mix of the descendants of the early Celtic natives (in Scotland, Ireland, Wales, and Cornwall), descendants of the invading Anglo-Saxons who took southeast England in the Dark Ages, and descendants of the conquering Normans of the 11th century...not to mention more recent immigrants from around the world (explained below). Cynics call the United Kingdom an English Empire ruled by London, whose dominant Anglo-Saxon English (49 million) far outnumber their Celtic brothers and sisters (8 million).

Politically, Britain is ruled by the House of Commons, with some guidance from the mostly figurehead Queen and House of Lords. Just as the United States Congress is dominated by Democrats and Republicans, Britain's Parliament is dominated by two parties: Labour and Conservative ("Tories"). (George W. Bush would fit the Conservative Party and Bill Clinton the Labour Party like political gloves.)

The prime minister is the chief executive. He's not elected directly by voters; rather, he assumes power as the head of the party that wins a majority in Parliamentary elections. Instead of imposing term limits, the Brits allow their prime ministers to choose when to leave office. The ruling party also gets to choose when to hold elections, as long as it's within five years of the previous one—so prime ministers carefully schedule elections for times during which (they hope) their party will win.

In the 1980s, Conservatives were in charge under Prime Minister Margaret Thatcher and Prime Minister John Major. As proponents of traditional, Victorian values—community, family, hard work, thrift, and trickle-down economics—they took a Reaganesque approach to Britain's serious social and economic problems.

In 1997, a huge Labour victory brought Tony Blair to the prime minister's office. Labour began shoring up a social-service system (health care, education, the minimum wage) undercut by years of Conservative rule. Blair's Labour Party was "New Labour"—akin to Clinton's "New Democrats"—meaning they were fiscally conservative but attentive to the needs of the people. Conservative Party fears of old-fashioned, big-spending, bleeding-heart, Union-style liberalism have proved unfounded. The Liberal Parliament has proved to be more open to integration with Europe.

Tony Blair—relatively young, family-oriented, personable, easy-going, and forever flashing his toothy grin—started out as a respected and well-liked PM. But after he followed US President

From Blair to Brown: Britain's New PM

On June 27, 2007, Tony Blair stood on the stoop at #10 Downing Street (the prime minister's residence) and waved good-bye to his country, clutching his four children and flashing his trademark ear-to-ear grin. Just before getting into their car, Blair's wife, Cherie, said to the press, "Goodbye. I don't think we will miss *you*." Within minutes, Gordon Brown presented himself at Buckingham Palace for an audience with Queen Elizabeth II, then came to stand in front of #10 and said, "I have just accepted the invitation of Her Majesty the Queen to form a government."

Brown, who comes from a humble fishing village in Scotland, is the yin to Blair's yang. When their Labour Party was gaining popularity in the mid-1990s, the two had to decide which one would lead. After the pair reached a legendarily mysterious deal, Blair went on to a successful 10-year run as prime minister, while Brown bided his time playing second fiddle as chancellor of the exchequer (who controls the budget). Unlike the gregarious, lovable Blair, Brown is a staid and gruff policy wonk. At first accused of being shifty-eyed (and therefore untrustworthy), Brown later revealed he was actually blind in his left eye from an old rugby injury. While Blair is married to the beloved daughter of a popular acting family, Brown remained a bachelor well into his forties; his wife Sarah (whom he married in 2000) prefers to avoid the limelight. Of the Browns' three children, one lived only 10 days, and another has been diagnosed with cystic fibrosis—one of the few aspects of Brown's personal life that has garnered him sympathy.

At Blair's last appearance before parliament, he received a rousing ovation, and earned cheers and plaudits even from his political enemies; meanwhile, Brown was received only with a polite smattering of applause. The next day, the press seized on one typically well-meaning but uninspiring snippet from Brown's speech at #10: his old school motto, "I will try my utmost."

George W. Bush into an unnecessary and costly war with Iraq, his popularity took a nosedive. The 2005 elections were a virtual referendum on whether Blair could be trusted. His Labour party won a slim majority, but Blair's prime ministership was doomed. In May of 2007, Blair announced he would resign his post; a few weeks later, his chancellor of the exchequer and longtime colleague, Gordon Brown, was sworn in as Britain's new prime minister. Burdened with managing Britain's involvement in the Iraq War—and lacking Blair's charisma—Brown's struggle is to keep

Labour in power through the next parliamentary elections (which must occur sometime before June of 2010).

Looking to the future, London is gearing up to host the 2012 Olympic Games.

Challenges Facing Today's Britain

Great as Britain is, the country has its share of challenges. You'll likely hear people talking about some of the following hot-button topics during your visit: terrorism, immigration, and binge-drinking.

Like the US, Britain has been coping with its own string of terrorist threats and attacks. On the morning of July 7, 2005, London's commuters were rocked by four different bombs that killed dozens across the city. In the summer of 2006, authorities foiled a plot to carry liquid bombs onto a plane (resulting in the liquid ban air travelers are still experiencing today). On June 29, 2007—just two days after Gordon Brown became prime minister—two car bombs were discovered (and defused) near London's Piccadilly Circus, and the next day, a flaming car drove into the baggage-claim level at Glasgow Airport. Most Brits have accepted that they now live with the possibility of terrorism at home—and that life must go on.

Britain has taken aggressive measures to prevent future attacks, such as installing "CCTV" (close-captioned) surveillance cameras everywhere, in both public and private places. (You'll frequently see signs warning you that you're being filmed.) These cameras have already proved helpful in piecing together the events leading up to an attack, but as Brits trade their privacy for security, many wonder if they've given up too much.

The recent terrorist threats have also highlighted issues relating to Britain's large immigrant population (nearly 2 million). Second-generation Muslims—born in Britain, but who strongly identify with other Muslims rather than their British neighbors—were responsible for the July 2005 bombs. Some Brits reacted to the event known as "7/7" as if all the country's Muslims were to blame. At the same time, a handful of radical Islamic clerics began to justify the bombers' violent actions. Unemployment and other economic factors further stretch the already strained relations between communities within Britain.

The large Muslim population is just one thread in the tapestry of today's Britain. While nine out of ten Brits are white, the country has large minority groups, mainly from Britain's former overseas colonies: India, Pakistan, Bangladesh, Africa, the Caribbean, and many other places. But despite the tensions between some groups, for the most part Britain is well-integrated, with minorities represented in most (if not all) walks of life.

Recently another wave of immigration has hit Britain. Throughout the British Isles, you'll see lots of Eastern Europeans (mostly Poles, Slovaks, and Lithuanians) working in restaurants, cafés, and B&Bs. These transplants—who started arriving after their home countries joined the EU in 2004—can make a lot more money working here than back home. British small-business owners tell me they find these new arrivals to be polite, responsible, and affordable. While a few Brits complain that the new arrivals are taking jobs away from the natives, and others are frustrated that their English is often far from perfect, for the most part Britain has absorbed this new set of immigrants gracefully.

Over the last several years, Britain has seen an epidemic of binge-drinking among young people. A 2007 study revealed that one out of every three British men, and one out of every five British women, routinely drinks to excess. It's become commonplace for young adults (typically from their mid-teens to mid-20s) to spend every weekend night drinking at pubs and carousing in the streets. (And they ratchet up the debauchery even more when celebrating a "stag night" or "hen night"—bachelor and bachelorette parties.) While sociologists and politicians scratch their heads about the causes and effects of this phenomenon, tourists are complaining about weekend noise and obnoxious (though generally harmless) young drunks on the streets.

Basic British History for the Traveler

When Julius Caesar landed on the misty and mysterious isle of Britain in 55 B.C., England entered the history books. The primitive Celtic tribes he conquered were themselves invaders (who had earlier conquered the even more mysterious people who built Stonehenge). The Romans built towns and roads, establishing their capital at Londinium. The Celtic natives in Scotland and Wales—consisting of Gaels, Picts, and Scots—were not easily subdued. The Romans built Hadrian's Wall near the Scottish border as protection against their troublesome northern neighbors.

As Rome fell, so fell Roman Britain, a victim of invaders and internal troubles. Barbarian tribes from Germany and Denmark, called Angles and Saxons, swept through the southern part of the island, establishing Angle-land. These were the days of the real King Arthur, possibly a Christianized Roman general who fought valiantly, but in vain, against invading barbarians. The island was plunged into 500 years of Dark Ages—wars, plagues, and poverty—lit only by the dim candle of a few learned Christian monks and missionaries trying to convert the barbarians. The sightseer sees little from this Anglo-Saxon period.

Modern England began with yet another invasion. William the Conqueror and his Norman troops crossed the English

Channel from France in 1066. William crowned himself king in Westminster Abbey (where all subsequent coronations would take place), and began building the Tower of London. French-speaking Norman kings ruled the country for two centuries. Then followed two centuries of civil wars, with various noble families vying for the crown. In one of the most bitter feuds, the York and Lancaster families fought the Wars of the Roses, so-called because of the white and red flowers the combatants chose as their symbols. Battles, intrigues, kings, nobles, and ladies imprisoned and executed in the Tower—it's a wonder the country survived its rulers.

England was finally united by the "third-party" Tudor family. Henry VIII, a Tudor, was England's Renaissance king. He was handsome, athletic, highly sexed, a poet, a scholar, and a musician. He was also arrogant, cruel, gluttonous, and paranoid. He went through six wives in 40 years, divorcing, imprisoning, or beheading them when they no longer suited his needs.

Henry also "divorced" England from the Catholic Church, establishing the Protestant Church of England (the Anglican Church) and setting in motion years of religious squabbles. He also "dissolved" the monasteries (circa 1540), left just the shells of many formerly glorious abbeys dotting the countryside, and pocketed their land and wealth for the crown.

Henry's daughter, Queen Elizabeth I, who reigned for 45 years, made England a great trading and naval power (defeating the Spanish Armada) and presided over the Elizabethan era of great writers (such as William Shakespeare) and scientists (such as Francis Bacon).

The longstanding quarrel between England's divine-right kings and Parliament's nobles finally erupted into a civil war (1643). Parliament forces under the Protestant Puritan farmer Oliver Cromwell defeated—and beheaded—King Charles I. This civil war left its mark on much of what you'll see in Britain. Eventually, Parliament invited Charles' son to take the throne. This "restoration of the monarchy" was accompanied by a great colonial expansion and the rebuilding of London (including Christopher Wren's St. Paul's Cathedral), which had been devastated by the Great Fire of 1666.

Britain grew as a naval superpower, colonizing and trading with all parts of the globe. Admiral Horatio Nelson's victory over Napoleon's fleet at the Battle of Trafalgar secured her naval superiority ("Britannia rules the waves"), and 10 years later, the Duke of Wellington stomped Napoleon on land at Waterloo. Nelson and Wellington—both buried in London's St. Paul's Cathedral—are memorialized by many arches, columns, and squares throughout England.

Economically, Britain led the world into the Industrial Age with her mills, factories, coal mines, and trains. By the time of

Royal Families: Past and Present

Royal Lineage

802–1066	Saxon and Danish kings
1066–1154	Norman invasion (William the Conqueror), Norman kings
1154–1399	Plantagenet (kings with French roots)
1399–1461	Lancaster
1462–1485	York
1485–1603	Tudor (Henry VIII, Elizabeth I)
1603–1649	Stuart (civil war and beheading of Charles I)
1649–1653	Commonwealth, no royal head of state
1653–1659	Protectorate, with Cromwell as Lord Protector
1660–1714	Restoration of Stuart monarchy
1714–1901	Hanover (four Georges, Victoria)
1901–1910	Edward VII
1910–present	Windsor (George V, Edward VIII, George VI, Elizabeth II)

The Royal Family Today

It seems you can't pick up a British newspaper without some mention of the latest scandal or oddity involving the royal family. Here is the cast of characters:

Queen Elizabeth II wears the traditional crown of her great-great grandmother, Victoria. Her husband is Prince Phillip, who's not considered king.

Their son, Prince Charles (the Prince of Wales), is next in line to become king. In 1981, Charles married Lady Diana Spencer (Princess Di) who, after their bitter divorce, died in a car crash in 1997. Their two sons, William and Harry, are next in line to the throne after their father. In 2005, Charles married his longtime girlfriend, Camilla Parker Bowles, who is trying to gain respectability with the Queen and the public.

The Queen Mother (or Queen Mum) is the late mother of Queen Elizabeth II. Prince Charles' siblings are often in the news for their marital or dating escapades: Princess Anne, Prince Andrew (who married and divorced Sarah "Fergie" Ferguson), and Prince Edward (who married Di look-alike Sophie Rhys-Jones). For more on the monarchy, see www.royal.gov.uk.

Queen Victoria's reign (1837–1901), Britain was at its zenith of power, with a colonial empire that covered one-fifth of the world.

The 20th century was not kind to Britain. Two world wars devastated the population. The Nazi blitzkrieg reduced much of London to rubble. The colonial empire dwindled to almost nothing, and Britain lost its superpower economic status. The war over the Falkland Islands in 1982 showed how little of the British Empire was left—and how determined the British are to hang on to what remains. The "Irish Troubles"—calmer today than they have been in the past—still flare up on occasion, as the Catholic inhabitants of British-ruled Northern Ireland fight for the independence their southern neighbors won decades ago.

But the tradition (if not the substance) of greatness continues, presided over by Queen Elizabeth II, her husband Prince Philip, and Prince Charles. With economic problems, the marital turmoil of Charles and the late Princess Diana, and a relentless popular press, the royal family has had a tough time. But the queen has stayed above it all, and most British people still jump at an opportunity to see royalty. With the death of Princess Diana and the historic outpouring of grief, it's clear that the concept of royalty was still alive and well as Britain entered the third millennium.

Queen Elizabeth marked her 50th year on the throne in 2002 at age 76. While many wonder who will succeed her, the case is fairly straightforward: The queen sees her job as a lifelong position, and legally, Charles (who wants to be king) cannot be skipped over for his son, William. Given the longevity in the family (the queen's mum, born in August of 1900, made it to 101 before she died in 2002), Charles is in for a long wait.

Architecture in Britain

From Stonehenge to Big Ben, travelers are storming castle walls, climbing spiral staircases, and snapping the pictures of 5,000 years of architecture. Let's sort it out.

The oldest ruins—mysterious and prehistoric—date from before Roman times back to 3000 B.C. The earliest sites, such as Stonehenge and Avebury, were built during the Stone and Bronze ages. The remains from these periods are made of huge stones or mounds of earth, even man-made hills, and were created as celestial calendars and for worship or burial. Britain is crisscrossed with lines of these mysterious sights (ley lines). Iron Age people (600 B.C.–A.D. 50) left desolate stone forts. The Romans thrived in Britain from A.D. 50 to 400, building cities, walls, and roads. Evidence of Roman greatness can be seen in lavish villas with ornate mosaic floors, temples uncovered beneath great English churches, and Roman stones in medieval city walls. Roman roads sliced across the island in straight lines. Today, unusually straight rural roads are very likely laid directly on these ancient roads.

As Rome crumbled in the fifth century, so did Roman Britain. Little architecture survives from Dark Ages England, the Saxon period from 500 to 1000. Architecturally, the light was switched on with the Norman conquest in 1066. As William earned his title "the Conqueror," his French architects built churches and castles in the European Romanesque style.

English Romanesque is called Norman (1066–1200). Norman churches had round arches, thick walls, and small windows; Durham Cathedral and the Chapel of St. John in the Tower of London are prime examples. The Tower of London, with its square keep, small windows, and spiral stone stairways, is a typical Norman castle. You'll see plenty of Norman castles—all built to secure the conquest of these invaders from Normandy.

Gothic architecture (1200–1600) replaced the heavy Norman style with light, vertical buildings, pointed arches, soaring spires, and bigger windows. English Gothic is divided into three stages. Early English (1200–1300) features tall, simple spires; beautifully carved capitals; and elaborate chapter houses (such as the Wells Cathedral). Decorated Gothic (1300–1400) gets fancier, with more elaborate tracery, bigger windows, and ornately carved pinnacles, as you'll see at Westminster Abbey. Finally, the Perpendicular style (1400–1600, also called "rectilinear") returns to square towers and emphasizes straight, uninterrupted vertical lines from ceiling to floor, with vast windows and exuberant decoration, including fan-vaulted ceilings (King's College Chapel at Cambridge). Through this evolution, the structural ribs (arches meeting at the top of the ceilings) became more and more decorative and fanciful (the most fancy being the star vaulting and fan vaulting of the Perpendicular style).

As you tour the great medieval churches of Britain, remember that nearly everything is symbolic. For instance, on the tombs of knights, if the figure has crossed legs, he was a Crusader. If his feet rest on a dog, he died at home, but if the legs rest on a lion, he died in battle. Local guides and books help us modern pilgrims understand at least a little of what we see.

Wales is particularly rich in English castles, which were needed to subdue the stubborn Welsh. Edward I built a ring of powerful castles in Wales, including Conwy and Caernarfon.

Gothic houses were a simple mix of woven strips of thin wood, rubble, and plaster called wattle and daub. The famous black-and-white Tudor (or half-timbered) look came simply from filling in heavy oak frames with wattle and daub.

The Tudor period (1485–1560) was a time of relative peace (the Wars of the Roses were finally over), prosperity, and renaissance. Henry VIII broke with the Catholic Church and "dissolved" (destroyed) the monasteries, leaving scores of Britain's greatest churches as gutted shells. These hauntingly beautiful abbey ruins (Glastonbury, Tintern, Whitby, Rievaulx, Battle, St. Augustine's in Canterbury, and lots more) surrounded by lush lawns are now pleasant city parks.

Although few churches were built during the Tudor period, this was a time of house and mansion construction. Heating a home was becoming popular and affordable, and Tudor buildings featured small square windows and many chimneys. In towns, where land was scarce, many Tudor houses grew up and out, getting wider with each overhanging floor.

The Elizabethan and Jacobean periods (1560–1620) were followed by the English Renaissance style (1620–1720). English architects mixed Gothic and classical styles, then Baroque and classical styles. Although the ornate Baroque never really grabbed Britain, the classical style of the Italian architect Andrea Palladio did. Inigo Jones (1573–1652), Christopher Wren (1632–1723), and those they inspired plastered Britain with enough columns, domes, and symmetry to please a Caesar. The Great Fire of London (1666) cleared the way for an ambitious young Wren to put his mark on London forever with a grand rebuilding scheme, including the great St. Paul's Cathedral and more than 50 other churches.

The celebrants of the Boston Tea Party remember Britain's Georgian period (1720–1840) for its lousy German kings. Georgian architecture was rich and showed off by being very classical. Grand ornamental doorways, fine cast-ironwork on balconies and railings, Chippendale furniture, and white-on-blue Wedgwood ceramics graced rich homes everywhere. John Wood Jr. and Sr. led the way, giving the trendsetting city of Bath its crescents and circles of aristocratic Georgian row houses. "Georgian" is English for "Neoclassical."

The Industrial Revolution shaped the Victorian period (1840–1890) with glass, steel, and iron. Britain had a huge new erector set (so did France's Mr. Eiffel). This was also a Romantic period, reviving the "more Christian" Gothic style. London's Houses of Parliament are Neo-Gothic—just 100 years old but looking 700, except for the telltale modern precision and craftsmanship. Whereas Gothic was stone or concrete, Neo-Gothic was often red brick. These were Britain's glory days, and there was more building in this period than in all previous ages combined.

The architecture of modern times obeys the formula "form follows function"—it worries more about your needs than your eyes. Britain treasures its heritage and takes great pains to build tastefully in historic districts and to preserve its many "listed" buildings. With a booming tourist trade, these quaint reminders of its past—and ours—are becoming a valuable part of the British economy.

British TV

British television is so good—and so British—that it deserves a mention as a sightseeing treat. After a hard day of castle climbing, watch the telly over tea in the living room of your village B&B.

There are currently five free channels that any television can receive. BBC-1 and BBC-2 are government regulated and commercial free. Broadcasting of these two channels (and of the five BBC radio stations) is funded by a mandatory £132-per-year-per-household television and radio license (hmmm, 70 cents per day to escape commercials and public-broadcasting pledge drives). Channels 3, 4, and 5 are privately owned, are a little more lowbrow, and have commercials—but those commercials are often clever and sophisticated, providing a fun look at British life. In addition, about 65 percent of households now receive digital cable or satellite television, which offer dozens of specialty channels, similar to those available in North America.

Britain is about to leap into the Digital Age ahead of the rest of the TV-watching world. Beginning in 2008, a few areas will receive only a digital signal, which will require a digitally equipped set. More regions will gradually follow, and by 2013 the old analog signals will be switched off and only digital signals will be broadcast. Ultimately every house will enjoy literally hundreds of high-definition channels with no need for cable or satellites.

Whereas California "accents" fill our airwaves 24 hours a day, homogenizing the way our country speaks, Britain protects and promotes its regional accents by its choice of TV and radio announcers. See if you can tell where each is from (or ask a local for help).

Commercial-free British TV, while looser than it used to be, is still careful about what it airs and when. But after the 21:00 "watershed" hour, when children are expected to be in bed, some nudity and profanity is allowed, and may cause you to spill your tea.

American programs (such as *Desperate Housewives, Lost, Oprah,* and trash-talk shows) are very popular. The visiting viewer should be sure to tune the TV to a few typical British shows, including a dose of British situation- and political-comedy fun, and the top-notch BBC evening news. British comedies have tickled the American funny bone for years, from sketch comedy *(Monty Python's Flying Circus)* to sitcoms (such as *Are You Being Served?, Fawlty Towers,* and *Absolutely Fabulous*). A more recent cross-the-pond mega-hit, *The Office,* has made its star Ricky Gervais *the* top name in British comedy today, and has spawned successful adaptations in the US, Germany, France, and French Canada. Quiz shows and reality shows are taken very seriously here (*Who Wants to Be a Millionaire?, American Idol,* and *Dancing with the Stars* are all based on British shows). Michael Parkinson is the Johnny Carson of Britain for late-night talk. For a tear-filled, slice-of-life taste of British soaps dealing in all the controversial issues, see the popular *Emmerdale, Coronation Street,* or *EastEnders.*

APPENDIX

CONTENTS

RESOURCES

Tourist Information Offices

The **Visit Britain** office in the US is a wealth of knowledge. Check it out: tel. 800-462-2748, www.visitbritain.com, travelinfo@visitbritain.org. Ask for free maps of London and Britain and any specific information you may want (such as regional information, a garden-tour map, urban cultural activities brochures, and so on).

Virtually every city in Britain has a tourist information office; the best is the **Britain and London Visitors Centre** in London (see page 44). Note that tourist information offices are abbreviated "TI" in this book.

Resources from Rick Steves

Guidebooks and Online Updates

This book is updated every year in person. The telephone numbers and hours of sights listed in this book are accurate as of mid-2007—but even with annual updates, things change. For the very latest, visit www.ricksteves.com/update. Also at my website, you'll find a valuable list of reports and experiences—good and bad—from fellow travelers (www.ricksteves.com/feedback).

This book is one of more than 30 titles in my series on European travel, which includes country guide-books (such as my England guide), city and regional guidebooks (including London), and my budget-travel skills handbook, *Rick Steves' Europe Through the Back Door.* My phrase books—for French, Italian, German, Spanish, and Portuguese—are practical and budget-oriented. My other books are *Europe 101* (a crash course on art and history, newly expanded and in full color), *European Christmas* (on traditional and modern-day celebrations), and *Postcards from Europe* (a fun memoir of my travels over 25 years). For a complete list of my books, see the inside of the last page of this book.

Public Television and Radio Shows

My TV series, *Rick Steves' Europe,* covers European destinations in 70 shows, with 10 episodes on Great Britain. My weekly public radio show, *Travel with Rick Steves,* features interviews with travel experts from around the world, including several hours on Great Britain and British culture. All the TV scripts and radio shows (which are easy and free to download to an MP3 player) are at www.ricksteves.com.

Free Audiotours

If your travels take you beyond Britain to France or Italy, take advantage of the free, self-guided audiotours I offer of the major sights in Paris, Florence, Rome, and Venice. The audiotours, produced by Rick Steves and Gene Openshaw (the co-author of seven books in the Rick Steves series) are available through iTunes and at www.ricksteves.com (Italy tours available after January 2008). Simply download them onto your computer and transfer them to your iPod or MP3 player. (Remember to bring a Y-jack and extra set of ear buds for your travel partner.)

Begin Your Trip at www.ricksteves.com

At our travel website, you'll find a wealth of free information on European destinations, including fresh monthly news and helpful tips from thousands of fellow travelers.

Our **online Travel Store** offers travel bags and accessories specially designed by Rick Steves to help you travel smarter and lighter. These include Rick's popular carry-on bags (wheeled and rucksack versions), money belts, totes, toiletries kits, adapters, other accessories, and a wide selection of guidebooks, planning maps, and DVDs.

Choosing the right **railpass** for your trip—amidst hundreds of options—can drive you nutty. We'll help you choose the best pass for your needs, plus give you a bunch of free extras.

Rick Steves' Europe Through the Back Door travel company offers **tours** with more than two dozen itineraries and 450 departures reaching the best destinations in this book... and beyond. We offer several tours that include London, such as our seven-day in-depth London city tour; our eight-day Paris and London tour, featuring the highlights of both great cities; and our 15-day Best of Britain tour. You'll enjoy great guides, a fun bunch of travel partners (with small groups of generally around 25), and plenty of room to spread out in a big, comfy bus. You'll find European adventures to fit every vacation length. For all the details, and to get our Tour Catalog and a free Rick Steves Tour Experience DVD (filmed on location during an actual tour), visit www.ricksteves.com or call the Tour Department at 425-608-4217.

Maps

The black-and-white maps in this book, drawn by Dave Hoerlein, are concise and simple. Dave, who is well-traveled in London and Britain, designed the maps to help you quickly orient yourself and get to where you want to go painlessly.

If you'll be lingering in London and want more detail, buy a city map at a London newsstand; the red *Bensons Mapguide* (£3) is excellent. Even the vending-machine maps sold in Tube stations are good. The *Rough Guide* map to London is well-designed (£5, sold at London bookstores). The *Rick Steves' Britain, Ireland &*

London City Map has a good map of London ($6, www.ricksteves .com). Many Londoners, along with obsessive-compulsive tourists, rely on the highly detailed *London A–Z* map book (generally £5–7, called "A to Zed" by locals, available at newsstands).

If you're driving, get a road atlas (1 inch equals 3 miles) covering all of Britain. Ordnance Survey, AA, and Bartholomew editions are all available for about £7 at tourist information offices, gas stations, and bookstores. Drivers, hikers, and cyclists may want more in-depth maps for the Cotswolds and the Lake District. Before you buy a map, look at it to make sure it has the level of detail you want.

Other Guidebooks

If you're like most travelers, this book is all you need. But racks of fine guidebooks are sold at bookstores throughout Britain and in the US. You may want some supplemental travel guidebooks, especially if you're traveling beyond my recommended destinations. When you consider the improvements they'll make in your $3,000 vacation, $30 for extra maps and books is money well spent. Especially for several people traveling by car, the extra weight and expense are negligible.

The following books are worthwhile, though not updated annually; check the publication date before you buy. The *Lonely Planet* and *Let's Go* guidebooks on London and on Britain are fine budget-travel guides. *Lonely Planet*'s guidebooks are more thorough and informative; *Let's Go* books are youth-oriented, with good coverage of nightlife, hostels, and cheap transportation deals. For cultural and sightseeing background, look into Michelin and Cadogan guides to London, England, and Britain. The readable Access guide for London is similarly well-researched. *Secret London* by Andrew Duncan leads the reader on unique walks through a less-touristy London. If you're a literature fan, consider picking up *The Edinburgh Literary Companion* (Lownie).

If you'll be focusing on London or traveling only in England, consider *Rick Steves' London 2008* or *Rick Steves' England 2008*.

Recommended Books and Movies

To get the feel of Great Britain past and present, consider reading some of these books or seeing these films:

Nonfiction

For a better understanding of the British, check out *A History of Britain, Volumes I, II & III* (by Schama; a companion series is also available on DVD). *A Traveller's History of England* (Daniell), *A Traveller's History of Scotland* (Fisher), and *A History of Wales* (Davies) provide good, succinct summaries of British history.

Appendix

Other possibilities include the humorous *Notes from a Small Island* (Bryson), *The Matter of Wales* (Morris), and Susan Allen Toth's *My Love Affair with England; England As You Like It;* and *England For All Seasons.*

If you'll be visiting Scotland, consider reading *Crowded with Genius* (Buchan) or *How the Scots Invented the Modern World* (Herman), which explains the influence the Scottish Enlightenment had on the rest of Europe. *The Guynd* is a memoir of a woman who married into a historic Highlands estate.

Fiction

Much British fiction is already familiar to North American readers, but here are a few you might have missed.

Classics such as *Mapp & Lucia* (Benson), *The Warden* (Trollope), and *Brideshead Revisited* (Waugh) are always a good place to start. Add to this group anything by Charles Dickens, Jane Austen, the Brontë sisters, Thomas Hardy, Agatha Christie, and P.G. Wodehouse. *Kidnapped*, by Robert Louis Stevenson, is a fantastic adventure story set in Scotland.

Historical fiction is a fun and easy way to learn about your destination. *The Pillars of the Earth* (Follett), *Sarum* (Rutherfurd), and *Stonehenge* (Cornwell) are all set in and around Salisbury. The heroines of Philippa Gregory's novels (*The Other Boleyn Girl* and *The Queen's Fool,* among others) witness intrigue at the courts of Henry VIII and Elizabeth I, while *Restoration* (Tremain) celebrates the excesses of King Charles II. Sharon Kay Penman brings 13th-century Wales to life in *Here Be Dragons.* And in the romantic, swashbuckling *Outlander* (Gabaldon), the heroine time travels between the Scotland of 1945 and 1743.

Mystery novels have a long tradition in Britain. *A Morbid Taste for Bones* (Peters) features a Benedictine monk-detective in 12th-century Shropshire. Agatha Christie's Miss Marple was introduced in 1930 in *The Murder at the Vicarage.* And Ian Rankin's troubled Inspector Rebus first gets his man in *Knots and Crosses,* set in modern-day Edinburgh. For a modern mystery, try any of the books in the Inspector Lynley series by Elizabeth George.

Films

Goodbye, Mr. Chips (1939) looks back on a schoolteacher's life in Victorian England. *Mrs. Miniver* (1942), a sentimental WWII picture, won the Academy Award for Best Picture, as did *How Green Was My Valley* (1941), set in a 19th-century Welsh mining village.

If Scotland is on your itinerary, consider viewing the Hitchcock mystery *The 39 Steps* (1935); *I Know Where I'm Going!* (1945), a charming love story filmed on the Island of Mull; the musical *Brigadoon* (1954); the horror film *The Wicker Man* (1973);

and/or the funny, fish-out-of-water flick *Local Hero* (1983).

The Wicker Man (1973), a horror flick, shows a different side of a small Scottish town. *Monty Python and the Holy Grail* (1975) brings the famous comedy troupe's irreverence to Arthurian legend. *Chariots of Fire* (1981) tells the tale of British runners at the 1924 Paris Olympics.

A Room with a View (1985), an adaptation of the E. M. Forster novel, sets half of the film in rural England. The all-star *Gosford Park* (2001) is part comedy, part murder mystery, and part critique of British class stratification in the 1930s. *Hope and Glory* (1987) is a semi-autobiographical story of a boy growing up during WWII's Blitz.

In 1995, Scottish history had a mini-renaissance, with *Braveheart,* winner of the Best Picture Oscar, and *Rob Roy*, which some historians consider the more accurate of the two films. The UK television series *Monarch of the Glen* (2000) features stunning Highland scenery and the eccentric family of a modern-day Laird.

Harry Potter Sights

Harry Potter's story is set in a magical Britain, and all of the places mentioned in the books except London are fictional, but you can visit many real film locations. Some of the locations are closed to visitors, though, or can be an un-magical disappointment in person. But quicker than you can say "Lumos," let's shine a light on where to get your Harry Potter fix if you're a die-hard fan.

Spoiler Warning: Information in this section will ruin surprises for those who haven't yet read the Harry Potter series or seen the movies.

London

In the first film, Harry first realizes his wizard powers when talking with a boa constrictor, filmed at the **London Zoo's Reptile House** in Regent's Park (Tube: Great Portland Street).

London bustles along oblivious to the parallel universe of wizards, hidden in the magical Diagon Alley (filmed, like many of the other fictional settings, on a set at Leavesden Studios, north of London). The goblin-run Gringotts Wizarding Bank, though, was filmed in the real-life marble-floored Exhibition Hall of **Australia House** (Tube: Temple), home of the Australian Embassy.

Harry catches the train to Hogwarts at **King's Cross Station.** Inside the glass-roofed train station, on a **pedestrian sky bridge** over the tracks, Hagrid gives Harry a train ticket. Harry heads to platform 9¾. You'll find a fun re-creation—complete with a *Platform 9¾* sign and a luggage cart that appears to be disappearing into the wall—on the way to platform 9. (Walk towards the pedestrian bridge and make a left at the arch.)

In film #3, Harry careens through London's lamp-lit streets on a purple three-decker bus that dumps him at The Leaky Cauldron. In this film, the pub's exterior was shot on rough-looking Stoney Street at the southeast edge of **Borough Street Market,** by The Market Porter pub (Tube: London Bridge).

In film #5, the Order of the Phoenix takes to the sky on broomsticks over London, passing by plenty of identifiable landmarks at night. Far beneath them glow the **London Eye, Big Ben,** and **Buckingham Palace.**

Cinema buffs can visit **Leicester Square** (Tube: Leicester Square), where Daniel Radcliffe and other stars strolled past paparazzi and down red carpets to the Odeon Theater to watch the movies' premieres.

Near Bath

The mysterious side of Hogwarts is often set in the elaborate, fan-vaulted corridors of the **Gloucester Cathedral** cloisters, 50 miles north of Bath. When Harry and Ron set out to save Hermione, they look down a long, dark Gloucester hallway and spot a 20-foot troll at the far end. And it's here that the walls whisper ominously to Harry, and letters in blood warn: "Enemies of the heir, beware."

The scene showing Harry being chosen for Gryffindor's Quidditch team was shot in the halls of the 13th-century **Lacock Abbey,** 13 miles east of Bath. Harry attends Professor Snape's class in one of the Abbey's bare, peeling-plaster rooms—appropriate to Snape's temperament. (Mad Max tours include Lacock on its day-trip itinerary; for details, see page 176.)

Oxford

Hogwarts, Harry's prestigious wizarding prep school, is a movie creation. But it's made from a number of locations, many of them real places in Oxford.

Christ Church College—with plenty of Harry-related sights that you can tour—inspired two film sets familiar to Potter fans. In the first film, the kids are ferried to Hogwarts, and then ascend a **stone**

staircase that leads into the Great Hall. The high-ceilinged **dining hall** used throughout the films—looking like a much larger version of what you see in Oxford—is filled with students at long rows of tables (as it is today at lunchtime, minus the weightless candles and flaming braziers).

Later in the first film, Harry sneaks into the restricted book section of Hogwarts Library under a cloak of invisibility. This scene was filmed inside Oxford's **Duke Humfrey's Library.** Hermione reads about the Sorcerer's Stone here, too.

At the end of the first film, Harry awakens from his dark battle into the golden light of the Hogwarts infirmary, filmed in a big-windowed **Divinity School** (downstairs). In film #4, Mad-Eye Moody turns Draco into a ferret on the grounds of **Bodleian Library.**

Durham and Northeast England
In the first film, Harry walks with his white owl, Hedwig, through a snowy cloister courtyard located in **Durham Cathedral.** The bird soars up and over the church's twin 13th-century towers.

Harry first learns to fly a broomstick on the green grass of Hogwarts school grounds, filmed inside the walls of **Alnwick Castle,** located 30 miles from Newcastle. In film #2, this is where the Weasleys' flying car crashes into the Whomping Willow.

Scotland
A lot of what you'll see in the exterior shots in the Harry Potter movies—especially scenes of the Hogwarts grounds—was filmed in craggy, cloudy, mysterious Scotland.

The **Hogwarts Express train** that carries Harry, Ron, and Hermione to school each year is filmed along an actual steam-train line. The movies show the train chugging across the real-life **Glenfinnan Viaduct,** where—in film #4—the Dementors stall the train and torture Harry.

Steal Falls, a waterfall at the base of Ben Nevis, is the locale for Harry's battle with a dragon for the Triwizard Tournament in film #4.

Other scenes filmed in the Highlands include a desolate hillside with Hagrid's stone hut in **Glencoe,** which was the main location for outdoor filming in *Azkaban*. Hagrid skips stones across the water at **Loch Eilt,** west of Fort William.

MONEY MATTERS

Damage Control for Lost Cards

If you lose your credit, debit, or ATM card, you can stop people from using it by reporting the loss immediately to the respective global customer-assistance centers. Call these 24-hour US numbers collect: Visa (410/581-9994), MasterCard (636/722-7111), and American Express (623/492-8427). Diner's Club has offices in the US (702/797-5532, call collect) and Britain (0870-1900-011).

At a minimum, you'll need to know the name of the financial institution that issued you the card, along with the type of card (classic, platinum, or whatever). Providing the following information will allow for a quicker cancellation of your missing card: full card number, whether you are the primary or secondary cardholder, the cardholder's name exactly as printed on the card, billing address, home phone number, circumstances of the loss or theft, and identification verification (your birth date, your mother's maiden name, or your Social Security number—memorize this, don't carry a copy). If you are the secondary cardholder, you'll also need to provide the primary cardholder's identification-verification details. You can generally receive a temporary card within two or three business days in Europe.

If you promptly report your card lost or stolen, you typically won't be responsible for any unauthorized transactions on your account, although many banks charge a liability fee of $50.

Tipping

Tipping in Britain isn't as automatic and generous as it is in the US, but for special service, tips are appreciated, if not expected. As in the US, the proper amount depends on your resources, tipping philosophy, and the circumstance, but some general guidelines apply.

Restaurants: At pubs where you order at the counter, you don't have to tip. (Regular customers ordering a round sometimes say, "Add one for yourself" as a tip for drinks ordered at the bar—but this isn't expected.) At a pub or restaurant with wait staff, check the menu or your bill to see if the service is included; if not, tip about 10 percent.

Taxis: To tip the cabbie, round up. For a typical ride, round up to a maximum of 10 percent (to pay a £4.50 fare, give £5; or for a £28 fare, give £30). If the cabbie hauls your bags and zips you to the airport to help you catch your flight, you might want to toss in a little more. But if you feel like you're being driven in circles or otherwise ripped off, skip the tip.

Special Services: It's thoughtful to tip a pound to someone who shows you a special sight and who is paid in no other way.

Tour guides at public sites often hold out their hands for tips after they give their spiel; if I've already paid for the tour, I don't tip extra, though some tourists do give a pound, particularly for a job well done. I don't tip at hotels, but if you do, give the porter about 50p for carrying bags and leave a pound in your room at the end of your stay for the maid if the room was kept clean. In general, if someone in the service industry does a super job for you, a tip of a pound or two is appropriate...but not required.

When in doubt, ask. If you're not sure whether (or how much) to tip for a service, ask your hotelier or the TI; they'll fill you in on how it's done on their turf.

Getting a VAT Refund

As is the case throughout the European Union, wrapped into the purchase price of your British souvenirs is a Value Added Tax (VAT) of about 17.5 percent. If you purchase more than £20 (about $40) worth of goods at a store that participates in the VAT-refund scheme, you're entitled to get most of that tax back. Getting your refund is usually straightforward and, if you buy a substantial amount of souvenirs, well worth the hassle. If you're lucky, the merchant will subtract the tax when you make your purchase. (This is more likely to occur if the store ships the goods to your home.) Otherwise, you'll need to:

Get the paperwork. Have the merchant completely fill out the necessary refund document, called a "Tax-Free Shopping Cheque." You'll have to present your passport at the store.

Get your stamp at the border or airport. Process your cheque(s) at your last stop in the EU (e.g., at the airport) with the customs agent who deals with VAT refunds. It's best to keep your purchases in your carry-on for viewing, but if they're too large or dangerous (such as knives) to carry on, track down the proper customs agent to inspect them before you check your bag. You're not supposed to use your purchased goods before you leave. If you show up at customs wearing your new kilt, officials might look the other way—or deny you a refund.

Collect your refund. You'll need to return your stamped document to the retailer or its representative. Many merchants work with a service, such as Global Refund (www.globalrefund.com) or Premier Tax Free (www.premiertaxfree.com), which have offices at major airports, ports, or border crossings. These services, which extract a 4 percent fee, can refund your money immediately in your currency of choice or credit your card (within two billing cycles). If the retailer handles VAT refunds directly, it's up to you to contact the merchant for your refund. You can mail the documents from home, or quicker, from your point of departure (using a stamped, addressed envelope you've prepared or one that's been provided by the merchant)—and then wait. It could take months.

Customs for American Shoppers

You are allowed to take home $800 worth of items per person duty-free, once every 30 days. The next $1,000 is taxed at a flat 3 percent. After that, you pay the individual item's duty rate. You can also bring in duty-free a liter of alcohol (slightly more than a standard-size bottle of wine; you must be at least 21), 200 cigarettes, and up to 100 non-Cuban cigars. Food in cans or sealed jars is permissible as long as no meat is included. Some, but not all, types of cheese are allowed. Fresh fruits and vegetables are prohibited. Note that you'll need to carefully pack any bottles of wine and other liquid-containing items in your checked luggage, due to the three-ounce limit on liquids in carry-on baggage. To check customs rules and duty rates before you go, visit www.cbp .gov, and click on "Travel," then "Know Before You Go."

TELEPHONES, EMAIL, AND MAIL

Telephones

Smart travelers learn the phone system and use it daily to reserve or reconfirm rooms, get tourist information, reserve restaurants, confirm tour times, or phone home.

Types of Phones

You'll encounter various kinds of phones in Britain:

British public pay phones are easy to find and easy to use, but relatively expensive. They take major credit cards (which you insert into the phone—minimum charge for a credit-card call is 50p) or coins. Phones clearly list which coins you can use (usually from 10p to £1, with a minimum toll of 40p; some new phones even accept euro coins), and a display shows how your money supply's doing. Only completely unused coins will be returned, so put in biggies with caution. (If money's left over, rather than hanging up, push the "make another call" button.)

The only tricky public pay phones you'll use are the expensive, coin-op ones in bars and B&Bs. Some require money before you dial, while others wait until after you're connected. Many have a button you must push before you begin talking. But all have clear instructions.

Hotel room phones, rare in B&Bs, can be fairly cheap for local calls, but expensive for international calls—unless you use an international phone card (see below).

American mobile phones work in Europe if they're GSM-enabled, tri-band (or quad-band), and on a calling plan that includes international calls. They're convenient but pricey. For example, with a T-Mobile phone, you'll pay $1 per minute for calls. If your phone works in Europe, ask about getting it "unlocked" so you can buy a British SIM card (a fingernail-sized chip that holds the phone's information, available at mobile-phone stores) to make calls cheaply abroad.

British mobile phones are sold with prepaid calling time, which you can "top up" as you use up your credit. (For example, Britain's Carphone Warehouse sells pay-as-you-go mobile phones for as little as £10 plus £10 for calling time.) Incoming calls are free, and outgoing domestic calls generally run about 15–20p per minute—less than from a pay phone. If you're traveling to multiple countries within Europe, make sure the phone is electronically "unlocked," so that you can swap out its SIM card for a new one when you cross the border. Some London hotels will lend you a free mobile phone, but you'll pay  a 50 cents-a-minute usage fee. Ask your hotel about this service if you're interested.

For more information on mobile phones, see www.ricksteves .com/plan/tips/mobilephones.htm.

Americans, who generally pay the same no matter how many calls they make, think nothing of asking a stranger (or B&B owner) if they can use their phone. But most British people pay for each call (whether from a fixed line or a mobile phone), and rates are expensive. Therefore, to be polite, ask to use someone's phone only in an emergency—and offer to use an international calling card or to pay for the call.

Using Phone Cards

Prepaid **international calling cards** are the cheapest way to make international calls from Britain (less than 10 cents a minute to the US). But there's a catch: British Telecom now charges a hefty surcharge for using international calling cards from a pay phone (so instead of 100 minutes for a £5 card, you'll get less than 10 minutes—a miserable deal). But they're still a good deal if you use them when calling from a fixed-line or a mobile phone.

International calling cards are sold at many post offices, newsstands, mini-marts, and exchange bureaus in denominations of £5, £10, and £20. Some are rechargeable (you can call up the number on the card, give your credit-card number, and buy more time). There are many different brands, so ask the clerk which one has the best rates to the States. Because cards are occasionally duds, avoid

---

The British Accent

In the olden days, a British person's accent indicated his or her social standing. Eliza Doolittle had the right idea—elocution could make or break you. Wealthier families would send their kids to fancy private schools to learn proper pronunciation. But these days, in a sort of reverse snobbery that has gripped the nation, accents are back. Politicians, newscasters, and movie stars have been favoring deep accents over the Queen's English. While it's hard for American ears to pick out all of the variations, most Brits can determine where a person is from based on their accent...not just the region, but often the village, and even the part of a town.

---

the high denominations.

You can use these cards from anywhere, including most hotel rooms (if your phone is set on "pulse," switch it to "tone"), avoiding pricey hotel rates. Make sure, however, that your hotel isn't overcharging you to dial the access number.

To use a card, scratch off the back to reveal your code. After you dial the access phone number, the message tells you to enter your code and then dial the phone number you want to call. (If you have several access numbers listed on your card, you'll save money overall if you choose the toll-free one starting with 0800, rather than 0845, 0870, or 0871, which cost around 10p per minute.) To call the US, see "Dialing Internationally," on the following page. To make calls within Britain, dial the area code plus the local number; when using an international calling card, the area code must be dialed even if you're calling across the street. These cards work only within the country of purchase (e.g., one bought in Britain won't work in France).

To make numerous, successive calls with an international calling card without having to redial the long access number each time, press the keys (see instructions on card, usually ##) that allow you to launch directly into your next call. Remember that you don't need the actual card to use a card account, so it's sharable. You can write down the access number and PIN (Personal Identification Number) in your notebook and share it with friends.

Using Hotel-Room Phones, VoIP, or US Calling Cards

The phone in your **hotel room** is convenient...but expensive. While incoming calls (made by folks back home) can be the cheapest way to keep in touch, charges for *outgoing* calls can be a very unpleasant surprise. Make sure you understand all the charges and fees associated with outgoing calls before you pick up that receiver.

Dialing direct from your hotel room—without using an international phone card (described above)—is usually quite pricey for international calls. Always ask first how much you'll be charged, even for local and (supposedly) toll-free calls.

If your family has an inexpensive way to call Europe, either through a long-distance plan or prepaid calling card, have them call you in your hotel room. Give them a list of your hotels' phone numbers before you go. Then, as you travel, send them an email or make a quick pay-phone call to set up a time for them to give you a ring.

If you're traveling with a laptop, consider trying **VoIP (Voice over Internet Protocol)**. With VoIP, two computers act as phones, allowing for a free Internet-based call. The major providers of this service are Skype (www.skype.com) and Google Talk (www.google.com/talk).

US Calling Cards (such as the ones offered by AT&T, MCI, or Sprint) are the worst option. You'll nearly always save a lot of money by paying with a phone card (see above).

How to Dial

Calling from the US to Britain, or vice versa, is simple—once you break the code. The European calling chart on page 642 will walk you through it.

Dialing Within Britain

Britain, like much of the US, uses an area-code dialing system. If you're dialing within an area code, you just dial the local number to be connected; but if you're calling outside your area code, you have to dial both the area code (which starts with a 0) and the local number.

Area codes are listed by city on phone-booth walls or are available from directory assistance (dial 118-500, 42p/min). It's most expensive to call within Britain from 8:00–13:00 and cheapest from 17:00–8:00. Still, a short call across the country is inexpensive; don't hesitate to call long distance.

Dialing Internationally

If you want to make an international call, follow these three steps:

1) Dial the international access code (00 if you're calling from Britain, 011 from the US or Canada).

2) Dial the country code of the country you're calling (44 for Britain, or 1 for the US or Canada).

3) Dial the area code (without its initial 0) and the local number.

For example, London's area code is 020. To call one of my recommended London B&Bs from the US, dial 011 (US international access code), 44 (Britain's country code), 20 (London's area code without its initial 0), then 7730-8191 (the B&B's number).

To call my office from Britain, I dial 00 (Britain's international access code), 1 (US country code), 425 (Edmonds' area code), then 771-8303.

Useful Phone Numbers

Understand the various prefixes—numbers starting with 09 are telephone-sex–type expensive. As mentioned earlier, 0800 numbers are toll-free, but numbers with prefixes of 0845, 0870, and 0871 cost around 10p per minute. If you have questions about a prefix, call 100 for free help.

Embassies and Consulates

US Embassy: tel. 020/7499-9000, passport info tel. 020/7894-0563, passport services available Mon–Fri 8:30–12:30 (24 Grosvenor Square, Tube: Bond Street, www.usembassy.org.uk)
Canadian Consulate: tel. 020/7258-6600, passport services available Mon–Fri 9:30–13:30 (Trafalgar Square, Tube: Charing Cross, www.international.gc.ca)

Emergency Needs

Police and Ambulance: tel. 999

Dialing Assistance

Operator Assistance: tel. 100 (free)
Directory Assistance: tel. 118-500 (42p/min, plus 24p/min connection charge from fixed lines)
International Directory Assistance: tel. 118-505 (£1.50/min, plus 75p connection charge)

Trains

Train information for trips within Britain: tel. 0845-748-4950
Eurostar (Chunnel Info): tel. 08705-186-186 (www.eurostar.com)
Trains to all points in Europe: tel. 08705-848-848 (www.raileurope.com)

Airports

For online information on the first three airports, check www.baa.co.uk.
Heathrow (flight info): tel. 0870-000-0123
Gatwick (general info): tel. 0870-000-2468 for all airlines, except British Airways—tel. 0870-551-1155 (flights) or tel. 0870-850-9850 (booking)
Stansted (general info): tel. 0870-000-0303
Luton (general info): tel. 01582/405-100 (www.london-luton.com)
London City: tel. 020/7646-0088 (www.londoncityairport.com)

European Calling Chart

Just smile and dial, using this key:
AC = Area Code, LN = Local Number.

European Country	Calling long distance within ...	Calling from the US or Canada to ...	Calling from a European country to ...
Austria	AC + LN	011 + 43 + AC (without the initial zero) + LN	00 + 43 + AC (without the initial zero) + LN
Belgium	LN	011 + 32 + LN (without initial zero)	00 + 32 + LN (without initial zero)
Bosnia-Herzegovina	AC + LN	011 + 387 + AC (without initial zero) + LN	00 + 387 + AC (without initial zero) + LN
Britain	AC + LN	011 + 44 + AC (without initial zero) + LN	00 + 44 + AC (without initial zero) + LN
Croatia	AC + LN	011 + 385 + AC (without initial zero) + LN	00 + 385 + AC (without initial zero) + LN
Czech Republic	LN	011 + 420 + LN	00 + 420 + LN
Denmark	LN	011 + 45 + LN	00 + 45 + LN
Estonia	LN	011 + 372 + LN	00 + 372 + LN
Finland	AC + LN	011 + 358 + AC (without initial zero) + LN	999 + 358 + AC (without initial zero) + LN
France	LN	011 + 33 + LN (without initial zero)	00 + 33 + LN (without initial zero)
Germany	AC + LN	011 + 49 + AC (without initial zero) + LN	00 + 49 + AC (without initial zero) + LN
Greece	LN	011 + 30 + LN	00 + 30 + LN
Hungary	06 + AC + LN	011 + 36 + AC + LN	00 + 36 + AC + LN
Ireland	AC + LN	011 + 353 + AC (without initial zero) + LN	00 + 353 + AC (without initial zero) + LN

European Country	Calling long distance within ...	Calling from the US or Canada to ...	Calling from a European country to ...
Italy	LN	011 + 39 + LN	00 + 39 + LN
Montenegro	AC + LN	011 + 382 + AC (without initial zero) + LN	00 + 382 + AC (without initial zero) + LN
Netherlands	AC + LN	011 + 31 + AC (without initial zero) + LN	00 + 31 + AC (without initial zero) + LN
Norway	LN	011 + 47 + LN	00 + 47 + LN
Poland	LN	011 + 48 + LN (without initial zero)	00 + 48 + LN (without initial zero)
Portugal	LN	011 + 351 + LN	00 + 351 + LN
Slovakia	AC + LN	011 + 421 + AC (without initial zero) + LN	00 + 421 + AC (without initial zero) + LN
Slovenia	AC + LN	011 + 386 + AC (without initial zero) + LN	00 + 386 + AC (without initial zero) + LN
Spain	LN	011 + 34 + LN	00 + 34 + LN
Sweden	AC + LN	011 + 46 + AC (without initial zero) + LN	00 + 46 + AC (without initial zero) + LN
Switzerland	LN	011 + 41 + LN (without initial zero)	00 + 41 + LN (without initial zero)
Turkey	AC (if no initial zero is included, add one) + LN	011 + 90 + AC (without initial zero) + LN	00 + 90 + AC (without initial zero) + LN

- The instructions above apply whether you're calling a land line or mobile phone.
- The international access codes (the first numbers you dial when making an international call) are 011 if you're calling from the US or Canada, or 00 if you're calling from virtually anywhere in Europe (except Finland, where it's 999).
- To call the US or Canada from Europe, dial 00, then 1 (the country code for the US and Canada), then the area code and number. In short, 00 + 1 + AC + LN = Hi, Mom!

Airlines

Aer Lingus: tel. 0870-876-5000 in UK, 800-474-7424 in US (www.aerlingus.ie)

Air Canada: tel. 0870-524-7226 (www.aircanada.ca)

Alitalia: reservations tel. 0870-544-8259, Heathrow tel. 020/8745-5812 (www.alitalia.com)

American: tel. 0845-789-0890 (www.aa.com)

British Airways: reservations tel. 0870-850-9850, flight info tel. 0870-551-1155 (www.britishairways.com)

bmi british midland: reservations tel. 0870-607-0555, flight info tel. 020/8745-7321 (www.flybmi.com)

Continental Airlines: tel. 0845-607-6760 (www.continental.com)

easyJet (cheap fares): tel. 0871-244-2366 (www.easyjet.com)

KLM Royal Dutch/Northwest Airlines: tel. 0870-507-4074 (www.klm.com)

Lufthansa: tel. 0870-837-7747 (www.lufthansa.co.uk)

Ryanair (cheap fares): tel. 0871-246-0000 (www.ryanair.com)

Scandinavian Airlines (SAS): tel. 0870-607-27727 (www.scandinavian.net)

United Airlines: tel. 0845-844-4777, tel. 07626/915-500 (www.ual.com)

US Airways: tel. 0845-600-3300 (www.usairways.com)

Heathrow Car-Rental Agencies

Avis: tel. 0870-157-8700

Budget: tel. 0870-608-6313

Europcar: tel. 020/8897-0811

Hertz: tel. 020/8897-2072

National: tel. 020/8750-2800

Email and Mail

Email: Many travelers set up a free email account with Yahoo, Microsoft (Hotmail), or Google (Gmail). Internet cafés are easy to find in big cities. Most of the towns where I've listed accommodations in this book also have Internet cafés. Many libraries offer free access, but they also tend to have limited opening hours, restrict your online time to 30 minutes, and may require reservations. Look for the places listed in this book, or  ask the local TI, computer store, or your B&B host. Some hotels have a dedicated computer for guests' email needs. Small places are accustomed to letting clients (who've asked politely) sit at their desk for a few minutes just to check their email.

If you're traveling with a laptop, you'll find that Wi-Fi, or wireless Internet access, is gradually being installed in many hotels and progressive B&Bs. Most are free, while others charge by the minute.

Mail: Get stamps at the neighborhood post office, newsstands within fancy hotels, and some mini-marts and card shops. To arrange for mail delivery, reserve a few hotels along your route in advance and give their addresses to friends. Allow 10 days for a letter to arrive. Phoning and emailing are so easy that I've dispensed with mail stops altogether.

TRANSPORTATION

By Car or Train?

Cars are best for three or more traveling together (especially families with small kids); those packing heavy; serious photographers (who want to get off the beaten path); and those scouring the countryside. Trains and buses are best for solo travelers, blitz tourists, and city-to-city travelers.

Britain has a great train-and-bus system, and travelers who don't want (or can't afford) to drive a rental car can enjoy an excellent tour using public transportation. Britain's 100-mph train system is one of Europe's best. Buses pick you up when the trains let you down. In Britain, my choice is to connect big cities by train and to explore rural areas (the Cotswolds, North Wales, Lake District, and the Highlands) footloose and fancy-free by rental car. The mix works quite efficiently (e.g., London, Bath, Edinburgh, and York by train with a rental car for the rest). You might consider a BritRail & Drive Pass, which gives you various combinations of rail days and car days to use within two months' time.

Deals on Rails, Wheels, and Wings in Britain

Regular tickets on Britain's great train system (15,000 departures from 2,400 stations daily) are the most expensive per mile in all of Europe. Those who save the biggest are those who book in advance, leave after rush hour (after 9:30), or ride the bus.

Note that it can be tricky to track down all your options; a single bus or train route can be operated by several companies.

As with airline tickets, there can be many different prices for the same train journey. A clerk at any station (or the helpful National Rail folks at tel. 0845-748-4950, 24 hours daily) can figure out the cheapest fare for your trip. Savings can be significant. For a London–Edinburgh round-trip (standard class), the full fare, with no date stipulated for the return trip, is £234; if you book the day of departure for travel after 9:30, it's £98; and the cheapest fare, booked a couple of months in advance as two one-way tickets, is £42.

Sample Train Journey

Here is a typical example of a personalized train schedule printed out by Britain's train stations. At the Llandudno Junction station in North Wales, I told the clerk I wanted to leave after 16:30 for Moreton-in-Marsh in the Cotswolds.

Stations	Arrive	Depart	Class
Llandudno Junction	—	16:41	Standard
Crewe	17:56	18:11	Standard
Smethwick	19:20	19:33	Standard
Worcester	20:20	20:58	1st/Standard
Moreton-in-Marsh	21:37	—	

Even though the trip involved three transfers, this schedule allowed me to easily navigate the rails. It's helpful to ask at the information desk (or any conductor) for the final destination of your next train so you'll be able to figure out quickly which platform it's departing from (e.g., upon arrival at Worcester, I looked for "Oxford" on the station's overhead train schedule to determine where to catch my train to Moreton-in-Marsh; often the conductor on your previous train can even tell you the platform your next train will depart from, but it's wise to confirm). Note that on the smaller runs, only standard (second) class is available. If you're exploring Britain's backcountry with a BritRail pass, rather than invest the extra money in first class, buy standard class—because that's how you'll travel.

Lately Britain's train system has experienced a lot of delays, causing more and more travelers to miss their connections. Don't schedule your connections too tightly if you need to be at your destination at a specific time.

For schedules, visit http://bahn.hafas.de/bin/query.exe/en (Germany's excellent all-Europe timetable), www.nationalrail.co.uk, or www.thetrainline.com. While not required on British trains, reservations are free, and a good idea for long journeys or any train travel on Sunday. Make them at any train station before 18:00 on the day before you travel.

Railpasses

Buying Train Tickets in Advance: The best fares go to those who book their trips well in advance of their journey. (While only a 7-day minimum advance booking is officially required for the cheapest fares, these go fast—especially in summer—so a 6–8 week advance booking is often necessary.) Keep in mind that

Public Transportation Routes in Britain

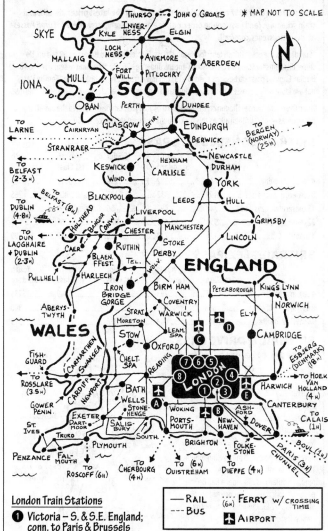

London Train Stations

❶ Victoria – S. & S.E. England; conn. to Paris & Brussels

❷ Charing Cross – S.E. England

❸ Waterloo – S. England;

❹ Liverpool Street – E. England; conn. to Amsterdam

❺ King's Cross – E. England, N.E. England, E. Scotland

❻ St. Pancras – Central England; Eurostar to Paris

❼ Euston – N. & N.W. England, N. Wales, W. Scotland

❽ Paddington – W. England, S. Wales

Legend:
— RAIL
--- BUS
(6н) FERRY w/ crossing time
✈ AIRPORT

London Airports

🅐 Heathrow

🅑 Gatwick

🅒 Luton

🅓 Stansted

🅔 London City

Railpasses

Prices listed are for 2007 and are subject to change. For the latest prices, details, and train schedules (and easy online ordering), see my comprehensive *Guide to Eurail Passes* at www.ricksteves.com/rail.

"Standard" is the polite British term for "second" class. "Senior" refers to those age 60 and up. No senior discounts for standard class. "Youth" means under age 26. For each adult or senior BritRail or BritRail England pass you buy, one child (5–15) can travel free with you (ask for the "**Family Pass,**" not available with all passes). Additional kids pay the normal half-adult rate. Kids under 5 travel free.

Note: Overnight journeys begun on the final night of your pass can be completed the day after your pass expires—only BritRail allows this trick. A bunk in a twin sleeper costs $60.

BRITRAIL CONSECUTIVE PASS

	Adult 1st Class	Adult Standard	Senior 1st Class	Youth 1st Class	Youth Standard
4 consecutive days	$349	$232	$296	$279	$185
8 consecutive days	499	332	425	400	265
15 consecutive days	748	499	636	599	400
22 consecutive days	950	631	808	760	505
1 month	1124	748	956	899	599

BRITRAIL FLEXIPASS

	Adult 1st Class	Adult Standard	Senior 1st Class	Youth 1st Class	Youth Standard
4 days in 2 months	$436	$293	$370	$349	$235
8 days in 2 months	638	425	542	510	340
15 days in 2 months	960	644	816	768	515

BRITRAIL & DRIVE PASS

Any 4 rail days and 2 car days in 2 months.

	1st Class	Standard Class	Extra Car Day
Mini car	$526	$370	$48
Economy car	535	379	58
Compact car	546	390	68
Intermediate car	556	400	79
Minivan	678	522	200

Prices are per person, two traveling together. Third and fourth persons sharing car buy a regular BritRail pass. To order a Rail & Drive pass, call your travel agent or Rail Europe at 800-438-7245. *This pass is not sold by Europe Through the Back Door.*

Map key:

Approximate point-to-point one-way standard-class fares in US dollars by rail (solid line) and bus (dashed line). First class costs 50 percent more. Add up fares for your itinerary to see whether a railpass will save you money.

BRITRAIL ENGLAND CONSECUTIVE PASS

	Adult 1st Class	Adult Standard	Senior 1st Class	Youth 1st Class	Youth Standard
4 consecutive days	$279	$185	$237	$223	$148
8 consecutive days	399	265	339	319	212
15 consecutive days	599	399	509	479	319
22 consecutive days	760	505	646	608	404
1 month	898	599	763	719	479

Covers travel only in England, not Scotland, Wales, or Ireland.

BRITRAIL ENGLAND FLEXIPASS

Type of Pass	Adult 1st Class	Adult Standard	Senior 1st Class	Youth 1st Class	Youth Standard
4 days in 2 months	$349	$235	$296	$279	$188
8 days in 2 months	510	340	434	408	272
15 days in 2 months	769	515	653	615	412

Covers travel only in England, not Scotland, Wales, or Ireland.

BRITRAIL LONDON PLUS PASS

	Adult 1st Class	Adult Standard
2 out of 8 days	$113	$74
4 out of 8 days	187	140
7 out of 15 days	249	187

Formerly called BritRail Southeast Pass and Days Out of London Pass. Covers much of SE England (see coverage map at www.ricksteves.com/rail). No Heathrow Express. Many trains are standard class only. The 7 p.m. rule for night trains does not apply. With this pass, you'll pay about $30 more to Bath or $15 more to Stratford. Kids 5–15 half price.

BRITRAIL SCOTTISH FREEDOM PASS

4 out of 8 days	$217
8 out of 15 days	292

Valid in Scotland only, standard class only. Not valid on trains that depart before 9:15am, Mon–Fri. Covers Caledonian MacBrayne and Strathclyde ferry service to Scotland's most popular islands. Discounts on some P&O ferries, some Citylink buses & more. Kids 5–15 half fare; under 5 free.

BRITRAIL PASS PLUS IRELAND

	First Class	Standard Class
5 days in 1 month	$636	$462
10 days in 1 month	1040	733

This pass covers the entire British Isles (England, Wales, Scotland, Northern Ireland, and the Republic of Ireland) including a round-trip Stena Line ferry crossing between Wales or Scotland and the Emerald Isle during the pass's validity (okay to leave via one port and return via another). Reserve boat crossings a day or so in advance—sooner for holidays. Kids 5-15 pay half fare; under 5 free. No Family Pass, Party Pass, nor Off-Peak Special. Before buying the 10-day pass, consider the cost of two separate passes plus flight or ferry ticket.

when booking in advance, return (round-trip) fares are not always cheaper than buying two single (one-way) tickets. Also note that cheap advance tickets often come with the toughest refund restrictions, so be sure to nail down your travel plans before you reserve. To book ahead, you can go in person to any station, book online at www.nationalrail.co.uk, or call 0845-748-4950 (from the US, call 011-44-845-748-4950, phone answered 24 hours) to find out the schedule and best fare for your journey; then you'll be referred to the appropriate number to call—depending on the particular rail company—to book your ticket. If you order online, be sure you know what you want; it's tough to reach a person who can change your online reservation. You'll pick up your ticket at the station (unless your order was lost—this service still has some glitches). If you want your ticket mailed to you in the US, you need to allow a couple of weeks and cover the shipping costs. Note that BritRail passholders cannot use the Web to make reservations.

Buying Train Tickets en Route: If you'd rather have the flexibility of booking tickets as you go, you can save a few pounds by buying a round-trip ticket, called a "return ticket" (a same-day round-trip, called a "day return," is particularly cheap); buying before 18:00 the day before you depart; traveling after the morning rush hour (this usually means after 9:30 Mon–Fri); and going standard class instead of first class. Preview your options at www.nationalrail.co.uk or www.thetrainline.com.

Senior, Youth, and Family Deals: To get a third off the price of most point-to-point rail tickets, seniors can buy a Senior Railcard (for age 60 and above, www.senior-railcard.co.uk), and young people can buy a Young Persons Railcard (for ages 16–25, or for full-time students 26 and above with a valid ISIC card; www.youngpersons-railcard.co.uk). Each card costs £20. A Family Railcard allows adults to travel cheaper (about 33 percent) while their kids age 5 to 15 receive a 60 percent discount for most trips (£20, maximum of 4 adults and 4 kids, www.family-railcard.co.uk). Any of these cards are valid for a year on virtually all trains except special runs such as the Heathrow Express and Eurostar (fill out application at station, brochures on racks in info center, need to show passport). Youths also need to submit a passport-type photo for the Young Persons Card.

Railpasses: Consider getting a railpass. The BritRail pass comes in "consecutive day" and "flexi" versions, with price breaks for youths, seniors, off-season travelers, and groups of three or more. If you're exploring Britain's backcountry with a BritRail pass, standard class is a good choice since many of the smaller train lines don't even offer first-class cars. BritRail passes cover England as well as Scotland and Wales.

BritRail options include England-only passes, Britain/Ireland passes, "London Plus" passes (good for travel in most of southeast England but not in London itself), and BritRail & Drive passes (which offer you some rail days and some car-rental days). These BritRail passes, as well as Eurailpasses, get you a discount on the Eurostar train that zips you to continental Europe under the English Channel. These passes are sold outside of Europe only. For specifics, contact your travel agent or see www.ricksteves.com/rail.

Buses: Although buses are about a third slower than trains, they're also a lot cheaper. Round-trip bus tickets usually cost less than two one-way fares (e.g., London–York one-way costs £23; round-trip costs £30). And buses go many places that trains don't. Budget travelers can save a wad with a bus pass. The National Express sells Brit Xplorer bus passes for unlimited travel on consecutive days (£79/7 days, £139/14 days, £219/28 days, sold over the counter, non-UK passport required, tel. 0870-580-8080, www .nationalexpress.com). Check their website to learn about online Funfare deals; senior/youth/family cards and fares; and discounts for advance booking.

If you want to take a bus from your last destination to the nearest airport, you'll find that National Express often offers airport buses. Bus stations are normally at or near train stations (in London, the bus station is a block southwest of Victoria Station). The British distinguish between "buses" (for local runs with lots of stops) and "coaches" (long-distance express runs).

A couple of companies offer **backpackers' bus circuits.** These hop-on, hop-off bus circuits take mostly youth hostellers around the country super-cheap and easy with the assumption that they'll be sleeping in the hostels along the way. For instance, **Backpacker Tours** offers 1–19-day excursions through England and other destinations in Great Britain (from about £65/1 day, £90/3 days, £243/5 days, tel. 0870-745-1046, www.backpackertours.co.uk, email@backpackertours.co.uk).

Renting a Car

To rent a car in Britain, you must be at least 23 years old with a valid license. Drivers under the age of 25 may incur a young-driver surcharge, and some rental companies do not rent to anyone 75 and over. If you're considered too young or old, look into leasing, which has less-stringent age restrictions (see "Leasing," on page 653).

Although an International Driving Permit is not required if your driver's license has been renewed within the last year, play it safe and get one anyway ($15 through AAA, plus two passport photos, www.aaa.com).

A British Automobile Association membership comes with most rentals. Understand its towing and emergency-road-service benefits.

Research car rentals before you go. It's cheaper to arrange most car rentals from the US. Call several companies and look online to compare rates, or arrange a rental through your hometown travel agent. Two reputable companies among many are Auto Europe (www.autoeurope.com) and Europe by Car (www.europebycar.com). Rent by the week with unlimited mileage. I normally rent the smallest, least-expensive model with a stick-shift. Remember, minibuses are a great budget way to go for five to nine people.

If you want an automatic, reserve the car at least a month in advance and specifically request an automatic. Cars with automatic transmissions are generally larger, making them less than ideal for narrow, winding roads (such as in the Cotswolds). An automatic transmission is going to add at least 40 percent to the car rental cost over a manual transmission. Weigh this against the fact that in Britain you'll be sitting on the right side of the car, and shifting with your left hand...while driving on the left side of the road. The floor pedals are in the same locations as in the US, and the gears are found in the same basic "H" pattern as at home (i.e., first gear, second, etc.).

For a three-week rental, allow $900 per person (based on two people sharing a car), including gas and insurance. Consider leasing to save money on insurance and taxes; see below. Compare pick-up costs (downtown can be cheaper than the airport) and explore drop-off options. For a trip covering both Britain and Ireland, you're better off with two separate car rentals.

When you pick up the car, check it thoroughly and make sure any damage is noted on your rental agreement. Find out how your car's lights, turn signals, wipers, and gas cap function.

If you pick up the car as you leave a smaller city such as Bath, you'll more likely survive your first day on the British roads. If you drop the car off early or keep it longer, you'll be credited or charged at a fair, prorated price.

Returning a car at a big-city train station can be tricky; get precise details on the car drop-off location and hours. Note that rental offices usually close from midday Saturday until Monday. When you return the car, make sure the agent verifies its condition with you.

Car Insurance Options

When you rent a car, you are liable for a very high deductible, sometimes equal to the entire value of the car. There are various ways you can limit your financial risk in case of an accident. For Britain, you have three options: buy Collision Damage Waiver (CDW) coverage from the car-rental company, get coverage through your credit card (free, if your card automatically includes zero-deductible coverage), or buy coverage through Travel Guard.

CDW includes a very high deductible (typically $1,000–1,500). When you pick up the car, you'll be offered the chance to "buy down" the deductible to zero (for $10–30/day; this is often called "super CDW").

If you opt instead for credit-card coverage, there's a catch. You'll technically have to decline all coverage offered by the car-rental company, which means they can place a hold on your card for the full deductible amount. In case of damage, it can be time-consuming to resolve the charges with your credit-card company. Before you decide on this option, quiz your credit-card company about how it works and ask them to explain the worst-case scenario.

Buying CDW insurance (plus "super CDW") is the easier but pricier option. Using the coverage that comes with your credit card saves money, but can involve more hassle.

Finally, you can buy CDW insurance from Travel Guard ($9/day plus a one-time $3 service fee covers you up to $35,000, $250 deductible, tel. 800-826-4919, www.travelguard.com). It's valid throughout Europe, but some car-rental companies refuse to honor it (especially in the Republic of Ireland and in Italy). Oddly, residents of Washington State aren't allowed to buy this coverage.

For more fine print about car-rental insurance, see www.ricksteves.com/cdw.

Leasing

For trips of two and a half weeks or more, leasing (which automatically includes CDW-like insurance) is the best way to go. By technically buying and then selling back the car, you save lots of money on tax and insurance. Leasing provides you a brand-new car with unlimited mileage and a 24-hour emergency assistance program. You can lease for as little as 17 days to as long as 6 months. Car leases must be arranged from the US. One of many reliable companies offering affordable lease packages is Europe by Car (US tel. 800-223-1516, www.europebycar.com).

Driving

Driving in Britain is basically wonderful—once you remember to stay on the left and after you've mastered the roundabouts.

But be warned: Every year I get a few notes from traveling readers advising me that, for them, trying to drive in Britain was a nerve-racking and regrettable mistake. If you want to get a little slack on the roads, drop by a gas station or auto shop and buy a green "P" (probationary driver with license) sign to put in your car window (don't get the red "L" sign, which means you're a learner driver without a license and thus prohibited from driving on motorways).

Many Yankee drivers find the hardest part isn't driving on

the left, but steering from the right. Your instinct is to put yourself on the left side of your lane, which means you may spend your first day or two constantly drifting off the road to the left. It can help to remember that the driver always stays close to the center line.

Roundabouts are circular intersections found on non-motorway roads throughout Britain and much of Europe but only occasionally in the US. Instead of the traffic lights Americans are used to finding when two or more roads meet, roundabout traffic flows clockwise around a center island. They work effi-

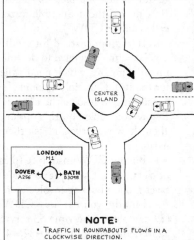

A Typical Roundabout

NOTE:
- TRAFFIC IN ROUNDABOUTS FLOWS IN A CLOCKWISE DIRECTION.
- VEHICLES ENTERING A ROUNDABOUT MUST YIELD TO VEHICLES IN THE ROUNDABOUT.
- LOOK TO YOUR RIGHT AS YOU MERGE!

ciently and safely as long as everyone follows a few simple rules. Traffic in roundabouts has the right-of-way; entering traffic yields (look to your right as you merge). There are a variety of roundabout types; many aren't even "round." You'll probably encounter "double-roundabouts"—figure-eights where you'll slingshot from one roundabout directly into another. Just go with the flow and track signs carefully. When approaching an especially complex roundabout, you'll first pass a diagram showing the layout and the various exits. And in many cases, the pavement is painted with which lane you should be in if you're heading for a particular road or town.

Seat belts are required by law. Speed limits are 30 mph in town, 70 mph on the motorways, and 50 or 60 mph elsewhere. The national sign for 60 mph is a white circle with a black slash. Note that road-surveillance cameras strictly enforce speed limits. Any driver (including foreigners renting cars) photographed speeding will get a nasty bill in the mail. (Cameras—you'll see the foreboding gray boxes—flash on your rear license plate in order not to invade the privacy of anyone sharing the front seat with someone they shouldn't be with.)

The shortest distance between any two points is usually the motorway. Road signs can be confusing, too few, and too late. Miss a motorway exit and you can lose 30 minutes. Buy a good map and study it before taking off, especially if you'll be driving solo. If you're traveling with a partner, you'll find that a competent

Britain by Car: Mileage and Time

85m • 2h
Inverness
35m 1h
Kyle of Lochalsh
90m • 2.5h
85m • 3h
SCOTLAND

m = miles
h = hours

Note: Your times may vary based on traffic, construction, and road conditions.

Glencoe
90m • 2.75h
90m • 1.75h
Pitlochry
35m • 1h
Oban
120m • 3h
60m • 1.5h
70m • 1.5h
St. Andrews
125m • 3.25h
100m • 2.5h
50m • 1.5h
Glasgow
50m • 1h
Edinburgh
75m • 2h
Holy Island
90m • 2.25h
130m • 3h
125m • 2.75h
80m • 1.75h
Stranraer
135m • 2.5h
100m • 2.5h
145m • 3h
Hadrian's Wall (Housesteads Fort)
65m • 1.5h
50m • 1h
Durham
Keswick (N. Lake Dist.)
20m • .5h
120m • 3h
85m • 2h
Windermere (S. Lake Dist.)
60m • 1.25h
90m • 1.75h
75m • 1.5h
Whitby
35m • 1h
Blackpool
55m 1.25h
120m • 2.5h
York
40m • .75h
Holyhead
60m • 1.25h
Liverpool
130m • 3.5h
160m • 3h
25m • .5h
Conwy
30m • 1.25h
15m • .5h
30m 1h
75m • 2h
145m • 2.75h
220m • 4h
Caernarfon
Ruthin
25m • .75h
Snowdonia (Betws-y-Coed)
30m 1h
60m • 1.5h
Ironbridge Gorge
ENGLAND
170m • 4h
150m • 3.5h
Warwick
10m • .25h
110m
Stratford
↓2h
Cambridge
WALES
100m • 2h
10m • .5h
Cotswolds (Chipping Campden)
90m • 2h
60m • 1.25h
Cardiff
65m • 1.75h
55m • 1.25h
20m • .75h
Bath
115m • 2.5h
London
Wells
40m • 1h
10m • .25h
Glastonbury
50m • 1.25h
100m • 2h
75m • 1.5h
Salisbury (Stonehenge)
Dover

copilot makes life much easier. Know the cities you'll be lacing together, since road numbers are inconsistent. British road signs are never marked with compass directions (e.g., "A30 West"); instead, you need to know what major town or city you're heading toward ("A30 Penzance"). The driving directions in this book are intended to be used with a good local map. A British road atlas, easily purchased at gas stations in Britain, is money well spent (see "Maps," page 629).

STOP AND LEARN THESE ROAD SIGNS

Speed Limit (km/hr)	Yield
No Passing	End of No Passing Zone
One Way	Intersection
Main Road	Freeway
Danger	No Entry
No Entry for cars	All Vehicles Prohibited
Parking	No Parking
Customs	Peace

Gas (petrol) costs around $7 per gallon and is self-serve. Green pumps are unleaded.

Whenever possible, don't drive in cities. Be warned that London assesses a congestion charge (see page 54). Most cities have modern ring roads to skirt the congestion. Follow signs to the parking lots outside the city core—most are a five- to ten-minute walk to the center—and avoid what can be an unpleasant network of one-way streets (as in Bath).

Outside of the big cities and the motorways, British roads tend to be narrow and often lack shoulders. In towns, you may have to cross over the center line just to get past parked cars. Sometimes both directions of traffic can pass parked cars simultaneously, but frequently you'll have to take turns—follow the locals' lead and drive defensively. Similarly, some narrow country lanes are barely wide enough for one car. Go slowly, and if you encounter an oncoming car, look for the nearest pullout (or "passing place")—the driver who's closest to one is expected to use it, even if they have to back up to reach it. British drivers are quick to offer a friendly wave to thank you for letting them pass (and they appreciate it if you reciprocate).

Parking can be confusing. One yellow line marked on the pavement means no parking Monday through Saturday during work hours. Double yellow lines mean no parking at any time. Broken yellow lines mean short stops are OK, but you should always look for explicit signs or ask a passerby. White lines mean you're free to park.

Armed with a good map, a navigator (if possible), and a sense of humor, most drivers will do just fine in Britain.

In towns, rather than look for street parking, I generally just pull into the most central and handy "pay and display" parking lot I can find. To "pay and display," feed change into a machine, receive a timed ticket, and display it on the dashboard or stick it to the driver's-side window. Rates are reasonable by US standards, and locals love to share stickers that have time remaining. If you stand by the machine, someone on their way out with time left on their sticker will probably give it to you. Keep a bag of coins in the ashtray or glove box for these machines and for parking meters.

Set your car up for a fun road trip. Establish a cardboard-box munchies pantry. Buy a rack of liter boxes of juice for the trunk, and some Windex and a roll of paper towels (called a "kitchen roll" in Britain) for cleaner sightseeing.

Cheap Flights

If you're visiting one or more cities on a longer European trip, you might want to look into the affordable intra-European airlines. While trains are still the best way to connect places that are close together, a flight can save both time and money on long journeys.

London is the hub for many cheap, no-frills airlines, which affordably connect the city with other destinations in the British Isles and throughout Europe. Although bmi british midland has been around the longest, the other small airlines generally offer cheaper flights. A visit to www.skyscanner.net sorts the numerous options offered by the many discount airlines, enabling you to see the best schedules for your trip and come up with the best deal. Other comparison search engines include www.kayak.com, www.mobissimo.com, www.sidestep.com, and www.wegolo.com.

Be aware of the potential drawbacks of flying on the cheap: nonrefundable and nonchangeable tickets, rigid baggage restrictions (and fees if you have more than what's officially allowed), use of airports far outside town, tight schedules that can mean more delays, little in the way of customer assistance if problems arise, and, of course, no frills. To avoid unpleasant surprises, read the small print—especially baggage policies—before you book.

With **bmi british midland,** you can fly inexpensively to destinations in the UK and beyond (fares start at about £30 one-way to Edinburgh, Paris, Brussels, or Amsterdam; or about £50 one-way to Dublin; prices can be higher, but there can also be much cheaper midweek or via Internet specials—check online). For the latest, call British tel. 0870-607-0555 or US tel. 800-788-0555 (check www.flybmi.com and their subsidiary, bmi baby—which has hubs at Manchester, Gatwick, and Cardiff—at www.bmibaby.com). Book in advance. Although you can book right up until the flight departs, the cheap seats will have sold out long before, leaving the most expensive seats for latecomers.

With no frills and cheap fares, **easyJet** flies from London (Luton, Stansted, and Gatwick), as well as Liverpool. Prices are based on demand, so the least popular routes make for the cheapest fares, especially if you book early (tel. 0905-821-0905 to book by phone, 10p per minute, or do it free online at www.easyjet.com).

Ryanair is a creative Irish airline that prides itself on offering the lowest fares. In the UK, it flies from London (mostly Stansted airport), Liverpool, and Glasgow, to often obscure airports in Dublin, Frankfurt, Stockholm, Oslo, Venice, Turin, and many other places. Sample fares: London–Dublin—£60 round-trip (sometimes as low as £15), London–Frankfurt—£50 round-trip (Irish tel. 0818-303-030, British tel. 0871-246-0000, www.ryanair.com). Because they offer promotional deals any time of year, you can get great prices on short notice. There is a cost of £5 per checked bag (if you prepay online), and you can carry on only a small day bag. Each checked bag can weigh up to 15 kilograms—about 33 pounds (up to five bags per passenger allowed). If you're traveling with lots of bags, a cheap Ryanair flight can quickly become a bad deal because of these £5-a-pop fees.

Brussels Airlines (formerly Virgin Express) is a Brussels-based company with good rates and hubs in Bristol, Birmingham, Gatwick, Manchester, and Newcastle (book by phone and pick up ticket at airport an hour before your flight, www.brusselsairlines.com). From its primary hub in Brussels, you can connect cheaply to Barcelona, Madrid, Nice, Málaga, Copenhagen, Rome, or Milan.

HOLIDAYS AND FESTIVALS

This list includes major festivals in major cities, plus national holidays observed throughout Great Britain. Many sights and banks close down on national holidays—keep it in mind when planning your itinerary. Note that this isn't a complete list; holidays can strike without warning.

Many British towns have holiday festivals in late November and early December, with markets, music, and entertainment in the Christmas spirit. Two of these include York's St. Nicholas Fayre (www.yuletideyork.com) and Keswick's Victorian Fayre.

For specifics and a more comprehensive list of festivals, contact the Visit Britain office in the US (listed at the beginning of the appendix) and check www.visitbritain.com and www.travelbritain.org.

Here's a partial list of events:
> **Jan 1** New Year's Day
> **Jan 2** New Year's Holiday (Scotland)

2008

JANUARY

S	M	T	W	T	F	S
		1	2	3	4	5
6	7	8	9	10	11	12
13	14	15	16	17	18	19
20	21	22	23	24	25	26
27	28	29	30	31		

FEBRUARY

S	M	T	W	T	F	S
					1	2
3	4	5	6	7	8	9
10	11	12	13	14	15	16
17	18	19	20	21	22	23
24	25	26	27	28	29	

MARCH

S	M	T	W	T	F	S
						1
2	3	4	5	6	7	8
9	10	11	12	13	14	15
16	17	18	19	20	21	22
23/30	24/31	25	26	27	28	29

APRIL

S	M	T	W	T	F	S
		1	2	3	4	5
6	7	8	9	10	11	12
13	14	15	16	17	18	19
20	21	22	23	24	25	26
27	28	29	30			

MAY

S	M	T	W	T	F	S
				1	2	3
4	5	6	7	8	9	10
11	12	13	14	15	16	17
18	19	20	21	22	23	24
25	26	27	28	29	30	31

JUNE

S	M	T	W	T	F	S
1	2	3	4	5	6	7
8	9	10	11	12	13	14
15	16	17	18	19	20	21
22	23	24	25	26	27	28
29	30					

JULY

S	M	T	W	T	F	S
		1	2	3	4	5
6	7	8	9	10	11	12
13	14	15	16	17	18	19
20	21	22	23	24	25	26
27	28	29	30	31		

AUGUST

S	M	T	W	T	F	S
					1	2
3	4	5	6	7	8	9
10	11	12	13	14	15	16
17	18	19	20	21	22	23
24/31	25	26	27	28	29	30

SEPTEMBER

S	M	T	W	T	F	S
	1	2	3	4	5	6
7	8	9	10	11	12	13
14	15	16	17	18	19	20
21	22	23	24	25	26	27
28	29	30				

OCTOBER

S	M	T	W	T	F	S
			1	2	3	4
5	6	7	8	9	10	11
12	13	14	15	16	17	18
19	20	21	22	23	24	25
26	27	28	29	30	31	

NOVEMBER

S	M	T	W	T	F	S
						1
2	3	4	5	6	7	8
9	10	11	12	13	14	15
16	17	18	19	20	21	22
23/30	24	25	26	27	28	29

DECEMBER

S	M	T	W	T	F	S
	1	2	3	4	5	6
7	8	9	10	11	12	13
14	15	16	17	18	19	20
21	22	23	24	25	26	27
28	29	30	31			

Feb (one week)	London Fashion Week (www.londonfashionweek.co.uk)
Feb 13–17	Jorvik Viking Festival (costumed warriors, battles, www.jorvik-viking-centre.co.uk), York
Feb 23–March 2	Literature Festival (www.bathlitfest.org.uk), Bath
March 21	Good Friday
March 23–24	Easter Sunday and Monday
May 5	Early May Bank Holiday
Mid-May	Jazz Festival, Keswick
May 16–June 1	International Music Festival (www.bathmusicfest.org.uk), Bath
Late May	Chelsea Flower Show, London (book tickets ahead for this popular event at www.rhs.org.uk/chelsea)

May 23–June 8	Fringe Festival, Bath (alternative music, dance, and theater; www.bathfringe.co.uk)
May 26	Spring Bank Holiday
Early June	Late Music Festival, York (www.latemusicfestival.org.uk)
Mid-June	Trooping the Colour, London (military bands and pageantry, Queen's birthday parade)
Mid-June	Royal Ascot Horse Race (www.ascot.co.uk), Ascot (near Windsor)
June 6–7	Beer Festival (music, shows, www.keswickbeerfestival.co.uk), Keswick
June 19–22	Royal Highland Show (Scottish county fair, www.royalhighlandshow.org), Edinburgh
June 23–July 6	Wimbledon Tennis Championship, London (www.wimbledon.org)
July 3–12	Early Music Festival (www.ncem.co.uk/yemf.shtml), York
July 31–Aug 3	Cambridge Folk Festival, Cambridge (buy tickets early at www.cambridgefolkfestival.co.uk)
July 8–13	International Eisteddfod (folk songs, dances, www.international-eisteddfod.co.uk), Llangollen
Late Aug	Notting Hill Carnival, London (costumes, Caribbean music)
Aug 1–23	Military Tattoo (massing of bands, www.edinburgh-tattoo.co.uk), Edinburgh
Aug 3–25	Fringe Festival (offbeat theater and comedy, www.edfringe.com), Edinburgh
Aug 4	Summer Bank Holiday (Scotland only, not England or Wales)
Aug 8–31	Edinburgh Festival (music, dance, shows, www.eif.co.uk), Edinburgh
Aug 25	Summer Bank Holiday (England and Wales only, not Scotland)
Aug 29–Nov 2	Illuminations (waterfront light festival), Blackpool
Sept (one week)	London Fashion Week (www.londonfashionweek.co.uk)
Late Sept	Festival of Food and Drink (www.yorkfestivaloffoodanddrink.com), York
Late Sept	Jane Austen Festival (www.janeausten.co.uk/festival), Bath
Nov 1	All Saints' Day

Nov 5	Bonfire Night, or Guy Fawkes Night (fireworks, bonfires, effigy burning of 1605 traitor Guy Fawkes), Britain
Dec 1	St. Andrew's Day, Scotland
Dec 24–26	Christmas holidays and Boxing Day (Dec 26)
Dec 31–Jan 2	Hogmanay (music, street theater, carnival, www.hogmanay.net), Scotland

CONVERSIONS AND CLIMATE

Numbers and Stumblers

- The British write a few of their numbers differently than we do. 1 = 1, 4 = 4, 7 = 7.
- In Europe, dates appear as day/month/year, so Christmas is 25/12/08.
- What Americans call the second floor of a building is the first floor in Britain.
- On escalators and moving sidewalks, Brits keep the left "lane" open for passing. Keep to the right.
- When pointing, use your whole hand, palm down.
- When counting with fingers, start with your thumb. If you hold up your first finger to request one item, you'll probably get two.
- To avoid the British version of giving someone "the finger," don't hold up the first two fingers of your hand with your palm facing you. (It looks like a reversed victory sign.)
- And please...don't call your waist pack a "fanny pack."

Metric Conversions (approximate)

1 foot = 0.3 meter	1 square yard = 0.8 square meter
1 yard = 0.9 meter	1 square mile = 2.6 square kilometers
1 mile = 1.6 kilometers	1 ounce = 28 grams
1 centimeter = 0.4 inch	1 quart = 0.95 liter
1 meter = 39.4 inches	1 kilogram = 2.2 pounds
1 kilometer = 0.62 mile	32°F = 0°C

Weights and Measures

1 British pint = 1.2 US pints
1 imperial gallon = 1.2 US gallons or about 4.5 liters
1 stone = 14 pounds (a 168-pound person weighs 12 stone)
Shoe sizes = about .5 to 1.5 sizes smaller than in the US

Britain's Climate

First line, average daily high; second line, average daily low; third line, days of no rain. For more detailed weather statistics for destinations throughout Britain (as well as the rest of the world), check www.worldclimate.com.

	J	F	M	A	M	J	J	A	S	O	N	D

LONDON

43°	44°	50°	56°	62°	69°	71°	71°	65°	58°	50°	45°
36°	36°	38°	42°	47°	53°	56°	56°	52°	46°	42°	38°
16	15	20	18	19	19	19	20	17	18	15	16

CARDIFF (SOUTH WALES)

45°	45°	50°	56°	61°	68°	69°	69°	64°	58°	51°	46°
35°	35°	38°	41°	46°	51°	54°	55°	51°	46°	41°	37°
13	14	18	17	18	17	17	16	14	15	13	13

YORK

43°	44°	49°	55°	61°	67°	70°	69°	64°	57°	49°	45°
33°	34°	36°	40°	44°	50°	54°	53°	50°	44°	39°	36°
14	13	18	17	18	16	16	17	16	16	13	14

EDINBURGH

42°	43°	46°	51°	56°	62°	65°	64°	60°	54°	48°	44°
34°	34°	36°	39°	43°	49°	52°	52°	49°	44°	39°	36°
14	13	16	16	17	15	14	15	14	14	13	13

Temperature Conversion: Fahrenheit and Celsius

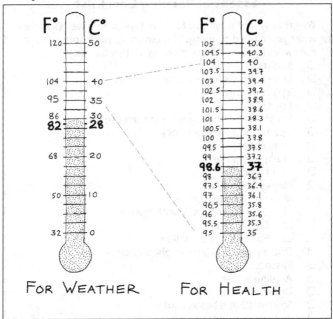

Britain uses both Celsius and Fahrenheit to take its temperature. For a rough conversion from Celsius to Fahrenheit, double the number and add 30. For weather, remember that 28°C is 82°F—perfect. For health, 37°C is just right.

Essential Packing Checklist

Whether you're traveling for five days or five weeks, here's what you'll need to bring. Remember to pack light to enjoy the sweet freedom of true mobility. Happy travels!

- ❏ 5 shirts
- ❏ 1 sweater or lightweight fleece jacket
- ❏ 2 pairs pants
- ❏ 1 pair shorts
- ❏ 1 swimsuit (women only—men can use shorts)
- ❏ 5 pairs underwear and socks
- ❏ 1 pair shoes
- ❏ 1 rainproof jacket
- ❏ Tie or scarf
- ❏ Money belt
- ❏ Money—your mix of:
  - ❏ Debit card for ATM withdrawals
  - ❏ Credit card
  - ❏ Hard cash in US dollars
- ❏ Documents (and backup photocopies)
- ❏ Passport
- ❏ Airplane ticket
- ❏ Driver's license
- ❏ Student ID and hostel card
- ❏ Railpass/car-rental voucher
- ❏ Insurance details
- ❏ Daypack
- ❏ Sealable plastic baggies
- ❏ Camera and related gear
- ❏ Empty water bottle
- ❏ Wristwatch and alarm clock
- ❏ Earplugs
- ❏ First-aid kit
- ❏ Medicine (labeled)
- ❏ Extra glasses/contacts and prescriptions
- ❏ Sunscreen and sunglasses
- ❏ Toiletries kit
- ❏ Soap
- ❏ Laundry soap (if liquid and carry-on, limit to 3 oz.)
- ❏ Clothesline
- ❏ Small towel
- ❏ Sewing kit
- ❏ Travel information
- ❏ Necessary map(s)
- ❏ Address list (email and mailing addresses)
- ❏ Postcards and photos from home
- ❏ Notepad and pen
- ❏ Journal

Hotel Reservation

To: _____   _____
                hotel   *email or fax*

From: _____   _____
                name   *email or fax*

Today's date: _____ / _____ / _____
                    day   *month*   *year*

Dear Hotel _____ ,

Please make this reservation for me:

Name: _____

Total # of people: _____ # of rooms: _____ # of nights: _____

Arriving: _____ / _____ / _____   My time of arrival (24-hr clock): _____
              day month year   (I will telephone if I will be late)

Departing: _____ / _____ / _____
                day month year

Room(s): Single ____ Double ____ Twin ____ Triple ____ Quad ____

With: Toilet ____ Shower ____ Bath ____ Sink only ____

Special needs: View ____ Quiet ____ Cheapest ____ Ground Floor ____

Please email or fax confirmation of my reservation, along with the type of
room reserved and the price. Please also inform me of your cancellation
policy. After I hear from you, I will quickly send my credit-card information
as a deposit to hold the room. Thank you.

_____
Name

_____
Address

_____
City   *State*   *Zip Code*   *Country*

*Before hoteliers can make your reservation, they want to know the informa-
tion listed above. You can use this form as the basis for your email, or you can
photocopy this page, fill in the information, and send it as a fax (also available
online at www.ricksteves.com/reservation).*

British–Yankee Vocabulary

advert–advertisement

afters–dessert

anticlockwise–counterclockwise

aubergine–eggplant

banger–sausage

bangers and mash–sausage and mashed potatoes

bank holiday–legal holiday

bap–small roll

bespoke–custom-made

billion–a thousand of our billions (a million million)

biro–ballpoint pen

biscuit–cookie

black pudding–sausage made from dried blood

bloody–damn

blow off–fart

bobby–policeman ("the Bill" is more common)

Bob's your uncle–there you go (with a shrug), naturally

boffin–nerd, geek

bolshy–argumentative

bomb–success or failure

bonnet–car hood

boot–car trunk

braces–suspenders

bridle way–path for walkers, bikers, and horse riders

brilliant–cool

brolly–umbrella

bubble and squeak–cabbage and potatoes fried together

bum–butt

candy floss–cotton candy

caravan–trailer

car boot sale–temporary flea market, often for charity

car park–parking lot

casualty–emergency room

cat's eyes–road reflectors

ceilidh (KAY-lee)–informal evening of song and folk fun (Scottish and Irish)

cheap and cheerful–budget but adequate

cheap and nasty–cheap and bad quality

cheers–good-bye or thanks; also a toast

chemist–pharmacist

chicory–endive

chippie–fish-and-chip shop; carpenter

chips–French fries

chock-a-block–jam-packed

chuffed–pleased

cider–alcoholic apple cider

clearway–road where you can't stop

coach–long-distance bus

concession–discounted admission

cos–romaine lettuce

cotton buds–Q-tips

courgette–zucchini

craic (pronounced "crack")–fun, good conversation (Irish and spreading to England)

crisps–potato chips

cuppa–cup of tea

dear–expensive

dicey–iffy, risky

digestives–round graham cookies

dinner–lunch or dinner

diversion–detour

donkey's years–ages, long time

draughts–checkers

draw–marijuana

dual carriageway–divided highway (four lanes)

dummy–pacifier

elevenses–coffee-and-biscuits break before lunch

elvers–baby eels

face flannel–washcloth

fag–cigarette
fagged–exhausted
faggot–meatball
fancy–to like, to be attracted to (a person)
fanny–vagina
fell–hill or high plain (Lake District)
first floor–second floor
fizzy drink–pop or soda
flutter–a bet
football–soccer
force–waterfall (Lake District)
fortnight–two weeks
fringe–hair bangs
Frogs–French people
fruit machine–slot machine
full Monty–whole shebang; everything
gallery–balcony
gammon–ham
gangway–aisle
gaol–jail (same pronunciation)
gateau (or gateaux)–cake
gear lever–stick shift
geezer–"dude" (slang for young man)
give way–yield
glen–narrow valley (Scotland)
goods wagon–freight truck
green fingers–green thumbs
half eight–8:30 (not 7:30)
heath–open treeless land
hen night–bachelorette party
holiday–vacation
homely–homey or cozy
hoover–vacuum cleaner
ice lolly–Popsicle
interval–intermission
ironmonger–hardware store
ish–more or less
jacket potato–baked potato
jelly–Jell-O
Joe Bloggs–John Q. Public
jumble sale–rummage sale
jumper–sweater

just a tick–just a second
kipper–smoked herring
knackered–exhausted (Cockney: cream crackered)
knickers–ladies' panties
knocking shop–brothel
knock up–wake up or visit (old-fashioned)
ladybird–ladybug
lady fingers–flat, spongy cookie
lady's finger–okra
lager–light, fizzy beer
left luggage–baggage check
lemon squash–lemonade, not fizzy
lemonade–lemon-lime pop, fizzy
let–rent
licenced–restaurant authorized to sell alcohol
lift–elevator
listed–protected historic building
loo–toilet or bathroom
lorry–truck
mac–mackintosh raincoat
mangetout–snow peas
marrow–summer squash
mate–buddy (boy or girl)
mean–stingy
mental–wild, memorable
mews–former stables converted to two-story rowhouses (London)
mobile (MOH-bile)–cell phone
moggie–cat
motorway–freeway
naff–dorky
nappy–diaper
natter–talk on and on
neep–Scottish for turnip
newsagent–corner store
nought–zero

noughts & crosses–tic-tac-toe

off-licence–liquor store

on offer–for sale

panto, pantomime–fairy-tale play performed at Christmas (silly but fun)

pants–underwear, briefs

pasty (PASS-tee)–crusted savory (usually meat) pie from Cornwall

pavement–sidewalk

pear-shaped–messed up, gone wrong

petrol–gas

pillar box–mailbox

pissed (rude), paralytic, bev-vied, wellied, popped up, trollied, ratted, rat-arsed, pissed as a newt–drunk

pitch–playing field

plaster–Band-Aid

publican–pub manager (old-fashioned)

public school–private "prep" school (e.g., Eton)

pudding–dessert in general

pull, to be on the–looking for love

punter–customer, especially in gambling

put a sock in it–shut up

queue–line

queue up–line up

quid–pound (money, worth about $2)

randy–horny

rasher–slice of bacon

redundant, made–laid off

Remembrance Day–Veterans' Day

return ticket–round trip

ring up–call (telephone)

roundabout–traffic circle

rubber–eraser

rubbish–bad

sausage roll–sausage wrapped in a flaky pastry

Scotch egg–hard-boiled egg wrapped in sausage meat

self-catering–accommodation with kitchen

Sellotape–Scotch tape

services–freeway rest area

serviette–napkin

setee–couch

shag–intercourse (cruder than in the US)

shandy–lager and 7-Up

silencer–car muffler

single ticket–one-way ticket

skip–Dumpster

sleeping policeman–speed bumps

smalls–underwear

snogging–kissing, making out

sod–mildly offensive insult

sod it, sod off-screw it, screw off

soda–soda water (not pop)

solicitor–lawyer

spanner–wrench

spend a penny–urinate

stag night–bachelor party

starkers–buck naked

starters–appetizers

state school–public school

sticking plaster–Band-Aid

sticky tape–Scotch tape

stone–14 pounds (weight)

stroppy–bad-tempered

subway–underground walkway

suet–fat from animal rendering (sometimes used in cooking)

sultanas–golden raisins

surgical spirit–rubbing alcohol

suspenders–garters

suss out–figure out

swede–rutabaga

ta–thank you

take the mickey–tease

tatty–worn out or tacky

taxi rank–taxi stand
telly–TV
tenement–stone apartment house (not necessarily a slum)
tenner–£10 bill
theatre–live stage
tick–a check mark
tight as a fish's bum–cheapskate (watertight)
tights–panty hose
tin–can
tip–public dump
tipper lorry–dump truck
top hole–first rate
top up–refill a drink
torch–flashlight
towel, press-on–panty liner
towpath–path along a river
trainers–sneakers

trousers–pants
Tube–subway
twee–quaint, cute
twitcher–bird watcher
Underground–subway
verge–grassy edge of road
verger–church official
way out–exit
wee (adj)–small
wee (verb)–urinate
Wellingtons, wellies–rubber boots
whacked–exhausted
whinge (rhymes with hinge)–whine
wind up-tease, irritate
witter on–gab and gab
yob–hooligan
zebra crossing–crosswalk
zed–the letter Z

INDEX

Travel smart...carry on!

The latest generation of Rick Steves' carry-on travel bags is easily the best—benefiting from two decades of on-the-road attention to what really matters: maximum quality and strength; practical, flexible features; and no unnecessary frills. You won't find a better value anywhere!

Rick Steves' Convertible Carry-On $99.95

Our roomy, versatile 9" x 21" x 14" carry-on has a large 2600 cubic-inch main compartment, plus four outside pockets (small, medium and huge) that are perfect for often-used items. Wish you had even more room to bring home souvenirs? Pull open the full-perimeter expando-zipper and its capacity jumps from 2600 to 3000 cubic inches. When you want to use it as a suitcase or check it as luggage (required when "expanded"), the straps and belt hide away in a zippered compartment in the back. It weighs just 3 lbs.

Rick Steves' Classic Back Door Bag $79.95

This ultra-light (1½ lbs.) version of our Con-vertible Carry-On features the same 9" x 21" x 14" dimensions and hideaway straps, but does not include a waistbelt or expandability. This is the bag that Rick lives out of for three months a year!

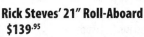

Rick Steves' 21" Roll-Aboard $139.95

Our sturdy 21" Roll-Aboard is rucksack-soft in front, but the rest is lined with a hard ABS-lexan shell to give maximum protection to your belongings. We've spared no ex-pense on moving parts, splurging on an extra-long button-release handle and big, tough inline skate wheels for easy rolling on rough surfaces. It features the same 9" x 21" x 14" carry-on di-mensions, pocket configuration and expandability as our Convertible Carry-On—and at 7 lbs. it's the lightest roll-aboard in its class.

Prices and features are subject to change.

For great deals on a wide selection of travel goodies, begin your next trip at the Rick Steves Travel Store!

Visit the Rick Steves Travel Store at
www.ricksteves.com

FREE-SPIRITED TOURS FROM

Rick Steves

Small Groups
Great Guides
No Grumps

Best of Europe ■ Family Europe
Italy ■ Village Italy ■ South Italy
Sicily ■ France ■ Eastern Europe
Adriatic ■ Prague ■ Scotland
Britain ■ Ireland ■ Scandinavia
Germany-Austria-Switzerland ■ Spain ■ Turkey ■ Greece
London-Paris ■ Paris ■ Rome ■ Venice-Florence-Rome...and more!

Looking for a one, two, or three-week tour that's run in the Rick Steves style?
Check out Rick Steves' educational, experiential tours of Europe.

Rick's tours are an excellent value compared to "mainstream" tours. Here's a taste
of what you'll get...

- **Small groups:** With just 24-28 travelers, you'll go where typical groups of
  40-50 can only dream.

- **Big buses:** You'll travel in a full-size 40-50 seat bus, with plenty of empty
  seats for you to spread out and be comfortable.

- **Great guides:** Our guides are hand-picked by Rick Steves for their wealth of
  knowledge and giddy enthusiasm for Europe.

- **No tips or kickbacks:** To keep your guide and driver 100% focused on giving
  you the best travel experience, we pay them well—and prohibit them from
  accepting tips and merchant kickbacks.

- **All sightseeing:** Your tour price includes all group sightseeing, with no
  hidden extra charges.

- **Central hotels:** You'll stay in Rick's favorite small, characteristic, locally-run
  hotels in the center of each city, within walking distance of the sights you
  came to see.

- **Visit www.ricksteves.com:** You'll find all our latest itineraries, dates and
  prices, be able to reserve online, and request a free copy of our Rick Steves Tour
  Experience DVD!

Rick Steves' Europe Through the Back Door, Inc.
130 Fourth Avenue North, PO Box 2009, Edmonds, WA 98020 USA
Phone: (425) 771-8303 ■ Fax: (425) 771-0833 ■ www.ricksteves.com

Start your trip at
www.ricksteves.com

**Rick Steves' website
is packed with over
3,000 pages of timely
travel information. It's
also your gateway to
getting FREE monthly
travel news from
Rick—and more!**

Free Monthly Travel News

Fresh articles on Europe's most interesting destinations and happenings.
Rick will even send you an email every
month (often direct from Europe) with
his latest discoveries!

Timely Travel Tips

Rick Steves' best money-and-stress-
saving tips on trip planning, packing,
transportation, hotels, health, safety,
finances, hurdling the language barrier…and more.

Travelers' Graffiti Wall

Candid advice and opinions from thousands of travelers on everything listed
above, plus whatever topics are hot at
the moment (discount flights, politics,
nude beaches, scams…you name it).

Rick's Guide to Eurail Passes

The clearest, most comprehensive
guide to the confusing array of railpass
options out there, and how to choo-
choose the railpass that best fits your
itinerary and budget.

Great Gear at Our Travel Store

In the past year alone, more than
50,000 travelers have enjoyed great
online deals on Rick's guidebooks,
maps, DVDs—and his custom-
designed carry-on bags, day packs,
and light-packing accessories.

Rick Steves Tours

This year, 12,000 lucky travelers will
explore Europe on a Rick Steves tour.
Learn about our 28 different one- to
three-week itineraries, read uncen-
sored feedback from our tour alums,
and get our free Tour Experience DVD.

Rick on TV, Radio and Podcasts

Read the scripts from the popular Rick
Steves' Europe TV series, and listen to or
download your choice of over 100 hours
of our Travel with Rick Steves radio show.

Respect for Your Privacy

Whether you buy something from us
or subscribe to Rick's monthly Travel
News emails, we'll never share your
name or email address with anyone
else. You won't be spammed!

Have fun raising your Travel I.Q. at
www.ricksteves.com

Rick Steves®

More *Savvy*. More *Surprising*. More *Fun*.

COUNTRY GUIDES

Croatia & Slovenia
England
France
Germany & Austria
Great Britain
Ireland
Italy
Portugal
Scandinavia
Spain
Switzerland

CITY GUIDES

Amsterdam, Bruges & Brussels
Florence & Tuscany
Istanbul
London
Paris
Prague & The Czech Republic
Provence & The French Riviera
Rome
Venice

BEST OF GUIDES

Best of Eastern Europe
Best of Europe

PHRASE BOOKS & DICTIONARIES

French
French, Italian & German
German
Italian
Portuguese
Spanish

MORE EUROPE FROM RICK STEVES

Europe 101
Europe Through the Back Door
Postcards from Europe

RICK STEVES' EUROPE DVDs

All 70 Shows 2000–2007
Britain
Eastern Europe
France & Benelux
Germany, The Swiss Alps & Travel Skills
Ireland
Italy
Spain & Portugal

PLANNING MAPS

Britain & Ireland
Europe
France
Germany, Austria & Switzerland
Italy
Spain & Portugal

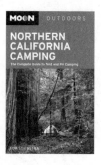
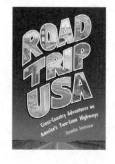

CREDITS

Researchers

To help update this book, Rick relied on…

Cameron Hewitt

Cameron leads tours and writes guidebooks in Eastern Europe for Rick Steves. For this book, he drove 2,119 miles—all on the left—to explore Britain's forgotten stone circles, stately white cliffs, moody lochs and glens, and tongue-twisting Welsh words. He lives in Seattle with his wife Shawna.

Jennifer Hauseman

Jennifer, a researcher and senior editor for Rick Steves, originally hails from the East Coast but has since become an honorary Seattleite. If Jen had her way, she'd be sampling high tea in London right now.

Sarah Murdoch

Sarah loves all things English, particularly cream tea and Rowntree's Fruit Pastilles. While plotting ways to get back to England, she lives in Seattle with her husband Patrick and son Lucca.

Lauren Mills

Lauren, a map editor and in-house search engine at Rick Steves, was an ardent Anglophile even before bringing home her British husband as a souvenir. They live in Seattle with their cat Keswick.

Contributor

Gene Openshaw

Gene is the co-author of seven Rick Steves books. For this book, he wrote material on Europe's art, history, and contemporary culture. When not traveling, Gene enjoys composing music, recovering from his 1973 trip to Europe with Rick, and living everyday life with his wife and daughter.

IMAGES

Location	Photographer
Front color matter: Village of Stanton	Nik Wheeler
Front color matter: Bagpipe player at Loch Ness	Randy Wells
England: Salisbury Cathedral	Cameron Hewitt
London: Houses of Parliament	Rick Steves
Greenwich, Windsor, and Cambridge: Windsor's Changing of the Guard	Lauren Mills
Bath: Pulteney Bridge	Lauren Mills
Near Bath: Avebury Stone Circle	David C. Hoerlein
The Cotswolds: Typical Cotswold Scene	Dominic Bonuccelli
Stratford-upon-Avon: Anne Hathaway's Cottage	Rick Steves
Ironbridge Gorge: The Iron Bridge	Lauren Mills
Wales: Snowdonia	Cameron Hewitt
North Wales: Snowdonia	David C. Hoerlein
Blackpool and Liverpool: Blackpool	Rick Steves
The Lake District: Derwentwater	Rick Steves
York: York Minster	Rick Steves
Durham and Northeast England: Durham Cathedral	David C. Hoerlein
Scotland: Neist Point	Cameron Hewitt
Edinburgh: Edinburgh Castle	Rick Steves
St. Andrews: The Old Course	Cameron Hewitt
Glasgow: Cityscape with the Lighthouse	David C. Hoerlein
Oban and the Southern Highlands: Oban	Jennifer Hauseman
Isle of Skye: Kyleakin Harbor	Cameron Hewitt
Inverness and the Northern Highlands: Inverness	Jennifer Hauseman
Between Inverness and Edinburgh: View from Stirling Castle	Cameron Hewitt

Rick Steves' Guidebook Series

Country Guides

Rick Steves' Best of Europe
Rick Steves' Croatia & Slovenia
Rick Steves' Eastern Europe
Rick Steves' England
Rick Steves' France
Rick Steves' Germany & Austria
Rick Steves' Great Britain
Rick Steves' Ireland
Rick Steves' Italy
Rick Steves' Portugal
Rick Steves' Scandinavia
Rick Steves' Spain
Rick Steves' Switzerland

City and Regional Guides

Rick Steves' Amsterdam, Bruges & Brussels
Rick Steves' Florence & Tuscany
Rick Steves' Istanbul
Rick Steves' London
Rick Steves' Paris
Rick Steves' Prague & the Czech Republic
Rick Steves' Provence & the French Riviera
Rick Steves' Rome
Rick Steves' Venice

Rick Steves' Phrase Books

French
German
Italian
Spanish
Portuguese
French/Italian/German

Other Books

Rick Steves' Europe Through the Back Door
Rick Steves' Europe 101: History and Art for the Traveler
Rick Steves' Postcards from Europe
Rick Steves' European Christmas

(Avalon Travel Publishing)

Avalon Travel Publishing
a member of the Perseus Books Group
1400 65th Street, Suite 250
Emeryville, CA 94608

Avalon Travel Publishing is an Imprint of Avalon Publishing Group, Inc.
Text © 2008 by Rick Steves
Maps © 2008 by Europe Through the Back Door. All rights reserved.

Printed in the USA by Worzalla
First printing November 2007

ISBN (10) 1-56691-858-8
ISBN (13) 978-1-56691-858-9
ISSN 1090-6843

Thanks to my wife, Anne, for making home my favorite travel destination. Thanks also to
Cameron Hewitt for his original work on several of the Scotland chapters (particularly
St. Andrews and the Isle of Skye), to Jennifer Hauseman for the original version of the
Glasgow chapter, and to friends listed in this book who put the "Great" in Britain.

For the latest on Rick's lectures, guidebooks, tours, public radio show, and public television
series, contact Europe Through the Back Door, Box 2009, Edmonds, WA 98020, 425/771-
8303, fax 425/771-0833, www.ricksteves.com, rick@ricksteves.com.

Europe Through the Back Door Managing Editor: Risa Laib
ETBD Senior Editors: Cameron Hewitt, Jennifer Hauseman
ETBD Editors: Cathy McDonald, Jennifer Madison Davis
Avalon Travel Publishing Senior Editor and Series Manager: Madhu Prasher
Avalon Travel Publishing Project Editor: Kelly Lydick
Research Assistance: Cameron Hewitt, Jennifer Hauseman, Sarah Murdoch, Lauren Mills
Copy Editor: Patrick Collins
Proofreader: Judith Brown
Indexer: Carl Wikander
Production and Layout: McGuire Barber Design
Cover Design: Kari Gim, Laura Mazer
Cover Art Manager: Laura VanDeventer
Maps and Graphics: David C. Hoerlein, Laura VanDeventer, Lauren Mills, Barb Geisler,
Mike Morgenfeld
Front matter color photos: p. i, Village of Stanton © Nik Wheeler; p. viii, Bagpipe player
in Loch Ness © Randy Wells
Front Cover Photos: front image, Stow-on-the-Wold ©Jennifer Hauseman; back image:
The North Lakes District © Rick Steves
Additional Photography: Rick Steves, Gene Openshaw, Bruce VanDeventer, Lauren Mills,
David C. Hoerlein, Jennifer Hauseman, Jennifer Schutte, Ken Hanley, Sarah Murdoch,
Darbi Macy